2005-2006

EVANGELICAL SUNDAY SCHOOL LESSON COMMENTARY

FIFTY-FOURTH ANNUAL VOLUME
Based on the
Evangelical Bible Lesson Series

Editorial Staff
Lance Colkmire — Editor
Tammy Hatfield — Editorial Assistant
Bill George — Editor in Chief
M. Thomas Propes — General Director of Publications

Lesson Exposition Writers

Lance Colkmire	Joshua Rice
Jerald Daffe	Glenda Walter
Rodney Hodge	Richard Keith Whitt

Published by

PATHWAY PRESS   Cleveland, Tennessee

* To place an order, call 1-800-553-8506.
* To contact the editor, call 423-478-7597.

Lesson treatments in the *Evangelical Sunday School Lesson Commentary* for 2005-2006 are based upon the outlines of the Pentecostal-Charismatic Bible Lesson Series prepared by the Pentecostal-Charismatic Curriculum Commission.

Copyright 2005

PATHWAY PRESS, Cleveland, Tennessee

ISBN: 1-59684-036-6

Printed in the United States of America

TABLE OF CONTENTS

INTRODUCTION TO THE 2005-2006 COMMENTARY

The *Evangelical Sunday School Lesson Commentary* contains in a single volume a full study of the Sunday school lessons for the months beginning with September 2005 and running through August 2006. The 12 months of lessons draw from both the Old Testament and the New Testament in an effort to provide balance and establish relationship between these distinct but inspired writings. The lessons in this 2005-2006 volume are drawn from the seventh year of a seven-year cycle, which will be completed in August 2006. (The cycle is printed in full on page 15 of this volume.)

The lessons for the *Evangelical Commentary* are based on the Evangelical Bible Lesson Series Outlines, prepared by the Pentecostal-Charismatic Curriculum Commission. (The Pentecostal-Charismatic Curriculum Commission is a member of the National Association of Evangelicals.) The lessons in this volume are drawn from the Old and New Testaments; and taken together with the other annual volumes of lessons in the cycle, they provide a valuable commentary on a wide range of Biblical subjects. Each quarter is divided into two units of study.

The 2005-2006 commentary is the work of a team of Christian scholars and writers who have developed the volume under the supervision of Pathway Press. All the major writers, introduced on the following pages, represent a team of ministers committed to a strictly Evangelical interpretation of the Scriptures. The guiding theological principles of this commentary are expressed in the following statement of faith:

1. WE BELIEVE the Bible to be the inspired, the only infallible, authoritative Word of God.

2. WE BELIEVE that there is one God, eternally existing in three persons: Father, Son, and Holy Spirit.

3. WE BELIEVE in the deity of our Lord Jesus Christ, in His virgin birth, in His sinless life, in His miracles, in His vicarious and atoning death through His shed blood, in His bodily resurrection, in His ascension to the right hand of the Father, and in His personal return in power and glory.

4. WE BELIEVE that for the salvation of lost and sinful men, personal reception of the Lord Jesus Christ and regeneration by the Holy Spirit are absolutely essential.

5. WE BELIEVE in the present ministry of the Holy Spirit by whose cleansing and indwelling the Christian is enabled to live a godly life.

6. WE BELIEVE in the personal return of the Lord Jesus Christ.

7. WE BELIEVE in the resurrection of both the saved and the lost—they that are saved, unto the resurrection of life; and they that are lost, unto the resurrection of damnation.

8. WE BELIEVE in the spiritual unity of believers in our Lord Jesus Christ.

USING THE COMMENTARY

The *Evangelical Sunday School Lesson Commentary* for 2005-2006 is presented to the reader with the hope that it will become his or her weekly companion through the months ahead.

The fall quarter 2005 continues a seven-year cycle of lessons which will be completed with the summer quarter 2006. The 28 quarters of studies, divided into two or more units each, have been drawn from both the Old and New Testaments. Also a number of studies have been topical in nature. A complete listing of the themes that have been included in the seven-year cycle is printed on page 15 of this volume.

Quarterly unit themes for the 2005-2006 volume are as follows:
• Fall Quarter—Unit One: "God's Word in the Minor Prophets (Nahum to Malachi)"; Unit Two: "Parables of Jesus"
• Winter Quarter—Unit One: "Peter and Jude"; Unit Two: "Numbers"
• Spring Quarter—Unit One: "Roots of Christian Formation"; Unit Two: "Fruit of Christian Formation"
• Summer Quarter—Unit One: "Living in Light and Love (1, 2 and 3 John)"; Unit Two: "Christ in the Revelation"

The lesson sequence used in this volume is prepared by the Pentecostal-Charismatic Curriculum Commission.

The specific material used in developing each lesson is written and edited under the guidance of the editorial staff of Pathway Press.

INTRODUCTION: The opening of each week's lesson features a one-page introduction. It provides background information that sets the stage for the lesson.

CONTEXT: A time and place is given for most lessons. Where there is a wide range of ideas regarding the exact time or place, we favor the majority opinion of conservative scholars.

PRINTED TEXT: The printed text is the body of Scripture designated each week for verse-by-verse study in the classroom. Drawing on the study text the teacher delves into this printed text, exploring its content with the students.

CENTRAL TRUTH and FOCUS: The central truth states the single unifying principle that the expositors attempted to clarify in each lesson. The focus describes the overall lesson goal.

DICTIONARY: A dictionary, which attempts to bring pronunciation and clarification to difficult words or phrases, is included with many lessons. Pronunciations are based on the phonetic system used by Field Enterprises Educational Corporation of Chicago and New York in *The World Book Encyclopedia*. Definitions are generally based on *The Pictorial Bible Dictionary*, published by Zondervan Publishing Company, Grand Rapids, Michigan.

EXPOSITION and LESSON OUTLINE: The heart of this commentary—and probably the heart of the teacher's instruction each week—is the exposition of the printed text. This exposition material is preceded by a lesson outline, which indicates how the material is to be divided for study.

QUOTATIONS and ILLUSTRATIONS: Each section of every lesson contains illustrations and sayings the teacher can use in connecting the lesson to daily living.

TALK ABOUT IT: Questions are printed throughout the lesson to help students explore the Scripture text and how it speaks to believers today.

CONCLUSION: Each lesson ends with a brief conclusion that makes a summarizing statement.

GOLDEN TEXT CHALLENGE: The golden text challenge for each week is a brief reflection on that single verse. The word *challenge* is used because its purpose is to help students apply this key verse to their life.

DAILY BIBLE READINGS: The daily Bible readings are included for the teacher to use in his or her own devotions throughout the week, as well as to share with members of their class.

SCRIPTURE TEXTS USED IN LESSON EXPOSITION

Numbers

3:5-10, 44-49	February 12
11:4-6, 10	February 19
11:25, 29	June 4
14:2-5, 11, 12	February 19
21:4-9	February 26

Isaiah

9:6	April 9
53:7, 8	May 21

Nahum

1:2, 3, 5-7, 12-15	September 4
2:13	September 4
3:4, 5	September 4

Habakkuk

1:2-5, 12, 13	September 11
2:1-4	September 11
3:2, 17, 18	September 11

Zephaniah

1:14-18	September 18
2:3	September 18
3:8, 17-20	September 18

Haggai

1:4-8, 12-14	September 25
2:11-15, 19	September 25

Zechariah

1:8-10, 12	October 2
3:1-4	October 2
5:1-4	October 2
9:9-11, 16	October 9
10:6	October 9

Zechariah (cont.)

13:7-9	October 9
14:3, 4, 8, 9	October 9

Malachi

1:6-12	October 16
2:5, 6, 8-10	October 16
2:17	October 23
3:1-4, 7-9, 13, 14	October 23
4:1-4	October 23

Matthew

4:1-10	May 28
5:23-25	March 19
6:5, 6	March 12
6:14, 15	March 19
6:25, 26, 33, 34	April 9
8:5-10, 13	May 14
11:28-30	May 21
13:31-33, 37-50	October 30
21:28-32	November 6
22:2, 3, 8-10, 14	November 6
25:1, 2, 6-9, 13	November 6
25:14, 19-21, 29, 31, 34, 37-40	November 13
26:48-53	May 21
27:57-60	April 16
28:1-10, 18-20	April 16

Mark

1:35-39	March 12
11:25, 26	March 19
13:33-37	November 13
18:23, 26-28, 32, 34, 35	November 20

Luke

2:1, 4-12, 22, 25-32	December 25
10:30-37	May 7
10:40-42	March 26
11:1-4	March 12
15:3-14, 20-24	November 27
16:10-13	November 20
17:7-10	November 20
23:33-37, 39-43	March 26

John

3:14-21	February 26
8:3-5, 7-11	April 30
10:11-15	April 30
11:40-44	May 14
14:6, 7, 11, 12, 15-21	March 5
14:27	April 9
15:1-7	March 5
15:9-11	April 2
16:33	April 9
17:1-5, 13	March 12
19:25-27	May 7

Acts

2:4, 16, 17, 42	June 4
2:42-47	April 2
4:31	June 4
7:55-60	May 21

Romans

8:1-6	April 9
12:10	May 7

1 Corinthians

9:25-27	May 28
10:6, 10-13	February 19
13:4-8, 13	March 26

2 Corinthians

3:5, 6	June 4
4:17, 18	April 2

Galatians

5:16, 22-25	May 28
5:22, 23	June 4

Ephesians

4:25, 29, 31, 32	May 7
5:18-21	June 4

Philippians

3:12-17	April 23
4:4-8	April 2

Colossians

3:13	March 19

1 Thessalonians

2:7, 8, 10-12	April 30

2 Timothy

2:2-5	April 23
2:20-22	February 12

Hebrews

9:22-28	March 19
11:1-3, 6	May 14

James

5:7-11	April 23

1 Peter

1:1-12	December 4
1:13-23	December 11
2:6-9	December 11
2:13-17, 20-25	December 18
2:21	April 23
3:1, 2, 7-9	December 18
3:13-17	January 1
4:1, 2	January 1
4:8-11	January 8
4:12-19	January 1
5:1-11	January 8

2 Peter

1:1-11	January 15
1:19-21	January 22
2:1-4, 9, 17, 19-22	January 22
3:1-14	January 29

1 John

1:1-10	June 11

1 John (cont.)

2:1-6	June 11
2:17-19	June 18
3:1-3, 7, 10, 14-18	June 25
4:1-4	July 2
4:7-21	June 18
5:1-5, 7-13	July 2
5:14-16, 19, 20	June 25

2 John

4-11	July 9

3 John

4-6, 8-12	July 9

Jude

3-7, 15, 16, 19-25	February 5

Revelation

1:1, 4-11, 17-20	July 16
2:2-10	July 23
3:2, 3, 7, 8, 11, 12, 16, 19	July 23
4:2, 3	July 30
5:1-7, 9-13	July 30
6:1-8	August 6
7:9, 10	August 6
10:5-7	August 6
11:15-18	August 20
12:7-10	August 13
14:6, 7, 13, 14	August 13
17:13, 14	August 13
19:11, 15, 16	August 13
20:1-4, 7, 8, 10	August 20
21:1, 4, 5, 7, 9-11, 22, 23	August 27
22:1-5	August 27

SCRIPTURE TEXTS USED IN GOLDEN TEXT CHALLENGE

Isaiah

40:11	April 30

Micah

6:8	October 23

Nahum

1:3	September 4

Habakkuk

3:18	September 11

Zephaniah

3:17	September 18

Haggai

1:5	September 25

Zechariah

2:11	October 2
14:9	October 9

Malachi

1:11	October 16

Matthew

6:33	October 30
11:29	May 21
22:37	November 6
28:6	April 16

Mark

11:25	March 19

Luke

2:11	December 25
11:1	March 12
15:7	November 27
16:10	November 20

John

3:14, 15	February 26
14:27	April 9
15:5	March 5
15:11	April 2

1 Corinthians

10:11	February 19
13:13	March 26
15:25	August 13

2 Corinthians		2 Peter	
5:10	November 13	1:4	January 15
		1:21	January 22
Galatians		3:13	January 29
5:16	May 28		
		1 John	
Ephesians		1:7	June 11
4:32	May 7	3:24	June 25
5:18, 19	June 4	4:7	June 18
		5:11	July 2
2 Timothy			
2:21	February 12	**3 John**	
4:1	August 6	4	July 9
Hebrews		**Jude**	
11:6	May 14	21	February 5
1 Peter		**Revelation**	
1:3	December 4	1:18	July 16
2:9	December 11	2:7	July 23
2:17	December 18	5:9	July 30
2:21	April 23	11:15	August 20
4:10	January 8	21:5	August 27
4:19	January 1		

ACKNOWLEDGMENTS

Many books, magazines and newspapers have been used in the research that has gone into the 2005-2006 *Evangelical Commentary*. The major books that have been used are listed below.

Bibles
King James Version, Oxford University Press, Oxford, England
Life Application Study Bible, Zondervan Publishing House, Grand Rapids
New American Standard Bible (NASB), Holman Publishers, Nashville
New International Version (NIV), Zondervan Publishing House, Grand Rapids
New King James Version (NKJV), Thomas Nelson Publishers, Nashville
The Nelson Study Bible, Thomas Nelson Publishers, Nashville
Word in Life Study Bible, Thomas Nelson Publishers, Nashville

Commentaries
Adam Clarke's Commentary, Abingdon-Cokesbury, Nashville
Apocalypse!, David C. Cooper, Pathway Press, Cleveland, TN
Barnes' Notes, BibleSoft.com
Be Resolute, Warren Wiersbe, Victor Books, Colorado Springs
Commentaries on the Old Testament (Keil & Delitzsch), Eerdmans Publishing Co., Grand Rapids
Ellicott's Bible Commentary, Zondervan Publishing House, Grand Rapids
Ephesians, The Mystery of the Body of Christ, R. Kent Hughes, Crossway Books, Wheaton, IL
Exploring Hebrews, John Phillips, Kregel Publications, Grand Rapids
Expositions of Holy Scriptures, Alexander MacLaren, Eerdmans Publishing Co., Grand Rapids
Expository Thoughts on the Gospels, J.C. Ryle, Baker Books, Grand Rapids
Hebrews: Finding the Better Way, Ron Phillips, Pathway Press, Cleveland, TN
Jamieson, Fausset and Brown Commentary, BibleSoft.com
Life Application Commentary, Tyndale House, Carol Stream, IL
The Broadman Bible Commentary, Volumes 10 and 11, Broadman Press, Nashville
The Expositor's Greek Testament, Eerdmans Publishing Co., Grand Rapids
The Interpreter's Bible, Abingdon Press, Nashville
The Letters to the Corinthians, William Barclay, Westminster Press, Philadelphia
The Letters to Timothy, Titus, and Philemon, Westminster Press, Philadelphia
The Pulpit Commentary, Eerdmans Publishing Co., Grand Rapids
The Wesleyan Commentary, Eerdmans Publishing Co., Grand Rapids
The Wycliffe Bible Commentary, Moody Press, Chicago
Zondervan NIV Bible Commentary, Zondervan Publishing House, Grand Rapids

Illustrations
A-Z Sparkling Illustrations, Stephen Gaukroger and Nick Mercer, Baker Books, Grand Rapids
Knight's Master Book of New Illustrations, Eerdmans Publishing Co., Grand Rapids

Notes and Quotes, The Warner Press, Anderson, IN
1,000 New Illustrations, Al Bryant, Zondervan Publishing Co., Grand Rapids
Quotable Quotations, Scripture Press Publications, Wheaton
The Encyclopedia of Religious Quotations, Fleming H. Revell Co., Old Tappan, NJ
The Speaker's Sourcebook, Zondervan Publishing House, Grand Rapids
3,000 Illustrations for Christian Service, Eerdmans Publishing Co., Grand Rapids
Who Said That?, George Sweeting, Moody Press, Chicago

General Reference Books
Biblical Characters From the Old and New Testament, Alexander Whyte, Kregel
    Publications, Grand Rapids
Harper's Bible Dictionary, Harper and Brothers Publishers, New York
Pictorial Dictionary of the Bible, Zondervan Publishing House, Grand Rapids
Pronouncing Biblical Names, Broadman and Holman Publishers, Nashville
The Interpreter's Dictionary of the Bible, Abingdon Press, Nashville

Evangelical Bible Lesson Series (1999-2006)

Fall Quarter September, October, November	Winter Quarter December, January, February	Spring Quarter March, April, May	Summer Quarter June, July, August
1999 Unit One—Beginnings (Genesis) Unit Two—Personal Ethics	**1999-2000** Unit One—Gospel of the King (Matthew) Unit Two—Growing Spiritually	**2000** Unit One—Ruth & Esther Unit Two—Divine Healing Unit Three—Great Prayers of the Bible	**2000** Unit One—Acts (Part 1) Unit Two—Family Relationships
2000 Unit One—Providence (Exodus) Unit Two—Spiritual Warfare Unit Three—Worship	**2000-2001** Unit One—Faith for the 21st Century Unit Two—Jesus the Servant (Mark)	**2001** Unit One—The Kingdom of God Unit Two—Law & Gospel (Leviticus-Deuteronomy)	**2001** Unit One—Acts (Part 2) Unit Two—Evangelism
2001 Unit One—Christian Living (Romans & Galatians) Unit Two—Christian Discipleship	**2001-2002** Unit One—The Gospel According to Luke Unit Two—Message of the Early Church	**2002** Unit One—Leadership (Joshua & Judges) Unit Two—The Church	**2002** Unit One—Psalms (Part 1) Unit Two—Learning From Samuel, Elijah & Elisha
2002 Unit One—Wisdom From Job, Proverbs, & Ecclesiastes Unit Two—God's Great Promises	**2002-2003** Unit One—Jesus the Son of God (John) Unit Two—Gifts of the Spirit	**2003** Unit One—Kings of Israel (Samuel, Kings, Chronicles) Unit Two—Second Coming	**2003** Unit One—Heaven & Hell Unit Two—Psalms (Part 2)
2003 Unit One—Judgment & Comfort (Isaiah) Unit Two—Values & Priorities	**2003-2004** Unit One—1 & 2 Corinthians Unit Two—Lesser-Known People of the Bible	**2004** Unit One—Jeremiah & Lamentations Unit Two—Out of Exile (Ezra & Nehemiah)	**2004** Unit One—Prison Epistles Unit Two—Revival & Renewal
2004 Unit One—God's Sovereignty (Ezekiel) Unit Two—James	**2004-2005** Unit One—1 & 2 Thessalonians Unit Two—Pastoral Epistles	**2005** Unit One—Minor Prophets I (Hosea-Micah) Unit Two—Redemption	**2005** Unit One—Faith (Hebrews) Unit Two—Daniel
2005 Unit One—Minor Prophets II (Nahum—Malachi) Unit Two—Parables of Jesus	**2005-2006** Unit One—Peter & Jude Unit Two—Numbers	**2006** Unit One—People Who Met Jesus Unit Two—Christian Formation (inc. Fruit of the Spirit)	**2006** Unit One—1, 2, 3 John Unit Two—Studies in Revelation

Introduction to Fall Quarter

S elected writings from six of the minor prophets—Nahum, Habakkuk, Zephaniah, Haggai, Zechariah and Malachi—comprise Unit 1 (lessons 1-8). Expositions were written by Lance Colkmire (lessons 1, 2, 7, 8), Glenda Walter (lessons 3, 4) and Joshua Rice (lessons 5, 6)

Reverend Lance Colkmire (B.A., M.A.) is editor of the *Evangelical Sunday School Lesson Commentary* and young adult curriculum for Pathway Press. He is a graduate of Lee University and the Church of God Theological Seminary, and has taught courses at both institutions.

Glenda Walter is a Bible teacher and freelance writer who served as the Christian education director for Bethel Assembly of God in Sedro Woolley, Washington. Glenda has numerous certificates of completion in Bible subjects. She has also completed her certification for the Assemblies of God ACTS Training Program, specializing in Sunday school administration.

Joshua Rice (B.A., M.A.Th.) is regional director of youth and Christian education for the Great Lakes Region. He is a graduate of Lee University and Columbia Theological Seminary.

The studies for Unit 2 (lessons 9-13), "Parables of Jesus," were written by Joshua Rice. This unit addresses parables concerning God's kingdom, Christ's return, servanthood and salvation.

Additional resource available from Pathway Press:

Malachi: Hope at the End of an Age
by Ron Phillips
$11.99
Item # 087148-3785

Call 1-800-553-8506 or go to *www.pathwaybookstore.com*

The Justice of God (Nahum)

Nahum 1:1 through 3:19

INTRODUCTION

The name *Nahum* has a double meaning—"compassion" and "vengeance." His name proved to be prophetic in his own life, which began in the village of Elkosh. It is believed this village was located in Galilee, though this is uncertain.

The Book of Nahum has two parts: first, a poem lifting up God and His greatness (1:2-15); second, a longer poem detailing the fall of Nineveh (2:1—3:19).

Nahum's name symbolized consolation for God's people and vengeance upon their enemies, the Assyrians. In the first chapter these two themes alternate. As the prophecy advances, vengeance upon Nineveh, the capital of Assyria, becomes the dominant theme. Nahum's goal was to inspire and comfort his people with the assurance that however alarming their situation might appear, the Assyrians would not only fail to capture Jerusalem, but they would be destroyed.

More than a century earlier, the Lord had sent another messenger, Jonah, to the Assyrians. When Jonah finally obeyed the Lord and went to Nineveh, he preached, "Yet forty days, and Nineveh shall be overthrown" (Jonah 3:4). The Assyrians believed Jonah's message, repented of their violent and cruel ways, and God forgave them.

However, the Assyrians' repentance was short-lived. They returned to their terrible practices, cruelly oppressing God's people, and so divine judgment was going to fall on them. This time there would be no opportunity for repentance and forgiveness. History tells us that Nineveh was conquered by the Babylonians, Medes, and Scythians in 612 B.C.

Unit Theme:
God's Word in the Minor Prophets (Nahum to Malachi)

Central Truth:
God is completely just in all He does.

Focus:
To affirm and find encouragement in the just nature of God.

Context:
Nahum prophesied in Judah around 700 B.C., during the reign of King Hezekiah.

Golden Text:
"The Lord is slow to anger, and great in power, and will not at all acquit the wicked" (Nahum 1:3).

Study Outline:
I. Warning of Judgment (Nahum 1:1-11)

II. Promise of Deliverance (Nahum 1:12—2:2)

III. Judgment of the Wicked (Nahum 2:13 through 3:7)

I. WARNING OF JUDGMENT (Nahum 1:1-11)
A. The Burden of Nineveh (vv. 1, 2)
1. The burden of Nineveh. The book of the vision of Nahum the Elkoshite.

2. God is jealous, and the Lord revengeth; the Lord revengeth, and is furious; the Lord will take vengeance on his adversaries, and he reserveth wrath for his enemies.

Talk About It:
1. Explain "the burden of Nineveh" (v. 1).
2. What makes God "jealous"? What makes Him "furious"?

The heavy "burden" (v. 1) of the message Nahum had to deliver concerning God's judgment imposed a grave responsibility on him. Every true teacher and preacher of Christ feels likewise burdened by the necessity of proclaiming both the wrath and the love of God.

The word *burden* here also means "message" or "oracle." The message Nahum had to proclaim resulted from the *vision*—"authoritative revelation"—God had given him.

Three times in verse 2 God declares He will take vengeance on His enemies, and the reason can be traced to His jealousy. The Lord God is jealous over people because He loves them, but if they reject His wooing, His wounded honor finally demands that He judge them.

God had offered mercy to the cruel Assyrians in the days of Jonah, and they had received it; but then they turned their backs on God again. The Lord had used the Assyrian oppression in judging the Jews for their sins, but now it was time for the oppressors to be oppressed.

B. The Power of God (vv. 3-7)
3. The Lord is slow to anger, and great in power, and will not at all acquit the wicked: the Lord hath his way in the whirlwind and in the storm, and the clouds are the dust of his feet.

4. He rebuketh the sea, and maketh it dry, and drieth up all the rivers: Bashan languisheth, and Carmel, and the flower of Lebanon languisheth.

5. The mountains quake at him, and the hills melt, and the earth is burned at his presence, yea, the world, and all that dwell therein.

6. Who can stand before his indignation? and who can abide in the fierceness of his anger? his fury is poured out like fire, and the rocks are thrown down by him.

7. The Lord is good, a strong hold in the day of trouble; and he knoweth them that trust in him.

Talk About It:
1. Why is the Lord "slow to anger" (v. 3)?

God is "slow to anger" because He is infinitely good and great. For a hundred years He had endured the wickedness of the Assyrians. Their judgment was delayed not for lack of power, for God is all-powerful, but because of abundant mercy. Sinners are sometimes allowed to pursue wrong, not because God is unaware of their sins, but because He is patient and

The Justice of God

loving. A lack of punishment is not to be mistaken for acquittal.

Nahum describes the greatness of God in nature as a reminder that He is sovereign. The One who can control storms, causing them to rise up or cease, was about to send a deadly whirlwind against Nineveh. The One who walks on clouds like humans walk on dust was about to walk into Assyria to deliver unstoppable judgment. The One whose word of rebuke can cause an ocean or a river to dry up was about to rebuke Nineveh. The One who controls earthquakes was about to shake Assyria to its core.

When it is time for divine judgment to go forth, nothing and no one can stand against the anger of God. Though calm and deliberate, His judgment is overwhelming. Expulsion from Eden, the Flood, and the destruction of Sodom and Gomorrah are examples of it. How ridiculous for the strongest and brashest sinner to think he or she can stand against the power of God's wrath!

For those who trust in God, there is comfort and security in the day of distress. And it's the Lord himself who is our refuge! The reason is that God is good all the time, and all the time, God is good. His promise to help His people is as certain to be fulfilled as His threat to punish those who reject Him.

C. The Justice of God (vv. 8-11)

8. But with an overrunning flood he will make an utter end of the place thereof, and darkness shall pursue his enemies.

9. What do ye imagine against the Lord? he will make an utter end: affliction shall not rise up the second time.

10. For while they be folden together as thorns, and while they are drunken as drunkards, they shall be devoured as stubble fully dry.

11. There is one come out of thee, that imagineth evil against the Lord, a wicked counsellor.

The destruction of proud Nineveh, as it will be with all of God's enemies, was complete and irretrievable (v. 8). Its very location was unknown for ages, and no city has ever been raised up on its site.

The "wicked counsellor" of verse 11 was Assyria's King Sennacherib. He and the Assyrians thought the people of Judah were weak (which they were in their own power), but Sennacherib failed to take Judah's God into account (v. 9). The Assyrians invaded Judah, captured 40 of its cities, and deported over 200,000 Jews. Meanwhile, Judah's King Hezekiah tried striking a deal with Sennacherib to save his throne and the capital city of Jerusalem. Hezekiah paid tribute to Sennacherib by stripping the Temple of its riches. But this didn't stop Sennacherib, who laid siege to Jerusalem.

2. Answer the questions in verse 6: "Who can stand before his indignation? And who can abide in the fierceness of his anger?"

3. How is the Lord like a "strong hold" (v. 7)?

"You have laughed God out of your schools, out of your books, and out of your life, but you cannot laugh Him out of your death."
—**Dagobert Runes**

Talk About It:

1. What does it mean to be pursued by darkness (v. 8)?

2. What does it mean to "imagine" against the Lord (vv. 9, 11), and what will come of it?

However, through Nahum the Lord prophesied that the powerful Assyrian army would somehow be defeated. The defeat would be so total that it would never need to be repeated (v. 9). They would be tangled up as if in thorns, caught in a drunken stupor, and defeated as easily as dry stubble is burned (v. 10).

II. PROMISE OF DELIVERANCE (Nahum 1:12—2:2)
A. Broken Bonds (1:12-14)

12. Thus saith the Lord; Though they be quiet, and likewise many, yet thus shall they be cut down, when he shall pass through. Though I have afflicted thee, I will afflict thee no more.

13. For now will I break his yoke from off thee, and will burst thy bonds in sunder.

14. And the Lord hath given a commandment concerning thee, that no more of thy name be sown: out of the house of thy gods will I cut off the graven image and the molten image: I will make thy grave; for thou art vile.

Though Sennacherib's army lay confidently in its camp outside Jerusalem, it was already doomed to be cut down like grass before the sickle. How often has it happened that sinners, confident in their own strength, only prepared themselves for doom. In announcing the fate of the Assyrians, God assured His people that their day of affliction was past.

As Sennacherib prepared to pounce on Jerusalem, King Hezekiah prayed. Through the prophet Isaiah, God promised, "By the way that he came he will return; he will not enter this city. . . . I will defend this city and save it" (2 Kings 19:33, 34, *NIV*). That night the Lord's angel swept through the Assyrian camp and put to death 185,000 soldiers. So Sennacherib broke camp and returned to Nineveh, where he soon was assassinated.

In verse 14 of the text, Nahum prophesies that not only would the power of Assyria be destroyed, but its very name and fame would perish. Idols would be thrown down, and the city of Nineveh would become as a graveyard.

B. Good News (v. 15)

15. Behold upon the mountains the feet of him that bringeth good tidings, that publisheth peace! O Judah, keep thy solemn feasts, perform thy vows: for the wicked shall no more pass through thee; he is utterly cut off.

When Sennacherib triumphed in his initial attacks against Judah, every Jewish messenger brought bad news from that land. However, when the Assyrian army was supernaturally routed, breaking the long siege against Jerusalem, couriers raced away with good news of peace. And better news was

---

no more of thy name be sown (v. 14)—There will be no descendants to carry on your name.

Talk About It:
1. Why were the Assyrians quietly confident, and why was this a mistake (v. 12)?
2. What did God promise to do for His people (v. 13)?

In His Hands
The citizens of Feldkirch, Austria, didn't know what to do. Napoleon's army was preparing to attack. It happened to be Easter Sunday, and the people had gathered in church. The pastor said, "As this is the day of our Lord's resurrection, let us just ring the bells, have our services as usual, and leave the matter in His hands." The people agreed and the church bells rang.

The Justice of God

coming! When Nineveh was completely crushed a century later (as predicted in verse 14), that good news would be proclaimed on the mountains.

With Jerusalem no longer under siege, the people were urged to honor God by keeping all the religious ceremonies He had established and by carrying out all the vows they had made to the Lord. Many of those promises to God likely came under the duress of the siege, yet God expected His people to keep those promises.

In Ecclesiastes 5 we are warned, "When you make a vow to God, do not delay in fulfilling it. He has no pleasure in fools; fulfill your vow. It is better not to vow than to make a vow and not fulfill it. Do not let your mouth lead you into sin" (vv. 4-6, *NIV*).

The enemy, hearing the sudden peal, concluded that the Austrian army had arrived during the night to defend the town. Before the service ended, the enemy broke camp and left.
—*Sermon Illustrations.com*

C. Renewed Splendor (2:1, 2)

1. He that dasheth in pieces is come up before thy face: keep the munition, watch the way, make thy loins strong, fortify thy power mightily.

2. For the Lord hath turned away the excellency of Jacob, as the excellency of Israel: for the emptiers have emptied them out, and marred their vine branches.

munition (v. 1)—fortress

Verse 1 makes a mockery of Nineveh. Those fierce warriors who had been so cruel to other peoples were going to be under siege themselves. The Assyrians are warned, "Guard the fortress, watch the road, brace yourselves, marshal all your strength!" (*NIV*). Of course, nothing they did would save them, for Almighty God would be their pursuer.

Verse 2 refers to the Assyrian army as "emptiers." Through the providence of God, He had allowed Nineveh to "empty" His people of their security, material goods and pride, as well as letting them ruin Judah's produce. But now God promised restoration to His people, identifying Himself as their Restorer.

When God allows emptiness to invade the lives of His people today, it is for a redemptive purpose—to draw us back to God. We can't understand the fullness God can bring to our lives until we recognize how empty we are without Him.

Talk About It:
1. Why would Nineveh need to be on the alert (v. 1)?
2. What had the Assyrians done to Judah, and what would God do for Judah (v. 2)?

III. JUDGMENT OF THE WICKED (Nahum 2:13—3:7)

A. God's Enemy (2:13)

13. Behold, I am against thee, saith the Lord of hosts, and I will burn her chariots in the smoke, and the sword shall devour thy young lions: and I will cut off thy prey from the earth, and the voice of thy messengers shall no more be heard.

In chapter 2, Nahum's graphic description of Nineveh's fall includes these pictures:
- Assyria's best soldiers stumbling as they rush to protect their city walls (v. 5).

Talk About It:
1. Explain the title "Lord of hosts."

2. What does it mean to have the Lord of Hosts against you?

- Nineveh's palace collapsing (v. 6).
- Nineveh's life being drained away like a pool losing its water (v. 8).
- The capital is "pillaged, plundered, stripped!" (v. 10, NIV).
- Hearts melting, knees collapsing, and bodies trembling in fear (v. 10).

The reason for this scene of total chaos and destruction is sounded in verse 13—the Lord Almighty is against Nineveh. What a horrible condition! In Romans 8:31, Paul asks, "If God be for us, who can be against us?" But if God is against us, who can be for us?

"Though the mills of God grind slowly, yet they grind exceedingly small; though with patience He stands waiting, with exactness grinds He all."
—Friedrich von Logau

The prophet refers to Assyria's soldiers as "young lions" (Nahum 2:13) who have been devouring other nations. Now, however, their prey will no longer be found. With Assyria's weapons of war being wiped out, the hunter will become the hunted. No longer will the nation's messengers go from place to place proclaiming victory. Instead, they will be silenced.

B. Sounds of War (3:1-4)

(Nahum 3:1-3 is not included in the printed text.)

4. Because of the multitude of the whoredoms of the wellfavoured harlot, the mistress of witchcrafts, that selleth nations through her whoredoms, and families through her witchcrafts.

the prey departeth not (v. 1)—never without victims

Talk About It:
1. Describe the sounds of judgment that would be heard in Nineveh.
2. Describe the sights of judgment that would be seen.
3. Why would Nineveh's punishment be so extreme?

The beautiful poetry in these verses is marred by the picture it describes. The city with blood on its hands because of its viciousness toward others will now be filled with its own blood. The city filled with plunder from foreign lands will be plundered by others. The nation known for its military might will hear the noises of whips snapping, wheels rattling, horses prancing, chariots jolting, and swords clanging as Assyria is invaded. There will be "many casualties, piles of dead, bodies without number, people stumbling over the corpses" (v. 3, NIV).

The reason for Assyria's horrible judgment is explained in verse 4, where Assyria is referred to as a harlot who practices sorceries. Barnes wrote that Nineveh's "being was one vast idolatry of self and of 'the god of this world.' All art, fraud, deceit, protection of the weak against the strong (2 Kings 16:7-9; 2 Chronicles 28:20, 21), promises of good (Isaiah 36:16, 17), were employed, together with open violence, to absorb all nations into it. The one end of all was to form one great idol-temple, of which the center and end was man, a rival worship to God, which should enslave all to itself and the things of this world. Nineveh and all conquering nations used fraud as well as force, enticed and entangled others, and so sold and deprived them of freedom."

C. Utter Humility (vv. 5-7)

5. Behold, I am against thee, saith the Lord of hosts; and I will discover thy skirts upon thy face, and I will shew the nations thy nakedness, and the kingdoms thy shame.

6. And I will cast abominable filth upon thee, and make thee vile, and will set thee as a gazingstock.

7. And it shall come to pass, that all they that look upon thee shall flee from thee, and say, Nineveh is laid waste: who will bemoan her? whence shall I seek comforters for thee?

Again the Lord declares that He is against Nineveh; then He declares His plans to humiliate them for their horrible sins. The Assyrians prided themselves in wearing expensive clothing that was obtained through robbery and deceit. However, no matter how beautifully they adorned themselves outwardly, God saw their soiled hearts which He could no longer abide.

In ancient lands, sometimes a prisoner of war or a prostitute would be paraded through the street with his or her skirt lifted over their head to publicly shame them. This would be Nineveh's fate. The world would scorn as the Assyrians' nakedness was revealed. They would be a spectacle, with people pelting them with dirt and filth. No one would mourn for Nineveh. Instead, people would run from her, lest they were to meet a similar fate.

Talk About It:
1. Why would Nineveh's shame be exposed to the nations?
2. What would people say about Nineveh (v. 7)?
3. Why do people today apparently feel so little shame for their sins?

CONCLUSION

"The cruelty of the Assyrians is almost beyond belief. Their policy seems to have been one of calculated terror. Their own pictures show captives staked to the ground and being skinned alive! No wonder Nahum exulted at the overthrow of the proud, rich, cruel empire of Assyria" (*Zondervan Pictorial Bible Dictionary*).

The Assyrians would have never imagined their kingdom falling, yet that is exactly what happened. Likewise, people today who are leading self-consumed lives are rushing head-long to destruction, whether or not they realize it.

GOLDEN TEXT CHALLENGE

"THE LORD IS SLOW TO ANGER, AND GREAT IN POWER, AND WILL NOT AT ALL ACQUIT THE WICKED" (Nahum 1:3).

This one verse presents three great truths about God. First, He is not a quick-tempered God who acts irrationally. Instead, He is patient, merciful, and slow to anger.

Second, we must not think God's patience is a sign of weakness, for His power is awesome. He is able to do anything at any moment, but His actions will never violate His nature.

Third, while God's grace leads Him to extend mercy as far as possible, His holiness demands that those who reject His grace will one day be condemned.

Daily Devotions:
M. God Turns From Judgment
Jonah 3:1-10
T. God Explains His Mercy
Jonah 4:1-11
W. Supernatural Deliverance
2 Kings 19:32-36
T. God Judges Pride
Acts 12:20-24
F. Judgment Begins in God's House
1 Peter 4:12-19
S. God Rescues the Godly
2 Peter 2:4-9

Trust in God's Sovereignty (Habakkuk)

Habakkuk 1:1 through 3:19

Unit Theme:
God's Word in the Minor Prophets (Nahum to Malachi)

Central Truth:
Through faith in the Sovereign God, Christians find strength and joy for living.

Focus:
To realize that God is faithful regardless of our circumstances and rejoice in every situation.

Context:
Scholars differ on the time of Habakkuk's ministry, but generally agree it took place between 627 and 586 B.C.

Golden Text:
"I will rejoice in the Lord, I will joy in the God of my salvation" (Habakkuk 3:18).

Study Outline:
I. Complaining About Injustice (Habakkuk 1:1-11)
II. Lamenting Over Wickedness (Habakkuk 1:12—2:5)
III. Praying With Confidence (Habakkuk 3:1-19)

INTRODUCTION

We know very little about the personal life of the prophet Habakkuk. He is mentioned twice in the book that bears his name; apart from this, he is not mentioned in any other Old Testament book.

Habakkuk means "to fold the hands, to embrace." Martin Luther said his name "speaks as one who took his nation to his heart, comforted it and held it up, as one embraces and presses to his bosom a poor weeping child, calming and consoling it with good hope—if God so will" (Cunningham Geike, *Hours With the Bible*).

Apparently Habakkuk was a member of the Temple court and qualified to sing in the worship of the Temple. This would make him a member of one of the Levitical families who were responsible for music in the Temple.

Habakkuk was commissioned to show Judah that punishment was waiting them at the hands of the Chaldeans (neo-Babylonians), although they had not yet realized the threat Babylon posed. However, the prophet Isaiah had forewarned that the treasury of Judah's King Hezekiah would be carried to Babylon and Hezekiah's sons would be servants in the palace of Babylon's king (see Isaiah 39:5-7).

The prophecy of Habakkuk is given in two parts. The first part is a dialogue between God and the prophet concerning the judgment coming upon Judah through the Chaldeans. The second is an ode celebrating the punishment of God's enemies and the salvation of the righteous.

I. COMPLAINING ABOUT INJUSTICE (Habakkuk 1:1-11)

A. Perplexing Questions (vv. 1-3)

1. The burden which Habakkuk the prophet did see.

2. O Lord, how long shall I cry, and thou wilt not hear! even cry out unto thee of violence, and thou wilt not save!

3. Why dost thou shew me iniquity, and cause me to behold grievance? for spoiling and violence are before me: and there are that raise up strife and contention.

The word *burden* literally refers to a heavy load to be carried or lifted up. In verse 1 and in other writings of the prophets, it means a message or oracle from God—a proclamation, an utterance or prophecy. In this case, the message was burdensome because it denounced the sins of the people and pronounced a severe judgment on them and their place of habitation.

Habakkuk was burdened about the wickedness of the age in which he lived. Violence was epidemic, the law of God was forgotten, and human justice was perverted. Under the pressure of such corruption, Habakkuk apparently had cried often for the Lord to intervene, but no answer had come.

The prophet's complaint was that God would not save (v. 2). But Jehovah does not violate human will by directly interfering. He appeals through the moral urging of His law and the word of His prophets. When this fails, He interferes by judgment.

In verse 3, Habakkuk asked how God could look on Judah's condition without bringing it to an end. The prophet specifically mentioned five manifestations of sin he witnessed:

* *Iniquity*—troubling persons and troubling thoughts of Habakkuk's time
* *Grievance*—mischief and perversity used by those in political power
* *Spoiling*—destruction
* *Violence*—malicious action designed to injure another person
* *Strife and contention*—disputes

Habakkuk was a man of integrity and courage. His integrity was such that he was sincerely concerned about the silence and inaction of God. His courage was such that he did not hesitate to ask God, "Why?"

B. Honest Complaint (v. 4)

4. Therefore the law is slacked, and judgment doth never go forth: for the wicked doth compass about the righteous; therefore wrong judgment proceedeth.

There is a relationship between the horrors of the unstable society of verse 3 and the fact that the Law had lost its force in verse 4. The word *slacked* means being "feeble, faint, ineffective." The Law—which was meant to be the soul and the heart

Talk About It:
1. Why was Habakkuk angry with God?
2. Is it appropriate for us to pray such a prayer today? Why or why not?

"I have been driven many times to my knees by the overwhelming conviction that I had nowhere else to go. My own wisdom, and that of all about me, seemed insufficient for the day."
—**Abraham Lincoln**

Talk About It:
1. According to Habakkuk, why was injustice ("wrong judgment") prevailing?

2. How available is the Word of God in our society? How much is it read and taught? How much is it obeyed? What is the result?

of political, religious and domestic life—was paralyzed through the moral and spiritual apathy of the nation. There was no response and no obedience to what God had said.

The minority of righteous people were unable to effect meaningful change in society because of the widespread perversion among the people. Thus, injustice had become the norm.

C. Revealed Enemy (vv. 5-11)

(Habakkuk 1:6-11 is not included in the printed text.)

5. Behold ye among the heathen, and regard, and wonder marvellously: for I will work a work in your days, which ye will not believe, though it be told you.

Talk About It:
1. How was God going to amaze Habakkuk (vv. 5-9)?
2. Why were the Chaldeans so bold and arrogant? Where was their trust (vv. 10, 11)?

The Lord God answered Habakkuk's complaint by saying He was going to do something amazing—something the people of Judah would not believe even if He told them. Then God revealed His plan: He was raising up the Chaldeans, who would sweep across nations—including Judah—to claim them as their own.

The Chaldean army is compared to various animals: swifter than leopards, fiercer than ravenous wolves, swooping like vultures (v. 8). "They are a feared and dreaded people; they are a law to themselves and promote their own honor" (v. 7, *NIV*).

Bent on violence and certain that nothing could stop them, the Lord said the Chaldeans would mock and scoff at kings and princes. They would build earthen mounds that would enable them to capture fortified cities. The Chaldeans would attack like a stinging, suffocating desert wind, and capture more prisoners than they could count.

Rather than recognizing it was the living God who enabled them to wield such power, the Chaldeans would honor themselves and their god, Bel, so that they would "pass over" (v. 11)—move beyond all laws and restraints—and set the stage for their own eventual defeat. As Proverbs 16:18 says, "Pride goeth before destruction, and an haughty spirit before a fall."

II. LAMENTING OVER WICKEDNESS (Habakkuk 1:12—2:5)

A. Incomparable God (1:12-17)

(Habakkuk 1:14-17 is not included in the printed text.)

12. Art thou not from everlasting, O Lord my God, mine Holy One? We shall not die. O Lord, thou hast ordained them for judgment; and, O mighty God, thou hast established them for correction.

13. Thou art of purer eyes than to behold evil, and canst not look on iniquity: wherefore lookest thou upon them that deal treacherously, and holdest thy tongue when the wicked devoureth the man that is more righteous than he?

Even though the people of Judah would undergo severe punishment at the hands of the Chaldeans, Habakkuk declared, "We shall not die" (v. 12). The Lord was appointing the Chaldeans to carry out judgment and punishment against His people, but for the purpose of changing them, not destroying them.

God's eyes could not continue to "behold evil" (v. 13) without acting on it. The evil acts of Judah were bringing them to judgment, and the ensuing evil acts of the Chaldeans would also be judged in God's time. Even though God would use the Chaldeans for His purposes, He would not forever ignore their pride, worship of idols, and reckless violence.

Because Judah had rejected the ways of God, they had become "as the fishes of the sea" (v. 14) with no one to guide them. The Chaldeans were like fishermen using hooks and nets to easily capture Judah as well as other nations. Then they bragged on themselves and their god for their fishing success. Habakkuk asked, "Is he to keep on emptying his net, destroying nations without mercy?" (v. 17, *NIV*).

Talk About It:
1. Describe the significance of the three descriptions of God the prophet gives in verse 12.
2. What troubled Habakkuk regarding God's plan to use the Chaldeans (v. 13)?
3. How were the Chaldeans like fishermen (vv. 14-17)? Who were the fish? Whom did the Chaldeans praise for their victories?

B. Watching for God (2:1)

1. I will stand upon my watch, and set me upon the tower, and will watch to see what he will say unto me, and what I shall answer when I am reproved.

No doubt the prophet was overwhelmed by the voices of injustice and oppression around him; he was troubled by the foreign voices of the Chaldeans on the distant hills; he was stressed by his own voice raising questions with God. Yet, he had the spiritual maturity to move himself to a place where he could hear God speak.

Commentators are divided as to whether Habakkuk actually went to a high tower or in his spirit ascended to a high quiet place where he could hear from God. Either way, he prepared himself to listen for God's response to his complaint.

Talk About It:
1. What did the prophet decide to do?
2. Where should you go and what should you do when you need an answer from God?

C. Vision From God (vv. 2, 3)

2. And the Lord answered me, and said, Write the vision, and make it plain upon tables, that he may run that readeth it.

3. For the vision is yet for an appointed time, but at the end it shall speak, and not lie: though it tarry, wait for it; because it will surely come, it will not tarry.

In response to the prophet's plea, the Lord told him to write the vision he would receive. A vision is a revelation from God made known by the Holy Spirit. The "tables" to be used for recording the vision were tablets or plates. Such tablets were used to record messages to be placed in public places so the general public would have access to them.

Talk About It:
1. What is a vision from God, and why was it important for Habakkuk to receive a divine vision?

2. Why is it important
for the church today
to have vision?

"Visions in the Bible
were gifts of God.
They most often
were divine revela-
tions to a prophet.
Visions were sent by
God—not by mar-
keters or consultants
or demographers.
And at times eye-
sight was bad and
'there were not many
visions' (1 Samuel
3:1, *NIV*)."
—Leonard Sweet

Talk About It:
1. Why is the prideful
person "not upright"
(v. 4)?
2. How does some-
one "live by faith"
(v. 4)?

This message was written so people could quickly read it,
understand it, and run with it.

The vision would not be fulfilled immediately, but at God's
appointed time. When it was fulfilled, people would recognize
God's word had come to pass.

Waiting has always been a part of living for God. More than
25 times David spoke of his waiting for God. The thrust of the
Old Testament message is waiting the coming of the Messiah.
In the New Testament, the wait for Christ's second coming
begins, and we still wait expectantly for His return.

D. Trusting in God (vv. 4, 5)

**4. Behold, his soul which is lifted up is not upright in
him: but the just shall live by his faith.**

**5. Yea also, because he transgresseth by wine, he is a
proud man, neither keepeth at home, who enlargeth his
desire as hell, and is as death, and cannot be satisfied, but
gathereth unto him all nations, and heapeth unto him all
people.**

The Chaldean approach to life is distorted by pride and has
no meaning. It is irrational, unsatisfying and unreasonable. The
more that is gained, the more is wanted. This person drinks
wine and thirsts for more wine; he greedily takes from others
one day and then gathers more to himself the next day.

In contrast, the righteous person lives by his faith.
Possessing confidence in God, he is preserved and protected,
and his life has purpose. This person doesn't see and understand everything, but he trusts the One who sees and understands all.

A purposeless approach to life produces victims—cynics,
skeptics, pessimists, and often suicides. A faith approach produces victors—triumphant, radiant, wholesome, optimistic individuals.

III. PRAYING WITH CONFIDENCE (Habakkuk 3:1-19)
A. A Plea (vv. 1, 2)

1. A prayer of Habakkuk the prophet upon Shigionoth.

**2. O Lord, I have heard thy speech, and was afraid: O
Lord, revive thy work in the midst of the years, in the midst
of the years make known; in wrath remember mercy.**

One commentator explains the musical term *shigionoth*
(v. 1) to mean "in an impassioned or triumphal strain, with rapid
change of emotion." The idea is that this psalm was written
under strong emotion.

His complaints having been answered by the Lord,
Habakkuk wrote a psalm. He recognized that Judah and
Jerusalem must be punished for their sins. He accepted that

Talk About It:
1. What did
Habakkuk recall,
and what did he ask
God to do?

God was going to use the Chaldeans for His work of judgment, and then He would punish the Chaldeans for their wickedness.

"The whole picture of what is about to take place wrings from the prophet a confession, 'O Jehovah, I have heard the report of thee, and am afraid.' The report makes the prophet tremble, but his fear draws him closer to God. He calls upon Jehovah to revive His 'work in the midst of the years,' to carry out His purpose now as He has in the past. 'In the midst of the years' would be at the present time, the time between the announcement of judgment and its execution. Out of this fear comes the urgent plea of the prophet, 'In wrath remember mercy'" (Homer Hailey, *The Minor Prophets: A Commentary*).

2. Have you heard about or witnessed great deeds of God that you long to see manifested again today? Is this something you should pray for? Why or why not?

B. Memories (vv. 3-15)

(Habakkuk 3:6-15 is not included in the printed text.)

3. God came from Teman, and the Holy One from mount Paran. Selah. His glory covered the heavens, and the earth was full of his praise.

4. And his brightness was as the light; he had horns coming out of his hand: and there was the hiding of his power.

5. Before him went the pestilence, and burning coals went forth at his feet.

Habakkuk recalled God's past actions and revelations as a way of expressing faith that He would intervene mightily on Judah's behalf.

God's glory covered the heavens, His praise filled the earth, and His power radiated from His hands. As He walked on the earth, it shook, causing mountains to fall and hills to collapse. Plagues went before Him and pestilence followed Him, leaving His enemies in distress. In verses 8-10, God is pictured as using the rivers, streams and oceans of the earth for His purposes.

In verses 11-15, Habakkuk recalls that nothing was able to stop God when He set out to rescue His people. When God "came out to deliver" (v. 13, *NIV*), the sun and moon stood still, lightning served as God's weapon, the sea was trampled, and His enemies were crushed.

Talk About It:
1. From verses 3-15, list at least five acts of God that displayed His powers.
2. How is the Lord manifesting His power in the world today?

C. Hope (vv. 16-19)

16. When I heard, my belly trembled; my lips quivered at the voice: rottenness entered into my bones, and I trembled in myself, that I might rest in the day of trouble: when he cometh up unto the people, he will invade them with his troops.

17. Although the fig tree shall not blossom, neither shall fruit be in the vines; the labour of the olive shall fail, and the fields shall yield no meat; the flock shall be cut off from the fold, and there shall be no herd in the stalls:

1. Have you ever been physically affected by the words and deeds of God, as was Habakkuk (v. 16)? If so, what was the result?

2. How could Habakkuk maintain his faith in God even if his eyes saw no reason to do so?

"Sight is not faith, and hearing is not faith, neither is feeling faith; but believing when we neither see, hear, nor feel is faith; and everywhere the Bible tells us our salvation is to be by faith. Therefore we must believe before we feel, and often against our feelings."
—Hannah Whitall Smith

Daily Devotions:
M. God Will Avenge His Servants Deuteronomy 32:39-43
T. Rejoice in God's Victory 2 Chronicles 20:13-23
W. Trust in God to Defend Psalm 5:1-12
T. Rejoice When Persecuted Luke 6:20-26
F. Rejoicing Is a Witness Acts 16:25-34
S. Rejoice in God's Keeping Power Romans 8:28-39

18. Yet I will rejoice in the Lord, I will joy in the God of my salvation.
19. The Lord God is my strength, and he will make my feet like hinds' feet, and he will make me to walk upon mine high places. To the chief singer on my stringed instruments.

As Habakkuk reflected on the judgment that God's people and then the Chaldeans would suffer as part of God's ultimate victory, he said, "My heart pounded, my lips quivered . . . decay crept into my bones, and my legs trembled" (v. 16, *NIV*). This shaking of the flesh had a purpose: it brought the prophet to the rest in God that is available in the day of trouble. He would have patient confidence in God.

Verse 17 echoes the noise of desolation begun in verse 16. Habakkuk had no illusions about what his faith would accomplish. In an agrarian society, the failing of crops and the loss of livestock symbolized the worst of times. Yet, even when such calamity came to pass, the prophet would find joy in God.

Habakkuk reached the peak of faith in verse 19. In the midst of disappointment and in the absence of every sign of God's blessing, the prophet could rejoice, for God was his strength. Communion with God had enabled him to rise above his circumstances and lift his voice in praise. "Where there is no vision, the people perish" (Proverbs 29:18), but Habakkuk affirmed that where there is vision, the people may flourish.

CONCLUSION

Centuries after Habakkuk's day, Paul wrote similar words from a Roman prison. Paul said that even when he found himself in hunger and in need, he would be content because he could "do all things through Christ" (Philippians 4:11-13).

GOLDEN TEXT CHALLENGE

"I WILL REJOICE IN THE LORD, I WILL JOY IN THE GOD OF MY SALVATION" (Habakkuk 3:18).

Even while he trembled because of fear of the coming judgment, the prophet rejoiced in the Lord, whom he knew would save him. Shouldn't this same tension be part of the life of every believer today? We should be somber as we look at the world around us, knowing that God is going to bring severe judgment against every sinner, including those in our community, our neighborhood, and even our own family if they don't first turn to Him.

At the same time, we should rejoice in the knowledge that God will deliver us from the coming judgment because of our faith in Jesus Christ. Our salvation is secure in Him.

The Day of the Lord (Zephaniah)

Zephaniah 1:1 through 3:20

INTRODUCTION

The Hebrew word *Zephaniah* (ZEF-uh-NY-uh) translates as "God has hidden" or "God has treasured." It carries with it the same idea of Mary hiding or treasuring in her heart certain things concerning her beloved Son, Christ the Savior (see Luke 2:19).

In a time when nearly all of God's chosen people had turned from Him to the idolatrous worship of other gods, Zephaniah was counted among the few whose love and loyalty remained true to the Lord. Because of this, as his name suggests, God held the prophet as a beloved treasure hidden in His heart.

Zephaniah's royal and prophetic lineage possibly traces back to King Hezekiah, who was one of Judah's more righteous kings. The two kings who succeeded the throne after Hezekiah's death—Manasseh and Amon—were so wicked that by the time Josiah inherited the throne, Judah was overrun with every kind of evil imaginable. Moral and spiritual corruption, as well as apostasy and idolatry, were widespread.

King Josiah, who was a cousin of the prophet Zephaniah, purged the nation of every form of idol worship. Afterward, he began the work of repairing God's holy temple. Zephaniah prophesied to Judah during Josiah's reign (641-609 B.C.).

During Josiah's restoration of the Temple, Hilkiah the high priest found a copy of the Book of the Law. King Josiah was so profoundly moved after hearing and confirming the scroll's contents that he took great measures to lead God's people in a national revival.

Scriptures reveal that God moved through four key men during that time to bring His beloved people back to Him. Besides King Josiah, God also worked through the high priest Hilkiah and the prophets Jeremiah and Zephaniah. It is believed that Zephaniah delivered his prophecy sometime during the early part of King Josiah's reign, about 620 B.C., before Judah's great revival. No doubt, Zephaniah's stirring prophecy helped to inspire Judah's reformation.

Unit Theme:
God's Word in the Minor Prophets (Nahum to Malachi)

Central Truth:
God seeks to reconcile people to Himself.

Focus:
To investigate the Day of the Lord and live in right relationship with God.

Context:
Zephaniah prophesied to Judah during Josiah's reign.

Golden Text:
"The Lord thy God in the midst of thee is mighty; he will save, he will rejoice over thee with joy" (Zephaniah 3:17).

Study Outline:
I. Day of God's Wrath (Zephaniah 1:1-18)
II. Day of Repentance (Zephaniah 2:1-3; 3:8-13)
III. Day of Restoration (Zephaniah 3:14-20)

I. DAY OF GOD'S WRATH (Zephaniah 1:1-18)

God's prophets often voiced the phrase "the Day of the Lord." It points to a specific time in history and in the future when God intervenes in the affairs of people bringing judgment and punishment for sin. Zephaniah expresses a fearful description of this "day" which reveals God's wrath. It is a day, he warns, that will come soon.

A. Idolatry Rebuked (vv. 1-9)

(Zephaniah 1:7-9 is not included in the printed text.)

2. I will utterly consume all things from off the land, saith the Lord.

3. I will consume man and beast; I will consume the fowls of the heaven, and the fishes of the sea, and the stumbling blocks with the wicked: and I will cut off man from off the land, saith the Lord.

4. I will also stretch out mine hand upon Judah, and upon all the inhabitants of Jerusalem; and I will cut off the remnant of Baal from this place, and the name of the Chemarims with the priests;

5. And them that worship the host of heaven upon the housetops; and them that worship and that swear by the Lord, and that swear by Malcham;

6. And them that are turned back from the Lord; and those that have not sought the Lord, nor enquired for him.

Talk About It:

1. Describe everything God said He would "consume" (vv. 2, 3). What does this mean?

2. List the people God was going to judge (vv. 4-6).

3. Describe the event the Lord would "bid his guests" to attend (vv. 7-9).

The first chapter in the Book of Zephaniah is similar to Genesis 6. There we read how the "wickedness of man" was so great that "every imagination" of their heart was continually evil (v. 5). God was so moved with righteous anger that He "was sorry that He made man" (v. 6, *NKJV*). He then pronounced His coming judgment on all those who refused to repent.

Centuries later, Zephaniah bears God's heart showing us that He is again grieved at idolatrous sin. The prophet clearly defines his message as "the word of the Lord." Vividly, he describes God's impending judgment toward those who chose to continue their evil practices of idol worship.

The fact that throughout history God sent forth His prophets warning His chosen people of His impending judgment reveals His immeasurable grace toward them. No matter how great the sin, God is ever willing to extend His all-encompassing forgiveness to those who seek Him with a penitent heart.

Zephaniah raised his prophetic voice first against God's chosen people, who chose not to totally abandon the worship of the one true God. Instead, they tried to combine their worship of Him with the worship of pagan gods. Judah went so far as to import statues or images of false gods for the purpose of practicing pagan worship. Idol worship was so widespread in

Zephaniah's day that nearly every Judean home housed a statue of a false god.

Modern-day believers may not own miniature statues of false gods. However, it is possible to allow other types of idols to interfere with the quality of our worship of God. Money, health, television, the Internet, and even ministry can become idols. This happens when more time and effort is unnecessarily given to these things than to giving God quality time in prayer, Bible study, church fellowship, and other aspects of the Christian life.

One of the primary reasons for God's fierce wrath toward pagan worship was the evil and grotesque rituals practiced by pagans. When King Josiah began to reign, the Judean people were participating in the worship practices of three main pagan gods: the Canaanite god Baal, the goddess Ashtoreth, and the Ammonite god Malcham or Molech.

Modern-day Satan worship traces its roots back to Baal worship. In fact, the New Testament word *Beelzebub*, the prince of demons (Mark 3:22) is rendered *Baal-Zebub* in the Old Testament (2 Kings 1). To worship Baal was to worship Satan, for Baal-Zebub was known as the supreme evil spirit in Old Testament times. The satanic priests of Baal were known as *Chemarims* (Zephaniah 1:4)—some think this is because of the black robes they wore, which are still worn today.

Along with Satan or Baal worship, the Judeans also worshiped *Ashtoreth*, believed by many to be Baal's wife. Ritual worship of Ashtoreth involved the forbidden practice of astrology (the worship of the sun, moon and stars). Both Baal and Ashtoreth worship included gross exhibitions of sexual immorality.

A third deity worshiped in this day was *Malcham* (Milcom or Molech). Among other abominations, the Judeans sacrificed their young children to this deity on fiery altars. As stated earlier, King Josiah went to great lengths to rid Judah of these false gods. Around the same time, Zephaniah harshly rebuked God's people for proclaiming allegiance to and practicing worship rituals of these three pagan gods along with the worship of God (Zephaniah 1:4, 5).

Zephaniah also prophesied God's judgment toward the cultic priests responsible for corrupting His people (vv. 4, 8). They were the ones who originally set the traps (stumbling blocks) that lured His people to commit forbidden abominations. They too would experience His day of wrath. Like a flash flood, God would sweep away even the symbols of nature the pagan idols represented.

Finally, Zephaniah turned his attention toward "those who have turned back from following the Lord, and have not sought the Lord, nor inquired of Him" (v. 6, *NKJV*). Just like a grieving

"Belief in an ultimate judgment and belief in the immortality of the soul" are the "two necessary stimuli" for people endeavoring to lead ethical lives.

—Wernher von Braun

parent, hurt and angered over a child's horrid behavior, God cautions His children through Zephaniah to keep silent (v. 7). Emphatically, he declares, "Hold thy peace at the presence of the Lord." There are times when it is necessary to go before God with a trembling and humble spirit of the fear of the Lord and just silently weep for God's grieving heart for our sins. Zephaniah called for just such a time for all of God's chosen people.

B. Judgment Predicted (vv. 10-18)

(Zephaniah 1:10-13 is not included in the printed text.)

14. The great day of the Lord is near, it is near, and hasteth greatly, even the voice of the day of the Lord: the mighty man shall cry there bitterly.

15. That day is a day of wrath, a day of trouble and distress, a day of wasteness and desolation, a day of darkness and gloominess, a day of clouds and thick darkness,

16. A day of the trumpet and alarm against the fenced cities, and against the high towers.

17. And I will bring distress upon men, that they shall walk like blind men, because they have sinned against the Lord: and their blood shall be poured out as dust, and their flesh as the dung.

18. Neither their silver nor their gold shall be able to deliver them in the day of the Lord's wrath; but the whole land shall be devoured by the fire of his jealousy: for he shall make even a speedy riddance of all them that dwell in the land.

Talk About It:

1. Why would the Lord "search Jerusalem with candles" (v. 12)?

2. In verse 12, what were the complacent people saying about the Lord? Is this a common philosophy today?

3. Who would "walk like blind men" (v. 17)? Why?

4. How valuable will material wealth be on Judgment Day (v. 18)?

The remaining verses of this chapter describe God's forthcoming day of judgment. Zephaniah's prophecy of this terrible event serves also as a reminder of God's future and final judgment day. The prophet boldly declares that a day is soon coming when God's judgment will be so severe that people of position and power will bitterly weep because of the anguish of utter ruin.

In that terrible day, they will discover that even their wealth will be of no use. God will cause it to be taken from them. Also, God will lift His hand of protection from Judah. Their dreaded enemy, the Chaldeans, will seize them. Nebuchadnezzar's massive army will storm through the Fish Gate on the northern side of the city and break down their fortified walls (v. 10). Some will die. Most, however, will be taken captive. Judah's beloved homeland will be reduced to a charred heap of rubble.

In that terrible day, no one will escape God's judgment. Deceitful merchants, evil extortionists, and even the spiritually complacent will experience the wrath of God's righteous anger at wickedness and sin (vv. 11, 12).

Zephaniah's graphic portrayal of Jerusalem's utter destruction was purposed by God to be a preventative measure. We

The Day of the Lord

need to realize that when everything else has failed, God might use a spiritual shock treatment, if necessary, as a wake-up call.

Zephaniah declares that the overwhelming devastation of God's judgment day will cause people to walk as blind men (v. 17). In other words, they won't know what hit them. His judgment will be so great that, like a wildfire, it will spread and consume everything in its path.

The prophet explains all of this will happen because God's people refused to repent. The seed of God's Word through His prophets habitually fell on the stony ground of His chosen people's hearts, taking no root. Genesis 6:3 warns us that God's Spirit "shall not strive with man forever" (*NKJV*). Though God's grace is immeasurable, even He has His limits.

II. DAY OF REPENTANCE (Zephaniah 2:1-3; 3:8-13)

It is never God's will for anyone to perish. Although His wrath is great and terrible, His mercy and forgiveness is even greater. God always provides every opportunity for repentance. He exhorts His people everywhere to escape His judgment for sin by seeking His forgiveness.

A. Appeal for National Repentance (2:1-3)

1. Gather yourselves together, yea, gather together, O nation not desired;

2. Before the decree bring forth, before the day pass as the chaff, before the fierce anger of the Lord come upon you, before the day of the Lord's anger come upon you.

3. Seek ye the Lord, all ye meek of the earth, which have wrought his judgment; seek righteousness, seek meekness: it may be ye shall be hid in the day of the Lord's anger.

This chapter opens with God's prophet making an urgent appeal to the people of Judah for national repentance. The Judean nation had fallen into such a state of utter apostasy that Zephaniah called for a national spiritual gathering. It was time to fall before God in humble repentance. This was the only way Judah could avert His coming judgment for their sins.

The nation's spiritual decline had caused the people of Judah to become calloused in their affections toward God. Though they were a people who belonged to a holy God, they had lost their sense of shame toward sin. They had also lost any fear of the consequences of sin. Because of their lack of shame, no sin was hidden to them. Worse still, their sins were tolerated by everyone else around including Judah's spiritual leaders, who were also steeped in sinful behavior.

The years spent indulging in unrepentant sins caused God's people to experience a spiritual separation from Him. In fact, Zephaniah described Judah as "a nation not desired" (v. 1).

Talk About It:
1. Why did Zephaniah call Judah "a nation not desired" (v. 1)?
2. For whom did the prophet hold out hope, and what did he urge them to do?

The lack of sorrow for sin and the lack of the fear of the Lord also meant the lack of God's presence. This is the saddest of all human conditions.

For this reason, the prophet Zephaniah makes one final plea for God's chosen people to repent of their sins and renew their devotion to God. His urgent plea highlights the fact that if God was so willing to forgive His people of such wicked behavior in the Old Testament, He is just as willing to forgive those who ask Him today. Obeying His will is our only assurance, as well, of escaping the coming Judgment Day.

The faithful few in Zephaniah's day—those who had not hardened their hearts against God—would be spared from His wrath. God promised that He would protect His righteous remnant in a special way. Like the meaning of His prophet's name, they too would be treasure hidden in Him. In Psalm 83:3, David also describes those faithful to God as His "hidden ones." God's divine protection is guaranteed to all who hide in God through Christ (Colossians 3:3).

B. A Call to Wait (3:8-13)

(Zephaniah 3:9-13 is not included in the printed text.)

to the prey (v. 8)—
to plunder

8. Therefore wait ye upon me, saith the Lord, until the day that I rise up to the prey: for my determination is to gather the nations, that I may assemble the kingdoms, to pour upon them mine indignation, even all my fierce anger: for all the earth shall be devoured with the fire of my jealousy.

Talk About It:
1. Why was Judah's righteous remnant encouraged to wait?
2. Compare the people who would be condemned (v. 11) with those whom God would bless (v. 12).
3. What can take away fear (v. 13)? Why?

Here God speaks through His prophet to Judah's righteous remnant. He encourages them to wait upon Him and watch for His completed restoration work in His people. God promises that at His appointed time He will gather and judge all nations. He will then purify His people and take away all pride from them. They will trust in the Lord.

All throughout Scripture, God expresses His jealous love for His people. God's chosen Judean nation, however, had made herself an enemy of God because of her sins. Therefore, God would also rise up as Judah's enemy and allow His righteous judgment to descend on her.

The Gospels reveal to us that Christ's physical enemies nailed Him to the cross of Calvary. Hebrews 6:6 says that if we fall away from the Christian faith, as Judah fell away from her faith, and remain in sin, as she did, then we too make ourselves God's enemy. In a spiritual sense we crucify Christ again because our sin exposes His name to shame and disgrace. Therefore, those who fall away must be brought back to God through repentance.

Zephaniah prophesies in verse 9 that God will restore to the people "a pure language," meaning they will return to worshiping the Lord God alone. God's divine purification of His people will cause their devotion to be undivided. They will honor God as did His servant King David, who declared, "Their sorrows shall be multiplied that hasten after another god: their drink-offerings of blood will I not offer, nor take up their names into my lips" (Psalm 16:4).

Speaking through His prophet, God promises to purge from His people all the arrogant and prideful spiritual leaders. Only an afflicted and poor people purified of sin are promised the peace of His divine presence in their midst. The progression of God's glorious promise is also extended to all New Testament believers who remain faithful to Him. The prophet's message assures us that a day is soon coming when all of God's dispersed people will be brought into God's land and bring Him the offering of praise. He again will dwell in their midst, this time for eternity.

III. DAY OF RESTORATION (Zephaniah 3:14-20)

Zephaniah began his prophetic ministry with a harsh message from God, but he now shows us the softer side of God. It is God mending broken relationships with Him through His merciful love.

A. God's Rapturous Love (vv. 14-17)

14. Sing, O daughter of Zion; shout, O Israel; be glad and rejoice with all the heart, O daughter of Jerusalem.

15. The Lord hath taken away thy judgments, he hath cast out thine enemy: the king of Israel, even the Lord, is in the midst of thee: thou shalt not see evil any more.

16. In that day it shall be said to Jerusalem, Fear thou not: and to Zion, Let not thine hands be slack.

17. The Lord thy God in the midst of thee is mighty; he will save, he will rejoice over thee with joy; he will rest in his love, he will joy over thee with singing.

The trembling child who once faced the wrath of a hurt and angry Parent over his offenses would now experience that same Parent's complete forgiveness. Zephaniah prophesies that God's judgments of Judah's sins have come to an end. God's forgiveness and grace also meant the end of the nation's suffering.

Twice in this passage God assures His people that He is in their midst (vv. 15, 17). God's holy presence is Judah's assurance of His divine protection from her enemies. It is only in the presence of God that His people need not fear anything. God's power drives away His people's enemies, thereby silencing all of His children's fears. He allows nothing to come near to hurt those who are embraced in His holy arms.

Talk About It:
1. What should cause God's people to sing and rejoice (vv. 14, 15)?
2. Instead of one's hands being "slack" (*limp*, v. 16), what should they do?
3. What causes God to sing, and why (v. 17)?

Zephaniah's poetic words open our mind's eye to a scene of God's parental love. As any parent would be, God is also pleased when His children are genuinely sorrowful over a wrong they have committed. The temporary separation from a parent's approval proves to be more than enough chastisement for most children.

The feeling of being alone often causes a child to seek the security of his parent's loving embrace. In order to secure the reassurance of his parent's love, the child tearfully expresses both his apology and his love. He then seals his words with his own tender embrace.

Because of God's intimate relationship with Judah, God's presence was, in effect, His divine way of embracing His beloved people. Zephaniah shows us how God embraced, caressed, and adoringly brooded over His penitent children. It was as if God gently rocked them in His arms while He held them close to His heart. His covenant relationship with Judah was once again restored.

God's own heart, once so full of grief and hurt, was now flooded over with joy and love. The tender embrace of the Judean nation and God sealed their bond of love. In this tender moment God quieted His people with His love. The blessedness of God's love for His own fills His holy being with joy. God breaks the silence of this precious moment with a song of love rooted in the depth of His innermost being.

To know this secret place in God's heart means to abide in His covenant love. Those who share His love, share His joy.

> "If you have no joy, there's a leak in your Christianity somewhere."
> —Billy Sunday

B. Divine Promises Restored (vv. 18-20)

18. I will gather them that are sorrowful for the solemn assembly, who are of thee, to whom the reproach of it was a burden.

> her that halteth (v. 19)—the lame

19. Behold, at that time I will undo all that afflict thee: and I will save her that halteth, and gather her that was driven out; and I will get them praise and fame in every land where they have been put to shame.

20. At that time will I bring you again, even in the time that I gather you: for I will make you a name and a praise among all people of the earth, when I turn back your captivity before your eyes, saith the Lord.

In these last verses, Zephaniah foretells of a future time that God's people have yet to fully experience. Their forthcoming years spent in Babylonian captivity would prevent the Judean nation from gathering together for the purpose of worshiping God. Because of this, the nation would one day long for their sacred, solemn assembly.

God promises His beloved people that He will turn their

Talk About It:
1. What would God "undo" (v. 19)?
2. What did God promise to do for the scattered and suffering remnant people?

The Day of the Lord

longing into joy. He will gather them together and make them an object of His praise. His chosen nation's fame will quickly spread throughout all other nations in the world.

God also promises the Judean people that He will undo all that has afflicted them. In other words, God will break their enemy's yoke of bondage that has caused His people such great suffering.

The prophet Zephaniah declares that God himself will bring His dispersed people together and lead them back to their promised land. There they will experience His presence and His many blessings. Both God's divine presence amid His people and the repossession of their beloved homeland means the restoration of God's favor. This will be cause for great joy for the Judean nation.

The last words of Zephaniah's prophecy were only partially fulfilled in his day. The complete fulfillment will come in the millennial future. At that time, every nation in the millennial period will look upon God's chosen nation and share His beloved people's joy because of Him who is in their midst lovingly watching over them.

This latter part of Zephaniah's prophecy is a message of hope to all who believe. The forgiveness and deliverance God promised through Zephaniah is still extended to any who turn to Him in faith.

CONCLUSION

If God's wrath and judgments for sin prevent anyone from perishing, then His judgments have served their purpose. God desires all people to live in a covenant relationship with Him. Only then will we have divine rest in His love.

GOLDEN TEXT CHALLENGE

"THE LORD THY GOD IN THE MIDST OF THEE IS MIGHTY; HE WILL SAVE, HE WILL REJOICE OVER THEE WITH JOY" (Zephaniah 3:17).

Here's the scene: The people of God have turned to Him wholeheartedly, and their time of suffering is over. The presence of Almighty God is with them; they know they are safe, so they are shouting praises to God, rejoicing with all their heart.

What is the Lord's response? He takes "great delight" (NIV) in His people, just as a groom is thrilled with his new bride. He quiets His people with the calm, reassuring security of His love. And then the Lord himself breaks into song, rejoicing over His children! This brings to mind Jesus' description of the joy that breaks out in heaven when one unbeliever comes to Christ (see Luke 15:7, 10).

When we rejoice in God, He rejoices in us!

From Mess to Masterpiece

J. Stuart Holden tells of an old Scottish mansion close to his summer home. The walls of one room were filled with sketches made by distinguished artists. The practice began after a pitcher of soda water was spilled on a freshly decorated wall and left an unsightly stain. At the time, a noted artist was a guest in the house. One day with a few masterful strokes of a piece of charcoal, the artist transformed that ugly spot into the outline of a beautiful waterfall, bordered by trees and wildlife.

—Charles Swindoll, *The Quest for Character*

Daily Devotions:
M. Day of Judgment
  Joel 2:1-11
T. Repent and Turn
  to God
  Joel 2:12-20
W. God Restores
  His People
  Joel 2:28-32
T. God Saves the
  Nations
  Romans 11:5-12
F. Ministry of
  Reconciliation
  2 Corinthians
  5:11-21
S. Reconciled to
  God
  Ephesians
  2:11-22

Bible Insight

WRITING PROPHETS

Some of the greatest prophets, such as Elijah and Elisha, never committed their prophecies to writing. The prophetic message was principally an oral message, intended for proclamation rather than writing, and effective immediately rather than a delayed response.

But there were 16 prophets who did write, and it is from their writings that we learn most about the prophetic ministry. Four are called Major Prophets, for no reason except the length of their writings. These are Isaiah, Jeremiah, Ezekiel and Daniel.

Twelve are called Minor Prophets, not because they were less important or effective than those called Major, but because their writings were shorter. These are Hosea, Joel, Amos, Obadiah, Jonah, Micah, Nahum, Habakkuk, Zephaniah, Haggai, Zechariah and Malachi.

These 16 literary prophets lived over a period of some 425 years which covered a large, important stretch of Israelite history. There is no way of dating the work of individuals with unquestioned certainty. Such dating is a tedious process of comparing persons and circumstances mentioned in the books with known historical dates and records.

The writing prophets all lived after David and Solomon's united kingdom was divided into the southern kingdom (Judah) under Rehoboam and the northern kingdom (Judah) under Jeroboam in 930 B.C.

- Seven of the prophets ministered before the conquest of the northern kingdom by Assyria in 721 B.C. They were Obadiah, Joel, Jonah, Hosea, Amos, Isaiah and Micah.
- Four others lived during the 150 years that the southern kingdom survived alone, before Judah was conquered and its people taken captive to Babylon in 597 B.C. They were Nahum, Zephaniah, Jeremiah and Habakkuk.
- Two prophets—Daniel and Ezekiel—preached during the exile in Babylon.
- The Jews were restored to their homeland in 536 B.C., after which three final prophets—Haggai, Zechariah and Malachi—did their work.

(From *The Living Book*, by Charles W. Conn)

TIMELINE OF THE MINOR PROPHETS

Name & Meaning	Probable date (B.C.)	Audience	Main Theme
Obadiah: Servant of Yahweh	840-830	Edom	Edom to be judged for mistreating the Jews
Joel: Yahweh is God	830-750	Israel	The Day of the Lord
Jonah: Dove	786-746	Nineveh	God's desire to save all people
Hosea: Salvation	760-720	Israel	God's unending love for people
Amos: Burden-bearer	760-753	Israel, Judah, other nations	God's call for justice and righteousness
Micah: Who is like Yahweh?	735-700	Samaria, Jerusalem and whole earth	Call for mercy and justice
Nahum: Comfort	686-620	Assyrians— mainly those in Nineveh	God jealously protects His people.
Zephaniah: Hidden by Yahweh	640-621	All people	The Day of the Lord
Habakkuk: Embrace	608-598	Babylon	Divine call for faithfulness
Haggai: Festival	520	The returned remnant	Prioritizing the house of God
Zechariah: Yahweh remembers	520-514	The returned remnant	God will rule the earth.
Malachi: My messenger	433-400	Israel	Honor God and wait for His righteousness.

Consider Your Ways (Haggai)

Haggai 1:1 through 2:23

Unit Theme:
God's Word in the Minor Prophets (Nahum to Malachi)

Central Truth:
God's blessings come to those who live to please Him.

Focus:
To examine the importance we place on the things of God and put Him first in all we do.

Context:
Haggai prophesied to the Jews in 520 B.C.

Golden Text:
"Thus saith the Lord of hosts; Consider your ways" (Haggai 1:5).

Study Outline:
I. Put God First (Haggai 1:1-11)
II. Live in God's Presence (Haggai 1:12-15; 2:1-9)
III. Experience God's Blessings (Haggai 2:10-23)

INTRODUCTION

The Temple that lay in ruins in Haggai's day once stood as the glory of all Israel. Its splendor far surpassed even King David's expectations for a magnificent sanctuary. Prior to his death, David provided Solomon with much of the materials necessary for building the Temple. Experts estimate that David's contribution of the gold and silver alone was worth nearly $3 million.

King Solomon used his architectural skills in such an exemplary fashion that, during its seven-and-a-half year construction, not a single tool used by the 180,000 laborers was ever heard inside the Temple. The Temple's stone walls and floors were then paneled with cedar and overlaid with gold. The entire Temple was so elaborate that its fame spread throughout the world.

Pagan religions often built temples to house statues of their false gods. Solomon knew, however, that the one true God could never be housed. His dual purpose for building such a grand sanctuary was merely to provide a dwelling place for God's name, symbolizing His presence, and to serve as the Israelites' central place of worship.

After its completion, Solomon dedicated the Temple to God with a humble prayer (see 2 Chronicles 6; 7). He acknowledged that if the highest heavens couldn't contain God, then how much less could the house he built. Solomon concluded his dedication prayer with an exhortation for the Israelites to fully commit to God through obedience.

During a second visitation, God assured Solomon that He accepted the Temple and consecrated it as a permanent dwelling place for His name. However, God warned Solomon of the Temple's destruction if he or His people disobeyed Him and followed after other gods. God also warned that without His divine presence, His people would be captured in war and deported to foreign lands.

All of the Israelites, including Solomon, failed to heed God's warning. Less than 500 years after King Solomon's death the Babylonians, under Nebuchadnezzar's leadership, raided and burned the Temple, destroyed the land, and took captive all but a remnant of God's people.

I. PUT GOD FIRST (Haggai 1:2-11)

A. 'The Time Is Not Come' (vv. 2-4)

2. Thus speaketh the Lord of hosts, saying, This people say, The time is not come, the time that the Lord's house should be built.

3. Then came the word of the Lord by Haggai the prophet, saying,

4. Is it time for you, O ye, to dwell in your cieled houses, and this house lie waste?

After 70 years in Babylonian captivity, King Cyrus of Persia liberated the Israelites. He made a decree that they were to return to their homeland and rebuild the Temple. He also ordered that the Persian treasury pay the expenses of the restoration work. When God desires His people to complete a work, He always provides every necessity to complete the task.

God prophesied through Isaiah, 200 years earlier, that a king named Cyrus would play a major role in the deliverance of His people and in the restoration of His Temple (see Isaiah 44:28). Our omniscient God knew His people would turn from Him to follow after other gods. Yet, because of His love for them, He planned centuries in advance for their deliverance.

What was true for the Israelites then is true for God's people today. His love for us and His willingness to forgive us is not a license to sin. However, if we do sin, God has provided a Mediator, Jesus Christ. He is our deliverance from sin's penalty once we have confessed and repented of sin.

Cyrus was made aware of Isaiah's prophecy. He recognized that God had chosen him to accomplish His will for the Temple's restoration. God used Isaiah's prophecy to stir the king to return the Temple's gold and silver vessels which Nebuchadnezzar had taken to adorn his own pagan temple.

In addition, King Cyrus abundantly supplied the Israelites with the necessary means for the long 700-mile journey back to Jerusalem (see Ezra 1). When God chooses to bless, His blessings are often greater than our expectations.

Some of the Israelites decided to remain in Babylon where they had grown accustomed to their captive lifestyle. Those who chose to return to Jerusalem were mostly leaders from the tribe of Judah. Because of this, the Israelites were called Jews from this point on in history.

After reaching their homeland, the Jews returned to their own cities. However, under Joshua's and Zerubbabel's leadership, all of the Jews gathered in Jerusalem to rebuild the Temple's sacrificial altar (Ezra 3:1-3). Before we can experience God's abiding presence, we must kneel before His altar and experience His holy presence. Only then can we know the joy of being forgiven and spiritually restored.

cieled houses (v. 4)—paneled houses

Talk About It:
1. Why were people saying the time had not yet come for God's house to be rebuilt?
2. Is Haggai's challenge in verse 4 a message Christians need to hear today? Why or why not?

"O Lord, let us not live to be useless, for Christ's sake."
—**John Wesley**

During their captive years the Jews were not able to worship at the Temple's altar. Because of their deliverance, the Jews now enjoyed a lengthy time of worship celebrating the Feast of Tabernacles. Experts agree it was approximately one year later that the Jews began the actual work of restoring the Temple. Their zeal was short-lived, however, when heavy opposition discouraged them from continuing the restoration work.

History reveals that whenever God's people begin a work for Him, opposition meets them head on. Discouragement is one of the Enemy's greatest weapons. Sadly, many testify of its effectiveness.

Disillusioned, the Jews soon abandoned their restoration project. Instead, they focused their efforts on rebuilding their own houses. For the next 16 years the Jews endured hardships and poverty. In 520 B.C. God sent His prophet Haggai to them with a strong word of rebuke for abandoning His ruined Temple.

B. 'Consider Your Ways' (vv. 5-7)

5. Now therefore thus saith the Lord of hosts; Consider your ways.

6. Ye have sown much, and bring in little; ye eat, but ye have not enough; ye drink, but ye are not filled with drink; ye clothe you, but there is none warm; and he that earneth wages earneth wages to put it into a bag with holes.

7. Thus saith the Lord of hosts; Consider your ways.

In order to arouse the Jews' conscience concerning their apostasy, God allowed them to go through seasons of drought and poverty. Yet, the Jews still failed to regard the obvious. They continued to show more interest in building their own houses than in building God's house. The prophet Haggai's harsh message from the Lord opened their eyes for the reason God had allowed so much suffering. God wanted His people to return to their first love for Him.

"There is no contradiction between the description of poverty here and the description of the ceiled, expensive houses of verse 4. As in other societies, the wealthy were found along with the poorer class. That age, as every age in man's history, proved the truth of Matthew 6:33. When God is forgotten, all labor is without profit. Materialistic civilizations of this day need to ponder this truth as much as any other" (Wycliffe).

C. 'Build the House' (vv. 8-11)

8. Go up to the mountain, and bring wood, and build the house; and I will take pleasure in it, and I will be glorified, saith the Lord.

9. Ye looked for much, and, lo it came to little; and when ye brought it home, I did blow upon it. Why? saith the Lord

Talk About It:
1. Why were the people sowing, drinking and working, yet hungry, thirsty and in financial need?
2. Why did the Lord twice say, "Consider your ways"?

Consider Your Ways

of hosts. Because of mine house that is waste, and ye run every man unto his own house.

10. Therefore the heaven over you is stayed from dew, and the earth is stayed from her fruit.

11. And I called for a drought upon the land, and upon the mountains, and upon the corn, and upon the new wine, and upon the oil, and upon that which the ground bringeth forth, and upon men, and upon cattle, and upon all the labour of the hands.

The Jews' physical suffering mirrored their spiritual suffering from the years of neglect of worshiping God. He desired His people to renew their spiritual zeal and fervently pursue the rebuilding of His Temple. In other words, God longed for worship to be restored.

The apostle Paul wrote, "It is good to be zealously affected always in a good thing" (Galatians 4:18). Allowing spiritual zeal to wane only gives rise to spiritual apathy. When God's people lose their Christian zeal, their priorities are out of order.

Haggai's message for the Jews to put God first was not restricted to his day alone. Centuries later Christ elaborated on a similar message. In Matthew 6:25-33 He encouraged New Testament believers to also experience God's covenant promises by making His desires their first priority.

The prophet Haggai's first task was to caution the Jews to consider their ways and put their priorities in order. His second task was to incite God's people to fulfill God's desire. God's powerful Word, spoken through His servant Haggai, accomplished both.

In 2 Chronicles 7:14, God made a covenant promise to His people: "If my people, which are called by my name, shall humble themselves, and pray, and seek my face, and turn from their wicked ways; then will I hear from heaven, and will forgive their sin, and will heal their land."

This promise is just as applicable to His people today. Backsliding in one's heart is as serious an offense as backsliding in one's actions. Yet, God's forgiveness is equally serious. His ears are ever open to the prayers of those who repent. He calls backsliders to return.

II. LIVE IN GOD'S PRESENCE (Haggai 1:12-14; 2:1-9)
A. God's Promised Presence (1:12-14)

12. Then Zerubbabel the son of Shealtiel, and Joshua the son of Josedech, the high priest, with all the remnant of the people, obeyed the voice of the Lord their God, and the words of Haggai the prophet, as the Lord their God had sent him, and the people did fear before the Lord.

13. Then spake Haggai the Lord's messenger in the Lord's message unto the people, saying, I am with you, saith the Lord.

Talk About It:
1. Why did God want His people to rebuild the Temple?
2. What did God "blow away" (v. 9, NIV), and why?
3. How did God use nature to speak to His people (vv. 10, 11)?

Zerubbabel (*zuh-RUB-uh-buhl*) (v. 12)—the governor of the Jews when they returned to their homeland

14. And the Lord stirred up the spirit of Zerubbabel the son of Shealtiel, governor of Judah, and the spirit of Joshua the son of Josedech, the high priest, and the spirit of all the remnant of the people; and they came and did work in the house of the Lord of hosts, their God.

Talk About It:
1. Why was a fear of the Lord (v. 12) so important at this time?
2. What stirred the people to action?
3. What does it take to motivate believers today to get busy for God?

In John 10:4, Christ explained that God's people know His voice. This was certainly true of the Jews to whom Haggai spoke. They recognized immediately the voice of the Lord expressed through His prophet. The Jews responded to God's stirring word for them with a renewed holy fear.

God's message to His people resulted in a national conviction for the neglect of their spiritual priorities. The Jews acknowledged the truth of God's stern rebuke through Haggai. God would no longer tolerate their leaving His Temple in a charred heap of ruins.

God's chosen people knew His requirements for receiving His blessings and of His chastisements for disobedience. Yet, for years God's Temple lay in ruins. Therefore, God was just in chastening His people by allowing suffering and hardship. The Jews acknowledged their sins and, in the weeks following, went through the required purification to be cleansed of them.

Our heavenly Father never allows any of His erring children to stray very far without cautioning them with a word of correction. His methods of bringing that word vary. Whatever method He chooses, however, He reasons with love.

God desires all of His children to live in a close and abiding fellowship with Him. This is reflected in the second part of God's message spoken through Haggai: "I am with you, saith the Lord." This word had an equally powerful effect on the Jews.

"To some men who follow Him, God gives not only a vision of unlimited horizons, but a strong back and a determined mind to push on toward those horizons. As always, the horizons are ever moving ahead of them—ever out of reach—yet God's men stride on!"
—Victor E. Cory

The assurance of His divine presence motivated God's beloved nation to act with one heart and mind to obey His will. The Jews corporately set out to restore God's Temple, the symbol of His presence.

Even to this day, the voice of the Lord pierces our hearts with the most reassuring of all of God's promises. He declares to His people, "I am with you." What a motivational truth! Philippians 2:13 says it is God who inspires and enables each of us to fulfill His will and to do His good pleasure. No matter if it is corporate or individual, spiritual zeal is a direct result of God's presence. His abiding presence is the surest guarantee of the success of any task or ministry. It is also the greatest of all God's blessings toward us.

B. God's Promised Glory (2:1-9)
(Haggai 2:1-5 is not included in the printed text.)
6. For thus saith the Lord of hosts; Yet once, it is a little while, and I will shake the heavens, and the earth, and the sea, and the dry land;

Consider Your Ways

7. And I will shake all nations, and the desire of all nations shall come: and I will fill this house with glory, saith the Lord of hosts.

8. The silver is mine, and the gold is mine, saith the Lord of hosts.

9. The glory of this latter house shall be greater than of the former, saith the Lord of hosts: and in this place will I give peace, saith the Lord of hosts.

God spoke through His prophet Haggai, infusing Zerubbabel, the governor of Judah, with a powerful message to "be strong." Haggai then effectively ministered the same word from the Lord to Joshua, the high priest. Finally, Haggai exhorted all of God's chosen people to "be strong . . . and work" (v. 4).

This thrice-repeated word from God acted like a healing tonic to His disheartened people. Upon hearing these words, the Jews were fortified with spiritual energy for the task ahead.

God's Word continues to have the same effect on His servants today. Whenever He assigns a challenging task, God confirms the work with a promise from His Word. His Word has life-giving power to stir up the necessary faith to act.

God's promise to the Jews was a stirring reminder that His presence was with His people when He delivered them from Egypt. The assurance of His presence would also see them through the awesome task of restoring the Temple. The Jews listened attentively to God's promise, "So my Spirit remaineth among you: fear ye not" (v. 5).

Such encouraging words from God dislodged the fear of failure as the Jews believed God's Word. Christian history reminds us that great ministries are wrought through faith in God. Men and women who listen to God's Word and believe what He says are able to succeed in their God-given tasks.

Rather than allow His people to rely on their physical and material resources, God desired that the Jews draw their strength from Him. Therefore He quickened them with the fact that the wealth used to build the original Temple belonged to Him. Though the former Temple's splendor was great, this latter one would possess something of far greater value. The Messiah—"the desire of all nations" (v. 7)—would fill this latter Temple with a spiritual glory unknown to the former one.

Scripture reminds us that God's ways are always higher than ours and for this reason we are not to judge the eternal value of His work through us, past or present, great or small. It is more important that what His servants do for Him is appointed by Him. Only then can we be certain of success in ministry.

For the first time in 16 years, the Jews took their eyes off their past failure and looked only to God's abiding presence in the present. Their submission to His will opened the way for God's

Talk About It:
1. What command is repeated three times in verse 4? Why?
2. In what sense had the original Temple been greater than the present one (v. 3), and in what sense would "the glory of this latter house . . . be greater than of the former" (v. 9)?
3. Why did God declare that the silver and gold of the earth is His (v. 8)?

promised peace to fill their hearts. His inner peace is also our confirmation that the service we do for Him is of His divine will.

III. EXPERIENCE GOD'S BLESSINGS (Haggai 2:10-23)
A. The Key to God's Blessings (vv. 10-19)
(Haggai 2:10, 16-18 is not included in the printed text.)
11. Thus saith the Lord of hosts; Ask now the priests concerning the law, saying,
12. If one bear holy flesh in the skirt of his garment, and with his skirt do touch bread, or pottage, or wine, or oil, or any meat, shall it be holy? And the priests answered and said, No.
13. Then said Haggai, If one that is unclean by a dead body touch any of these, shall it be unclean? And the priests answered and said, It shall be unclean.
14. Then answered Haggai, and said, So is this people, and so is this nation before me, saith the Lord; and so is every work of their hands; and that which they offer there is unclean.
15. And now, I pray you, consider from this day and upward, from before a stone was laid upon a stone in the temple of the Lord.
19. Is the seed yet in the barn? yea, as yet the vine, and the fig tree, and the pomegranate, and the olive tree, hath not brought forth: from this day will I bless you.

holy flesh (v. 12)—
consecrated meat
pottage (v. 12)—
stew

Talk About It:
1. According to verse 14, who and what were unclean? Why?
2. "From this day [on]" (v. 19), what would change (vv. 15-19)? Why?

Since Haggai's first stirring message four months earlier, the Jews began the difficult task of restoring God's Temple and a regular pattern of worship. Yet, in spite of their obedience, the Jews still saw none of the blessings God had promised them.

Therefore, God sent His prophet Haggai to them with a third message that seized their attention. God would not release His blessings on His chosen nation until His people were cleansed of their previous years of sin and disobedience toward Him. Because of their defilement through sin, their work on the Temple as well as their sacrificial offerings were defiled.

To reinforce the necessity for purification from their sins, God commanded that the priests be asked specific questions on the transmittal of holiness and impurity. According to the law of Moses, it was the duty of priests to explain God's ordinances and the rules for observing His Law.

Speaking through Haggai, God used the priests' answers to illustrate how serving Him without confession and repentance of sins only contaminates any work done for Him. He also pointed out that the required sacrifices used in the worship of Him were also polluted through the uncleanness of sin. This made purification necessary.

This passage in Haggai emphasizes the fact that even today when Christians do not confess and repent of sin, it acts

Consider Your Ways

like a spreading cancer contaminating everything it touches. This includes any works of service or ministry. According to Scripture, God never will allow His children to cover sin with good works done in His name.

Confession and repentance of sins is God's chosen way to secure His approval for acceptable worship and for the fullness of His anointing for Christian service. Only by turning to God and seeking His forgiveness can we expect to experience His peace and His blessings.

God declares in Zechariah 1:3, "Turn ye unto me, saith the Lord of hosts, and I will turn unto you." In order to drive home this truth, God asked the Jews to think about the suffering and hardship they experienced throughout the previous years. He repeatedly chastised His chosen nation for sins and disobedience of His command to rebuild the Temple. Even though they suffered much, they still refused to turn back to Him. Instead, His people stubbornly focused their attention on their own self-centered ambitions.

However, now, because they chose to obey and turned back to Him, God promised that His countenance would once again shine on His beloved people. He said, "From this day will I bless you" (Haggai 2:19). This promise is extended to today's believers as well. In James 4:8, God assures us that if we draw near to Him, He will draw near to us. This nearness to God will bring us His inner peace and other blessings as well.

"Manifold simply means 'many folds.' Manifold grace means that it is not just one blessing, but there are thousands to come, one after another."
—Paul Rader

B. The Greatness of God's Blessings (vv. 20-23)

(Haggai 2:20-23 is not included in the printed text.)

God's fourth and final message was given on the same day as the preceding message. This time God's prophet spoke directly to Governor Zerubbabel.

Haggai prophesied, as he had in verse 6, that God would shake the heavens and the earth, and He would overthrow all future opposing kingdoms. Though these kingdoms would surely fall, Christ's future kingdom would reign supreme throughout eternity.

God then spoke a personal prophecy to Zerubbabel. He promised to make him like a signet ring which was used as a stamp or mark of guarantee. To better understand the meaning of this promise, it is necessary to read Jeremiah 22:24-30. Here we read how God brought judgment against Zerubbabel's grandfather, King Jehoiakim, for his unrepentant sins.

At that time, Jeremiah prophesied that, like a valued signet ring taken off and cast aside, God would cast Jehoiakim into exile. He also prophesied that none of King Jehoiakim's descendants would occupy the throne of David. Only a few months after this prophecy was given, Jerusalem fell at the hands of Nebuchadnezzar. From that point on, King David's royal lineage was cut off.

Talk About It:
1. Describe the promises God made to Zerubbabel.
2. God chose Zerubbabel to be like His signet ring. What has He chosen you to be and do?

However, because of Zerubbabel's faithfulness and obedience, God overpowered much of His curse with His pronounced blessing on Zerubbabel. Symbolically speaking, God chose Zerubbabel to be His guaranteed signature mark. Through Zerubbabel's royal lineage, God guaranteed His promise of a future Messiah-King who would rule an eternal kingdom.

In its final completion, the Temple was not as physically impressive as King Solomon's. Yet, as noted earlier, its spiritual glory far exceeded the former Temple's physical glory. Similarly, our Christian service and ministries may not seem very impressive in our eyes. However, in God's eyes the eternal value He places on our service unto Him far exceeds our human expectations. Unlike so many of us, God does not look so much at the visible aspects of our Christian service. Nor does He compare the greatness of one ministry with another.

He is more interested in the heart's attitude of those who serve Him. It is there that He applies the seal of the Holy Spirit. As the Book of Haggai reveals to us, God will only bless and anoint that which is truly His.

CONCLUSION

The Book of Haggai reveals two great promises from God. First, we are assured of His blessings if we obey His Word and seek His kingdom first in all we do. Second, only God is allowed to judge the importance of the work we do to advance His kingdom. He is more concerned with the heart's spiritual condition than with the physical works of ministry. He promises to abundantly bless our faithfulness as we continue to serve Him.

Daily Devotions:
M. Love God
   Completely
   Deuteronomy
   6:1-8
T. Challenge to Be
   Dedicated
   Isaiah 53:1-5
W. God's Powerful
   Presence
   Psalm 114:1-8
T. Expectancy in
   God's Presence
   Acts 10:30-33,
   44-48
F. Faith Brings
   Blessings
   Galatians 3:6-14
S. Spiritual
   Blessings in
   Christ
   Ephesians 1:3-12

GOLDEN TEXT CHALLENGE

"THUS SAITH THE LORD OF HOSTS; CONSIDER YOUR WAYS" (Haggai 1:5).

"Consider your ways" literally means to set your heart on what you are doing. Hence, the Lord was telling His people to think through and unravel the series of events that brought them into their present plight and then formulate a plan to rise above the distressing situation. The Lord said the Jews had come to this crisis "because my house lies in ruins, while each of you has a house that he can run to" (1:9, *NEB*).

God's admonition to "consider your ways" is predicated on our ability to reason and think through the dilemmas that separate us from fellowship with God, and upon the work of the Holy Spirit to establish a course of action that can reconcile us to God. When we consider the error of our ways—whether it is neglect of God's house, neglect of personal prayer and Scripture reading, or not giving God first place in our lives—the Holy Spirit can help us develop a strategy that will renew our fellowship with God.

Consider Your Ways

Visions of Assurance (Zechariah)

Zechariah 1:7 through 6:15

INTRODUCTION

Prophets such as Joel and Obadiah are not always easy to locate within Israel's history. Zechariah, like Haggai, identifies his place on the time line in the book's first verse. In fact, his prophetic ministry began within two months of Haggai's, in the eighth month in the second year of the reign of Persia's King Darius.

Darius' predecessor on the Persian throne, Cyrus, had officially ended the period of exile for the Jews, allowing them to return to their land and begin rebuilding God's Temple (2 Chronicles 36:21-23; Ezra 1:1-7). However, steady opposition from neighboring rulers eventually stopped the building campaign. The Jews' appeal reached Darius in the second year of his rule (Ezra 4:24), and he quickly restarted the Temple construction, even blessing the effort with funds from the royal treasury (6:8-10). It was during this period of uncertainty and eventual triumph for Israel that Zechariah ministered alongside Haggai. For this reason, their books are placed beside one another in the order of the Old Testament.

In the first half of Zechariah (chs. 1-6), the prophet explains eight visions. Although such images may seem strange to the modern mind, prophets often communicated distinct revelations God had shown them. These visions are highly symbolic, and usually are given with the help of an angelic mediator. It is typical for the vision to be interpreted either by the prophet, the angel, or even by God himself. Such "visionary preaching" remained common through the time of the New Testament, as the Book of Revelation portrays.

The first three visions are prophecies of national restoration. In these, Zechariah is most concerned with assuring Israel that her status as a nation, torn apart by the Babylonian exile, will soon be completed because of Darius' declaration. The next two are visions of spiritual restoration, in which a renewed and holy priesthood is promised for the Temple. Because Zechariah is a priest himself, he respects the priesthood as the critical leaders who will bring the nation back to God. The final three visions highlight God's sovereignty over Israel's past, present and future. From the book's introduction, in which the people are blamed for bringing the exile upon themselves, God's supremacy is preached.

Unit Theme:
God's Word in the Minor Prophets (Nahum to Malachi)

Central Truth:
Because God is sovereign, everything He has promised will be fulfilled.

Focus:
To acknowledge that God has ultimate control and rely on His sovereignty.

Context:
In 519 B.C., Zechariah urged the Israelites to complete the Temple restoration.

Golden Text:
"Many nations shall be joined to the Lord in that day, and shall be my people: and I will dwell in the midst of thee" (Zechariah 2:11).

Study Outline:
I. Visions of National Restoration (Zechariah 1:7–2:12)
II. Visions of Spiritual Restoration (Zechariah 3:1–4:14)
III. Visions of God's Sovereignty (Zechariah 5:1-4; 6:1-15)

I. VISIONS OF NATIONAL RESTORATION
(Zechariah 1:7—2:12)

In 1:1, Zechariah is introduced as a prophet, the son of Berechiah, who was the son of Iddo. In the Book of Ezra, Zechariah is referred to as "a descendant of Iddo" (5:1; 6:14). This could indicate that Iddo was once a person of prominence, possibly even the prophet of 2 Chronicles (9:29; 12:15; 13:22). Most scholars consider Zechariah both a prophet and a priest, since several of his visions deal directly with the ordering of the new Temple. Some Old Testament prophets, like Jeremiah, are known for speaking directly against the Temple worship when it had become corrupt. Zechariah is emphatically committed to the Temple as God's principal dwelling place in Jerusalem. In this respect, the Temple represents not only spiritual renewal but also national restoration. Such zeal for the Temple probably identifies him as a priest by vocation.

The first six verses locate the beginning of Zechariah's prophetic ministry firmly within the second year of Darius' reign, which would have been about 520 B.C. In fact, the dates given in the Book of Zechariah indicate an approximate two-year time frame in which his prophetic ministry took place. Of course, Zechariah was undoubtedly a major Israelite leader for much longer, but the visions and messages he preached throughout his lifetime derive from this two-year span.

Over 60 years before, in 586 B.C., the Babylonians had completely destroyed Jerusalem (however, they had been invading it since 598 B.C.) and forced many of its inhabitants to move into Babylon. This period is known as the Exile. It is this era that Zechariah rehearses in verses 2-6, as he begins his ministry by recounting Israel's unfaithfulness that brought about the Exile.

Not until the Babylonian Empire was defeated by Cyrus and the Persian Empire were the Israelites allowed to return to their native land. Nonetheless, prophets such as Haggai, Nehemiah and Zechariah did not consider the Exile truly terminated until the Temple was rebuilt. It is important to remember that the Temple represented national unity for Israel, in some ways like our present White House. Because at this time Israel did not have a king, and has not had one since, the Temple was the seat of total power, both spiritual and political.

Sebat (she-BAT) (v. 7)—the 11th month of the Jewish year, corresponding with February

Zechariah (ZEK-uh-RYE-uh) (v. 7)—the Old Testament prophet whose name means "God remembers" or "God is renowned"

A. God Will Lead the Rebuilding of Jerusalem (1:7-17)

(Zechariah 1:7, 11, 13-17 is not included in the printed text.)

8. I saw by night, and behold a man riding upon a red horse, and he stood among the myrtle trees that were in the bottom; and behind him were there red horses, speckled, and white.

9. Then said I, O my lord, what are these? And the angel that talked with me said unto me, I will shew thee what these be.

Visions of Assurance

10. And the man that stood among the myrtle trees answered and said, These are they whom the Lord hath sent to walk to and fro through the earth.

12. Then the angel of the Lord answered and said, O Lord of hosts, how long wilt thou not have mercy on Jerusalem and on the cities of Judah, against which thou hast had indignation these threescore and ten years?

About four months pass between Zechariah's initial call to Israel to return to the Lord, and the first vision he recounts. Zechariah's first vision takes place at night, which is typical for Biblical visionaries in both testaments (see Daniel 2:19; Acts 16:9). His vision of four colored horses is similar to the white, red, black and pale horses seen in Revelation 6:2-8. In both places the horses are sent out into the earth at the command of God. The number four is significant, as it orders the visions of horns and craftsmen and the chariots (Zechariah 1:18-21; 6:1-8). Here the number probably serves to highlight the way in which the horsemen are sent "throughout the earth," given that the earth is sometimes said to have "four corners" (Ezekiel 7:2; Revelation 7:1; 20:8).

The angel serves as the sole mediator in Zechariah's vision. The angel confers with the horsemen, and then speaks to Zechariah and to God. The chief finding of their journey throughout the earth is explained in verse 11—the world is "still, and is at rest." This message upsets the angel, who immediately beseeches the Lord for a reason. To make sense of this, we must recall the conclusion of Haggai's prophecy: "Tell Zerubbabel governor of Judah that I will shake the heavens and the earth. I will overturn royal thrones and shatter the power of the foreign kingdoms. I will overthrow chariots and their drivers; horses and their riders will fall, each by the sword of his brother" (2:21, 22, *NIV*).

This initial vision of Zechariah points to his impatience with God's timing in fulfilling the promise to Haggai that God would bring major disruption to those nations who had oppressed Israel. Israel is still under foreign rule. After the Lord speaks words of comfort to the angel and to Zechariah, the angel commands that a fiery word be proclaimed. In order that Haggai's prophecy might be fulfilled, God himself will return to Jerusalem to lead the national rebuilding (v. 16). God's jealousy for Zion will bring comfort and prosperity to the city. This should serve as a rallying cry to forge a new sense of national unity for the fragmented Jewish people.

B. God Will Defend Jerusalem (1:18—2:12)
(Zechariah 1:18-21; 2:1-7 is not included in the printed text.)

8. For thus saith the Lord of hosts; After the glory hath he sent me unto the nations which spoiled you: for he that toucheth you toucheth the apple of his eye.

Talk About It:
1. What was the angel concerned about, and how did the Lord respond (vv. 11-13)?
2. Explain the "great jealousy" of the Lord. Why is this jealousy righteous?
3. What promises did God make regarding Jerusalem (vv. 16, 17)?

Koinonia Farm

In 1942, Biblical scholar Clarence Jordan founded Koinonia Farm—a small, Christian farming community outside of Americus, Georgia. His vision was a Christian community bringing people of all races and statuses together in the service of God and each other. In the segregated South, his mission was not eagerly accepted. Upon the destruction of his farming community by racists, his enemies were amazed to find him working the fields the next day, beginning the process of restoration.

It takes only a strong faith in God's promises to have the strength to restore that which has been devastated by forces hostile to God.

9. For, behold, I will shake mine hand upon them, and they shall be a spoil to their servants: and ye shall know that the Lord of hosts hath sent me.

10. Sing and rejoice, O daughter of Zion: for, lo, I come, and I will dwell in the midst of thee, saith the Lord.

11. And many nations shall be joined to the Lord in that day, and shall be my people: and I will dwell in the midst of thee, and thou shalt know that the Lord of hosts hath sent me unto thee.

12. And the Lord shall inherit Judah his portion in the holy land, and shall choose Jerusalem again.

Talk About It:

1. Why did God need to be a "wall of fire" (2:5) for Jerusalem? How is God a fiery wall for Christians today?

2. What does it mean to be the "apple of his [God's] eye" (v. 8)?

3. What is God's will for the nations (v. 11)?

Like the first vision, Zechariah's second vision includes a grouping of four that symbolizes the worldwide nature of the vision. The four horns, however, are not servants of God like the four horsemen. Instead, they are those responsible for the destruction of Jerusalem and the exile of the Jewish nation. Although the first vision presents a peaceful world, the second vision proclaims that the days of this peace are numbered. Just like skilled craftsmen might destroy a poorly built or damaged item, those guilty nations can also look forward to ultimate judgment.

In one sense, this prophecy spoken by Zechariah could have been considered partially fulfilled. Babylon, headed by the ruthless Nebuchadnezzar, had been defeated and replaced with Cyrus, then Darius; both leaders being friends of Israel. Yet Zechariah and his contemporaries were in the middle of rebuilding the city of Jerusalem, and even the authorization by King Darius did not stop forceful opposition from neighboring peoples. In the Books of Ezra and Nehemiah, these opponents include powerful leaders such as Sanballat, Xerxes and Artaxerxes. Perhaps it is this struggle that Zechariah targets as Israel's conflict with "the horns." *Horns* symbolized the strength of a given nation, just like a ram's horns symbolize the age and fighting power of the animal. Though such nations may seem strong, God was raising up craftsmen to repay them for harm done to Israel.

In Zechariah's third vision (2:1-13), a man with a measuring apparatus stands before him. He claims to be an architect, heading toward Jerusalem to plan the dimensions of its walls. As he goes, an angel commands Zechariah to declare that his task of measuring is futile; Jerusalem will not even need walls. For God himself will serve as a wall of fire around the city, and its glory inside it. This was an astonishing notion in Zechariah's times, for the most important structure in a city were its walls. They were the city's ultimate form of protection from foreign invaders. So then, God claims total protective responsibility over Jerusalem.

Not only will God act as Jerusalem's walls, but in verses 6-9

Visions of Assurance

the Lord again promises vengeance on Israel's enemies. In fact, Zechariah claims that his identity as a prophet sent from God will be ultimately vindicated by God's judgment of these nations (v. 9). Yet in the end, these nations will not be destroyed but will in fact be united with the people of God (v. 11). Verses 12 and 13 restate God's passionate commitment to dwell again in Jerusalem. What remarkable words of assurance to broken Israel! They easily call to mind the New Jerusalem in the Book of Revelation, in which the nations are represented in the city of God's dwelling (21:24). Although his initial prophecy communicates the discouragement of God's pace in fulfilling Haggai's prophecy to judge the nations, by Zechariah's third vision God deals with the nations and brings them into His very fold.

II. VISIONS OF SPIRITUAL RESTORATION (Zechariah 3:1—4:14)
Zechariah's first three visions lay a broad framework of national restoration for Israel, but the following visions focus that promise by identifying how this will come to pass. In visions four and five, Zechariah is concerned with the spiritual restoration of the nation. As discussed, this spiritual restoration is centered on rebuilding and reorganizing the Temple. However, the word of the Lord to Zechariah pinpoints the precise figures to lead this spiritual revival. The prophet validates Joshua the high priest and Zerubbabel the governor as servants of God called to restore spiritual fervor to the Jews.

A. Spiritual Renewal Through Joshua (3:1-10)
(Zechariah 3:5-10 is not included in the printed text.)
1. And he shewed me Joshua the high priest standing before the angel of the Lord, and Satan standing at his right hand to resist him.

Satan (3:1)— means "accuser"

2. And the Lord said unto Satan, The Lord rebuke thee, O Satan; even the Lord that hath chosen Jerusalem rebuke thee: is not this a brand plucked out of the fire?
3. Now Joshua was clothed with filthy garments, and stood before the angel.
4. And he answered and spake unto those that stood before him, saying, Take away the filthy garments from him. And unto him he said, Behold, I have caused thine iniquity to pass from thee, and I will clothe thee with change of raiment.
Zechariah's vision of Joshua specifies God's intentions for Israel's spiritual renewal. Although he has experienced strong opposition, Joshua is still "God's man." This vision takes the form of an intense courtroom drama. Both Joshua and Satan (literally translated "the Accuser") stand before the angel of God. Note that when verse 2 states, "The Lord said unto

Talk About It:
1. Compare Zechariah 3:1, 2 with Revelation 12:10. Who accuses God's people? What

does he accuse them about? Who rebukes the accuser?

2. Describe how God ministered to Joshua and describe the charge God gave to him (vv. 3-7).

3. Why is "the Branch" (v. 8) an appropriate name for the Messiah?

Satan," Zechariah is probably referring to the angel doing the speaking. Because the Hebrew word *angel* also means "messenger," the prophets often saw no difference between God's words and an angel's. Thus, the angel uses the name of the Lord to rebuke Satan. Although Satan has been at work stirring up opposition to Joshua's spiritual leadership, Zechariah's vision reinforces Joshua's calling from God. As a burning stick is snatched from the fire, so Joshua has been handpicked to intensely purify Israel's spirituality.

The tension in the vision comes as a result of Joshua's filthy clothes. How could he be wearing rags in the presence of a holy God? Such an image could represent three things. First, filthy clothes were used for mourning. In this respect, Joshua's clothes represent the discouragement of the nation of Israel, as they have been oppressed some 70 years during the Exile. Second, filthy clothes could symbolize a national catastrophe. Recall the city of Nineveh, who donned rags at the prospect of God's judgment upon the city (Jonah 3:4, 5). Likewise, Israel was still reeling from God's judgment during the Exile. Last, wearing filthy garments was a way to acknowledge guilt. In Joshua's case, this is national guilt. Yet God's declaration is that his filthy clothes—the nation's guilt—be replaced with clean garments. That is, the sin of the priesthood and the people that resulted in the Exile is forgiven by God. Israel would be given yet another chance as a nation to walk in the Lord's ways.

After the angel's charge to Joshua in verses 6 and 7, the scope of Zechariah's message widens. In verse 8 he reveals that Joshua's importance is not only for the present, but also for future Israel. He is symbolic of One coming later—"the Branch." This is the first mention of the Messiah in Zechariah, and the second half of the book greatly expounds on this prophecy. Here, however, Zechariah uses the language of one of his predecessors, Isaiah (11:1): "A shoot will come up from the stump of Jesse; from his roots a Branch will bear fruit" (*NIV*).

In verse 9 of the text, Joshua's calling is further magnified by an engraved stone with seven eyes. In 4:10, we are told that the seven eyes represent God's watchfulness over the entire world. Therefore, with regards to the Branch, Joshua's leadership has a universal quality. The entire sin of the land will be removed within a day, and 3:10 illustrates the peace that Israel will experience with its neighbors as a result. So then, this Branch that Zechariah speaks of will hold a priestly role like Joshua, will exercise a universal ministry, and will be responsible for the complete removal of sin in Israel. Given that the name *Jesus* is simply the Greek form for the Hebrew *Joshua*, Zechariah's prophecies about the coming Messiah are some of the most pronounced in the Old Testament.

> "I'm not afraid of the devil. The devil can handle me—he's got judo I've never heard of. But he can't handle the One to whom I'm joined; he can't handle the One to whom I'm united; he can't handle the One whose nature dwells in my nature."
> —A.W. Tozer

B. Spiritual Renewal Through Zerubbabel (4:1-14)
(Zechariah 4:1-5, 8-14 is not included in the printed text.)
6. Then he answered and spake unto me, saying, This is the word of the Lord unto Zerubbabel, saying, Not by might, nor by power, but by my spirit, saith the Lord of hosts.
7. Who art thou, O great mountain? before Zerubbabel thou shalt become a plain: and he shall bring forth the headstone thereof with shoutings, crying, Grace, grace unto it.

By Zechariah's fifth vision, perhaps the prophet is so tired from the weight of his ministry that he must be awakened by the angel. He describes an image of a solid gold lampstand (envision a Jewish menorah such as is often visible during Hanukkah/ Christmas) enclosed by two olive trees. The lampstand has seven lights with a bowl on top that channels oil to them. Oil was often crushed from olives and used for lamp fuel, which would have been perfectly familiar to Zechariah. The angel seems surprised that the prophet does not understand the vision's meaning, and proceeds to explain it. He proclaims that Zerubbabel has been handpicked by the Lord to complete the Temple (v. 9). We know from Haggai 2:21 that Zerubbabel is the political governor over the land who had led the Jews out of captivity. His name is obviously Babylonian (*Zerub-Babel*), meaning he was likely born under Babylonian rule. So then, the angel declares that Zerubbabel is one of the two who are anointed to do the Lord's work. One olive tree stands for Joshua's priestly leadership, the other for Zerubbabel's political office (v. 14).

III. VISIONS OF GOD'S SOVEREIGNTY (Zechariah 5:1-4; 6:1-15)
The visions in chapters 5 and 6 answer questions regarding not only Israel's future, but God's universal rule. These were pressing issues for Zechariah, given that Israel was still under a pagan empire.

A. God Will Purge the Land (5:1-4; 6:1-8)
(Zechariah 6:1-8 is not included in the printed text.)
1. Then I turned, and lifted up mine eyes, and looked, and behold a flying roll.
2. And he said unto me, What seest thou? And I answered, I see a flying roll; the length thereof is twenty cubits, and the breadth thereof ten cubits.
3. Then said he unto me, This is the curse that goeth forth over the face of the whole earth: for every one that stealeth shall be cut off *as* on this side according to it; and every one that sweareth shall be cut off *as* on that side according to it.

Talk About It:
1. Explain the significance of Zechariah 4:6 for Christians today.
2. How would Zechariah's prophetic ministry be confirmed?
3. What is the meaning and significance of the question "Who despises the day of small things?" (v. 10, *NIV*).

Twenty cubits, and . . . ten cubits (v. 2)
—30 feet long and 15 feet wide

Talk About It:
1. Who would be affected by the "curse" (3:3) announced by the Lord, and how would they be affected?
2. How is the sovereignty of God expressed by the four horses (6:1-8)?

God's Providence

A blind man taps the pavement with his stick on a New York street corner, then shouts, "How about it, Charley?"

The traffic officer sees the blind man, holds up his hand, and blows his whistle. "All right, Ben, you can cross now," the officer says, and the blind man walks fearlessly between the lines of vehicles held up for him.

It's a picture of the way God's providence "hoids up traffic" for us.

—*King's Business*

4. I will bring it forth, saith the Lord of hosts, and it shall enter into the house of the thief, and into the house of him that sweareth falsely by my name: and it shall remain in the midst of his house, and shall consume it with the timber thereof and the stones thereof.

In the sixth vision, the dimensions of a massive, flying scroll actually match those of the portico of Solomon's temple (1 Kings 6:3). The scroll is double-sided, with thieves listed on one side and liars on the other. Zechariah may have had in mind something like the formal list of curses in Deuteronomy 27:14-26. In this case, the thief and the liar are representative of all sinners, and the scroll signifies God's imminent judgment on such persons. Perhaps the greatest sin of thievery and falsity is that of idolatry. Idolaters sought to steal the image of God and impute a gross lie to that image. In this respect, Zechariah's prophecy came to pass with remarkable specificity, as the Exile thoroughly purged the Jews of idolatry until this very day.

Of course, the Jewish people are not the only targets of this purging. As a dominated people, they hoped for God's judgment against their enemies. The vision of the woman in the basket (vv. 5-11) illustrates this judgment, as the Babylonian Empire is repressed and replaced, never to rise again.

Zechariah's eighth vision recalls his first (1:7-17), in which four horsemen travel throughout the earth to find it at rest, and so leave Haggai's prophecy unfulfilled. In 6:1-8, however, the horsemen have been armed with war chariots, and they are again sent to the four corners of the world. The unrest of God's Spirit gives them the power to overcome the difficulty of their journey, and the black horse finally gives God's Spirit rest in the land of the north—Babylon. Zechariah is declaring that the prophecy given in Haggai 2:22 has been fulfilled, in part, by the destruction of Babylon. Therefore, God's Spirit has been given rest because the judgment written on the flying scroll has already been carried out against Babylon.

B. God Will Raise Up "The Branch" (6:9-15)
(Zechariah 6:9-11, 14, 15 is not included in the printed text.)

12. And speak unto him, saying, Thus speaketh the Lord of hosts, saying, Behold the man whose name is The Branch; and he shall grow up out of his place, and he shall build the temple of the Lord:

13. Even he shall build the temple of the Lord; and he shall bear the glory, and shall sit and rule upon his throne; and he shall be a priest upon his throne: and the counsel of peace shall be between them both.

At this point, a marked shift takes place in Zechariah's prophesying. Visions are no longer the mode of God's word. Instead, the material is introduced by the familiar prophetic expression, "The word of the Lord came unto me." This declaration is the first straightforward prophecy of Zechariah that does not require an angelic mediator. God's word to the prophet commands that gold be given by three prominent people returning from Babylon, in order that a crown might be made for Joshua, the high priest. Although the names Heldai and Tobijah are not recognized in the Biblical books surrounding the return from exile, Jedaiah may, in fact, be the priest mentioned in Nehemiah 7:39 and 12:6. We can only assume that they were prominent spiritual and political leaders during this time, as they are commanded to give authority to Joshua, the high priest, through the symbolic ritual of crowning.

In verse 12, Zechariah again announces that the Branch will come through Joshua's lineage (see 3:8). This Branch will ultimately build the temple of the Lord, and He will be both priest and governor. Zechariah looks forward to the fusion of these two offices, presently occupied by Joshua and Zerubbabel, in the coming Branch. When He comes, 6:15 shows how people will be brought to God from far away, as the nation obeys God. The visions of national and spiritual unity are effectively combined in the prophecy of the coming Messiah, who will be a leader not just for the Jews, but for all nations.

CONCLUSION

Although Zechariah's visions may seem mysterious to contemporary readers, he utilizes literary methods that were quite common in his day. When his symbolic visions are "decoded," they reveal God's extraordinary mission to rebuild broken Israel, and to ultimately heal a broken world. Although this process begins by raising up spiritual and political leaders in Jerusalem, its glorious conclusion is the coming of the Branch. The second half of the Book of Zechariah is consumed with this promise, used to encourage the Jews to continue work on Jerusalem and the Temple.

GOLDEN TEXT CHALLENGE

"MANY NATIONS SHALL BE JOINED TO THE LORD IN THAT DAY, AND SHALL BE MY PEOPLE: AND I WILL DWELL IN THE MIDST OF THEE" (Zechariah 2:11).

This verse is a powerful reminder that God has sovereign control over all nations. In a world where Islam is dominant in many lands, where Hinduism has sway in other nations, where secularism rules numerous countries, and where other peoples are nominally Christian, we need to be reminded that in God's way and time, "many nations will be joined with the Lord . . . and will become [His] people" (*NIV*). Meanwhile, we who love God must serve Him wholeheartedly and influence other people to do the same.

Talk About It
1. Describe the Messiah's role as priest and king.
2. How are believers the temple of the Lord?

Daily Devotions:
M. See God's Salvation
Isaiah 52:1-10
T. Seek God and Find Him
Jeremiah 29:10-14
W. Promise of Spiritual Cleansing
Ezekiel 36:22-28
T. Restoration of Israel
Romans 11:25-36
F. Convinced of God's Keeping Power
2 Timothy 1:8-14
S. Hope Anchors the Soul
Hebrews 6:13-20

Prophecies About the Messiah (Zechariah)

Zechariah 9:9 through 14:9

Unit Theme:
God's Word in the Minor Prophets (Nahum to Malachi)

Central Truth:
The Messiah came to bring salvation and will return to establish His kingdom.

Focus:
To review the promises of redemption through the Messiah and find hope in Christ's first and second comings.

Context:
These events took place in and around Jerusalem after 517 B.C.

Golden Text:
"The Lord shall be king over all the earth: in that day shall there be one Lord, and his name one" (Zechariah 14:9).

Study Outline:
I. The Messiah Will Come (Zechariah 9:9-17)
II. The Messiah Will Redeem (Zechariah 10:6-10; 13:7-9)
III. The Messiah Will Reign (Zechariah 14:1-9)

INTRODUCTION

In the second half of the Book of Zechariah, the prophet turns his focus to the coming Messiah, who will completely reestablish Israel. He looks forward to the promised Branch of 3:8 as the One to end Israel's suffering and change their present status as an oppressed people. Zechariah has already proven God's total commitment to Israel's situation at the end of the Exile. Now he shifts to God's heart for Israel's future as a nation. That future's hope is a mighty King that the Lord will send to redeem Israel and to eventually reign over the whole earth.

It is not surprising that by the time of Christ, over 500 years later, the Jews were still clinging to the words of Zechariah. After all, up to this time the prophecies had yet to be fulfilled, as Judea remained dominated by a foreign power. The Romans, however, proved to be much less merciful than Persia. It is no surprise, then, to see references to Zechariah popping up throughout the New Testament. In fact, references to Zechariah appear in each of the four Gospels.

In Matthew 21:5, Jesus' triumphal entry into Jerusalem on a colt includes a quotation of Zechariah 9:9. In Mark 14:27, Jesus himself quotes Zechariah 13:7 to explain to His disciples how they would desert Him after His arrest. In Luke 11:51, Jesus pronounces woe on the Pharisees for the murder of Zechariah. And in John 19:37, the apostle cites Zechariah 12:10 to explain why Jesus' side was pierced with a spear. It is clear that Zechariah held a central place in the early Christians' understanding of Jesus Christ, particularly in chapters 9-14.

I. THE MESSIAH WILL COME (Zechariah 9:9-17)

Zechariah begins chapter 9 by announcing judgment on Israel's surrounding hostile peoples, specifically identifying cities in Syria, Phoenicia and Philistia. Notice that Persia is not mentioned, because they have been friendly to the Jews and provided protection and funds for the rebuilding of Jerusalem. Nevertheless, by the end of Zechariah there is no doubt that in the future all nations will be subdued under the rule of God. This will come about after the arrival of a great King in Jerusalem, known elsewhere as "the Messiah." The word comes from the Hebrew verb *masah*, meaning "to anoint," and is literally translated "the Anointed One." Isaiah, Daniel and Habakkuk use this designation. Interestingly, Zechariah does not use the word *Messiah* to describe this coming King. His choice to leave out this traditional title parallels his distinctive prophecies about the nature of the Messiah.

A. A Nonviolent Arrival (vv. 9-13)

(Zechariah 9:12, 13 is not included in the printed text.)

9. Rejoice greatly, O daughter of Zion; shout, O daughter of Jerusalem: behold, thy King cometh unto thee: he is just, and having salvation; lowly, and riding upon an ass, and upon a colt the foal of an ass.

10. And I will cut off the chariot from Ephraim, and the horse from Jerusalem, and the battle bow shall be cut off: and he shall speak peace unto the heathen: and his dominion shall be from sea even to sea, and from the river even to the ends of the earth.

11. As for thee also, by the blood of thy covenant I have sent forth thy prisoners out of the pit wherein is no water.

An amazing contrast exists between the beginning of Zechariah's formal prophecies regarding the Messiah and his preceding material. As mentioned, verses 1-8 pronounce God's judgment against Israel's enemies. Then, in verse 9, Israel is commanded to rejoice at the coming of the One to consummate this judgment. Surprisingly, He will be gentle and nonviolent (vv. 9-11).

"See, your king comes to you!" (v. 9, *NIV*). There were likely no words more encouraging to the people of Zechariah's day. Could a king come to officially crush their enemies, completely end the Exile, and restore their political power once again? Throughout Biblical times, only the educated elite were literate, so the Scriptures were read aloud publicly. Verse 9 would surely have functioned as a climactic point in the book, at which the listeners anticipated a final solution to the problem of the Exile. Yet the King that Zechariah presents is not a general riding a majestic military stallion at the head of a massive

Talk About It:
1. Explain the description of the Messiah in verse 9.
2. What would God take away, and what would He pronounce (v. 10)? Why?
3. Explain the phrase "prisoners of hope" (v. 12).

army, but a humble man on a slow donkey's back. In His hand is not a gleaming sword or a ruler's scepter, but righteousness and salvation. He does not come to bring revolution through battle, but through gentleness. He will not be like the previous kings in Jerusalem who depended on chariots, soldiers and weapons, but will gather all nations under His rule of peace.

Zechariah seems to be pointing to this coming King as the fulfillment of previous prophecy stretching all the way back to the concluding chapters of Genesis: "The scepter will not depart from Judah, nor the ruler's staff from between his feet, until he comes to whom it belongs and the obedience of the nations is his. He will tether his donkey to a vine, his colt to the choicest branch; he will wash his garments in wine, his robes in the blood of grapes" (49:10, 11, *NIV*).

The similarities between the passages are striking. Both speak of this coming King's rule over Israel and the nations, His gentleness in riding a donkey, and His blood. In verse 11, however, Zechariah further identifies this figure as One who will free prisoners from death through a blood covenant. This not only references the previous blood covenant between the Lord and Israel inaugurated at the Passover, but the coming new covenant through Christ. "This cup is the new covenant in my blood, which is poured out for you" (Luke 22:20, *NIV*). Such is the meekness and humility of this coming King.

> "The world is full of experiments for bringing deliverance to the race, but on the authority of the New Testament and in the light of history, I declare my conviction that the only hope of this world is the return of Christ to reign over the earth and to establish universal peace."
> —A.J. Gordon

B. A Divine Arrival (9:14-17)

14. And the Lord shall be seen over them, and his arrow shall go forth as the lightning: and the Lord God shall blow the trumpet, and shall go with whirlwinds of the south.

15. The Lord of hosts shall defend them; and they shall devour, and subdue with sling stones; and they shall drink, and make a noise as through wine; and they shall be filled like bowls, and as the corners of the altar.

16. And the Lord their God shall save them in that day as the flock of his people: for they shall be as the stones of a crown, lifted up as an ensign upon his land.

17. For how great is his goodness, and how great is his beauty! corn shall make the young men cheerful, and new wine the maids.

Talk About It:
1. Describe the sights and sounds depicted in verses 14 and 15.
2. What are the jewels in God's crown? Why?

The arrival of this King will be validated by none other than God himself. Verse 14 points to God's sudden appearance during the time of the King, using the language of battle. When the King arrives, God's presence will be evident, and Israel will be fully delivered (v. 16). Salvation will come in the day of the King, and Israel will be the visible sign of it, like jewels in a crown identify the presence of royalty. The imagery is identical

Prophecies About the Messiah

to Isaiah's description of God's plan for Jerusalem: "The nations will see your righteousness, and all kings your glory; you will be called by a new name that the mouth of the Lord will bestow. You will be a crown of splendor in the Lord's hand, a royal diadem in the hand of your God" (62:2, 3, *NIV*).

God chose the land and people of Israel to display His glory in the coming King. The Book of Hebrews opens by recognizing this fact: "In the past God spoke to our forefathers through the prophets at many times and in various ways, but in these last days he has spoken to us by his Son" (vv. 1, 2, *NIV*). Zechariah is clear: the arrival and reign of this coming King are to come not from political situations, but from the action of God alone.

II. THE MESSIAH WILL REDEEM (Zechariah 10:6-10; 13:7-9)

Throughout the Scriptures, God is known as Redeemer. In the terminology of ancient business, *redemption* referred to the process by which a property or person was released to a new owner after payment had been made (Leviticus 25:54; 27:20). Therefore, the children of Israel were constantly reminded that God had *redeemed* them from slavery in Egypt, and could consequently claim authority over them (Deuteronomy 7:8; 2 Samuel 7:23; Psalm 74:2). In the New Testament, the blood of Christ made redemption possible, as a person's former life was transformed by his or her new allegiance to Christ (Galatians 3:13; 1 Peter 1:18, 19). It is no surprise, then, that Zechariah looked forward to a coming King who would redeem not only Israel but the nations for the glory of God.

A. Redeeming a Scattered People (10:6-10)

6. And I will strengthen the house of Judah, and I will save the house of Joseph, and I will bring them again to place them; for I have mercy upon them: and they shall be as though I had not cast them off: for I am the Lord their God, and will hear them.

7. And they of Ephraim shall be like a mighty man, and their heart shall rejoice as through wine: yea, their children shall see it, and be glad; their heart shall rejoice in the Lord.

8. I will hiss for them, and gather them; for I have redeemed them: and they shall increase as they have increased.

9. And I will sow them among the people: and they shall remember me in far countries; and they shall live with their children, and turn again.

10. I will bring them again also out of the land of Egypt, and gather them out of Assyria; and I will bring them into the land of Gilead and Lebanon; and place shall not be found for them.

hiss (v. 8)—signal

increase as they have increased (v. 8)—"be as numerous as before" (*NIV*)

Talk About It:

1. What do the words *strengthen* and *save* (v. 6), *redeem* and *increase* (v. 8) have in common in this passage?

2. Explain God's actions of sowing (scattering) and gathering, and their purpose (vv. 9, 10).

"A few years ago, an angry man rushed through the Rijks Museum in Amsterdam until he reached Rembrandt's famous painting *Nightwatch*. Then he took out a knife and slashed it repeatedly before he could be stopped. What did officials do? Throw [it] out and forget about [it]? Absolutely not! Using the best experts, who worked with the utmost care and precision, they made every effort to restore the treasure."
—Charles Swindoll

In the opening verses of chapter 10, Zechariah laments the leadership responsible for the Exile. The people wander like sheep because no loving shepherd guides them. Verse 4, however, points to a "cornerstone" (*NKJV*) from Judah that will reverse this trend by redeeming and restoring fallen Israel. Verse 6 poignantly illustrates the redemption God will bring. He will so completely restore Israel that the Exile will be just a distant memory, as though it didn't even happen. In fact, this redemption will be so powerful that the nation will be united for the first time in centuries. We find this in Zechariah's references to the houses of Judah and Joseph.

"Judah" refers to the southern kingdom (Judah), and "Joseph" to the northern kingdom (Israel). They had divided shortly after the death of Solomon, due to the rebellion of Jeroboam, and existed as separate nations from about 924 to 722 B.C. In 722 B.C., the northern kingdom was brought to an end by Assyrian conquest. The Babylonians invaded the southern kingdom in 598 B.C. and were responsible for the Exile. The coming era of redemption that Zechariah looks forward to will unite these halves and encompass all Israel. Jeremiah also prophesied about this when the Exile had just begun: "Hear the word of the Lord, O ye nations, and declare it in the isles afar off, and say, He that scattered Israel will gather him, and keep him, as a shepherd doth his flock" (31:10). Israel will be split no longer, but reunited because of God's compassion.

In Zechariah 10:7-10, the prophet continues the theme of redemption. In verse 8, God's redemption will replenish Israel's population, severely decimated by the Exile. Even though they have been scattered among the nations, verses 9 and 10 promise the Israelites will be blessed and God will bring them back to their homeland, where they will flourish. Verse 11 mentions Assyria and Egypt, promising that God will open a way through the "sea of trouble" (*NIV*), a direct reference to the parting of the Red Sea. Even from the most distant places of exile, God will gather the Jews and bring them back to Jerusalem, punishing those who have ruined them.

In chapter 11, Zechariah is commanded to prophetically "act out" God's word for Israel. His dramatic performance represents God's intense disdain for errant leadership in Israel. Zechariah takes on the role of shepherd for a flock marked for slaughter, but is met with conflict from both shepherds and sheep. After he rejects his payment of 30 pieces of silver, the Lord pronounces judgment on foolish shepherds. This scene seems to mirror the treatment the coming King may expect. Because the Messiah will shepherd God's people during a time of great political and spiritual tumult, He will be misunderstood and rejected by many, both Israelite leaders and commoners.

Prophecies About the Messiah

This parallels Isaiah's understanding of the coming Messiah as one "despised and rejected of men" (53:3). Although God will ultimately triumph through the coming King, He will undergo a time of rejection before the divine plan is accomplished.

B. Redeeming Israel From Sin (13:7-9)
   7. Awake, O sword, against my shepherd, and against the man that is my fellow, saith the Lord of hosts: smite the shepherd, and the sheep shall be scattered: and I will turn mine hand upon the little ones.
   8. And it shall come to pass, that in all the land, saith the Lord, two parts therein shall be cut off and die; but the third shall be left therein.
   9. And I will bring the third part through the fire, and will refine them as silver is refined, and will try them as gold is tried: they shall call on my name, and I will hear them: I will say, It is my people: and they shall say, The Lord is my God.
   In chapter 12, Zechariah pictures a final siege against Jerusalem, with the nations gathered against the city. This scene is resolved by the Lord himself, who throws the armies into a panic and delivers Judah. Verse 7 offers the final solution to errant leadership, as God restores the leaders of Judah.

Talk About It:
1. In what context did Christ quote from verse 7 in Matthew 26:31? Explain the meaning.
2. Why would God take His people through a "refiner's fire"?

   The remainder of chapter 12 depicts an outpouring of God's grace that causes mourning throughout Jerusalem. Central to this mourning is the One "they have pierced" (v. 10), the One whom John identifies as the crucified Jesus (see John 19:37). Zechariah 13 explains the ramifications of this event, namely that it will result in the people being purged from sin, specifically idolatry and false prophecy. Verses 7-9 then focus the prophecy on the coming Messiah.
   Redemption from sin will not come without great cost. The sword will be drawn against the very Shepherd that God is sending (v. 7). Jesus himself references this verse on the night of His arrest, explaining to His disciples how they will abandon Him (Matthew 26:31). However, although most will reject the Shepherd, some will be refined by the Lord to live in communion with Him (Zechariah 13:9). This "third" is a remnant of God-followers who stay true to Him despite overwhelming odds. Such a remnant always existed in Israel, from Noah's family to Elijah and the 7,000 faithful followers of God (1 Kings 19:17, 18). Zechariah looks for that remnant even in the dark times of the Shepherd's rejection, for it is through them that the nation will be delivered.

III. THE MESSIAH WILL REIGN (Zechariah 14:1-9)
   Zechariah's opening visions (chs. 1-6) center on particular leaders of Israel in his day. Chapters 7-13 predict the coming of

the Messiah to redeem the sin of the nation and its leadership. In chapter 14, the prophet's scope widens to not only include the judgment of the nations, but their total subjugation under the complete rule of God. In this respect, the book mirrors the movement in the Book of Revelation. John's Revelation initially addresses the contemporary church of his day, then explains its future destiny, and then broadens until the entire world confesses Jesus' lordship. The two books essentially conclude with the same result—a redeemed people dwelling in the peace of God's presence with no further threat of foreign oppression.

A. The Decisive Conquest of the Messiah (vv. 1-5)
(Zechariah 14:5 is not included in the printed text.)

1. Behold, the day of the Lord cometh, and thy spoil shall be divided in the midst of thee.

2. For I will gather all nations against Jerusalem to battle; and the city shall be taken, and the houses rifled, and the women ravished; and half of the city shall go forth into captivity, and the residue of the people shall not be cut off from the city.

3. Then shall the Lord go forth, and fight against those nations, as when he fought in the day of battle.

4. And his feet shall stand in that day upon the mount of Olives, which is before Jerusalem on the east, and the mount of Olives shall cleave in the midst thereof toward the east and toward the west, and there shall be a very great valley; and half of the mountain shall remove toward the north, and half of it toward the south.

Verse 1 introduces a term—"the day of the Lord"—that appears in the prophecies of Isaiah, Ezekiel, Joel, Amos, Obadiah, Zephaniah and Malachi. These different prophets invest the term with various implications, but they agree on the major concept of a time in which God accomplishes His purposes with finality. These purposes include judging God's enemies and restoring Israel to perfect peace under the reign of God. In fact, the last passage of the Old Testament predicts this era: "Behold, I will send you Elijah the prophet before the coming of the great and dreadful day of the Lord" (Malachi 4:5). That day is always considered great for God's followers but dreadful for His enemies. Zechariah's final prophecy draws together the future redemption of Israel and the reign of the Messiah by employing the theme of "the day of the Lord."

Verse 2 cautions the Israelites concerning the nature of the Day of the Lord. It will begin with a horrible siege of Jerusalem. Amos also warned the people of the coming day's turbulence: "Woe to you who long for the day of the Lord! Why do you long for the day of the Lord? That day will be darkness, not light. It

---

Uzziah (you-ZI-uh) (v. 5)—This king assumed the throne of Judah at age 16 and reigned 52 years.

Talk About It:
1. How will sinners suffer because of their sins (vv. 1, 2)?
2. How will the Lord vindicate His people on the Day of the Lord (vv. 3-5)?

The Right Side
A child from the city traveled to a rural area for the first time and saw the amazing night sky, unaffected by man-made lights. He immediately exclaimed to his father, "Oh Daddy, if heaven is so pretty on this

Prophecies About the Messiah

will be as though a man fled from a lion only to meet a bear, as though he entered his house and rested his hand on the wall only to have a snake bite him. Will not the day of the Lord be darkness, not light—pitch-dark, without a ray of brightness?" (Amos 5:18-20, *NIV*). Zechariah seems to be explaining that the Day of the Lord *already began* with the Babylonian conquest of Jerusalem and the chaos of the Exile. However, Israel could hope in the fact that God would act decisively (14:3, 4).

The nations responsible for the Exile will punish Israel no longer, for the Lord's feet will span the breadth of Jerusalem. The splitting of the Mount of Olives is symbolic of God's protection, as He will defend the city like two mountains at its side. Jesus may have been referring to this prophecy in Matthew 17:20, where, disappointed at His disciples' lack of faith, He exclaims, "I tell you the truth, if you have faith as small as a mustard seed, you can say to this mountain, 'Move from here to there' and it will move" (*NIV*). Perhaps Jesus is pointing to Zechariah's prophecy, explaining to His disciples that His coming is the messianic fulfillment of the promised Day of the Lord. In Zechariah 14:5, God's decisive defense of Jerusalem causes all enemies and armies to flee, as in the days of the earthquake in Uzziah's time (see Amos 1:1–2:3).

side, it must be incredible on the right side!"

Unfortunately, there is much on "this side" that is anything but heavenly. The Old Testament prophets ministered amid war, chaos and exile. Still, they were able to hope in the promise of God's coming kingdom. That promise can help us maintain our spiritual fervor until that day.

B. The Universal Conquest of the Messiah (vv. 6-9)

6. And it shall come to pass in that day, that the light shall not be clear, nor dark:

7. But it shall be one day which shall be known to the Lord, not day, nor night: but it shall come to pass, that at evening time it shall be light.

8. And it shall be in that day, that living waters shall go out from Jerusalem; half of them toward the former sea, and half of them toward the hinder sea: in summer and in winter shall it be.

9. And the Lord shall be king over all the earth: in that day shall there be one Lord, and his name one.

As Zechariah's prophecy closes, it again parallels the Book of Revelation. The conclusion of the Day of the Lord will result in a heavenly utopia, in which no manmade light or heat source is needed. Note the New Jerusalem in Revelation 21:23: "The city had no need of the sun, neither of the moon, to shine in it: for the glory of God did lighten it, and the Lamb is the light thereof."

Zechariah prophesies about the kingdom of God on earth. Even time will take on a new definition, as daytime and nighttime cease their normal patterns. Instead of streams from the Dead (eastern) and the Mediterranean seas (western) bringing nutrients and food into the city, Jerusalem will be so prosperous

Talk About It:
1. What will be supernaturally different about the coming Day of the Lord (vv. 6-8)?
2. Describe the future reign of the Lord (v. 9).

that new rivers from its foundation will feed the great seas year round. Plus, these waters will be "living," teeming with life. Again, perhaps Jesus references Zechariah when He proclaims Himself the bearer of "living water" (John 4:10). At this culmination of human history, other gods will be nonexistent; the Lord himself will reign over the entire cosmos.

CONCLUSION

Over 500 years before the birth of Jesus of Nazareth, Zechariah ministered within a community of prophets that looked forward to the coming of the Day of the Lord—that time in which God would ultimately reveal Himself in human history and provide absolute salvation for His people. Although many details of God's plan were hidden from him, Zechariah speaks with remarkable clarity about the nature of the Messiah. He was to come as a nonviolent Redeemer and be rejected by many. However, the remnant believing in Him would hasten the day of His return to rule over the entire world. In this way, Zechariah solves the problem of the Exile not only in his contemporary situation, but for all who long for God's final appearing.

GOLDEN TEXT CHALLENGE

"THE LORD SHALL BE KING OVER ALL THE EARTH: IN THAT DAY SHALL THERE BE ONE LORD, AND HIS NAME ONE" (Zechariah 14:9).

Zechariah prophesies that the kingdom of God will be universal and united.

Universal: "The Lord shall be King over all the earth." He is, and ever was, so of right, and in the sovereign disposals of His providence His kingdom does rule over all and none are exempt from His jurisdiction; but it is here promised that He shall be so by actual possession of the hearts of His subjects; He shall be acknowledged King by all in all places; His authority shall be owned and submitted to, and allegiance sworn to Him. This will have its accomplishment with that word in Revelation 11:15—"The kingdoms of this world are become the kingdoms of our Lord."

United: "There shall be one Lord, and His name one." All shall worship one God only, and not idols, and shall be unanimous in the worship of Him. All false gods shall be abandoned, and all false ways of worship abolished; and as God shall be the center of their unity, in whom they shall all meet, so the scripture shall be the rule of their unity, by which they shall all walk.—*Matthew Henry*

Daily Devotions:
M. The Messiah Foretold
   Deuteronomy 18:15-18
T. The Messiah Suffers
   Isaiah 53:1-12
W. The Messiah Anointed
   Isaiah 61:1-11
T. The Messiah Worshiped
   Luke 19:28-38
F. The Messiah Followed
   John 1:35-42
S. The Messiah Conquers
   Revelation 19:11-16

Prophecies About the Messiah

October 16, 2005

Honor God (Malachi)

Malachi 1:1 through 2:16

INTRODUCTION

Malachi is the unknown prophet with the angelic name. Nothing is known of him. Some scholars believe the name *Malachi* is only a title descriptive of his official position, meaning "my angel" or "my messenger."

The exact date of the writing of the Book of Malachi is not known. It is generally agreed that it belongs in the period between 460 B.C. and 400 B.C. This would make Malachi a contemporary with Ezra and Nehemiah.

Malachi's content deals with conditions as they existed about 100 years after the first arrival of exiles under Zerubbabel. The people and their leaders had not only lost much of their initial enthusiasm for rebuilding Jerusalem and the Temple, but they had also become lukewarm in their faith. They began to question the love of God and the justice of His rule. They saw evildoers prospering in the sight of the Lord. So there seemed to be no profit in trying to keep His commandments. Even the priests were negligent in the performance of their duties. They permitted the people to corrupt the Lord's worship.

Jewish men were violating the tradition regarding marriage and its sanctity. They divorced the wives of their youth in order to marry foreign and pagan wives. Even high-ranking officials were guilty of this practice along with the common people. In such an environment comes Malachi—God's messenger with a bold message.

Unit Theme:
God's Word in the Minor Prophets (Nahum to Malachi)

Central Truth:
God is honored when Christians please Him through their worship, attitudes and actions.

Focus:
To examine and practice principles for honoring God.

Context:
The events took place in Judah and Jerusalem following the Jews' return from captivity.

Golden Text:
"From the rising of the sun even unto the going down of the same my name shall be great among the Gentiles" (Malachi 1:11).

Study Outline:
I. Honor God With Your Worship (Malachi 1:1-9)
II. Honor God With Your Attitudes (Malachi 1:10-14; 2:1, 2)
III. Honor God With Your Actions (Malachi 2:3-16)

I. HONOR GOD WITH YOUR WORSHIP (Malachi 1:1-9)
A. Speaking to the People (vv. 1-5)

1. The burden of the word of the Lord to Israel by Malachi.

2. I have loved you, saith the Lord. Yet ye say, Wherein hast thou loved us? Was not Esau Jacob's brother? saith the Lord: yet I loved Jacob,

3. And I hated Esau, and laid his mountains and his heritage waste for the dragons of the wilderness.

4. Whereas Edom saith, We are impoverished, but we will return and build the desolate places; thus saith the Lord of hosts, They shall build, but I will throw down; and they shall call them, The border of wickedness, and, The people against whom the Lord hath indignation for ever.

5. And your eyes shall see, and ye shall say, The Lord will be magnified from the border of Israel.

Haggai and Zechariah had predicted God's blessings were about to be poured out on a people redeemed and cleansed. But several decades had passed, and these prophecies of hope were still unfulfilled. The days had become increasingly drab and dreary. It was a time of disappointment, disillusionment and decay. Hopes and hearts were broken.

The people had become bitter, but their bitterness was only delaying God's promised blessings! They sounded almost sarcastic and flippant in their attitude toward God. Probably the long days of waiting had left the people dull and doubting.

In the first five verses of his book, Malachi reminded the people of God's love and provided Exhibit A—Edom. God had chosen Jacob and rejected Esau. Observe what happened to the Edomites, the descendants of Esau. Soon after the beginning of the Jewish captivity, the Nabatean Arabs had pushed the Edomites out of their land and laid it waste. Now would they be allowed to return to their own land as Israel had? No. So Israel's misfortunes were minor compared to Edom's. God still loved His own chosen nation.

B. Speaking to the Priests (vv. 6-9)

6. A son honoureth his father, and a servant his master: if then I be a father, where is mine honour? and if I be a master, where is my fear? saith the Lord of hosts unto you, O priests, that despise my name. And ye say, Wherein have we despised thy name?

7. Ye offer polluted bread upon mine altar; and ye say, Wherein have we polluted thee? In that ye say, The table of the Lord is contemptible.

8. And if ye offer the blind for sacrifice, is it not evil? and if ye offer the lame and sick, is it not evil? offer it now unto

---

Talk About It:
1. How did God answer Israel's question, "Wherein hast thou loved us?" (v. 2).
2. What happens to the plans of people who rebel against God (v. 4)?

polluted bread (v. 7)—defiled food

Honor God

thy governor; will he be pleased with thee, or accept thy person? saith the Lord of hosts.

9. And now, I pray you, beseech God that he will be gracious unto us: this hath been by your means: will he regard your persons? saith the Lord of hosts.

After responding to the people, Malachi turned his attention to the priests. He criticized them for their low esteem of God's majesty. They did not even show their God the respect that a son would show his father or a servant would show his master.

The Law had been very specific concerning the son and his father. Some infractions even carried the death penalty. It was also generally accepted that a servant should respect his master. But instead of honoring God, the priests had despised His name.

When God answered their first rejoinder with "You place defiled food on my altar," they came right back at Him, saying, "How have we defiled you?" (v. 7, *NIV*). When people respond to God so sharply, it's a sign that sin has hardened their heart.

The priests had polluted God and His house by saying the table of the Lord was contemptible. When spiritual leaders despise sacred things, the people they serve are surely in trouble!

The priests showed their contempt for God by offering blind, lame and sick animals for sacrifice. They certainly would not offer such animals to the governor, the Lord said. Nor would the governor accept them. Why then should they offer them to God?

The priests had developed an attitude that was so bad they could not expect God to hear and answer their prayers. They were in such a state of indifference toward God that He would not accept them or their offerings.

II. HONOR GOD WITH YOUR ATTITUDES
(Malachi 1:10-14; 2:1, 2)

A. Mercenary Attitude (1:10-14)

10. Who is there even among you that would shut the doors for nought? neither do ye kindle fire on mine altar for nought. I have no pleasure in you, saith the Lord of hosts, neither will I accept an offering at your hand.

11. For from the rising of the sun even unto the going down of the same my name shall be great among the Gentiles; and in every place incense shall be offered unto my name, and a pure offering: for my name shall be great among the heathen, saith the Lord of hosts.

12. But ye have profaned it, in that ye say, The table of the Lord is polluted; and the fruit thereof, even his meat, is contemptible.

13. Ye said also, Behold, what a weariness is it! and ye have snuffed at it, saith the Lord of hosts; and ye brought that which was torn, and the lame, and the sick; thus ye

Talk About It:
1. How is God like a father? Like a master? How does He expect us to respond to Him as Father and Master?
2. Why did the priests have contempt for the very item God provided for their salvation? If this still happens today, how and where does it happen?
3. Do you think the priests really thought God would accept their sickly sacrifices?
4. What kind of sad sacrifices do some believers offer God today?

brought an offering: should I accept this of your hand? saith the Lord.

14. But cursed be the deceiver, which hath in his flock a male, and voweth, and sacrificeth unto the Lord a corrupt thing: for I am a great King, saith the Lord of hosts, and my name is dreadful among the heathen.

Talk About It:
1. Why did God tell the priests to shut the Temple doors (v. 10)?
2. What was God's plan regarding people of other nations, and how had Israel's sins hindered that plan (vv. 11, 12)?
3. Whom does God deem "cursed" (v. 14)? Why?

These verses suggest that wrong worship is worse than no worship at all. It was better for the people to keep their sorry animals for themselves than to bring them to the Temple to be sacrificed, for God would refuse such an offering. The Hebrew word translated "for nought" (v. 10) means "without results."

"Wrong worship will one day be practically repudiated. . . . A modern expositor expresses the idea [of verse 11] thus: 'Since ye Jewish priests and people "despise my name" (v. 6), I shall find others who will magnify it (Matthew 8:11). Do not think I shall have no worshipers because I have not you, for from the east to the west my name shall be great among the Gentiles, those very peoples whom ye look down on as abominable" (*Pulpit Commentary*).

The ministry of the priests had become a burden of routine that they found distasteful. They arrogantly *snuffed* (Malachi 1:13) at the Lord's table, which is a metaphor taken from cattle that do not like their fodder. The cattle blow strongly through their nose upon it; and after this neither they nor any other cattle will eat it.

"A rather pompous-looking deacon was endeavoring to impress upon a class of boys the importance of living the Christian life. 'Why do people call me a Christian?' the man asked. After a moment's pause, one youngster said, 'Maybe it's because they don't know you.'"
—*Sermon Illustrations.com*

In verse 14 the Lord uses the term *deceiver* ("cheat," *NIV*) to describe the person who vows to bring an acceptable sacrifice to the Lord but instead brings a crippled, injured or diseased animal to the Temple, leaving the acceptable animal at home. Such a person is *cursed*—he will be judged by God.

This brings to mind the account of Ananias and Sapphira, who willingly sold a piece of property and pretended to give the entire sale price to the Lord, but who secretly kept some of the money. It wasn't such a secret—God saw what they did—and they were immediately judged by Him for their deception (see Acts 5:1-11).

B. Cursed Blessings (2:1, 2)

1. And now, O ye priests, this commandment is for you.

2. If ye will not hear, and if ye will not lay it to heart, to give glory unto my name, saith the Lord of hosts, I will even send a curse upon you, and I will curse your blessings: yea, I have cursed them already, because ye do not lay it to heart.

The Lord God was fed up with the attitudes of the priests, so He sent them the sternest of warnings. He told them to listen to Him and determine in their heart to honor His name. That was the source of the priests' unfaithfulness—their heart. Unless change began there, no outward actions would make any difference. Genuinely listening to God involves the ear, the heart and the hands.

If the priests did not listen, God said He would curse their blessings. God had blessed the priests so they would honor the name of the Lord, but they had turned His honor to dishonor by the way they performed their duties in His house and in His name. Because of their heart condition, the priests were already under a curse. And now the blessings of serving the Lord as His priests would turn around and become a curse to them as God judged them. Their position of honor would become their dishonor.

Talk About It:
1. Why is it so important for our lives to bring glory to God?
2. How can a blessing become a curse?

III. HONOR GOD WITH YOUR ACTIONS (Malachi 2:3-16)
A. Unfaithful Priests (vv. 3-9)

3. Behold, I will corrupt your seed, and spread dung upon your faces, even the dung of your solemn feasts; and one shall take you away with it.

4. And ye shall know that I have sent this commandment unto you, that my covenant might be with Levi, saith the Lord of hosts.

5. My covenant was with him of life and peace; and I gave them to him for the fear wherewith he feared me, and was afraid before my name.

6. The law of truth was in his mouth, and iniquity was not found in his lips: he walked with me in peace and equity, and did turn many away from iniquity.

equity (v. 6)— uprightness

7. For the priest's lips should keep knowledge, and they should seek the law at his mouth: for he is the messenger of the Lord of hosts.

8. But ye are departed out of the way; ye have caused many to stumble at the law; ye have corrupted the covenant of Levi, saith the Lord of hosts.

9. Therefore have I also made you contemptible and base before all the people, according as ye have not kept my ways, but have been partial in the law.

base (v. 9)—humiliated

Verse 3 explicitly describes the shame the priests would experience because of their contempt for the sacrifices of worship. First, He would "corrupt [their] seed," which translates as "restrain your arm. God would 'tie the hands' of those officiating at the altar, and there would be no fruit from altar, and there would be no fruit from their labors" (Wycliffe).

In addition, the unworthy sacrifices the priests placed on the altar would be thrown back at them. Not only would their sacrifices be rejected, but the unfaithful priests themselves would be rejected. God would sweep them away just as animal dung

Talk About It:
1. Why would the priests be treated with such disrespect (vv. 3, 4)?
2. Describe the character and activities that should mark a minister's life (vv. 4-7).

3. Why is the fall of a minister so destructive (vv. 8, 9)?

would be swept out. In essence, the priests would be taken out with the trash.

In verse 5, God begins to lay out the covenant He made with the tribe of Levi when the priesthood was begun. It was "a covenant of peace" and "a covenant of a lasting priesthood" (Numbers 25:12, 13, *NIV*). The priest was responsible for teaching God's precepts and laws to His people, and offering sacrifices on their behalf (Deuteronomy 33:10).

Through the priest's ministry, people were brought into a relationship of peace with God, and the priest himself had life and peace from the Lord. Being a priest demanded the highest level of reverence and awe of God, for the priest represented God to the people. The priest was "the messenger of the Lord of hosts" (Malachi 2:7).

The faithful priest was noted for teaching God's truth to His people, and "nothing false was found on his lips" (v. 6, *NIV*). In other words, the priest knew the Law of God and spoke it to the people. More importantly, God's priest lived an upright life, thereby teaching God's ways through word and example. As a result, he "did turn many [people] away from iniquity" (v. 6).

"In great measure, according to the purity and perfections of the instrument, will be the success [of the minister]. It is not great talents God blesses so much as great likeness to Jesus. A holy minister is an awful weapon in the hand of God."
—Robert McCheyne

Tragically, the priests in Malachi's day were having the opposite effect on the people. They taught things that were contrary to the Law, causing people to stumble. And they lived in disobedience to the Law, setting a ruinous example. As Jesus later said, "Can a blind man lead a blind man? Will they not both fall into a pit? A student is not above his teacher, but everyone who is fully trained will be like his teacher" (Luke 6:39, 40, *NIV*).

The priests had broken their covenant with God, thus God was breaking covenant with them. They had labeled God's ways "contemptible," but now the priests themselves were becoming hated and humiliated before the nation. This was the result of flouting God's laws and misrepresenting God by showing favor to some people rather than treating all people equally.

B. Unfaithful People (vv. 10-16)
(Malachi 2:11-16 is not included in the printed text.)

10. Have we not all one father? hath not one God created us? why do we deal treacherously every man against his brother, by profaning the covenant of our fathers?

Talk About It:
1. How can believers "deal treacherously" (break faith) with other believers?
2. How does a person's marriage relationship affect his/her relationship with God (vv. 13-15)?

Now Malachi brings charges against the people of Judah. Though they had been betrayed by the priesthood, God still held them responsible for their choices and actions.

The people were living as though they had forgotten that the same God had created each one of them. Rather than living as one national family serving Father God, they had broken faith with Him and one another. How?

First, in violation of God's command, they were marrying foreigners who worshiped idols. Thus they were trying to mix the worship of Jehovah with the religion of strange gods (v. 11). Second, they were continuing to offer sacrifices in the Temple even though they were living in violation of God's Law, and they wept and wailed because God would not accept their sacrifices (vv. 12, 13). Third, when a man would tire of the wife of his youth, he would break his marriage covenant with her in favor of marrying someone else.

By violating God's marriage laws, the people were breaking covenant with God, and the Lord himself was the witness against them (v. 14). In fact, the Lord was both eyewitness and judge. Malachi reminded the readers that when a couple is united in marriage, they "make one" (v. 15). God wants the husband and wife to live in accordance with His covenant and to rear their children in His ways. This is still how God expects the faith to be passed on, from generation to generation.

God declared that He hates divorce (v. 16). And He sees right through individuals who try to hide their thoughts and their deeds, as if they can hide their sins with a garment. But even the garment itself is stained with sin until the people confess their faults and turn to God.

3. What is God's attitude toward divorce? Why?

"What the church needs most desperately is holy fear. The passion to please God more than the culture and community in which we spend these few, short years."
—Charles Colson

CONCLUSION

At the end of verse 16, God gives a command that is as relevant today as it was when Malachi proclaimed it some 2,400 years ago: "So guard yourself in your spirit, and do not break faith" (2:16, *NIV*).

The priests' unguarded spirit grew into a bitter attitude toward God and His ways, while the people's unguarded spirit led to broken marriage vows and a shattered covenant with God Almighty. We don't have to follow their paths. Instead, let's heed the words of Hebrews 12:15: "See to it that no one misses the grace of God and that no bitter root grows up to cause trouble and defile many" (*NIV*).

GOLDEN TEXT CHALLENGE

"FROM THE RISING OF THE SUN EVEN UNTO THE GOING DOWN OF THE SAME MY NAME SHALL BE GREAT AMONG THE GENTILES" (Malachi 1:11).

It was God's plan for the priests and the people of Israel to be shining examples of God's power and grace so the nations of the world would be drawn to life with God. He wanted their worship, their attitudes and their actions to testify of His grace and greatness.

Israel repeatedly failed in this calling until the Savior was born. However, the compelling beauty of Christ's perfection in worship, attitude and actions became the Light of the World. And we as His children are to be reflections of the Light, leading people to the Cross.

Daily Devotions:
M. Failure to Honor God
  1 Samuel 2:27-36
T. Worship the Creator
  Psalm 96:1-9
W. Amend Your Ways
  Jeremiah 7:1-7
T. Loving Actions Honor God
  Romans 12:9-21
F. Proper Attitude Toward Service
  Philippians 1:12-18
S. Proper Attitude Toward Life
  Philippians 1:19-30

What God Expects of Us (Malachi)

Malachi 2:17 through 4:6

Unit Theme:
God's Word in the Minor Prophets (Nahum to Malachi)

Central Truth:
Christians must faithfully fulfill their commitments to God and people.

Focus:
To identify what God expects of His people and live to please Him.

Context:
The events took place in Judah and Jerusalem following the Jews' return from captivity.

Golden Text:
"He hath shewed thee, O man, what is good; and what doth the Lord require of thee, but to do justly, and to love mercy, and to walk humbly with thy God?" (Micah 6:8).

Study Outline:
I. God Expects Purity (Malachi 2:17; 3:1-5)
II. God Expects Obedience (Malachi 3:6-18)
III. God Expects Reverence (Malachi 4:1-6)

INTRODUCTION

The final book of the Old Testament is a fitting conclusion to the story of God's people who are waiting for their promised salvation. This book was written during a time of relative inactivity in the life of the Jewish nation. Priests and people had become lethargic and cynical in their relationship with God. They questioned if God listened to them or cared for them. Evildoers had arisen in their midst and seemed to suffer little consequence for their actions. Von Rad writes, "The man who addresses us is exclusively concerned with abuses practiced by the community. He attacks priests who are careless in ritual matters, divorce, and, above all, blasé skepticism in religious matters" (*Old Testament Theology,* Volume 2, Harper & Row).

Malachi records seven complaints to the Lord against Israel during the restoration period. And the opening words of the book prove that every complaint was motivated by divine love: "I have loved you, saith the Lord" (1:2). They had doubted God's love (v. 2), despised His name (v. 6), profaned His worship (v. 7), questioned His justice (2:17), spurned His invitation (3:7), repudiated His claim (v. 7), and blasphemed His character (v. 13).

However, there was a faithful remnant to whom those charges did not apply, and in them God's love triumphed. These people "feared the Lord and honored his name" (v. 16, *NIV*). This loyalty was pleasing to the Lord, for He heard them, honored them, claimed them, and saved them from judgment.

I. GOD EXPECTS PURITY (Malachi 2:17; 3:1-5)

A. The Question (2:17)

17. Ye have wearied the Lord with your words. Yet ye say, Wherein have we wearied him? When ye say, Every one that doeth evil is good in the sight of the Lord, and he delighteth in them; or, Where is the God of judgment?

The people of Judah were gossiping about God! As they watched evildoers prosper, they decided God must be pleased with those sinners and their sins. The people were asking each other, "Where is the God of justice?" (*NIV*). They were questioning the integrity of God and even His very existence. It's as if they were saying, "We're not sure if God exists. If He does exist, He must not be a just God."

Of course, God was hearing everything they said, and their words *wearied* Him: "He has borne with [them] so long, and has been provoked so often, that He will bear it no longer. It is not fit that He should" (Adam Clarke).

Talk About It:
1. What does it mean to weary God, and how can we do it?
2. Compare the scoffers of our time (2 Peter 3:3-9) with the doubters described in Malachi 2:17.

B. The Forerunner (3:1)

1. Behold, I will send my messenger, and he shall prepare the way before me: and the Lord, whom ye seek, shall suddenly come to his temple, even the messenger of the covenant, whom ye delight in: behold, he shall come, saith the Lord of hosts.

This verse speaks of two different *messengers* God would send to His people. "My messenger" speaks of one who would precede the Messiah and prepare the way for Him. "The messenger of the covenant" refers to the Messiah himself, who would come in fulfillment of the covenant God made with Abraham.

The messenger who would be the Messiah's forerunner was John the Baptist. Isaiah prophesied about him: "The voice of him that crieth in the wilderness, Prepare ye the way of the Lord, make straight in the desert a highway for our God" (40:3).

The statement "whom ye delight in" referred to the Jewish attitude regarding the coming Messiah. They looked for Him, dreamed of Him, and longed for Him through hundreds of years of various kinds of oppression. The irony is that when He finally came, only a small minority received Him.

Talk About It:
1. Why did the Messiah need a forerunner?
2. What was John the Baptist's message (Matthew 3:1-3)?
3. What did Jesus say about John in Luke 7:26-29?

C. The Messiah (vv. 2-5)

2. But who may abide the day of his coming? and who shall stand when he appeareth? for he is like a refiner's fire, and like fullers' soap:

3. And he shall sit as a refiner and purifier of silver: and he shall purify the sons of Levi, and purge them as gold and silver, that they may offer unto the Lord an offering in righteousness.

October 23, 2005

4. Then shall the offering of Judah and Jerusalem be pleasant unto the Lord, as in the days of old, and as in former years.

5. And I will come near to you to judgment; and I will be a swift witness against the sorcerers, and against the adulterers, and against false swearers, and against those that oppress the hireling in his wages, the widow, and the fatherless, and that turn aside the stranger from his right, and fear not me, saith the Lord of hosts.

The coming Messiah was to be so splendid and magnificent that human beings would scarcely be able to stand in His presence. His power and influence would be so cleansing that He was likened to a refiner's fire and a launderer's soap. A refiner's fire would melt metal until all the dross and impurities were carried away. A launderer's soap was not soap as we know it, but lye or potash—a cleansing agent made from wood ashes that could whiten and purify garments and other items.

Verse 3 says the Lord would act as "a refiner and purifier of silver." He would purify the priests ("the sons of Levi") and purge them as gold and silver. Judgment must begin at the house of God, with the people of God and for the purposes of God. Just as the Messiah would come to the Jews first, so He would purify and cleanse them first.

God's judgment would first fall on Israel's priests because they were the most highly privileged and the most responsible and therefore held to the highest standard. James 3:1 says, "Not many of you should presume to be teachers, my brothers, because you know that we who teach will be judged more strictly" (*NIV*).

When God's judgment completed its work of purification, Judah's offerings would be acceptable once again (Malachi 3:4). The Lord looked back to the ideal periods in Israel's checkered past, and said it could be like that again.

In verse 5 the Lord moves from speaking to the priests to speaking to the people. The people were scarcely less guilty than the priests in disobeying the Lord's commands. As Ezekiel had done in Ezekiel 22, Malachi observed that the people had followed the priests in their sins. They were guilty of sorcery, adultery, perjury, and exploitation of the poor and defenseless. Sorcery meant they had followed false gods and occult practices; adultery was both physical and spiritual; they had lied against and taken advantage of neighbors, widows and orphans.

All of these sins grieved the Lord, and they all had their root in the people's lack of reverence for the Lord. The fear of the Lord leads a person to live righteously, but a lack of reverence removes restraints.

Talk About It:
1. How does Jesus Christ refine and purify people, and why?
2. What kind of offering does God expect from people today, and how can that offering be acceptable?
3. How are the sins listed in verse 5 taking place today? Is God currently judging people for those sins? What judgment awaits them in the future?

Always Pure
It is said that at Saint Margaret's Bay, in the southeast of England, there is a well which is always covered by the sea at high tide. Strangely enough, its water remains fresh and pure, uncontaminated by the salty sea water. Fed from the hills above, it has a constant supply of fresh water pouring into it, which effectively prevents the ocean from flowing in. How like the Christian who is dominated by the Holy Spirit!
—1,000 New Illustrations

II. GOD EXPECTS OBEDIENCE (Malachi 3:6-18)

A. Robbery (vv. 6-9)

6. For I am the Lord, I change not; therefore ye sons of Jacob are not consumed.

7. Even from the days of your fathers ye are gone away from mine ordinances, and have not kept them. Return unto me, and I will return unto you, saith the Lord of hosts. But ye said, Wherein shall we return?

8. Will a man rob God? Yet ye have robbed me. But ye say, Wherein have we robbed thee? In tithes and offerings.

9. Ye are cursed with a curse: for ye have robbed me, even this whole nation.

In verse 6 God refers to Himself by His covenant name, Jehovah, which expresses His eternal, independent and unchangeable being. His patience in executing judgment does not infer that He has changed. He has ever been holy, and He ever will be. He is ever faithful in fulfilling His promises, hence the wicked will be judged and the righteous will be rewarded. Because His eternal purpose must stand, His people may be chastened, but not wholly consumed.

The disobedience of the children of Israel was no new offense (v. 7). But God's call to repentance and return is met with the pharisaical spirit of self-righteousness. How could they return when they acknowledged no wrong and therefore no need of repentance? No confession of sin means no salvation from God.

Verse 8 contains God's sixth complaint against Israel in the Book of Malachi. He charges them with defrauding Him. It is not clear whether they had actually withheld their tithe or given it by measure out of a selfish and miserly spirit. In any case, they were guilty of fraud before God. Whether Christians in the church must give their tenth or more, it must be done cheerfully in a spirit of love for the Lord and His cause, or else one might be guilty of fraud even in that which is given. The primary requirement is to give ourselves to the Lord and then to give of our substance willingly as God has prospered us (1 Corinthians 16:2; 2 Corinthians 8:5).

The penalty for defrauding God is the divine curse (Malachi 3:9). From the two verses that follow, we gather that the effect of this curse was scarcity and barrenness. The last clause of verse 9 gives the reason for the curse. The whole nation had robbed God, hence a national chastening. From history, ancient and modern, it is evident that God will deal with both nations and individuals as they deserve.

Talk About It:
1. Why is it so comforting to know God never changes?
2. What offer does God make in verse 7? Does He still make this offer today?
3. Why is it so important to give tithes and offerings to the Lord?

B. Blessings (vv. 10-12)

10. Bring ye all the tithes into the storehouse, that there may be meat in mine house, and prove me now herewith, saith the Lord of hosts, if I will not open you the windows

of heaven, and pour you out a blessing, that there shall not be room enough to receive it.

11. And I will rebuke the devourer for your sakes, and he shall not destroy the fruits of your ground; neither shall your vine cast her fruit before the time in the field, saith the Lord of hosts.

12. And all nations shall call you blessed: for ye shall be a delightsome land, saith the Lord of hosts.

Talk About It:
1. How would God bless Israel for faithfully bringing their tithes to His house?
2. How would Israel's faithful giving be a blessing to other nations?

Although the covenant people had broken their covenant with God and suffered chastisement, He graciously invited them to a renewal through obedience. He asked for the full tenth as a proof that they trusted Him and recognized His love toward them. To bring "all the tithes" means more than a mathematical part; it includes the inner intention as motivated by love for the Lord.

God challenged the people to *prove* Him. That is, they were to do their part, perform their duty, and trust the Lord to pour out a blessing "that there shall not be room enough to receive it" (v. 10). God would "rebuke the devourer" (v. 11) for their sakes, meaning He would destroy the devouring locust and every agency that could hurt the crops, assuring that there would be an abundant harvest.

"When we come to the end of life, the question will be, 'How much have you given?' not 'How much have you gotten?'"
—George Sweeting

As a consequence of their blessings, Israel's reputation would be exalted among the nations (v. 12). Other peoples would admit that Israel's obedience to the true God had brought them prosperity. This verse is evidently prophetic of that prosperity to be enjoyed by Israel and the nations of the world at the second advent of Christ to set up His literal kingdom on earth. We can be part of that blessed population.

C. Complaints (vv. 13-15)

stout (v. 13)—harsh

13. Your words have been stout against me, saith the Lord. Yet ye say, What have we spoken so much against thee?

14. Ye have said, It is vain to serve God: and what profit is it that we have kept his ordinance, and that we have walked mournfully before the Lord of hosts?

15. And now we call the proud happy; yea, they that work wickedness are set up; yea, they that tempt God are even delivered.

Talk About It:
What accusation did the people bring against the Lord?

The people had been defiant toward God. The implication is that the people had been speaking not directly to God, but of God to one another. Many had been the defiant speeches and blasphemies spoken against the Lord. But He will ultimately judge all blasphemers (Jude 15). This charge the people were unwilling to accept.

Among themselves the people had questioned the usefulness of serving God loyally, and had imagined it was the evildoers who were prospering. It seems the Jews had known

What God Expects of Us

material prosperity. So when adversity came they blamed God for being unjust, and that was because their hopes for blessings were confined to temporal things.

D. Remembrance (vv. 16-18)
(Malachi 3:16, 17 is not included in the printed text.)

18. Then shall ye return, and discern between the righteous and the wicked, between him that serveth God and him that serveth him not.

The Lord's response here is to that devoted remnant of the Jews who, in contrast to the blasphemers described above, spoke among themselves about God's righteous dealings with people both righteous and unrighteous. The Lord took special notice of those conversations. He not only heard them, but had their words recorded in a book of remembrance, to reward them for their loyalty in due time.

In verse 17, the Lord said He would claim the righteous remnant as His own peculiar treasure on the Day of Judgment. They will be spared from the punishment because they are His sons and because they have served Him.

III. GOD EXPECTS REVERENCE (Malachi 4:1-6)
A. Judgment and Healing (vv. 1-3)
1. For, behold, the day cometh, that shall burn as an oven; and all the proud, yea, and all that do wickedly, shall be stubble: and the day that cometh shall burn them up, saith the Lord of hosts, that it shall leave them neither root nor branch.

2. But unto you that fear my name shall the Sun of righteousness arise with healing in his wings; and ye shall go forth, and grow up as calves of the stall.

3. And ye shall tread down the wicked; for they shall be ashes under the soles of your feet in the day that I shall do this, saith the Lord of hosts.

Malachi foresaw the coming of the Day of the Lord as a time when the proud and the wicked would be destroyed. Like all the Old Testament prophets, Malachi did not speak of two separate advents of the Lord, but only of one. Some things we now know will happen at His second coming were included with prophecies of His first coming.

The Day of the Lord is described as having a twofold effect. For the wicked, it will be a day of burning and destruction. For the righteous, it will be a day of healing and salvation. Verse 3 says God will give the righteous dominion over the wicked.

As the rising sun quickly spreads a canopy of light from the east to the west, so will the Lord's coming spread light over the nations, riding on wings of grace (v. 2). Malachi carried the

Talk About It:
1. How did God promise to minister to the minority who faithfully served Him?
2. How would the distinction "between the righteous and the wicked" be made clear (v. 18)?

"In every age there has been a remnant that feared the Lord."
—Matthew Henry

as calves of the stall (v. 2)—as calves released from their pen

Talk About It:
1. Why is an oven an appropriate analogy for the Day of Judgment?
2. Who will be rewarded on Judgment Day, and how?

"You only go around once in life—and after that the judgment."
—Dan Cory

metaphor by declaring there will be healing in these wings. The Lord will heal every kind of infirmity and need.

B. Moses and Elijah (vv. 4-6)

4. Remember ye the law of Moses my servant, which I commanded unto him in Horeb for all Israel, with the statutes and judgments.

5. Behold, I will send you Elijah the prophet before the coming of the great and dreadful day of the Lord:

6. And he shall turn the heart of the fathers to the children, and the heart of the children to their fathers, lest I come and smite the earth with a curse.

If the people were to avert divine judgment and instead receive eternal reward, they were to remember and follow the decrees and laws God gave to Moses. Remembering the Law was especially critical now because Israel was about to enter a 400-year period when the prophetic ministry would be quiet as they awaited the coming of the Messiah.

In verse 5 the prophet again predicts the coming of the forerunner of Christ, who would be a bold "Elijah" preaching repentance and restoration. This promise was fulfilled in John the Baptist, who paved the way for the Lord Jesus. With this promise to sustain Israel for four centuries, the Old Testament written record came to a close.

CONCLUSION

At the close of Malachi, Israel was under the domination of Persia, and remained so for about another hundred years. Beginning in 332 B.C. the Persian Empire was destroyed by Alexander the Great. At Alexander's death his empire was divided between his generals, and Judea was ultimately ruled by the Seleucids, who were cruel, arrogant and hostile toward the Jews. This led to the Maccabean revolt, when a small guerilla band freed Judea and introduced a period of prosperity and peace. The Romans arrived in 63 B.C. They were occupying Judea when Christ was born.

GOLDEN TEXT CHALLENGE

"HE HATH SHEWED THEE, O MAN, WHAT IS GOOD; AND WHAT DOTH THE LORD REQUIRE OF THEE, BUT TO DO JUSTLY, AND TO LOVE MERCY, AND TO WALK HUMBLY WITH THY GOD?" (Micah 6:8).

The *good* God requires is the doing of His will. To *do justly* is to act toward God and people according to the divine standard of righteousness revealed in His law. To *love mercy* is to show a compassionate warmheartedness toward others. To *walk humbly* before God is to recognize the absolute holiness and righteousness of God and to walk in submissive obedience to Him.

Talk About It:
1. What did God call the people to remember, and what does the church today need to remember?
2. The last verse of the Old Testament describes the hearts of fathers and children being turned toward each other. Why was this so important then? Why is it so important now?

Daily Devotions:
M. Obey God's Commands
Deuteronomy 30:15-20
T. Learn to Fear the Lord
Deuteronomy 31:9-13
W. Prayer for Purity
Psalm 19:7-14
T. Christ's Lordship Demands Obedience
Luke 6:46-49
F. Vessels of Honor
2 Timothy 2:20-26
S. Serve With Godly Fear
Hebrews 12:25-29

What God Expects of Us

The Kingdom of God

Matthew 13:24-50

INTRODUCTION

The subject Jesus taught about most frequently was the "kingdom of God," or "kingdom of heaven." Throughout the four Gospels there are over 70 direct references to this kingdom in His teaching. In fact, the religious leaders' chief charge against Jesus was that He claimed to be a king—a claim that Jesus fully accepted.

Jesus answered, "My kingdom is not of this world: if my kingdom were of this world, then would my servants fight, that I should not be delivered to the Jews: but now is my kingdom not from hence. Pilate therefore said unto him, Art thou a king then?" (John 18:36, 37).

Jesus' ministry began with the simple proclamation, "The kingdom of heaven is at hand" (Matthew 4:17) and ended with the simple sign on His cross that read "This is Jesus the king of the Jews" (27:37). How then do we understand this kingdom Jesus preached?

In Jesus' day, the word *kingdom* was full of political and religious vigor. Whereas people in His day might speak about governments in terms of *kingdoms* or *empires*, examples of similar words we presently use are *nation, country* or *culture*. So it is easy to see how Pilate could have misunderstood Jesus' notion of His kingship. To suddenly declare oneself a king posed a threat to the ruling Roman Empire! Even during the growth and expansion of the early church, Roman rulers mistook the cause of Christ, fearing a possible political insurgency against Roman power. Of course, Jesus had no such intention. Instead, He spoke of an inner, invisible kingdom far beyond the reach of political authority: "Once, having been asked by the Pharisees when the kingdom of God would come, Jesus replied, 'The kingdom of God does not come with your careful observation, nor will people say, "Here it is," or "There it is," because the kingdom of God is within you'" (Luke 17:20, 21, *NIV*).

Yes, the kingdom of God is a real kingdom, with its own citizens, values and boundaries, but it stretches far beyond this earth. While Jesus offers it to the world, its origin and destination is ultimately heaven itself.

A short definition of the *kingdom of God* is simply "the full reign of God in the lives of people." It encompasses every gift given to believers in Christ. When people are living in the kingdom of God—that is, under the full reign of God—they have total access to salvation, Holy Spirit baptism, and the fruit of the Spirit. Jesus used parables to depict the citizens, growth, and value of His kingdom.

Unit Theme:
Parables of Jesus

Central Truth:
Kingdom parables reveal characteristics of God's kingdom.

Focus:
To study the nature of the kingdom of God and value the Kingdom above all else.

Context:
Sitting in a boat, Jesus teaches about the kingdom of heaven.

Golden Text:
"Seek ye first the kingdom of God, and his righteousness; and all these things shall be added unto you" (Matthew 6:33).

Study Outline:
I. Citizens of the Kingdom (Matthew 13:24-30, 36-43, 47-50)
II. Growth of the Kingdom (Matthew 13:31-33)
III. Value of the Kingdom (Matthew 13:44-46)

I. CITIZENS OF THE KINGDOM (Matthew 13:24-30, 36-43, 47-50)

As with any nation, the kingdom of God is made up chiefly of its citizens. Without citizens, a kingdom cannot exist, much less grow. For this reason, citizenship in any nation requires a pledge of allegiance and a commitment to the values of that nation. How does this relate to a heavenly kingdom?

A. Weeds and Wheat (vv. 24-30)

24. Another parable put he forth unto them, saying, The kingdom of heaven is likened unto a man which sowed good seed in his field:

25. But while men slept, his enemy came and sowed tares among the wheat, and went his way.

26. But when the blade was sprung up, and brought forth fruit, then appeared the tares also.

27. So the servants of the householder came and said unto him, Sir, didst not thou sow good seed in thy field? from whence then hath it tares?

28. He said unto them, An enemy hath done this. The servants said unto him, Wilt thou then that we go and gather them up?

29. But he said, Nay; lest while ye gather up the tares, ye root up also the wheat with them.

30. Let both grow together until the harvest: and in the time of harvest I will say to the reapers, Gather ye together first the tares, and bind them in bundles to burn them: but gather the wheat into my barn.

Talk About It:
1. How are Christians like wheat?
2. How are unbelievers like weeds?

Jesus tells two important parables to illustrate the values of citizenship in the kingdom of God. The first is the story of the weeds. It depicts a sower who plants wheat seed in a field, but in the middle of the night an enemy comes and sows weeds ("tares") in that same field. Rather than pulling the weeds and risking damage to the wheat, the sower declares that both the wheat and the weeds will grow together until the harvest, at which time the weeds will be burned and the wheat harvested. Interestingly, this parable is told immediately following a lengthier parable of a farmer who sowed seed on different types of ground. Here, however, Jesus is not concerned with the way people receive the message of the kingdom of God, but the way its citizens are identified.

B. Kingdom Citizenship on Earth (vv. 36-43)

36. Then Jesus sent the multitude away, and went into the house: and his disciples came unto him, saying, Declare unto us the parable of the tares of the field.

37. He answered and said unto them, He that soweth the good seed is the Son of man;

The Kingdom of God

38. The field is the world; the good seed are the children of the kingdom; but the tares are the children of the wicked one;

39. The enemy that sowed them is the devil; the harvest is the end of the world; and the reapers are the angels.

40. As therefore the tares are gathered and burned in the fire; so shall it be in the end of this world.

41. The Son of man shall send forth his angels, and they shall gather out of his kingdom all things that offend, and them which do iniquity;

42. And shall cast them into a furnace of fire: there shall be wailing and gnashing of teeth.

43. Then shall the righteous shine forth as the sun in the kingdom of their Father. Who hath ears to hear, let him hear.

Upon being asked by His disciples, Jesus offers an explanation of the parable of the weeds. Although the harvest occurs at the end of the parable, the story is chiefly concerned with what happens in the field, which symbolizes the world. In this world two distinct types of seed have been planted by two distinct leaders—the Son of Man (Jesus) and the devil. Interestingly, the two types of seed are referred to as children of either the Kingdom or the Evil One. Therefore, Jesus takes Kingdom citizenship beyond committed allegiance to a community or a set of values. Also, there are no peasant citizens in the Kingdom. No, membership in God's kingdom means living as one of "the children of the kingdom," an accepted member of the family of God.

Although the ultimate separation of the wheat and the weeds will not take place until "the end of the age" (*NKJV*), their citizenship is decided by clear characteristics of their earthly lifestyles. Notice there is no mention of those who have formally confessed Jesus Christ as Lord and those who haven't. Instead, it is assumed that their confession is evidenced by their character. The weeds, therefore, are easily identified as "them which do iniquity" (v. 41). Their actions betray their citizenship. Contrarily, the wheat are simply named *the righteous*, those who "shine forth as the sun in the kingdom of their Father" (v. 43). Again, Jesus equates citizenship in the kingdom of God with family. The righteous do not serve a distant king, but a loving Father.

Jesus closes the explanation of the parable with His familiar request for everyone to "hear"—to pay close attention to the meaning of the parable. Its main message is clear: *Citizenship in the kingdom of God is not only the promise of eternal life with God in heaven, but it is clearly evidenced by one's earthly way of life*. Throughout His teaching, Jesus reiterates this truth. He

Talk About It:
1. From this passage, list everything you can learn about the fate of unbelievers.

2. Explain the phrase "gnashing of teeth" (v. 42).

"Fire is evidently the only word in human language which can suggest the anguish of perdition. It is the only word in the parable of the wheat and the tares which our Lord did not interpret. . . . The only reasonable explanation is that fire is not a symbol. It perfectly describes the reality of the eternal burnings."

—**Richard Baxter,** *The Free Gift*

observes that discerning a person's loyalty toward or against God is basic, because "a tree is recognized by its fruit" (Matthew 12:33, *NIV*). Paul also picks up this theme in Galatians 6:7, 8: "Do not be deceived: God cannot be mocked. A man reaps what he sows. The one who sows to please his sinful nature, from that nature will reap destruction; the one who sows to please the Spirit, from the Spirit will reap eternal life" (*NIV*).

Although God alone ultimately knows the eternal destiny of individuals, their kingdom citizenship is discernable and active during their earthly life. In fact, *eternity* is simply the consequence of which kingdom was sown into during one's living years. For this reason, salvation or entrance into the kingdom of God is not only a claim for eternal life, but equally an expression of citizenship on earth.

C. Kingdom Citizenship in Heaven (vv. 47-50)

47. Again, the kingdom of heaven is like unto a net, that was cast into the sea, and gathered of every kind:

48. Which, when it was full, they drew to shore, and sat down, and gathered the good into vessels, but cast the bad away.

49. So shall it be at the end of the world: the angels shall come forth, and sever the wicked from among the just,

50. And shall cast them into the furnace of fire: there shall be wailing and gnashing of teeth.

Jesus has already used several parables that employ contemporary farming practices to communicate truth, and He now moves onto the fishing profession. Such teaching must have captured the minds of His audience, as several of His disciples were called from a previous life of professional fishing. Now that Jesus has declared the earthly aspects of citizenship in the kingdom of God versus the kingdom of the Enemy, He moves onto plain teaching regarding citizenship's consequences for eternity.

In this parable, a sobering insight into eternal damnation is explained in terms of the discerning quality of the kingdom of heaven. Although citizenship is open to all, as the kingdom of heaven is compared to an empty net that is cast almost indiscriminately into the sea of humanity, avoiding the choice of allegiance will one day be impossible. Jesus relates the "end of the age" to a final sweeping of the earth, in which citizenship in the kingdom of God is completely determined. God's angels will separate the citizens of the kingdom of God from the citizens of the kingdom of the Enemy, whose fate is graphically described as one of weeping and pain.

Interestingly, the destiny of the righteous is not mentioned. They are simply likened to "good fish" collected in baskets.

Talk About It:
1. Who is able to separate the wicked from the righteous?
2. What modern analogy could be used to explain the division of believers and sinners?

The Kingdom of God

Jesus' emphasis is on the eternal separation between the wicked and the righteous.

II. GROWTH OF THE KINGDOM (Matthew 13:31-33)

The very nature of creation teaches us that healthy life will always grow. Because Jesus preached a kingdom comprised of the family of God, He often emphasized its propensity to multiply. In Jesus' parables, this growth took two forms—visible and invisible, external and internal.

A. Visible Growth (vv. 31, 32)

31. Another parable put he forth unto them, saying, The kingdom of heaven is like to a grain of mustard seed, which a man took, and sowed in his field:

32. Which indeed is the least of all seeds: but when it is grown, it is the greatest among herbs, and becometh a tree, so that the birds of the air come and lodge in the branches thereof.

Jesus frequently taught on the power of small commitments to be multiplied into effective use in the kingdom of God. He likened the work of the Kingdom to investing small sums of money effectively (25:14-18), and praised the rewards that even a tiny seed of faith can produce (17:20). These spiritual laws are possible because of the nature of anything—even a mustard seed—that comes under the full reign of God to multiply in great measure.

Talk About It:
What makes God's kingdom "the greatest" (v. 32)?

How thrilling the parable of the mustard seed was to the early followers of Christ! When these words were spoken, their movement must have seemed like a mustard seed. They were a small band of simple peasants following a miracle-working Messiah, being criticized and persecuted at every turn. Jesus' ministry itself seemed to embody this process of seed planting. He never ventured outside of a small area in Israel. He occasionally ministered among crowds but more often invested into His 12 disciples and other individuals who He came across. Many times He even *commanded* beneficiaries of His power to tell no one (8:4; 16:20; 17:9). Christ was committed to the careful nurture of the small seeds of the kingdom of God. If He could plant their roots deeply in the hearts of a few, they could not help but eventually gain momentum and become a force to be reckoned with throughout the world.

In the Book of Acts, we see Jesus' promise in this parable come to pass. He reiterates the promise in concrete terms in 1:8: "But ye shall receive power, after that the Holy Ghost is come upon you: and ye shall be witnesses unto me both in Jerusalem, and in all Judaea, and in Samaria, and unto the uttermost part of the earth."

This promise was inaugurated in Acts 2, as the coming of

"The mustard seed was employed proverbially by the Jews, as it was by Jesus, to denote anything very minute. The common mustard of Palestine is black mustard. It grows wild, attaining the height of a horse and rider."

—Westminster Bible Dictionary

the Holy Spirit transformed a small group of followers into a Christian movement that quickly spread throughout Jerusalem. The persecution of the church in Acts 8 began the next step, as the movement was scattered throughout the empire. From that point, Paul was called by Christ to take the gospel exclusively to the Gentiles, truly "to the ends of the earth" (1:8, *NIV*). In this way, the Kingdom which began as a mustard seed with the people Jesus touched eventually became so large as to spread like a mighty tree throughout the earth.

B. Invisible Growth (v. 33)

33. Another parable spake he unto them; The kingdom of heaven is like unto leaven, which a woman took, and hid in three measures of meal, till the whole was leavened.

Talk About It:
1. Why can leaven not be hidden?
2. In what sense is the kingdom of heaven hidden? How is it not hidden?

Of course, Jesus was not simply talking about the growth of the Christian movement. That was a broad view of the Kingdom, but the movement at large was the sum total of thousands of individuals who experienced the growth of a grain of faith into a life-changing force.

Not only was the kingdom of God going to visibly work its way throughout the earth; it would do so in an invisible way, like yeast is mixed into flour. Remember, "the kingdom of God is within you" (Luke 17:21), therefore its outward expression is the consequence of an inner reality. A faithless individual first encounters the kingdom of God as a small mustard seed, or a small amount of yeast. It may take no obvious, outward effect on the person's life initially, but the message of the Kingdom never stagnates. Jesus compares it to yeast that causes inactive flour to rise, to become nourishing. So it is with the person who allows the kingdom of God to take root in his or her life.

Kingdom Authority
Almost everyone at some time gets pulled over by a police officer because of a traffic violation. What is it about the officer's presence that humbles us? Is it their gun, their siren, or their handcuffs? In reality, their authority comes only from their badge—the symbol that they are operating according to the power of the state.
So, too, our authority in Christ is not ours to possess, but is rather a symbol of our basic citizenship in the kingdom of God. When we immerse ourselves

The disciples are remarkable examples of this truth. Only Jesus would have picked such rugged men! Early on, they showed so little insight into the kingdom of God that their rise to church leadership is nothing short of miraculous. Nathanael wondered out loud how the Messiah could come from Nazareth (John 1:46). James and John, the brothers whom Jesus called "Sons of Thunder" (Mark 3:17), asked for Jesus' permission to call down fire on an unwelcoming village (Luke 9:54). Later, these two recruited their mother to request that they be given the most prominent status when Jesus inaugurated His earthly kingdom (Matthew 20:20, 21). And Peter, the rock upon whose confession the church was built, denied all knowledge of Jesus the night before His crucifixion. Even after the Resurrection, the disciples failed to understand the Kingdom, asking Jesus if He was finally going to raise it up within Israel (Acts 1:6).

It took years of discipling, experience, and the power of the

The Kingdom of God

Holy Spirit for the yeast of the Kingdom to work its way through the lives of these men, but eventually it yielded the church's greatest leaders. What anticipation must have been in Jesus' voice as He spoke this truth! Like a mustard seed and a batch of yeast, the Kingdom was always on the move, its invisible power eventually resulting in an unstoppable force.

in the promises and values of the Kingdom, the authority we possess to overcome obstacles is insurmountable.

III. VALUE OF THE KINGDOM (Matthew 13:44-46)

In the parables surveyed so far, Jesus has utilized common images to describe the kingdom of God. He makes use of the language of farming, gardening, fishing and baking to best communicate with His audience, who undoubtedly practiced these necessities on a daily basis. When discussing the value of the Kingdom, however, Jesus shifts away from metaphors that depend on mundane realities. Instead, He compares the Kingdom to a priceless treasure and an invaluable pearl.

Talk About It:

1. Why is God's kingdom so valuable?

2. What have you "sold" to be part of His kingdom?

Here Jesus brings out the hidden nature of the Kingdom. Whereas His other parables emphasize the Kingdom's openness to all, Jesus now portrays an important new dimension to Kingdom living—it often must be searched for. This is evident even in the Sermon on the Mount, which could be called a blueprint for life in God's kingdom. There Jesus promises, "Ask and it will be given to you; seek and you will find; knock and the door will be opened to you" (Matthew 7:7, *NIV*). Jesus is not saying that God is reluctant to disclose His kingdom, but simply that it does require asking, seeking and knocking.

The most valuable items are often hidden. It may not seem that way, given that many of the world's most valuable objects are now displayed in museums; but even these are usually protected by elaborately designed security systems, or armed guards. When a thief breaks into a home, he or she usually searches for places where valuables are hidden. In fact, fireproof safes are commonly owned today, as people secure their most treasured possessions from intrusion.

Similarly, there is a hidden nature to the invaluable truths of the kingdom of God. At one point, Jesus even explained He used parables so the "mystery of the kingdom of God" would not be unveiled too easily (Mark 4:11). The Kingdom is too valuable to be treated lightly.

A. Joyful Sacrifice (v. 44)

44. Again, the kingdom of heaven is like unto treasure hid in a field; the which when a man hath found, he hideth, and for joy thereof goeth and selleth all that he hath, and buyeth that field.

People have been known to make incredible sacrifices for great rewards. In the parable of the hidden treasure, Jesus describes just such a situation.

Here Jesus first portrays the hidden nature of the treasure that necessitates a search. The fortune was buried in a field, apparently discovered by a lone treasure-hunter. Telling no one, he quickly sells everything to purchase the field and possess this great reward. He thinks nothing of sacrificing everything he owned, because the treasure gained is worth far more.

How poignantly this must have resonated with the disciples! They had left everything to follow Christ and pursue the kingdom of God, urged on by Jesus' promise of reward (Matthew 19:29). They had left families, homes, fields and professions after hearing the call of the Kingdom. Later they would give their very life's blood for its cause, as would thousands of other nameless believers who discovered the hidden treasure worth far more than life itself. The church of Jesus Christ was born out of joyful sacrifice right from Pentecost: "And all that believed were together, and had all things common; and sold their possessions and goods, and parted them to all men, as every man had need" (Acts 2:44, 45).

Jesus lays a firm foundation for the carefree joy of the early church. Riches, honor and even life itself are valueless compared with the possession of the kingdom of God.

B. The Longing of the Heart (vv. 45, 46)
45. Again, the kingdom of heaven is like unto a merchant man, seeking goodly pearls:
46. Who, when he had found one pearl of great price, went and sold all that he had, and bought it.

In the parable commonly called "the pearl of great price," Jesus significantly changes His focus. He is still summarizing the great value of the Kingdom, but He shifts to the metaphor of professional merchants, who traded in fine jewels.

Whereas selling everything to own a diverse treasure full of valuables worth far more than the owner's previous possessions makes financial sense, for a pearl merchant to trade everything for a single pearl is absurd! The business of merchants was to make profits by selling goods for slightly more than their purchase price. For a pearl dealer to own nothing but one pearl severely handicapped his ability to make a living!

With this parable, Jesus goes beyond the infinite value of the kingdom of God to the inherent and deep need that it meets in the human heart. In fact, it is this need that gives the Kingdom its pricelessness. The merchant finds a pearl that makes the entire business of searching for valuable pearls obsolete. His life is too changed to look elsewhere. The deepest desire of his heart has been satisfied. The kingdom Jesus preached is not simply the best decision because of all its

Talk About It:
1. Name some faux "pearls" people are seeking after.
2. What makes God's kingdom so valuable?

"Christ is not valued at all unless He is valued above all."
—Augustine

promises—it is the only decision that quenches the longing thirst of the human heart to be complete, to be free, to be a part of the family of God.

CONCLUSION
The kingdom of God represents the full reign of God over a life, both on earth and in heaven. This Kingdom maintains promises for citizenry, constant growth and priceless value. Jesus used parables to explain these Kingdom principles. Citizenship in the kingdom of God is an earthly reality with heavenly rewards, and is primarily defined by inclusion into the family of God, whereby we are named children of God. The growth of the Kingdom took place slowly in the lives of early believers, until internal reality eventually exploded into visible enlargement as the early church spread throughout the world. The value of the Kingdom is portrayed in its hidden nature, whereby it produces joyful sacrifice as it meets the deepest longing of the human heart. For this reason the kingdom of God continues to grow mightily in the hearts of people all over the world today.

GOLDEN TEXT CHALLENGE
"SEEK YE FIRST THE KINGDOM OF GOD, AND HIS RIGHTEOUSNESS; AND ALL THESE THINGS SHALL BE ADDED UNTO YOU" (Matthew 6:33).

The verse is both a command and a promise. The clause which tells us to seek first the kingdom of God is a no-nonsense order. It speaks to the ordering of our priorities.

The second clause is a promise. It says that if we put God first, the more tangible aspects of life will be taken care of. The implication is that the very things which we are tempted to put ahead of God will turn out all right if we keep them in their proper place.

Daily Devotions:
M. A Just Kingdom
   Psalm 45:1-7
T. God's Kingdom
   Rules Over All
   Psalm 103:19-22
W. An Everlasting
   Kingdom
   Daniel 7:9-14
T. Supreme Value
   of the Kingdom
   Luke 18:18-30
F. Enter the
   Kingdom
   Through Rebirth
   John 3:1-8
S. The Wicked
   Won't Inherit the
   Kingdom
   1 Corinthians
   6:9-11

Bible Insight

PARABLES OF JESUS

Witnessing

1. Tasteless Salt	Matthew 5:13; Mark 9:50; Luke 14:34, 35
2. Shining Light	Matthew 5:14-16; Mark 4:21-23; Luke 8:16-18

Right and Wrong Attitudes

1. A Speck and a Log	Matthew 7:3-5
2. Children in the Market	Matthew 11:16-19
3. Unclean Spirit	Matthew 12:43-45; Luke 11:24-26
4. A Humbled Guest	Luke 14:7-11
5. A Pharisee and a Tax Collector	Luke 18:9-14

Salvation

1. Two Ways	Matthew 7:13, 14
2. Wise and Foolish Builders	Matthew 7:24-27
3. The Door	Luke 13:24, 25

Relationship With Jesus

1. Bridegroom's Friends	Matthew 9:14, 15; Mark 2:18-20; Luke 5:33-35
2. New Cloth	Matthew 9:16
3. New Wine	Matthew 9:17
4. Two Debtors	Luke 7:41-43
5. Bread of Life	John 6:31-38
6. Good Shepherd	John 10:1-18
7. Vine and Branches	John 15:1-7

Prayer

1. Harvest Workers	Matthew 9:37, 38; Luke 10:2
2. A Friend at Midnight	Luke 11:5-8
3. An Unjust Judge	Luke 18:1-8

The Kingdom of God

1. The Sower	Matthew 13:3-8; Mark 4:4-8; Luke 8:5-8
2. The Wheat and the Tares	Matthew 13:24-30
3. The Mustard Seed	Matthew 13:31, 32; Mark 4:3-32; Luke 13:18, 19
4. The Leaven	Matthew 13:33; Luke 13:20, 21

5. The Hidden Treasure   Matthew 13:44
6. The Pearl of Great Price   Matthew 13:45, 46
7. The Net of Fish   Matthew 13:47-50
8. The Growing Seed   Mark 4:26-29

Service and Rewards
1. Workers in the Vineyard   Matthew 20:1-16
2. The Talents   Matthew 25:14-30
3. The Pounds   Luke 19:11-27
4. Unprofitable Servants   Luke 17:7-10

Judgment
1. Two Sons   Matthew 21:28-32
2. Wicked Vine-growers   Matthew 21:33, 34;
                                 Mark 12:1-12; Luke 20:9-18
3. Barren Fig Tree   Luke 13:6-9
4. Rich Man and Lazarus   Luke 16:19-31
5. Marriage Feast   Matthew 22:1-14
   of the King's Son
6. Unforgiving Servant   Matthew 18:23-25

Watching for Christ's Return
1. Budding Fig Tree   Matthew 24:32-35;
                                 Mark 13:28-32; Luke 21:29-33
2. Faithful and Unfaithful   Matthew 24:45-51;
   Servants   Luke 12:42-48
3. The Ten Virgins   Matthew 25:1-13
4. Watchful Porter   Mark 13:34-37

Loving Others
1. The Good Samaritan   Luke 10:30-37
2. Feast Invitations   Luke 14:12-14

Worldly Wealth
1. Rich Fool   Luke 12:16-21
2. Great Supper   Luke 14:15-24
3. Unjust Steward   Luke 16:1-9

Discipleship
1. The Tower   Luke 14:28-30
2. War Plans   Luke 14:31-33

God's Love for the Lost
1. The Lost Sheep   Luke 16:1-9
2. The Lost Coin   Luke 15:8-10
3. The Lost Son   Luke 15:11-32

November 6, 2005

Responding to God

Matthew 21:28-32; 22:1-14; 25:1-13

Unit Theme:
Parables of Jesus

Central Truth:
God desires people to respond to Him in obedience.

Focus:
To identify ways people respond to God, and bear the fruit of righteousness by faith and obedience to God.

Context:
In Jerusalem, Jesus teaches about the kingdom of God.

Golden Text:
"Jesus said unto him, Thou shalt love the Lord thy God with all thy heart, and with all thy soul, and with all thy mind" (Matthew 22:37).

Study Outline:
I. Unrighteous or Repentant?
   (Matthew 21:28-32)
II. Indifferent or Receptive?
   (Matthew 22:1-14)
III. Foolish or Wise?
   (Matthew 25:1-13)

INTRODUCTION

The Bible is filled with diverse stories of people's response to God. Adam and Eve hid themselves. Sarah laughed. Abraham raised the knife above his only son. Moses questioned and begged. Israel would later find themselves in a cycle of distinct responses to the Lord—from sin, to outcry, to deliverance, to repentance, and back to sin. Perhaps Joshua best summed up the Old Testament decision with which Israel constantly struggled: "And if it seem evil unto you to serve the Lord, choose you this day whom ye will serve; whether the gods which your fathers served that were on the other side of the flood, or the gods of the Amorites, in whose land ye dwell: but as for me and my house, we will serve the Lord" (Joshua 24:15). The Bible's characterization of the Lord as a jealous God necessitates a clear-cut response from His people.

The coming of Christ amplified this demand from God for His people to choose a response, as it became focused on the person of Jesus. Whereas the religious leaders of His day called for the Jews' loyalty to the Law and the Temple as proof of their commitment to God, Jesus went beyond this by challenging people to dedicate themselves to the kingdom of God and to honor His own claim to its throne. Jesus' radical claims of messiahship and His own sacrificial lifestyle for the Kingdom produced a *crisis of belief* among those who encountered Him. The nature of the decision for or against Christ was so extreme that they were compelled to choose.

For Jesus' disciples, this choice meant leaving their professions, their families, and their sources of income (Matthew 4:18-22). For the rich young ruler, this choice meant shedding his wealth (19:21). For the religious leaders, this choice necessitated that Jesus be killed. Incredibly, Jesus understood that this crisis of belief He produced meant that many would choose against Him, a consequence He accepted: "And another also said, Lord, I will follow thee; but let me first go bid them farewell, which are at home at my house. And Jesus said unto him, No man, having put his hand to the plough, and looking back, is fit for the kingdom of God" (Luke 9:61, 62).

God chose to send His only Son into the world. The people of the world must choose their response to Him.

I. UNRIGHTEOUS OR REPENTANT? (Matthew 21:28-32)

Jesus' parables in Matthew 21 are spoken in the Temple in response to criticism by "the chief priests and the elders of the people" (v. 23). They wanted to know where Jesus got His authority; that is, how could He possess the audacity and the boldness to walk straight into *their* sanctuary and draw crowds of people to *His* teaching. In response, Jesus told a series of parables beginning with that of a man with two sons who make opposing decisions concerning the work of their father's vineyard. So then, Jesus took the charge of the religious leaders and effectively turned it against them. He might be guilty of acting under a bold authority that drew crowds, but they were the guilty party for neglecting the work of the Father altogether! They were obligated to spiritually nourish the throngs of the Temple, but instead they were serving their own prideful purposes.

A. Requires Total Commitment (vv. 28-31a)

28. But what think ye? A certain man had two sons; and he came to the first, and said, Son, go work to day in my vineyard.

29. He answered and said, I will not: but afterward he repented, and went.

30. And he came to the second, and said likewise. And he answered and said, I go, sir: and went not.

31a. Whether of them twain did the will of his father? They say unto him, The first.

Jesus' parable carefully lays out for the religious leaders the nature of the response that God requires. Here He is portraying two types of people. Both are sons of the father, and both receive the same command to do the father's work. Yet the first son rejects his father's request then later carries through with it, while the second son heartily agrees to his father's work yet does nothing. Jesus points out the obvious truth that the father's command to work in the vineyard was not just a matter of verbal commitment, but action! God expects more than a mere confession of His authority, more than a commitment of the mouth or mind, but a *total* commitment to His work. To simply agree that God's work should be done while not doing it is disobedience to God's commands. Likewise, someone who refuses God's call at one point of life but later answers yes wholeheartedly will always be welcomed into the Kingdom and its work.

This parable calls to mind Jesus' constant conflict with the religious leaders. In Matthew 15:8, He describes them by quoting from the prophet Isaiah: "This people draw near me with their mouth, and with their lips do honour me, but have removed their heart far from me" (29:13). He categorizes them as those who respond to God like the second son—though

Talk About It:
1. How do we know the will of the heavenly Father?
2. Is it possible to think we are obeying God's will when we are not? Explain.

dedicated to God in words, appearance and even doctrine, they reject the work of His vineyard. They are not involved in cultivating the work of the Father, but are quickly falling behind the true workers.

B. Overshadows Past Responses (vv. 31b, 32)
31b. Jesus saith unto them, Verily I say unto you, That the publicans and the harlots go into the kingdom of God before you.
32. For John came unto you in the way of righteousness, and ye believed him not: but the publicans and the harlots believed him: and ye, when ye had seen it, repented not afterward, that ye might believe him.

Talk About It:
1. Why were prostitutes and tax collectors more apt to put their faith in Jesus than were the Pharisees?
2. Who are today's "Pharisees," and how can they be saved?

The religious leaders frequently criticized Jesus on the basis of His company. "This man welcomes sinners and eats with them," they mutter in Luke 15:2 (*NIV*). In the parable of the two sons, Jesus portrays the folly of their arrogance.

How shocking it must have been to these leaders of Israel to suddenly be put in a place of spiritual inferiority to sinners! Tax collectors were among the most despised Jews of that day. Considered traitors for taxing God's people to support the oppressive Roman Empire, they grew wealthy by profiting off overtaxation. The only class inferior to these was the prostitutes, who had for economic reasons rejected the faith of the Jews entirely. The religious leaders often stoned such sexual offenders (John 8:5). However, now such persons were becoming children of God. They had previously rejected the Father's call to work in His vineyard, but since John the Baptist prepared the way for Christ, some of them were responding wholeheartedly.

Such a response was possible under the Kingdom principle Jesus communicates in the parable. The vineyard has been made open to those who rejected God in the past. However, even a person with a religious or even righteous background could not expect to please the Father without responding to the *present* call of Jesus' kingdom. In this way, the tax collectors and prostitutes became beneficiaries, while the religious leaders squandered their heritage.

The kingdom of God can be considered a place where the past is irrelevant, overshadowed by the choice of *today*. Paul put this principle to work in his own life: "This one thing I do, forgetting those things which are behind, and reaching forth unto those things which are before, I press toward the mark for the prize of the high calling of God in Christ Jesus" (Philippians 3:13, 14). Although the two sons in Jesus' parable had previously responded in opposite ways to the call of their father, yesterday's choice was not determinative of today. Whether obedience or disobedience, our response *right now* matters most to God.

"To reject God's Son is to slam the door of hope."
—Anonymous

II. INDIFFERENT OR RECEPTIVE? (Matthew 22:1-14)

In the parable of the wedding banquet, Jesus significantly expands His teaching on the human response to God. This time, the main character in the story is not calling his sons to work, but calling guests to a joyful banquet. By presenting the thorough responses of the invited guests, Jesus reveals another dimension to the manner in which people react to His message. Although "both good and bad" (v. 10) are allowed into the banquet hall, the indifferent are completely shut out. In this sense, Jesus praises a person's receptivity to the kingdom of God as the first step toward a total commitment to it.

A. A Wedding Banquet (vv. 1-7)

1. And Jesus answered and spake unto them again by parables, and said,

2. The kingdom of heaven is like unto a certain king, which made a marriage for his son,

3. And sent forth his servants to call them that were bidden to the wedding: and they would not come.

4. Again, he sent forth other servants, saying, Tell them which are bidden, Behold, I have prepared my dinner: my oxen and my fatlings are killed, and all things are ready: come unto the marriage.

5. But they made light of it, and went their ways, one to his farm, another to his merchandise:

6. And the remnant took his servants, and entreated them spitefully, and slew them.

7. But when the king heard thereof, he was wroth: and he sent forth his armies, and destroyed those murderers, and burned up their city.

Jesus likened the Kingdom to a lavish wedding banquet prepared by a king for his son, fully furnished with fresh meat. Jewish wedding receptions of Jesus' day were no small affairs, often lasting up to seven days. They were filled with music, dancing, eating and drinking—a joyful celebration for all invited! Recall Jesus' first miracle (John 2), which was necessitated by the crisis of a wine shortage at a wedding in Cana. Jesus acted to save the reputation of the groom's party, because in that society cutting short a wedding banquet was a massive insult toward the bride's family. In this parable in Matthew 22, the offense is much greater. After the enormous banquet is prepared, those on the distinguished guest list simply refuse to attend, citing various other priorities. The king is undaunted, and sends out a second invitation by additional servants, this time describing the delicacies that await them (v. 4). They continue in their indifference, and some even resort to violence against the king's servants.

Talk About It:
1. Why did Jesus use so many parables in His teaching?
2. How were the responses to the wedding invitation similar to people's response to Christ's invitation to be saved?

Remember that Jesus was still addressing the religious leaders. Their presence framed this parable (see 21:45, 46; 22:15), and Jesus was accusing them of acting like the delinquent guests. His criticism is especially sharp in verses 6 and 7, as the king fights against those invitees who had mistreated his servants. This connects to Jesus' teaching in the Beatitudes about believers who are persecuted (Matthew 5:10). He instructed His disciples to expect such persecution, apparently from the religious leaders, because "in the same way they persecuted the prophets who were before you" (v. 12, *NIV*). This is later echoed in 23:31, where Jesus identifies the religious leaders as "the descendants of those who murdered the prophets" (*NIV*), and thus sharers of guilt.

What a stark contrast between the king's joyful preparation for the banquet honoring his son and the invited guests' violent reaction! In this way the parable foreshadows the violence that the religious leaders would ultimately direct against Jesus himself.

B. An Open Invitation (vv. 8-10)

8. Then saith he to his servants, The wedding is ready, but they which were bidden were not worthy.

9. Go ye therefore into the highways, and as many as ye shall find, bid to the marriage.

10. So those servants went out into the highways, and gathered together all as many as they found, both bad and good: and the wedding was furnished with guests.

Despite the king's wrath toward the first set of invitees to his banquet, yet another call is issued. The invitation becomes indiscriminate—everyone the servants can find are brought to the king's palace. Even the sinful have a place at this open-invitation banquet, which symbolizes the kingdom of God. Indeed, the criterion for entrance into the King's banquet is not one's *past history* but one's *present receptivity*.

Paul goes to great lengths in his letter to the Romans to explain this truth. Whereas before the coming of Jesus Christ the family of God consisted of Israel and all who became converts to the faith of Israel, the gospel declares that since all of humanity lies in bondage to sin, everyone is in need of God's grace (Romans 3:23, 24). This transforms the family of God into an open invitation. This act of God does not replace God's covenant with Israel, but rather enlarges it to include all who will respond and confess to God's work in Christ (9:6-9). This invitation no longer makes a distinction between those Jews who adhere to the Law and Gentiles who have found Christ outside of the Law: "For there is no difference between the Jew and the Greek: for the same Lord over all is rich unto all that call upon him. For whosoever shall call upon the name of the Lord shall be saved" (10:12, 13).

Talk About It:
1. Describe the various "highways" used by today's evangelists and missionaries.
2. Why does Christ invite "both bad and good" (v. 10) to come to Him today?

"The King wants you to come to the great feast. He has sent you an invitation. He has taken care of everything, even the wedding garment. He has invited both good and bad and is fully

Responding to God

To the religious leaders, this banquet is nothing short of scandalous. For the king, who symbolized a holy God, to allow *just anyone* to enter his presence was offensive. They resented Jesus' message of inclusion and grace toward sinners and outcasts. Jesus caps off the parable with a grave warning both for them and for any who respond to God lightly. Though the invitation to the king's banquet is fully open to all, it is not without obligations on the part of the guests.

> prepared to make all necessary provision, so that all, of every class, may meet the heavenly standard. The robe of His righteousness can cover every deficiency."
> —W.G. Williams

C. A Key Requirement (vv. 11-14)

11. And when the king came in to see the guests, he saw there a man which had not on a wedding garment:

12. And he saith unto him, Friend, how camest thou in hither not having a wedding garment? And he was speechless.

13. Then said the king to the servants, Bind him hand and foot, and take him away, and cast him into outer darkness, there shall be weeping and gnashing of teeth.

14. For many are called, but few are chosen.

Despite the packed banquet hall, the king is alarmed to find a guest not dressed for the occasion. The man is addressed cordially and asked how he has been admitted without proper attire. His speechlessness incurs the king's wrath. The marked shift in the parable is dramatic: after the king finally fills his wedding hall and the jubilant celebration begins, a single guest is bound and thrown outside. His crime is simply the failure to properly prepare for the banquet. He had not changed his clothes, and had somehow sneaked in past the attendants. Although the king was heartbroken toward those who had rejected his invitation, he is enraged at this intruder. Here Jesus finally steps outside of the parable, wrapping it up with a closing sentence (v. 14).

Talk About It:
Why do the "few" say yes to God's calling to salvation?

Jesus explains that while everyone is called to become part of His kingdom, few enter it. Many simply ignore the invitation, while others try to slip in without putting on the right clothes— they seek to enter the Kingdom while neglecting the necessity of change. Recall the early preaching of Jesus: "Repent, for the kingdom of heaven is near" (4:17, *NIV*). The Kingdom is near to all, and its entry requirement is repentance. As Paul urged the Romans, "So let us put aside the deeds of darkness and put on the armor of light. Let us behave decently, as in the day-time, not in orgies and drunkenness, not in sexual immorality and debauchery, not in dissension and jealousy. Rather, *clothe yourselves with the Lord Jesus Christ*, and do not think about how to gratify the desires of the sinful nature" (13:12-14, *NIV*).

We enter God's joyful kingdom only when we clothe ourselves with Christ.

III. FOOLISH OR WISE? (Matthew 25:1-13)

In the parable of the 10 virgins, Jesus was addressing His disciples, elaborating on His second coming. In 24:44 He encouraged them to understand and to discern the times surrounding His return: "So you also must be ready, because the Son of Man will come at an hour when you do not expect him" (*NIV*).

This parable accentuates how imperative it is to be prepared for His arrival. Whereas in the story of the wedding banquet, preparation is likened to changing into wedding clothes, here it is explained in greater detail.

A. Wise Living (vv. 1-5)

1. Then shall the kingdom of heaven be likened unto ten virgins, which took their lamps, and went forth to meet the bridegroom.

2. And five of them were wise, and five were foolish.

3. They that were foolish took their lamps, and took no oil with them:

4. But the wise took oil in their vessels with their lamps.

5. While the bridegroom tarried, they all slumbered and slept.

Talk About It

1. Why do you think there is no reference to the bride in this parable?

2. Spiritually speaking, are there more "wise" or "foolish" people in the world today? Why?

The introduction "at that time" (v. 1, *NIV*) reveals the parable is describing Jesus' future return. The story had an immediate impact on its hearers, as it depicts a prominent Jewish custom of that day. Unlike our society, Jewish wedding dates were not set to the hour. Instead, the bridal party would go through several days of waiting for the bridegroom to suddenly arrive. He customarily did so at night, whisking his bride away to the ceremony and the banquet. In Jesus' parable, the bridal party consists of 10 virgins—the main characters. It is their response that provides the insight Jesus is communicating.

Despite the fact that the parable is referring to Jesus' future return, He spends the majority of it explaining the virgins' *preparation* for the bridegroom's coming, not the coming itself. This is because the bridal party is divided into two distinct groups—the foolish and the wise. Each group has lamps and oil. Each group is concerned with the bridegroom's return. Each group recognizes it as a coming event. Yet only one group regards this future experience in such a way as to shape wise living in their present situation. It is this mind-set that separates the wise from the foolish. Although many may expect the return of Christ, that expectation is valueless unless it produces wise living in one's present circumstances.

B. Constant Readiness (vv. 6-9)

6. And at midnight there was a cry made, Behold, the bridegroom cometh; go ye out to meet him.

7. Then all those virgins arose, and trimmed their lamps.
8. And the foolish said unto the wise, Give us of your oil; for our lamps are gone out.
9. But the wise answered, saying, Not so; lest there be not enough for us and you: but go ye rather to them that sell, and buy for yourselves.

It was typical of the bridegroom, or one of his attendants, to loudly announce his arrival in the middle of the night. The parable portrays this, as the virgins wake and light their lamps. The foolish group seems surprised at their lack of oil. While they were asleep, it slowly burned away. Yet the wise virgins refuse to divide their portion, afraid of being left behind in the darkness should their source of light be extinguished.

The wise were prepared at all times for the bridegroom's coming. The foolish took no reserve supply of oil, and consequently were prepared for only a short interval of waiting. Jesus' message, then, centers on the period of waiting for His return. The period of life before His return is crucial, as it calls for wise living. Those who choose to live foolishly and then expect to somehow be prepared for Christ at His coming are acting irresponsibly. It is the Christian's duty not to simply believe in the Son's return, but to *live* in readiness for it.

C. Limited Opportunity (vv. 10-13)
10. And while they went to buy, the bridegroom came; and they that were ready went in with him to the marriage: and the door was shut.
11. Afterward came also the other virgins, saying, Lord, Lord, open to us.
12. But he answered and said, Verily I say unto you, I know you not.
13. Watch therefore, for ye know neither the day nor the hour wherein the Son of man cometh.

The final segment of the parable consists of a chilling warning. The foolish virgins are left in the darkness while the wise virgins are taken into the wedding banquet. Though they plead for entrance, the bridegroom refuses. It is too late. Jesus closes with a word of instruction (v. 13). The foolish virgins misjudged the time of the bridegroom's arrival. When He delayed, they failed to stay alert.

Although the Kingdom is open to all, it will not be so forever. This parable ultimately points to a time at which changing one's response to Christ has expired. Only God knows the time set for this event (24:36), but it is one of supreme importance for present believers. Even in the early church, believers were questioning the delay of Christ's coming, wondering if His promise could be untrue. Peter addressed this problem:

Talk About It:
1. How will the return of Christ be like a "midnight cry"?
2. Is it possible for a Christian's "lamp to go out" without his or her knowledge? What could prevent this?

"A Christian, like a candle, must keep cool and burn at the same time."
—Merv Rosell

Talk About It:
1. What does it mean to "watch" for Christ's return?
2. Why didn't God reveal the time of Christ's second coming?

The Lord is not slow in keeping his promise, as some understand slowness. He is patient with you, not wanting anyone to perish, but everyone to come to repentance. But the day of the Lord will come like a thief. The heavens will disappear with a roar; the elements will be destroyed by fire, and the earth and everything in it will be laid bare. Since everything will be destroyed in this way, what kind of people ought you to be? You ought to live holy and godly lives as you look forward to the day of God and speed its coming (2 Peter 3:9-12, *NIV*).

Here Peter echoes the exhortation of Jesus, cautioning us against recklessness and urging us to live every day in readiness for His return.

CONCLUSION

The message of the kingdom of God requires a response on the part of people. Jesus' claims are too radical, His personhood too miraculous to be met with indecision. His parables offer the promise of acceptance into the Kingdom for all, regardless of their past, who come to Christ with a repentant heart, a receptive stance, and a wise response. It is these persons who work productively in the Father's vineyard, who celebrate joyfully at His wedding feast, and who will one day join Him at His coming.

GOLDEN TEXT CHALLENGE

"JESUS SAID UNTO HIM, THOU SHALT LOVE THE LORD THY GOD WITH ALL THY HEART, AND WITH ALL THY SOUL, AND WITH ALL THY MIND" (Matthew 22:37).

Daily Devotions:

M. Repentance Brings Forgiveness
1 Kings 8:46-53

T. Pride Causes Indifference Toward God
Psalm 10:1-11

W. God Commands Obedience
Jeremiah 7:21-23

T. Repent or Perish
Luke 13:1-5

F. Foolishness of Rejecting God
Romans 1:18-25

S. Invite Christ In
Revelation 3:14-22

The words "the Lord thy God" indicate three things. The term *Lord* expresses the authority of God in the believer's life. *Thy* (your) expresses the personal relationship between the Christian and the Lord. The term *God* indicates the deity of our Lord. All three in combination present a rather full description of the covenant relationship of the child of God with the one true God.

The believer's love for the Lord must come from the *heart*—the seat of consciousness and emotions. The affections of the Christian are to be set on the Lord.

The word *soul* emphasizes the source of inner life and strength in the believer. The believer is to perceive life as depending on the Lord and no one else.

The word *mind* indicates the ability to think something through. The thought life of the Christian is to be committed to and centered in the Lord.

The word *all* is used with *heart, soul* and *mind* to express depth of commitment. Full and total love for God is the only acceptable level of commitment.

Living With Eternity in Mind

Matthew 25:14-46; Mark 13:32-37

INTRODUCTION

Perhaps no other Christian doctrine stands at such sharp odds with our surrounding culture than our belief in eternity. In a world governed by immediacy, the idea that our decisions carry eternal consequences is hard for many to accept. The notion of death is something to be avoided at all costs. The medical industry continues to devise more potent drugs and new surgical procedures to delay death as long as possible. Plastic surgeons rake in billions of dollars per year for their attempts at reversing the natural aging process. The advertising industry consistently utilizes images of youth and vitality, as if using a certain product could make one feel younger. Whereas previous cultures, including the people of God in the Old Testament, prized old age as the path to wisdom and honor, and death as the passage to eternity, our present world champions youth and strives to avoid death.

Even so, Christ consistently calls our attention to the afterlife, and specifically to His future return. Occasionally in the body of Christ, this has resulted in pockets of believers denying their earthly responsibilities in anticipation of the Rapture. Such believers are "too heavenly-minded for earthly good."

Thankfully, Jesus did not teach that our longing for heaven should diminish our commitment to His work on earth. On the contrary, He declared that being conscious of heaven should spur a believer on toward an *active* life of service in the Kingdom. In fact, when Jesus refers to "eternal life," He is not only speaking of life after death. Instead, the term *eternal life* indicates a level of life available as a *present* possession on earth that carries with it the promise of heaven!

Peter continues Jesus' teaching concerning eternity, urging the same commitment: "But the day of the Lord will come like a thief. . . . Since everything will be destroyed in this way, what kind of people ought you to be? You ought to live holy and godly lives as you look forward to the day of God and speed its coming" (2 Peter 3:10-12, *NIV*). Living with eternity in mind means a commitment to holiness and godliness here on earth. Several of Jesus' parables further explain these earthly responsibilities that hold eternal significance.

Unit Theme:
Parables of Jesus

Central Truth:
Eternal rewards await those who faithfully serve Christ.

Focus:
To consider and heed imperatives for godly living.

Context:
At the Mount of Olives, Jesus teaches about His second coming.

Golden Text:
"We must all appear before the judgment seat of Christ; that every one may receive the things done in his body, according to that he hath done, whether it be good or bad" (2 Corinthians 5:10).

Study Outline:
I. Use Your Resources for God (Matthew 25:14-30)
II. Serve Christ by Serving Others (Matthew 25:31-46)
III. Watch for Christ's Coming (Mark 13:32-37)

I. USE YOUR RESOURCES FOR GOD (Matthew 25:14-30)

Jesus frequently used metaphors involving money and labor to describe life in the kingdom of God (Matthew 18:23-35; 20:1-16; 21:33-44). In the parable of the talents, Jesus effectively connects the two, and compares handling God's resources to making earthly investments.

A. Being Entrusted With Kingdom Resources (vv. 14-18)

14. For the kingdom of heaven is as a man travelling into a far country, who called his own servants, and delivered unto them his goods.

15. And unto one he gave five talents, to another two, and to another one; to every man according to his several ability; and straightway took his journey.

16. Then he that had received the five talents went and traded with the same, and made them other five talents.

17. And likewise he that had received two, he also gained other two.

18. But he that had received one went and digged in the earth, and hid his lord's money.

Talk About It:

1. Why does God entrust different abilities and responsibilities to different individuals?

2. Who owns the "goods" God has entrusted to us? Why is this important?

3. How did the two-talent person do "likewise" (v. 17), and what was the result?

Probably the most important word in this parable is found in its opening sentence. Incredibly, the wealthy master "delivered" (entrusted) his great resources to his servants, those who lived and worked in his household. The Greek word may also be translated "gave," or, more specifically, "handed over." While it was typical for prosperous leaders to travel in the New Testament world, thereby leaving their property to the care of employees, Jesus is painting a different picture. This master actually handed over his resources to the servants! He took an incredible risk, knowing the different degrees of character and ability between them. Yet he did so with profound trust, assuming they would put his resources to good use.

Jesus' message in this parable is defined and particular. He begins it with the word *for*, which connects the story to the previous one—the parable of the 10 virgins (vv. 1-13). That parable begins simply, "Then shall the kingdom of heaven be likened . . ." and follows Jesus' discourse on His second coming. Therefore, in our present parable, Jesus is again illustrating how to give proper attention to His future return. Whereas His previous teaching is concerned with being constantly ready for His arrival, the issue at hand here is how we are to act *before* this time.

The characters in the parable each receive an allotment of talents. A talent was a unit of currency based on weight. In the Old Testament, a talent equaled the weight of about 3,000 shekels, or approximately 125 pounds. In the New Testament world, a talent of gold was worth around $30,000 in today's currency, and a talent of silver was valued at about $2,000 in today's currency. The story does not pinpoint whether the talents were gold or silver, but regardless, the servants are obviously entrusted with sizeable sums, even though they are plainly unequal. The first servant receives five times the total of the third!

The application of the first part of the parable is plain. Although Christ has departed, God has entrusted His followers with Kingdom resources to be put to immediate use. The issue is not how many of God's resources one has at his or her disposal. While some have been given great means to be useful in many areas of Kingdom service, others have been assigned just one area in which to be productive. Later on in the New Testament, Jesus' teaching of the talents is complemented by instruction on spiritual gifts: "There are different kinds of gifts, but the same Spirit. There are different kinds of service, but the same Lord. There are different kinds of working, but the same God works all of them in all men. Now to each one the manifestation of the Spirit is given for the common good" (1 Corinthians 12:4-7, *NIV*). In the form of spiritual gifts, God's resources have been divided unevenly among believers so as to maximize their use throughout the body of Christ.

In the parable of the talents, the first two servants were equally productive, for they both doubled what they had received. However, the third servant dug a hole in the ground and hid the master's money. He hoped that simply protecting what he had received would satisfy the master.

> "Too often we attempt to work for God to the limit of our incompetency, rather than to the limit of God's omnipotency."
> —J. Taylor

B. Investing Kingdom Resources (vv. 19-28)
  (Matthew 25:22-28 is not included in the printed text.)
  19. After a long time the lord of those servants cometh, and reckoneth with them.
  20. And so he that had received five talents came and brought other five talents, saying, Lord, thou deliveredst unto me five talents: behold, I have gained beside them five talents more.
  21. His lord said unto him, Well done, thou good and faithful servant: thou hast been faithful over a few things, I will make thee ruler over many things: enter thou into the joy of thy lord.

The second segment of the parable details the return of the master and his reaction to the servants' individual work. The language of business transactions describes the master's return. He is not only interested in the upkeep and condition of his household, but also the growth of his *accounts* ("reckoneth," v. 19). Interestingly, the Greek word used here is the same word found in Romans 14:12: "So then every one of us shall give *account* of himself to God." The master's return in the

Talk About It:
1. What will please the Lord regarding our use of the opportunities and abilities He gives us?
2. What excuses did the one-talent person make?

3. What excuses do ability-wasting believers use today?

parable is a day of joy for some servants, but a day of despair for others. For all, though, it is a day of *reckoning*—the master comes to calculate the use of his resources.

For the first servant, his reunion with the master erupts in joy. He proudly displays the profit he has made on the master's initial investment, and the master responds with glee and great reward. His meeting with the second servant is identical to the first one. Even though the amount is smaller than the first servant's, the second servant receives the same praise. He is commended as a faithful servant and is therefore rewarded with greater leadership in the household.

The master's reunion with the third servant, however, is absolutely chilling. The jubilant meetings with the first two servants are brought to an abrupt end, as the final servant approaches with only the master's initial investment in hand. What is more, he blames the master himself for his laziness, expressing his fear of failing the master's requirements. The master states the obvious—that at the very least a trip to the bank would have brought some profit, and this would have been sufficient. But because no effort was exercised at all, his talent is stripped and transferred to the first servant.

Jesus illustrates two important principles here. First, He communicates that a servant's present accomplishment ensures a future reward. Although Christ's followers should be ready for His return, they should not simply inactively *wait*. They have been given Kingdom resources to employ! Their degree of faithfulness with those resources carries eternal consequences. Second, faithfulness has nothing to do with the amount of one's resources. The last servant was not judged for his inability to double his talent, but his failure to earn *any* interest whatsoever. Jesus does not expect 10 talents from everyone, but He does expect profit from all His servants.

"Jesus will never say 'Well done' to anyone unless his work has been 'done well.'"

—G. Campbell Morgan

C. Receiving Kingdom Rewards (vv. 29, 30)

29. For unto every one that hath shall be given, and he shall have abundance: but from him that hath not shall be taken away even that which he hath.

30. And cast ye the unprofitable servant into outer darkness: there shall be weeping and gnashing of teeth.

In the final section of the parable, Jesus explains the reason for such harsh treatment toward the lazy servant, whose only talent is given to the servant who already holds 10. On first glance, this teaching seems incredibly unfair! The one with the most talents to spare receives more, while the one lacking loses all. However, Jesus is still talking about the use of Kingdom resources, and here lies the important principle. Those who effectively put God's resources to good use may

Talk About It:
1. Why was the 10-talent person given another talent?
2. Why was the one-talent person treated so harshly?

Living With Eternity in Mind

expect an award that is *not* in proportion with what they have done, but is *dis*proportionate in their favor! Jesus emphasizes the incredible abundance of the faithful servant's reward, contrasted with the infinite sorrow of the lazy one. The message is clear: As we look forward to Christ's return, we must remember that He will come to reward those who have been faithful with God's resources, and His reward is beyond what we could ever earn.

II. SERVE CHRIST BY SERVING OTHERS
(Matthew 25:31-46)

Now that Jesus has outlined the necessity of being faithful with God's resources, He defines specifically how to do just that. The teaching on the sheep and the goats draws yet another picture of Christ's return and, similarly to the parable of the talents, calls believers to faithfulness. In the previous parable, faithfulness is defined in terms of exercising available Kingdom resources. Here, however, that same faithfulness is applied to service toward others.

A. Glorious Judge (vv. 31-36)

31. When the Son of man shall come in his glory, and all the holy angels with him, then shall he sit upon the throne of his glory:

32. And before him shall be gathered all nations: and he shall separate them one from another, as a shepherd divideth his sheep from the goats:

33. And he shall set the sheep on his right hand, but the goats on the left.

34. Then shall the King say unto them on his right hand, Come, ye blessed of my Father, inherit the kingdom prepared for you from the foundation of the world.

35. For I was an hungred, and ye gave me meat: I was thirsty, and ye gave me drink: I was a stranger, and ye took me in:

36. Naked, and ye clothed me: I was sick, and ye visited me: I was in prison, and ye came unto me.

Whereas in the previous verses Jesus has already likened His return to a wealthy master and a bridegroom, in the teaching of the sheep and the goats He speaks in plainer language. Although the teaching is still in parable form, it appears less metaphoric than the previous parables. They begin with Jesus' common introduction, "The kingdom of heaven is like . . .," but here Jesus begins, "When the Son of man shall come in his glory . . ." (v. 31). Jesus suddenly shifts to the incredible scene of majesty at His return, at which the heavenly host joins Him at His throne. This is an actual scene from heaven itself, the

Talk About It:
1. When will God's Son be seen "in his glory" (v. 31)? What does this mean?
2. What plan did God have in mind, and what did He know "from the foundation of the world" (v. 34)?

3. Why is there so much emphasis on works in this judgment scene?

Kingdom which Jesus has explained and illustrated using various parables. Now He clarifies heaven's character and His own role as "the Son of Man."

Oftentimes Jesus was hesitant to proclaim His divinity. When the Pharisees asked for a miraculous sign, He would give none (Matthew 12:38, 39). He frequently commanded those whom He healed to tell no one (8:4), as He similarly instructed His disciples after the Transfiguration (17:9) and Peter's famous confession (16:20). Obviously, Jesus had no interest in arrogantly displaying His power and identity. However, there were times, such as this teaching, where He did disclose His majesty. In fact, it was this disclosure that incurs the wrath of the Sanhedrin during His first trial: "The high priest said to him, 'I charge you under oath by the living God: Tell us if you are the Christ, the Son of God.' 'Yes, it is as you say,' Jesus replied. 'But I say to all of you: In the future you will see the Son of Man sitting at the right hand of the Mighty One and coming on the clouds of heaven'" (26:63, 64, *NIV*).

While Jesus' first descent to earth was in the form of a humble servant, His second coming will be completely different. He will return as a righteous, glorious King ready to judge all peoples of the earth.

Even as Jesus the mighty King begins the judgment process, He is not likened to an all-powerful tyrant but a shepherd. How fitting, given that in John 10 He describes Himself as "the good shepherd." His hearers certainly knew the language of shepherding, and they knew that both sheep and goats were valued by shepherds. One provided wool, while the other provided milk. So then, Jesus is not separating the two because of a lack of love for the goats, but doing so because of the distinction in their lifestyles. The sheep are immediately praised: "Come, you who are blessed by my Father" (Matthew 25:34, *NIV*).

It is the Father who deems them "blessed," and who decides their entrance into the kingdom of heaven. Reminiscent of the Prodigal Son, whose squandered inheritance was restored upon his return to his father, the Kingdom is described as the ultimate inheritance. It has been created and prepared for just this time.

After inviting the sheep into the Kingdom, the King lets them know His reasons. They have been judged worthy based upon their relationship to the King himself! They have treated Him as a friend.

"Common humanity would move a man to relieve his bitterest foe when perishing by hunger or thirst. . . . But to clothe the naked implies a liberal and loving spirit, to visit the sick is an act of spontaneous self-sacrifice, to go to the wretched outcasts in prison was perhaps an unheard-of act of charity in those days; it was to enter places horrible and foul beyond description."

—A. Carr

B. Perfect Justice (vv. 37-46)
(Matthew 25:41-46 is not included in the printed text.)
37. Then shall the righteous answer him, saying, Lord, when saw we thee an hungred, and fed thee? or thirsty, and gave thee drink?

38. When saw we thee a stranger, and took thee in? or naked, and clothed thee?

39. Or when saw we thee sick, or in prison, and came unto thee?

40. And the King shall answer and say unto them, Verily I say unto you, Inasmuch as ye have done it unto one of the least of these my brethren, ye have done it unto me.

Jesus radically defines service in the kingdom of God as charity toward the hungry, the thirsty, the estranged, the poor, the sick and the imprisoned. He effectively revolutionizes every part of life, taking a massive leap beyond an understanding of working in the kingdom of God as something we do *for* the Lord. Whereas in the parable of the talents, workers are commended for what they do on behalf of their master, here workers are rewarded for their ministry directed *toward* the Master. In this sense, Jesus clearly defines Kingdom work as ministry to Christ that is consistently reflected by service to people. The two cannot be separated.

The remainder of the teaching portrays the alternate judgment of the group on the King's left. The outcome is the polar opposite than that of the group on His right. The "goats" are condemned to eternal punishment based on their neglect of the King, as evidenced in their disregard for the hungry, the thirsty, the estranged, the poor, the sick and the imprisoned.

This passage has long been troubling to Christian teachers, due to its apparent emphasis on works as the main criteria for Kingdom entrance. However, three things should be considered. First, the teaching is in the form of a parable that, although having some literal components, uses earthly images to convey heavenly truth. Second, the context of Matthew 25 instructs Jesus' disciples on how to act *presently* in a way that is faithful to the Second Coming. His teaching here is concerned primarily with their current lifestyle and only secondarily with His future return. Third, judgment takes place based on one's relationship to the King, *as reflected by* their service to others. Jesus does not simply judge according to how each group treated others, but how this reflected their treatment of Him.

III. WATCH FOR CHRIST'S COMING (Mark 13:32-37)

In Matthew's Gospel, the teaching on the sheep and the goats formally closes Jesus' teaching ministry. It serves as the culmination of instruction concerning the end times beginning in chapter 24, just before Jesus' impending trial and crucifixion. In Mark's Gospel, Jesus' teaching ministry similarly closes with a chapter on the Second Coming, but His final parable centers on the unknown time of this event, coupled with the command to His followers to be ever mindful of it.

Talk About It:
1. Why does Jesus identify Himself with the stranger, the sick and the prisoner?
2. Who are the "least of these" in our society?
3. What does our treatment of needy people reveal about our relationship with Christ? Why?

A. An Unknown Time (vv. 32, 33)

32. But of that day and that hour knoweth no man, no, not the angels which are in heaven, neither the Son, but the Father.

33. Take ye heed, watch and pray: for ye know not when the time is.

Talk About It:

1. Has God already determined the timing of Christ's return? Why does it matter?

2. How does a believer "watch and pray" for Christ's return?

In verse 32, Jesus makes the statement, "No one knows about that day or hour, not even the angels in heaven, nor the Son, but only the Father" (*NIV*). This statement has created much controversy among scholars. How could the all-knowing Son of God not know when He will return to earth? Two common explanations are given below:

1. The Greek word translated *know* sometimes means "reveal." Thus, Jesus did not reveal the time of His coming. However, this raises the question, When did the Father reveal the time of Christ's coming?

2. This statement "is to be understood in the light of His self-limitation during the days of His humiliation (cf. Philippians 2:5-8). He had assumed a position of complete subjection to the Father, exercising His divine attributes only at the Father's bidding (cf. John 8:26-29)" (Wycliffe).

Many times since Jesus spoke these words, various people have claimed a special revelation of the exact date of the Second Coming. Some teachers have made a career out of searching the Scriptural prophecies in the attempt to unlock this secret from the Bible. Such an effort is fruitless, as Jesus has already declared. True, we can and must be familiar with the signs of the end times proclaimed by Jesus himself and other authors of Scripture, but we cannot know the exact date. We must not think that the signs of the end times will lead us to a piece of knowledge not even given to the angels.

> "Trying to second-guess the [time of the] return of Christ is dangerous business because it tends toward sensationalism and immobilizes the church in its mission of world evangelism."
>
> —David Cooper

Rather than speculating about the date of Christ's return, believers are to "watch and pray" for His return. The apostle John prayed, "Even so, come, Lord Jesus" (Revelation 22:20).

B. A Sudden Event (vv. 34-37)

porter (v. 34)— doorkeeper

34. For the Son of man is as a man taking a far journey, who left his house, and gave authority to his servants, and to every man his work, and commanded the porter to watch.

35. Watch ye therefore: for ye know not when the master of the house cometh, at even, or at midnight, or at the cockcrowing, or in the morning:

36. Lest coming suddenly he find you sleeping.

37. And what I say unto you I say unto all, Watch.

Talk About It:

1. What authority and responsibility did the master give to his servants?

Like the parable of the talents, a master assigns the care of his property to his servants before departing for an unspecified amount of time. In this scenario, however, it is their watchfulness, not their work, that is emphasized. In the New Testament world, if a master returned and found his property and household in disarray, the servants would undoubtedly find themselves out of a job. They were to be ready for their master's return at any point by keeping the household in order at all times.

Jesus is not encouraging His followers to do nothing but watch for His return, but to prove their watchfulness by being consistently ready for this event. The household of faith must be kept in order; the Kingdom must be advanced. When we heed Jesus' call to watch, we get actively involved in ministry as a consciousness of eternity fills and fulfills our earthly tasks.

2. What authority and responsibilities has God given His children?

CONCLUSION

The Christian lifestyle necessitates living with eternity in mind. This takes several forms, which Jesus illustrates in parables. In the parable of the talents, He commands us to be mindful of His coming by multiplying the resources given to us for the betterment of the Kingdom. In the teaching on the sheep and the goats, He identifies the chief way we are faithful in this task—by serving others. In His discourse regarding the unknown time of His coming, He urges an active alertness on the part of His followers. In each of these, two extremes are avoided. Jesus cautions us against being lazy while we wait for Him, but also commands that our active work for Him never lose sight of His imminent return. It is only when faithful service is combined with watchfulness that the kingdom of God is fully served.

GOLDEN TEXT CHALLENGE

"WE MUST ALL APPEAR BEFORE THE JUDGMENT SEAT OF CHRIST; THAT EVERY ONE MAY RECEIVE THE THINGS DONE IN HIS BODY, ACCORDING TO THAT HE HATH DONE, WHETHER IT BE GOOD OR BAD" (2 Corinthians 5:10).

Every man produces one masterpiece—himself. Day and night, year in and year out, in conscious and unconscious moments, his words and deeds, his secret desires, what he permits or refuses, every hope, every fear, every purpose—all are strokes of the brush, all help to produce the painting.

One day the canvas is finished. Death frames it and puts it on exhibition. Then not a line can be erased or changed, not a feature retouched or altered. The work is finished. There is the masterpiece—a masterpiece because it is absolutely true to life.—**Clarence Edward**

Daily Devotions:
M. God Gives Abilities
  Exodus 31:1-11
T. Serving God Brings Provision
  1 Kings 17:8-16
W. The Lord Will Return
  Zechariah 14:1-5
T. Fulfill the Law of Christ
  Galatians 6:1-10
F. Patient Until Christ's Coming
  James 5:7-11
S. Glorify God With Your Abilities
  1 Peter 4:7-11

Teachings on Servanthood

Matthew 18:23-35; Luke 16:1-15; 17:7-10

Unit Theme:
Parables of Jesus

Central Truth:
A servant of Christ will be forgiving, trustworthy, and humble.

Focus:
To study illustrations of servanthood and develop a servant's heart.

Context:
Jesus tells His disciples three parables about servanthood.

Golden Text:
"He that is faithful in that which is least is faithful also in much: and he that is unjust in the least is unjust also in much" (Luke 16:10).

Study Outline:
I. Be Forgiving
   (Matthew 18:23-35)
II. Be Trustworthy
   (Luke 16:1-15)
III. Do Your Duty
   (Luke 17:7-10)

INTRODUCTION

It is impossible to study the parables and teachings of Jesus without being struck by His profound emphasis on servanthood. The word *servant* or *servants* is used almost 100 times in the four Gospels! Many of the parables studied in previous lessons include the presence of servants—the parables of the weeds, the wedding banquet, and the talents. Such constant references to servanthood point to its importance in Kingdom living. Whereas the world's system of power means that the greater dominates the lesser, in the kingdom of God the greater becomes the servant of the lesser.

This is illustrated perfectly in the exchange between Jesus and the mother of James and John in Matthew 20. Her request almost seems honorable: she asks that her sons may be given positions of greatness in the Kingdom. Jesus' response, however, completely turns the tables on her way of thinking, and radically redefines power for His followers: "But Jesus called them unto him, and said, Ye know that the princes of the Gentiles exercise dominion over them, and they that are great exercise authority upon them. But it shall not be so among you: but whosoever will be great among you, let him be your minister; and whosoever will be chief among you, let him be your servant" (vv. 25-27).

Imagine the shock of Jesus' disciples as He spoke these words! Slavery as a path to honor was undoubtedly beyond anything they had ever heard. It took the lifestyle of Jesus to show them the path to servanthood—the way in which He humbly taught, healed, and connected with others. Through daily following and imitating His ministry of servanthood, they were slowly transformed into true servants. By the time they were leading the church in the Book of Acts, they had learned to minister with a servant's heart.

In the parables of this lesson, Jesus demonstrates the qualities of servanthood. A servant of Christ will be forgiving, trustworthy and humble. All of the traits of servanthood are bound together by an unflinching faithfulness to the Lord, the One we are really serving whenever we minister to others.

I. BE FORGIVING (Matthew 18:23-35)

The parable of the unmerciful servant is introduced by Peter's simple question. He asks Jesus how often a brother who sins against him should be forgiven, proposing that surely seven times is more than gracious. The Jewish rabbis of Jesus' day taught that such an offending brother should be forgiven three times, but beyond this, no clemency was called for. Although Peter considered his proposal generous, Jesus tells a shocking parable that illustrates the true nature of forgiveness.

A. Overwhelming Debt (vv. 23-25)

23. Therefore is the kingdom of heaven likened unto a certain king, which would take account of his servants.

24. And when he had begun to reckon, one was brought unto him, which owed him ten thousand talents.

25. But forasmuch as he had not to pay, his lord commanded him to be sold, and his wife, and children, and all that he had, and payment to be made.

Our responsibility to forgive others is based on God's remarkable forgiveness toward us. Here Jesus uses the metaphor of the payment of a great debt to describe this act of God. He employs similar language in Luke 7:36-50, where Simon the Pharisee is taught the important connection between forgiveness and worship. Here, however, Jesus is communicating the dramatic nature of forgiveness itself.

The opening verse of the parable calls to mind the similar context in the parable of the talents, where the business terminology of "settling accounts" similarly sets up Jesus' teaching. Likewise, the Greek word used is again the same one found in Romans 14:12, and refers not only to a financial account but can indicate an explanation of one's situation. Here, the servant's financial debt is astronomical and his explanation unstated. His debt (10,000 talents) would amount to tens of millions of dollars in today's currency, and literally tons of coinage. Such a debt would have been hard for even a wealthy person to comprehend, but this man is a lowly servant! No wonder he does not try to explain his mismanagement; he has no self-defense. Instead, he and his family are ordered to be sold to another master, so that at least a tiny fraction of the debt might be paid, and that his banishment from the king's house would prevent such an offense in the future.

Just like this servant, the New Testament teaches that we also are crushed under an enormous debt. The thought of somehow working hard enough to earn our place back in God's kingdom is outrageous—the debt of sin is too large. Because of this, we, like the servant, deserve punishment. Romans 3:23 states this clearly: "For all have sinned, and come short of the

Talk About It:
1. What was the master's order regarding his servant? Why?
2. How are we like the servant?

glory of God." Every single person has failed in managing the King's account; our sin has indebted us beyond anything we can solve on our own. Romans 6:23 states the result of this: "For the wages of sin is death." Ejection from God and His kingdom are the natural consequences of this debt of sin. Jesus' parable illustrates the enormity of this debt in order to highlight the magnificence of the King's forgiveness.

B. Unforgiving Spirit (vv. 26-31)
(Matthew 18:29-31 is not included in the printed text.)

26. The servant therefore fell down, and worshipped him, saying, Lord, have patience with me, and I will pay thee all.

27. Then the lord of that servant was moved with compassion, and loosed him, and forgave him the debt.

28. But the same servant went out, and found one of his fellowservants, which owed him an hundred pence: and he laid hands on him, and took him by the throat, saying, Pay me that thou owest.

Although the debt is beyond the servant's imagination, he throws himself before the king in a display of humility. Incredibly, the king completely wipes out his servant's debt with one word of compassion! Instantly, the servant's record is clean and the threat of slavery is lifted.

The next part of the story is intended to produce shock and horror. In an appalling twist, the forgiven servant finds an equal servant who owes him just a few days' wages. He physically assaults his debtor and insists on immediate repayment. When he is begged for mercy with the precise plea he had just given to the king, he refuses. He irrationally orders his debtor thrown into prison, as if imprisonment would speed repayment.

Jesus is undoubtedly illustrating the foolish nature of unforgiveness, since the man would obviously have no way to earn money in jail. What is more, the unmerciful servant's behavior cannot be kept a secret. The other servants find out and quickly relay the matter to their master. The outrage that this story would evoke is similar to the parable of the tenants (21:33-46), in which Jesus plays off His audience by making them angry and then turns the story against them. Likewise, here Jesus clearly portrays the audacity of unforgiveness in the wake of God's abundant mercy toward us.

Interestingly, the descriptions of the debt of sin in Romans 3:23 and 6:23 are immediately followed by God's magnificent act of cancellation: "All . . . being justified freely by His grace through the redemption that is in Christ Jesus" (3:23, 24); "The gift of God is eternal life through Jesus Christ our Lord" (6:23).

The enormity of our debt of sin only magnifies God's act of

Talk About It:
1. What does verse 27 reveal about the master's character?
2. What do verses 28-30 reveal about the servant's character?
3. Why did the other servants "tattle" on the unforgiving servant (see v. 31)?

Power of Forgiveness
Ronald Reagan's attitude after the 1982 attempt on his life made an impression on his daughter, Patti Davis:
"The following day my father said he knew his physical healing was directly dependent on his ability to forgive John Hinckley. By

forgiveness. This truth alone makes unforgiveness on our part inexcusable. Paul puts it succinctly in Colossians 3:13: "Forgive as the Lord forgave you" (*NIV*). Any other option is unthinkable for a true servant of God.

C. Certain Judgment (vv. 32-35)

32. Then his lord, after that he had called him, said unto him, O thou wicked servant, I forgave thee all that debt, because thou desiredst me:

33. Shouldest not thou also have had compassion on thy fellowservant, even as I had pity on thee?

34. And his lord was wroth, and delivered him to the tormentors, till he should pay all that was due unto him.

35. So likewise shall my heavenly Father do also unto you, if ye from your hearts forgive not every one his brother their trespasses.

Enraged, the king confronts the servant, calling him "wicked." His fury is completely understandable. How could the servant who was shown such great grace not extend similar mercy to the other servants?

Jesus' final summary of the parable is chilling. The servant will in fact be responsible for his huge debt, and his payment will take the form of physical punishment. What is worse, we can expect divine judgment when we harbor unforgiveness.

Perhaps this is the sharpest point of Jesus' parable. Whereas the unmerciful servant seeks to imprison the man who owes him money, he instead ends up imprisoned. In a sense, the unmerciful servant's behavior is perfectly fair. His fellow servant legitimately owes him money and he therefore has a right to demand it back. Here lies the destructive power of unforgiveness. When we harbor grudges, we may believe we are hurting the person who legitimately owes us something. In fact, we are only isolating and imprisoning ourselves, while probably having little affect on them whatsoever.

Forgiveness is not a matter of fairness, but a matter of unfairness. Because God has chosen to act completely unfairly in our favor, we are absolutely responsible to act graciously toward those who sin against us. If we do not, we invite the painful effects of unforgiveness mentally, spiritually, and even physically into our lives. The intensity of Jesus' final warning calls us away from these consequences to the freedom of forgiveness. A faithful servant of the generous King must extend mercy to others.

II. BE TRUSTWORTHY (Luke 16:1-15)

The parable of the shrewd manager (or "unjust steward") is yet another teaching about proper servanthood in the Kingdom. In this parable the spiritual truth is directly related to the way God's servants manage real earthly possessions. Jesus connects a believer's ability to handle worldly wealth to his capacity to be trusted with heavenly riches.

A. Are We Trustworthy? (vv. 1-12)
(Luke 16:1-9 is not included in the printed text.)

10. He that is faithful in that which is least is faithful also in much: and he that is unjust in the least is unjust also in much.

mammon (v. 11)—
riches

11. If therefore ye have not been faithful in the unrighteous mammon, who will commit to your trust the true riches?

12. And if ye have not been faithful in that which is another man's, who shall give you that which is your own?

Talk About It:

1. How and when is it good to be "shrewd" (v. 8, *NIV*)?

2. What is the main point of this parable?

3. Explain the principle in verse 10.

At first glance, the parable of the shrewd manager is a strange tale indeed. Just like the parable of the unmerciful servant and the parable of the talents, it begins with a wealthy man settling accounts with someone he had entrusted with his property. In this parable, however, the one entrusted is not a servant, but a "steward" (manager). He is a professional employee of the wealthy boss.

After being accused of managing ineffectively, an account of his administration is demanded. Rather than idly accept his fate, the manager quickly goes to work. Calling two of his master's chief debtors, he cancels part of their debt. The first receives a 50 percent discount, while the second receives a 20 percent reduction in their balance due. The reason? If the manager cannot retain his position, he hopes he will be taken care of by those whose debts he had reduced. The manager is too lazy to be a common laborer and too proud to be a beggar.

When the master realizes what his manager has done, he commends him for his shrewd actions, and the parable abruptly ends. Rather than letting us know whether the master actually restores his manager to his previous position, Jesus immediately explains the master's reasoning. In the financial system of the world, acting in a self-serving fashion for personal gain is highly commendable. If only Jesus' followers would stick to a Kingdom outlook toward money with the same tenacity as the world does to a self-seeking point of view, much more could be accomplished in the Kingdom! Worldly wealth would win many more people to eternity.

In the kingdom of God, the handling of one's finances becomes a litmus test that determines ability to manage spiritual riches. It is not the amount of resources one has at his disposal, but his honesty with whatever is given him. To the worldly master in the parable, dishonesty on the part of the manager displayed his ability to turn a quick dollar. To God, dishonesty

Teachings on Servanthood

with money is proof of one's *inability* to be trusted with higher treasures. As verse 12 illustrates, all financial resources belong to the Lord; and if a person mismanages God's resources, why should they be trusted with any assets of their own?

In 2 Corinthians 9, Paul instructs his congregation concerning this issue of managing finances properly. After encouraging them to participate in his offering for Jerusalem, he communicates an important principle: "Remember this: Whoever sows sparingly will also reap sparingly, and whoever sows generously will also reap generously" (v. 6, *NIV*). Paul practically echoes Jesus' words in Luke 16—anyone who abundantly sows financially into the Kingdom can expect to reap spiritually from it, but the stingy should anticipate no such reward. The New Testament calls us to prove our trustworthiness as servants of God through financial skill, integrity and generosity.

B. Who Is Our Master? (vv. 13-15)
(Luke 16:14, 15 is not included in the printed text.)
13. No servant can serve two masters: for either he will hate the one, and love the other; or else he will hold to the one, and despise the other. Ye cannot serve God and mammon.

This matter of managing money is no less than a lordship issue. God will not tolerate the worldly and dishonest approach of the shrewd manager among His followers. He demands total allegiance to Himself, which may mean forsaking wealth entirely. After a rich young man rejected Jesus' invitation to do just that, Jesus lamented this dilemma in Matthew 19:23, 24: "I tell you the truth, it is hard for a rich man to enter the kingdom of heaven. Again I tell you, it is easier for a camel to go through the eye of a needle than for a rich man to enter the kingdom of God" (*NIV*). He went on to explain that with God anything is possible, but this does not diminish His hard truth regarding servanthood.

When the Pharisees sneered at Jesus' teaching in Luke 16:14, He was unapologetic, exclaiming, "That which is highly esteemed among men is abomination in the sight of God" (v. 15). For a person to compromise his or her integrity as a servant of God for the sake of money is absolutely detestable to the Lord. The Christ-follower is forced to a critical decision whenever tempted to improperly handle worldly wealth, and this decision indicates his or her true master.

III. DO YOUR DUTY (Luke 17:7-10)
In response to His disciples' emphatic request, "Increase our faith" (v. 5), Jesus gives two short teachings. The first is a proclamation of the power of great faith—"as a grain of mustard seed" (v. 6); through it, He validates the value of their appeal for more faith. He then provides a scenario that portrays the challenge of living out such faith.

"It is a greater compliment to be trusted than to be loved."
—**George MacDonald**

Talk About It:
1. Why can't someone serve both God and money?
2. How does Christ contrast God's values with the world's values?

He Served Elijah
After marching through the desert for seven days, the armies of Judah and Israel were out of water. Judah's king asked whether there was a prophet they could consult. An officer of the king identified Elisha, saying, "He used to pour water on the hands of Elijah" (2 Kings 3:11, *NIV*). Elisha then performed a great miracle for the troops.

It was only because Elisha served Elijah that he was recognized as a great prophet. Likewise, our greatness is completely dependent on those we have served.

A. Servanthood Requires Consistency (vv. 7, 8)

7. But which of you, having a servant plowing or feeding cattle, will say unto him by and by, when he is come from the field, Go and sit down to meat?

8. And will not rather say unto him, Make ready wherewith I may sup, and gird thyself, and serve me, till I have eaten and drunken; and afterward thou shalt eat and drink?

Jesus' teaching here is not in His typical parable format, but it still qualifies as a parable, given that He tells a story for the purpose of comparison. In most parables, the comparison occurs at the beginning of the story, usually introduced by "The kingdom of heaven is like. . . ." Here the comparison occurs at the end and is solely directed toward His disciples (v. 10). Even so, the teaching reflects Jesus' ability to communicate in vivid images that were certainly understandable to His audience.

As a response to the disciples' request for greater faith, Jesus communicates a strong teaching. Although a servant may be faithful in the field, he is still expected to cook and wait on his master, even after a hard day's work. Jesus clearly depicts the hierarchical nature between master and servant, one that may make our modern tastes quite uncomfortable. But His command is unambiguous—a servant is owned by his master and therefore subject to his duty at all times.

Perhaps this servant-master relationship is better explained in terms of slavery. In reality, the same Greek word is used for both "servant" and "slave," so their use in Jesus' parables is interchangeable. Whereas a servant could possibly be hired for work in a master's household or business, a slave was considered the sole property of that household. At this juncture, it is important to refrain from importing our understanding of the early American slave system into the New Testament world. In Jesus' day, being a slave was often very desirable, as slaves could rise to great prominence in a household. Occasionally, slaves were known to reject their freedom in order to stay within a particular master's household. Jesus' notion of slavery in God's kingdom refers to such an arrangement.

So then, Jesus' story clearly calls us to consistent servanthood, because of our status as slaves of God. This is a critical distinction—we are not called to serve, but to take on the identity of servants. Someone who chooses to serve can just as easily choose not to upon becoming distracted or tired. Someone who takes upon himself the yoke of slavery has no choice; his vocation requires a constant response to duty, no matter when it calls. This is Jesus' calling to His followers.

B. Servants Should Be Thankful (vv. 9, 10)

9. Doth he thank that servant because he did the things that were commanded him? I trow not.

Talk About It:

1. Can one be a Christian without being a servant? Why or why not?

2. Describe some of the servant tasks of believers.

"At the close of life, the question will be, not how much have you got, but how much have you given? Not how much have you won, but how much have you done? Not how much have you saved, but how much have you sacrificed? It will be, how much have you loved and served, not how much were you honored?"

—Nathan Schaeffer

trow (v. 9)—think

Teachings on Servanthood

10. So likewise ye, when ye shall have done all those things which are commanded you, say, We are unprofitable servants: we have done that which was our duty to do.

What remarkable humility Jesus requires from the servant's heart! After toiling in the service of the master, it is still the servant that owes thankfulness for the opportunity to fulfill his duty. Jesus challenges His disciples to focus on servanthood regardless of the reward involved. Of course, we know from Jesus' other teachings that God is not an unappreciative master, for the Gospels are full of promises of reward for His faithful servants. Nevertheless, we do not serve God for any reward, but because the choice is not ours. Once we become slaves of the Kingdom, our duty is sworn. Paul says it powerfully in 1 Corinthians 6:19, 20: "You are not your own; you were bought at a price" (*NIV*). When we truly comprehend God's ownership of our lives, a servant's heart will guide everything that we do. We are nothing less than property of the kingdom of God.

Talk About It:
Why doesn't our service to God earn us any merit with Him?

CONCLUSION

Jesus' parables on servanthood reveal the vital components of the true servant's heart. The parable of the unmerciful servant shows us the terrible consequences of unforgiveness, and communicates the necessity of forgiveness for servants of God. The parable of the shrewd manager portrays the importance of faithful stewardship in becoming truly trustworthy in God's kingdom. Jesus' teaching on duty conveys our obligation to faithful and thankful service in the Master's house. In each of these teachings, Jesus calls us to a life of greatness in the Kingdom by our serving others. It is by maturing into a slave of His kingdom that we develop a true servant's heart.

GOLDEN TEXT CHALLENGE

"HE THAT IS FAITHFUL IN THAT WHICH IS LEAST IS FAITHFUL ALSO IN MUCH: AND HE THAT IS UNJUST IN THE LEAST IS UNJUST ALSO IN MUCH" (Luke 16:10).

The principle expressed here is repeatedly fleshed out in the lives of Biblical personalities. For instance, David faithfully cared for his father's sheep, even protecting them against lions and bears, so God empowered him to take down a giant. . . . Mordecai refused to bow to a human ruler, so God brought him into a royal position. . . . An unknown widow gave her last pennies to the Lord, so God made her into a person still talked about 2,000 years later.

God's economy works like this: Those who sweep the floor may one day own the store!

Daily Devotions:
M. Joseph Forgives His Brothers Genesis 50:15-21
T. A Person's Duty to God Ecclesiastes 12:9-14
W. Daniel Is Trustworthy Daniel 6:1-10
T. Forgiveness Necessary to Be Forgiven Matthew 6:9-15
F. Faithfulness Will Be Rewarded Luke 19:15-26
S. Our Spiritual Duty Romans 8:12-17

November 27, 2005

What Makes Heaven Rejoice?

Luke 15:1-32

Unit Theme:
Parables of Jesus

Central Truth:
God earnestly desires all people to be saved.

Focus:
To recognize the value God places on sinners and diligently seek to win the lost to Christ.

Context:
Jesus relates three salvation parables to the Pharisees, teachers, tax collectors and sinners.

Golden Text:
"Likewise joy shall be in heaven over one sinner that repenteth, more than over ninety and nine just persons, which need no repentance" (Luke 15:7).

Study Outline:
I. A Lost Sheep Rescued (Luke 15:1-7)
II. A Lost Coin Recovered (Luke 15:8-10)
III. A Lost Son Returns (Luke 15:11-32)

INTRODUCTION

What made the New Testament church so focused on evangelism? At the church's inception on the Day of Pentecost in Acts 2, Peter's sermon effected the salvation of 3,000 souls (v. 41), and this number immediately began to increase on a daily basis (v. 47). After the church in Jerusalem began experiencing persecution in Acts 8, the Christians scattered throughout the Roman Empire, winning converts and planting churches in every city they touched. In this way Jesus' promise to them in Acts 1:8 is fulfilled at the end of the book where Paul preaches in Rome.

We often look to the coming of the Spirit at Pentecost, or to Jesus' great commission (Matthew 28:18-20) as the apostles' "springboard" for evangelistic outreach. In both, the emphasis is on taking the message of Christ to those who have not yet heard. Later on in the New Testament, this call to win souls is amplified by every writer, culminating in the cry of the Spirit at the end of John's Revelation (22:17): "The Spirit and the bride say, Come. . . . And let him that is athirst come. And whosoever will, let him take the water of life freely."

This evangelistic zeal that so quickly swept over the empire did not originate after Christ had risen. No, the charge to reach the lost was present throughout the teaching of Jesus. The parables of the sower (Luke 8:4-15), the wedding banquet (Matthew 22:1-14), and the workers in the vineyard (20:1-16) illustrate the necessity of bringing unreached people into the Kingdom. In Luke 15, this necessity becomes the specific call to reach those that are lost, whether they are aware of their state or not. Jesus gives three parables that exemplify this passion for evangelism, using the images of a lost sheep, coin and son. The conclusion of each is great rejoicing over a missing part of the household being found. Here Jesus is only secondarily concerned with calling believers to witness, and primarily interested in giving them a theological basis for such witnessing. This basis is simple—God is the originator of evangelism, and we are called to join Him in His work of finding the lost.

I. A LOST SHEEP RESCUED (Luke 15:1-7)

Jesus' three great parables on the importance of evangelism are actually a direct response to an accusation of the Pharisees and teachers of the Law. As Jesus taught the people, verse 1 says that both tax collectors and sinners were pressing around Him, paying close attention to His words. These two groups were among the most despised throughout Israel.

Tax collectors were true traitors of their own people. They purchased the expensive rights to collect taxes for the Romans, and often accumulated great wealth by overtaxing the Jews and keeping the profits. "Sinners" were a class one step down the social ladder. Usually for economic reasons, they had all but renounced the faith of Israel altogether. In the case of women, this was often due to their husband's death pushing them into a life of prostitution in order to survive. In the case of men, this category comprised the very poor who resorted to thievery and crime. Incredibly, Jesus not only entertained their company, but offered no objection to the Pharisees' accusation that He ate with them! In that society, to share a meal with someone else solidified a strong bond of friendship, as it communicated familiarity and equality. Jesus therefore went far beyond simply tolerating sinners; He welcomed them with open arms into the community of the kingdom of God.

Because of the religious leaders' complete misunderstanding of Jesus' ministry to the lost, He explains His actions using three parables. Each one communicates the absolute priority of evangelism in a different way, and each illustrates heaven's bias toward those still unreached with the gospel.

A. Evangelism Begins With Leadership (vv. 1-4)

1. Then drew near unto him all the publicans and sinners for to hear him.

2. And the Pharisees and scribes murmured, saying, This man receiveth sinners, and eateth with them.

3. And he spake this parable unto them, saying,

4. What man of you, having an hundred sheep, if he lose one of them, doth not leave the ninety and nine in the wilderness, and go after that which is lost, until he find it?

Jesus' first defense of His stance toward sinners is a commonsense story about basic shepherding practices of His day. Undoubtedly His rural listeners would have been quite familiar with the keeping of animals, as they often constituted the only real wealth a commoner might accumulate. For this reason, shepherds were constantly on guard for threats to their flocks, and did everything possible to keep them together. Still, the weather and openness of the countryside was such that the animals often strayed, and Jesus depicts such a scenario to

Talk About It:
1. Why is God so concerned for lost people?
2. Does our church focus enough attention on the lost "one"?

perfectly represent God's heart for human sinners.

What great initiative on the part of this compassionate shepherd! Whether because of weather or wandering, a single sheep has become hopelessly separated from the sizeable flock. It cannot survive long alone in a countryside filled with predators and other shepherds who might lay claim to a stray. Because of this, Jesus explains that any good sheep owner is perfectly willing to leave the 99 and begin a search in the direction of their day's grazing.

Perhaps the most striking feature of Jesus' teaching here is that the priority of evangelism begins with God himself, and therefore evangelism is the primary responsibility of spiritual leadership. Remember, Jesus is illustrating the character of God for religious leaders who misunderstand Jesus' open arms to sinners. The shepherd, then, signifies God and His heart for lost people. It is God who initiates the search, finds the sheep, and begins the celebration.

This leadership-driven approach to evangelism flows throughout the early church and the New Testament writings. Perhaps it is most clearly demonstrated by the apostle Paul, who, though being a church planter and pastor, saw the primary characteristic of his ministry to be one of soulwinning. He consistently engaged in encounters with unbelievers in the hopes of winning some who would help build an evangelistic church in their city. Though a disciple maker, Paul made his passion known at the close of his letter to the Romans: "It has always been my ambition to preach the gospel where Christ was not known, so that I would not be building on someone else's foundation" (15:20, *NIV*). As leaders in the church, we are not *primarily* obligated to the business of the membership—the 99 safe sheep—but to the needs of the lost.

> "Being an extrovert isn't essential to evangelism—obedience and love are."
> —Rebecca Pippert

B. Evangelism Should Be a Joyful Search (vv. 5, 6)

5. And when he hath found it, he layeth it on his shoulders, rejoicing.

6. And when he cometh home, he calleth together his friends and neighbours, saying unto them, Rejoice with me; for I have found my sheep which was lost.

Talk About It:
Who should be involved in the search for lost people?

Retrieving the lost sheep requires great effort in Jesus' parable. The shepherd must find adequate supervision for the 99 before commencing his journey. The sheep may have wandered in any direction, so the shepherd has much ground to cover. He does not find a neutral spot and wait on the lost sheep to arrive; he aggressively searches out the sheep and actually carries it home. Even though the search for the sheep is hard and mostly uneventful work, its discovery is cause for communal rejoicing.

This parable teaches us several truths about winning the lost. First, it can be difficult work. When a child is declared missing by the authorities, search parties begin the painstaking job of finding that child. Evangelism, too, often necessitates a long process in winning someone to Christ. Second, it should be joyful work. The shepherd does not express anger at the sheep's condition, but he joyfully carries it back home for further rejoicing. Third, it should be done in community. The shepherd rallies his friends and neighbors around the discovery of that which was lost.

C. Evangelism Is Focused on Heaven (v. 7)

7. I say unto you, that likewise joy shall be in heaven over one sinner that repenteth, more than over ninety and nine just persons, which need no repentance.

While demonstrating the way in which the community of faith should rejoice at the turning of a sinner to God, Jesus also describes the rejoicing that breaks out in heaven. Obviously, the math of the kingdom of heaven is completely different than earthly thinking.

It was the religious leaders whom Jesus was addressing that prized and comprised the 99 righteous persons. They sought to exclude the unrighteous from the family of God. But Jesus teaches that heaven is radically inclusive of outsiders, throwing a party for every sinner who joins its number. He does not say heaven is *not* joyous over those righteous persons already bound for its gates, but that its most enthusiastic joy comes from a new sinner who repents.

In this first parable, then, Jesus effectively communicates the priority of evangelism for His followers. Because heaven's priority is lost sheep, so must the church's be. A church that does not participate in God's great search for the lost is depriving itself of great rejoicing both presently on earth and later in heaven.

II. A LOST COIN RECOVERED (Luke 15:8-10)

8. Either what woman having ten pieces of silver, if she lose one piece, doth not light a candle, and sweep the house, and seek diligently till she find it?

9. And when she hath found it, she calleth her friends and her neighbours together, saying, Rejoice with me; for I have found the piece which I had lost.

10. Likewise, I say unto you, there is joy in the presence of the angels of God over one sinner that repenteth.

On first glance, the parable of the lost coin may seem to be identical both in form and meaning to the parable of the lost sheep. They both include the search for something valuable coupled with great rejoicing at its discovery. However, there is a

Talk About It:
1. Why is the salvation of one soul the cause of such rejoicing in heaven?
2. Can a church that does not emphasize soulwinning be a joyous church? Why or why not?

Talk About It:
1. How and where should the church be searching for lost people?
2. What does it mean for a sinner to "repent" (v. 10), and why does this cause angels to rejoice?

critical difference. In the first story, the lost sheep knows it is lost yet does not know how to find its way back to the shepherd. An animal would be completely conscious of such a predicament. In the second story, though, the inanimate coin is obviously not aware of either being lost or of finding a way back to its owner. So this parable provides yet a fuller picture of God's heart for successful evangelism.

The silver coin referred to is a *drachma*, which was worth about a day's wages in Jesus' day. Most Jews needed every one they could earn to survive, so this story definitely resonated in the ears of its hearers. The item lost is of great worth to the woman, the product of much labor. Because of this, an investment of time and resources is immediately mobilized to find the lost coin. A lamp is lit, using costly oil, and the woman uses as much time as it takes. She does so because any investment necessary will pay off when the coin is discovered.

This is an important Kingdom principle Jesus is teaching on evangelism. Winning the lost is a costly endeavor! For the shepherd, it meant risking his entire flock and livelihood to find a single sheep. For the woman, it meant spending valuable time and lamp oil to uncover the coin's whereabouts. Yet by the end of the story, all of her work is completely worth the sacrifice. Like the shepherd, her entire community erupts in joy. So we also must view evangelism as an investment. Our initial search for a lost person may turn up little progress, but we must keep searching. Any sacrifice along the way will be soon forgotten in the rejoicing salvation will bring.

In the parable of the sheep, the search for the lost is broad and spacious, involving a journey. The search for the lost coin, however, is localized in a home. It requires careful, tedious searching. Again, this is the case when someone is not aware of his or her lost status. Such evangelism often takes place on the mission field overseas, where ministers must be careful not to offend the culture of the unreached people. They must delicately search for ways the gospel connects with that culture's particular way of life as a bridge for sharing Christ. If our evangelism is done without sensitivity and care, the lost may not be found.

III. A LOST SON RETURNS (Luke 15:11-32)

At this point in Luke 15, Jesus has emphasized the fact that God has lost something. The parables of the lost sheep and the coin illustrate the desperation of God, who cannot stand for His possessions to be incomplete. In the third parable, the story of the lost son, this longing on the part of God to be reconnected with His lost children focuses on human characters. Here no search takes place, because the parable's context is different. Unlike the lost coin, the son understands he is lost;

Praying for Opportunity

Each of us should ask ourselves, "Are there people for whom I am praying by name every day, asking God the Holy Spirit to open their eyes, enlighten them, and bend their wills until they receive Jesus Christ as Lord and Savior? Are there any people with whom I am building bridges and seeking opportunities to show the love of Christ?" . . . If we discover an absence of vital contact with non-Christians, we may simply ask God to show us even one person whom He wants us to befriend, pray for, love and eventually bring to the Savior, and He will show us that one.

—Paul Little
(How to Give Away Your Faith)

What Makes Heaven Rejoice?

unlike the lost sheep, the son knows the way back home to his father. Just like God, the father chooses not to interfere with his son's free will. It is up to the son to choose to return. Yet when he does, Jesus illustrates the heart of God in a way unprecedented throughout Scripture. The story is not centered on a fallen son but on an incredible father.

A. Lost People Are Destructive (vv. 11-13)
11. And he said, A certain man had two sons:
12. And the younger of them said to his father, Father, give me the portion of goods that falleth to me. And he divided unto them his living.
13. And not many days after the younger son gathered all together, and took his journey into a far country, and there wasted his substance with riotous living.

Because the story concerns people instead of animals or objects, it is more than twice the length of the first two parables combined. Jesus portrays human nature in its brutally fallen state, sparing no degree of detail. The wandering son symbolizes the person who finds himself far from God. Jesus spent time with such people because He understood their sinful deeds as symptoms of a deeper need. Unlike the religious leaders, though, Jesus looked past these symptoms to focus on the true illness—separation from the Father's house.

The parable introduces not just one, but two sons. The older son does not appear until the end of the parable, but provides a vital contrast that Jesus is applying to His audience. The younger one represents those the religious leaders are judging—tax collectors and sinners. Jesus does not justify the behavior of such persons, but explains it in terms of this young son, who was rebellious, as all lost people are.

Lost people are in rebellion against God and will be destructive. We should expect them to act that way. They are damaging both to themselves and to others. The younger son in Jesus' parable is immediately depicted as a dishonorable character. First, he selfishly demands his share of the household's inheritance right away. Typically, such wealth would be transferred upon the father's death and its passing on was considered a sacred honor to the memory of the father. The egotistical son has no regard for his father's honor, and quickly leaves the house, and the country, foolishly wasting his inheritance on sin and debauchery.

Such is the allure of sin. The younger son has a great inheritance, a productive place in his household, and a loving relationship with his father. Yet he trades all of these for an alternative lifestyle. We should not gasp either at his behavior or the consequences thereof. Those who decide against a relationship with God for whatever reason are sure to act destructively.

Talk About It:
1. In what sense is the Prodigal Son like all people?
2. Why, like the father in the parable, does God allow us to make choices that He knows will harm us?

B. Lost People Are in Great Need (vv. 14-19)

14. And when he had spent all, there arose a mighty famine in that land; and he began to be in want.

15. And he went and joined himself to a citizen of that country; and he sent him into his fields to feed swine.

16. And he would fain have filled his belly with the husks that the swine did eat: and no man gave unto him.

17. And when he came to himself, he said, How many hired servants of my father's have bread enough and to spare, and I perish with hunger!

18. I will arise and go to my father, and will say unto him, Father, I have sinned against heaven, and before thee,

19. And am no more worthy to be called thy son: make me as one of thy hired servants.

Talk About It:

1. Describe how unbelievers are "in want" (v. 14).

2. List some of the things people "join" with (v. 15) when in want.

3. In verses 17-19, what change took place in the Prodigal's heart? Why was this important?

Only a few sentences into Jesus' parable, the younger son's destructive lifestyle turns against him and he finds himself "in want." What a statement of the son's plight! This son who just one verse ago had a wealthy inheritance at his disposal now begins to lack. In countries far from the father's house, famine is the routine, and Jesus tells of the son's further descent into a pig's pen, where he hungers for the very food the pigs ate out of a trough. The irony is astonishing—the son lives with pigs yet lies starving for meat!

We must never be surprised at the neediness of lost people. Some may seem to have all the tools to better themselves right in front of them, yet they are incapable of helping themselves. The old adage "God helps those who help themselves" is difficult to apply to the lost. Just like the lost son, their distance from the Father often isolates them from others, keeping them from life-giving relationships. It is vital that we understand this need before trying to meet it.

When he can take it no longer, the son constructs a plan to work his way back into the father's household. Resigned to the fact that he will never regain his place as a son, he remembers the provision made for the servants. Because their lives were of much greater quality than his, he composes a speech and sets off for home. *Notice that it is not a renewed love for his father that drives him, but his own hunger.* Lost people may not recognize that their true need is God when they seek to better their lives.

> "If a man in vision could see the kind of being he was intended to be, he would never again be content to be what he has been."
> —Gypsy Smith

C. God Accepts the Return of the Lost (vv. 20-24)

20. And he arose, and came to his father. But when he was yet a great way off, his father saw him, and had compassion, and ran, and fell on his neck, and kissed him.

21. And the son said unto him, Father, I have sinned

What Makes Heaven Rejoice?

against heaven, and in thy sight, and am no more worthy to be called thy son.

22. But the father said to his servants, Bring forth the best robe, and put it on him; and put a ring on his hand, and shoes on his feet:

23. And bring hither the fatted calf, and kill it; and let us eat, and be merry:

24. For this my son was dead, and is alive again; he was lost, and is found. And they began to be merry.

The most gripping part of the parable begins when the son makes the critical decision to return to the father. Through the language of repentance, the son "turns back" to the father. Such repentance is all the father needs. As if waiting for him all this time, upon catching a glimpse of the son staggering home, his father takes off running. This alone was an affront to the sense and sensibilities of honorable Jews. The authoritative and respectable Jewish father would never bless a son that had mocked the family name, much less run to him! Yet this father, who symbolizes the heart of God, takes center stage in the parable, converting it from one of a lost son into a story of an amazing father.

The son speaks only one sentence before his father begins the process of restoring him to his place of sonship. In his excitement, he orders his servants to make haste. The father's expensive robe replaces the son's haggard clothing. New sandals are placed on the boy's blistered feet. Not only this, but a ring which stood for official family authority is set on his finger. As the feast begins, there is no doubt that the son has been completely reinstated.

D. We Must Accept the Return of Lost People (vv. 25-32)

(Luke 15:25-32 is not included in the printed text.)

The father's faithful older son hears the celebration while performing household work in the fields. Incredibly, he shows no concern about the return of his brother and is instead angry with his father, scorning his graciousness. The father lovingly responds to his outburst, explaining that his place in the house is not being diminished in any way by the return of his younger brother. It is not cause for alarm, but for celebration at the discovery of that which was lost!

The "older brother" principally refers to the religious leaders Jesus was addressing. They claimed to be faithful to God's house yet wanted to keep out the sinners who were turning to the Kingdom. Jesus did not address them harshly, but showed them that God wants everyone in His kingdom—those who have been faithful and those who have been lost. This stands as a charge to us also—we must not envy God's graciousness

Talk About It:
1. Compare God's compassion with the compassion of the Prodigal's father.
2. What is available to us when we realize we are unworthy to be called God's children?

Fatherly Connection

Among children placed into unconventional families, there often lies an inner need to connect with their biological parents. Something in the human psyche longs for the connection of a real parent.

Thankfully, such a connection is realized when we come into a relationship with Jesus Christ. Until this happens, an unfulfilled longing stands in every human heart. Though some may try to fill this longing with selfishness, materialism, or destructive living, only when the lost are reconnected with their heavenly Father will they be made whole.

Talk About It:
1. Explain the older son's attitude.

2. Why do church members sometimes have a similarly negative attitude toward new converts?

3. How does God want the church to respond to the salvation of lost people?

Daily Devotions:
M. A Saved People
   Deuteronomy
   33:26-29
T. No Savior but
   God
   Isaiah 43:8-13
W. God Delights to
   Save
   Ezekiel 18:21-32
T. Strive to Enter
   Luke 13:22-30
F. Christ Came to
   Save Sinners
   John 3:16-21
S. Salvation Only
   Through Christ
   Acts 4:5-12

toward even the most destructive sinner. Because the Father stands ready to forgive, we must be jubilant, not judgmental.

CONCLUSION

As long as there are people who live outside of the Kingdom, God is missing something He infinitely values. As a follower of Jesus, reaching the lost is not an option; it is a mandate. If God values sinners, so must we. If God searches out those separated from Him, so must we. Such work requires seeking out the lost with desperation, carefulness and compassion. Heaven hinges on our success, since its most joyous celebration takes place at the repentance of one sinner.

GOLDEN TEXT CHALLENGE

"LIKEWISE JOY SHALL BE IN HEAVEN OVER ONE SINNER THAT REPENTETH, MORE THAN OVER NINETY AND NINE JUST PERSONS, WHICH NEED NO REPENTANCE" (Luke 15:7).

So significant is the redemption of a sinner that heaven itself joins in the rejoicing. Perhaps the reason for that holy company's joy is their knowledge of the future which awaits the redeemed one. Also, they know (in a way we cannot know) the degree of love and sacrifice inherent in Christ's coming to buy us back.

It is not that the heavenly host is displeased and unconcerned about those who are redeemed already. However, this verse points up the extreme importance of redemption and to the marked, crucial difference between the lost and the saved. It is not a matter of degree—it is a matter of life or death!

Introduction to Winter Quarter

S tudies from the epistles of 1 Peter, 2 Peter and Jude are the focus of Unit 1 (lessons 1-10). The topics include salvation, sanctification, submission, suffering, service, standing firm, and the Second Coming. Lesson 4 is the Christmas emphasis, based on Luke 2.

Editor Lance Colkmire (see biographical information on page 16) compiled lessons 1-6, while the Reverend Richard Keith Whitt wrote lessons 7-10.

Keith Whitt (B.A., M.Div., Ph.D. cand.) has earned degrees from Lee University and the Church of God Theological Seminary; he is completing the doctor of philosophy at the University of Nottingham (England). An ordained bishop in the Church of God, Keith has served his denomination as a pastor for 23 years, district overseer for 12 years, and as a member of various boards and committees. He has taught courses for the Church of God Theological Seminary and Lee University External Studies.

The second unit (lessons 11-13)—three lessons from the Book of Numbers—was written by the Reverend Dr. Jerald Daffe (B.A., M.A., D.Min.). Dr. Daffe earned his degrees from Northwest Bible College, Wheaton College Graduate School, and Western Conservative Baptist Seminary. An ordained minister in the Church of God, Dr. Daffe has served in the pastoral ministry for 10 years and has been a faculty member at Northwest Bible College and Lee University for 30 years. Dr. Daffe received the Excellence in Advising Award (1999) at Lee University. His two latest books are *Life Challenges for Men* and *Revival: God's Plan for His People*.

December 4, 2005
Salvation of the Believer
1 Peter 1:1-12

Unit Theme:
Peter and Jude

Central Truth:
God provided salvation from sin through the death and resurrection of Jesus Christ.

Focus:
To understand and appreciate God's wonderful provision of salvation through Jesus Christ.

Context:
Written to churches in Asia Minor around A.D. 64

Golden Text:
"Blessed be the God and Father of our Lord Jesus Christ, which according to his abundant mercy hath begotten us again unto a lively hope by the resurrection of Jesus Christ from the dead" (1 Peter 1:3).

Study Outline:
I. Saved by Abundant Mercy
(1 Peter 1:1-4)
II. Kept by God's Power
(1 Peter 1:5-9)
III. Salvation Revealed
(1 Peter 1:10-12)

INTRODUCTION

The apostle Peter is well known to all Christians. He was certainly one of the most vibrant and energetic persons in the life of our Lord. His life divides into four general areas. The first area—from his birth to the time he met Jesus—we know little about. We do know that he was married and his mother-in-law was still living (Mark 1:30). He was a Galilean fisherman who lived in Capernaum, and had a brother named Andrew (v. 16).

The second area of his life is given in some detail for us. This is his life following his conversion up until the Day of Pentecost. The records are clear in the Gospels and in Acts.

The third area of his life is that of the period from the Day of Pentecost to the Jerusalem Council. This is found in Acts 1—15 and Galatians 2. It covered a time frame from about A.D. 33 to 49.

The final period is from the Jerusalem Council to his death. The records are meager, and we have only his two epistles and brief references in the remainder of the New Testament: 1 Corinthians 9:5 and John 21:18, 19.

Church tradition had always held that Peter had a close relationship with the congregation at Rome. The Roman church later made extravagant claims for this relationship which Protestants have rejected. In all probability, the martyrdom described in John 21:18, 19 took place in Rome.

Peter's first letter is addressed to a mixture of Jewish and Gentile Christians in five areas of Asia Minor. It was probably written from Rome in the early to middle part of the decade of the 60s. It is clear that these Christians in Asia Minor were beginning to be persecuted for their faith. In light of this, the apostle Peter wrote in an exhortation style (called "hortatory") with "a powerful appeal to courage, purity and faithfulness to Christ amid the sufferings which they are experiencing" (Hiebert, *An Introduction to the Non-Pauline Epistles*).

I. SAVED BY ABUNDANT MERCY (1 Peter 1:1-4)

A. Chosen by God (vv. 1, 2)

1. Peter, an apostle of Jesus Christ, to the strangers scattered throughout Pontus, Galatia, Cappadocia, Asia, and Bithynia,

2. Elect according to the foreknowledge of God the Father, through sanctification of the Spirit, unto obedience and sprinkling of the blood of Jesus Christ: Grace unto you, and peace, be multiplied.

In this salutation Peter introduced himself simply as "an apostle of Jesus." He was apparently well known to the readers and did not need to further identify himself.

He wrote this letter to congregations settled in five areas of Asia Minor. "Strangers" (v. 1) is better rendered "exiles." Peter could have been writing to the Jews who were scattered around the Mediterranean world and not settled in Palestine. He also could have been speaking to Gentile Christians whose new citizenship was in heaven. "Scattered" here does not refer to persons who were fleeing; rather, it indicates that the churches covered a wide range of territory. The order of the areas mentioned corresponds to the natural movement a person would take in delivering the letter to each area so it could be read.

Each of the places is of some significance. Together they formed four Roman provinces with Pontus and Bithynia together as one province. Pontus was located in the northern part of Asia Minor on the south coast of the Black Sea. Aquila, the Christian orator (Acts 18:2), was from this area. Bithynia was located near Pontus by the Black Sea. In Acts 16:7 there is an interesting note regarding a proposed visit by Paul to this area that was prohibited by the Spirit of Jesus.

Galatia was in the central part of Asia Minor. This area was evangelized by the apostle Paul during his first missionary tour described in Acts 13 and 14. Cappadocia was east of Galatia and south of Pontus. This area probably heard the gospel early as Jews from here were present in Jerusalem on the Day of Pentecost (2:9).

Asia was on the western coast of Asia Minor. In this province were located the seven churches mentioned in the Book of Revelation. These churches underwent intense persecution some 30 years later.

Verse 2 of the text is one of the most powerful verses in Holy Scripture. It stresses the majesty and sovereignty of God and His power to save. The people addressed in these Asian provinces are described as the "elect according to the foreknowledge of God the Father." Note carefully what Peter wrote.

These people had been chosen according to God's foreknowledge. The word foreknowledge is the Greek prognosis. It

---

Pontus, Galatia (*guh-LAY-she-uh*), Cappadocia (*cap-uh-DOE-she-uh*), Bithynia (*bi-THIN-e-uh*), Asia (v. 1)— regions of Asia Minor

Talk About It:
1. Why did Peter call fellow believers in Christ "strangers"?
2. Whom does God "elect," and for what purpose?
3. Why do believers need "multiplied grace and peace" (see v. 2)?

---

was a medical term (as it is today) and Peter used it in his Pentecost sermon in Acts 2:23 to describe the death of Jesus.

God's ability to prognosticate leaves us dumbfounded in our weak minds. God is not an elevated human being. He created the human race and is thus free to exercise His lordship according to His holy character and holy purposes.

Thus, Peter spoke of this election as being accomplished through *sanctification*. This corresponds to the position of Paul in Romans 6:22, "But now being made free from sin, and become servants to God, ye have your fruit unto holiness, and the end everlasting life." This sanctification is wholly the work of the Spirit of God. This is not legalism nor self-righteousness. This is the true liberty that the children of God have in the Spirit of God. As men and women certain of our calling, we are free to live wholly (holy) for Him. This sanctifying work of the Spirit is done in relationship to the shed blood of Jesus Christ. We are sprinkled with His blood. The image of "sprinkling" is drawn from Exodus 24:7, 8 with the establishment of the covenant at Sinai. This sprinkling by Jesus and the sanctifying work of the Spirit leads to obedience.

Thus, election is made secure in our hearts because of our love of His Word and His commandments. Our entire life shifts to obedience to His will. We no longer seek excuses for disobedience, but we seek to love Him more.

Peter joyfully concluded this verse with "Grace unto you, and peace, be multiplied." So confident was he of the loving mercy of Jesus that he called for the grace of Jesus to be given "in abundance" (*NIV*). Two things come to mind when we think of this multiplying of grace. The first is Paul's similar comments in Romans 5:18-21, which show the overwhelming triumph of grace over sin. The second is the personal experience of Peter in those terror-filled hours when he betrayed his Lord. Yet Peter discovered that his Lord loved him and gave Himself for a person like him. He learned the meaning of the foreknowledge of God and the powerful work of the Holy Spirit in sanctification and obedience.

"God has foreordained each of us—that includes you, no matter how shattered your life may be—to be conformed to the image of His Son."
—David Morris
(A Lifestyle of Worship)

B. Filled With Hope (vv. 3, 4)

3. Blessed be the God and Father of our Lord Jesus Christ, which according to his abundant mercy hath begotten us again unto a lively hope by the resurrection of Jesus Christ from the dead,

4. To an inheritance incorruptible, and undefiled, and that fadeth not away, reserved in heaven for you.

Peter gave praise to God because of what God had accomplished in Jesus. The real focus of praise in the death and resurrection of Jesus is God the Father. He has been shown as righteous. He has been shown as the God of love and holiness.

Salvation of the Believer

God's mercy has proved to be abundant. He had birthed us to new life and hope through the resurrection of Jesus.

Note the focus of our being born again. We are born to a "lively hope." Salvation means we have a purpose for living. Our horizons of the world are viewed through the cross of Jesus, and life is lived to its fullest because we have experienced new life in Christ. The resurrection of Jesus has provided this possibility. Thus, we as Christians enter the world with a new song, a new confession, a new lifestyle, a new worldview, a newness that attracts all who are claimed by death and sets people free from bondage.

This lively hope that is ours through the Resurrection has content. It is not speculative philosophy. It is a real hope which God has set for us, making it "incorruptible." This is the same word used in 1 Corinthians 15:52 to speak of the resurrection body. It is a pure, "undefiled" hope. In other words, this hope is untouched by the power of sin and death.

To many, the Easter story is the bright point of the year, but their commitment fades as the days progress. The lively hope we have does not fade and is not tarnished. It shines pure and bright, and every day and night is the beacon call of our inheritance in heaven. This inheritance is "reserved" for us. The perfect tense of this verb means the "reservation still holds good; for it is in heaven, beyond the reach of earthly accidents" (*Interpreter's Bible*).

II. KEPT BY GOD'S POWER (1 Peter 1:5-9)
A. A Shielding Power (v. 5)
5. Who are kept by the power of God through faith unto salvation ready to be revealed in the last time.

The "who" of verse 5 refers to the "for you" of verse 4. Just as God has given us a "lively hope" through the Resurrection, He has also promised to keep us by His power. The word *kept* is a present participle that connotes the ongoing "keeping" quality of God. The word was used in the sense of a protective garrison watching over the city gates from the inside. Thus, faith keeps us in the power of God. This is a marvelous source of comfort and strength. God has promised to preserve us with His mighty power for the salvation that is to be revealed; namely, the return of Jesus in the last day.

Because we *were saved* at the moment we put our faith in Christ, and because we *are being saved* through the indwelling Holy Spirit day by day, we know we *will be saved* after we leave this life. Heaven will be our eternal home.

Think of stepping on shore,
And finding it heaven;
Think of taking hold a hand,

Talk About It:
1. Why do we need "abundant mercy"?
2. How is the Christian's hope "lively"?
3. Describe the inheritance awaiting God's children.

And finding it God's hand.
Think of breathing new air,
And finding it celestial air.
Think of feeling invigorated,
And finding it immortality;
Think of passing from storm and tempest,
To an unknown calm;
Think of waking up,
And finding it home!

B. A Purified Faith (vv. 6-9)

6. Wherein ye greatly rejoice, though now for a season, if need be, ye are in heaviness through manifold temptations:

7. That the trial of your faith, being much more precious than of gold that perisheth, though it be tried with fire, might be found unto praise and honour and glory at the appearing of Jesus Christ:

8. Whom having not seen, ye love; in whom, though now ye see him not, yet believing, ye rejoice with joy unspeakable and full of glory:

9. Receiving the end of your faith, even the salvation of your souls.

After presenting wonderful truths of the promise we have in Christ, Peter shifted to deal with the earthly realities these Christians faced. It was clear they had many reasons for rejoicing. But it was also clear there were reasons for heaviness. The "if need be" of verse 6 should be remembered. Not all Christians at all times undergo major stresses on their faith. There are many believers living in very pleasant and safe circumstances who are sheltered from direct onslaughts from Satan. We should not envy them for that. God's purposes are beyond our comprehension.

Peter reminds us that if onslaughts come our way, we are to be mindful of God's promises. In the midst of temptations our faith grows. The "trial of . . . faith" (v. 7) refers to the genuineness of our faith. Note how important faith is: it is more valuable than gold. Nothing earthly compares with the value of our saving faith in Christ.

Our faith abounds unto praise to God. This praise is that of the adoration of a coming monarch—the appearing of Jesus Christ—to establish His kingdom. He will reign as King. The connection of praise, honor and glory is found in Revelation 4:11 and 5:12, 13 in the context of praise to God for our coming salvation.

The concluding line of 1 Peter 1:8 is familiar to most Christians. Indeed, in Christ we have "joy unspeakable and full of glory." This glory and joy is related to Jesus Christ and His

Talk About It:
1. What is the importance of the phrase "now for a season" (v. 6)?
2. What is the purpose of "the trial of your faith" (v. 7)?
3. Why can believers have such confidence in the Savior we have not yet seen?

By God's Appointment
First, He brought me here; it is by His will I am in this [difficult] place: in that fact I will rest. Next, He will keep me here in His love, and give me grace to behave as His child. Then, He will make the trial a blessing, teaching me the lessons He intends me to learn, and working in me the grace He means to bestow. Last, in His good time He can bring me out again—how and when He knows.

134

coming. While Peter was able to see Jesus in His earthly ministry, we are part of that multitude of faith who have not yet seen Him but nevertheless believe. Peter may have been thinking of the event recorded in John 20:29 where Jesus told Thomas, "Because thou hast seen me, thou hast believed; blessed are they that have not seen, and yet have believed."

This Lord whom we have not seen, we love. If we love the One whom we have not seen, then we are able to love those around us. Our rejoicing is that of joy that has no possibility of language. In light of this joy, we are able to know and receive the "end" (fullness) of our faith, the salvation of our souls. Faith in Jesus leads us to a point in divine-human history: the day of ultimate salvation.

III. SALVATION REVEALED (1 Peter 1:10-12)
A. Diligent Search (vv. 10, 11)
   10. Of which salvation the prophets have inquired and searched diligently, who prophesied of the grace that should come unto you:
   11. Searching what, or what manner of time the Spirit of Christ which was in them did signify, when it testified beforehand the sufferings of Christ, and the glory that should follow.
   The prophets searched diligently to understand salvation in Christ. To them, however, the prophecies of Christ were a mystery—"the mystery that has been kept hidden for ages and generations, but is now disclosed to the saints," Paul wrote. "To them God has chosen to make known among the Gentiles the glorious riches of this mystery, which is Christ in you, the hope of glory" (Colossians 1:26, 27, *NIV*).
   The prophets knew they would not see Christ in their generation, but they had faith in Him nevertheless. It ought to be much easier for us today, with the complete canon of Scripture, and all of the facts of history and the discoveries of archaeology at our disposal, to believe in Christ.
   Not only did the Holy Spirit indicate to the prophets the details of the Messiah's birth, but also insights into the plan of salvation. Christ's sufferings, for example, are described in detail in Isaiah 53. The prophets possessed as great a hope before Christ as the apostles did after Christ. They looked for His first coming, while we look for His second coming. Our hope will be rewarded as was theirs.
   When Peter spoke of the glory that followed the suffering of Christ, he greatly encouraged the believers to whom he wrote. Although they were suffering persecution and trials at the present time, they could be assured that glory and blessing would follow.

Talk About It:
1. What did the Old Testament prophets know about the coming salvation, and what did they not know?
2. Describe the relationship between sufferings and glory.

B. Divine Revelation (v. 12)

12. Unto whom it was revealed, that not unto themselves, but unto us they did minister the things, which are now reported unto you by them that have preached the gospel unto you with the Holy Ghost sent down from heaven; which things the angels desire to look into.

Here Peter continued to show that the Old Testament prophets did not minister to their own generations about Christ. Their visions of His glory were signposts along the way of Israel's disobedience. These visions point out that God still has a purpose for Israel. That purpose will be fulfilled in Christ.

However, the things they saw and recorded were certainly for our benefit. When we read in Isaiah the passages of our Lord's suffering, we cannot help but be moved to compassion and service to Him.

The things which have been handed down to us through the preaching of the apostles are the revelations of the gospel of God. Peter related effective preaching with the Holy Spirit. This was his own experience as seen in Acts 2 and 3.

Peter said even the angels seek to look into the mysteries of God's holy gospel. The word *look* could be translated "peep." While the angels cannot experience redemption, they still marvel at the power of God to redeem sinful people and they look in wonder at this mighty salvation.

CONCLUSION

The Asian Christians to whom Peter wrote had never personally seen the Lord; yet, they had steadfast faith in Him. To have this faith in One whom they had never seen brought to them a joy beyond description. If those who had seen Jesus were blessed by having seen Him, then those who believed without having seen Him were doubly blessed. This is an assurance to all of us who have lived in subsequent generations. Christ in us is our hope of glory (Colossians 1:27).

GOLDEN TEXT CHALLENGE

"BLESSED BE THE GOD AND FATHER OF OUR LORD JESUS CHRIST, WHICH ACCORDING TO HIS ABUNDANT MERCY HATH BEGOTTEN US AGAIN UNTO A LIVELY HOPE BY THE RESURRECTION OF JESUS CHRIST FROM THE DEAD" (1 Peter 1:3).

The Christian hope is not static or passive, for its basis is upon a living Lord. The hope is not in the words of Christ or even the death of Christ, but in the fact that He arose from the dead and extends His life to all who receive Him. Believers have been "begotten," or born again, through the abundant mercy which He has provided.

Talk About It:

1. Describe the relationship between the gospel preacher and the Holy Spirit.

2. Why is gospel preaching necessary?

"A sermon born in the head reaches only the head; a sermon born in the emotions reaches only the emotions; a sermon full of imagination reaches only the imagination. But a sermon born of the Spirit of God captivates the heart of the listening ones."

—Leonard Ravenhill

Daily Devotions:

M. Joseph Models the Savior
Genesis 45:1-7

T. God's Great Deliverance
Exodus 12:29-41

W. Salvation Comes From the Lord
Psalm 3:1-8

T. The Promised Savior
Luke 1:67-79

F. Salvation for All People
Romans 1:8-16

S. Confession of Salvation
Romans 10:9-15

Salvation of the Believer

December 11, 2005

Sanctification (Holiness) of the Believer

INTRODUCTION

The Biblical concept of holiness centers in the verbs *qadash* and *hagiazo* and their derived forms in the Hebrew and Greek languages respectively. Both sources mean, generally, "to make holy," and, more specifically, "to separate" and "to cleanse." The Hebrew root word in its various and versatile inflections is applied in the Old Testament to *places* (to Jerusalem in Nehemiah 11:1 and to the Temple in 1 Kings 9:3), to *times* (to the Sabbath in Exodus 20:8 and to the 50th year in Leviticus 25:10), and to *persons* (to the firstborn in Exodus 13:2 and to the priests in 28:41).

God himself was regarded as "holy," One who from His nature, position and attributes was to be set apart and revered as distinct from all others. Israel, too, was to separate herself from the world because God was thus separated (Leviticus 11:44; 19:2). In accordance with this teaching, therefore, the Lord was to be "sanctified"; that is, regarded as occupying a unique position both morally and essentially (Leviticus 10:3; Psalm 111:9; Isaiah 6:3). The Hebrew word connotes both position and relationship, and furthermore, both the act and the process whereby that relationship is realized (Judges 17:3; 2 Samuel 8:11).

The New Testament says the life of the individual Christian should be "a living sacrifice, holy [*hagia*], acceptable unto God" (Romans 12:1). The fundamental idea, then, of both Old and New Testament concepts of "the holy" is separation for the purpose of consecration and devotion to the service of the deity.

According to Hebrews 12:14, the pursuit of the personal and practical dimension of holiness is mandatory: "Follow peace with all men, and holiness, without which no man shall see the Lord." *Holiness* (sanctification) refers to the work whereby one becomes separated unto God in his entire life and conduct. He who is already holy by faith (justification, regeneration) is ever to continue in pursuit of holiness in daily experience.

F.F. Bruce reminds us that "'the sanctification without which no man shall see the Lord' is, as the words themselves make plain, no optional extra in the Christian life but something which belongs to its essence" (*The Epistle to the Hebrews*).

Unit Theme:
Peter and Jude

Central Truth:
God's people glorify Him by living holy and loving others.

Focus:
To realize believers are God's chosen people and live to glorify Him.

Context:
Written to churches in Asia Minor around A.D. 64

Golden Text:
"Ye are a chosen generation, a royal priesthood, an holy nation, a peculiar people; that ye should shew forth the praises of him who hath called you out of darkness into his marvellous light" (1 Peter 2:9).

Study Outline:
I. Be Holy
   (1 Peter 1:13-21)
II. Love Others
   (1 Peter 1:22 through 2:3)
III. Live as God's People
   (1 Peter 2:4-12)

I. BE HOLY (1 Peter 1:13-21)

A. Obedient Children (vv. 13, 14)

gird up the loins of your mind (v. 13)— "prepare your minds for action" (NIV)

13. Wherefore gird up the loins of your mind, be sober, and hope to the end for the grace that is to be brought unto you at the revelation of Jesus Christ;

14. As obedient children, not fashioning yourselves according to the former lusts in your ignorance.

Talk About It:
1. Where should believers place their hope? Why?
2. Describe the life lived in "ignorance."
3. How does God call us to live?

Peter's exhortation to holiness of life was based on the praises for salvation that preceded verse 13, as "joy unspeakable and full of glory" (v. 8) would indicate. His proposition was clear: his readers' whole manner of life was to be holy, even as the God whose praises they sang was holy.

He admonished that they "gird up," "be sober," and "hope to the end." To "gird up the loins of your mind" is a metaphor referring to the long, loose robes worn by Easterners, which were drawn up and belted at the waist when one wanted to work or walk energetically. The point that the writer was pressing was this: Make up your minds decisively! To "gird up the loins" is really to mean business, to take positive action, to be committed totally to accomplishing something.

Soberness is the opposite of infatuation with the momentary attractions of the world, a steady state of mind allowing responsible decision making. The grace about which we are to be so mindful and on which we are to affix our hope is the same as that mentioned earlier in verses 2 and 10, which is brought to us now in the Word of God and by the ministry of the Holy Spirit. This grace which we constantly receive points us to the glory and the inheritance at the "revelation [return] of Jesus Christ."

"Hope and holiness are closely associated in the Scriptures and must not be separated in life" (Lenski). Indeed, John declared that "every man that hath this hope [of Christ's return and the Christian's transformation] in him purifieth himself, even as he is pure" (1 John 3:3).

So Peter here described the character and constitution of God's children: They were obedient to God's saving will as projected in the gospel. In their former life this was not so; for their pagan ignorance engendered pagan lusts totally opposite to the Christian life.

> "Christian sanctification is the only road to true spirituality."
> —Henry Holloman

David's ancient insight is relevant here: "The entrance of thy words giveth light; it giveth understanding unto the simple" (Psalm 119:130).

B. Holy Walk (vv. 15-17)

all manner of conversation (v. 15)— all that you do

15. But as he which hath called you is holy, so be ye holy in all manner of conversation;

16. Because it is written, Be ye holy; for I am holy.

17. And if ye call on the Father, who without respect of

**persons judgeth according to every man's work, pass the
time of your sojourning here in fear.**

Since God is holy, all those who are called must also be
"holy in all manner of conversation." The Greek word here
translated "conversation" is actually much broader in range
than the spoken word, and the idea is better rendered as "in all
kinds of life situations." An Old Testament statement is cited
here to strengthen Peter's injunction (see Leviticus 11:44), and
it is a constraining one, indeed!

Lenski notes, "What God asked of Israel when he made that
people his own he now asks and must ask of us whom he has
called by Jesus Christ. . . . Only the pure in heart shall see God,
and without holiness it is impossible to see him. Christ died, not
to save us *in* our sins, but *from* our sins."

God, who is holy, has called us to be holy. This holiness is
to affect every area of our conduct. Holiness is not an aspect of
life that we can take on or off. Through the indwelling of Christ,
holiness becomes our renewed nature. Thus, every area of life
is ultimately directed by His holiness.

In verse 17, the fear of God is related to our calling upon the
Father. Coming to God in prayer is a privilege graciously afford-
ed us by God himself—never to be taken for granted—and a
holy fear is required of us as "obedient children" (v. 14) lest at
any time we lift up to the Holy One hands that are not holy (see
1 Timothy 2:8). Not only is God the Father who graciously
extends an invitation to intimacy, but He is also the Father who
critiques our every action. He is not an indulgent "grandfather"
in the heavens; He is, rather, the loving One who relates to us
with a holy impartiality, showing favoritism to no person.

C. Spotless Lamb (vv. 18-21)

**18. Forasmuch as ye know that ye were not redeemed
with corruptible things, as silver and gold, from your vain
conversation received by tradition from your fathers;**

**19. But with the precious blood of Christ, as of a lamb
without blemish and without spot:**

**20. Who verily was foreordained before the foundation
of the world, but was manifest in these last times for you,**

**21. Who by him do believe in God, that raised him up
from the dead, and gave him glory; that your faith and
hope might be in God.**

These marvelous verses locate another reason for the fear
prescribed above. We walk carefully not only because God will
sit in judgment of our conduct, but because our salvation has
been procured at such precious price (cf. 1 Corinthians 6:20).
The force of these words is all the more compelling when we
reflect upon the historical circumstances provoking the letter.

Talk About It:
1. What does it
mean to say God is
holy?
2. How is it possible
for us to be holy?
3. On what basis
does God judge
people, and what
should our response
be?

Talk About It:
1. What cannot redeem us from sin, and what can redeem us?
2. When was the plan of salvation established? What does this reveal about God's love for humanity?
3. Why can we have "faith and hope . . . in God" (v. 21)?

The price so dearly paid should have prompted in the benefactors a holy fear sufficient to guard them from ever disdaining their calling and going back into their old manner of conduct.

To be *redeemed* is "to be bought back" from bondage by payment of a ransom sufficient to effect the release. Christ Jesus "gave himself a ransom for all" (1 Timothy 2:6). Even the most costly earthly metals are perishable because they have value only for time, but Jesus' blood, shed in substitutionary sacrifice, is eternally effective.

The "vain conversation received by tradition from your fathers" (1 Peter 1:18) may have referred to Jewish legalists and their message of bondage. However, it is more likely that since Peter was addressing Christians who, for the most part, had come out of paganism, he had in mind the whole range of pagan experience. These considerations were "vain" in that they were unfruitful presently and led, ultimately, to nothingness.

From eternity, God ordained that His Son, having been incarnated, would suffer vicariously for the sins of the race, be resurrected from the dead, ascend to intercede while in session with the Father, and return to claim His own in the world. Peter's express understanding was that Jesus was "delivered by the determinate counsel and foreknowledge of God" (Acts 2:23) and that "God before had shewed by the mouth of all his prophets, that Christ should suffer" (3:18).

There was a cross in eternity, then, before one appeared in time. Calvary was the historical outworking of an event decreed before the foundation of the world. And nothing could have deterred God's plan, for what He decreed had to come to pass.

Continuing the "for you" of verse 20 in verse 21, Peter made personal application of all that Christ had done. It was for our sakes that God raised Him from the dead and glorified Him above all principalities and powers. Our faith and hope alike look toward these two actions of God with respect to His Christ.

II. LOVE OTHERS (1 Peter 1:22—2:3)
A. Sincere Love (1:22-25)

"No one can make you again but He who made you the first time."
—W.Y. Fullerton

unfeigned (v. 22)—sincere

22. Seeing ye have purified your souls in obeying the truth through the Spirit unto unfeigned love of the brethren, see that ye love one another with a pure heart fervently:

23. Being born again, not of corruptible seed, but of incorruptible, by the word of God, which liveth and abideth for ever.

24. For all flesh is as grass, and all the glory of man as the flower of grass. The grass withereth, and the flower thereof falleth away:

25. But the word of the Lord endureth for ever. And this is the word which by the gospel is preached unto you.

Love among believers follows upon the fear of God. Having the same heavenly Father makes believers brothers and sisters in the faith. Their spiritual condition is made strong by acceptance of the truth in faith and submission to it in life.

Peter had in mind here one feature of obedience that is especially required: "unfeigned love"—unhypocritical, sincere, honest affection. *Unfeigned* means "not wearing a mask," such as ancient actors wore on the stage to represent fictitious character. Peter discerned the possible danger that saints might pretend affection for one another rather than genuinely offer it.

In verse 23, Peter emphasized the divine seed and the sowing by which that new birth had been effected. *Corruptible* is the same word used in verse 18, the point being that the Word of God—the written and spoken message of the resurrection of Jesus Christ—generated through the Holy Spirit a new birth unto life everlasting. The exalted nature of the new life implanted in believers is borne out by the fact that the Word of God "liveth and abideth for ever." Jesus affirmed that "heaven and earth shall pass away, but my words shall not pass away" (Matthew 24:35).

New birth inaugurates believers upon a new and noble fellowship, the company of the redeemed. It is incumbent upon them to respond accordingly—loving one another with a pure heart fervently.

In 1 Peter 1:24, "all flesh" refers to all people in their natural state as born to earthly parents. All that of which humanity may be proud—the "glory" of existence, beauty, strength, wealth, honor, art, learning achievement—is but the bloom of the grass, and no more. But God's Word—the agency of the begetting Spirit—endures interminably.

B. Growing Faith (2:1-3)

1. Wherefore laying aside all malice, and all guile, and hypocrisies, and envies, all evil speakings,

2. As newborn babes, desire the sincere milk of the word, that ye may grow thereby:

3. If so be ye have tasted that the Lord is gracious.

The "wherefore" of verse 1 indicates this is a conclusion based upon truths given earlier. The earlier facts are fourfold: (1) the resurrection of Jesus; (2) our hope of His glorious return; (3) the call to be holy even as He is holy; (4) the love of the body of Christ and the authority of His Word.

On the basis of these things, Peter calls us to "lay aside" several things. The tense suggests "putting aside" these things once and for all with a decisive action. We call this action "sanctification." This is holiness brought into real life.

In Romans 13:12, Paul used this phrase (*laying aside*) to speak of "*casting off* the works of darkness." The things mentioned

Talk About It:
1. According to verse 22, what does a holy heart produce?
2. How is the born-again person like the Word of God (vv. 23, 24)?

Talk About It:
1. Why must believers lay aside the things listed in verse 1? What will happen if they don't?
2. How do Christians mature?

in 1 Peter 2:1 are the things of darkness. Colossians 3:8 says to "*put off* all these; anger, wrath, malice, blasphemy, filthy communication out of your mouth." James 1:21 says to "*lay apart* all filthiness and superfluity of naughtiness."

Note Peter's emphasis on "all." There is no compromising of the moral magnitude of our faith. The person who has been claimed by God has been totally claimed by Him. Nowhere in the Bible will we find God wanting simply a part of a person's life. God desires that our entire lives be filled with His love, holiness and Spirit.

The first vice listed in 1 Peter 2:1 is *malice*. This is a "special kind of moral inferiority, a deficiency" (*Bauer Lexicon*). It is "ill will"—seeking to bring harm to a neighbor. When professing Christians seek to harm one another, they live in darkness and the light of God is not in them!

Guile comes from the Greek word *dolos*, which has the meaning of "deceit, cunning, treachery." The *Interpreter's Bible* speaks of guile as the person who seeks to take advantage of another unfairly. This would cover an area of Christian life from slander to economic opportunity.

The next moral issue is *hypocrisy*. The Greek word refers to "playacting." In a positive sense, a good actor is a hypocrite; he is pretending to be something he is really not. The word is used often in the New Testament because the gospel calls us from a life of pretending to a life in the truth. In Christ we are liberated to truly be ourselves. We do not have to playact any longer. God accepts us and has called together a people who are willing to be genuine to one another for the sake of His kingdom.

Envy is the state by which we seek no longer to please God but to please people. We thus look at how others are doing and compare ourselves to them. If we come up lacking (in our minds), then we envy them for their approval by others. If we come up ahead of them (in our minds), then we feel superior to them and put ourselves above them. In either case, envy begins as we take our eyes off God. There is a close relationship between hypocrisy and envy. Both are based on "falseness." Both are destructive because they fail to take seriously the worth of the other person and the worth of oneself as seen by God. The key for successful living is to look at one another through the Spirit of Jesus.

The last item mentioned is *evil speaking* (slander). How do Christians slander one another? One way is to see a person doing something we think is wrong and then to tell everyone about it before we have actually talked about it with the person himself! Another way is to find out a person's past sin which has been forgiven and to try to remove the cover of the blood from that sin. Another way is to talk about a brother in sin rather than to follow our Lord's instructions on how we deal with this (see Matthew 18:15-17).

We should not think Peter is speaking to new converts in these verses. What he is calling for by the metaphor of "newborn babes" is an attitude of reception and nurture. It is God's Word that nourishes us as babes. We are dependent upon the Word for life. The Word is trustworthy and never fails.

The King James Version does not give a full translation of the Greek in verse 2. The words "unto salvation" should be added to complete the thought—"that ye may grow thereby unto salvation." *Salvation* is a comprehensive term for our total redemptive life in Christ. It means being freed from the encumbrances of life and made available for God. It means discovering the goodness and grace of God.

III. LIVE AS GOD'S PEOPLE (1 Peter 2:4-12)
A. Living Stones (vv. 4, 5)

4. To whom coming, as unto a living stone, disallowed indeed of men, but chosen of God, and precious,

5. Ye also, as lively stones, are built up a spiritual house, an holy priesthood, to offer up spiritual sacrifices, acceptable to God by Jesus Christ.

Believers live in daily contact with Christ, who is our constant source of life and power. He is called "a living stone." This is an interesting metaphor. We think of stones as inanimate objects with no life. Exposed to the elements, in time they are washed away. But Peter knew Jesus of Nazareth was solid and constantly stable. While people rejected Jesus as that foundation of life, He was chosen (elected) by God and is precious.

Even as Christ is "a living stone," so we are to be "living stones." This is a reminder of 1:3 regarding our "lively hope" in the Resurrection. As living stones, our purpose in life is to be joined with other living stones for the work of the church. We become people built into a "spiritual house." The church becomes that place where we gather in one accord as brothers and sisters through our common bloodline of Jesus. In this part of 1 Peter we see some of the elements of this household of God.

This household also has a "holy priesthood." A criticism of an "unholy" priesthood that failed to provide for God's people is found in Ezekiel 34:1-10. In 1 Peter 2 this holy priesthood is not limited just to a select few, but includes every person who belongs to Jesus Christ. As a holy priesthood, all believers are to offer up spiritual sacrifices that are acceptable to God. The thought is similar to Romans 12:1: "I beseech you therefore, brethren, by the mercies of God, that ye present your bodies a living sacrifice, holy, acceptable unto God, which is your reasonable service."

Talk About It:
1. Who is the "living Stone," and what does this title mean? What is the world's opinion of Him? What is God's opinion?
2. What is God building, and what are the building materials?
3. What is an "acceptable spiritual sacrifice"?

B. The Cornerstone (vv. 6-8)

6. Wherefore also it is contained in the scripture, Behold, I lay in Sion a chief corner stone, elect, precious: and he that believeth on him shall not be confounded.

7. Unto you therefore which believe he is precious: but unto them which be disobedient, the stone which the builders disallowed, the same is made the head of the corner,

8. And a stone of stumbling, and a rock of offence, even to them which stumble at the word, being disobedient: whereunto also they were appointed.

The *cornerstone* was "the stone at the corner of two walls that unites them; specifically, the stone built into one corner of the foundation of an edifice as the actual . . . starting point of a building" (*Unger's Bible Dictionary*). Thus, Christ as the Cornerstone is the source of everything His church should be. As we allow ourselves to be built upon Him, we shall grow into a solid and mature spiritual house which will last into eternity for His work.

Peter concluded verse 6 (a quote from Isaiah 28:16) by saying our belief in Christ will not lead us to shame or disappointment. However, in Mark 8:38 Jesus warned, "Whosoever . . . [is] ashamed of me and of my words in this adulterous and sinful generation; of him also shall the Son of man be ashamed."

That Christ is "precious" (1 Peter 2:7) means the honor of God has been acknowledged by us as being upon Him. His willing death for us, even while we were sinners, is what makes Him precious for us. Eternal life is found *only* in Him; thus, by its rarity, it is precious. No doubt Peter remembered numerous incidents in His earthly ministry that revealed just how precious Jesus was, and is.

For those who believe, His life is near and full of salvation. But Peter quickly changed gears and spoke of those who rejected Him. He certainly had in mind those Jews and Gentiles who refused to acknowledge His messiahship and lordship.

Note that this disbelief is called *disobedience*. Rejecting Christ is disobedience to the call of God. To reject Christ is to reject God. Thus, God chose to make the cornerstone of His salvation out of the One whom the Jews rejected.

Peter then went on to relate how God turned the stone they rejected into the stone over which they stumbled. Verse 8 is based on Isaiah 8:14. The ministry of Jesus was seen as a scandal by His own people. John wrote, "He came unto his own, and his own received him not" (1:11).

Christ's words were a scandal because in Him was the truth of God incarnate. Sinful people cannot accept such a clear encounter with Christ. Yet, Jesus confronts us with His claim and insists we believe and obey.

Talk About It:

1. What purpose does a "cornerstone" serve, and why is Christ given this title?

2. Describe the blessings that come to those who believe in Christ.

3. Why do so many people "stumble" over Jesus?

"The same blessed Jesus who is the author of salvation to some is to others the occasion of their sin and destruction."

—Matthew Henry

Sanctification (Holiness) of the Believer

C. A Royal Priesthood (vv. 9-12)

9. But ye are a chosen generation, a royal priesthood, an holy nation, a peculiar people; that ye should shew forth the praises of him who hath called you out of darkness into his marvellous light.

10. Which in time past were not a people, but are now the people of God: which had not obtained mercy, but now have obtained mercy.

11. Dearly beloved, I beseech you as strangers and pilgrims, abstain from fleshly lusts, which war against the soul;

12. Having your conversation honest among the Gentiles: that, whereas they speak against you as evildoers, they may by your good works, which they shall behold, glorify God in the day of visitation.

Peter contrasts the state of the Christians with that of those who rejected Christ. Unbelievers acted out their role even as it had been ordained, while those who belong to Jesus are chosen by God. God has spoken and these people have obeyed. They are indeed children of faith.

Peter used names that applied to Israel, presenting the church as the new Israel of God. This does not mean God has dropped His promises to Abraham (see Romans 9:6-8); but it does mean the church has a special relationship to Him as His covenant people.

A "chosen generation" was used of Israel in Isaiah 43:20 and Exodus 19:5, 6. It is based on God's covenant-making power to align Himself with His people. God has chosen us; we have not chosen Him. When we hear the gospel message of His election in Christ, we respond in faith through the Holy Spirit, and His love and holiness fills us with life anew.

We are also a "royal priesthood"—priests of the King. This is the basis of our "royalty." A similar expression is found in Revelation 5:10, "[Thou] hast made us unto our God kings and priests: and we shall reign on the earth."

Our role as holy and royal priests gives us opportunity to intercede for our world and church. As priests we have discarded our own righteousness and taken Christ's righteousness upon ourselves. Our holiness comes from Him. We are His loyal servants and we serve the Mighty One. Thus, our intercession is one of boldness and faith.

God's people make up a "holy nation." As the church, we relate to our world not from its standards and values but from the standards of our holy God. Thus, we become a different pattern for the world to see.

Peter then wrote that we are "a peculiar people." The English word *peculiar* comes from the Latin *peculium*, which refers to a slave held as private property. The passage in

Talk About It:
1. What are the roles to which God calls His children, and why (v. 9)?
2. According to verse 10, how has God transformed His followers?
3. Describe the "war" (v. 11) believers must fight.
4. What should Christians expect from the unbeliever, and how can they overcome?

1 Peter reflects Isaiah 43:21, where the Lord speaks of a people He has formed for Himself. Thus, *peculiar* does not mean odd; rather, it means a people who belong exclusively to God. Such people are to give praises to God who has brought us from darkness into light.

In verse 10, Peter quoted from Hosea 1:6, 9, 10; 2:1, 23. Here he indicated that the Gentiles in these Asian provinces who once lived in darkness of sin now were children of light and belonged to God. The church is that collection of people who were scattered with no identity and no salvation but are now caught up in the new language of God, which is mercy and love. The church is made up of people who were the outcast, but are now God's "living stones."

The word *strangers* (v. 11) means "foreign settlers" or "dwellers in a strange land." The word *pilgrims* means "visitors" or "those who tarry for a time in a foreign country, those who do not settle permanently." The apostle is using these terms to indicate that his readers were just sojourners on earth; they were actually citizens of the heavenly country.

Peter's warning to his readers was to avoid those sinful practices that were evident in the country in which they were visiting. The lusts of the flesh would be those desires that are a result of man's depraved nature.

The word *Gentiles* is used by Peter as a synonym for unsaved people (v. 12). The suggestion is that unsaved people are watching Christians, speaking against them, and looking for excuses to reject the gospel. Therefore, if unsaved people are to receive a witness from Christ, Christians must live honest lives. We must not only talk, but we must also walk the Christian life.

"Lighthouses don't ring bells and fire guns to call attention to their light . . . they just shine."
—*Christian Digest*

Daily Devotions:
M. Holiness and Majesty of God
 Exodus 19:16-25
T. Set Apart for Service
 Leviticus 8:1-13
W. Integrity of Character
 Job 31:1-8
T. Holy and Without Blame
 Ephesians 1:1-12
F. Pursue Holiness
 Hebrews 12:5-14
S. Holiness Rewarded
 Revelation 22:8-14

CONCLUSION

The Christian's greatness lies not in himself but in the fact that God, through Christ, has chosen him to do His work in this world. A Christian is chosen for three things:

1. *Obedience.* The Christian is not chosen to do as he likes but to do as God likes.

2. *Privilege.* This means a new and intimate relationship and fellowship with God through Christ will exist.

3. *Service.* A Christian's honor is that he is a servant of God, and this privilege is that he will be used for the purpose of God.

December 18, 2005

Submission of the Believer

1 Peter 2:13 through 3:9

INTRODUCTION

Our first two lessons on 1 Peter dealt with some important theological foundations: our lively hope in the Resurrection, Jesus Christ the cornerstone of the church, and the priesthood of the believers. In this lesson we move to some practical issues confronting the Asian Christians. The faith of these people cut them off from normal situations of living. They were forced to grapple with the implications of their new faith as it related to every sphere of life: from slavery to family relationships.

Peter referred to his readers as "strangers" and "pilgrims" (2:11). The word *stranger* indicated a person who lived in a foreign country and had no rights as a citizen in that country. It was used of ancient Israel to describe their status as "strangers" in the world (see Hebrews 11:9; Acts 7:6). The word *pilgrim* is used in Hebrews 11:13 and indicated a person who was visiting for a time in a foreign country with no intentions of actually remaining. It is clear that Peter wanted believers to think of themselves as citizens of another commonwealth.

Since believers are strangers and pilgrims in this world, they are not to be partakers of the fleshly life of this world. While all people are born sinners into a world of lust, believers have been reborn into the reality of another world: the kingdom of God. Thus, these things are not to have a claim upon their lives. We should not think of "fleshly lusts" (1 Peter 2:11) only in a sexual sense. The Greek word *sarx* ("flesh") refers to anything that is of this world. Thus, fleshly existence involves power, manipulation, money, prestige—anything that is not of the Spirit of God.

Today's lesson focuses on three principles of godly living that Christian "strangers and pilgrims" are to follow: (1) submit to authority, (2) follow Christ's example, and (3) honor one another.

Unit Theme:
Peter and Jude

Central Truth:
The believer in Christ is called to live in submission to God.

Focus:
To know that submission is necessary in a Christian's life and follow Christ's example.

Context:
Written to churches in Asia Minor around A.D. 64

Golden Text:
"Honour all men. Love the brotherhood. Fear God. Honour the king" (1 Peter 2:17).

Study Outline:
I. Submit to Authority (1 Peter 2:13-17)
II. Follow Christ's Example (1 Peter 2:18-25)
III. Honor One Another (1 Peter 3:1-9)

I. SUBMIT TO AUTHORITY (1 Peter 2:13-17)

A. Free Servants (vv. 13-16)

13. Submit yourselves to every ordinance of man for the Lord's sake: whether it be to the king, as supreme;

14. Or unto governors, as unto them that are sent by him for the punishment of evildoers, and for the praise of them that do well.

15. For so is the will of God, that with well doing ye may put to silence the ignorance of foolish men:

16. As free, and not using your liberty for a cloke of maliciousness, but as the servants of God.

cloke (v. 16)— cover

Talk About It:

1. Why does God want His children to submit to government authorities?

2. According to verse 14, who establishes authorities, and why?

3. Describe what it means to live in Christian liberty.

This is one of two major passages in the New Testament that speak positively to the issue of the Christian and the state. The other one is found in Romans 13:1-7. Both reflect situations in which the Roman Empire was taking an ambivalent position toward the Christian movement. The movement was perceived as a fanatical part of Jewish religion and was thus given certain privileges in the Empire.

The only negative references regarding the state are found in the brief comment by Jesus in Mark 12:13-17 and by John in Revelation 13:1-18. The Mark passage has Jesus setting limits upon the state in terms of what it can require. It can require nothing that belongs to God. The Revelation passage, written some 30 years after Romans and 1 Peter, reflected a situation in which the state was demanding worship. Thus, by claiming prerogatives that were not divinely ordained, the state was functioning as the apocalyptic "beast" toward believers.

It is important that these diverse elements of Scripture be kept in mind. The Bible does not give credence to religious/political theology that gives uncritical allegiance to the state (government). At the same time, the Bible makes it clear that orderly government is ordained by God to provide a foundation for meaningful life. Thus, even pagan rulers can rule effectively within this sphere of God's ordained will in order to provide an atmosphere of peace in the world. It is no accident that Christ came into the world during the height of the *Pax Romana*, the peace of Rome. This was indeed the "fullness of time," and the message was allowed to spread and ultimately claim control of the empire itself.

First-century Christians faced a serious problem. They recognized Jesus was the King of the world. Thus, their allegiance was to His kingdom. What did that have to say to their relationship to the physical kingdom of Rome? Peter wrote that, for the sake of Jesus, Christians were to maintain order and good relations with the Roman state. Christians were to remember that the Roman empire, like every human state, will not last forever. They were to remember their lives were established in a Kingdom that was forever.

"Every ordinance of man" (v. 13) means "every human institution" or "every institution ordained for men." If a law of the state required the Christian to do something contrary to God's law, then Peter would make allowance for disobedience and the probable persecution it would bring.

The first of those whom Christians were to respect was the king (emperor). The word used to describe the emperor, *supreme*, is used in Christian writing to refer to that which exceeds or is superior (Philippians 2:3; 4:7). In nonbiblical Greek the word had the sense of "to hold over." Thus, the emperor was in a position of power to hold sway with what he demanded (Kittel, *Theological Dictionary of the New Testament*).

In verse 14, Peter said governors were to be obeyed. The reason is that government has a twofold purpose. The first is negative: government brings about order and law by punishing those who violate the social dictates of peaceful society. The second is positive: government commends those who preserve the law and add to the commonwealth.

At the time 1 Peter was written, the probable emperor was Nero. Nero did not become a violent ruler until later in his reign. The early years of his reign were benevolent, and it is apparently this period that reflects the contents of 1 Peter.

Verse 15 looks back to verse 12 and the Gentiles who speak against Christians. It is God's will that Christians respond by doing good things—such as obeying government authorities—for His glory. His glory is served by the heathen being silenced. There are some Pauline passages that relate to this principle. The first is in Romans 12:17, 20, 21, where Paul argued that Christians are to repay evil by doing good. The second is in Ephesians 2:10, where Paul wrote that we have been created by God to do the good works which He had created from the beginning of time. God has clearly ordained how believers are to relate to the world: by good works. In verse 16, Peter describes Christians as "free" people; on the other hand, he calls them "servants [bondslaves] of God."

How Christians are to exercise their freedom has always been a problem area. This issue is discussed by Paul in Romans 14 and 15. Love takes precedence over an expression of Christian freedom. Yet, the efforts of those who would seek to establish bondage over our freedom are to be rejected, but in a way that fosters love for the brother.

In our text Peter is obviously dealing with Christian freedom in relation to non-Christians. In such a case, we are to exercise our freedom as witnesses of God to the world. Thus, our liberty is never to be used as a "cover-up for evil" (v. 16, *NIV*). Apparently, Peter knew of instances here some Christians were using their freedom in such a regard. The key for

"There is one chain of command, and the ultimate authority is God at the top."

—Billy Graham

Christians is that we remember we are servants of God. Therefore, we should let the world know that we belong to God.

B. Four Laws (v. 17)

17. Honour all men. Love the brotherhood. Fear God. Honour the king.

These four sayings are meant to be understood in pairs. We are called to give honor to all people. We acknowledge that every person is ultimately a child of God by virtue of creation. Yet, the "brotherhood" refers to those in the church. We are to love our brothers and sisters in Christ.

The same applies to our relationship between God and the king (government). We are to fear God—acknowledge His authority over every situation on earth. But we are to honor the king as he is due such honor. Again, such honor comes as the king obeys his God-ordained responsibilities.

How do these verses relate to us who live in a democratic society? In Peter's day there was little democracy. Even in Greece democracy was reserved for the upper classes. We are still to honor those in positions of worldly power over us. Such honor never means an uncritical view of them or their policies. But it does mean our acceptance of the institution of government as God's way of providing order for human life.

II. FOLLOW CHRIST'S EXAMPLE (1 Peter 2:18-25)
A. Unjust Suffering (vv. 18-20)

18. Servants, be subject to your masters with all fear; not only to the good and gentle, but also to the froward.

19. For this is thankworthy, if a man for conscience toward God endure grief, suffering wrongfully.

20. For what glory is it, if, when ye be buffeted for your faults, ye shall take it patiently? but if, when ye do well, and suffer for it, ye take it patiently, this is acceptable with God.

Slavery was common in the ancient world. Peter discusses how Christians who were slaves should relate to their masters. The newfound freedom in Christ created complex situations for both slave and owner, especially when both were Christians.

The word used for *servants* (v. 18) is the usual word for a household slave. The word for *masters* is where our English word *despots* originates. In this instance, it does not have the negative connotations it has in modern language. "Be subject to your masters with all *fear*" means they are to be respected. It is the same word used in verse 17 for "fear God." This does not suggest paralysis, but respect for one's place in life.

The end of verse 18 begins the transition for dealing with unjust suffering. It is easy to be respectful toward those who treat us properly; it is very different to be respectful to those

Talk About It:
1. How are these four commands related to one another?
2. Which of these commands is easiest to follow, and which is the most difficult? Why?

froward (v. 18)— harsh

Talk About It:
1. How should believers respond to different types of bosses (v. 18)?
2. What kind of suffering will be rewarded (vv. 19, 20)?

Submission of the Believer

who treat us in an overbearing manner. The word *froward* means "crooked, dishonest."

A slave did not have any options regarding place of employment, nor did he have review boards for worker-employer disputes. Christians today can respond to abusive employers by such boards or by changing jobs. However, the apostle's point is still relevant for us in the modern world. Christian employees are to relate differently to their employers. Even if we discover we are being cheated, we are still to act toward that person as a Christian who seeks the salvation of his or her soul. That may mean—in certain circumstances as the Lord directs—we have to forego our rights for the sake of promoting the gospel. Such a policy is seldom advocated in our modern world; but our modern world needs Christians who will make a difference in every aspect of life.

Verse 19 refers to a person who receives grace for willingly suffering wrongdoing for the sake of his or her obligation toward God. In Luke 6:32-35, our Lord spoke to this kind of dilemma:

> "If you love those who love you, what credit is that to you? Even 'sinners' love those who love them. And if you do good to those who are good to you, what credit is that to you? Even 'sinners' do that. And if you lend to those from whom you expect repayment, what credit is that to you? Even 'sinners' lend to 'sinners,' expecting to be repaid in full. But love your enemies, do good to them, and lend to them without expecting to get anything back. Then your reward will be great, and you will be sons of the Most High, because he is kind to the ungrateful and wicked" (*NIV*).

The principle of verse 19 of the text is restated in verse 20. Peter is making the obvious point that if we suffer punishment because we have committed an offense, and receive our punishment patiently, what glory is there for God? We are simply getting what we deserve and our good behavior really has no significance. But if we suffer patiently under duress for good things we have done, then God is given glory.

"If a man is called to be a street sweeper, he should sweep streets even as Michelangelo painted, or Beethoven composed music, or Shakespeare wrote poetry. He should sweep streets so well that all the hosts of heaven and earth will pause to say, 'Here lived a great street sweeper who did his job well.'"

—**Martin Luther King Jr.**

B. Perfect Example (vv. 21-23)

21. For even hereunto were ye called: because Christ also suffered for us, leaving us an example, that ye should follow his steps:

22. Who did no sin, neither was guile found in his mouth:

guile (v. 22)—deceit

23. Who, when he was reviled, reviled not again; when he suffered, he threatened not; but committed himself to him that judgeth righteously.

Two key concepts in verse 21 are "suffered" and "example."

Talk About It:
1. Can a person be a Christian without experiencing suffering? Why or why not?
2. What does Christ teach us about handling undeserved criticism?

Suffered refers to the type of suffering described in verse 20. Suffering is rough treatment which may be undeserved. The concept was used to describe the lashing that a slave may endure. In this case, it refers to a lashing given undeservingly. Christ suffered pain and punishment while being eternally innocent. One may be able to understand suffering that comes with an explainable or justifiable reason. The suffering which Christ endured, however, was completely unjust.

Example literally means "copy" or "outline." In the Greek literature contemporary with Peter, this word was used to refer to the outline an artist drew and then filled in with a painting. It also referred to the letters that a schoolboy copied in learning to write. Christ's suffering is not merely the object of adoration, but it is the prototype of the attitude we are to maintain in the midst of suffering. Christ is our example in the way He suffered. Not only is He the firstfruits of the resurrection, not only does Christ lead with power, not only does Christ provide healing, but He also provides the model for us to follow in enduring suffering that is undeserved.

The way Christ endured unjust treatment is presented in verses 22 and 23. First, He "did no sin." The evil treatment He received was not used as an excuse to let down His holy standard. Second, no "deceit was found in his mouth" (v. 22, *NIV*). Christ not only refused to "do" sin, but even controlled His words. The evil mistreatment He received did not cause Him to utter a curse back to those who were persecuting Him.

Third, when people "reviled" Christ, He did not "revile" them. The word *revile* means "to verbally abuse." Though people were extremely abusive of Christ, He did not retaliate with abuse. The grammatical form of the first "revile" indicates His abusers reviled Him over and over again. Still, Christ did not retaliate wrongfully. Fourth, when Christ received suffering, He did not threaten. When we are wronged, the temptation is often to wish wrong and threaten others. Christ did not even do this.

The fifth response by Christ is the foundation for all of His endurance. Christ rested His confidence in God Almighty. Christ acted with the assurance that the God of justice would see that justice was done. The pain was great. The wrong done to Him was overwhelming. The shame before people was monumental. Yet Christ knew true justice comes by the hand of Almighty God.

Our task is not only to adore Christ for His suffering and endurance, we are also to follow "in His steps" (see v. 21). Christ maintained a holy and pure life in the face of great opposition. Our call is to maintain a holy and pure life no matter how great the temptation or human justification for lowering our standards.

"He who fears to suffer cannot be His who suffered."
—Tertullian

C. Healing Shepherd (vv. 24, 25)

24. Who his own self bare our sins in his own body on the tree, that we, being dead to sins, should live unto righteousness: by whose stripes ye were healed.

25. For ye were as sheep going astray; but are now returned unto the Shepherd and Bishop of your souls.

In verse 24 Peter dealt with the implication of the death of Jesus. First, He has borne our sins in His body. That means sin has been taken on by the Savior and our archenemy has been defeated. Second, it means that we are to consider ourselves dead to sin, even as He brought death to sin. We are now alive to righteousness. Third, by His stripes we have been healed.

The word *stripes* refers to the bloody blows Christ received from the soldiers' cruel whips. By those "wounds you have been healed" (*NIV*). Christ's suffering has paid the price for our healing once and for all. We merely need to appropriate this healing by faith.

Regarding verse 25, Wycliffe said, "Peter has been urging upon his readers a sharing of Christ's sufferings. Even as He commanded, they are to follow Him, taking up the cross (Luke 14:27). But they have already made an initial step in this sharing of the cross; once wayward sheep, they have been converted to the Shepherd and Bishop (caretaker) of their soul."

III. HONOR ONE ANOTHER (1 Peter 3:1-9)
A. Words to Wives (vv. 1-6)

1. Likewise, ye wives, be in subjection to your own husbands; that, if any obey not the word, they also may without the word be won by the conversation of the wives;

2. While they behold your chaste conversation coupled with fear.

3. Whose adorning let it not be that outward adorning of plaiting the hair, and of wearing of gold, or of putting on of apparel;

4. But let it be the hidden man of the heart, in that which is not corruptible, even the ornament of a meek and quiet spirit, which is in the sight of God of great price.

5. For after this manner in the old time the holy women also, who trusted in God, adorned themselves, being in subjection unto their own husbands:

6. Even as Sara obeyed Abraham, calling him lord: whose daughters ye are, as long as ye do well, and are not afraid with any amazement.

Women in the ancient world were treated as property. They had no rights and men were free to divorce them with little or no reason (provided he return the dowry). Even in more conservative Jewish circles, men were given much higher privileges than women.

Talk About It:
1. What did Christ's suffering afford us (v. 24)?
2. Why do our souls need a "Shepherd and Bishop"?

chaste conversation (v. 2)—pure and reverent life

1. How can a Christian wife best influence an unsaved husband for Christ?

2. What makes a woman beautiful in God's eyes?

With their newfound freedom in Christ, women had to come to terms with living as effective witnesses in a world that had little regard for them. The "likewise" of verse 1 connects these verses to the model of the suffering of Jesus found at the end of chapter 2. What at first seems odd in our day—that wives be subject to their own husbands—was actually liberating. It meant that the woman was responsible to no other man other than her husband to direct her life. Even if the husband was not a believer, she was still to be subject to him.

This may reflect a situation where wives were coming to church and meeting men who were believers. Peter gives instruction that a marriage is not to be disbanded for the sake of two Christians as husband and wife. The unsaved husband was the primary mission field of the wife. If the husband would not respond to preaching (the Word), he just might respond to the godly life ("conversation") of his wife.

The reason the husband might be saved was that he would see the holy life of his wife and be converted. The "fear" of verse 2 is not fear toward the husband; rather, it is fear as respect toward God. Peter's advice is not much different from that of the apostle Paul in 1 Corinthians 7:1-16.

In verses 3 and 4 of the text, Peter calls for the women to be sure their lives reflect the inner qualities of peace and the Spirit as they minister to their husbands rather than focusing on outward appearance.

> "Some women are not beautiful—they only look as though they are."
> —Bob Phillips

Verses 5 and 6 indicate that women of faith have existed from the beginning of time. The example of Sarah and Abraham is given: they are the models of faith.

B. Words to Husbands (v. 7)

7. Likewise, ye husbands, dwell with them according to knowledge, giving honour unto the wife, as unto the weaker vessel, and as being heirs together of the grace of life; that your prayers be not hindered.

After speaking to the wives, Peter addresses the Christian men in these congregations. In all likelihood, these Christian husbands had entire Christian families. We know from Acts 10 that the entire household of Cornelius was converted and baptized by Peter. The wife and children usually followed suit with the religion of the husband. Thus, Peter addresses husbands who had Christian wives (although we should not press this point far because there were exceptions—see 1 Corinthians 7:12).

"According to knowledge" means the husband is sensitive to the needs and claims of his wife. Paul made it clear in 1 Corinthians 7 that the husband and wife had a mutual claim upon one another regarding sexual life. The husband is to treat his wife as another human being, not as the property of the pagan world.

Submission of the Believer

The man is to honor his wife as "the weaker vessel." The word *weaker* implies "powerless." This was true in the ancient world. The woman was powerless in the general run of society. In spite of her powerlessness, she was to be treated with honor and respect. Paul used the same word in 2 Corinthians 10:10 to describe his own physical appearance.

Peter then described married couples as "heirs together of the grace of life." The word for "heirs together" (one Greek word) is used in Romans 8:17 to refer to our joint heirship with Christ; it is used in Hebrews 11:9 to show Abraham and Isaac were joint heirs in the covenant promises of God. Peter wrote that unity and proper treatment of the wife by the husband will result in their prayers being effective.

C. Words to the Church (vv. 8, 9)

8. Finally, be ye all of one mind, having compassion one of another, love as brethren, be pitiful, be courteous:

9. Not rendering evil for evil, or railing for railing: but contrariwise blessing; knowing that ye are thereunto called, that ye should inherit a blessing.

In sentiment, aim and purpose, Christians are to be like-minded. Nothing will so impress the world about us, nor be so good for us, as unity. To act on one's own agenda contrary to the rest is to harm oneself and others.

Then, Peter called for showing compassion to one another. In adversity and in prosperity, we are to identify with our fellow believers. This quality calls for us to go beyond care for ourselves and have regard for what benefits others. This is a trait found in other New Testament passages (see Romans 12:15; 1 Corinthians 12:26).

Next, the apostle urged believers to love as family. If God is our Father, we are brothers and sisters in Christ. Barclay wrote, "The simplest test of the reality of the Christianity of a man or a church is whether or not it makes them love their fellowmen."

To be "pitiful" and "courteous" means to be merciful and humble. We are not only to help our fellow believers and relieve their miseries, but we are also to bear with their weaknesses. We can best do so when we think modestly and humbly of ourselves. There is nothing that produces more discord than when we think too highly of ourselves. So Peter calls upon us to be humble-minded, lest pride and haughtiness should lead us to despise others.

Believers are not to retaliate or take revenge when we have been wronged. The opposite is true. We are to seek to bless, calling down good on those who wrong us. God called us to inherit His infinite blessing; therefore, we are to bless others regardless of the circumstances.

pitiful (v. 8)—compassionate

Talk About It:
1. Describe the proper relationship between Christians (v. 8).
2. How should we respond to insult or maltreatment, and what will the result be?

"We will only be weak and stumbling believers and a crippled church unless and until we truly apply God's Word—that is, until we truly love Him and act on that love."
—Charles Colson

CONCLUSION

It sounds contradictory, but the key to having spiritual authority is to submit oneself to authority. When a Roman centurion (leader of a hundred soldiers) came to Jesus on behalf of his dying servant, the Roman said, "I myself am a man under authority, with soldiers under me" (Luke 7:8, *NIV*). Because this man yielded to the authorities in his life, he was placed in a position leading others.

Recognizing the authority of Jesus, the centurion said, "Say the word, and my servant will be healed" (v. 7, *NIV*). Jesus said He had not found such great faith even in Israel, and He healed the man's servant (vv. 9, 10).

If we will submit ourselves to Christ's authority, which also involves submitting to the other authorities in our lives, we will find ourselves walking in blessing and power.

Daily Devotions:

M. Submission
   Tested
   Genesis 2:15-17
T. Submission
   Commanded
   1 Kings 2:1-4
W. Jonah Finally
   Submits
   Jonah 3:1-5
T. Submit to God
   Romans 12:1-10
F. Submit to Civil
   Authority
   Romans 13:1-17
S. Submit to God's
   Spirit
   Romans 13:8-14

GOLDEN TEXT CHALLENGE

"HONOUR ALL MEN. LOVE THE BROTHERHOOD. FEAR GOD. HONOUR THE KING" (1 Peter 2:17).

These small sentences summarize four of the Christian's key relationships. First, we are called to honor all people, which means to treat others as having value. We are to affirm the universal worth and dignity of all people.

Second, we are called to love fellow believers with the divine love that exists only among Christians. Third, we are to fear God, which is the starting point of wisdom and righteousness. Finally, Peter returns to the word *honor* in relation to the king. We are to treat political leaders with respect and dignity even if they are not believers or God-fearing people.

December 25, 2005

The Savior Is Born (Christmas)

Luke 2:1-40

INTRODUCTION

The second chapter of Luke presents a picture of Romans and angels and shepherds and parents and a baby—not just any baby, but the infant Jesus. What do we learn from these individuals concerning the coming of Christ?

The Romans. From the Romans we see the government of that ancient world continued to make its demands even when the birth of Christ was imminent. The ruling authorities were only concerned with the functioning of government; it had not been revealed to them that the birth of the Messiah was imminent. And even if Caesar himself had been aware of the impending birth of a Savior in one small part of his empire, it is doubtful he would have blinked. Similarly today, we should not expect secular government to pay much attention to Jesus Christ or His claims. It is up to the church to lift up Jesus Christ as Lord.

The Angels. The message of eternal hope was delivered by the angels in the announcement that Jesus had been born. Their supernatural appearance and communication with the shepherds reminds us God does whatever it takes to get His message to humanity. He primarily speaks through His written Word and His Spirit, but God also speaks through people, circumstances, miracles, angels and many other means.

The Shepherds. The perfect response to the gospel message was evidenced by the shepherds, who believed the angels' amazing message, went to see the evidence for themselves, and then spread the good news to others. This is the same pattern God wants His children to follow today: believe His message, draw close to Jesus, and take the good news to other people.

The Parents. Mary and Joseph provided the tender and special care that any infant should receive and which this infant especially deserved. They set the example which every parent and everyone else who deals with holy things should follow.

The Baby. Unlike the image depicted in some paintings, there was no halo encircling the head of the baby Jesus. There was nothing extraordinary about His appearance, and His resting place was the humblest of beds—a feeding trough. Yet angels led shepherds to Him, and they went away "praising God for all the things that they had heard and seen" (Luke 2:20). Today God is still revealing Himself in the mundane aspects of life, and it takes spiritual ears to hear His voice and learn His lessons.

Unit Theme:
Christmas

Central Truth:
Jesus was born to be the Savior of the world.

Focus:
To examine the events surrounding Christ's birth and accept Him as Savior.

Context:
Bethlehem in 5 B.C. It seems strange to say Christ was born four years "Before Christ," but this is due to a four-year error in our calendar.

Golden Text:
"Unto you is born this day in the city of David a Saviour, which is Christ the Lord" (Luke 2:11).

Study Outline:
I. Humble Birth
   (Luke 2:1-7)
II. Angelic Announcement
   (Luke 2:8-20)
III. Seeing God's Salvation
   (Luke 2:21-38)

I. HUMBLE BIRTH (Luke 2:1-7)

A. The Decree (vv. 1-3)

(Luke 2:2, 3 is not included in the printed text.)

all the world (v. 1)—the sphere of Roman rule

Talk About It:
1. Why would God's Spirit inspire Luke to record historical details?
2. Where did everyone have to go to be taxed?

1. And it came to pass in those days, that there went out a decree from Caesar Augustus, that all the world should be taxed.

Censuses were carried out in the Roman world for two reasons: to assess taxes and to discover who was eligible for military service. Since the Jews were exempt from military service, a census conducted in Palestine would be for taxation purposes.

Discoveries have been made which provide definite information about the censuses. The information has come from actual census documents written on papyrus and discovered in the dustheaps of Egyptian towns and villages and in the sands of the desert. It is almost certain that what happened in Egypt happened in Syria, too, and Judea was part of the province of Syria.

At one time, critics questioned the thought of every person going to his own city to be enrolled, but now people possess actual documents proving that this is what happened. We have here another instance of additional knowledge confirming the accuracy of the New Testament record.

Christianity is sometimes accused of being behind the times and the Bible of being irrelevant. The facts are that the Bible and Christianity are very much up-to-date and speak to the burning issues of the day. Instead of disproving the message of Scripture, modern discoveries confirm what the Word says. This should be a source of special encouragement to the believer. The truths we have known all along are now attested by sources outside Christendom.

B. The Journey (vv. 4, 5)

4. And Joseph also went up from Galilee, out of the city of Nazareth, into Judaea, unto the city of David, which is called Bethlehem; (because he was of the house and lineage of David:)

5. To be taxed with Mary his espoused wife, being great with child.

Talk About It:
1. Despite Mary's condition, how did Joseph and Mary respond to the decree?
2. Why does God often ask His children to do difficult tasks?

Actors on the stage of the world don't always know how to evaluate their role. Caesar Augustus, the first Roman emperor, issues a decree; it is obeyed and he is in control. Joseph and Mary, peasants from Nazareth, answer his decree and make their way to Bethlehem. How insignificant they seem amid the many who are returning to their hometown. Yet this woman, marching under the orders of Caesar, is carrying in her womb the Son of God. This man traveling by her side is protecting her.

The significance of the actors in this drama changes when you read the words of the prophet Micah: "But thou, Bethlehem Ephratah, though thou be little among the thousands of Judah, yet out of thee shall he come forth unto me that is to be ruler in Israel; whose goings forth have been from of old, from everlasting. Therefore will he give them up, until the time that she which travaileth hath brought forth: then the remnant of his brethren shall return unto the children of Israel. And he shall stand and feed in the strength of the Lord, in the majesty of the name of the Lord his God; and they shall abide: for now shall he be great unto the ends of the earth" (Micah 5:2-4).

No longer is the big man in the city on seven hills, Caesar Augustus, the main character in this drama. Joseph and Mary become the most significant personalities on the stage. Caesar is only an instrument that God is using to prepare the way for the fulfillment of prophecy. Things are not always as they appear to be.

C. The Birth (vv. 6, 7)

6. And so it was, that, while they were there, the days were accomplished that she should be delivered.

7. And she brought forth her firstborn son, and wrapped him in swaddling clothes, and laid him in a manger; because there was no room for them in the inn.

Prior to this time, Mary had been living at the wrong address for the birth of the Christ child. Caesar's decree had changed all of that. She arrived in Bethlehem in the nick of time. Soon upon her arrival, the time of her delivery came.

Jesus was born in a stable. It is probable that the stable was built out of a cave. Travelers put up in such places, that is, in the open areas, while the back parts were used for animals. When the child was born, Mary wrapped Him in swaddling clothes, which consisted of a square of cloth with a long bandagelike strip coming diagonally off from one corner. The infant was first wrapped in the square of cloth and then the long strip was wound around Him. Jesus was then laid in a manger—a place where animals feed.

The reason Jesus was born in a stable was that when Joseph and Mary arrived in Bethlehem, there was no room for them in the inn. In Mary's condition the journey was a very slow one. By the time they arrived, the rooms in the inn were already occupied. This experience anticipated the reception He would receive from people. John recorded, "He came unto his own, and his own received him not" (1:11). Then he added: "But as many as received him, to them gave he power to become the sons of God, even to them that believe on his name" (v. 12). And some came to the stable reverently. God sent visitors of

Talk About It:

1. How important was the location (town and bed) where Christ was born? Why?

2. Why was there "no room for them in the inn"? Name some of the places Christ is crowded out of today.

Let not our hearts
be busy inns
That have no room
for Thee,
But cradles of the
living Christ
And His nativity.
—*Pulpit Helps*

His own to pay homage to the newborn King. And in every generation some have come and bowed before Him.

II. ANGELIC ANNOUNCEMENT (Luke 2:8-20)
A. The Shepherds (vv. 8, 9)

8. And there were in the same country shepherds abiding in the field, keeping watch over their flock by night.

9. And, lo, the angel of the Lord came upon them, and the glory of the Lord shone round about them: and they were sore afraid.

Talk About It:
1. How ordinary is the scene in verse 8? Why is this meaningful?
2. What terrified the shepherds, and why?

Now enter the shepherds into this drama. They were tending their flocks. Most Biblical scholars agree these were probably Temple shepherds, watching flocks intended for sacrifice. Whether this is the case or not, at least they were men in pursuit of their own calling; they were doing their own work.

The announcement of the birth of Jesus came at night as the shepherds watched over their flocks, in the discharge of their duty. This shows us God's regard for people of every station in life. The message did not come to Caesar's palace, nor to the Temple, but to lowly shepherds. When at a later time Jesus described His mission, He declared: "The Spirit of the Lord is upon me, because he hath anointed me to preach the gospel to the poor; he hath sent me to heal the brokenhearted, to preach deliverance to the captives, and recovering of sight to the blind, to set at liberty them that are bruised, to preach the acceptable year of the Lord" (Luke 4:18, 19).

As the shepherds were busy at their task, an angel of the Lord appeared to them, and the glory of the Lord shone around them. The immediate reaction of the shepherds was one of fear; they were terrified.

B. The Angel (vv. 10-12)

10. And the angel said unto them, Fear not: for, behold, I bring you good tidings of great joy, which shall be to all people.

11. For unto you is born this day in the city of David a Saviour, which is Christ the Lord.

12. And this shall be a sign unto you; Ye shall find the babe wrapped in swaddling clothes, lying in a manger.

Talk About It:
1. What was "good" and "great" (v. 10), according to the angel?
2. What do Jesus' three titles—Savior, Christ, Lord (v. 11)—mean?

The angel's first act was to still the fear that was in the heart of the shepherds. The angel said, "Do not be afraid." The shepherds mistakenly feared that hurt would come to them from the one who had come to help. How often do we make that same mistake? How often do we misinterpret God's hand in our lives? We must learn "that all things work together for good to them that love God, to them who are the called according to his purpose" (Romans 8:28).

The Savior Is Born

The message of the angel was good news for all people of all time. It was the joyful news that the Savior had been born. That Savior is Christ the Lord, the Messiah. He would confront all the sin of the world with regal authority, based on redeeming power. Of Him, the angel told Joseph, "And she [Mary] shall bring forth a son, and thou shalt call his name Jesus: for he shall save his people from their sins" (Matthew 1:21). Christ has confronted all the chaos of the world as the Messiah and has established the true kingdom of God. He is Lord and as such confronts all eternity and all ages, and does so triumphantly.

3. Why were the shepherds given a "sign"?

The angel announced to the shepherds that the Baby could be found "wrapped in swaddling clothes, lying in a manger" (Luke 2:12).

C. The Heavenly Host (vv. 13, 14)

13. And suddenly there was with the angel a multitude of the heavenly host praising God, and saying,

14. Glory to God in the highest, and on earth peace, good will toward men.

The terrified shepherds hardly had time to respond before the angel was joined by a great company of the heavenly host, praising God and shouting praise unto Him. What a picture! All heaven breaking forth, sweeping down, and hovering over Bethlehem's plains to declare the meaning of the coming of the Child.

The anthem is twofold. It speaks of heaven and earth. It exalts God who is above. The expression is a descriptive word for heaven, the dwelling place of God: "Glory to God in the highest." The message it bears for earth is one of peace—not just any kind of peace, but the peace which God alone can give. His peace comes only to people in whom He is well pleased, those on whom His favor rests.

Peace comes through Jesus Christ. It will come to the earth when people are like Him. That is the way to peace, and there is no other way. Negotiations, disarmament, peace treaties, and the like will never produce lasting peace. We applaud the efforts of world leaders in their quest for peace, but we put our hope for ultimate and complete peace in the Prince of Peace—Jesus Christ.

Talk About It:
1. What is God's desire for humanity?
2. How was that desire expressed in the birth of Christ?

"The coming of Christ by way of a Bethlehem manger seems strange and stunning. But when we take Him out of the manger and invite Him into our hearts, then the meaning unfolds and the strangeness vanishes."

—C. Neil Strait

D. The Response (vv. 15-20)

(Luke 2:15, 20 is not included in the printed text.)

16. And they came with haste, and found Mary, and Joseph, and the babe lying in a manger.

17. And when they had seen it, they made known abroad the saying which was told them concerning this child.

---

18. And all they that heard it wondered at those things which were told them by the shepherds.

19. But Mary kept all these things, and pondered them in her heart.

Talk About It:
1. How did the shepherds confirm the angel's message?
2. How did people respond to the shepherds' testimony?
3. Explain Mary's response to all these events.

The message to the shepherds was that God in Christ had begun His earthly sojourn. The Babe they would find in the manger is the Son of God. So, as soon as the angels had departed, the shepherds said, "Let's go to Bethlehem, and see for ourselves what the Lord has told us" (see v. 15).

The shepherds hurried off to Bethlehem, and when they had seen Jesus they spread the word concerning Him. What was their message? "Unto you is born this day . . . a Savior." Joseph Parker wrote: "The world did not want an adviser. The world had advised itself almost into hell. The world did not ask for a speculator. Everything that man could do had been done, and men sat in the darkness of their own wisdom. The world did not want a reformer, a man who could change his outward and transient relations, an engineer that would continually devote his time (for appropriate remuneration) to the readjustment of the wheels and the pulleys and the various mechanical forces of society. The world wanted a Savior."

It is not surprising that all who heard what the shepherds said to them were amazed. The story they conveyed was good news of the highest order. We can easily understand that Mary treasured in her heart and pondered over the heavenly messages. And what is more natural than that the shepherds would return to their tasks with gratitude and praise? In their memories, there lingered a song that expresses still the hope of all humanity.

III. SEEING GOD'S SALVATION (Luke 2:21-38)
A. Fulfillment of the Law (vv. 21-24)
(Luke 2:23, 24 is not included in the printed text.)

21. And when eight days were accomplished for the circumcising of the child, his name was called JESUS, which was so named of the angel before he was conceived in the womb.

22. And when the days of her purification according to the law of Moses were accomplished, they brought him to Jerusalem, to present him to the Lord.

When Jesus was eight days old, He was circumcised according to Jewish law and given the name Jesus (v. 21). The Hebrew form of *Jesus* was *Joshua*, meaning "savior." This name was given to Jesus by the angel Gabriel even before He was conceived (Matthew 1:21; Luke 1:31).

The period of purification for the mother of a newborn child was 40 days. At the expiration of this 40-day period, Mary and

The Savior Is Born

Joseph took Jesus to Jerusalem for dedication in the Temple. There He would be "called holy [set apart] to the Lord" (2:23; see also Exodus 13:2, 12).

A lamb was the usual sacrifice as a burnt offering. Persons too poor to offer a lamb were allowed to bring two turtledoves or two pigeons, which cost considerably less than a lamb (Leviticus 12:8). The fact that Joseph and Mary offered doves or pigeons instead of a lamb indicates the degree of their poverty. Joseph was a carpenter, not a prosperous merchant or landowner. For God's purposes, Jesus began His earthly life in the most ordinary and humble station of life.

B. Simeon's Prophecy (vv. 25-35)
   (Luke 2:33-35 is not included in the printed text.)
   25. And, behold, there was a man in Jerusalem, whose name was Simeon; and the same man was just and devout, waiting for the consolation of Israel: and the Holy Ghost was upon him.
   26. And it was revealed unto him by the Holy Ghost, that he should not see death, before he had seen the Lord's Christ.
   27. And he came by the Spirit into the temple: and when the parents brought in the child Jesus, to do for him after the custom of the law,
   28. Then took he him up in his arms, and blessed God, and said,
   29. Lord, now lettest thou thy servant depart in peace, according to thy word:
   30. For mine eyes have seen thy salvation,
   31. Which thou hast prepared before the face of all people;
   32. A light to lighten the Gentiles, and the glory of thy people Israel.

Few people in the Temple would likely have paid any attention to the infant in Mary's arms. The fact that His parents had given the offering of the poor would have made Him even less noticed by either the people or religious leaders. One who did notice Him, however, was Simeon, a man of deep devotion, who lived in anticipation of the Messiah. This is the meaning of "waiting for the consolation of Israel" (v. 25). The fact that "the Holy Ghost was upon him" means he frequently prophesied and spoke by revelation of the Spirit.

It had been revealed to this devout man that he would not see death until he had seen the Messiah. Although the Scripture does not indicate Simeon's age, it has been believed from earliest time he was a very old man.

Just as Simeon came into the Temple by the Holy Spirit, so

Talk About It:
1. What is the significance of the name *Jesus*?
2. Why did they "present him [the Savior] to the Lord" (v. 22)?
3. Explain the irony of Mary and Joseph presenting a sacrifice.

consolation of Israel (v. 25)—the expected Messiah

Talk About It:
1. Describe Simeon's relationship with the Holy Spirit.
2. How did Simeon realize Jesus was the Messiah?
3. Describe the ministry of Jesus as pictured in verse 32.

he recognized Jesus by the same Spirit. He took the infant in his arms and blessed the Lord with a beautiful hymn of praise. His words "Now lettest thou thy servant depart in peace" (v. 29) meant he could now conclude his life without regret or sense of incompleteness. His life had been perfectly fulfilled, and Simeon yielded his place to the infant in his arms. Simeon was like a guard whose responsibility was to hold the fort in faith and prayer until the Deliverer arrived; he then could end his vigil and retire in peace.

Simeon recognized in Jesus the salvation that was to come to all people. The Jews had long awaited their Messiah, who would be their salvation and their glory. They expected Him to be strictly a Jewish redeemer and ruler, taking vengeance on all except themselves. Simeon's prophecy was far more inclusive and showed deep spiritual insight. This was the greatest lesson the Jews had to learn: the messianic salvation could not be held to themselves alone. There had now come together a light that would lighten the world.

Joseph and Mary's amazement (v. 33) was twofold. First, they marveled that a devout stranger such as Simeon should recognize the divine nature of their Son. Then, they marveled at such deep insight into the things He was destined to do.

In verse 34 Simeon blessed both Joseph and Mary, and then emphasized to Mary that her child was the great hope of Israel. What the Jewish people had awaited for more than three centuries, she had brought into the world. Yet, His ministry would bring division to the nation. Those who would reject Him would fall, and those who would accept Him would rise to great glory. This child was a sign to Israel, a clear evidence of God's visitation to humanity.

> "Unless we see the Cross overshadowing the cradle, we have lost the real meaning of Christ's birth."
> —*Pulpit Helps*

Simeon further revealed that the child would be cruelly treated, and that the sword of His suffering would pierce into Mary's heart as well (v. 35). This is a prediction of the sacrifice of Christ's life for the salvation of all people. Simeon foretold the sorrow that would come to Mary when she saw the suffering of her child (see John 19:25-27).

C. Anna's Praise (vv. 36-38)

Phanuel (*fuh-NEW-el*) (v. 36)—father of Anna

36. And there was one Anna, a prophetess, the daughter of Phanuel, of the tribe of Aser: she was of a great age, and had lived with an husband seven years from her virginity;

37. And she was a widow of about fourscore and four years, which departed not from the temple, but served God with fastings and prayers night and day.

38. And she coming in that instant gave thanks likewise unto the Lord, and spake of him to all them that looked for redemption in Jerusalem.

The Savior Is Born

There was a woman in the Temple who, like Simeon, was endowed with the spirit of prophecy. Anna had been a woman of importance; the mention of her father's name indicates he had been a man of some renown. She was an extraordinary woman about 84 years of age, of such great age, in fact, that she no longer left the Temple. She very likely lived in a small chamber of the Temple. The kingdom of God has been advanced greatly by saintly women who make precious their declining years with fasting and prayers. Such women have always been choice handmaidens of the Lord.

Like Simeon, Anna spoke praise to the Lord for the dawning of the day of redemption. It is not likely that she saw the extent of this redemption, but she clearly saw the beginning of the messianic age. She recognized in Jesus the redemption for which Israel had been waiting.

Talk About It:
1. Describe Anna's relationship with God.
2. What was Anna's prophecy concerning Jesus?

CONCLUSION

There was a European monarch who worried his court by often disappearing and walking incognito among his people. When he was asked not to do so for security's sake, he answered, "I cannot rule my people unless I know how they live." It is the great thought of the Christian faith that we have a God who knows the life we live because He too lived it and claimed no special advantage over common people.

GOLDEN TEXT CHALLENGE

"UNTO YOU IS BORN THIS DAY IN THE CITY OF DAVID A SAVIOUR, WHICH IS CHRIST THE LORD" (Luke 2:11).

A baby was born in Bethlehem many years ago. His parents were poor, and He had no unusual advantages. He raised no army, He conquered no kingdoms, He owned no real estate, and He had no bank account. Neither did He write books or paint pictures or compose music. He was mocked by the great and died a criminal's death. Yet this Man has revolutionized the civilized world.

Multitudes have lived and died triumphantly by the power of their faith in Him and obedience to the doctrines He inculcated, and He has more followers in the world today than ever before. His maxims are acknowledged, even by those who reject His authority, to be the noblest and purest that ever have been uttered, and no man has ever been able to pick a flaw with His character. What will you do with Jesus who is called the Christ?—**Phillips Brooks**

Daily Devotions:
M. Sure Prophecy
Isaiah 9:2-7
T. Source of Our Peace
Isaiah 53:1-5
W. God's Anointed Son
Psalm 2:1-12
T. Miraculous Conception Foretold
Luke 1:26-35
F. Virgin Birth
Matthew 1:18-25
S. Cause for Rejoicing
Matthew 2:1-11

Suffering of the Believer

1 Peter 3:13-17; 4:1-7, 12-19

Unit Theme:
Peter and Jude

Central Truth:
Suffering can serve a divine purpose in a Christian's life.

Focus:
To learn that believers suffer according to the will of God and rejoice in identifying with Christ.

Context:
Written to churches in Asia Minor around A.D. 64

Golden Text:
"Let them that suffer according to the will of God commit the keeping of their souls to him in well doing, as unto a faithful Creator" (1 Peter 4:19).

Study Outline:
I. Suffering for Righteousness' Sake (1 Peter 3:13-17)
II. Living in God's Will (1 Peter 4:1-7)
III. Rejoicing in Trials (1 Peter 4:12-19)

INTRODUCTION

Simon Peter knew firsthand what it meant to live through trials, loss and suffering. Consider some of his personal experiences recorded in the Gospels and Acts.

Peter lost it all. When Jesus called him, Peter and his brother Andrew "at once . . . left their nets and followed him" (Matthew 4:20, *NIV*). He left everything familiar to him—his career, his home, his security—to follow Christ.

Peter had a near-death experience. In the midst of a storm-tossed lake, Peter became frightened and began to sink. He cried out, "Lord, save me" (14:30).

Peter suffered rebuke. When Peter declared Jesus would never be killed by the religious leaders, Jesus said to him, "Get thee behind me, Satan: thou art an offence unto me" (16:23).

Peter miserably failed Christ. As Jesus was being tried, three times Peter denied knowing Him. "And he went out, and wept bitterly" (26:75).

Peter suffered physically. Peter was arrested, beaten and threatened for preaching in the name of Jesus (Acts 5:40, 41).

Peter experienced criticism. Fellow Christians accused Peter of doing wrong by winning Gentiles to Christ (11:1-3).

Peter faced certain death. When he was again arrested for preaching the gospel, Peter was chained, locked up, and a date was set for trial (12:4-6).

In looking back at Peter's life, we can see the purposes served in his difficulties:

• By losing it all he gained everything.

• In his near drowning he witnessed Christ's power over nature.

• In Christ's rebuke he heard how even Christ's followers can hinder the purposes of God.

• After denying Christ three times, the Lord restored Peter with a three-part calling (John 21:15-17).

• Through the persecution of Peter and the other apostles, the gospel was spread and the church grew.

• In his willingness to face criticism, Peter helped open the door of the gospel to the Gentile nations.

• Through Peter's miraculous deliverance from prison, the early church's confidence in prayer was multiplied.

I. SUFFERING FOR RIGHTEOUSNESS' SAKE
(1 Peter 3:13-17)

A. Don't Be Fearful (vv. 13-15)

13. And who is he that will harm you, if ye be followers of that which is good?

14. But and if ye suffer for righteousness' sake, happy are ye: and be not afraid of their terror, neither be troubled;

15. But sanctify the Lord God in your hearts: and be ready always to give an answer to every man that asketh you a reason of the hope that is in you with meekness and fear.

The principle that people are not punished for doing good is universal, if at times inconsistent. Ignorance has occasioned many exceptions to this principle, but it is still true. This is definitely the case in Christian living. If the wrath of unbelievers sometimes perverts this principle, we can be sure their wrath will have a short life. Ultimately, we will be blessed for the good we do.

There is a special blessing for those who endure persecution, as Christ stated in Matthew 5:11, 12. On one occasion the apostles rejoiced that they were counted worthy to suffer for Christ (Acts 5:41). Peter now writes to those who might well face persecution in its fiercest form. They would be ordered to denounce the Christian faith or lose their lives. Peter called on them to have courage in the face of such danger.

A complete dedication to the Lord is the only possible way believers can stand in the face of persecution. The apostle quoted Isaiah 8:13, "Sanctify the Lord of hosts himself; and let him be your fear, and let him be your dread." Only our awe of God is able to overcome our dread of people. With a healthy fear of God, believers will be able to meet the expectations of courage laid upon them (Matthew 10:28).

Because the disciples lived in a time of persecution and injustice, they were given much instruction about how they should reply to the accusations brought against them. In Mark 13:11, Jesus instructed them, "But when they shall lead you, and deliver you up, take no thought beforehand what ye shall speak, neither do ye premeditate: but whatsoever shall be given you in that hour, that speak ye: for it is not ye that speak, but the Holy Ghost." Peter adds his similar instruction here.

B. Have a Good Conscience (vv. 16, 17)

16. Having a good conscience; that, whereas they speak evil of you, as of evildoers, they may be ashamed that falsely accuse your good conversation in Christ.

17. For it is better, if the will of God be so, that ye suffer for well doing, than for evil doing.

Once again the apostle calls his readers to a life of "good

Talk About It:
1. Why should believers "be not afraid" of fears that trouble unbelievers (v. 14)?
2. What does it mean to "sanctify the Lord God in your hearts" (v. 15)?
3. What is the "reason of the hope" believers have (v. 15)?

Talk About It:
1. How should believers live before those who speak maliciously of them?
2. Which kind of suffering brings reward? Why?

"I do not believe that sheer suffering teaches. If suffering alone taught, then all the world would be wise, since everyone suffers. To suffering must be added mourning, understanding, patience, love, openness and the willingness to remain vulnerable."

—Anne Morrow Lindbergh

the Gentiles (v. 3)—pagans
lasciviousness (v. 3)—lewdness
revellings (v. 3)—"orgies" (*NIV*)

Talk About It:
1. What are the attitude (v. 1) and lifestyle (v. 2) of the committed Christian?

conscience." If they were to suffer, then it should be as servants of the Lord and not as evildoers. Accusations will come against Christians, but our lives should be so exemplary that all accusations against us will be proven false.

Frequently those who are subjected to false accusations take the attitude that they would not mind suffering if they deserved it. A complaint heard in all ages is that we would not mind being ill-treated if we felt it was just. Peter contradicts this common opinion. It is better that our suffering be brought about by our good living than by our evil. When suffering comes as a result of good, then it is a temporary and peripheral experience. If it is occasioned by evil, then the penalties we suffer outwardly are less than our inner suffering of sin and guilt. Furthermore, suffering for righteousness' sake brings spiritual blessings to us both now and in eternity.

The prime example of all unjust suffering is that of the Lord Jesus Christ (v. 18). Yet, it was through His suffering that we have been brought to God. He is our great example: He who was infinitely holier than we are, suffered the greatest of unjust deaths. Not only did He die *because of* sin, but He died *for* sin. This means He was willing to suffer in order to forgive our sins and bring us unto Himself. Although Jesus was put to death in the flesh, He was quickened, or made alive, by the Spirit. If we live for Him, some of us may die *for* Him; and all should certainly die *in* Him. Then, like Him, we shall be made alive— quickened by the Holy Spirit.

II. LIVING IN GOD'S WILL (1 Peter 4:1-7)
A. Sins of the Past (vv. 1-3)
1. Forasmuch then as Christ hath suffered for us in the flesh, arm yourselves likewise with the same mind: for he that hath suffered in the flesh hath ceased from sin;
2. That he no longer should live the rest of his time in the flesh to the lusts of men, but to the will of God.
3. For the time past of our life may suffice us to have wrought the will of the Gentiles, when we walked in lasciviousness, lusts, excess of wine, revellings, banquetings, and abominable idolatries:

Christ suffered, and the believer must also suffer; but to suffer triumphantly, the Christian must have the mind of Christ. It is impossible to pattern one's life after Christ unless one thinks as Christ did. The believer might be in a great conflict, but he or she needs no other armor than "the mind of Christ." This is the temper of patient submission and unwavering trust in the wisdom and love of the Father.

Regarding the statement "He who has suffered in his body is done with sin" (v. 1, *NIV*), Barnes wrote, "So if a Christian becomes dead in a moral sense—dead to this world, dead by being crucified with Christ—he may be expected to cease from sin. The reasoning is based on the idea that there is such a union between Christ and the believer that His death on the cross secured the [believer's] death [to sin]."

In verse 2, Peter is referring more to the result of suffering than to its purpose. Here the "lusts," or desires, of people are pointedly contrasted with the "will of God"; the wild and restless cravings are contrasted with the calm and fixed purpose. Paul has said, "This is the will of God, even your sanctification" (1 Thessalonians 4:3). To be truly in His will, we must seek to live holy, or separated, lives. To do this we must "cleanse ourselves from all filthiness of the flesh and spirit, perfecting holiness in the fear of God" (2 Corinthians 7:1).

In verse 3 of the text, Peter is saying enough time had already been given to the world. Was it not well now to give some time to the Lord? The tense used in this verse implies that the course is closed and done. The Christian should look upon his or her life before salvation as a closed matter. The old is over and gone. The believer is a new creation in Christ Jesus.

The apostle enumerates some of the sins of the past from which his readers would have been separated:

Lasciviousness is from a Greek word which refers to "actions that incite disgust and shock the public decency." This refers to sensuality or debauchery. The word *lusts*, or "lustful desires," does not refer to sexual desires alone; it has to do with all unrestricted passions and desires.

Two Greek words are used to express *excess of wine*. These words mean "wine" and "bubble up"; the sin is drunkenness.

Revellings referred to the orgies held by the heathen devotees as they wildly and furiously worshiped their pagan deities. *Banquetings* had to do with the drinking bouts and feasts that were a part of the pagan rites.

Finally, Peter refers to *abominable idolatries*, or "idolatry that leads to lawlessness" (Williams). These illicit and criminal idolatries were against even the Roman law.

2. Name one word that summarizes the lifestyle of those who live according to their carnal desires.

"By nature I was too blind to know Him, too proud to trust Him, too obstinate to serve Him, too base-minded to love Him."

—John Newton

B. Judgment by God (vv. 4-6)

4. Wherein they think it strange that ye run not with them to the same excess of riot, speaking evil of you:

5. Who shall give account to him that is ready to judge the quick and the dead.

6. For for this cause was the gospel preached also to them that are dead, that they might be judged according to men in the flesh, but live according to God in the spirit.

It was only natural for the friends of the converted pagans to

Talk About It:
1. What is strange to unbelievers?
2. What motivates us to live right (v. 5)?

"wonder why" they "stopped running around with them" (v. 4, *CEV*), and to speak evil of them. These former pagans had been changed and now looked at all things in a different light (1 Corinthians 6:9-11). Their consciences were more sensitive now. Their standards of honesty and purity were much higher.

We know how strange our friends thought we were when we became Christians. It is therefore easy to imagine how the former friends of these onetime pagans felt when the converts began to refrain from contact with prostitutes, refuse invitations to idolatrous revelries, and reject alcoholism.

Because the believers wanted to live sanctified lives and would not partake of the "excesses" (a pouring forth or an overflowing), they found their erstwhile friends "speaking evil" of them. A better rendering would be "reviling" or even "blaspheming" them. Those who speak evil of God's children speak evil of Him as well.

The heathen may laugh, and the worldly person mock, but they both "will have to give account [for it] to him who is ready to judge the living and the dead" (1 Peter 4:5, *NIV*). Our former friends may think us strange and ask for an explanation of our actions, but they do not fully realize that they too will have to give an account to God. This accounting, or judging, will take place at His coming (2 Timothy 4:1).

Regarding verse 6 of the text, some theologians believe this is the gospel of a second chance, claiming that the gospel will yet be preached to people after death. Others believe that this judgment of the dead refers to believers already dead who have been saved by the same gospel now being preached. Then, there is the position that this verse alludes to those who heard Jesus preach while He was in Hades (hell). Peter mentions this event clearly in 3:19.

Those righteous ones who died before Calvary were "prisoners of hope." They were not given a second chance, but were released from the prison of the soul. Today the gates of hell do not prevail against the church, which Christ purchased with His blood. The soul that dies in Christ now ascends into His presence.

> "If what they are saying about you is true, mend your ways. If it isn't true, forget it, and go on and serve the Lord."
> —H.A. Ironside

C. Watchful Prayer (v. 7)

7. But the end of all things is at hand: be ye therefore sober, and watch unto prayer.

Peter recites the demands that must be met as we approach the coming judgment. First, we must be "sober" ("clear minded," *NIV*). This word could be translated "preserve your sanity." The insane person does not see things as they really are; he or she has lost the power of perception and is easily deceived, not knowing reality. So it is with those who have been so beguiled by Satan that they literally believe a lie (2 Thessalonians 2:11). In these last days there is much deception. We live in a society that is not able to see things as they are.

As we look for the Lord to come, we should think as sober people and not treat salvation and Christianity frivolously. We who look for His coming should realize the importance of a soul's salvation. The coming of the Lord is a sobering event, and all people should face that day with sane and self-controlled minds, for that is the day which will determine the destiny of us all.

The second demand is a call for prayer. Tyndale translates this, "Be apt to pray." A calm and collected spirit is conducive to the act of praying. The Christian whose mind is crowded with fears and worries, who is never at rest in his or her heart, cannot do much effective praying. Prayer is the mightiest weapon in the arsenal of the believer; it is tragic it is used so little.

III. REJOICING IN TRIALS (1 Peter 4:12-19)
A. The Certainty of Persecution (vv. 12, 13)

12. Beloved, think it not strange concerning the fiery trial which is to try you, as though some strange thing happened unto you:

13. But rejoice, inasmuch as ye are partakers of Christ's sufferings; that, when his glory shall be revealed, ye may be glad also with exceeding joy.

Peter addresses these words to his "beloved," which could be translated "divinely loved ones." The true believer has never been loved or appreciated by the world. Persecution is inevitable. That's because the Christian's ways are so different that only scorn and resentment are elicited from an unappreciative and misunderstanding world. Peter has already spoken of this matter earlier in his letter (1:6, 7; 2:19-21; 3:15-17), and his remarks here only emphasize the fact of persecution's presence in the life of the believer. Paul also speaks of the tribulations and trials that would beset the true child of God (2 Timothy 3:12; Acts 14:22).

The inevitable persecution of the Christian is really a test, or "fiery trial" (1 Peter 4:12). The word literally means "a burning," but is used here to refer to a smelting furnace and the smelting process in which gold or silver ore is purified. The believer should not "think it strange" if he is tested; he should rather wonder why he is *not* tested. God is refining us; and, as He accomplishes this, there must be some sacrifice and suffering on our part. The devotion of anyone to a principle can best be measured by his or her willingness to suffer for that principle. We will never wear the crown if we never bear the cross.

What a joy it is to know that if we suffer with Him we will be glorified with Him (Romans 8:17). By suffering with Him, we not

Talk About It:
1. Why should a "fiery trial" not catch a Christian off guard?
2. What is the connection between suffering and glory?

only walk as He walked, but we also share in the cross He carried. It must bring joy to the heart of the Savior to know that His followers love Him enough to suffer for Him.

B. The Blessedness of Persecution (vv. 14-16)

14. If ye be reproached for the name of Christ, happy are ye; for the spirit of glory and of God resteth upon you: on their part he is evil spoken of, but on your part he is glorified.

15. But let none of you suffer as a murderer, or as a thief, or as an evildoer, or as a busybody in other men's matters.

16. Yet if any man suffer as a Christian, let him not be ashamed; but let him glorify God on this behalf.

Peter now assures the persecuted believer of a great and present blessing. The Christian who is able to bear the reproach and abuse of a sinful world is not only being tested, but he is also showing forth the presence of God's glory.

The persecutors who looked on Stephen "saw his face as it had been the face of an angel" (Acts 6:15). All the fire of the persecutors cannot keep the glory of God from shining forth from the faces of His beloved.

The phrase "resteth upon you" (1 Peter 4:14) is the translation of a Greek word used as a technical term in agriculture. "The writer speaks of a farmer resting his land by sowing light crops upon it. He relieved the land of the necessity of producing heavy crops, and thus gave it an opportunity to recuperate its strength" (Wuest). The Spirit of God therefore rests the tormented and persecuted believer with His refreshing power. In spite of the venom and hatred of an evil world, we can live a life that pleases God and gives glory to Him as well.

In verse 15, it is easy to understand Peter's meaning regarding murder, theft and evildoing; the word translated "busybody" literally means "looking upon, or into, that which belongs to another." It could, first of all, mean "covetous of someone's property." Then, too, it could refer to those who pry into other people's affairs. Finally, it could mean that the Christian should not engage in any act or business that does not become a Christian. There are some things a true believer should not do.

To be a Christian in Peter's day meant that you were opposed to the Caesar cult. Christianity was a rival claimant to world worship and dominion. The followers of our Lord looked for Him to return and overthrow the Roman kingdom. For this hope the believers underwent 10 bloody persecutions during the early days of the church. Peter warned his friends not to be ashamed because of this tribulation. We should be glad to be numbered among His followers, regardless of the suffering it might entail.

Talk About It:
1. Who should be happy, and why (v. 14)?
2. What kind of suffering should be expected by the people listed in verse 15?
3. Why should a believer's suffering not bring shame?

"In the presence of trouble, some people grow wings; others buy crutches."
—*Quotable Quotes*

Suffering of the Believer

C. The Certainty of Our Safety (vv. 17-19)

17. For the time is come that judgment must begin at the house of God: and if it first begin at us, what shall the end be of them that obey not the gospel of God?

18. And if the righteous scarcely be saved, where shall the ungodly and the sinner appear?

19. Wherefore let them that suffer according to the will of God commit the keeping of their souls to him in well doing, as unto a faithful Creator.

God always judges most sternly where privilege has been greatest. Judgment should "begin at my sanctuary" (Ezekiel 9:6). God expects His children to walk uprightly; and, if He expects honor from them, how much more will be the terror of those who have not cared so much for Him as to even attempt to serve Him.

Today we live in a world that has lost the fear of God. Sin is rampant even in churches, and evil is not only tolerated, but loved. However, God, in His goodness, has chosen to redeem humanity. We merited only banishment forever; but God, who is Love, made a way of escape. He paid dearly for our salvation. He gave His best to redeem us from the power, presence and penalty of sin.

What can the ungodly person who laughs in the face of God and mocks at His offer of salvation expect? Love that is spurned can render an awful penalty. He who goes to hell has no one to blame but himself. It was a difficult task to save us from sin, and woe be to the person who makes a mockery of Calvary.

In verse 19, Peter uses a financial term to portray what he wants to say. In Peter's day there were no banks in which to deposit money, so when someone went on a trip, he left his money in the safekeeping of a friend. This friend was honor-bound to keep the funds and to return them when they were called for. So it is with our Lord. He and He alone can be trusted with the care of our souls. Did He not create the universe? Why then should we wince when it comes to committing our souls to Him?

Talk About It:
1. Why must judgment begin with the people of God?
2. "If it is hard for the righteous to be saved, what will become of the ungodly and the sinner?" (v. 18, *NIV*).
3. How does God prove Himself to be the "faithful Creator" (v. 19)?

CONCLUSION

Your pain has a purpose. I can't tell you what that purpose is—that is something you will discover in your own walk with God. It may be a marvelous discovery, a grace, like Paul's, which once received makes you glad you went down the road of suffering with God at your side.—**John Haggai**

GOLDEN TEXT CHALLENGE

"LET THEM THAT SUFFER ACCORDING TO THE WILL OF GOD COMMIT THE KEEPING OF THEIR SOULS TO

HIM IN WELL DOING, AS UNTO A FAITHFUL CRE-ATOR" (1 Peter 4:19).

In this verse Peter seems to sum up his exhortations and to return to the thoughts declared in 3:17. In times of adversity, as well as in times of prosperity, we are under the tender care of a loving heavenly Father. We should learn submission, not because suffering is inevitable, but because it is according to His will, and His will is salvation and sanctification. Let us make sure we are in the will of God, for "we know that all things work together for good to them that love God, to them who are the called according to his purpose" (Romans 8:28).

Service of the Believer

1 Peter 4:8-11; 5:1-11

INTRODUCTION

The Bible never attempts to gloss over the realities of living for Christ. Instead, it clearly lays out the challenges and blessings of being a Christ follower. This is especially true in the Spirit-inspired writings of Peter, a man known for his boldness and outspokenness.

If the scriptures in today's lesson had been written in the form of a classified ad, it would have looked something like this:

FULL-TIME POSITION AVAILABLE

The Chief Shepherd Group is looking for employees who can start immediately and work for the rest of their lives. Please read all of the following before applying:

Character: Loving, forgiving, hospitable, dependable, energetic, humble, alert, controlled, courageous, generous, faith-filled, service-oriented.

Duties: Deeply love other believers, open your home to them whenever necessary, use the gifts God has given you, willingly suffer for Christ, be an example to others, humble yourself under God's hand, resist the devil, and stand firm.

Experience and education: No experience and no education necessary. The Good Shepherd is willing to qualify every committed worker through on-the-job training.

Benefits: The covering of a multitude of sins; suffering in Christ's name; experiencing God's grace; receiving an eternal crown of glory.

How to apply: Humble yourself under God's mighty hand.

The life of service to which God calls His children is an adventurous one that cannot be fulfilled in our own power. He calls us to do things—love deeply, use our spiritual gifts, withstand sufferings, be humble, resist the devil—that we in ourselves cannot do. In fact, that's the point. The only way to genuinely minister to others, imitate Christ and live in humility is through the enabling grace of God. If we will live in His grace, we will be the people and do the works that fulfill our calling.

Unit Theme:
Peter and Jude

Central Truth:
The Christian is empowered to minister effectively within the body of Christ.

Focus:
To discover that Christian service requires love and humility, and find your place of service in the body of Christ.

Context:
Written to churches in Asia Minor around A.D. 64

Golden Text:
"As every man hath received the gift, even so minister the same one to another, as good stewards of the manifold grace of God" (1 Peter 4:10).

Study Outline:
I. Minister to Others
(1 Peter 4:8-11)
II. Serve Willingly
(1 Peter 5:1-4)
III. Humble Yourself
(1 Peter 5:5-11)

I. MINISTER TO OTHERS (1 Peter 4:8-11)

A. Fervent Love (v. 8)

8. And above all things have fervent charity among yourselves: for charity shall cover the multitude of sins.

Talk About It:
1. Why is fervent love needed "above all things" in a church?
2. Explain the statement, "Love covers over a multitude of sins" (*NIV*).

When the apostle speaks of "charity," this is not the love of a philanthropist who gives not of himself but of what he possesses. This is a "stretched-out love" that goes from heart to heart. Bengel translates it "vehement love." This love makes great demands and is not an easy sentimental reaction. The failure of the Ephesian church was a loss of this type of love (Revelation 2:4). Today, as never before, we should love with an intensity that reaches to all people.

The concluding phrase runs parallel with Proverbs 10:12, meaning that love does not expose the sins of others and, so, is contrasted with the "hatred [which] stirs up strife" (*NKJV*). We do not find it hard to forgive those whom we love, but the faults of those we do not love glare at us quite menacingly.

The verse could also mean that if we love others, God will overlook and forgive confessed sins in our lives. We can easily relate to our erring brother, because he is beset by the same evils as we are.

B. Selfless Giving (vv. 9, 10)

9. Use hospitality one to another without grudging.

10. As every man hath received the gift, even so minister the same one to another, as good stewards of the manifold grace of God.

Talk About It:
1. How do the words *hospitality* and *grudging* (grumbling) stand against each other?
2. What does "every man" receive from God, and for what purpose?

The true believer is not to live in isolation; he is to be "ungrudgingly hospitable" (Williams). The early church was composed of people who only recently had been either pagans or followers of Judaism. Now they were social outcasts and were unwelcome in the homes of their former friends and relatives. This is why we find several references to the importance of hospitality (Romans 12:13; 1 Timothy 3:2; Hebrews 13:2).

There were impostors in those days who posed as believers; so, traveling believers often carried letters of commendation. There were no church buildings in those early days. The homes of the believers became citadels of the faith and places of worship and accommodation. There was a church in the house of Aquila and Priscilla (Romans 16:3, 5; 1 Corinthians 16:19). There was also a church in the house of Philemon (Philemon 2). Widows lodged strangers, and a bishop was to be a lover of hospitality (1 Timothy 5:10; Titus 1:8). Thus, we see the early church as one great harmonious family.

Not only were the believers to open their homes to their Christian friends; they were enjoined to give of the gift they had received from God. "In whatever quality or quantity each one has received a gift, be ministering it among yourselves as good stewards of the variegated grace of God" (1 Peter 4:10, *Wuest*). The gifts referred to in this passage are those mentioned in 1 Corinthians 12 and Romans 12:3-8.

God, through the gracious operation of the Spirit, had endowed the believers with special gifts and enablements. These gifts were given not for the glory of the recipient but for the glory of God and the benefit of all. The gifted believer was only a steward. What he had belonged to his Master and was to be used at the Master's behest and for the Master's good.

The church needed these enabling benefits in apostolic times; the church needs them even more today. As a matter of fact, we are asked to "covet earnestly the best gifts" (1 Corinthians 12:31). Ordinary religion will not suffice in this day of scientism and rationalism. There must be a demonstration of the supernatural among His people if the world is to take any notice of their need of Him.

> "The desire to help others and minister to their needs is the underlying principle in the use of the spiritual gifts."
> —B.G. Hamon

C. Spiritual Service (v. 11)

11. If any man speak, let him speak as the oracles of God; if any man minister, let him do it as of the ability which God giveth: that God in all things may be glorified through Jesus Christ, to whom be praise and dominion for ever and ever. Amen.

oracles (v. 11)— words

In verse 11 Peter expands his comment concerning the gifts, which are in two categories. First, there are the gifts that have to do with preaching. "If any one is preaching, let him do it as one who utters the oracles of God" (Williams). These gifts are enumerated in 1 Corinthians 12—14. The person who possesses a gift that enables him or her to utter the mind of Christ must ever be subservient to the Spirit and completely dead to the flesh. The anointed preacher has the gift of prophecy, and he or she foretells as well as forthtells.

Talk About It:
1. How should believers use the spiritual gifts God has given them?
2. What will happen if the gifts are used properly?

If a person has the duty of preaching, let him or her preach not as someone offering their own opinions or propagating their own prejudices, but as a preacher with a message from God. It was said of one great preacher: "First he listened to God, and then he spoke to men." Spirit-filled people deliver God's message of hope and deliverance, for it is "not by might, nor by power, but by my spirit, saith the Lord of hosts" (Zechariah 4:6).

The second category of gifts has to do with practical ministry. The word *minister* means "rendering service to others." It is from the Greek word *diakonein*. This can hardly be limited to those who bear the name "minister" or "deacon," but it takes in all works of service, such as teaching, visiting the sick and needy, helping children, and aiding those who are in trouble. All that the believer has in talents, abilities and finances comes from God and is to be used to help others.

In the Western world we have a pagan concept of ownership and feel that what we have is ours and ours alone. Too often we fail to remember that He who gives can take away as well. The early church amazed a pagan world because of their service to others. Our Lord calls us to be shining lights so people might see our good works and glorify our Father who is in heaven (Matthew 5:16). Paul said we should "do all to the glory of God" (1 Corinthians 10:31).

II. SERVE WILLINGLY (1 Peter 5:1-4)

A. The Ministry of Elders (vv. 1, 2)

1. The elders which are among you I exhort, who am also an elder, and a witness of the sufferings of Christ, and also a partaker of the glory that shall be revealed:

2. Feed the flock of God which is among you, taking the oversight thereof, not by constraint, but willingly; not for filthy lucre, but of a ready mind.

Talk About It:

1. What was Peter "a witness of" and "a partaker of" (v. 1)? Why was this important?

2. Describe the characteristics a "shepherd of God's flock" should *not* have (see v. 2).

Elders were men whose age and experience led to spiritual responsibilities in the church. From a Jewish perspective the notion of elders can be traced from the wilderness wanderings. We know from Numbers 11:16-30 that Moses set apart 70 elders to aid in the administration of justice and leading the people. These men were given power by the Holy Spirit to assist Moses. In 2 Kings 6:32 elders are mentioned as being friends of the prophets. They were advisers to kings in 1 Kings 20:8; 21:11. Elders were in every village as they met at the city gates to decide issues of justice (Deuteronomy 25:7). During the time of Jesus they formed a part of the Sanhedrin (Matthew 16:21; 21:23; 26:3, 57). In the Book of Revelation, 24 elders are presented as being around the throne of God.

The office of elder was a basic office in the early church. We know from Acts 14:23 that Paul ordained elders in churches. He gave Titus specific instructions to ordain elders in Crete (Titus 1:5). Elders had financial ministry responsibilities (Acts 11:30). One of the most important sections on elders is found in Acts 20:17-38 with Paul's farewell address to the Ephesian elders.

In 1 Peter 5:1, Peter described himself as a fellow elder of the elders in Asia Minor. Although he could claim the office of apostle, Peter understood the call of God upon his life to "feed the flock of God." Thus, rather than exalting himself, Peter saw himself as a fellow member of God's leaders.

He did indicate he had seen the suffering and glory of Christ. This made him different from the elders in the provinces as well as different from elders today. The sufferings of Christ referred to Peter's seeing the bruised and beaten Savior at the time of denial (Luke 22:54-62). The "glory that shall be revealed" (1 Peter 5:1) probably has a double meaning. On the one hand, it referred to the Mount of Transfiguration (Luke 9:28-36); secondly, it referred to Peter's belief in the Second Coming.

In 1 Peter 5:2, the leader is given specific responsibilities among God's people. He is to "feed" God's flock. Certainly Peter was remembering his Lord's instructions in John 21 regarding his role of feeding His lambs and sheep. The apostle Paul used a similar expression in Acts 20:28 in his charge to the Ephesian elders. The Greek word for "feed" is also translated as "tend" or "shepherd."

There is to be no false humility nor refusal to serve this pastoral office. The Christian elder serves eagerly (ready mind) and not for shameful gain. Although "filthy lucre" usually refers to money, here it refers to any effort to gain advantage over someone else. The word indicated a certain "meanness" in the life of the elder. Peter made it clear that the elder is not to manifest such an attitude toward others.

There are parallel references in 1 Timothy 3:3, 8 and Titus 1:7, 11 that indicate the early church had to make a strong statement regarding the tendency for church leaders to be more concerned with private gain than spiritual service. As Barclay wrote, "The point that Peter is making . . . is that no man dare accept office or render service for what he can get out of it."

> "Do not trust proud, self-seeking leadership."
> —Harold Lundquist

B. The Example of Elders (vv. 3, 4)

3. Neither as being lords over God's heritage, but being ensamples to the flock.

4. And when the chief Shepherd shall appear, ye shall receive a crown of glory that fadeth not away.

The elder is not to dominate those whom he/she serves. The words "being lords" translate one Greek word that is used in Mark 10:42 by Jesus in addressing His disciples.

The setting of Mark 10 is the request of James and John for positions of power in the Kingdom. Jesus had just indicated that His role as the Son of Man was to suffer and die (vv. 32-34). In contrast, James and John sought to find glory. Jesus took issue with their approach to Kingdom service. They desired the glory without the service. Jesus called for them to be servants if they desired to be great among God's people. In this sense "greatness" is never sought; it comes as a spiritual gift in humble obedience.

Thus Peter teaches that spiritual leadership never gives the leader the opportunity to replace Jesus as the Lord in the lives of people. The reason is quite clear: the people belong to the Lord and Him alone. The word *heritage* means "allotment." The allotment of Christians belongs to God and He has placed it in the hands of spiritual leaders for earthly care.

Talk About It:
1. What is the difference between a *lord* and an *example*?
2. What is God's promise to faithful pastors and leaders?

Leaders are thus to lead by being examples and servants. One challenge facing Christian leaders is how to balance submission and authority. Many can testify to the pain caused by overzealous leaders and to the confusion caused by leaders afraid to act. The balance is found as spiritual leaders submit themselves to God's Word and use it as the guiding force for leadership. Such a balance becomes life-giving through prayer and the manifestation of the fruit of the Spirit.

Only here (v. 4) in the New Testament does the title "chief Shepherd" appear for Christ. However, the notion is familiar to the New Testament. In John 10:11, 14, Jesus is given the Shepherd title: "I am the good shepherd: the good shepherd giveth his life for the sheep. . . . I am the good shepherd, and know my sheep, and am known of mine." The same image is found in Hebrews 13:20: "Now the God of peace, that brought again from the dead our Lord Jesus, that great shepherd of the sheep . . ."

The imagery of Jesus as the Shepherd is connected to His return in glory. At His appearing He will gather in His flock from the Evil One. At the end of human history the crown of glory that does not fade will be conferred upon those leaders who have been faithful as shepherds.

There are many spiritual leaders who choose to receive their rewards in this life by prestigious titles and human recognition. However, the faithful servant will be that one who is not concerned about such recognition but instead lives in the fear of God in total obedience to His call. The fear of people does not dominate such a life. Such a life reflects the lordship of Jesus in compassion and power.

III. HUMBLE YOURSELF (1 Peter 5:5-11)
A. Mutual Submission (v. 5)

5. Likewise, ye younger, submit yourselves unto the elder. Yea, all of you be subject one to another, and be clothed with humility: for God resisteth the proud, and giveth grace to the humble.

Talk About It:
1. Why should younger believers submit to older Christians?
2. How is it possible for everyone to "be subject to one another"?
3. Why does God resist the proud?

There are two major elements to this verse. The first deals with the relationship between those younger in age and those older. The second deals with the relationship of mutual submission and humility.

Younger believers are to be submissive to the wisdom of the elders. However, we have just seen that elders in the church are to have the relationship of "servants" with all in the church. Thus, this submission on the part of the younger to the elders is one of mutuality and love. This is not an attempt to impose strict regulations or to suppress the energy and drive of the younger generation. Neither is it a license for the younger to rebel and offer contentious resistance to the call of God through the wisdom of the elders.

Regarding the call to mutual submission and humility, Peter quoted Proverbs 3:34 to speak to all age groups and social groups in the church. If the elders are proud, God will resist them through the striving of youth. If the young are proud, God will resist them through the authority of the elders. All believers are to submit themselves one to the other in humility for the sake of pleasing God.

The word translated *elder* in Greek is plural, and we should think of submission to all who are in spiritual positions of authority rather than just one person. The word for *submit* is used in four other places in 1 Peter (2:13, 18; 3:1, 5) and implies obedience. The tense of the verb has the connotation of making a onetime commitment to live a life of submission to those in authority in the church.

The word *clothed* describes a garment tied with a knot that was used as a slave's apron. The same idea is expressed in John 13:4, 5 to describe the towel Jesus wore when He washed His disciples' feet. It was the garment of humility and servanthood. All, young and old alike, are to wear this garment.

> "Nothing sets a person so much out of the devil's reach as humility."
> —*Marquee Messages*

B. Casting Cares (vv. 6, 7)

6. Humble yourselves therefore under the mighty hand of God, that he may exalt you in due time:

7. Casting all your care upon him; for he careth for you.

Even though we are to be humble in the sight of others, the source of humility is the power of God. The expression "the mighty hand of God" referred in the Old Testament to God's power (Exodus 13:9; Deuteronomy 3:24; 9:26). This is truly a life lived in the fear of the Lord. Proverbs 9:10 says, "The fear of the Lord is the beginning of wisdom." This fear does not paralyze our actions; rather, it sets us free to live totally for Him.

By humbling ourselves before God, He becomes finally responsible for our life. We can trust that He will exalt us in "due time," which refers to His special time. When we are able to trust Him so the incidentals of life are not so important to us, then we shall truly be used for His purposes.

In 1 Peter 5:7, the two words for "care" are different. The first "care" is better translated "worry, anxiety." It is found in Psalm 55:22, "Cast thy burden upon the Lord, and he shall sustain thee." This ability to place our worries upon Him is part of the call of humility in verse 6.

The final clause of verse 7 capsulizes what the gospel is about: God *cares* for us. He cares so much that He sent His Son to die for us, His Spirit is at work wooing us, and He has determined to defeat evil and establish His kingdom.

Talk About It:
1. When is the "due time" God will lift up the humble?
2. What does it mean to "cast" your cares on God? Which ones concern Him?

C. Resisting Satan (vv. 8, 9)

8. Be sober, be vigilant; because your adversary the

devil, as a roaring lion, walketh about, seeking whom he may devour:

9. **Whom resist stedfast in the faith, knowing that the same afflictions are accomplished in your brethren that are in the world.**

Talk About It:

1. How is the devil like a lion?

2. What is common to "your brethren that are in the world" (v. 9)? How is this an encouragement?

3. How can a Christian resist the devil?

The word *sober* has the sense of being "free from every form of mental and spiritual drunkenness, free from excess, rashness, confusion; to be well-balanced" (*Bauer Lexicon*). Peter used "sober" in 1:13 to refer to the attitude of the believer awaiting the return of the Lord. In 4:7 he used it to refer to our way of praying in the light of the impending end. Thus, being sober is a characteristic of those who live in the end time. It means that self-control and discipline are crucial elements as we await our Lord's return.

The word translated *vigilant* is often used in the New Testament in relationship to the return of the Lord. In Matthew 24:42 and 25:13, it indicates the state of "awakeness" that believers are to have as they await the Lord's return. In 1 Thessalonians 5:6 Paul used it in a similar fashion regarding the watchful state of Christians at the end. In 1 Peter we have seen numerous references regarding the return of the Lord (1:7, 13; 5:4). With the use of "vigilant" and "sober," Peter apparently is calling for Christians to be wary of Satan because the return of the Lord is near. Satan knows his days are limited, therefore he seeks with intense fervor to destroy humanity, especially those who claim to be servants of God. Thus, believers are called to be extra careful in these final days.

The simile of a "roaring lion" is used to describe the terror of the work of Satan. The image is drawn from Psalm 22:13, where the roaring indicates the rage of hunger of the devouring beast. Psalm 22 is a messianic psalm dealing with the suffering of Christ at the Cross. Thus, one easily pictures the conflict between Satan the adversary and Christ our advocate.

The term *adversary* was used by Christ in Matthew 5:25 referring to an accuser in the courts of law. Job 1:7 describes Satan as roaming over the earth and coming into the court of God, seeking to bring charges against God's people. This act of bringing charges against God's elect is also vividly portrayed in Romans 8:33.

There is one other incident in the life of Peter that made this reference to Satan so important. In Luke 22:31 Jesus told Peter that Satan had permission to "sift you as wheat." Although he would be sifted, the Lord said he would be converted, and his brethren would be strengthened (v. 32). Here in 1 Peter is the fulfillment of that prophecy. Peter was converted from his denial of Christ and was now offering strength and encouragement to his brothers and sisters in Christ.

Verse 9 says we are to resist the devil by our steadfastness in the faith. In Mark 11:22 Jesus spoke to Peter, "Have faith in God." The context was the cleansing of the Temple during Passion Week. Peter had noted that the cursed fig tree had withered. In response to this observation, Jesus told him to have faith in God. When the world is withering around us, when those things in which we trusted are decaying and losing their power, we can trust God.

Next, Peter drew the attention of his readers to their common lot of suffering in the world. The word *accomplished* implies that God's people pay the "tax" (the burden) of suffering around the world. This lesson has been hard for Western Christians to understand. Our society has made it convenient, even profitable, to be a Christian. But that is changing. The day is coming when suffering because we are Christians will be our lot. When that day comes, we must remember that our suffering is not unique. It simply makes us one with those millions of unnamed persons who have suffered for His sake.

> "There are two possible mistakes to be made. One is to overestimate the power of Satan, and the other is to underestimate it."
> —*Quotable Quotes*

D. Experiencing Victory (vv. 10, 11)

10. But the God of all grace, who hath called us unto his eternal glory by Christ Jesus, after that ye have suffered a while, make you perfect, stablish, strengthen, settle you.

11. To him be glory and dominion for ever and ever. Amen.

Peter seeks to show that suffering for the Christian is not the final word in the story of redemption. The final word is victory over suffering. The Resurrection follows the Cross. The martyrs of Revelation 6:10 will become the victorious children of righteousness (6:11).

Talk About It:
What is God's plan for the believer's life, and how will He accomplish it?

This victory over suffering takes place in the grace of God. This unmerited favor is revealed in His calling upon our lives. Election is the Biblical way of expressing God's powerful way of keeping us as His children from the destruction of Satan. As a roaring lion Satan may attempt havoc, but Christ has overcome and His claim upon us is certain. This calling and election calls for us to persevere in steadfast love toward Him.

Peter says God will make us anew in His image. As we were made by God in the beginning, so at the end of life God will remake us. God will make Christians "perfect." The Greek word translated "perfect" means "to restore to its former condition, put in order." It was used in Mark 1:19 of mending nets and in Galatians 6:1, which gives instruction on restoring a brother in a spirit of gentleness. It was also a medical term in Greek to describe the setting of a bone. Thus, the notion is one of restoring and making well. This certainly fits the experience of Peter as he was restored by Christ.

The word *stablish* is to "set up, support, confirm and strengthen," while *strengthen* has the basic meaning of "make strong." The word *settle* refers to the believers whom God has established. The word referred to the laying of foundation stones in a building. Thus, it meant the laying of a foundation upon which life is built. God has made provision for these areas of our lives. So Peter can joyfully conclude with the glory and dominion that belongs to Christ.

CONCLUSION
"There is no portion of our time that is our time, and the rest God's; there is no portion of our money that is our money, and the rest God's. It is all His; He made it all, gives it all, and He has simply entrusted it to us for His service."—**Adolphe Monod**

GOLDEN TEXT CHALLENGE

Daily Devotions:

M. Aaron Ministers for the People
Leviticus 16:1-10
T. David Shows Mercy
2 Samuel 9:1-13
W. Isaiah Humbled Before God
Isaiah 6:1-7
T. Serve One Another
John 13:3-16
F. Christ's Example of Humility
Philippians 2:5-11
S. Divine Grace for the Humble
James 4:6-12

"AS EVERY MAN HATH RECEIVED THE GIFT, EVEN SO MINISTER THE SAME ONE TO ANOTHER, AS GOOD STEWARDS OF THE MANIFOLD GRACE OF GOD" (1 Peter 4:10).

The grace of giving. Peter has been talking about ungrudging hospitality (v. 9). The homes of Christians were to be open to God's servants who in travel bare the good news. This ability to give to others is a gift received from God. God's children are to "minister" in temporal things to others as "good stewards."

The ministry of giving. God gives to us; we share with others. No one can truthfully claim, "I made it myself; it is for me and my family!" All we have, even when we work hard for it, comes from God. He allows us to have it so we can share.

When we selfishly consume our possessions, we live like the world. God's children give all they can. The needs are great—church, missions, the needy. Cheerfully we give because of the "manifold grace of God." It should be arranged so that when we are gone, our accumulated wealth will be distributed to the needs of others in Christ's kingdom. How else do we die as Christians?

Spiritual Growth

2 Peter 1:1-11

INTRODUCTION

If we are not careful, we can set up a canon, or standard, of accepted Scripture within the canon we know as the Bible. Certainly, we accept all the Biblical books as inspired, but it is easy to fall prey to the habit of favoring some books and ignoring others. Yet, all of God's Word is inspired and profitable (2 Timothy 3:16). Second Peter is one of those books often ignored by readers. Throughout history its authorship and value have been questioned. However, there is ample evidence to prove that it is the work of the apostle Peter and is profitable for all Christians, especially those living in a day and age when false teachers try to undermine the truths of the Word and scoffers make fun of those who believe in the second coming of Christ. Peter was writing to encourage, teach, and build up Christians facing these obstacles. The more things change, the more they stay the same.

This lesson focuses on the resources provided by God that enable Christians to grow in the wisdom and knowledge of Jesus Christ. It also examines the expectations God has for us. We are in a living relationship with God. There are some things we expect from Him, such as salvation, provision and His presence. There are also some things He expects from us, as this section of 2 Peter reveals. However, God never expects without giving us the ability to fulfill those expectations.

Spiritual growth is not an option for the child of God. Neither does it come without intentionality, determination and a plan. It helps to take a spiritual inventory of our lives to see where we are and what we need to move to a deeper, more intimate walk with God. This can be accomplished through prayer and meditation upon the Word. A specific plan must then be formulated to address the areas in our lives that need to be addressed. We plan our finances, careers, and other important areas of our lives. Can we afford to be neglectful in the spiritual realm? Scripture is full of examples of people who treated their walk with God carelessly and suffered the terrible consequences of their negligence. We can and must grow in His grace. It is the will of God.

Unit Theme:
Peter and Jude

Central Truth:
God provides resources to nurture spiritual growth in Christ.

Focus:
To identify the divine resources available to the believer and commit to grow in Christ.

Context:
A general epistle written by the apostle Peter around A.D. 67 to warn its readers of threatening apostasy.

Golden Text:
"Whereby are given unto us exceeding great and precious promises; that by these ye might be partakers of the divine nature" (2 Peter 1:4).

Study Outline:
I. Divine Resources for Growth (2 Peter 1:1-4)
II. Developing Christian Character (2 Peter 1:5-7)
III. Results of Spiritual Growth (2 Peter 1:8-11)

I. DIVINE RESOURCES FOR GROWTH (2 Peter 1:1-4)

A. Love, Leadership, Legacy and Lordship (vv. 1, 2)

1. Simon Peter, a servant and an apostle of Jesus Christ, to them that have obtained like precious faith with us through the righteousness of God and our Saviour Jesus Christ:

2. Grace and peace be multiplied unto you through the knowledge of God, and of Jesus our Lord.

Talk About It:

1. Why did Simon Peter identify himself as both "a servant and an apostle" (v. 1)?

2. What makes the Christian faith "precious"?

3. How do you suppose Peter would fare as a leader in today's church?

Often, we view the opening verses of an epistle as a common formulary that has little spiritual value for the modern day. However, these particular verses remind us of at least four resources God has given us.

Love. The greeting reminds us of God's love that causes Him to be interested in people—not just the Kingdom at large. Epistles were written to address specific needs in the first century and have the ability to speak to 21st-century Christians in an equally meaningful and authoritative way. The Word of God is alive and empowered by the Spirit to address our needs (Hebrews 4:12). In the midst of busyness, we must not miss what God is speaking today, even through common or normal things. The writer is Simon Peter (literally, Simeon Peter), a joining of his Jewish and Greek names (v. 1). It is a reminder of the inclusiveness of God's kingdom. It does not matter what our race, background or gender is; what matters is that we are saved by grace.

Leadership. This salutation informs us that spiritual leaders are divine gifts from God. These leaders provide an example to follow, contribute to the expansion of the kingdom of God, and have God-given talents, blessings ("grace and peace," v. 2), and words to share. Here, the earthly source of this message is Peter, one of the Twelve, a perfect example of a human spiritual leader. He was not perfect, often stumbling in times of pressure (Matthew 26:69-75), even after Pentecost (Galatians 2:11-14). His quick speech usually got him in trouble (Matthew 16:21-23), and his actions were often rash (John 18:10). Yet, he was God's chosen leader as an "apostle" (a messenger or representative from God) and a "servant" (one who ministers to others as unto the Lord). Peter was well aware of the tension between the two callings that become one ministry.

In this age of postmodernity, with its cynicism, skepticism and focus on the self, we can begin to question and resist our God-given leaders. Irresponsible behavior from leaders should not be tolerated. Scripture provides for the discipline of leaders (1 Timothy 5:19). We must look beyond the actions to see the heart of the individual (1 Samuel 16:7), and see how we, through Christian love and prayer, can help mold the vessel of clay into the leader of God. This requires examining our own hearts, being the vessels God has called us to be, and submitting to those whom God has placed in our lives (Hebrews 13:17). Although Simon Peter denied the Lord, he developed into a mature Christian leader and blessed the church with inspired wisdom and insight. Neither God nor the early church gave up on him.

Legacy. The recipients of this letter are "those who have received through a divine gift the faith that is equally precious and honorable as ours" (v. 1, author's translation). No matter how far in time we are removed from the cross of Christ and the proclamation of the witnesses thereto, we have the same standing in the sight of God as the apostles! Even the least in the Kingdom are as great as the greatest (Matthew 11:11; 25:40; Ephesians 3:8). The Enemy convinces too many that they cannot make a difference. The men and women of the New Testament were people just like us, who allowed the power of God to flow through them. It is His power that makes the difference, not us. We just need to be the willing instruments for His hand to use.

Lordship. The writer recognizes that both he and the readers owe all that they are and hope to become to the lordship of Jesus Christ. Peter acknowledges that he is a servant and apostle because he chose to respond to the call of Christ, not because of any inherent greatness. We are who and what we are because of the "righteousness [upright and just behavior] of God and our Saviour Jesus Christ."

The "grace" (undeserved favor) and "peace" (confidence in God despite the circumstances) promised are dependent on "the knowledge of God, and of Jesus our Lord" (v. 2). *Knowledge* is of great importance in this epistle (1:2, 3, 5, 6, 8; 2:20; 3:18). Knowledge has been treated with suspicion in some spiritual circles; however, knowledge that is from the Spirit (Exodus 31:3) should be sought (Psalm 119:66), will keep us from sin (Psalm 14:4), and enables us to "know" God (see Proverbs 2:5). It is a necessary spiritual sustenance (Job 36:12). Knowledge, like education, is a tool (Proverbs 15:2) and can be used for good (2 Corinthians 2:14) or evil (1 Corinthians 8). It is not evil in and of itself.

> "The great difference between present-day Christianity and that of which we read in these [Biblical] letters is that to us it is primarily a performance, to them it was a real experience. . . . To these men it is quite plainly the invasion of the lives by a new quality of life altogether. They do not hesitate to describe this as Christ 'living in' them."
>
> —J.B. Phillips
> *(Letters to Young Churches)*

B. Provision, Promise and Partaking (vv. 3, 4)

3. According as his divine power hath given unto us all things that pertain unto life and godliness, through the knowledge of him that hath called us to glory and virtue:

4. Whereby are given unto us exceeding great and precious promises: that by these ye might be partakers of the divine nature, having escaped the corruption that is in the world through lust.

January 15, 2006

Talk About It:

1. How do these verses answer the complaint "It is too hard to lead a Christian life in this world"?

2. Name some of the "great and precious promises" God's Word gives to empower believers.

"The Bible, God's inerrant Word, is forever true whether or not anyone reads or believes it; but it becomes of value to you when you get hold of it for yourself. Never leave a passage of Scripture until it has said something to you."

—Robert Cook

These verses are powerful reminders of God's unfailing provision that helps all believers in every aspect of life (physical and spiritual). Through the power of God, we have access to *everything* we need for "life and godliness" (v. 3). It is a promise to supply all of our needs for life upon the earth, as well as whatever we need to live in right relationship with God ("godliness"). We are called to reflect God's majesty ("glory") and goodness or excellence ("virtue") in the midst of the darkness, so that others might see the light and be drawn to Him. As in verse 2, our ability to participate in this provision of God is dependent upon our knowledge of Him. It is not just mental knowledge, but also encompasses the spirit, emotions and will. It is knowledge that willfully and intentionally experiences God. Some know Christ strictly as Savior. Others have moved to a deeper walk and allow Him to be Lord (Master) of every aspect of their lives. The goal is to know Him so intimately that we flow in and with His love and power.

The ability to grasp such a lofty goal is not left to our own abilities. We are the recipients of "very great and precious promises" (v. 4, *NIV*). The Old Testament is full of promises—promises of *deliverance* (Psalm 32:7), *healing* (Isaiah 61:1), and *hope* (Jeremiah 29:11), to name a few. Those promises are fulfilled in and through Jesus Christ (2 Corinthians 1:20), as are the New Testament promises of salvation (Acts 4:12), the Second Coming (John 14:3), and a new home (1 Thessalonians 4:17) for those who believe in Him. The message is clear: God promises to do whatever it takes to perfect that which He has begun in us. The proof and guarantee of this and all promises is Jesus Christ.

These promises enable us to be partakers (fellow participants) of His "divine nature." There are aspects of God's nature or attributes in which humanity cannot participate, such as His omnipresence and omnipotence. There are, however, qualities of God in which we can share, such as love, life, holiness and goodness. As a believer grows in grace and faith, participates in discipleship, and continually develops character consistent with the example of Jesus Christ, he or she partakes of the nature of God. This work of God in our lives enables us to "escape the corruption in the world caused by evil desires" (2 Peter 1:4, *NIV*). This escape is both present and future, giving us hope in freedom from sin now and escape from the influences of this world at the appearance of Jesus Christ.

II. DEVELOPING CHRISTIAN CHARACTER (2 Peter 1:5-7)
A. Inner Character (vv. 5, 6)
  5. And beside this, giving all diligence, add to your faith virtue; and to virtue knowledge;

Spiritual Growth

6. And to knowledge temperance; and to temperance patience; and to patience godliness.

The apostle moves from God's resources to the expected and natural response by Christians: "And so for this very reason, make every effort to earnestly add to your faith . . ." (v. 5, author's translation). He then addresses five inner values that define our character and Christian life ("faith"). *Character* is best understood as who we are when no one else is looking. It is who God knows us to be. Character governs conduct, so its development is crucial to the spiritual health of the believer. Each of these qualities builds upon the previously mentioned one. They all start with *faith*.

The first inner quality is *moral excellence* ("virtue"). God is not looking for people who simply do right; He is looking for people who do right because they are right with Him (see 2 Chronicles 25:2). This is holiness, being wholly affected by the nature of God to the point that we not only *want* to please Him, we *must* please Him. There is no simple formula that makes this work. It requires time spent in God's presence and a determination to be like Him.

The second inner quality is *insight and understanding.* It is "knowledge" that discerns God's nature, will and purpose, and continually develops from being immersed in the Word of God and the flowing of the Spirit. Thus, it is aware of the spiritual forces at work and knows how to effectively counteract them through the Spirit.

The third inner quality is *disciplined self-control* ("temperance"). The term originally pertained to sports. Athletes were expected to abstain from wine, unhealthy foods and sexual activity. The focus was on becoming the best athlete possible for the sake of winning. Paul identified self-control as a characteristic of the fruit of the Spirit (Galatians 5:23) and often used the sports imagery to teach Christians to lay aside unnecessary things (1 Corinthians 9:25). For the Christian, it is willfully placing the desires of the flesh in submission to God. The New Testament does not give a comprehensive list of "don'ts" in association with this term, but lists it as a quality for Christians to practice (v. 27). As we seek God, He will reveal the areas in our lives that lack this characteristic, but we must be willing to listen before we will hear His admonition.

The fourth inner quality is *persistent perseverance* ("patience"). The growing Christian must remain loyal to the faith and promises of God despite the circumstances. It is a mind-set that refuses to be turned from the course God has set. It is choosing not to look to the right or the left, but always to Jesus, the author and finisher of our faith, and His example (Hebrews 12:2).

Talk About It:
1. Why is faith the beginning point in Christian living?
2. What does the phrase "giving all diligence" say about the Christian life?
3. What kind of knowledge does the believer need?

The last inner quality listed here is *godliness*. This is a decision to live in a way that is always conscious of God's provision and presence. It is leading a life that is a visible testimony to God and brings Him glory.

The passage makes it clear it is within the believer's ability to cultivate and incorporate these qualities. It is a process that may take longer for some to develop in certain areas. We must be patient with ourselves *and* others as Christian character develops; however, patience must not be used as an excuse for failure to cultivate these qualities in our lives. We must lovingly encourage one another to develop into the person God has called us to be.

B. Outward Character (v. 7)

7. And to godliness brotherly kindness; and to brotherly kindness charity.

The passage progresses to qualities that are more outward in their expression. As we develop the inner person (attitudes), the outward person responds to that development (actions). For example, the heart governs what the mouth speaks (Luke 6:45). The thoughts upon which we dwell affect our behavior (Proverbs 23:7). It is a compelling reminder of how the spirit affects the flesh—both positively and negatively. Specifically, Peter calls for two types of love to be developed and shared. Together these types of love fulfill Jesus' summary of the Old Testament expectations (see Matthew 22:37-40).

"Brotherly kindness" is love for a brother or sister and is used in the New Testament for love between fellow believers—spiritual family members (see Romans 12:10). Jesus declares that our love for fellow believers serves as a powerful witness of our faith (John 13:35). Sometimes this can be difficult, especially when we have been hurt by a fellow believer. Those who are the closest to us can inflict the greatest pain. This pain can fester and result in bitterness and division. The lack of unity then can hinder the ministry of the entire congregation. True spiritual growth results from a nurturing atmosphere that requires healthy relationships. We need to do whatever is necessary to correct any problems so our love for one another shines brightly and purely.

The scope of our love is then extended beyond the church through what is often thought of as the highest degree of love (*agape*). It is a deep, devoted love that originates not from a feeling, but a decision. Jesus said, "Greater love has no one than this, than to lay down one's life for his friends" (John 15:13, *NKJV*). He chose to love us enough to lay down His life, so that we may find life. As believers develop in character, not only will we love God and His church, we will choose to love those who

"Even if you're on the right track, you'll get run over if you just sit there."

—Marquee Messages

Talk About It:

Why is love the greatest of Christian virtues?

Simple Truth

At one church I pastored, Chris blessed the community and us with insightful sayings on the church sign. One week the sign read, "For All You Do, His Blood's for You!" This particular saying brought a new family to the altar and the church. They realized they needed God's provision for salvation. Through the sign, another person came to understand that His blood provides the strength to do all that is expected of us. His blood is sufficient to save us and keep us walking forward in salvation.

—Keith Whitt

Spiritual Growth

are lost. It can be easier to preach against sin than it is to love those caught in its destructive power. This is not to belittle preaching against iniquity; this is a necessary aspect of the church's commission (Acts 2:38). However, without love, our preaching, evangelistic efforts, and testimonies are useless (1 Corinthians 13:1-3). This type of love values the object of that love. We must love sinners enough to value them as persons—and as souls that will spend eternity in heaven or hell. The decision to love others must include our enemies (Matthew 5:44). It is a resolution to allow the love of God to flow through us in spite of our feelings or past dealings. It is a determination to become an extension of God's nature. The church cannot win the people of the harvest it does not love.

III. RESULTS OF SPIRITUAL GROWTH (2 Peter 1:8-11)
A. The Necessity of Spiritual Growth (vv. 8, 9)

8. For if these things be in you, and abound, they make you that ye shall neither be barren nor unfruitful in the knowledge of our Lord Jesus Christ.

9. But he that lacketh these things is blind, and cannot see afar off, and hath forgotten that he was purged from his old sins.

These spiritual qualities (vv. 5-7) should be evident in our lives and "abound" in such a way that they are caused to increase continually (v. 8). Some people undertake spiritual disciplines only because they are required to do so. They usually do no more than is required—if that. These individuals are also usually unhappy and unfulfilled people. Others do the same things joyfully because they want to develop, mature, prepare themselves for further service, excel in the faith, and please God. The apostle says those who undertake spiritual growth willingly and with zeal ("abound") shall not be *barren*. This term literally means "not working." It is used in Scripture to describe those who are idle, busybodies and neglectful (1 Timothy 5:13). It also describes things (or people) that are unprofitable (James 2:20) or careless (Matthew 12:36). Neither shall we be "unfruitful." There is no fear of failing God nor of displeasing Him. The process guarantees our usefulness or profitableness for the cause of Christ and the kingdom of God. Fruit becomes a natural byproduct in our lives (John 15:8). Signs follow those who believe (Mark 16:17-20), and our "knowledge" of and intimacy with Jesus Christ increases, a theme repeated throughout the epistle.

Those who neglect or do not possess these qualities ("lacketh") are "nearsighted and blind" (2 Peter 1:9, *NIV*). The New Testament often illustrates loss of spiritual vitality through the imagery of blindness (Matthew 15:14). We can lose sight of that which is eternal and truly important. Here, the image is that

Talk About It:
1. What will the qualities listed in verses 5-7 do for the believer (v. 8)?
2. How can a believer become spiritually blind, and what is the consequence?

of one who tires of squinting and closes his or her eyes to the truth. The believer must be a willing participant in the growth process, even when it's uncomfortable.

Lost sight results in forgetting the importance of being "cleansed from . . . past sins" (2 Peter 1:9, NIV). This phrase reminds believers we are purified from sins and are now free. We are set free from sin and death (Romans 8:2) and receive eternal and abundant life (John 10:10). Also, it informs us that our participation carries with it eternal consequences. If we forget what God has done in the past, we will not expect cleansing in the present. If we are not cleansed in the present, we have no future. We either grow or we deteriorate.

> "It's a strange and tragic truth that spiritual things can be unlearned."
> —Art Glasser

B. The Assurance in Spiritual Growth (vv. 10, 11)

10. Wherefore the rather, brethren, give diligence to make your calling and election sure: for if ye do these things, ye shall never fall:

11. For so an entrance shall be ministered unto you abundantly into the everlasting kingdom of our Lord and Saviour Jesus Christ.

Peter sums up the teaching section by reminding his readers we are pilgrims on a journey. We can determine the outcome of that journey by working diligently to make certain our "calling and election" are steadfast. The image is that of an anchor holding a ship securely in the midst of a storm. We have been called to be saints of God and witnesses of His grace. Continual spiritual development enables us to walk without stumbling and assures acceptance at the appearing of Jesus Christ.

In *The Pilgrim's Progress*, John Bunyan tells of pilgrims seeing the doors of the heavenly city opened for a brief moment. What a pilgrim sees during the brief time encourages him to fight even harder the rest of the way. While we've not had a literal glimpse of heaven, God has given us "a seal, the promised Holy Spirit, who is a deposit guaranteeing our inheritance" (Ephesians 1:13, 14, NIV). The portion of God's power we have received through the presence of His Spirit should intensify our efforts to be with Him throughout eternity.

When Christ comes, we can enter His everlasting kingdom "abundantly," not merely by the skin of our teeth. If we have allowed Christ's virtues to flow through us, we can expect our works to survive God's testing by fire, revealing them to be as gold and silver, bringing us rewards (see 1 Corinthians 3:10-15).

> **Talk About It:**
> 1. What does it mean to be called by God and elected by Him?
> 2. To "never fall," what must a Christian do?

CONCLUSION

God has invested His life, His Son's life, and His nature in us. He provides whatever we need to succeed in our lives, both in and out of church (2 Peter 1:1-4). He wants us to develop

His character and nature in our lives (vv. 5-7). Our efforts benefit us and bless God (vv. 8-11). Jesus teaches us that God expects a return on that investment (Matthew 25:14-30). What kind of return are you giving Him on His investment in you?

GOLDEN TEXT CHALLENGE
"WHEREBY ARE GIVEN UNTO US EXCEEDING GREAT AND PRECIOUS PROMISES; THAT BY THESE YE MIGHT BE PARTAKERS OF THE DIVINE NATURE" (2 Peter 1:4).

God's promises are certified by Christ's ministry on earth, His redeeming death and resurrection, and the hope of His second coming. "His promises are precious because they are not mere empty words; they are exceeding great, because they point to the perfection and completion to which our present life is leading" (Andrew McNabb).

When Adoniram Judson was asked about the prospects of his ministry in Burma, he replied, "As bright as the promises of God." The object of these promises is to remake sinful people and have the lost image of God restored. When we become partakers of God's nature, we get both the desire and the power to do God's will and thereby escape the corruption of the world.

Daily Devotions:
M. Preserved by God
Exodus 2:1-10
T. Wise Living
Proverbs 1:8-15
W. Rewarded for Consecration
Daniel 1:8-17
T. Purpose of Spiritual Gifts
Ephesians 4:11-16
F. Rooted in Christ
Colossians 2:6-10
S. Keep Growing
2 Timothy 1:1-7

Standing for Truth and Righteousness

2 Peter 1:16 through 2:22

Unit Theme:
Peter and Jude

Central Truth:
The Bible is the authority for correct doctrine and right living.

Focus:
To acknowledge that God's Word is truth and guard against false teaching and unrighteousness.

Context:
A general epistle written by the apostle Peter around A.D. 67 to warn its readers of threatening apostasy.

Golden Text:
"The prophecy came not in old time by the will of man: but holy men of God spake as they were moved by the Holy Ghost" (2 Peter 1:21).

Study Outline:
I. The Foundation of Truth
   (2 Peter 1:16-21)
II. Warning Against False Teachers
   (2 Peter 2:1-10)
III. Consequences of Turning From Righteousness
   (2 Peter 2:11-22)

INTRODUCTION

In many of the Epistles, the apostles present a foundation of doctrinal truths that not only teach the readers but also encourage them in the faith. Often this is done while addressing specific needs known to the writer. After his opening greeting and encouragement, Peter addresses specific concerns that have come to his attention. He is aware that teachers are trying to impose heretical or false teachings and doctrine upon the readers (2 Peter 1:16; 2:1- 3). To establish their own doctrine, false teachers seek to distort or discredit the truth, then present their version of "the way it really is."

In this day and age multitudes of teachers, preachers and prophets have "a new word from the Lord." Certainly, God continues to give new insight into His ways, Word and will. Divine revelation is progressive and dynamic, not static. It is refreshing and exciting, not stale and boring. Part of the Spirit's work in the church today is to bring new understanding (John 16:13), fresh insight (Romans 7:6), direction for the times in which we live (see Acts 20:22, 23), life-giving power (John 6:63), and deeper knowledge of God (1 Corinthians 2:11- 13). Fresh moves of God and information are usually conveyed through willing human vessels. We must not become so accustomed with the way *we* think God should move that we place Him in a box and miss what He is doing in the church today. However, not everything new is from God (2 Corinthians 11:3, 4).

All Christians need to be able to discern truth from myth, and righteousness from ungodliness (John 8:32). We do that by becoming so familiar with the truth that any deviation becomes obvious to the mind and checked in the spirit. This is not just being uncomfortable with possible changes in the status quo, but certain knowledge that what we are hearing is contrary to God and His Word. The longer our journey with Christ and the deeper we go in the Word and the Spirit, the easier this becomes. It is a process that enhances our walk with the Lord and His church, matures our faith, enriches the Kingdom, and protects us from doctrinal error.

I. THE FOUNDATION OF TRUTH (2 Peter 1:16-21)
A. The Veracity of the Witnesses (vv. 16-18)

16. For we have not followed cunningly devised fables, when we made known unto you the power and coming of our Lord Jesus Christ, but were eyewitnesses of his majesty.

17. For he received from God the Father honour and glory, when there came such a voice to him from the excellent glory, This is my beloved Son, in whom I am well pleased.

18. And this voice which came from heaven we heard, when we were with him in the holy mount.

Peter informs the readers that their faith is not founded upon "cunningly devised fables" (v. 16). A fable is a myth that contains just enough truth to be enticing and believable, but twists the truth to present the ideas of the myth's teacher. The purpose is to impose the beliefs of the myth's presenter upon the hearers. Since a myth is a human invention, not divine revelation, it does not possess power to help anyone live according to the supposed teachings of the myth. This leads to discouragement and bondage (see 1 Timothy 1:4; Titus 1:14-16), as the hearer is unable to live out the expectations of the myth and is always dependent on the myth's teacher for further clarification and understanding.

These fables are contrasted to the truthful eyewitness accounts of the apostles and others who witnessed the powerful ministry of Jesus Christ. Peter is not presenting something he has heard or invented, but something he witnessed and experienced. Contrary to the powerless fables, the apostle reminds the readers of the power inherent within the gospel of Jesus Christ (see Romans 1:16). They too have experienced His redemptive and sustaining power (2 Peter 1:1-4). Further, knowledge of His imminent return produces (through the power of the Spirit) the desire and ability to live a godly life.

Jesus' role as the true revelation of God is solidified through Peter's recounting of the Transfiguration account (v. 17). Peter, James and John witnessed the special recognition ("honor") and radiant splendor ("glory") bestowed upon Jesus, especially upon the Mount of Transfiguration (see Matthew 17:1-10). *Honor* is something one achieves through accomplishment. *Glory* is a divine attribute that Christ shares with the Father. This verse not only emphasizes the importance of the redemptive work of Christ, but also His unity with the Father and His role in the Trinity. The declaration of the Father ("This is my beloved Son . . .") is a fulfillment of the Servant Song of Isaiah 42:1-7, a prophecy of the nature of Jesus' ministry on earth. In His pronouncement, the Father acknowledges that (1) He has

Talk About It:
1. What did Peter witness, and why was this significant?
2. How did God the Father publicly testify that Jesus is His Son?

Scattered Light
John Calvin once asked why God does not take all Christians and place us together in one protected place, if He were only concerned about our holiness. He noted instead that God scatters us in various places and situations in this sinful world, so that His holiness can be shared through our lives. We are to be beacons of light shining in the darkness, not lights hid under a basket (Matthew 5:14-16). Our influence in this world is founded on our relationship with God, and that relationship is revealed in part through our influence upon this world.
—Keith Whitt

sent the Son; (2) as the Son is loved, so are those who are in Him; (3) those who accept the Son receive His benefits; and (4) the redemptive work of the Son pleases the Father, therefore our salvation and standing are secure.

Peter reveals his Hebraic roots when he mentions the voice from "the Excellent Glory," (*NKJV*). The Jews were very careful to treat the name of God with care, honor and reverence; therefore, they often substituted other words to refer to God without using His name (called *circumlocution*). This is quite a contrast to those who use God's names as bywords, often without thinking. In Hebraic thought, the name was equal to the person, thus to invoke the name was to summons the person's presence. We must be careful that we do not become careless in our treatment of the divine names of the Godhead.

The apostle emphasizes that "we ourselves heard the declaration that came out of heaven" (v. 18, author's translation). Peter is not a creator of fables, but a credible eyewitness, willing to lay down his life for the cause of Christ (see vv. 13, 14). Because Peter calls the place "the holy mount," some have seen Mount Zion as the place of the Transfiguration. Others view mounts Hermon or Tabor as the place. Peter's emphasis is not on the physical location, but rather the Person honored and the manifestation of God's glory and presence which made the mountain (wherever it was) a sacred and holy place.

> "Reality is only one door—a narrow one—but it leads to life."
> —Paul Fromer

B. The Veracity of Scripture (vv. 19-21)

19. We have also a more sure word of prophecy; whereunto ye do well that ye take heed, as unto a light that shineth in a dark place, until the day dawn, and the day star arise in your hearts:

20. Knowing this first, that no prophecy of the scripture is of any private interpretation.

21. For the prophecy came not in old time by the will of man: but holy men of God spake as they were moved by the Holy Ghost.

Talk About It:
1. How is Biblical truth like "a light shining in a dark place" (v. 19, *NIV*)?
2. What is the source of genuine prophecy? What is not its source?

Peter emphasized the apostles' role (vv. 16, 18) as witnesses of Jesus Christ (God's perfect revelation) and the Father's own confirmation of the Beloved Son (v. 17) to contrast fables with true revelation. Now he emphasizes another aspect of divine revelation—the unfailing prophetic word (v. 19). He states that "the word of prophecy" is more "sure" (trustworthy) than the fables of the false teachers. The test of prophecy is its fulfillment (Deuteronomy 18:22). God has confirmed His Word through Jesus Christ (Acts 10:37-40), His messengers (Mark 16:20), and His Spirit (1 Thessalonians 1:5). The fables of the false teachers are contrasted with divine revelation.

Opinion is divided over whether the prophetic word is a reference to (1) the Old Testament, usually called "the Scriptures" in the New Testament; (2) the teachings and writings of the apostles; or (3) prophecies given by the Spirit to direct the church. At the time Peter wrote this epistle, the entire New Testament had not been completed and recognized as the inspired Word of God. Therefore, many believe Peter is emphasizing the role of the Old Testament in confirming the person and work of Jesus Christ. There is no doubt that He is the fulfillment of the Old Testament. With good reason Augustine declared, "The Old Testament is the New Testament concealed. The New Testament is the Old Testament revealed." It may be that Peter is intentionally comprehensive, allowing for the prophetic word to refer to God's communication with His people, no matter the source.

His command is clear. They must pay close attention to and obey ("heed") the real prophetic word. If it is of God, it must not be ignored. *Heed* originally meant "to bring a ship to its proper port." Apparently, the false teachers were telling the readers to ignore the teaching of Peter and the apostles, a common problem in the early church (see Galatians 1:7-9). It is also a problem that has not gone away and always results in a spiritual shipwreck. He informs them that the prophetic word is like "a light that shineth in a dark place." The word for *dark* occurs only here in the New Testament and carries the idea of a dirty, dismal place devoid of light. It speaks to the spiritual condition of those without the light of God. Light draws attention, pierces the darkness, illuminates its surroundings, and provides the ability for the eye to focus on reality rather than perception. This light will bring forth the dawn of a new day and the revelation of Jesus Christ ("day star") in their lives and hearts in the present, as well as in the future when He appears for His church.

Peter calls special attention to what follows through the phrase "knowing this first" (v. 20). He is not speaking of chronological order, but rather the priority of the information, that is, "First and foremost understand this" (author's translation). The apostle gives teaching that has been interpreted in two different but complementary ways.

First, verse 20 has been understood as saying no one person has the only interpretation of any scripture. The Lord is a God of relationship who wants to reveal Himself to all His people, not reserve the understanding of His Word for elite factions or select individuals. As well, God and His Word are multifaceted and can minister to each of us in different ways, based on where we are in our walk with Him and the situations we face. This does not mean we can interpret Scripture any way we choose. Our interpretations and applications of spiritual things are subject to critique and confirmation by other believers

"The Old Testament prophecies were not the result of human imagination but the result of the Holy Spirit's activity. In 2 Peter 2:20, 21 the prophets are likened to sailors who have raised the sails of their ships, and the Holy Spirit [is likened] to the wind which carries them along in the direction of His choosing."

—J. Christopher Thomas

(1 Corinthians 14:29) and must not violate other scriptures.

Second, the verse has been understood to say Scripture is God-breathed, not humanly inspired. It came solely through the will of God (v. 21). Holy men of God spoke from God only after they were moved by Him through the Holy Spirit (2 Samuel 23:2). This is a beautiful depiction of the symmetry that transpires in our spiritual walk with God. He calls, moves and inspires. We hear, respond and flow in the power of the Spirit. He does not violate our wills and we cannot usurp His. It is this networking of the divine and human wills that results in God's plan being accomplished.

II. WARNING AGAINST FALSE TEACHERS (2 Peter 2:1-10)
A. The Deceitfulness of Heresy (vv. 1-3)

1. But there were false prophets also among the people, even as there shall be false teachers among you, who privily shall bring in damnable heresies, even denying the Lord that bought them, and bring upon themselves swift destruction.

2. And many shall follow their pernicious ways; by reason of whom the way of truth shall be evil spoken of.

3. And through covetousness shall they with feigned words make merchandise of you: whose judgment now of a long time lingereth not, and their damnation slumbereth not.

Talk About It:
1. What identifies someone as a false prophet?
2. Why do many people follow false prophets?
3. According to verse 3, what is the motive of false prophets? What will their end be?

The apostle makes a deliberate shift ("but") in his teaching to address a serious issue (v. 1). He recalls Israel's almost continual struggle with false prophets to inform the readers that there are and shall be false teachers of the same kind. False prophets and teachers presumptively speak for God when He has not spoken (Deuteronomy 18:20). These false prophets promote rebellion against God (13:5), commit and promote spiritual adultery (Jeremiah 23:14), afflict the righteous through their lies (Ezekiel 13:22), and build illusions and false hope (22:28). The content of their message is *heresy*, a word that means "choice" or "option." It is not just the dissemination or spreading of blatantly false doctrine, though it certainly encompasses this. It is also a person choosing what he or she will believe without regard for the truth of God. It is an attitude that says, "I don't care what the Bible says; I know what I believe!" Heresies place those who embrace them in a path that leads to eternal hell ("destruction").

One heresy in particular is highlighted by Peter: denying Jesus Christ, the "sovereign Lord" (*NIV*). Jesus forewarned the apostles that this would happen and others would present themselves as the hope of the church (Matthew 24:4, 5). Apparently, these false teachers had been a part of the early church, for they had been redeemed ("bought") by the Lord.

Standing for Truth and Righteousness

This term carries the idea of being purchased or redeemed from the slave market (see 1 Corinthians 7:23; Revelation 5:9). Their foolish renunciation of Jesus Christ results in "swift destruction" or eternal punishment that they "bring upon themselves."

Their messages of deceit (Matthew 7:15) and destruction cause many to embrace a lifestyle that is enticing and gratifies the senses (see Hebrews 11:25), but result in their eternal punishment. Teaching and preaching do affect our conduct. Actions begin as thoughts (Proverbs 23:7). Thus, we must exercise care concerning whom we listen to. These heresies not only affect those who embrace them, but also bring a reproach upon Christ, Christianity and the church ("the way of truth," 2 Peter 2:2).

The motivation of these false teachers is greed (v. 3). They approach believers with appealing but fabricated stories, and bring them into bondage so they can exploit them financially. However, God is aware of their deeds and warns in very descriptive terms that the verdict and resulting destruction will not be indefinitely prolonged.

B. The Certainty of Judgment (vv. 4-10)

4. For if God spared not the angels that sinned, but cast them down to hell, and delivered them into chains of darkness, to be reserved unto judgment;

5. And spared not the old world, but saved Noah the eighth person, a preacher of righteousness, bringing in the flood upon the world of the ungodly;

6. And turning the cities of Sodom and Gomorrha into ashes condemned them with an overthrow, making them an ensample unto those that after should live ungodly;

7. And delivered just Lot, vexed with the filthy conversation of the wicked:

8. (For that righteous man dwelling among them, in seeing and hearing, vexed his righteous soul from day to day with their unlawful deeds;)

9. The Lord knoweth how to deliver the godly out of temptations, and to reserve the unjust unto the day of judgment to be punished.

10. But chiefly them that walk after the flesh in the lust of uncleanness, and despise government. Presumptuous are they, selfwilled, they are not afraid to speak evil of dignities.

To further emphasize the certainty of judgment, Peter uses three examples of previous judgments. First, the "angels that sinned" (v. 4) have already been cast into the abode for those who violated the will of God and now have no hope. Their abiding place is one of deep gloom and thick darkness. Their only reprieve is when they stand before God for final judgment.

> "First Timothy 4:1 warns us that in the last days deceiving spirits will teach the doctrines of demons. Today, religious cults and charlatans abound. The reason these deceivers draw many people is the power of the demonic that teaches them."
>
> —Ron Phillips

1. What was God's judgment against the angels who rebelled against Him? Against the world in Noah's day? Against Sodom and Gomorrah?
2. How did God intervene in Noah's and Lot's behalf? Why? What does this say to Christians today?
3. According to verse 10, who faces certain condemnation? Why?

Scripture does not provide many details of the angels' fall. Two possibilities have been offered: These angels are (1) the "sons of God" who cohabitated with the "daughters of men" and grieved God (Genesis 6:1-4) or (2) the ones who followed Satan when he rebelled against God's authority (Isaiah 14:12-15). The latter is preferable, as angels are spiritual beings and do not marry or procreate (Matthew 22:30).

Second, the Flood (Genesis 6:5–8:19; 2 Peter 2:5) is noted as an example of judgment upon the rampant wickedness of the ancient world. Only Noah, a proclaimer of righteousness, and seven other souls escaped. Third, the destruction of Sodom and Gomorrah into ashes (Genesis 19:24-29; 2 Peter 2:6, 7) is presented as a deterrent for those who would live apart from God.

In these three examples, Peter also emphasizes the vindication or exoneration of the righteous. Mercy always precedes judgment, and judgment is always redemptive. Final judgment may not be redemptive for those who ignored God's provision of salvation, but it is redemptive for the righteous in that they and their dependency upon God are vindicated. The angels who did not rebel against God, Noah and his family, and Lot and his family were vindicated through God's judgment of those who rejected His grace. The faith of the righteous, pilgrims in the midst of a world that lives contrary to God's Word, is vindicated (v. 8). The message is clear—God takes care of those who are His (v. 9; see also 1 Corinthians 10:13) and deals with those who are not, even those who are not afraid to blaspheme heavenly hosts ("dignitaries," 2 Peter 2:10, *NKJV*).

III. CONSEQUENCES OF TURNING FROM RIGHTEOUSNESS (2 Peter 2:11-22)
A. A Righteous Position (v. 11)
11. Whereas angels, which are greater in power and might, bring not railing accusation against them before the Lord.

Talk About It:
What lesson can we learn from angels?

Angels are lifted up as an example of how to be righteous in the midst of sinners. Though they are mightier than the false teachers and those who follow them, they do not pronounce a reviling judgment ("railing accusation") against them (or the fallen angels) before the Lord. They leave judgment to God, to whom it belongs (1 Corinthians 4:5).

B. The Nature of Unrighteousness (vv. 12-16)
12. But these, as natural brute beasts, made to be taken and destroyed, speak evil of the things that they understand not; and shall utterly perish in their own corruption;
13. And shall receive the reward of unrighteousness, as they that count it pleasure to riot in the day time. Spots they are and blemishes, sporting themselves with their

own deceivings while they feast with you;

14. Having eyes full of adultery, and that cannot cease from sin; beguiling unstable souls: an heart they have exercised with covetous practices; cursed children:

15. Which have forsaken the right way, and are gone astray, following the way of Balaam the son of Bosor, who loved the wages of unrighteousness;

16. But was rebuked for his iniquity: the dumb ass speaking with man's voice forbad the madness of the prophet.

The carnal nature of these false teachers is depicted through the comparison with animals devoid of spiritual understanding and rational thought (v. 12). It is a stark contrast between the spiritual and natural realms. God has created us as human beings, the crown jewel of His creation, which He pronounced as "very good" (Genesis 1:31). Only humanity is created in His image and has received the breath of God (1:26; 2:7). Yet, the false teachers have yielded to the baser nature of created order. They blaspheme, or slander ("speak evil") in areas of which they are ignorant. Their own depravity will bring about their eternal fate (2 Peter 2:12), the consequence ("reward of unrighteousness," v. 13) for injustice inflicted upon those whom they have led astray and fleeced, breaking the laws of God, and the lack of proper relationship with God. They are consumed with hedonistic pleasure, openly indulging in deceit and carousing. Their chosen lifestyle, however, has overtaken them and causes them to be addicted to illicit desires and insatiable sin, which results in their desire to ensnare others and bring them into the mire with them (v. 14).

Misery truly does love company. Such is the nature of sin. Its tentacles reach farther and hold longer than is humanly possible to escape. Sin is never satisfied, but requires a person to sink deeper and deeper into depravity for the "pleasure" or euphoria. Neither is it content to be practiced alone, but seeks to entangle others also.

The folly of these false teachers is highlighted through a comparison with Balaam (vv. 15, 16), whose own greed motivated him to attempt to curse the children of Israel (Numbers 22—24). A person who could have willingly been used by God to pronounce great spiritual blessings was rebuked by a voiceless donkey. The irony is anything but subtle—even one of the most stubborn animals had enough sense to listen to and be used by God, unlike these false teachers.

C. The Deceptive Bondage of Unrighteousness (vv. 17-22)

17. These are wells without water, clouds that are carried with a tempest; to whom the mist of darkness is reserved for ever.

18. For when they speak great swelling words of vanity,

Talk About It:
1. How are false leaders like "brute beasts" (v. 12)? What awaits them?
2. How are false teachers like "spots" (blots) and "blemishes" (vv. 13, 14)?
3. How did these false teachers once walk, and what drew them away?

"From the beginning of days to the present, the pattern of apostasy is the same: Satan does not stop worship—he perverts it, and turns it to error; he pollutes it, and makes it mean; he redirects it, from God to himself. He takes advantage of man's worshipful nature, twisting it to his own ends. That is the way of apostasy old and of apostasy new."

—Charles W. Conn

they allure through the lusts of the flesh, through much wantonness, those that were clean escaped from them who live in error.

19. While they promise them liberty, they themselves are the servants of corruption: for of whom a man is overcome, of the same is he brought in bondage.

20. For if after they have escaped the pollutions of the world through the knowledge of the Lord and Saviour Jesus Christ, they are again entangled therein, and overcome, the latter end is worse with them than the beginning.

21. For it had been better for them not to have known the way of righteousness, than, after they have known it, to turn from the holy commandment delivered unto them.

22. But it is happened unto them according to the true proverb, The dog is turned to his own vomit again; and the sow that was washed to her wallowing in the mire.

Talk About It:

1. How are false prophets "wells without water" (v. 17)?

2. How do false prophets entice people to follow them (vv. 18, 19)?

3. Explain the proverbs quoted in verse 22.

Peter continues his analysis of the unrighteous false teachers by showing the emptiness of their teaching and lives. One can hear his emotion and purposely emphatic concern in his writing. "*These people* are waterless springs and mist blown away by a gust of wind; *for these* the gloominess and darkness of hell stands waiting" (v. 17, author's translation). They carry the appearance of substance (refreshing water), but cannot back up the appearance with true life-giving teaching. The revelation of their deception and destruction is certain, if not imminent.

Their empty words appeal to the passions of the flesh and sensuality (v. 18). Their intent is to entice those who are weaker in their faith, because they have just begun their journey in Christ. The teachers promise freedom but deliver only bondage—a deathly bondage that has them ensnared as well (v. 19). Anything we allow to defeat us brings us into slavery. Peter graphically illustrates this in verses 20-22. It is a stark reminder that failure in our relationship with God has severe consequences (see Matthew 12:43-45). Thank God, Jesus Christ is the great Liberator for all who call upon Him, even Christians who succumb to sin's temptations!

CONCLUSION

We must be careful of the teaching we receive, and any teaching must agree with the Bible's presentation of truth (John 14:6), enable its readers to live according to the will of God (1 Peter 4:6), and not question the centrality and lordship of Jesus Christ (1 Corinthians 12:3). Our focus must be upon the power, prominence and position of Christ.

GOLDEN TEXT CHALLENGE

"THE PROPHECY CAME NOT IN OLD TIME BY THE WILL OF MAN: BUT HOLY MEN OF GOD SPAKE AS THEY

Standing for Truth and Righteousness

WERE MOVED BY THE HOLY GHOST" (2 Peter 1:21).

Bible prophecy did not proceed from the prophet's own knowledge or invention, nor was it the result of the prophet's calculation or conjecture. The prophecies of the Bible did not originate in the minds of men. They originated in the mind of God.

The kind of persons God used to be His mouthpieces were "holy men of God." God is particular about the quality of the people who work for Him. He chooses people who are holy, sincere and dedicated.

The prophecies which the "holy men of God" gave were God-inspired. The prophets were moved upon by the Holy Spirit to make the statements they made. They were "in the Spirit" and were directed by Him in what they wrote.

We should have total confidence in the Scriptures. They are the highest authority in matters of doctrine and behavior. We know this because holy men of God wrote the Bible in accordance with the direction they received from the Holy Spirit.

Daily Devotions:

M. Nurtured by Truth
Deuteronomy 6:1-9

T. Purified by the Word
Psalm 119:9-16

W. Turning From Righteousness Brings Judgment
Jeremiah 5:14-19

T. Abiding in God Brings Freedom
John 8:31-47

F. The Scripture Leads to Salvation
2 Timothy 3:10-16

S. Follow Sound Doctrine
2 Timothy 4:1-11

Anticipate Christ's Coming

2 Peter 3:1-18

Unit Theme:
Peter and Jude

Central Truth:
The believer lives in anticipation of Christ's coming.

Focus:
To realize that Christ's coming is certain and live in anticipation of His return.

Context:
A general epistle written by the apostle Peter around A.D. 67 to warn its readers of threatening apostasy.

Golden Text:
"Nevertheless we, according to his promise, look for new heavens and a new earth, wherein dwelleth righteousness" (2 Peter 3:13).

Study Outline:
I. Resist Indifference to Christ's Coming (2 Peter 3:1-7)
II. Accept the Certainty of Christ's Coming (2 Peter 3:8-10)
III. Look Forward to Christ's Coming (2 Peter 3:11-18)

INTRODUCTION

Biblical writers emphasize various themes. For example, Luke is concerned with the despised or forgotten people of society (the poor, slaves, publicans and women). Paul's letters call attention to the benefits of the redemptive work of Jesus Christ. Some themes are found in practically every New Testament book, such as the Second Coming. It is *the* prominent theme in 2 Peter.

Every Christian faces times of discouragement, weariness, troubling circumstances, or lack of motivation. Often, all it takes to help turn these difficult times around is a reminder that we are pilgrims, not permanent residents of this present age. The Martins recorded a song that reminds us "it came to pass, not to stay." This is true of circumstances *and* this world as we know it. God's plan will cause everything to change for the better.

In chapter 3, Peter focuses on the certainty of the return of Jesus Christ and its ability to motivate us, a theme he introduces early in this epistle (1:16). He presents it in language of power and ability. An awareness that Jesus can return at any time promotes righteousness and holiness in our lives. When we are in proper relationship with God, other relationships are affected positively as well. When there is wholeness of heart, our circumstances are less troubling.

The Second Coming often receives a lot of attention for brief periods, especially during times of crisis. For example, in the days following September 11, 2001, an awareness that we live in the end times motivated multitudes to get right with God. When people adjusted to this life-changing event and returned to normal routines, awareness of the times began to fade.

There are myriads of things in the Bible that need to be preached or taught; thus, it is not practical (nor even healthy) for ministers and teachers to focus solely on the Second Coming. However, the apostle's message reminds us we need to be so aware of the times (see 1 Chronicles 12:32) that we perform our ministries and live out our witness with an understanding that this could be the day Jesus returns. An awareness of the Second Coming needs to be inscribed into our spiritual consciousness, even during the mundane times. It will inspire us to follow the pattern of life set by the One to whom we belong.

I. RESIST INDIFFERENCE TO CHRIST'S COMING
(2 Peter 3:1-7)
A. Remembrance and Recall (vv. 1, 2)

1. This second epistle, beloved, I now write unto you; in both which I stir up your pure minds by way of remembrance:

2. That ye may be mindful of the words which were spoken before by the holy prophets, and of the commandment of us the apostles of the Lord and Saviour.

The apostle reveals a tender, pastoral side when he calls his readers "beloved." The term is used four times in this chapter concerning the readers (vv. 1, 8, 14, 17), and serves four purposes: (1) It invokes the image and example of Jesus Christ, who is the beloved Son of the Father, and all He has accomplished for them (1:17). (2) It communicates clearly that not only are they the recipients of Peter's love, but they are worthy of that love. (3) There is a bond between Peter and his readers that is unlike the greedy false teachers who do not have their interests at heart. (4) It also serves as a literary marker that signifies subsections of thought in this chapter. In reading Scripture, it helps to be aware of these types of indicators (e.g., "therefore," "but," and "thus") that emphasize pertinent information.

The writer states this is his "second epistle," a reminder that he also wrote 1 Peter. This reemphasizes his continued commitment to his readers and serves to bring to their minds the content of that letter, which encourages those facing persecution to live in obedience and anticipation of Christ's return.

In both epistles his intent is to "stir up your pure minds by way of reminder" (v. 1, *NKJV*). This has been understood in two ways. First, "pure minds" is viewed as a way of thinking that has been tested. Thus, he writes to awake within them the memory of the authentic doctrine they have received from apostolic teaching and writing. In times of crisis, it is helpful to reexamine the basics to reestablish proper thinking and perspective. Second, the phrase can be understood as a desire to arouse a pure disposition or attitude. No doubt, the false teachers' attitudes had infiltrated their minds and were affecting their personalities and relationships with Peter and other Christians.

Both understandings are possible, but the first is preferable in light of verse 2. Peter wanted them to recall that which they had received from the Old Testament ("holy prophets," who foretold of Christ), as well as the apostles, commissioned by and messengers of the Lord and Savior. They have also foretold the promise of the return of the One who is not just the Savior of their souls, but also the Lord to whom they must submit all things. This is the idea behind "the commandment." It is not a reference to one commandment, but the totality of the

Talk About It:
1. How should Christians think?
2. What must believers remember?

"When my gasoline tank registers empty, I know it is full—that is, it is full of air. But the automobile was not built to run on air. To displace the air, I must fill it with gasoline. God's cure for evil thinking is to fill our minds with that which is good."
—**George Sweeting**

apostles' teaching concerning Christ. If the readers remember the truth they have received, their theology will be pure, and it will fashion proper attitudes and forge godly character.

B. Scoffers as a Sign (vv. 3, 4)

3. Knowing this first, that there shall come in the last days scoffers, walking after their own lusts,

4. And saying, Where is the promise of his coming? for since the fathers fell asleep, all things continue as they were from the beginning of the creation.

The apostle continues his appeal to his readers' memories and knowledge. The false teachers have appealed to their emotions and have led some astray (2:1-3). These teachers are characterized and controlled by their own illicit desires. Peter appeals to the believers' minds and memory to help them regain their spiritual equilibrium, for emotions can deceive (Jeremiah 17:9). This does not, however, diminish the role of emotions in our spiritual walk. We are emotional beings and that should be a part of our worship and character. Emotions must have a proper foundation, and part of that foundation is a mind that has been transformed and maintains consciousness of God (see Luke 6:45). Proper knowledge and understanding are very important in this epistle (see 2 Peter 1:2, 3, 5, 6, 8; 2:12, 20; 3:18). Peter repeats a phrase used earlier, "knowing this first" (1:20), which serves to emphasize the importance of the information he is communicating.

Ironically, the false teachers who mock the belief of Christ's return are themselves a sign of the last days. Study of the future (the events associated with the end of the world) and the final destiny of humanity is known as *eschatology*. The New Testament makes it clear that we are living in the last days, just as the epistle's original readers were. These last days were ushered in by the ministry of Jesus Christ (Hebrews 1:2). Pentecost was a confirming sign that humanity is headed for the final hour (Acts 2:17).

Verse 4 of the lesson text is a direct citation of the false teachers' views. Their language is that of taunting and mockery, something God's people have endured in history (see Psalm 42:3; Jeremiah 17:15). In today's "civilized" world, the taunting might be less direct, but just as offensive. Christians are often depicted in the media as inept and ignorant buffoons who are committed more to a radical political ideology than their morals. We are in a hostile world and we must be careful of the image of Christ that we project. The false teachers' logic is, Since Christ has not yet returned, He is not coming; things will continue as they have. Jesus taught through parables that the master does not always return in the time frame anticipated by the servants

Talk About It:
1. Why do scoffers scoff?
2. Is the statement "All things continue as they were from the beginning" true? Why or why not?

Broken Barometer?
In 1938 a man with a home on the south shore of Long Island ordered a barometer from a sporting goods store. It arrived on the morning of September 21, and the owner hung it on the back porch. Half an hour later he peeked at this high-priced toy only to find the needle stuck at "Hurricane."
Quickly he wrote a letter demanding a new barometer. When he returned home from the post office from mailing the letter, both barometer and house were missing. September 21, 1938, it turned out, was the day of the worst hurricane to ever hit Long Island.
—Bits & Pieces

Anticipate Christ's Coming

(Matthew 24–25; see also 1 Thessalonians 4:13-18). The message of the New Testament is one of continual preparedness, "Therefore you also be ready, for the Son of Man is coming at an hour you do not expect" (Matthew 24:44, *NKJV*).

C. Certain Judgment (vv. 5-7)

5. For this they willingly are ignorant of, that by the word of God the heavens were of old, and the earth standing out of the water and in the water:

6. Whereby the world that then was, being overflowed with water, perished:

7. But the heavens and the earth, which are now, by the same word are kept in store, reserved unto fire against the day of judgment and perdition of ungodly men.

The false teachers' Stoic philosophy (common in the first century) of God's inability or lack of desire to intervene in the world order (v. 4) is one of willful ignorance of the fact that God spoke the universe into existence (v. 5). Peter draws from the Creation account. Out of the midst of watery chaos, God brought order (Genesis 1:2, 6, 7). When that world was disobedient, He brought judgment through the Flood (2 Peter 3:6). Through the sustaining Word of God, the world is reserved for judgment because of ungodliness. Peter's message can be summarized as such: If you want to know what God is going to do in the future, look at what He has done in the past. He has been active in the world, fulfilling His promises, redeeming His people, and judging the disobedient. He has not stopped just because the teachers do not understand His timing.

Talk About It:
1. What have scoffers forgotten (or not believed) about the past?
2. What do scoffers not know (or disbelieve) about the future?

II. ACCEPT THE CERTAINTY OF CHRIST'S COMING
(2 Peter 3:8-10)
A. Time and Eternity (v. 8)

8. But, beloved, be not ignorant of this one thing, that one day is with the Lord as a thousand years, and a thousand years as one day.

To help his readers understand the timing of the Second Coming from God's perspective, Peter draws from Old Testament teaching, "For a thousand years in Your sight are like yesterday when it is past, and like a watch in the night" (Psalm 90:4, *NKJV*). It reemphasizes what he has told them about learning from the prophets (see v. 2). As well, it provides a proper perspective from which to understand God's seeming delay and serves to warn that when Jesus returns, it will be suddenly, as humanity's understanding of time and God's eternal perspective do not always coincide. Thus, the problem of time is a human one, not God's.

Just as Psalm 90:4 has been used by Jewish writers as the

Talk About It:
What does verse 8 reveal about God's view of time?

formula for understanding earth's chronology, this verse has been used to predict the timing of Jesus' return. This view presupposes that there are seven "days" (7,000 years) in God's chronology for the earth, corresponding to the seven days of Creation. Such a view has been seriously challenged by modern scholars, even conservative ones. The apostle's point in 2 Peter 3:8 is that our understanding of time does not correspond to God's understanding. It is best to live our lives as though Jesus will return today, but conduct the business of the Kingdom wisely until He does come (Luke 19:13).

B. Delay or Mercy? (v. 9)

9. The Lord is not slack concerning his promise, as some men count slackness; but is longsuffering to usward, not willing that any should perish, but that all should come to repentance.

Talk About It:
1. What is the connection between God's patience and His promise?
2. What is God's will for all people?

Peter reveals the false teachers were ignorant of God's character. A perceived delay in the return of the Lord actually points to God's mercy and patience—characteristics seen in the Old Testament (Exodus 34:6; Jonah 4:2). Judgment and wrath are subject to God's ultimate desire to see repentance by those who are not in a proper relationship with Him. As noted, mercy always precedes judgment. God is not a tyrant who desires to punish people. Punishment is always His last resort and is not designed to be retributive or harmful, but to bring the person back to Him. God's desire is that absolutely no one spend eternity in hell, but that everyone find life in Christ. The language indicates He will do everything He can to accomplish this goal, except violate a person's will.

C. Judgment and Renewal (v. 10)

10. But the day of the Lord will come as a thief in the night; in the which the heavens shall pass away with a great noise, and the elements shall melt with fervent heat, the earth also and the works that are therein shall be burned up.

Talk About It:
1. How will "the day of the Lord . . . come as a thief in the night" (v. 10)?
2. How will God transform the earth?

The opportunity for repentance will only last for the period of time prescribed by the sovereignty of God. "The day of the Lord will come" quickly and unexpectedly (see also Matthew 24:42, 43; 1 Thessalonians 5:2). This phrase is drawn from the Old Testament and includes, but is more comprehensive than, the appearance of Jesus Christ for His church (Isaiah 13:9; Joel 2:11). It encompasses all of the climactic end-time events, but particularly emphasizes the outpouring of God's wrath upon evil (Obadiah 1:15). It signifies the end of this age and the preparation for the transformation of all things, including heaven and earth. Sin's presence and effects will be removed by

Anticipate Christ's Coming

fervent heat from earth (because of humanity's sin) and the heavens, presumably because of Satan's rebellion and dominion therein (Ephesians 6:12). Creation will be returned to its original sin-free state.

Most Pentecostals and Evangelicals have traditionally embraced a pre-Tribulation Rapture doctrine. In this view, first there will be the personal return of Jesus Christ in the clouds to resurrect the dead in Christ and rapture the church (John 14:1-3; Acts 1:10, 11; 1 Thessalonians 4:13-18). This ushers in the Tribulation, a period of seven years of God's wrath upon the sin of the world. During this Tribulation period, the Antichrist arises (2 Thessalonians 2:8; 1 John 2:18-22; Revelation 13). At the end of the Tribulation, the Battle of Armageddon is fought when Christ returns to the earth (Revelation 19:11-20). The return of Christ in the clouds and then to the earth is known as the Second Coming—one advent (arrival) with two events. Following this will come a thousand-year reign of Christ (20:6-10) and then the Great White Throne Judgment (vv. 11-15). The final scene in this scenario is the revelation of a new heaven and new earth (21:1-4). There may be differences concerning the chronology, but most conservative Christians agree these events will lead to the close of this age and the beginning of the new era of life as God designed it to be.

"Why predict what Christ has already promised? If you trust the promise of His return you won't be tempted to chase predictions [of His return]."
—David C. Cooper

III. LOOK FORWARD TO CHRIST'S COMING
(2 Peter 3:11-18)
A. Belief and Behavior (vv. 11-13)

11. Seeing then that all these things shall be dissolved, what manner of persons ought ye to be in all holy conversation and godliness,

12. Looking for and hasting unto the coming of the day of God, wherein the heavens being on fire shall be dissolved, and the elements shall melt with fervent heat?

13. Nevertheless we, according to his promise, look for new heavens and a new earth, wherein dwelleth righteousness.

In light of the awesomeness of this day, a day in which everything will be subject to God, the apostle asks his readers a very pointed question: "What manner of persons ought you to be in holy conduct and godliness?" (v. 11, *NKJV*). Peter understands that belief affects behavior. In fact, one could say that behavior is a true indicator of belief. If a person believes in the soon return of the Lord, it will be evident in behavior that reflects the holiness and character of God.

In a shift of focus ("nevertheless," v. 13) and a pastoral tone, Peter reminds them that on the basis of God's promise, they await the revelation of new heavens and a new earth (see

Talk About It:
1. How should the promise of Christ's coming influence our daily living?
2. What will characterize the "new heavens" and "new earth"?

Powerful Motivator
As a teenager, I came home one evening only to find our house unlocked with the lights and television on and nobody home. It was very uncharacteristic of my parents to do this. When I could find them nowhere, my heart began to pound with fear that Jesus had come and I was left behind. I picked up the phone and called the parsonage. When Pastor Haislip answered, I immediately hung up and breathed a sigh of relief! An awareness of Christ's sudden and soon return has been with me ever since. It is a powerful motivator.
—Keith Whitt

Talk About It:
1. What does it mean to "be found of him in peace" (v. 14)?
2. Explain the statement "Our Lord's patience means salvation" (v. 15, *NIV*).
3. What will happen to people who distort the Scriptures?

Isaiah 65:17; Revelation 21:1). The implication is that they will be the residents of the new world if they stand on the true foundation they have received and are not deceived by the false teachers' heresies. In this place God has designed for the redeemed, righteousness will be at home. In Scripture, righteousness is revealed as a power or force from God (Psalm 97:2) that enables right relationship (Isaiah 42:6) and empowers individuals to live life as God intended (Amos 5:24). Peter is informing them that not only has God provided the means whereby they can live a righteous life now, one day they will live where righteousness dwells because God dwells there (see Jeremiah 33:16).

B. Looking and Pressing Forward (vv. 14-16)
14. Wherefore, beloved, seeing that ye look for such things, be diligent that ye may be found of him in peace, without spot, and blameless.
15. And account that the longsuffering of our Lord is salvation; even as our beloved brother Paul also according to the wisdom given unto him hath written unto you;
16. As also in all his epistles, speaking in them of these things; in which are some things hard to be understood, which they that are unlearned and unstable wrest, as they do also the other scriptures, unto their own destruction.

The apocalyptic language of fire and destruction is not meant to scare people, but to motivate us to see things correctly—that is, from God's perspective. It also enables us to see the provision of God for believers, including the new heavens and earth, even in the midst of judgment. Consequently, we must make every effort with haste ("be diligent") to manifest four characteristics in particular when Jesus returns (vv. 14, 15): (1) be free from anxiety ("in peace"); (2) remain pure and uncorrupted ("without spot"); (3) be morally "blameless" and without reproach; and (4) manifest patient steadfastness in the midst of difficulty ("longsuffering"), which is a virtue of Christ. These things help assure final salvation and deliverance.

In a parenthetical section, Peter mentions "our beloved brother Paul" and his writings, which confirm what Peter is saying (vv. 15, 16). Subtly, it reminds the readers that people and situations can change. In Galatians 2:11-14, Paul confronted Peter concerning his actions, but now Paul is "beloved." God can turn even the most contentious of situations around.

Even at this early stage of the church, the writings of the apostles were recognized as the inspired Word of God. Yet even Peter had trouble understanding some of Paul's writings (v. 16). Like us, Peter needed the Holy Spirit to be his Teacher.

Anticipate Christ's Coming

C. Final Admonition and Praise (vv. 17, 18)

17. Ye therefore, beloved, seeing ye know these things before, beware lest ye also, being led away with the error of the wicked, fall from your own stedfastness.

18. But grow in grace, and in the knowledge of our Lord and Saviour Jesus Christ. To him be glory both now and for ever. Amen.

Peter closes out his epistle reminding his readers they have been warned and now they need to manifest the essence of his teaching and the provision and knowledge of "our Lord and Saviour Jesus Christ." He closes with a doxology, or declaration of praise, unto the One who saves and keeps us—and who shall return again! "To him be glory [and honor] both now and forever! Amen" (v. 18, *NIV*).

Talk About It:
1. What must Christians guard against?
2. How can believers "grow in grace, and . . . knowledge" (v. 18)?

CONCLUSION

Peter has warned of both the danger and error of the false teachers' heresy. The doctrine of the Second Coming serves to motivate Christians to live in a way that is consistent with the example of Jesus, through knowledge of Him as revealed in the Old and New Testaments. As well, God's mercy should not be construed as aloofness or delay, for He is sending His Son again and preparing a place for those who serve Him—a place in which He reigns supremely!

GOLDEN TEXT CHALLENGE

"NEVERTHELESS WE, ACCORDING TO HIS PROMISE, LOOK FOR NEW HEAVENS AND A NEW EARTH, WHEREIN DWELLETH RIGHTEOUSNESS" (2 Peter 3:13).

Christians are forward lookers. Rather than dwelling on past victories and failures, we are to deal with the challenges of today while always anticipating the return and reign of Christ. In fact, it is the hope of a new world where righteousness rules that motivates us to live holy today.

God's promises are certain: Jesus will return, He will establish a new heaven and a new earth, righteousness will prevail, and Christ's righteous people will reign with Him.

Daily Devotions:
M. The King of Glory
   Psalm 24:7-10
T. Day of God's
   Wrath
   Isaiah 13:6-13
W. Day of God's
   Glory
   Daniel 7:9-14
T. Jesus Prepares
   Our Heavenly
   Home
   John 14:13-18
F. Comfort One
   Another
   1 Thessalonians
   4:13-18
S. Come Quickly,
   Lord Jesus
   Revelation 22:16-21

Bible Insight

Two Words About Christ's Return

In the New Testament a number of words are used for the return of Christ. But two terms in particular throw special light on the Lord's return: *presence* and *revelation*.

Presence (*Parousia*)

In the Biblical world the word *parousia* was used to speak of the coming or visit of a distinguished person, such as a king or emperor, and emphasized his personal presence. It literally means "being nearby," combining the ideas of "approach" and "arrival." It was used for the coming of a person to visit a church, as in Paul's phrase "*my coming* to you again" (Philippians 1:26). Peter spoke of the first *coming* of our Lord (2 Peter 1:16). Frequently the term is seen in passages about the second coming of our Lord, as when the disciples asked Jesus, "What will be the sign of Your coming?" (Matthew 24:3, *NKJV*; also see 1 Corinthians 15:23; 1 Thessalonians 2:19; 3:13; 4:15; 5:23; 2 Thessalonians 2:1, 8).

Christ was received up into heaven at His ascension, and at His return He will come from heaven (Acts 1:11; 1 Thessalonians 4:16). The term *parousia* stresses the literal return of Jesus of Nazareth. John's writings emphasize the importance of being ready to see Christ at His coming and assures us that if we abide in Christ, we will "not be ashamed before Him at His coming" (1 John 2:28, *NKJV*).

Revelation (*Apocalypsis*)

The Second Coming is also described as the *revelation* of Jesus Christ—the uncovering of something that has been veiled or hidden. In the New Testament, *revelation* has reference to the last days. The eternal Christ is now hidden from view, but He will be unveiled when He comes the second time. The writer of Hebrews said He will be seen by "those who eagerly wait for Him" (9:28, *NKJV*).

Christ's first coming was a revelation of Himself in human form, so those with faith could believe in Him (John 1:14). Now He is hidden from our view, although He is spiritually present with us to the end of the age (Matthew 28:20). So we wait for the revelation of our Lord in power and majesty at His glorious coming (1 Corinthians 1:7; 2 Thessalonians 1:7; 1 Peter 1:7, 13; 4:13).—**French Arrington**

Standing in the Faith

Jude 1-25

INTRODUCTION

There are two primary topics addressed in the Epistle of Jude. First, the issue of perseverance (vv. 3, 17, 20, 21) and preservation (vv. 1, 5, 20, 21, 24) is emphasized. These are two aspects of one theme, or two sides of the same coin—standing strong in the faith. God has the ability to keep us safe from all evil (preservation), even in the last days. Yet, God requires our participation. We must press on in the midst of spiritual struggles and battles; we must take care in what we feed our souls and spirits (perseverance). We cannot be detracted from our goal by those who do not have our interests at heart.

Second, Jude exposes the ungodliness and deceptiveness of the false teachers who had reinfiltrated the church. These "wandering stars" (v. 13) were promoting false doctrine or heresy to the readers of Jude. This was causing many to question their faith, the teachings they received, and even the lordship of Jesus Christ. This confusion was causing Christians to stumble.

Jude and 2 Peter are similar in the material they present. They are both addressing the same basic concerns in the early church and probably were combating the same false teachers. Jude quotes from and extensively parallels 2 Peter, thus it was most likely written shortly after Peter's death, somewhere around A.D. 67-69. This similarity, however, does not mean Jude is a repeat of 2 Peter. The writer presents valuable information that is found nowhere else in the New Testament. There is a strong Pentecostal undertone to the letter. Its size is not indicative of its importance.

The mood of the epistle is one of urgency and deep concern—even righteous indignation! The characterization of the false teachers is descriptive, illuminating and forthright. It was probably written in haste after Jude received word of the false teachers' presence and damaging doctrine, though he intended to write the recipients anyway (v. 3). It was not, however, written without care. It reflects a broad knowledge of the Old Testament, other writings of the New Testament, oral tradition, and Jewish apocalyptic literature. The epistle reflects the heart of a strong godly leader who is passionate in his protection of the faith and compassionate for those in the midst of the struggle. The message is still relevant.

Unit Theme:
Peter and Jude

Central Truth:
The Christian remains firm in the faith by God's grace and truth.

Focus:
To acknowledge the call to stand firm in the faith and trust Christ's keeping power.

Context:
Written about A.D. 66.

Golden Text:
"Keep yourselves in the love of God, looking for the mercy of our Lord Jesus Christ unto eternal life" (Jude 21).

Study Outline:
 I. Contend for the Faith
    (Jude 1-4)
 II. Remember God's Judgments
    (Jude 5-19)
III. Remain in Christ
    (Jude 20-25)

I. CONTEND FOR THE FAITH (Jude 1-4)

A. Blessings in Christ (vv. 1, 2)

1. Jude, the servant of Jesus Christ, and brother of James, to them that are sanctified by God the Father, and preserved in Jesus Christ, and called:

2. Mercy unto you, and peace, and love, be multiplied.

Talk About It:

Explain the three words Jude uses to describe Christians: "sanctified," "preserved," and "called."

The writer introduces himself as "Jude." Several people are named Jude (or Judas) in the New Testament, including Judas Iscariot (Mark 3:19), Paul's friend (Acts 9:11), the prophet (15:22-33), the apostle (Luke 6:16; also called Thaddeus, Mark 3:18), and Judas the half-brother of Jesus and brother of James (Mark 6:3). The writer could either be the apostle of Jesus or the half-brother of Jesus. Tradition points to the latter as the writer of this epistle.

Jude describes himself as a *bondservant* of Jesus Christ" (v. 1, *NKJV*), not an apostle. The foundation for this term is found in Exodus 21:1-6, where a poverty-stricken Hebrew could sell himself into slavery to another Hebrew for six years, but had to be released the seventh year. If the servant decided to stay with the family, he was presented before witnesses to the agreement, then taken to the master's house, and had his ear placed against the doorjamb. The master pierced through the servant's ear into the doorjamb with a sharp tool, signifying that the servant was willingly and permanently joined to the household. Thus Jude's description of himself as Christ's bondservant was a powerful image that explained his authority to write the letter.

The letter is written to those who are *called*, a term used as a designation for Christians (2 Timothy 1:9). They are called by God from sin to salvation (1 Corinthians 1:2), from bondage into liberty (Galatians 5:13), from darkness into light (1 Peter 2:9), and from the masses into the chosen people of God (Matthew 22:14). As well, believers are *sanctified* by God, which here emphasizes God's love enveloping believers in deep intimacy. They are loved with such intensity that they choose to love God supremely and allow that love to be visible in every area of life. Finally, they are *preserved*—guarded and protected through their relationship with Christ. The word also conveys that they are never out of His sight. Their lives are "in Jesus Christ."

In his greeting (v. 2), Jude desires for them three specific blessings: (1) *mercy*, the manifestation of God's compassion; (2) *peace*, a calmness of soul and spirit from being in Christ that quells the anxious heart (Isaiah 26:3); and (3) *love*, God's everlasting love (Jeremiah 31:3). These blessings, which Jude desires to be increased and intensified in their lives, emanate solely from God's grace.

B. Warriors for the Faith (vv. 3, 4)

3. Beloved, when I gave all diligence to write unto you of the common salvation, it was needful for me to write unto you, and exhort you that ye should earnestly contend for the faith which was once delivered unto the saints.

4. For there are certain men crept in unawares, who were before of old ordained to this condemnation, ungodly men, turning the grace of our God into lasciviousness, and denying the only Lord God, and our Lord Jesus Christ.

As stated above, Jude originally intended to write a letter concerning our "common salvation." He does not use "common" in the sense of that which is ordinary, but rather, that which is mutually shared. Like Peter (2 Peter 1:1), he understands and wants to communicate that their salvation is no different than his. The Enemy attempts to convince us that our salvation and standing with God is somehow deficient or different from "real" Christians. However, the blood of Jesus cleanses us and gives us a new standing with God, whether we are an apostle or the "least" of the saints (see Hebrews 9:14).

Instead, the crisis demanded that Jude encourage them to "contend for the faith" (v. 3). This statement is a call to spiritual warfare that includes: (1) making every effort necessary to remain dedicated and consecrated in the faith (a preventative measure); (2) struggling, if necessary, to bring those deceived by the false teachers back to a correct relationship with God (a defensive effort); and (3) confronting the false teachers about their heretical doctrine (an offensive attack). "The faith" encompasses the body of beliefs given to the church. It includes all that has been designed by God the Father from the foundation of the world (Revelation 13:8), executed by God the Son on the cross (John 19:30), and effected in the hearts of repentant individuals by God the Spirit (1 Corinthians 6:11). It has been handed over ("delivered") to believers who are the holy ones of God ("saints") to be shared in the power of the Spirit (Acts 1:8).

An intentional contrast emerges between the "saints" (Jude 3), who are the rightful heirs of the heritage of the faith, and the "certain men" (v. 4) who have deceptively sneaked into the midst of the church. There is a disdainful tone to Jude's calling them "certain men." They are hindering the work of God, afflicting the saints, and deceiving the weak; they are not instruments of God, but "ungodly" instruments of the Enemy. These have previously been marked out for judgment ("ordained to this condemnation"). This is a difficult phrase to understand. It can mean they have already been identified by God as instruments of the Enemy and their continual unwillingness to repent has already assured certain judgment. It probably refers to traveling troublemakers, whose immorality, heresy and divisiveness have already been condemned by Christian leaders in

lasciviousness (v. 4)—"license for immorality" (*NIV*)

Talk About It:
1. What does it mean to "contend for the faith"?
2. What danger was facing Jude's readers? How is this danger still facing the church?

Polycarp's Example

Polycarp, a respected leader in the early church, was arrested for his faith. He was given the choice to recant his relationship with Jesus or die. He told his captors that for 86 years, Jesus Christ had blessed, provided for and sustained him. Therefore he would not deny Him. His captors burned him alive, tied to a stake. In the midst of his most trying hour, he was not abandoned and did not die alone (Psalm 23:4). If God can enable us to die for Him, He will empower us to live for Him.

other places (Matthew 7:15). Either way, their future is bleak. Posing as agents of God's grace, they promote flagrant immorality and deny the lordship of Jesus Christ. While it is probable that they taught against the deity and redemptive work of Jesus, it is also possible that their sensual lifestyle (one dedicated to pleasing the senses) indicates they had chosen not to acknowledge His lordship in their lives. Thus, it was a visible denial of who He is (see Titus 1:16).

II. REMEMBER GOD'S JUDGMENTS (Jude 5-19)
A. Examples of Judgment (vv. 5-7)
   5. I will therefore put you in remembrance, though ye once knew this, how that the Lord, having saved the people out of the land of Egypt, afterward destroyed them that believed not.
   6. And the angels which kept not their first estate, but left their own habitation, he hath reserved in everlasting chains under darkness unto the judgment of the great day.
   7. Even as Sodom and Gomorrha, and the cities about them in like manner, giving themselves over to fornication, and going after strange flesh, are set forth for an example, suffering the vengeance of eternal fire.

Talk About It:

1. What lesson should we learn from Israel's wilderness experience (v. 5) and the fallen angels (v. 6)?

2. Compare our society with that of Sodom and Gomorrah. How should the church respond?

After summarizing the activity of the false teachers (v. 4), Jude provides three examples of God's judgment upon ungodly behavior. He leaves no doubt that these individuals—and those who follow them—are headed for decisive and terrible judgment. It was information known to the church, but appears to have slipped from their consciousness. The first example (v. 5) addresses the disobedient and is drawn from the Exodus account. God delivered Israel from Egypt through His power and servant, Moses (Exodus 12—14). Yet, after seeing God's deliverance, provision and protection, an entire generation disobeyed God and perished in the wilderness (Numbers 14:1-38).

The second example, the fallen angels (Matthew 25:41; 2 Peter 2:4), speaks to rebellion (Jude 6). Their proper place was in the presence of God, but they chose to leave His presence and kingdom and are now "reserved in everlasting chains" for judgment.

The third example, Sodom and Gomorrah and other cities influenced by them (Genesis 19:1-29), deals with immorality (Jude 7). Their rampant desire for "fornication [sexual immorality] and . . . strange flesh" resulted in a fiery judgment. *Sexual immorality* is a broad term that encompasses any sexual behavior outside of God's prescribed boundaries and provision. The phrase "strange flesh" is usually understood as a reference to the homosexual desires of the Sodomites, who sought the angels visiting Lot (Genesis 19:5). God's judgment for unrepentant sin is severe and eternal.

Standing in the Faith

B. Coming Calamity (vv. 8-11)

(Jude 8-11 is not included in the printed text.)

Jude says that in a similar fashion to the Sodomites, the false teachers ("filthy dreamers") profane and pollute their bodies through activity not designed by God, reject the lordship of Jesus, and deny the authority of His leaders (v. 8). They also blaspheme without fear the heavenly host. To contrast the lack of respect of the teachers for spiritual beings, Jude provides an example from Michael's confrontation with the devil over Moses' body (v. 9). Michael the archangel understood that any rebuke had to be based solely on the authority of God. This is quite a contrast to the ignorant, immoral and greedy behavior of the teachers who follow after the examples of Cain, Balaam and Korah (vv. 10, 11). Distressing calamity ("woe") is reserved for them.

Talk About It:
1. Describe the characteristics of false teachers (vv. 8-10).
2. How are false teachers like Cain (Genesis 4:1-9)? How are they like Korah (Numbers 16:1-3, 28-35)?

C. Depravity and Disaster (vv. 12-16)

12. These are spots in your feasts of charity, when they feast with you, feeding themselves without fear: clouds they are without water, carried about of winds; trees whose fruit withereth, without fruit, twice dead, plucked up by the roots;

13. Raging waves of the sea, foaming out their own shame; wandering stars, to whom is reserved the blackness of darkness for ever.

14. And Enoch also, the seventh from Adam, prophesied of these, saying, Behold, the Lord cometh with ten thousands of his saints,

15. To execute judgment upon all, and to convince all that are ungodly among them of all their ungodly deeds which they have ungodly committed, and of all their hard speeches which ungodly sinners have spoken against him.

16. These are murmurers, complainers, walking after their own lusts; and their mouth speaketh great swelling words, having men's persons in admiration because of advantage.

In what has been described as a righteous denunciation, Jude provides descriptive metaphors—comparisons of two dissimilar objects—to reveal the true nature and effect of the false teachers afflicting the church (vv. 12, 13). They are "spots," or blemishes, that mar the "love feasts" (v. 12, *NKJV*). The early church often came together for fellowship suppers in connection with their services. The false teachers were exhibiting anything but love when they entered into these feasts without fear, profaning that which was sacred, and exhibited blatant selfishness. With good reason Jude calls them "spots." This term originally referred to reefs hidden under the surface of the sea that caused shipwreck to unsuspecting boats as they approached

Talk About It:
1. How are false teachers like waterless clouds? Like twice-dead trees? Like foaming waves? Like wandering stars?
2. Describe the thoroughness of the final judgment (vv. 14, 15).

3. What is the motive of false prophets (v. 16)?

land. The church has not yet realized the harm inflicted by these teachers.

They are "clouds without water," giving hope to farmers needing rain, but never producing anything valuable. Continuing the agricultural metaphors, Jude says they are like fruit trees that have produced no fruit in the summer; thus, to the farmer they are already dead. They are uprooted to make room for productive trees and laid on the ground to die; thus, they are "twice dead." The spiritual application is obvious. They produce false hopes but nothing of substance for those under their teaching. They have no fruit in their lives—which should have been noticed by those in the church (Matthew 7:16). It speaks not only to the failed character of the teachers, but also the lack of discernment in the church.

In a shift of metaphors, Jude compares the teachers to waves, which are unpredictable, violent, and pick up foam and debris (v. 13). They then scatter this trash and spoil the beauty of the landscape. Also, the doctrine of the heretics is like "wandering stars" or planets in the sky. Because of their drifting courses, they cannot be relied on for proper navigation. These have been reserved for a dark, dismal, gloomy, eternal punishment, prepared for the devil and his angels (Matthew 25:41).

In verses 14 and 15, Jude quotes from an apocryphal book, 1 Enoch, well known and respected at the time of Jude's writing. A few comments are in order. Nowhere does Jude recognize the material as authoritative Scripture, but truth is truth no matter where it is found. Jude was inspired to quote sections of the book. That does not make the rest of the book worthy to be included in Scripture. However, once the Holy Spirit directed Jude to include the quote in his epistle, the quote became inspired Scripture. Paul often quoted from material outside of Scripture to illustrate his point. The Holy Spirit is sovereign and free to draw truth from whatever source serves His purposes. The quotation itself confirms the second coming of Christ and judgment upon those who are disobedient and ungodly—a fate that awaits the manipulative, greedy and conniving teachers (v. 16).

> "The devil is very active in supplying false Christs, as well as false prophets, false angels, false doctrine, false miracles—total false religion. Satan's strategy is to 'flood the market' with the false, and thereby neutralize the true."
> —Charles W. Conn

D. Words to Remember (vv. 17-19)

17. But, beloved, remember ye the words which were spoken before of the apostles of our Lord Jesus Christ;

18. How that they told you there should be mockers in the last time, who should walk after their own ungodly lusts.

19. These be they who separate themselves, sensual, having not the Spirit.

Jude addresses the recipients again as "beloved" (v. 17), a term of endearment. It is a gentle reassurance that they are not the enemy. He then echoes the words of Peter (2 Peter 3:2, 3).

The apostles, under the direction of Jesus (Matthew 24:4, 5, 24, 25), warned the early church of "mockers," directed by ungodly, unrestrained illicit desires (Jude 18). These individuals actively destroy unity and promote discord ("separate themselves"), operate according to the whims of the unspiritual flesh ("sensual"), and are devoid of the Spirit of God (v. 19). They are apostates, who have no right influencing those directed by the Spirit. Jude advises his readers to "remember . . . the words" of warning (v. 17).

Talk About It:
How can we recognize religious people who "have not the Holy Spirit" (see v. 19)?

III. REMAIN IN CHRIST (Jude 20-25)
A. Edification (vv. 20, 21)
20. But ye, beloved, building up yourselves on your most holy faith, praying in the Holy Ghost,
21. Keep yourselves in the love of God, looking for the mercy of our Lord Jesus Christ unto eternal life.

In a dramatic shift of tone that contrasts those without the Spirit of God (v. 19), Jude admonishes the "beloved" to strengthen themselves through four exhortations. *First, they are to continue building on the strong foundation of the faith that endures.* It is the faith that has sustained them, not the false doctrine. And the faith will allow them to grow even stronger. They are to do this *themselves*, which suggests (1) they are to encourage themselves in the Lord (see 1 Samuel 30:6), and (2) they are to edify, or build up, one another.

Talk About It:
1. What is "praying in the Holy Ghost"? Why is such praying so effective?
2. How do you "keep yourselves in the love of God"?

Second, they are to continue praying in the Holy Spirit. Praying in the Spirit edifies. The Spirit comes alongside of us and walks with us, assisting and providing for us in our spiritual journey (John 16:13). There are some areas in our lives that defy words known to humanity. In those times, it is comforting to know that the Spirit intercedes for us according to the perfect will of God and protects us in our weaknesses (Romans 8:26, 27). Praying in the Spirit shields and makes us victorious in daily spiritual battle (Ephesians 6:18). Speaking in tongues is the initial evidence of baptism in the Spirit (Acts 2:1-4). Praying in tongues is continued evidence of that experience and sustains us in our daily walk.

Third, Jude commands them to guard themselves "in the love of God" (v. 21). They are to stay within the realm of the love of God. This can be a reference to either God's love for them (1 John 4:10) or their love for God (Matthew 22:37). It is taken as both. As they seek to understand more of God's love for them, it will cause their love for Him to increase (1 John 4:19). *Finally, they are to continue looking for the mercy of the Lord, accepting His loving-kindness.* We can be our own worst enemies. If we do not feel worthy of all God has for us, we will not anticipate or embrace His love and provision. Some wrongly

"The Christian has never known the real joy of prayer until he has prayed in the Spirit."
—Ray H. Hughes

see in this phrase an eschatological connotation; that is, they are to look for security in Christ in the midst of end-time events. However, if we embrace God's provision now, the future is secure.

B. Empathy and Evangelism (vv. 22, 23)
22. And of some have compassion, making a difference:
23. And others save with fear, pulling them out of the fire; hating even the garment spotted by the flesh.

Talk About It:
Describe two ways God calls us to minister to different people. Why are different approaches necessary?

Jude correctly teaches that the focus cannot be entirely inward, if they want to properly build up themselves in the faith. They must reach out to others. Verse 22 is difficult to interpret. It is best understood in light of the preceding phrase. Since they are receiving loving-kindness ("mercy"), they are to reach out with compassion to others who may be struggling, especially those who are doubting because of the false teachers' ability to persuade. True righteousness is a right relationship with God *and* a right relationship with humanity, starting with our brothers and sisters in the Lord.

However, our compassion should not remain in the house of the Lord. In descriptive language, Jude provides an image of those caught in the depths of sin (v. 23). This is drawn from Old Testament accounts of God delivering Israel out of the fire (Amos 4:11; also see Zechariah 3:1-9). It is a vivid reminder that if the church does not evangelize, lost souls are going to spend eternity in hell—a place to be feared. We must hate the sin ("garment spotted by the flesh"), but love the sinner enough to do whatever it takes to bring them to salvation.

C. Exaltation (vv. 24, 25)
24. Now unto him that is able to keep you from falling, and to present you faultless before the presence of his glory with exceeding joy,
25. To the only wise God our Saviour, be glory and majesty, dominion and power, both now and ever. Amen.

Talk About It:
1. Who wants to present us before God, and how?
2. If everything you knew about God is recorded in verse 25, exactly what would you know?

Jude concludes his letter with one of the finest doxologies ever composed. He praises the God who is able to guard us and keep us secure from moral failure. Unlike the false teachers, He will cause us to stand in the presence of God's glory with great joy—both now and the future. The only proper response to such love and power is praise to the One who reigns now and forever.

CONCLUSION
In powerful and provocative language, Jude informs the readers of God's preserving power, warns them of the effect

the false teachers are having upon them, and admonishes them to edify themselves and others. He reminds the readers of the power of the Spirit available to them in the midst of their struggles and leads them through praise into the presence of the King.

GOLDEN TEXT CHALLENGE
"KEEP YOURSELVES IN THE LOVE OF GOD, LOOKING FOR THE MERCY OF OUR LORD JESUS CHRIST UNTO ETERNAL LIFE" (Jude 21).

As believers we are to keep ourselves safe as in a fortress so we are not carried away by the evil influences of unbelief and apostasy in the world. The sphere of safety is the love of God; we are to live so that God can freely act toward us in love rather than in judgment. God's love never changes, but we need to keep in the conscious enjoyment of it by trust and obedience.

As we live in God's love, we should cherish the expectation of eternal life with Him. We live in hope for the fullness of life that only the return of Christ will bring.

Daily Devotions:
M. Call to Be
   Courageous
   Joshua 1:1-7
T. The Battle
   Belongs to God
   2 Chronicles
   20:14-25
W. Overcoming
   Discouragement
   Nehemiah 4:9-20
T. Little Is Much
   Matthew 13:31-
   33
F. Put On Christ
   Colossians 3:1-
   10
S. Author and
   Finisher of Faith
   Hebrews 12:1-4

February 12, 2006

Consecrated for Service

Numbers 3:1-13, 40-51; 2 Timothy 2:20-22

Unit Theme:
Numbers

Central Truth:
God calls and sets apart people for His service.

Focus:
To appreciate that God sets believers apart for His service and consecrate our lives to Him.

Context:
Selected Old and New Testament passages about consecration to God

Golden Text:
"If a man therefore purge himself from these, he shall be a vessel unto honour, sanctified, and meet for the master's use, and prepared unto every good work" (2 Timothy 2:21).

Study Outline:
I. Separated for Service
(Numbers 3:5-13)
II. Provision for Service
(Numbers 3:40-51)
III. Cleansed for Service
(2 Timothy 2:20-22)

INTRODUCTION

God sets believers apart for His service. However, God's calling and separation for service takes different forms. The nation of Israel demonstrates this. All the people of Israel's 12 tribes were predestined to be part of the chosen nation from whom the Messiah would eventually come. Yet only one of the tribes was selected for the purpose of being the ministering servants in charge of the Tabernacle and helping the people in their worship and service to the Lord.

All of the Israelites were God's people. They were chosen vessels of the Lord with a holy purpose. Though the Levites were chosen to serve in a different manner and location, it didn't make them better or more important than the others.

This concept still remains true today as we look at the Christian church with its designations of laity and clergy. In the early years of the church there was no such division. The 12 disciples provided the informal leadership and all the believers worked together using their individual gifts. Later we see the apostle Paul writing about the administrative positions of bishops and deacons. At this point individuals fulfilling these roles in the local churches were not considered clergy. They fulfilled their tasks as lay leaders.

It wasn't until the end of the first century when Clement, Bishop of Rome, wrote a letter to the church at Corinth indicating a distinction of function between clergy and laity. This initiated a dividing that eventually led to a hierarchy in which laity were secondary to clergy. However, the words themselves do not suggest any such division. The word *laity* in the Greek language simply means "people." Thus within the church, laity are the people of God. *Clergy* in Greek means "lot" or "inheritance." There's no sense of superiority, only a designation for a particular area. The word *minister* in the same language speaks of a servant or serving. Notice that none of these terms place one group higher than another. God wants all of His servants serving Him.

I. SEPARATED FOR SERVICE (Numbers 3:5-13)
A. Service in the Tabernacle (vv. 5-9)

5. And the Lord spake unto Moses, saying,

6. Bring the tribe of Levi near, and present them before Aaron the priest, that they may minister unto him.

7. And they shall keep his charge, and the charge of the whole congregation before the tabernacle of the congregation, to do the service of the tabernacle.

8. And they shall keep all the instruments of the tabernacle of the congregation, and the charge of the children of Israel, to do the service of the tabernacle.

9. And thou shalt give the Levites unto Aaron and to his sons: they are wholly given unto him out of the children of Israel.

While the Israelites are staying at Mount Sinai, God develops them into a nation. One aspect of this development is the religious dimension of the nation. God ensures the establishment and continuance of proper worship. He provides the means through designated sacrifices and offerings, prescribing specific procedures.

Of specific significance is God's provision for worship leadership through the selection of a group of people to serve as priests. They are specifically separated from the rest of the nation to serve in the Tabernacle and enable the people to worship. God sovereignly selects the tribe of Levi for service as the ministering tribe. He chooses to raise them from obscurity to a preeminent status.

Moses and Aaron are the dominant leaders of this tribe. Aaron begins as the "speaking assistant" to Moses. However, later God selects him for the position of high priest. Two of his sons, Eleazar and Ithamar, along with their sons will fulfill the priestly duties (see vv. 2-4). The remaining males within the tribe will serve as assistants to the priests and be responsible for tearing down, moving and setting up the Tabernacle as well as its general care.

Though God decrees the selection of the Levites for His service, there is still the distinct action of consecration. They come and stand before Aaron. In obedience to God's will they surrender to fulfill the prescribed duties of service. Their charge consists of two major areas of responsibility. First, they are responsible to help the people in their worship as the various sacrifices and offerings are brought to the Tabernacle. This reflects a definite change from when the head of the family served as the family priest.

The second area of responsibility is care for the Tabernacle and the furniture. They are responsible for cleaning the various pieces and repairing them when needed. And, as previously

Talk About It:
1. Describe the duties to which God called the Levites.
2. How does the term "wholly given" (v. 9) describe the calling of all believers today?

Moody's Ministry

Though D.L. Moody's ministry occurred during the middle and latter half of the 19th century, his examples of service live on. Here are two examples from his life:

1. Though well on his way to becoming one of the rich philanthropists of the Chicago area, he took a job at the local YMCA. This meant a reduction in salary of over 90 percent. He and Emma's first house became known as "poverty cottage."

2. Prior to this move to full-time service, he went to the neediest of the needy, the north side of Chicago, and reached out to the young and the old by starting Sunday school classes. He purchased a paint pony to bring attention to his work and promote attendance. Children were given rides and treats of candy.

matrix (v. 12)—
womb

Talk About It:
1. What restrictions did God put on the priestly ministry, and why (v. 10)?
2. How did the Levites replace the firstborn of Israel?

mentioned, when the nation moved they would be responsible for the packing, transporting and unpacking of the Tabernacle itself, the furniture and the utensils.

This separation of the Levites from the other tribes to serve the Lord, His house and His people becomes their full-time vocation. Their separation doesn't make them better than any of the other Israelites. It simply gives them a responsibility of service.

B. Service as Priests (vv. 10-13)

10. And thou shalt appoint Aaron and his sons, and they shall wait on their priest's office: and the stranger that cometh nigh shall be put to death.

11. And the Lord spake unto Moses, saying,

12. And I, behold, I have taken the Levites from among the children of Israel instead of all the firstborn that openeth the matrix among the children of Israel: therefore the Levites shall be mine;

13. Because all the firstborn are mine; for on the day that I smote all the firstborn in the land of Egypt I hallowed unto me all the firstborn in Israel, both man and beast: mine shall they be: I am the Lord.

Here we see the distinctiveness of God's selection. Aaron and his sons alone are to fulfill the priestly office. They alone have the responsibility and opportunity to minister in the Tabernacle. Anyone who is unauthorized and attempts this service will be put to death. This separation can also be seen in Numbers 1:51 and Leviticus 22:10.

This selection of the Levites for ministry service is, in reality, an adoption by God himself. The basis for this action has its roots in the Passover while the Israelites were in Egypt. At that time, God required them to dedicate all the firstborn sons for His service. Also, all the firstborn of the cattle were to be sacrificed to Him. Now God chooses the tribe of Levi to care for the service of the sanctuary instead of all firstborn males. Their cattle become His cattle. They alone will be the facilitators for worship and care for the Tabernacle.

II. PROVISION FOR SERVICE (Numbers 3:40-51)
A. Levitical Census (vv. 40-42)

40. And the Lord said unto Moses, Number all the firstborn of the males of the children of Israel from a month old and upward, and take the number of their names.

41. And thou shalt take the Levites for me (I am the Lord) instead of all the firstborn among the children of Israel; and the cattle of the Levites instead of all the firstlings among the cattle of the children of Israel.

42. And Moses numbered, as the Lord commanded him, all the firstborn among the children of Israel.

The Book of Numbers receives its name from the several censuses that are recorded. Initially, God directed Moses to number all the males of the 12 tribes who were 20 years old and healthy enough to go to war (see 1:2, 3). Notice there is no maximum age. Usually we refer to this as a military census.

God then directs Moses to do a separate census of Levi (3:15, 16). Here all males 1 month and older are counted. The significance of numbering every Levite male is due to the Levites being adopted in place of the firstborn of the other 11 tribes, who are ordered to be counted in verse 41. "The actual total of the male Levites is 22,300 (cf. Numbers 3:22, 28, 34); and the extra 300 (see v. 39) are considered by some to represent those who, being firstborn themselves in the tribe of Levi, could not be available to redeem the firstborn in other tribes" (*Barnes' Notes*).

Talk About It:
1. Why do you think the phrase "I am the Lord" is inserted in the middle of verse 41?
2. If you were to number the church-goers who are totally devoted to the Lord, what would the per-centage be? Would you be part of that number?

B. Firstborn Redemption (vv. 43-51)

43. And all the firstborn males by the number of names, from a month old and upward, of those that were numbered of them, were twenty and two thousand two hundred and threescore and thirteen.

44. And the Lord spake unto Moses, saying,

45. Take the Levites instead of all the firstborn among the children of Israel, and the cattle of the Levites instead of their cattle; and the Levites shall be mine: I am the Lord.

46. And for those that are to be redeemed of the two hundred and threescore and thirteen of the firstborn of the children of Israel, which are more than the Levites;

47. Thou shalt even take five shekels apiece by the poll, after the shekel of the sanctuary shalt thou take them: (the shekel is twenty gerahs:)

48. And thou shalt give the money, wherewith the odd number of them is to be redeemed, unto Aaron and to his sons.

49. And Moses took the redemption money of them that were over and above them that were redeemed by the Levites.

50. Of the firstborn of the children of Israel took he the money; a thousand three hundred and threescore and five shekels, after the shekel of the sanctuary:

51. And Moses gave the money of them that were redeemed unto Aaron and to his sons, according to the word of the Lord, as the Lord commanded Moses.

There were 273 more firstborn males in the other tribes than non-firstborn males in the tribe of Levi. This then necessitated a monetary redemption. The established price of redemption was 5 shekels. More than likely a shekel was unminted silver with a weight variance of 8 to 17 ounces. The weight and cost

Talk About It:
1. How were the 273 firstborn Israelites who exceeded the number of Levites to be "redeemed"?
2. What is the price of your redemption?

Talk About It:

1. How does someone become a "vessel of honor"?

2. Why does God want us to be honorable vessels?

involved here isn't nearly as important as the fact of there being a price which needed to be paid.

Who paid the price of redemption? Since it wouldn't be fair to simply single out a few families for payment while others experienced no obligation, more than likely the amount was taken from tribal treasuries. The total redemption price became the possession of Aaron and his sons.

What value does this account have for us today? Matthew Henry wrote, "The church is called the church of the firstborn, which is redeemed, not as these were, with silver and gold, but, being devoted by sin to the justice of God, is ransomed with the precious blood of Jesus Christ." As the ransomed ones, we should fully dedicate our lives in service to Him.

III. CLEANSED FOR SERVICE (2 Timothy 2:20-22)
A. Instruments for Service (vv. 20, 21)

20. But in a great house there are not only vessels of gold and of silver, but also of wood and of earth; and some to honour, and some to dishonour.

21. If a man therefore purge himself from these, he shall be a vessel unto honour, sanctified, and meet for the master's use, and prepared unto every good work.

To grasp the impact of what the apostle Paul writes to his son in the Lord, Timothy, one needs to review the previous context. Most of chapter 1 and part of chapter 2 contains an encouragement to be faithful. He reminds Timothy of his God-given gift and the need to be strong in the Lord (1:6; 2:1). Paul also encourages his spiritual son to "endure hardship, as a good soldier of Jesus Christ" (v. 3).

Paul then moves to the concept of a believer being a workman approved by God. He points to the need for correctly interpreting the Word of God and not being guilty of false teaching that spreads like gangrene and eventually causes death (vv. 15-17).

In marked contrast are those who have accepted Christ and turned away from unrighteousness. They have rejected sin and grasped holiness for the purpose of service (vv. 19-21). Paul paints a picture of this acceptance of service by using the home of a wealthy person as an illustration. He doesn't use the word *wealth*, but only those of considerable resources would have a "great" (large) home. Also, only individuals of considerable substance would have bowls, pitchers and various utensils made of precious metals. Yet, even in the homes of the rich some items were made of inexpensive materials such as wood and clay.

The major issue here isn't the material value of the items but rather the purpose each served. Those of precious metals were used for higher purposes. They were not used for everyday, humdrum needs. That's where the cheaper items served well. It's like having an expensive set of dishes for company and a cheaper one for the family's everyday use.

In contrast to the various items in a home which have no choice over their material or use, we believers can make a choice. If we choose to abandon the spots, stains and scars of the lower life, we will become precious instruments used for a higher purpose. Usefulness to the Master doesn't begin with the type or multitude of our talents. The key is our seeking to be holy. We must return even now to the directive the Lord gave to Israel through Moses: "Be holy: for I the Lord your God am holy" (Leviticus 19:2). As we strive to be Christlike and grow in sanctification, we become instruments that our Master can use to promote His kingdom.

It's so easy to become caught in the tangle of trying to be successful and noticed by *doing* rather than *being*. What is on the inside is by far more important. In the long run, it determines the quality and character of an individual. This can be seen in the words of Samuel to King Saul after the king foolishly offered a burnt offering, a task only a priest could perform. God rejected Saul's kingship because God was looking for "a man after his own heart" (1 Samuel 13:14).

The bottom line is this: Do we want to do a good work for the Lord? Do we want to be prepared properly in His sight? Then holiness is the first step. We must seek to be holy in our thoughts, words and actions.

B. Pursuit of Righteousness (v. 22)

22. Flee also youthful lusts: but follow righteousness, faith, charity, peace, with them that call on the Lord out of a pure heart.

As the recipient of this letter, Timothy doesn't fit the category of a teen or twenty-something. He is a mature man in his early to mid 30s. Yet Paul instructs him to flee from the evil desires of youth. There are some characteristics of youth that easily lead to the entrapment of sin. For example, the blossoming sexuality with its strong drives may lead to *illicit behavior* unless kept in check. Another characteristic is the desire to *experiment and discover*. This path can easily lead to false philosophies and harmful addictions. A third characteristic of youth is being *self-determining*—wanting to be the authority and do things one's own way. Then there's *selfishness*—wanting to be served rather than serving.

All of these characteristics do not just automatically leave us at a certain magic age. They can continue to be a plague as the decades mount up unless there is a choice to run "pell-mell" in the opposite direction. Cleansing for service isn't just the work of the Holy Spirit. We have to consciously be seeking

Talk About It:
1. Name some "youthful lusts" from which believers must flee.
2. What do pure-hearted people pursue, and how?

to shake away from those traits and actions that would cause us to be unfit vessels to serve in the Kingdom.

Paul specifically indicates how we are to seek after *righteousness*, or holy living. We are to strive to be a people of *faith* who will then exhibit a life of faithfulness. Instead of succumbing to dissension, hatred or ill feelings, we are to follow the pattern of *love* even toward those whose actions do not merit such kindness. And we should strive for *peace*. Inner peace comes initially through salvation and continues even in the middle of crises as we trust in the Peace Giver, the Lord Jesus Christ (see John 14:27).

The word *them* in 2 Timothy 2:22 indicates *company*. It's much easier to flee evil when there are others with us striving for the same goal. The fellowship of fellow believers enables us to be strengthened in our resolve and our lifestyle. Remember 1 Corinthians 15:33: "Do not be misled: 'Bad company corrupts good character'" (*NIV*).

CONCLUSION

When God chose the tribe of Levi to be the ministering or serving tribe, it was not because He saw them as better than the rest. In fact, the founding father of the tribe, Levi, was described by his own father, Jacob, as an "instrument of cruelty" (Genesis 49:5). Yes, the Levites did respond to Moses' question, "Who is on the Lord's side?" at Mount Sinai when the people demanded a visible god (Exodus 32:26). But it seems that the Levites' selection rests upon God's sovereign choice. And He continues the same separation today, calling some individuals into full-time ministry within the framework of a credentialed clergy. However, this doesn't make them extra special in the sight of God, or on a pedestal above other people. He calls all believers into His service.

GOLDEN TEXT CHALLENGE

"IF A MAN THEREFORE PURGE HIMSELF FROM THESE, HE SHALL BE A VESSEL UNTO HONOUR, SANCTIFIED, AND MEET FOR THE MASTER'S USE, AND PREPARED UNTO EVERY GOOD WORK" (2 Timothy 2:21).

While God calls believers to various ministries, He first calls each of His children to be "an instrument for noble purposes" (*NIV*). But there are many members of the church who are not set apart for God. They are more concerned about the affairs of this world than the kingdom of God, and it shows in their apathy, negligence and disobedience.

Being a vessel of honor begins by turning away from ignoble things through the cleansing power of Jesus Christ. Those who commit their lives to His holiness will be "useful to the Master and prepared to do any good work" (*NIV*).

Daily Devotions:

M. Joshua Commissioned to Lead
Numbers 27:15-23

T. Solomon Anointed King
1 Kings 1:32-40

W. Amos Called as a Prophet
Amos 7:10-15

T. A Glorious Church
Ephesians 5:25-29

F. Christ, Our High Priest
Hebrews 9:6-14

S. Service Before God's Throne
Revelation 7:13-17

Consecrated for Service

The Cost of Rebellion

Numbers 11:4-15; 14:1-12; 1 Corinthians 10:1-13

INTRODUCTION

What image comes to mind on hearing the word *rebellion*? Maybe it's a parent-child relationship in which the teen suddenly assumes a maturity and level of authority which supercedes that of their mother or father. This might be a passing challenge while it could develop into a separation of years.

Maybe you think of civil wars which divide and even destroy countries. The North/South struggle of the American Civil War still divides even though it ended by treaty nearly 140 years ago. Brother fought against brother. Atrocities and suffering took place on both sides.

Maybe the rebellion of church splits reluctantly pushes to the forefront. We refrain from dwelling on those situations in which the body of Christ becomes unnecessarily divided. Usually some type of rebellion can be found when it happens. It may range from rebellion against authority and structure to rebellion against doctrinal truth and Biblical ethics.

Many examples of rebellion are found in the Biblical record. They include the extremes of aggressive rebellion against God to the passive rebellion fostered by deceitful persuasion. Lucifer's rebellion against God and leaving the glory of the heavens with one-third of the angelic host readily stands out. How could they do that against God himself? Yet we humans seem to be equally skilled at rebellion. There's Eve's succumbing to Satan's deceit and choosing what she perceived to be truth. Cain chose his idea of the acceptable offering, and then committed the extreme sin of murdering his brother. Other incidents of rebellion follow. Some were on an individual level while many others were a group action.

Today's lesson provides us with two pictures of rebellion and punishment. The first one shows rebellion against God in the form of complaining against His provisions. The second account centers on a group of people rebelling by choosing not to believe God's ability to defeat an imposing enemy.

Unit Theme:
Numbers

Central Truth:
Rebellion brings God's judgment, but repentance leads to restoration.

Focus:
To learn from Israel's example of rebellion and accept God's provision of Christ.

Context:
Topical Old and New Testament passages

Golden Text:
"All these things happened unto them for examples: and they are written for our admonition, upon whom the ends of the world are come" (1 Corinthians 10:11).

Study Outline:
I. Complaint Against God's Provision (Numbers 11:4-15)
II. Results of Rebellion (Numbers 14:1-12)
III. Examples for Our Instruction (1 Corinthians 10:1-13)

I. COMPLAINT AGAINST GOD'S PROVISION
(Numbers 11:4-15)

A. The Complaint (vv. 4-9)

4. And the mixt multitude that was among them fell a lusting: and the children of Israel also wept again, and said, Who shall give us flesh to eat?

5. We remember the fish, which we did eat in Egypt freely; the cucumbers, and the melons, and the leeks, and the onions, and the garlick:

6. But now our soul is dried away: there is nothing at all, beside this manna, before our eyes.

7. And the manna was as coriander seed, and the colour thereof as the colour of bdellium.

8. And the people went about, and gathered it, and ground it in mills, or beat it in a mortar, and baked it in pans, and made cakes of it: and the taste of it was as the taste of fresh oil.

9. And when the dew fell upon the camp in the night, the manna fell upon it.

Talk About It:

1. Who were "the mixt multitude," and what influence did they have on the Israelites?

2. What did the people remember about Egypt, and what did they forget?

3. Describe the manna with which God was miraculously feeding them. Why were they dissatisfied with it?

The apostle Paul states, "Bad company corrupts good character" (1 Corinthians 15:33, *NIV*). How the people around us can greatly impact our thoughts and reactions! This can be seen among the Israelites after the final plague. As they left Egyptian bondage, a number of other people joined them (Exodus 12:38). There was no reason for them to stay in the devastated country of Egypt. Besides, the Hebrews' God had demonstrated His power over all the gods of Egypt, including Pharaoh. These people—"the mixt multitude" (Numbers 11:4)—were of a different culture and had no specific loyalty to God. They enjoyed His blessings, but in difficult times they willingly complained.

In verses 1-3 the Hebrews complained and God sent down fire and consumed those who lingered at the outskirts of the camp. Apparently this dynamic display of God's judgment did not have a lasting impact, for the other "rabble" (v. 4, *NIV*) began to crave for foods of Egypt and incite the Israelites to do the same. It didn't stop with a few "remember whens" or "wish we hads." No! It began to dominate them to the point of their audibly grieving loudly about the current state of their diet.

Follow the growth of their dietary complaint. It begins with a general desire of meat. Then it becomes very specific as they list some of the special foods they are missing. What's so amazing is their selective memory. Only the missed foods come to mind. Unmentioned is their unceasing hard work as slave laborers. Also, they demonstrate no anticipation for the foods of the Promised Land. Awaiting them there is wheat, barley, grapevines, fig trees, olives, honey and pomegranates.

The Cost of Rebellion

Short–sightedness and selfishness causes the Israelites to follow the complaints of the mixed crowd. All that seems to matter is their personal dissatisfaction with their God–given, daily provision of manna. When God first made this basic provision of food, the people called it *manna* ("What is it?") since they had never seen anything like it. And they were glad to have this food.

Verses 7-9 provide a description of the manna, the multiple ways of preparation and its taste. This heavenly provided food corresponds to no known earthly substance. It was not given to any other people groups. It was provided six days every week but not on the seventh. And it was available in all of the geographic areas where Israel traveled.

Verse 8 indicates the manna could be fixed in a variety of ways. (In our day someone surely would have come up with a cookbook titled "99 Ways to Fix Manna.") However, there seems to be a basic taste regardless of the process.

B. The Response (vv. 10-15)

10. Then Moses heard the people weep throughout their families, every man in the door of his tent: and the anger of the Lord was kindled greatly; Moses also was displeased.

11. And Moses said unto the Lord, Wherefore hast thou afflicted thy servant? and wherefore have I not found favour in thy sight, that thou layest the burden of all this people upon me?

12. Have I conceived all this people? have I begotten them, that thou shouldest say unto me, Carry them in thy bosom, as a nursing father beareth the sucking child, unto the land which thou swarest unto their fathers?

13. Whence should I have flesh to give unto all this people? for they weep unto me, saying, Give us flesh, that we may eat.

14. I am not able to bear all this people alone, because it is too heavy for me.

15. And if thou deal thus with me, kill me, I pray thee, out of hand, if I have found favour in thy sight; and let me not see my wretchedness.

The people become so upset and committed to being dissatisfied with their diet that they wail as though there is a death in the family. They make a public display by sitting in the doorway of their tents expressing intense displeasure. God's response to their behavior and lack of faith is predictable. How could He not be angry with them in view of His continued provision and demonstration of power? But the attention in this passage centers on Moses' response.

> "We have no more right to put our discordant states of mind into the lives of those around us and rob them of their sunshine and brightness than we have to enter their houses and steal their silverware."
>
> —**Julia Seton**

1. Why is a complaining, ungrateful spirit so troublesome to the Lord?

2. How did the people's rebellious attitude affect Moses, their leader?

3. How does a congregation's attitude affect their pastor?

"Why is all of this happening to me?" seems to be the underlying question he directs toward God. There are some settings in leadership where the actions of the people cause one to question his or her leadership role. Moses had not chosen to lead them, so why did he have to shoulder the whole burden? Moses was fatigued and "fed up" with people. He suggests this trouble may have been brought upon him due to God's displeasure with his leadership. He continues by pointing out that he isn't the one who birthed this people, so why should he have to nurse them on this journey? Moses felt like a parent caring for an infant—to be more precise, 2 to 3 million "infants."

In verse 14 Moses shares the bottom line. All the work and worry of this job has taken its toll, and he can't go on anymore. The burden is too heavy for one person to bear. So rather than continue any further, he prefers to die right now. It seems far more preferable than leading a nation which appears to be bent on its own ruin. Notice Moses doesn't demand death but would consider it a good change, if God agrees.

Though our lesson text doesn't go beyond verse 15, two observations from later verses need to made. First, God doesn't rebuke Moses for his questions and request. Second, God doesn't bother to reply to them either. He simply gives instructions for Moses to follow and informs him as to what will take place.

II. RESULTS OF REBELLION (Numbers 14:1-12)
A. The Problem (vv. 1-4)
(Numbers 14:1 is not included in the printed text.)
2. And all the children of Israel murmured against Moses and against Aaron: and the whole congregation said unto them, Would God that we had died in the land of Egypt! or would God we had died in this wilderness!
3. And wherefore hath the Lord brought us unto this land, to fall by the sword, that our wives and our children should be a prey? were it not better for us to return into Egypt?

4. And they said one to another, Let us make a captain, and let us return into Egypt.

The events of chapter 13 sets the stage for this rebellion. Israel arrives just outside the borders of Canaan. At the insistence of the people, God allows 12 men to spy out the land (Deuteronomy 1:22). These men give their report to the entire body of the nation. They all agree as to the abundance of the land and the strength of the people. On the basis of the latter, 10 state they cannot hope to overcome the odds. However, Joshua and Caleb state with assurance how victory is theirs for the taking.

The Cost of Rebellion

Our study text begins with the people's responses. Believing the 10 spies rather than the two, they immediately begin to sorrow regarding their plight. First, they weep and wail all night. Second, they begin to grumble against the leadership. When will these people ever learn to trust in the Lord? He promises to give them whatever portion of the land they step on (see Joshua 1:3); what more do they need?

Their despair reaches the depth of wishing death had overcome them while in Egyptian bondage, or that they had died in the wilderness. Then they get to the heart of the matter. The men believe they will die by the swords of the enemies. In turn, that will lead to their wives and children becoming the plunder of war.

In light of this perceived future, they suggest returning to Egypt. The bondage of Pharaoh and a land devastated by the plagues suddenly appears to be a brighter future. Under this illusion, they suggest choosing a leader to begin the return trip. Nehemiah records their actually selecting the person for the task (9:17).

The people assume their biggest problem is their inability to conquer the Promised Land and being defeated, if they attempt to enter. They fail to recognize the real problem. Walled cities and giants are a pushover for God. The biggest problem rests within themselves. It is faithless hearts pursuing rebellion against their God. Plus, they completely disregard the human leadership of Moses and Aaron whose sacrificial, humble leadership brought them through the multiple challenges of the past. No good can possibly come from their rebellious spirit.

B. The Plea (vv. 5-9)

5. Then Moses and Aaron fell on their faces before all the assembly of the congregation of the children of Israel.

6. And Joshua the son of Nun, and Caleb the son of Jephunneh, which were of them that searched the land, rent their clothes:

7. And they spake unto all the company of the children of Israel, saying, The land, which we passed through to search it, is an exceeding good land.

8. If the Lord delight in us, then he will bring us into this land, and give it us; a land which floweth with milk and honey.

9. Only rebel not ye against the Lord, neither fear ye the people of the land; for they are bread for us: their defence is departed from them, and the Lord is with us: fear them not.

Moses and Aaron respond to this rebellion by prostrating themselves on the ground in the presence of the entire assembly. This indicates their sorrow and anguish. The leaders do not even attempt to rebuke the Hebrews for this breach of faith and

2. Compare the people's current attitude (Numbers 14:2, 3) with their attitude when they crossed the Red Sea (Exodus 15:1, 2). What happened to their faith in God?

3. What foolish idea began circulating among the people (Numbers 14:4)?

Rebellion Personified

The decades of the '60s and '70s were a time of turmoil and rebellion. As some people repeatedly expressed their views against the various dimensions of the establishment, protests of all types became quite common.

One such rebel of this era lived in San Francisco and marched in any picket or protest line, regardless of the cause. So he didn't have to make a new sign for each protest, he repeatedly used a large placard which read "SHAME." When asked about it, he responded, "I figure it covers about everything and helps me feel like I belong."

Now that is an example of rebellion!

Talk About It:

1. Explain the reactions of Moses, Aaron and Joshua (vv. 5, 6).
2. Describe the faith statements of Israel's leaders (vv. 7-9).

outright rebellion. It reminds us how, in some situations, words of rebuttal or rebuke are a waste of time, energy and oxygen. The only response is to fall before the Lord.

Joshua and Caleb take a different approach (vv. 6-9). Immediately they tear their garments, symbolizing great sorrow and anguish. And they rightly choose to speak. After all, they were selected to search out the land. They have returned and are part of the group giving a report to the nation. Now they proceed to further present their case to enter the land rather than fail to fulfill God's plan. They repeat the positive nature of the land and the abundance of food awaiting them. They specifically point to God's leadership and His enabling them to possess Canaan. These two men understand their personal inability but are relying on God to continue displaying His sovereign power.

Joshua and Caleb are aware of the impact of fear on these people. In an attempt to calm them and bring assurance, they point to Canaan's vulnerability. The Canaanites have no protection because God is with Israel. With this in mind, no one should be willing to follow the path of rebellion against the Lord.

This part of the story brings us to a personal point of application. Are there aspects of our lives where we allow fear to dominate and thus hinder our ability to be people of faith?

C. The Possibility (vv. 10-12)

bade stone them (v. 10)—talked about stoning them

10. But all the congregation bade stone them with stones. And the glory of the Lord appeared in the tabernacle of the congregation before all the children of Israel.

11. And the Lord said unto Moses, How long will this people provoke me? and how long will it be ere they believe me, for all the signs which I have shewed among them?

12. I will smite them with the pestilence, and disinherit them, and will make of thee a greater nation and mightier than they.

Talk About It:

1. Why did the Lord make a glorious appearance?
2. What questions did God ask Moses (v. 11)?
3. What proposal did God present to Moses (v. 12)?

The situation really gets ugly. These people are totally opposed to the words of Joshua and Caleb. Unwilling to be a people of faith, the Israelites begin to discuss the need to stone the two men of faith. That's when God intervenes and brings a dramatic halt to their intentions. The appearance of the glory of the Lord in the Tabernacle silences the people. Exactly what they saw or even heard isn't described. It's possible, though, that the pillar of cloud descends on the Tabernacle in a dramatic manner signaling the Lord's immediate presence.

The Lord speaks to Moses in the form of questions. The questions center on Israel's continuing to fail in faith even though they have been the recipients of one miracle after another. Will they ever change?

Then God makes an unusual offer. He suggests the possibility of "killing off" these people. It would be an act of disinheriting, since they are doing nothing to demonstrate their identity with Him. Why continue a relationship the people do not value? This is another occasion when the heart of Moses shines clearly. God offers the option of destroying Israel and making a new nation of his descendants, but Moses points out this would be a negative testimony to the Egyptians and the people of Canaan (vv. 13-16).

The point we must emphasize is the result of rebellion. It would have been just for God to destroy the entire nation because of their sinfulness. They are the covenant breakers. God no longer has any obligation to them. However, because of His mercy and patience, God chooses to allow them to remain as a nation. But everyone 20 years of age and older will not enter the Promised Land (v. 29).

III. EXAMPLES FOR OUR INSTRUCTION
   (1 Corinthians 10:1-13)
A. The Past (vv. 1-5)
   1. Moreover, brethren, I would not that ye should be ignorant, how that all our fathers were under the cloud, and all passed through the sea;
   2. And were all baptized unto Moses in the cloud and in the sea;
   3. And did all eat the same spiritual meat;
   4. And did all drink the same spiritual drink: for they drank of that spiritual Rock that followed them: and that Rock was Christ.
   5. But with many of them God was not well pleased: for they were overthrown in the wilderness.

How should we view the past? One negative way is to seemingly live in its events and never grasp the reality and need of the present. Some glory in the past while others continue to sorrow because of failures and lost opportunities. Another negative way consists of attempting to forget past events as "ancient history" and failing to learn from them.

The past can have great value. For instance, it can be a standard to gauge one's progress. Another positive approach is to look at past mistakes and attempt to avoid repeating them. We can also review the past to see God's marvelous provision, love and even discipline.

In the initial verses of chapter 10, the apostle Paul encourages the Corinthian believers to look back at their heritage in terms of the actions of Israel. Paul briefly brings to their attention events dating more than 1,400 years before. Though Israel wasn't the blood heritage of the Corinthians, it was their spiritual heritage.

Talk About It:
1. List all the miraculous provisions named in verses 1-4.
2. In what sense were the Lord's provisions spiritual as well as material?
3. What happened to the Israelites who rebelled against God?

The Israelites had the privilege of living under the cloud of God's visible presence. It provided direction when to stay and when to continue on the journey (see Exodus 13:21). Everyone in the nation passed through the opened waters of the Red Sea and thereby escaped the pursuing Egyptian army.

In the wilderness, the Israelites were divinely provided manna six days a week for some 38 years. It didn't end until Israel crossed the Jordan River and ate from the produce of Canaan (Joshua 5:12). On two separate occasions God miraculously provided water from a rock—sufficient water to meet the needs of more than 2 million people and approximately 500,000 head of livestock. That took a river of water (Exodus 17:1-7; Numbers 20:1-13).

Paul uses the word *spiritual* in his description of these events (1 Corinthians 10:3, 4). This does not indicate the food and water had a spiritual impact on those participating. Rather, it appears to be Paul's way of saying these were divine provisions. This can also be seen as a symbolic way of pointing to the future spiritual provision through Christ, "that Rock."

In verse 5 we see the cost of rebellion. In spite of God's miraculous provision, He did not continue to overlook the people's repeated failures to trust and instead to readily complain. Finally they crossed the line from which there was no return. As a result, death rather than life dominated the life of an entire nation.

"Those who disregard the past are bound to repeat it."
—George Santayana

B. The Warning (vv. 6-12)

6. Now these things were our examples, to the intent we should not lust after evil things, as they also lusted.

7. Neither be ye idolaters, as were some of them; as it is written, The people sat down to eat and drink, and rose up to play.

8. Neither let us commit fornication, as some of them committed, and fell in one day three and twenty thousand.

9. Neither let us tempt Christ, as some of them also tempted, and were destroyed of serpents.

10. Neither murmur ye, as some of them also murmured, and were destroyed of the destroyer.

11. Now all these things happened unto them for ensamples: and they are written for our admonition, upon whom the ends of the world are come.

12. Wherefore let him that thinketh he standeth take heed lest he fall.

Paul wanted to shake people away from their lusting and grasping of evil. Just as the ancient Israelites had lusted toward evil, so this same lust for the "things of the world" was found in the Corinthian church.

In verse 7 Paul becomes very specific. He begins with idol-

The Cost of Rebellion

atry. This sin appeared in Israel while they camped at Mount Sinai. As Moses was on the mountain praying to God, the people were at the base worshiping a golden calf (Exodus 32). Celebrating with food and drink, they rose and gave homage to the image. In Corinth a similarity is found in only the believers who defiled their own conscience by choosing to eat meat that has been dedicated to idol gods.

The second concrete sin focuses on people participating in sexual acts outside the bonds of marriage. Some were involved to simply fulfill the sexual desire while others participated under the guise of a religious ritual. Israel stood guilty (Numbers 25:1-9) as some Corinthians did in the first century.

Paul then addressed being involved in sinful actions for the purpose of seeing how God would react, usually by complaining against His methods and timing. In verse 10 Paul refers to people murmuring and the consequences. On one occasion poisonous snakes invaded the camp and many Israelites died (Numbers 21:5, 6). On another, God sent down fire and consumed the grumblers (11:1-3). In response to the complaining of certain tribal leaders, God sent a consuming fire and opened the earth to swallow up the leaders and their families (ch. 16).

Knowing these examples of sin and God's response should serve as an incentive to keep away from sin. Verse 12 of the text provides a sobering warning. Life in Christ provides a marvelous liberty. However, this liberty can become the door to failure if we do not separate ourselves from ideas and actions that can entrap us and separate us from God. Our salvation isn't promised if we persist in a lifestyle God forbids!

C. The Promise (v. 13)

13. There hath no temptation taken you but such as is common to man: but God is faithful, who will not suffer you to be tempted above that ye are able; but will with the temptation also make a way to escape, that ye may be able to bear it.

What a promise! What a tremendous consolation! No believer needs to be overcome when tested by God or tempted by the devil! Yes, God tests His children. It is part of the faith growth process. Yes, our adversary the devil seeks to make sin so tempting that we will turn from salvation to the destruction of temporary satisfaction. Yet, in either situation we can remain strong. Regardless of what we face, God will provide the strength to overcome.

CONCLUSION

The devil will do his best to attack our weaknesses with temptations. Regardless of what comes our way, we have the

Talk About It:
1. What "evil things" are believers tempted to "lust after" (v. 6)?
2. How applicable is the statement "The people sat down to eat and drink, and rose up to play" (v. 7) to the church today?
3. How serious is the sin of fornication?
4. How can we "tempt Christ" (v. 9)?
5. Why did God preserve the Old Testament stories?
6. Restate verse 12 in your own words.

Talk About It:
1. Can you experience a temptation no one else has faced?
2. What does God provide amid every temptation?

assurance of God's faithfulness to help us overcome. Through the empowerment of the Holy Spirit, direction of the Word, and the fellowship of believers holding us accountable, we are more than conquerors!

GOLDEN TEXT CHALLENGE

"ALL THESE THINGS HAPPENED UNTO THEM FOR ENSAMPLES: AND THEY ARE WRITTEN FOR OUR ADMONITION, UPON WHOM THE ENDS OF THE WORLD ARE COME" (1 Corinthians 10:11).

When we read about the repeated failures by Israel always followed by divine judgment, we shake our head and wonder at their stupidity. Yet do we learn from their mistakes? Israel's rebellions are recorded as a warning of what can happen to us. Others have fallen, and so can we, since we live in a tempting world plagued with pitfalls and snares of the devil. Let's learn from Israel's mistakes instead of repeating them.

God Provides Deliverance

Numbers 21:4-9; John 3:14-21

INTRODUCTION

The word *deliverance* brings a variety of pictures to mind. For some it speaks of being freed from the oppression of a selfish dictator or political system which totally dominates people's lives. Only those who live and escape from it can fully understand the impact of newfound freedom.

Others may think of prisoners of war being freed from cruel captors. The recent national program of saving the stories of veterans from World War II, the Korean War, and Vietnam highlights not only the horrendous events of battle but also the struggles to survive imprisonment. They tell of scant clothing in winter conditions, forced marches and starvation conditions. Pictures of their gaunt bodies cause one to wonder how they ever regained health. And then they recount their joy in being freed!

Some may even reflect on deliverance from health problems. Through divine healing God dramatically brings deliverance. Others experience it through surgery or medicine. How marvelous to feel healthy and participate in activities previously prohibited!

Today's lesson reminds us of the need to be delivered from the curse of sin. Initially, the pleasures of sin provide a false sense of freedom. In the end, those involved become cognizant of the terrifying paradox. The sin which seems to free actually binds and brings judgment. God's people, Israel, repeatedly experienced this. Though the glory of God stood constantly before them in the pillar of cloud by day and the pillar of fire at night, they strayed from Him in pursuit of self-expression and self-indulgence.

Unit Theme:
Numbers

Central Truth:
God provides deliverance from the curse of sin through Jesus Christ.

Focus:
To recognize that sin leads to judgment and look to Christ for deliverance.

Context:
God's deliverance is experienced through a brass serpent, which typifies the deliverance later effected by the Cross.

Golden Text:
"As Moses lifted up the serpent in the wilderness, even so must the Son of man be lifted up: that whosoever believeth in him should not perish, but have eternal life" (John 3:14, 15).

Study Outline:
I. Sin Judged
  (Numbers 21:4-6)
II. Confession and
  Intercession
  (Numbers 21:7-9)
III. Deliverance
  Provided
  (John 3:14-21)

I. SIN JUDGED (Numbers 21:4-6)

A. The People's Sin (vv. 4, 5)

4. And they journeyed from mount Hor by the way of the Red sea, to compass the land of Edom: and the soul of the people was much discouraged because of the way.

5. And the people spake against God, and against Moses, Wherefore have ye brought us up out of Egypt to die in the wilderness? for there is no bread, neither is there any water; and our soul loatheth this light bread.

Let's put this event into context. All those individuals age 20 and older who had been condemned to die in the wilderness for their unbelief were now dead (Numbers 14:29). The nation of Israel now consists of those who escaped the death sentence or were born during the wilderness wandering. You would think they possess a more positive mind-set regarding God's provision. Also, God has just enabled them to overcome a Canaanite king, Arad (21:1-3), in their first battle in 38 years.

Yet, a few days later they have forgotten their great victory. So as to not engage the powerful army of their brother nation, Edom, Moses leads Israel in a detouring route. Yes, God could have enabled the Hebrews to defeat this army regardless of the odds. However, even though the Edomites have disallowed Israel from crossing into Canaan, God chooses a different route.

Notice the series of complaints that burst forth from Israel's discontent with the routing to the Promised Land. With little or no hesitation, they speak freely against both their God and Moses for bringing them here for the purpose of dying. How preposterous! If that were the case, this task could have been taken care of decades earlier and without enduring all the previous problems.

The whole issue rests on food and water. They desire bread made from grain. They say there is no water. And they despise the manna. Why don't they just request what they need from the Lord? Complaining blots out any prospect of praise and remembering His previous provision.

B. God's Judgment (v. 6)

6. And the Lord sent fiery serpents among the people, and they bit the people; and much people of Israel died.

How could a loving God send such an unusual judgment on His chosen people? Isn't it rather harsh? First, the reality of a gracious God doesn't preclude the necessity for swift judgment. Second, this event doesn't project a God just waiting up there to pounce on someone doing wrong.

The total picture must be seen. These are a people who regularly experience the presence and provision of God. But

---

Talk About It:

1. Contrast the victory of verses 1-3 with the discouragement of verse 4.

2. Whom were the people's complaints against, and what did they complain about?

3. Describe the manna with which God was miraculously feeding them. Why were they dissatisfied with it?

"It is generally true that all that is required to make men unmindful of what they owe God for any blessing is that they should receive that blessing often and regularly."

—Richard Whately

fiery serpents (v. 6)—poisonous snakes

Talk About It:

Why do you suppose God judged Israel so harshly?

God Provides Deliverance

do they humbly turn to Him and Moses regarding their needs? No! Instead, they flagrantly strike out against both God and their chosen leader.

God's choosing to send venomous snakes reminds us He isn't limited to just a few select methods of bringing punishment. Also, it speaks again of the seriousness of rebelling against the Creator. On a higher plain, this situation emphasizes how God continues to fulfill His plan even in the face of those whose faith falters and who resort to rebellion. He will take the necessary steps to enable the nation to complete His sovereign plan.

II. CONFESSION AND INTERCESSION (Numbers 21:7-9)
A. The People's Confession (v. 7)

7. Therefore the people came to Moses, and said, We have sinned, for we have spoken against the Lord, and against thee; pray unto the Lord, that he take away the serpents from us. And Moses prayed for the people.

Confession normally isn't an easy act; for in doing so, the individual or group openly admits guilt and inadequacy. It speaks of making wrong decisions and failing to have the right perspective. In some cases, it becomes even more complicated when part of the admission must be made to the persons wronged.

No time perspective appears in our Scripture text. It may have been a relatively short period of time due to the pain of the bites and the subsequent deaths. Besides, can you imagine the terror which resides in the camp with this reptile invasion? The possibility of snakebite surely places everyone on edge. Eventually the people come to a conclusion—they are experiencing this unusual form of judgment because of their sins.

Isn't it amazing how, in the time of trouble, they run to Moses for intercession! Previously they accused him of being a destroyer. Now they perceive him as the needed intermediary before God. Of course, this isn't anything new. The previous generation asked Moses to be their representative before God instead of hearing God speak and seeing the demonstration of His power (Exodus 20:18, 19). Even Moses' siblings found themselves appealing to Moses to be their intercessor. After Miriam received leprosy as punishment for her complaining against Moses, Aaron pleaded for his help. And as would be expected, Moses interceded on her behalf (Numbers 12:10-13).

In today's text, the people make no attempt to minimize their actions or offer extenuating excuses. They come right to the point, saying, "We have sinned." Notice how specifically their sin is described. Boldly they spoke against the Lord and

Talk About It:
1. How specific was the Israelites' repentance? Why does this matter?
2. How did Moses respond?
3. Who bears the ministry of intercession today?

against Moses. Now they desire his prayers on their behalf.

Does the request that the snakes be taken away suggest their actions are based only on a desire for self-preservation? There's no way for us to make such a judgment since we cannot determine the motive of their hearts. However, God sees their heart, and is willing to intervene when Moses intercedes for the people. Moses demonstrates the heart of a caring, non-retaliatory shepherd regardless of the people's straying, rebellious ways.

How should we respond when believers around us fall into sin and bring false accusations against us? In the middle of our pain and frustration it may become difficult to pray for the aggressors' forgiveness and relief. We may even find ourselves enjoying their problems and discomfort. And when we do so, we have fallen into a trap of sin ourselves. We must be reminded of the words of Jesus in Matthew 5:44: "Love your enemies . . . and pray for those who spitefully use you and persecute you" (*NKJV*).

B. God's Provision (vv. 8, 9)

8. And the Lord said unto Moses, Make thee a fiery serpent, and set it upon a pole: and it shall come to pass, that every one that is bitten, when he looketh upon it, shall live.

9. And Moses made a serpent of brass, and put it upon a pole, and it came to pass, that if a serpent had bitten any man, when he beheld the serpent of brass, he lived.

Talk About It:

1. Why do you suppose the Lord prescribed such an unusual remedy?

2. What did the victims have to do in order to live?

The Lord immediately responds. There's no time for delay. People's lives are at stake. The Lord tells Moses to have a brass (bronze) serpent constructed. Then this symbolic serpent is to be placed on a pole so the people can see it.

There are many details that the curious mind wants to know. How large is the metal image? How tall is the pole on which it is placed? The details are not given. However, we must assume it to be sufficient in size and height so the people of this large encampment can have access to deliverance.

The people's deliverance from these fatal bites rests upon their choosing to look up at the image. By obediently fixing their eyes on God's provision for healing, they will live. There is no other way! No amount of positive thinking will change the reality of sure death.

As we look backward, it's easy to understand the symbolism for the future—an Old Testament type of the salvation event. Christ's being lifted up on the cross of crucifixion becomes the means for the spiritual healing of humanity. Of course, the application comes only to those who look to Him as their Savior.

It's ironic how the metal symbol, which here provides healing,

God Provides Deliverance

would later become an object of sin. The Israelites preserved the object for centuries. Problems erupted when they began to see it as an object of worship rather than a spiritual reminder of the consequences of sin, the need for confession, and God's deliverance. For that reason, when King Hezekiah came to the throne and mounted a campaign against the idolatrous places, he broke the serpent into pieces (2 Kings 18:4).

A practical application still applies to us today. God doesn't instruct a church leader to make a particular object to assist our spiritual lives. However, care needs to be taken lest we give greater attention and adoration to particular places and favorite ministers and minimize our worship of Jesus Christ, our Savior and Lord!

> "It was not the sight of the brazen serpent that cured them, but, in looking up to it, they looked up to God as the Lord that healed them."
> —Matthew Henry

III. DELIVERANCE PROVIDED (John 3:14-21)
A. Life in the Son (vv. 14-18)

14. And as Moses lifted up the serpent in the wilderness, even so must the Son of man be lifted up:

15. That whosoever believeth in him should not perish, but have eternal life.

16. For God so loved the world, that he gave his only begotten Son, that whosoever believeth in him should not perish, but have everlasting life.

17. For God sent not his Son into the world to condemn the world; but that the world through him might be saved.

18. He that believeth on him is not condemned: but he that believeth not is condemned already, because he hath not believed in the name of the only begotten Son of God.

only begotten Son (v. 16)—"one and only Son" (*NIV*)

These verses are part of Jesus' encounter with Nicodemus, a serious inquirer. We tend to think of all Pharisees negatively due to their being so antagonistic to the ministry of Christ. Their desire to be pure developed a system in which the members valued their extra laws above God's law. No wonder Jesus rebuked them in strong words. He referred to them as a "generation of vipers" (Matthew 23:33) and "whited sepulchres . . . full of dead men's bones" (v. 27). Yet, a few Pharisees, such as Nicodemus, were good men seeking the truth.

In John 3, Nicodemus acknowledges Jesus must be a teacher sent from God, as evidenced by the miraculous signs (v. 2). Then the Master reveals there is a spiritual birth through belief in the Son of God which brings deliverance from sin. He knows this will be difficult for Nicodemus, who asks, "How can a man be born when he is old?" (v. 4). To help this sincere seeker, the Master refers to an event in Israel's history.

Jesus points Nicodemus to the provision of a bronze serpent to provide life to those who would surely die from the poi-

Talk About It:
1. How would "the Son of man be lifted up" (v. 14), and why was it necessary?
2. What does it mean to "believe in" Jesus Christ?
3. What brings condemnation to a person, and when does this condemnation take place?

sonous snakebites (Numbers 21). Lifted high enough for all to see, they could receive life if they chose to look and accept God's provision. In the same manner, the Son of Man (Jesus) must also be lifted up. This speaks of His sacrificial death by being placed on the cross and dying to bring life.

John 3:15 indicates a difference between the bronze serpent and Christ. Those looking to the bronze replica received temporal life that would eventually end. However, those who look to the crucified Christ will receive nonending eternal life.

We then come to the golden text of the Bible, verse 16, in which Jesus concisely packages the gospel for Nicodemus. It's quite simple: God the heavenly Father loves a sinful, unlovable people so much that He offers the ultimate sacrifice, His Son. Through the sacrificial death of the God-man, Jesus Christ, eternal death is exchanged for eternal life! This wonderful gift comes simply by choosing to believe on Jesus and accept Him as Savior and Lord.

Jesus doesn't stop there. He continues to press the point of the purpose of His coming to earth. God did not send His Son to condemn the world for its sinfulness. Rather, He came to bring salvation from the pit of sinful destruction. The only condemnation that occurs is self-determined. Condemnation is the result of choosing not to believe in Jesus as God's Son and the only means of life eternal.

Jesus indicates there's no reason for anyone to perish spiritually. The door of eternal life stands before us when presented with the claims of Christ. Each person makes the decision to accept or reject salvation.

B. Light in the World (vv. 19-21)

19. And this is the condemnation, that light is come into the world, and men loved darkness rather than light, because their deeds were evil.

20. For every one that doeth evil hateth the light, neither cometh to the light, lest his deeds should be reproved.

21. But he that doeth truth cometh to the light, that his deeds may be made manifest, that they are wrought in God.

Using the contrast of light and darkness, Jesus points to the contrast between the Savior who comes to bring deliverance and those who cling to their evil deeds. His purpose for bringing spiritual light isn't to condemn the sinner, but to bring salvation and the promise of life eternal.

The fallen state of humanity causes individuals to cling to the spiritual darkness and their evil ways. Also, sinful actions can bring great personal enjoyment for the moment. But consequences and repercussions will follow. While "things are

Talk About It:
1. Why do people love "darkness rather than light"?
2. How does a person come to truth, and what is the result?

God Provides Deliverance

going well" the sinner sees no reason to accept the spiritual light of Jesus Christ and change his or her ways. Besides, as indicated in verse 20, this process necessitates being convicted of one's sins, recognizing the error of one's ways, and then humbly presenting oneself to the Savior in repentance.

Verse 21 explains what occurs when a person chooses light rather than darkness. His or her life begins to follow the example and teachings of Jesus Christ. Their words and actions become transparent. It is hypocritical for someone to claim life in Christ and then live in opposition to the holiness of God. Light and truth go hand in hand. Just as Jesus brought the light of truth into the world, so believers should be the candles which go forth from the greater Light offering life in the darkness of spiritual death.

CONCLUSION

A father went into a toy store to buy his son a Christmas present. The salesman showed him a new educational toy. It came unassembled, but no matter how the child put the pieces together, they wouldn't fit. That's because the toy was designed to help children learn how to deal with life.

Such is the predicament of someone without God. He is never able to put his life together. A life without Christ is fatality. (Adapted from *Illustrations for Biblical Preaching*, Baker Books)

GOLDEN TEXT CHALLENGE

"AS MOSES LIFTED UP THE SERPENT IN THE WILDERNESS, EVEN SO MUST THE SON OF MAN BE LIFTED UP: THAT WHOSOEVER BELIEVETH IN HIM SHOULD NOT PERISH, BUT HAVE ETERNAL LIFE" (John 3:14, 15).

The simplicity of God's method of healing the snake-bitten Israelites is more noteworthy than the mysteriousness with which it has often been regarded. The most significant thing about the method was that it was God's. Much the same may be said for the whole Old Testament system of worship. The Israelites did not need to know all of the "whys" and "wherefores" for their ceremonies. The primary issue was that they were worshiping God as He had ordered. Recognizing God's sovereignty is the first step in pleasing Him.

The worship practices of the Old Testament only *represented* the great facts of redemption which would be revealed in Jesus Christ. Thus, Jesus pointed out the true meaning of the brazen serpent incident in referring to it as the type of His own suffering on the cross. Jesus repeated this reference shortly before His death, saying, "I, if I be lifted up from the earth, will draw all men unto me" (John 12:32).

Pardon Rejected

During President Andrew Jackson's administration, George Wilson was sentenced to be hanged for mail robbery and murder. President Jackson wrote out a pardon for Wilson. The condemned man refused it, saying, "If I refuse the pardon, it is not a pardon."

The Attorney General, the President and others were confused, unable to decide whether the pardon was valid if refused. The Supreme Court rendered this decision: "A pardon is a paper, the value of which depends upon its acceptance by the person implicated. It is hardly to be supposed that one under sentence of death would refuse to accept a pardon. But if it is refused, it is no pardon. George Wilson must hang."

—*A New Creation*

Daily Devotions:

M. Cain's Rebellion
Punished
Genesis 4:3-12
T. Israel's Sin
Confessed
Nehemiah 9:1-8
W. David's Sin
Forgiven
Psalm 32:1-5
T. Signs of
Deliverance
Mark 16:9-18
F. Anointed to
Deliver
Luke 4:16-21
S. Jesus Delivers
the Demoniac
Luke 8:26-40

Neither the brazen serpent nor the cross, however, were the cause of redemption. The cause is found in the Father's heart of love.

It is not the cross we are to worship; not even the cross of Christ. It is rather the Christ of the cross. It is He who reveals to us the eternal love of the Father, and it is He upon whom our hopes and desires must be centered. We now look for the return of a living Christ for the completion of our salvation.

Introduction to Spring Quarter

L esson expositions for the spring quarter center on two major themes: "Roots of Christian Formation" (Christian disciplines, prayer and forgiveness), Unit 1, and "Fruit of Christian Formation" (fruit of the Spirit), Unit 2.

Unit 1 (lessons 1-3) were compiled by Lance Colkmire, editor of the Evangelical Sunday School Lesson Commentary. He also wrote the Unit 2 lessons on love, joy and peace (4-6), as well as the Easter study (7, based on John 20).

The Reverend Rodney Hodge (A.B.) authored lessons 8-13. He is an ordained minister who has served as minister of music for 30 years at Northwood Temple Pentecostal Holiness Church in Fayetteville, North Carolina. He holds degrees from Emmanuel College and the University of Georgia and did graduate studies in history at the University of Georgia.

Reverend Hodge has written numerous Bible study programs, as well as dramas and music productions, and has produced an entire series of theater productions for church use.

Additional resource available from Pathway Press:

A Balanced Church
by Charles W. Conn
$9.99
Item # 087148-0174

Call 1-800-553-8506 or go to *www.pathwaybookstore.com*

Spirit of Christian Disciplines

John 14:6-26; 15:1-8

Unit Theme:
Roots of Christian Formation

Central Truth:
Loving Christ is the essence of the Christian disciplines.

Focus:
Grasp that the spirit of the Christian disciplines is to live in continual relationship with Christ, and abide in Him.

Context:
In April A.D. 30, just before His crucifixion, Jesus teaches and comforts His disciples in preparation for the troubling days ahead.

Golden Text:
"I am the vine, ye are the branches: He that abideth in me, and I in him, the same bringeth forth much fruit: for without me ye can do nothing" (John 15:5).

Study Outline:

I. Know Christ
   (John 14:6-14)
II. Rely on the Holy Spirit
   (John 14:15-26)
III. Stay Connected to the Vine
   (John 15:1-8)

INTRODUCTION

The comforting words of Jesus in John 14:1 set the stage for today's lesson: "Let not your heart be troubled: ye believe in God, believe also in me." Remembering that these words were spoken in the Upper Room at the Last Supper gives them special significance. Moments before, Jesus had predicted the betrayal by Judas and the denial by Peter. The Eleven were beginning to understand that Jesus' time with them was soon to end, and the Savior warned them and comforted them regarding the things to come.

Chapters 14 and 15 of John's Gospel address some of the cardinal teachings of Christ:

• Jesus will come again and take His children to heaven (14:1-3, 28-31).

• Jesus Christ is God, and He is the only way to the Father (vv. 4-11).

• God will perform mighty acts in response to the Christian's prayer of faith (vv. 12-14).

• The Holy Spirit will indwell and minister to believers (14:15-27; 15:26, 27).

• Jesus and His words will abide with believers (15:1-17).

• Christians will face persecution (vv. 18-25).

If we "believe in God," it should be easy to take the next step and "believe also" in His Son. The Jews believed in God. This was fundamental to their existence as a people. Jesus led His disciples from faith in God to belief in Himself as God's Son. This fortifying of their faith with the knowledge of His return, His preparation of an eternal home for them, and His promise of One to stand with them in the meantime was a sure foundation for their faith. It should be a firm foundation for us also.

I. KNOW CHRIST (John 14:6-14)

A. Show Us the Way (vv. 6, 7)

6. Jesus saith unto him, I am the way, the truth, and the life: no man cometh unto the Father, but by me.

7. If ye had known me, ye should have known my Father also: and from henceforth ye know him, and have seen him.

Jesus' words are a reply to the question of His disciple Thomas: "Lord, we do not know where You are going, and how can we know the way?" (v. 5, *NKJV*). What Jesus had taught concerning His destination and way of going was evidently not yet clear to His disciples, and Thomas was the one bold enough to express his doubts. Thomas acknowledged His ignorance and asked for an explanation.

Jesus' self-description in verse 6 is one of the greatest theological statements of all time. The pronoun *I* is emphatic and is intended to turn the thoughts of the disciples from a method to a Person. Jesus did not say He *knew* or *taught* the way, the truth, and the life, though He did. Instead, He claimed to *be* the way, the embodiment of truth, and the essence of life. He is the only *way* of reconciliation between sinful humanity and a holy God. He is the *truth* about God, humanity and salvation. He is the source and sustainer of *life*.

Since to know Jesus is to know the Father, the disciples already had knowledge of the way to the Father. Yet, though they knew Jesus personally as a man, their spiritual discernment regarding Him fell short. But with Jesus' full and clear affirmation of Himself here, their knowledge of Him and His relation to the Father was brought to a higher level. With the Cross, the Resurrection, and the Spirit's coming at Pentecost, their knowledge and relationship would vault even higher.

B.F. Westcott said, "The announcement which Christ made had placed the nature of the Father in a clear light. The disciples could no longer doubt as to His character or purpose. In this sense they had 'seen the Father'" (*The Gospel According to John*).

B. Show Us the Father (vv. 8-11)

8. Philip saith unto him, Lord, shew us the Father, and it sufficeth us.

9. Jesus saith unto him, Have I been so long time with you, and yet hast thou not known me, Philip? he that hath seen me hath seen the Father; and how sayest thou then, Shew us the Father?

10. Believest thou not that I am in the Father, and the Father in me? the words that I speak unto you I speak not of myself: but the Father that dwelleth in me, he doeth the works.

Talk About It:
1. Name some of the false "ways" and "truths" that are popular today. What makes Jesus' claim valid?
2. How is it that the person who knows Jesus also knows God the Father?

"Men occasionally stumble over the truth, but most of them pick themselves up and hurry off as if nothing happened."

—Winston Churchill

---

11. Believe me that I am in the Father, and the Father in me: or else believe me for the very works' sake.

Talk About It:
How did the works of Jesus agree with the words of Jesus? What did His words and works testify about Him?

Now it was Philip's turn to raise a question (v. 8). He asks for a visible manifestation of the invisible God, thinking that his mortal eyes can look on the infinite God and thereby witness indisputable proof of God's reality. Believing Jesus could bring this about, he would then be satisfied.

Philip apparently failed to recognize that Jesus' life and ministry had been a true revelation of the Father. Jesus asked him, "Have I been with you so long, and yet you have not known Me, Philip?" (v. 9, *NKJV*). Jesus then reassured Philip that to have witnessed the person, the teachings, and the works of Christ for some three years made for an adequate revelation of the Father.

Verse 10 is a continuation of the gentle rebuke of Philip. Jesus reinforced the concept of the close union between the Father and the Son. And He offered two proofs of that oneness between Himself and His Father; namely, His words and His works.

"The Gateway to Christianity is not through an intricate labyrinth of dogma, but by a simple belief in the person of Christ."

—**William Lyon Phelps**

In verse 11 the Lord evidently turns from Philip to urge all the disciples to believe in Him. He demands their faith in His oneness with the Father—a clear claim to deity. This mutual indwelling was such that everything Jesus said or did was the Father's saying or doing. Hence He requires their faith in His words, which really need no credentials. But if credentials are demanded, let *the works* convince them. His miracle-filled ministry was proof that His words were true.

C. Ask in My Name (vv. 12-14)

verily (v. 12)—"I tell you the truth" (*NIV*).

12. Verily, verily, I say unto you, He that believeth on me, the works that I do shall he do also; and greater works than these shall he do; because I go unto my Father.

13. And whatsoever ye shall ask in my name, that will I do, that the Father may be glorified in the Son.

14. If ye shall ask any thing in my name, I will do it.

The double *verily* is used to introduce an important truth. Having referred to His works as supporting His claims to deity, Jesus now predicts even greater works for His faithful disciples. *Greater works* refer to quantity rather than quality, and probably refer to the scope and success of the apostolic ministry after Pentecost. Christ's work was confined to Palestine, but the apostles spread the gospel in many different lands. Thus, Christ continued His ministry on a far greater scale from heaven through His Spirit-filled apostles.

Talk About It:
1. Describe how Jesus' promise in verse 12 is taking place today.
2. What does it mean to pray in Jesus' name? What does it *not* mean?
3. Why does Jesus delight in answering prayers?

These "greater works" are contingent upon prayers made to the ascended Christ. As for the power of prayer, anything that can rightly be asked in Jesus' name will be granted. Praying "in my name" means more than using the phrase as a formula in prayer; it implies praying "by the authority of" or "in harmony with the will of," or "by the sanction of" Christ.

In verse 14, the word *I* is emphatic. The prayer is regarded as addressed to the Father, but as granted by the Son, who is one with the Father. Believers are to pray to the Father with faith in Jesus' name.

II. RELY ON THE HOLY SPIRIT (John 14:15-26)
A. Another Helper (vv. 15-18)

15. If ye love me, keep my commandments.

16. And I will pray the Father, and he shall give you another Comforter, that he may abide with you for ever;

17. Even the Spirit of truth; whom the world cannot receive, because it seeth him not, neither knoweth him: but ye know him; for he dwelleth with you, and shall be in you.

18. I will not leave you comfortless: I will come to you.

Here Jesus begins teaching His disciples the role of the Holy Spirit during His own physical absence from them. The conjunction *and* at the beginning of verse 16 implies that the work of the Holy Spirit in the Christian's life is tied inseparably to the believer's obedience to Jesus' command that we love Him (v. 15). The Holy Spirit mandates and empowers that love. In the New Testament, love consistently appears not as an emotion but as a commitment—as the result of a mind motivated and empowered by the Holy Spirit.

Jesus refers to the Holy Spirit as the *Comforter* (v. 16), which means "one who strengthens." The Greek word (*Parakletos*) was often used with reference to an advocate for the defense in a court trial. By calling the Holy Spirit *another Comforter*, Jesus was saying He had been the disciples' Advocate, Teacher and Helper until this point, but the Holy Spirit would be with them *forever*.

The Comforter, to be sent by the Father at Jesus' request, is the *Spirit of truth* (v. 17). He would enable believers to understand and apply divinely revealed truths. He is not received by the world of unbelieving people because they are not spiritually enlightened and prepared for His ministry to them. But for the disciples who had already recognized the Spirit's presence in Christ, He gave the assurance that the Spirit would indwell them.

In verse 18 Jesus assured His disciples He would not abandon them, like orphans bereft of parents, but would come to them. He kept that promise through His postresurrection appearances to the disciples. Jesus gave them assurance and direction during the 40 days between the Resurrection and Ascension, readying them to carry forward His work on earth. Jesus also came to them by sending them the Holy Spirit on the Day of Pentecost, and Christ's presence has continued in the church since that day. Also, Christ will come to (and for) His followers visibly at the Second Coming.

Talk About It:
1. Why is obedience to Christ the evidence of genuine love for Him?
2. Describe everything Jesus reveals about the Holy Spirit in verses 16 and 17.
3. Why can't worldly people accept "the Spirit of truth"?

"It is impossible for that man to despair who remembers that his Helper is omnipotent."
—Jeremy Taylor

B. Proven Love (vv. 19-24)

(John 14:22-24 is not included in the printed text.)

19. Yet a little while, and the world seeth me no more; but ye see me: because I live, ye shall live also.

20. At that day ye shall know that I am in my Father, and ye in me, and I in you.

21. He that hath my commandments, and keepeth them, he it is that loveth me: and he that loveth me shall be loved of my Father, and I will love him, and will manifest myself to him.

Talk About It:

1. Explain Jesus' promise, "Because I live, ye shall live also" (v. 19).

2. What does it mean for Jesus to "manifest" Himself to someone (v. 21)? To whom does He manifest Himself, and why?

3. Describe God the Father's relationship with Christians (vv. 21, 23).

"Christianity does not think of a man finally submitting to the power of God; it thinks of him as finally surrendering to the love of God. It is not that man's will is crushed, but that man's heart is broken."

—William Barclay

Jesus again reminds His disciples that His departure is at hand, after which He would not appear to the world of unbelievers; no, not until the end of the age. His own, however, would see Him—a fact realized in His postresurrection appearances. Their beholding Him in His resurrection life was a pledge that they were also to share in that life.

Adam Clarke paraphrases verse 20, "After my resurrection, ye shall be more fully convinced of this important truth, that I and the Father are one; for I will live in you by the energy of my Spirit, and ye shall live in me by faith, love, and obedience."

In verses 21-24, love and obedience are emphasized as being characteristic of the age of the Holy Spirit. Here, too, the Lord assures His disciples He will *manifest*, or "disclose," Himself to those who love Him. There will be a continually growing and unfolding relationship of love between Jesus and His disciples. Unreserved love means unreserved commitment, which produces a deepening knowledge of Jesus.

Judas (or *Jude*) asks, "Lord, why do you intend to show yourself to us and not to the world?" (v. 22, *NIV*). Jesus ignored the obvious reference to an earthly existence and stated clearly the believers' relationship with God. Those who love Christ will obey Him; thus they will experience the presence of the Father and the Son. To reject Christ's words was to reject the Father, which is exactly what the world does. That's why Christ does not manifest Himself to the world.

C. Holy Teacher (vv. 25, 26)

25. These things have I spoken unto you, being yet present with you.

26. But the Comforter, which is the Holy Ghost, whom the Father will send in my name, he shall teach you all things, and bring all things to your remembrance, whatsoever I have said unto you.

Talk About It:

What has the Holy Spirit taught you? What has He brought to your memory?

"Jesus said the Holy Spirit would teach the disciples 'all things' it was needful for them to understand in the apostolic office, and particularly those things which they were not prepared then to hear or could not then understand," commented

Albert Barnes. "The Holy Spirit would seasonably remind them of the sayings of Jesus, which they might otherwise have forgotten. In the organization of the church, and in composing the sacred history, He would preside over their memories, and recall such truths and doctrines as were necessary either for their comfort or the edification of His people."

Also, "the Holy Spirit would teach them the meaning of those things which the Savior had spoken. Thus they did not understand that He ought to be put to death until after His resurrection, though He had repeatedly told them of it. So they did not until then understand that the gospel was to be preached to the Gentiles, though this was also declared before" (*Barnes' Notes*).

III. STAY CONNECTED TO THE VINE (John 15:1-7)

A. The True Vine (v. 1)

1. I am the true vine, and my Father is the husbandman.

Jesus in John 15 continued that long but enriching discourse started in chapter 13. At the end of chapter 14, Jesus and His disciples apparently left the Upper Room (see v. 31) in which they had celebrated the Passover and in which Jesus had instituted the Lord's Supper. The metaphor of the vine in John 15:1-17, then, might well have been communicated to the disciples while they were going to Gethsemane.

The vine is a living organism, nurtured by the sun and by nutrients in the soil. Here, Jesus himself is the vine; that is, He is the main trunk, connected with the rootage and essential to the continued life of any branch. Analogies are never perfect; hence Jesus cannot show through this metaphor the organic connection of God the Father to Himself and His followers. Instead, He will show another essential function of God the Father—that of gardener or vinedresser ("husbandman"). Hereby, Jesus can also show the ultimate authority of God the Father over Christ and His church. As vinedresser, the Father bears final responsibility for the health of the entire organism. His work determines the prevention of disease and fruitlessness.

B. The Pruned Branches (vv. 2-5)

2. Every branch in me that beareth not fruit he taketh away: and every branch that beareth fruit, he purgeth it, that it may bring forth more fruit.

3. Now ye are clean through the word which I have spoken unto you.

4. Abide in me, and I in you. As the branch cannot bear fruit of itself, except it abide in the vine; no more can ye, except ye abide in me.

5. I am the vine, ye are the branches: He that abideth in

Talk About It:
How does a person become part of "the true vine"?

me, and I in him, the same bringeth forth much fruit: for without me ye can do nothing.

Talk About It:

1. Describe the fruit God expects believers to bear.

2. How does someone "abide in" Christ (v. 4)?

Pain With Purpose

Jesus spoke to His disciples of first bearing *fruit*, then *more* fruit, and finally *much* fruit (John 15:2, 5). This statement not only attests to the increase of fruit-bearing in us, but it speaks of a pruning process responsible for the increase. This purging means cutting, or pruning, from our lives all that is unlike Christ or hinders our fruitfulness for Him. Purging or purifying is often a painful process, but it must be done. We must be purged of our fascination with the world, our carnal ambitions, our profane associations and our own base nature, in order that Christ and His nature may abide and abound in us. If we are not purged of unspiritual attitudes and habits, then we shall die—and no fruit grows on dead branches.

—Charles W. Conn

The key to the survival of any given branch lies in fruit-bearing. Now each branch is a disciple, and the fruit borne by a branch, the organic outgrowth of the life of the Vine, is listed in Galatians 5:22, 23: "love, joy, peace, patience, kindness, goodness, faithfulness, gentleness and self-control" (*NIV*). The fruit of a believer are the qualities of Christian character that appear as the disciple stays connected to the Vine, Jesus Christ.

As a vinedresser inspects the vine, he finds various conditions. Some branches are putting forth luscious grapes, beautiful to behold and tempting to the palate. These are the pride of the vinedresser. Other branches contain shoots (small outgrowths), which are drawing valuable nutrients from the branch without contributing to the function of the organism. These the vinedresser cuts away. Some branches, through disease or whatever other means, have withered and are no longer drawing life from the vine. These the vinedresser cuts off and piles up for burning.

Even essentially healthy believers, however, require pruning, and God mercifully works on them, molding them through circumstance, sometimes to the point of temporary pain, but always with their spiritual fruitfulness and ultimate preservation in mind.

The word *clean* (v. 3) refers to the result of the purging process. Jesus' disciples had benefited already from their constant association with Christ, during which He could give detailed attention to their lives, observing weaknesses one by one. Now He could say, "You are clean. You are free from impurities and weaknesses which, had they been allowed to remain, might ultimately have cost you your spiritual life."

That interrelationship with Christ essential to spiritual life becomes clear in verse 4. The primary precondition for survival of the branch is remaining attached to the Vine. Jesus is the believer's source of life. Only as we draw from Him those spiritual nutrients essential to life can we remain healthy Christians. And how does this nurturing relationship occur? Basically through prayer when we tell Him our need, express to Him our love, and listen to Him speak to us in turn; and through God's Word as we absorb from its pages those spiritual principles which are made alive within our heart by the Holy Spirit. This enables us to withstand pressures from the world and operate properly as a part of the body of Christ. Extended means of nurture from our source of life occur during corporate worship, fellowship with other believers, and expression of faith in Christian activity (for instance, various avenues of witnessing).

Abiding in Christ produces "much fruit." Connected to the

main trunk, the branch absorbs its life-giving nutrients and behaves as it must as a productive part of the organism, putting forth delectable fruit. Some Christians fail to apply the lesson of this metaphor and, as a result, fail to remain connected. The result is evident in the absence of truly Christlike character. There may be in its place an attempt to deliberately create a pious image through religious routines, a perpetual artificial smile, special "Christian" jargon, and careful attention to certain highly visible external practices. However, if the disciple (the branch) is connected to Jesus (the trunk), genuine holiness of character (the fruit) will be evident in all roles, relationships, and activities of that believer's life.

C. The Plight of the Fruitless (v. 6)

6. If a man abide not in me, he is cast forth as a branch, and is withered; and men gather them, and cast them into the fire, and they are burned.

Five distinct things happen to the nonproductive branch according to verse 6: (1) It is severed from the vine and thrown aside; (2) it withers because it is cut off from its source of life; (3) a worker in the vineyard collects it; (4) it is cast into a pile of burning branches; (5) it is consumed by the flames.

Any disciple who is cut off from his source of spiritual life withers. The changes in his character soon are evident to those around him. No longer can Christ be clearly seen in his life; instead, the ugliness of sin—the antithesis of life—appears. Ultimately all evidence of his having once been connected with life is gone, and he suffers the final result—total alienation from God and good—in the fires of hell.

Talk About It:
What causes some people to no longer "abide" (remain) in Christ? What are the consequences?

D. The Promise of Answered Prayer (v. 7)

7. If ye abide in me, and my words abide in you, ye shall ask what ye will, and it shall be done unto you.

Jesus is not offering here a blank check to carnal, immature Christians so they might satisfy desires and impulses which do not further the kingdom of God. In James 4:2, 3 the Word speaks plainly to such persons: "Ye lust, and have not: ye kill, and desire to have, and cannot obtain: ye fight and war, yet ye have not, because ye ask not. Ye ask, and receive not, because ye ask amiss, that ye may consume it upon your lusts." A person, then, who prays with selfish motives or without regard to what should be his primary motive—the kingdom of God—will not receive a positive response, however much he may believe (within his own spirit) that he is going to receive.

However, the person who abides in Christ, whose will has been subordinated to His will, whose desires are wholly focused upon Christ and His kingdom, and whose mind and

Talk About It:
1. What does it mean for Christ's words to "abide in you"?
2. Describe some prayers Christ will not answer.

spirit are permeated by His Word, will indeed receive whatever he asks since he will want nothing contrary to God's will and since his entire life will be absorbed in doing God's will.

CONCLUSION

If the Christian is not careful, he will become so absorbed in religious activity—good activity—that he will leave no time for cultivation of the spiritual life. As a result, he will fail to remain in intimate spiritual relationship with Jesus. Then he will bear even less spiritual fruit (which, remember, is not Christian *activity* but Christian *character*, the automatic result of the life of Jesus functioning within us). And as he bears less fruit, his Father in heaven will receive less glory—most regrettably since the primary aim of the Christian should be to glorify God. If the Christian disciple would realize his necessary aim of giving the maximum amount of glory to God, he must be fruitful—through interrelationship with Jesus the Son and God the Father. Jesus said, "This is to my Father's glory that you bear much fruit" (John 15:8, *NIV*).

GOLDEN TEXT CHALLENGE

"I AM THE VINE, YE ARE THE BRANCHES: HE THAT ABIDETH IN ME, AND I IN HIM, THE SAME BRINGETH FORTH MUCH FRUIT: FOR WITHOUT ME YE CAN DO NOTHING" (John 15:5).

The *identification* of the organism is a simple statement of fact: "I am the vine, ye are the branches." The vine is everything: root, trunk, branches, twigs, leaves, fruit. The branches are one part of the vine.

The *integration* of the organism is reciprocal: "He that abideth in me, and I in him. . . ." The branches remain or continue in the vine, and the vine abides in the branch. Believers, as branches, remain in the Vine by faith; the Vine continues in the branch by the Holy Spirit.

The *inspiration* of the organism is demonstrated by fruit. To the degree that the vine and branch are in vital connection, there will be fruit; for fruit is the visible evidence of the flow of life through the branch.

The *immobilization* of the organism can be accomplished by separation of the branch from the vine. "For without me"—that is, apart from Christ, with space between the Vine and the branch which interrupts the flow of life from the Vine through the branch—"ye can do nothing."

Daily Devotions:
M. Obedience Better Than Sacrifice
1 Samuel 15:20-25
T. Desiring to Do God's Will
Psalm 40:1-9
W. Holy Union
John 17:20-26
T. Living Sacrifices
Romans 12:1-11
F. Disciplines for Holy Living
Colossians 3:1-11
S. Life in the Son
1 John 5:1-12

Prayer: Conversations With the Father

Matthew 6:5-7; Mark 1:35-39; Luke 11:1-4; John 17:1-5, 13-21, 25, 26

INTRODUCTION

Prayer is a nearly universal human activity. Across the globe countless men and women offer it to diverse gods, in various attitudes, from different stances, and for every conceivable reason. It seems almost instinctive in times of great stress. In fact, people who engage in no other religious activity will pray when under pressure. So important is prayer that within the various religions of the world numerous guides and manuals have been created as means to increase its effectiveness. It is offered as a part of complex religious ritual, it exists in various formulas, and precise verbal behavior is often demanded in its practice.

It is also a person's noblest activity—when offered from a sincere heart to the living God.

What is prayer? Valid prayer is intimate communication with God, vital to spiritual life. Jesus prayed to His Father continually. The Gospel of Luke, for example, repeatedly presents Jesus in prayer: during His baptism (3:21), as a matter of habit in the wilderness (5:16), on a mountain before choosing the 12 apostles (6:12), just before His clear-cut revelation to His disciples of His full identity (9:18), in praise to His Father upon the return of the Seventy from their mission of ministry (10:21), in Gethsemane (22:41, 42), and during His physical and spiritual agony on the cross (23:34, 46).

Jesus, moreover, taught His disciples how to pray effectively. In the Sermon on the Mount He counseled secrecy, cautioned against meaningless repetition, and gave in its fullest form His model prayer (Matthew 6:1-15). In Luke 18:1-14 He encouraged persistence in prayer and showed the necessity of honesty with oneself before God. The New Testament in these and other passages enunciates several simple principles: recognition of divine authority, sincerity, simple faith, and persistence. Our lesson for this week emphasizes those principles as Jesus teaches about prayer.

Unit Theme:
Roots of Christian Formation

Central Truth:
Prayer is transforming dialogue with the heavenly Father.

Focus:
Study the prayer life of Christ and learn to pray as He did.

Context:
Selected New Testament passages in which Jesus tells and shows believers how to pray.

Golden Text:
"As he [Christ] was praying in a certain place, when he ceased, one of his disciples said unto him, Lord, teach us to pray" (Luke 11:1).

Study Outline:
I. Solitude: A Place of Prayer
(Mark 1:35-39; Matthew 6:5-7)
II. Conversing With God
(John 17:1-5, 13-21, 25, 26)
III. The Model Prayer
(Luke 11:1-4)

I. SOLITUDE: A PLACE OF PRAYER (Mark 1:35-39; Matthew 6:5-7)

A. Jesus Alone at Prayer (Mark 1:35)

35. And in the morning, rising up a great while before day, he went out, and departed into a solitary place, and there prayed.

Talk About It:
How should Jesus' example in verse 35 apply to our prayer life?

Having demonstrated His divine authority and power in the synagogue, in the home, and on the street in Capernaum on one memorable Sabbath, Jesus had become known and famous throughout Galilee. Crowds gathered to see and hear Him. Therefore He found it necessary to seek spiritual replenishment and communion alone with His heavenly Father in the early morning.

It is surely extraordinary that Jesus, after such a busy day and at the time when He must have known crowds would soon be thronging to see Him, would rise early in the morning and quietly find His way out of the city to a place of solitude for prayer. "It was when men most sought Him that He most sought God" (W.G. Scroggie). Because He was not only the Son of God but also a man dependent on the Father's will and the Spirit's enabling for His work, He had need to pray. And while the city was still asleep, Jesus rose up and went out to a solitary place to pray—or more accurately stated, "He continued in prayer," as though He had been in an attitude of prayer for some time.

"The moment you wake up each morning, all your wishes and hopes for the day rush at you like wild animals. And the first job each morning consists in shoving it all back; in listening to that other voice, taking that other point of view, letting that other, larger, stronger, quieter life come flowing in."
—C.S. Lewis

The word for *praying* here involves more than asking. "It suggests the going forward in desire to God, not for God's gift only, but for God. It is the word for true worship, the word that describes the soul moving toward God, desiring Him, and all He has to give" (G.C. Morgan).

If then Jesus—who taught with authority, delivered the demoniacs, and healed the sick with divine power—had need of prayer, surely we must also pray if we are to minister effectively and serve God with results. While prayer is a heart attitude, it is also an act and requires a time and place conducive for communion with God.

B. Jesus Sought by Many People (vv. 36, 37)

36. And Simon and they that were with him followed after him.

37. And when they had found him, they said unto him, All men seek for thee.

Talk About It:
Why is it that the more people "seek for" us, the more we need to pray?

Our Lord, however, even in the place of solitude, was never safe from interruption. Simon and the other disciples, evidently concerned about Jesus' absence and the gathering of the seeking people, set out to find Him. The words mark the anxiety and eagerness of their search. They "followed after him"—they pursued Him and hunted Him down.

Having found Him, they promptly informed Him that He was being sought by the crowds. Perhaps the disciples were disturbed by the seeking crowds in the city and felt Jesus was wasting His precious time and passing up golden opportunities to help the needy. But while there is a time to work, there must also be a time to pray and to recharge the spiritual battery that may have run down from hours of work. And Jesus knew how to budget His time and refresh His soul for the tasks of the day.

C. Jesus Powerful in Ministry (vv. 38, 39)

38. And he said unto them, Let us go into the next towns, that I may preach there also: for therefore came I forth.

39. And he preached in their synagogues throughout all Galilee, and cast out devils.

The Lord did not seem irritated by this interruption of His secret communion with God, for He responded to the intruders with gentleness and love. True fellowship with God is never selfish, but is willing to be interrupted when others need help. He did not request more time to pray; His early rising had anticipated the later demands upon Him. But He did take the occasion to explain to His disciples the further reason for His withdrawal from Capernaum. This city had been given one great opportunity to hear His message and receive His healing ministry. It must have no monopoly on His time, for other towns and communities more needy must have opportunity to receive His blessing.

The purpose of Christ's mission was to preach and minister to all who had need. He had come forth from the place of communion with God to minister under God's authority and providence to the lost, the sick, and the poor. It was His divine mission, essential and eternal.

Talk About It:
1. What was Jesus' purpose in coming to earth?
2. How did Jesus' words and works declare His identity?

D. The Hypocrite's Reward (Matthew 6:5)

5. And when thou prayest, thou shalt not be as the hypocrites are: for they love to pray standing in the synagogues and in the corners of the streets, that they may be seen of men. Verily I say unto you, They have their reward.

A primary motive in prayer is sincerity. The Pharisees manifested the same spirit about prayer as they did in giving; it was done in public places so as to be seen by people. They sought publicity and had come to regard the publicity they received as evidence of their great piety. Prayer had been reduced to a systematic schedule among the Jews, so that the hour of prayer might overtake a person anywhere. It is suggested that the hypocritical Pharisees might want to be so overtaken, especially in some public place where they could display their pretentious piety. The synagogues were, of course, places of

Talk About It:
1. Is the "praying" Jesus describes here genuine prayer? Why or why not?
2. What is the reward for "look-at-me" praying?

prayer, so here it would not be the place that mattered, but the manner, motive and intent. Unlike the practice of the Pharisees, which has the limited reward of the admiration of people, Christians are exhorted to seek divine approval rather than human admiration.

"Since 'that they may be seen of men' constitutes the evil, we may fairly say that Christ is not here prescribing the place where, but the spirit in which, we ought to pray; that what He condemned is not the fact of praying where we can be seen, but of picking out the place in order that we may be seen; that, in a word, the contrast here is between ostentation and sincerity" (Alexander MacLaren).

E. The Seeker's Reward (vv. 6, 7)

6. But thou, when thou prayest, enter into thy closet, and when thou hast shut thy door, pray to thy Father which is in secret; and thy Father which seeth in secret shall reward thee openly.

7. But when ye pray, use not vain repetitions, as the heathen do: for they think that they shall be heard for their much speaking.

Secrecy in prayer, as here exhorted, is meant to emphasize concentration, a sincere seeking after the divine Presence rather than human attention. The *closet* is the secret place of prayer, the place where all distractions are excluded from one's thoughts in realization of the heavenly Father's spiritual presence.

The Lord did not imply, however, that social or public prayer is ruled out, whether it be in the church or on the street corner. But it does imply that such public prayer will be effective only in proportion as it comes from a gathering of persons accustomed to private prayer. While secrecy in prayer may not get the admiration of people, it will surely have the Father's recognition, for He sees our inner motive for prayer as well as our secret place of prayer.

The Lord does not specify the times for such secret prayer and devotions. However, such times for prayer are needful. It may be in the morning, after a night's rest, preceding the activities of the day; or in the evening, when the day is done and we are thankful for the divine protection and leading. It may be in times of perplexity and embarrassment, in times of strong temptation. Then too, we should pray when the Holy Spirit moves us to seek God.

Simplicity in prayer is to avoid using vain repetitions (v. 7), and to concentrate on our needs and the Father's readiness to hear and answer. We are warned to avoid wordiness and empty phrases in prayer as being heathenish and useless. The pagans thought that by endless repetitions and many words

Talk About It:

1. Do you have a "prayer closet"? If so, how often do you occupy it?

2. According to verse 7, what wrong idea do some Christians have about prayer?

Prayer: Conversations With the Father

they would inform their gods as to their needs and weary them into granting their requests. An example of this may be found in the Baal worshipers of Elijah's day: "They . . . called on the name of Baal from morning even until noon, saying, O Baal, hear us" (1 Kings 18:26). It is possible, even for believers with good intentions, to become habitual in praying and to repeatedly use certain words and phrases till they lose their significance.

The Pharisees were open to the same censure as the heathen, for they made long prayers in a showy display of devotional zeal. It is not, however, the length of time spent in prayer or the fervent or reasonable repetition of forms of prayer that is forbidden, but the mechanical repetition of set words, and the belief that the efficacy of prayer consists in such repetition.

> "Is there any place in any of our rooms where there is a little bit of carpet worn by our knees?"
> —Alexander MacLaren

II. CONVERSING WITH GOD (John 17:1-5, 13-21, 25, 26)

A. Jesus Prays for Himself (vv. 1-5)

1. These words spake Jesus, and lifted up his eyes to heaven, and said, Father, the hour is come; glorify thy Son, that thy Son also may glorify thee:

2. As thou hast given him power over all flesh, that he should give eternal life to as many as thou hast given him.

3. And this is life eternal, that they might know thee the only true God, and Jesus Christ, whom thou hast sent.

4. I have glorified thee on the earth: I have finished the work which thou gavest me to do.

5. And now, O Father, glorify thou me with thine own self with the glory which I had with thee before the world was.

John 17 is the longest recorded prayer Jesus offered during His public ministry on earth. It has been justly designated the High Priestly Prayer. It was offered in the presence of His disciples after the institution and celebration of the Lord's Supper. It followed immediately the discourses recorded in chapters 14-16. Matthew Henry appropriately said of it, "The most remarkable prayer followed the most full and consoling discourse ever uttered on earth."

"The hour" Jesus was speaking of in verse 1 was the same as that referred to in 7:30 and 8:20. There John had said "his hour was not yet come." Now Jesus said "the hour is come." He meant, of course, His exaltation through death. Jesus had been preparing for this hour since the beginning of His earthly life. He had anticipated it in all His teachings, as well as in the miracles He performed. This hour had constituted the underlying purpose of His life on earth.

In verse 1, as noted by G. Campbell Morgan, "Jesus was expressing His desire that the Son might be glorified. What for? That the Son may glorify the Father. The deepest passion of His heart was the glory of God. The deepest passion of the heart of Jesus was not the saving of men, but the glory of God;

Talk About It:
1. What did Jesus mean by saying, "The hour is come" (v. 1)?
2. What authority did Jesus Christ have (vv. 2, 3)?
3. How had Jesus brought glory to the heavenly Father (v. 4)?
4. Describe the glory Jesus requested (v. 5). Why did He want this glory?

and then the saving of men, because that is for the glory of God" (*The Gospel According to John*).

Through His coming death and resurrection, Jesus would have the power to grant eternal life to unsaved humanity. Everyone who responds to the Father's wooing love is *given* to the Son, who gives the believer everlasting life.

Jesus defined *eternal life* as knowing the only true God and Jesus Christ His messenger (v. 3). This new life begins now, here on earth. To know God is to experience eternal life. It means knowing God and His Son personally—becoming intimately acquainted with Him.

Verse 4 says Jesus had glorified the Father on earth. How? Through His life, His teachings, His miracles, His obedience and His sufferings. And He would glorify the Father even more through His death and resurrection.

According to verse 5, the Son had an essential glory with the Father before the foundation of the world. For a time He emptied Himself of that which He received again. Philippians 2:8, 9 says the Son "humbled himself, and became obedient unto death, even the death of the cross. Wherefore God also hath highly exalted him, and given him a name which is above every name."

B. Jesus Prays for His Disciples (vv. 13-19)

13. And now come I to thee; and these things I speak in the world, that they might have my joy fulfilled in themselves.

14. I have given them thy word; and the world hath hated them, because they are not of the world, even as I am not of the world.

15. I pray not that thou shouldest take them out of the world, but that thou shouldest keep them from the evil.

16. They are not of the world, even as I am not of the world.

17. Sanctify them through thy truth: thy word is truth.

18. As thou hast sent me into the world, even so have I also sent them into the world.

19. And for their sakes I sanctify myself, that they also might be sanctified through the truth.

To this point Christ had been with His disciples and watching over them; but now it was to be so no longer. The old relation was about to be terminated, for He was already on His way to the Father. Still in the world, however, He was praying audibly so the disciples might be encouraged from His words. He prayed, too, that they might share in the joy of His completed mission on earth.

The pronoun *I* (v. 14) is emphatic and indicates the Lord, in

> "Prayer is surrender—surrender to the will of God and cooperation with that will. If I throw out a boat hook from the boat and catch hold of the shore and pull, do I pull the shore to me, or do I pull myself to the shore? Prayer is not pulling God to my will, but the aligning of my will to the will of God."
>
> —E. Stanley Jones

Talk About It:

1. Why is it important for Christians to have the joy Christ prayed we would have (v. 13)?

Prayer: Conversations With the Father

opposition to the world, in His gift of God's revelation to His own. Time and again they had heard His gracious and authoritative words as the Word of God. Now this revelation was entrusted to them. And because they had received this revelation of God in Christ, they were recognized as separate from the world even as Christ was separate, and had, therefore, become the objects of the world's hatred. As Jesus had encountered the undeserved hatred of civil and religious leaders, so His disciples were destined to know a similar fate.

It may have seemed to be desirable to have removed the disciples from the world, the scene of conflict and trouble. But not so, for this would have defeated the divine purpose. Although physically and psychologically in the world, true believers are not of the world, even as Christ was not of the world. Christians have a different standing, a different nature, a different Master, a different aim, a different citizenship, a different life, and a different destiny.

It was not enough for the apostles to be kept from evil in the world. They must be sanctified, or consecrated, for their advance against evil and for the cause of Christ. Thus, Christ prayed that His own be set apart from the profane and the evil in the world so they might be effective witnesses to the world. This sanctification is in, or by, the *truth* (v. 17)—God's Word.

The sanctification of the apostles was related to two areas: (1) their work for Christ and (2) Christ's work for them. As Christ was "sent" by His Father as a missionary to this world, so Christ "sent" His apostles as missionaries into the same world (v. 18). *Apostle* is the Greek term and *missionary* is the Latin term for "one who is sent." Christ had represented the Father to the world, and now the disciples were commissioned to represent Christ to the world.

In verse 19 Christ refers to His work for His apostles and to the mission entrusted to them. Jesus dedicated ("sanctified") Himself as a sacrifice in behalf of His disciples so they too could be sanctified.

C. Jesus Prays for All Believers (vv. 20, 21, 25, 26)
(John 17:25, 26 is not included in the printed text.)
20. Neither pray I for these alone, but for them also which shall believe on me through their word;
21. That they all may be one; as thou, Father, art in me, and I in thee, that they also may be one in us: that the world may believe that thou hast sent me.
"Their word" (v. 20) is the message of salvation in Christ, entrusted to the apostles by the Lord, and is the means of the larger harvest of believers anticipated in Jesus' prayer. The transmission of the divine word is, then, from the Father to the Son,

2. According to verse 16, how are believers like Christ? What challenge does this bring (v. 14)? How can believers lead Christlike lives (vv. 15, 17)?

3. According to verse 18, how else are believers like Christ?

4. What does it mean to be sanctified? How did Jesus sanctify Himself on the behalf of believers?

1. Why does Jesus want Christians to be unified (vv. 20-23)?
2. How does Jesus reveal His love for people in verse 24?
3. What is Jesus' desire for the world (vv. 25, 26)?

from the Son to believers, and from believers to an unbelieving world. For this unbelieving world the Lord now begins to pray.

In verse 21 the Lord prays for the spiritual unity of all believers, and that this unity may be a counterpart of the unity of Father and Son. This is not uniformity or necessarily organizational unity, but rather a spiritual unity which transcends denominational barriers. It is a oneness based on divine truth and spiritual life. The result of this unity is a world convinced of the Son's redeeming mission.

Verses 25 and 26 comprise a summary of the whole High Priestly Prayer. The term *righteous Father* may be considered as an appeal to the justice of God, knowing that He will surely do what is absolutely right. Two facts are then stressed: knowledge and love. Although the world had not known the Father, Christ knew Him, and His disciples knew the Father had sent the Son. This knowledge Christ had revealed to His own as He declared God's name and the divine attributes represented in that name.

In conclusion, Christ desires that the divine love exemplified by the Father may be evident in His followers through the mediation of the Son. That is Christ's desire for us.

III. THE MODEL PRAYER (Luke 11:1-4)
A. The Request for Instruction (v. 1)
1. And it came to pass, that, as he was praying in a certain place, when he ceased, one of his disciples said unto him, Lord, teach us to pray, as John also taught his disciples.

Talk About It:
What prompted a disciple to ask, "Lord, teach us to pray"?

Jesus was on His way to Jerusalem, moving slowly toward that city since He was stopping continually to minister in the towns and villages along the way. At some unnamed spot He stopped to pray. Apparently there were qualities in His prayer life—perhaps the sense of intimacy with His Father, fervency of spirit, verbal fluency, or the presence of the Holy Spirit—which impressed greatly one of His disciples who chanced to overhear. After Jesus had finished praying, the disciple—who either had not been present when Jesus delivered the Sermon on the Mount or who had not been spiritually prepared to absorb the lesson on prayer—asked Jesus to teach the disciples to pray.

"God wants us to seek Him more than anything else, even more than we seek answers to prayer. When we come to God in prayer, sometimes our hearts are so full of what we want that we leave God out."
—Charles Stanley

This particular disciple was aware that John the Baptist had given instructions regarding prayer to his followers (he might even previously have been one of John's disciples), and perhaps, sensing a difference in Jesus' prayer life, wished to know its secret. Jesus, of course, responded graciously to the request of His follower and gave the relatively simple, though profound, instructions found in Luke 11.

B. Our Father (v. 2)
2. And he said unto them, When ye pray, say, Our Father which art in heaven, Hallowed be thy name. Thy

kingdom come. Thy will be done, as in heaven, so in earth.
This model for prayer had been given by Jesus in the Sermon on the Mount at the beginning of His ministry (Matthew 6:9-13). He repeated it here, though it is nearly the same in substance. (It indeed is likely that Jesus often repeated His teaching on different occasions and in different forms, thus they ended up in the four Gospels in variant forms. The substance, of course, is never contradictory.)

The first phrase of the Lord's Prayer establishes the essential attitude for efficacious praying—"Our Father." The Old Testament prophets had acknowledged God as Father of the nation of Israel but had not recognized the fatherhood of God as operative on an individual level. Jesus demonstrated to His disciples that intimacy of communion with God is best characterized as that of a child with his father. In those prayers of Jesus recorded in the Bible, He speaks to God in terms of precious intimacy, teaching His followers thereby that great degree of closeness with which our heavenly Father wishes to relate to His children.

Praying the second aspect of the prayer—"Hallowed be thy name"—is an act of reverence and of worship. The name of God represents—indeed embodies—all those qualities and characteristics which compose His divine nature; therefore, in praying "Hallowed be thy name," we worshipfully give homage to His omnipotence, omniscience, omnipresence, infinite benevolence, and limitless grace, ever reaching toward us. In fact, as we learn more about Him, our worship becomes ever richer because we understand His wondrous qualities more fully, though always very incompletely.

If the Christian believer walks in such intimate fellowship with God, he eagerly awaits the consummation of God's plan in this world. At that time the kingdom of God will be realized in its fullness during Christ's millennial reign on earth. Then and afterward, believers will enjoy incomprehensible communion with Deity. Hence, every knowledgeable Christian prays "Thy kingdom come" with intense earnestness and with great eagerness.

When the dedicated believer addresses God as Father, reverences His name, and expresses a desire for His kingdom to be fully realized, he or she has already implicitly acknowledged the rightness of the fulfillment of God's will in heaven and in earth. The praying believer thereby implicitly agrees with God, putting himself in harmony with the divine plan for the universe; seeing himself, however small, as meshing with other parts of God's great design; and being willing to be an instrument of God in the realization of God's perfect will.

C. Our Daily Bread (v. 3)
3. Give us day by day our daily bread.

Talk About It:
1. How significant is it that we can join Jesus in beginning our prayer with "Our Father"?
2. If God is all-powerful and sovereign, why must we pray, "Thy will be done"?

Ten Years
Two Christian women, whose husbands were unconverted, agreed to spend one hour each day in united prayer for their salvation. This continued for seven years. When they debated whether they should pray longer, they decided to persevere till death; and, if their husbands went to destruction, it would be in spite of their prayers. They prayed three years longer. One night one of the women was awakened by her husband, who was under conviction. As soon as the day dawned, she hurried to tell her praying companion that God was about to answer their prayers. To her surprise, she met her friend coming to her on the same errand! After 10 years of united prayer, both husbands were saved on the same day.

Do prosperous
believers need to
pray, "Give us day
by day our daily
bread"? Why or why
not?

It may appear that the descent from so lofty a spiritual level to something so mundane as material provision for the day is inappropriate. However, man is a unity—neither totally spirit nor totally flesh, but a union of the two. Hence it is completely proper for us to ask God to supply our physical needs. Indeed, God urges the individual to bring all his needs before God, trusting that He will meet them "according to his riches in glory by Christ Jesus" (Philippians 4:19).

D. Our Spiritual Battles (v. 4)

4. And forgive us our sins; for we also forgive every one that is indebted to us. And lead us not into temptation; but deliver us from evil.

Talk About It:
1. What integrity issue is raised here?
2. How often should we pray for deliverance from evil and temptation? Why?

Our Lord invites us to honestly submit our weaknesses, our failures, and our sins to Him as we pray, with the expectation of forgiveness and restoration to fellowship—with one condition: we must have a forgiving heart. Our failure to forgive, itself an unconfessed sin, will cut off our fellowship with the Lord and destroy our spiritual life. Hence, recognizing our frailty, we pray for forgiveness while freely forgiving those who have offended us.

Also in recognition of human weakness, Jesus included the petition "Lead us not into temptation." While there is no implication in the Lord's Prayer that God is responsible for our temptation to sin, yet it is proper for us to ask God not to put us in situations where our weaknesses might more easily result in sin. And does not the Christian properly petition God to keep that hedge around him alleged by Satan to have been placed around Job (Job 1:10)? And is not the Christian who so prays asking for grace to so walk with God that he will avoid improper paths and thereby remain eligible for God's divine protection from evil?

"God is not the slightest bit interested in our prayers when we harbor sin in our lives, except for our prayers of repentance. We must make things right horizontally before we can have much impact vertically."
—Charles Stanley

The adjoining petition, "Deliver us from evil," is intimately related to "Lead us not into temptation," for the Christian is fighting a moral battle against Satan and constantly needs the aid of the Holy Spirit to remain separated from evil. Hence, the Lord ends the model prayer with petitions which underscore the basic nature of the Christian pilgrimage. As C.S. Lewis has stated, the devil is always just outside our skin. Is it not highly comforting to know that the Holy Spirit, the third person of the Trinity, is "inside our skin" in His fullness if we allow Him to be?

CONCLUSION

In a summary glance at Jesus' great model prayer (Luke 11:1-4), we observe five stages: *adoration, thanksgiving, petition, contrition* and *intercession*. Adoration and thanksgiving mesh in verse 2; petition occurs in verses 3 and 4; contrition and intercession occur in verse 4. Too, as a result of the plural pronouns ("our Father," "our sins," etc.), intercession occurs throughout the prayer. By employing these five stages in our prayers, we can enrich our worship and more intelligently present to God the needs we have and the needs of others.

GOLDEN TEXT CHALLENGE

"AS HE [CHRIST] WAS PRAYING IN A CERTAIN PLACE, WHEN HE CEASED, ONE OF HIS DISCIPLES SAID UNTO HIM, LORD, TEACH US TO PRAY" (Luke 11:1).

Prayer is an important part of the life of a disciple. If he does not know how to pray, he must learn. Where is a better source to turn to than Jesus? His disciples had heard Him pray, and they knew their prayers fell short of the effectiveness of the Master. When they approached Him about the matter, He gladly shared His knowledge about prayer with them.

How does Jesus teach His followers to pray today? He does so through the Word. The Bible contains many passages that shed light on the subject of prayer. He also teaches by His example. A careful study of what He says about prayer and an examination of His prayers will open a new world of power and effectiveness to the believer. Jesus also teaches by the Holy Spirit, who "intercedes for us" (Romans 8:26, *NIV*).

Daily Devotions:

M. Prayer Glorifies God
2 Samuel 7:18-29

T. A Powerful Prayer
1 Kings 18:36-39

W. Pray Throughout the Day
Psalm 55:16-23

T. How to Pray
Matthew 6:9-15

F. Prayer Is Submission of Will
Matthew 26:36-46

S. Prayer for Fellow Believers
Philippians 1:3-11

Forgiveness: Essential for Staying Connected

Matthew 5:23-25; 6:14, 15; Mark 11:25, 26; Colossians 3:12-14; Hebrews 9:22-28

Unit Theme:
Roots of Christian Formation

Central Truth:
Forgiveness is essential for staying connected to God and others.

Focus:
Discover that forgiveness is essential for right relationships and be forgiving.

Context:
Various New Testament passages concerning forgiveness

Golden Text:
"When ye stand praying, forgive, if ye have ought against any: that your Father also which is in heaven may forgive you your trespasses" (Mark 11:25).

Study Outline:
I. Forgiven by God (Hebrews 9:22-28)
II. Forgiving Others (Matthew 5:23-25; 6:14, 15)
III. Forgive and Be Forgiven (Mark 11:25, 26; Colossians 3:12-14)

INTRODUCTION

Forgiveness of that which has caused pain is essential to recovery from the pain. Held inside without being resolved, an injury festers into an infection of the soul that may cause serious problems. *The Encyclopedia of Biblical and Christian Ethics* says, "God's forgiveness and human forgiveness interlock. Man's being forgiven entails his having a forgiving spirit. . . . The righteousness of God is more than legal rectitude, for it embraces mercy and grace. For this reason Jesus urges His followers to practice love and forgiveness rather than stark justice (an eye for an eye) or vindictiveness" (Thomas Nelson Publishers).

Forgiveness is not always sought by the offender, or even accepted, but it is important to the victim that he or she forgive. Forgiving is not always easy, but we need to remember that God's forgiveness comes through Christ's death for our sins.

The victim must forgive whether the offender seeks it, wants it, or even feels he needs it. This is a fine point, but it needs to be understood. Repentance is the offender's road to restoration. Forgiveness is the victim's road to healing.

If the victim withholds forgiveness until the offender repents, then the offender remains in control of the victim's life. By refusing to repent, he consigns the victim to a life of bitterness and hate. The absence of forgiveness turns a person who has been hurt into a perpetual victim. It is in the forgiving that he is set free from bondage to that which hurts him.

God says, "I, even I, am he that blotteth out thy transgressions for mine own sake, and will not remember thy sins" (Isaiah 43:25). The God who forgives and forgets our sins will give us the power to forgive what we still remember. He can enable us to put offenses and hurts behind us as if they had never happened.—Charles W. Conn

I. FORGIVEN BY GOD (Hebrews 9:22-28)

A. Blood Required (v. 22)

22. And almost all things are by the law purged with blood; and without shedding of blood is no remission.

Under the Old Testament law "almost all things" were ceremonially cleansed by the sprinkling of blood. The fact that the word *almost* is used implies there were some things that were not so cleansed.

F.F. Bruce says: "There are certain exceptions. For example an impoverished Israelite might bring a tenth of an ephah (four pints) of fine flour to the priest as his sin-offering instead of a lamb or even instead of two turtle doves or young pigeons (Leviticus 5:11). In Numbers 16:46 atonement was made for the congregation of Israel, after the destruction of Korah and his company, by means of incense; in Numbers 31:22f, metal objects captured in war were to be purified by fire; in Numbers 31:50 the Israelite commanders in the fighting against Midian brought the gold objects which they had captured 'to make atonement for our souls before Jehovah,' but such exceptions were rare; the general rule was that ceremonial cleansing or atonement had to be effected by means of blood" (*New International Commentary on the New Testament*).

There may have been a few exceptions to purging by blood, but there were no exceptions for the remission of sins. Under the Law sin required the offering of sacrifice, and only blood had the power for this requirement. Blood alone was efficacious for the deepest spiritual needs of humanity.

B. The Best Offered (vv. 23, 24)

23. It was therefore necessary that the patterns of things in the heavens should be purified with these; but the heavenly things themselves with better sacrifices than these.

24. For Christ is not entered into the holy places made with hands, which are the figures of the true; but into heaven itself, now to appear in the presence of God for us.

Having viewed the Old Testament and its pattern of worship, the writer now shows us that Jesus Christ is the fulfillment of all the Old Testament promised. The blood of animals sufficed for ritualistic cleansing, but it did not remove inward and spiritual defilement. Jesus, by His blood, purified "the heavenly things."

"The use of the word *purified*, applied to heaven, does not imply that heaven was before 'unholy,' but it denotes that it is now made accessible to sinners; or that they may come and worship there in an acceptable manner. The ancient tabernacle was purified or consecrated by the blood of the victims slain, so that people might approach with acceptance and worship; the

remission—forgiveness

Talk About It:
Why does God require the shedding of blood for the forgiveness of sin?

"The word *blessed* comes from an Anglo-Saxon word for *blood*, and conveys the idea that in order to bless someone else you must part with your life or with some of your life. There was no way humanity could be eternally blessed except through the shed blood of Jesus Christ."
—**Ray Hughes**

Talk About It:
What is Jesus now doing on our behalf?

heavens by purer blood are rendered accessible to the guilty. The necessity for 'better sacrifices' in regard to the latter was, that it was designed to make the conscience pure, and because the service in heaven is more holy than any rendered on earth" (*Barnes' Notes*).

Jesus did not enter the Holy Place and the Holy of Holies, which, after all, were but figures of the true holy place in heaven. Jesus did not enter a material sanctuary for us, but He went into the presence of God to mediate for us and to draw us into the presence of God. What all high priests symbolized when they went into the Holy of Holies, Jesus did for His followers in reality. His blood was sprinkled upon the heavenly mercy seat in the eternal sanctuary of God.

C. Redemption Secured (vv. 25, 26)

25. Nor yet that he should offer himself often, as the high priest entereth into the holy place every year with blood of others;

26. For then must he often have suffered since the foundation of the world: but now once in the end of the world hath he appeared to put away sin by the sacrifice of himself.

Christ's superiority over the high priests was manifest in two ways. Whereas the priests went annually into the Holy of Holies to offer sacrifice, Christ entered the heavenly sanctuary for eternity. Those who entered the material Holy of Holies had to do so annually on the Day of Atonement. Their work was never done, for each time a priest went into the Holy of Holies he had to come out immediately. But when Jesus entered the heavenly sanctuary, He remained there as perpetual mediator for the sins of humanity. He does not periodically enter and then leave the sanctuary; rather His service on our behalf is both perpetual and eternal.

A second point of distinction and superiority is the sacrificial blood. The Jewish priests carried into the sanctuary the blood of sacrificed animals, but the token of Jesus' priesthood was His own blood shed for our sins. He secured our redemption by offering Himself.

If the sacrifice of Jesus were not eternal, then it would have been necessary for Him to die many times. This was not necessary, for His blood was powerful for the redemption of all people of all time. The one offering of Himself far outweighed the many offerings that had to be made before Him.

D. Return Guaranteed (vv. 27, 28)

27. And as it is appointed unto men once to die, but after this the judgment:

28. So Christ was once offered to bear the sins of

Talk About It:

1. Compare the frequency of the high priest's offering with the sacrifice made by Jesus.

2. What did Jesus' sacrifice accomplish that animal sacrifices could not accomplish?

Old and New

Once when Lord Tennyson was on vacation in a country village, he asked an old Methodist woman, "Is there any news?"

"Well, she replied, "there is only one piece of news that I know, and that is that Christ died for my sins."

Tennyson replied, "That is old news, good news, and new news."

—George Sweeting

Forgiveness: Essential for Staying Connected

many; and unto them that look for him shall he appear the second time without sin unto salvation.

By divine appointment, all people die once and their death is followed by judgment. In the case of Jesus, He also died once but there was no judgment afterward. His death was the basis of salvation for all who received Him.

Just as the Israelites watched their high priest enter the sanctuary with the tokens of their redemption and then emerge again, so the followers of Christ watched Him ascend to heaven where He entered the eternal sanctuary on our behalf. In like manner also, we shall see Him return for the completion of our redemption. It is the hope of all Christians today that this Mediator who sits at the right hand of God will return for us and that our salvation will be eternal. He will not return to deal with sin again—He has done that for all time—but He will return to draw us into the presence of God.

Talk About It:
1. Why do all people have an appointment with death?
2. Compare the purpose of Christ's first coming with the purpose of His second coming.

II. FORGIVING OTHERS (Matthew 5:23-25; 6:14, 15)
A. Leaving the Altar (5:23, 24)

23. Therefore if thou bring thy gift to the altar, and there rememberest that thy brother hath ought against thee;

24. Leave there thy gift before the altar, and go thy way; first be reconciled to thy brother, and then come and offer thy gift.

ought (v. 23)— something

The Pharisees believed if a person conformed to the external rites of religion such as bringing gifts to the altar which stood in front of the Temple—no matter how much envy and malice and hatred that person might harbor—he was doing well. But Jesus emphasizes a right relationship with one's God and other people as prerequisite to acceptance at the place of worship.

There must be reconciliation before sacrifice; there must be morality before religious exercise. Thus, if a Christian is on his way to the place of worship and is reminded and convicted of having offended someone, he is to interrupt his religious exercise and attempt reconciliation. This is his way of confessing and correcting his sin. Then that person can return to the place of worship, offer his gift, and be graciously accepted by God.

Talk About It:
Why do you suppose a problem in a relationship with another person might come to mind when we kneel before God?

B. Avoiding the Courtroom (v. 25)

25. Agree with thine adversary quickly, whiles thou art in the way with him; lest at any time the adversary deliver thee to the judge, and the judge deliver thee to the officer, and thou be cast into prison.

"Agree . . . quickly" emphasizes the brevity of time in which to make things right with another believer. The imagery here is taken from a lawcourt. While you are on the way to court, before the hearing takes place, it is your duty, if possible, to come to agreement. In other words, settle your case of disagreement

Talk About It:
Why is it important to settle disagreements as quickly as possible?

and complaint out of court (see Luke 12:58, 59). Do everything in your power to avoid a confrontation in a court of law.

The apostle Paul took the Christians at Corinth to task for this very thing. "Dare any of you, having a matter against another, go to law before the unjust, and not before the saints?" (1 Corinthians 6:1). These warnings from the apostle must be taken seriously (vv. 1-8).

Should the party in the complaint refuse out-of-court settlement, the verdict of the judge might be "guilty" and the sentence "imprisonment." This fate can be avoided by early agreement and reconciliation.

> "If you've been to Calvary and received the forgiveness of God, then adopt the heart of God and let the forgiven become the forgiver."
> —Woodrow Kroll

C. Forgiving Offences (6:14, 15)

14. For if ye forgive men their trespasses, your heavenly Father will also forgive you:

15. But if ye forgive not men their trespasses, neither will your Father forgive your trespasses.

Sin is an offense against God. Since this is the case, we must seek forgiveness at His hands. That forgiveness involves more than the removal of sin from our heart; it involves the removal from God's mind of His displeasure against us on account of sin; it involves the wiping or crossing out from His "book of remembrance" of all entries against us on this account.

Talk About It:

1. Why is *trespass* a good word in defining sin?

2. Why won't God forgive people who won't forgive others?

In our text, Jesus spoke about offenses given and received between people. He made a connection between our forgiving others and our own forgiveness. No one who is deliberately and habitually unforgiving toward others can expect to enjoy the wonder of divine forgiveness. God expects His children to possess a forgiving disposition. He sees His own image reflected in His forgiving children. On the other hand, to ask God for what we ourselves refuse to give others is to insult Him.

Macartney wrote: "The language spoken in heaven by the angels and the redeemed is the language of forgiveness. It will be the only language spoken there. No other language will be understood. It will be spoken by the cherubim and the seraphim and the whole angelic host as they praise God, the author of forgiveness and of eternal salvation. It will be spoken by all the redeemed as they greet one another on the banks of the River of Life and gather round the throne of the Lamb and sing their song unto Him who loved them and washed them from their sins. But no one can learn that language after he gets to heaven. It must be learned here upon earth—in this world, and in this life."

> "He who won't forgive others breaks the bridge over which he must pass himself."
> —George Herbert

III. FORGIVE AND BE FORGIVEN (Mark 11:25, 26; Colossians 3:12-14)

A. The Forgiving Forgiven (Mark 11:25, 26)

25. And when ye stand praying, forgive, if ye have

Forgiveness: Essential for Staying Connected

ought against any: that your Father also which is in heaven may forgive you your trespasses.

26. But if ye do not forgive, neither will your Father which is in heaven forgive your trespasses.

The answers to our prayers are linked with our forgiveness of those who offend us. This relates directly to the Lord's promise to give us the desires of our heart (v. 24). We cannot hold enmity and malice in our hearts and still exercise pure faith and holy desires. The opposing elements simply will not mix. We must be as willing to forgive those who wrong us as the Lord has been willing to forgive us. This points up to us how interwoven our lives are.

The efficacy of our praying is bound up in our readiness to forgive others. God will not measure blessings to us if we measure resentment and malice toward others. No one who refuses to forgive has any right to expect forgiveness from the Lord. An unforgiving heart cannot be forgiven; and a forgiven heart will also be a forgiving heart.

No one can reach for forgiveness in one direction while withholding his hand from forgiveness in the other. This was the sin of the Jewish leaders, and in a way it was the "sin" of the fig tree (vv. 12-14). The priests expected to receive good things from God while dealing in evil toward their fellowman. The fig tree expected to enjoy the blessings of sunshine and rain without providing the benefit of fruit to people. In each instance they expected to be receivers without being givers; they expected blessings without blessing. These things make us guilty in the work of the Lord, for the Christian way is to give to others as we receive from the Lord.

B. The Well-Dressed Christian (Colossians 3:12, 13)

12. Put on therefore, as the elect of God, holy and beloved, bowels of mercies, kindness, humbleness of mind, meekness, longsuffering;

13. Forbearing one another, and forgiving one another, if any man have a quarrel against any: even as Christ forgave you, so also do ye.

Christians must "put on" the new person, which involves putting on a new nature, with new attitudes and a new direction. There are specific effects of the new life in Christ. The new creation is called "the elect of God, holy and beloved" (v. 12). Men and women who were once strangers to God are now the elect of God, meaning they have been redeemed from the masses of unregenerate people, separated to God and beloved by Him. Here Paul resorts to his practice of enumerating the characteristics of a spiritual life. In much the same fashion as he did in Galatians 5:22, 23 (the fruit of the Spirit), Paul lists various ways in which the new life will express itself.

Talk About It:
How is it possible to forgive those who have wounded us deeply yet refuse to admit their wrongdoing?

bowels of mercies (v. 12)—compassion

Talk About It:
1. Who are the "elect of God"?
2. How can God's people "put on" the traits listed in verse 12?
3. What "quarrel" did Christ have against us, and how did He handle it?

"Men and women who are God's chosen people—His choice souls, whom He has set apart for Himself and on whom He has placed His love—should inevitably exhibit something of His nature. . . . Paul tells his readers to 'put on a compassionate heart, kindness, humility, gentleness, and patience'— graces that were perfectly blended in the character and conduct of Christ" (F.F. Bruce, *The Epistle to the Colossians*).

Believers will sometimes have grievances with each other, yet we are called upon to manifest mutual forbearance, mutual tolerance, and mutual forgiveness. This is premised upon the forgiveness Jesus Christ manifested toward us. This is similar to Paul's admonition to the Ephesians, "Be ye kind one to another, tenderhearted, forgiving one another, even as God for Christ's sake hath forgiven you" (4:32).

The entire Christian ethic is based upon the example of the Lord Jesus Christ. The lesson is clear: if we expect the forgiveness of God, then we must be ready to forgive one another and not harbor wrath or malice in our heart (Colossians 3:8).

> "When people were at their worst, Jesus was at His best, saying, 'Father, forgive them.'"
>
> —Woodrow Kroll

Talk About It:
1. Why must love be our priority?
2. What can love accomplish?

C. Above All (v. 14)

14. And above all these things put on charity, which is the bond of perfectness.

There is still another quality that Christians should "put on"—it is love, the crowning grace of all Christian qualities. Paul introduces this by saying, "Above all these things . . . ," which makes the exhortation to love primary among all Christian expectations. He emphasizes this fact further by calling it "the bond of perfectness." In 1 Corinthians 13:13, love is declared to be supreme Christian grace. In Romans 13:9, 10, love is the fulfillment of the Law. In Galatians 5:6, love is the motivation of faith. It is clear then that love is the supreme Christian virtue and the fountainhead of all others.

CONCLUSION

Jesus teaches we are to be forgiving toward those who have offended us. But He is *not* teaching that our forgiveness of others is the basis of God's forgiveness of us. The opposite is true. Christians forgive because they have been forgiven.

The importance of forgiving is underscored by these words from John Owens: "Our forgiving of others will not procure forgiveness for ourselves, but our not forgiving others proves that we ourselves are not forgiven."

GOLDEN TEXT CHALLENGE

"WHEN YE STAND PRAYING, FORGIVE, IF YE HAVE OUGHT AGAINST ANY: THAT YOUR FATHER ALSO WHICH IS IN HEAVEN MAY FORGIVE YOU YOUR TRESPASSES" (Mark 11:25).

The context of this verse is worship. This implies that the worship life of the Christian must be especially concerned with forgiveness. Petitions and praise cannot be offered genuinely from an unforgiving heart. The reason for this inability is that the lack of forgiveness by the worshiper interferes with his or her relationship with God. Thus when the unforgiving person comes to God, he or she does not have the access to the presence of the Father that is known when all is right with the Lord.

On the other hand, one whose heart has forgiven others feels the warmth of God's Spirit in times of prayer. That person has the assurance of the advocacy of the Lord for their petitions. So forgiveness of others stands at the center of the believer's worship and prayers.

Daily Devotions:

M. Forgiving Family Members
Genesis 50:15-21

T. Forgiveness Brings Restoration
Job 42:1-10

W. A Forgiving God
Psalm 86:1-10

T. Love Even Your Enemies
Matthew 5:43-48

F. Forgive as We Are Forgiven
Matthew 18:21-33

S. Christ, the Supreme Example
Luke 23:33-43

Bible Insight

Are You Bearing the Fruit of the Spirit?

The "works of the flesh" are deeds people do in disobedience to God (Galatians 5:19- 21). The "fruit of the Spirit" is the produce or harvest of Christian virtues or graces which result from the work of the Holy Spirit in our lives (vv. 22, 23). The virtues which are the harvest of the Spirit are so admirable, noble and intrinsically good that they are recognized universally as being of God. Against these virtues there is no condemning law (v. 23). To put it another way, the Spirit produces a life that is lawful—in harmony with the good will of God.

In Galatians 5, nine virtues are listed as being the harvest of the Spirit. Doubtlessly, the apostle Paul did not intend this list to be exhaustive but representative of the virtues produced by the Holy Spirit.

In Relation to God—Love, Joy, Peace

While the love, joy and peace produced in our life by the Spirit may be experienced as emotions, they are more than emotions. The love, joy and peace of the Christian rise from a right relationship with God. In this relationship, love is more than a feeling; it is an attitude and deeds which express to others the goodwill God has shown to us in Christ. Love is fellowship and friendship. In like manner, the joy and peace of the Christian are not feelings merely determined by our outward circumstances but by our inward relationship with God. This is "joy unspeakable and full of glory [God's presence]" (1 Peter 1:8). This is "the peace of God, which passeth all understanding" (Philippians 4:7).

In Relation to Others—Longsuffering, Gentleness, Goodness

These graces have to do primarily with our relationships with other people. We can have right relationships with people because we are right with God. The Holy Spirit enables the Christian to be longsuffering. This is a passive grace, meaning the capacity to suffer long or patiently the injuries or insults hurled upon us by others. The other two, gentleness and goodness, are active graces. In relationships with other people, the Holy Spirit enables the Christian to be both *gentle* (considerate, humane, fair) and *good* (morally honorable and beneficial).

In Relation to Self—Faith, Meekness, Temperance

The last three graces of the Spirit mentioned have to do with the regulation and conduct of our own life as Christians. *The*

Christian life is preeminently a life of faith in God. We are saved by faith, and we continue in Christian living by faith. The Holy Spirit produces and nurtures faith in us by enabling us to believe the Word of God.

Meekness is, above all things, an attitude of humility and reverence toward God which governs our attitude toward ourselves. Meekness is spiritual strength—the self- discipline that keeps us from becoming proud or thinking ourselves to be more important than we are. Meekness will keep us from being arrogant and will free us from status seeking.

Finally, the grace of temperance helps us to live a balanced Christian life. Temptations always seek to pull us away from the middle ground of God's perfect will for our life. Temptations to sin pull us either toward laxness and carelessness about right living or toward extremism and fanaticism resulting in ridiculous or impossible demands upon us. Either way, we are drawn away from God's perfect will. Temperance produced by the Holy Spirit will keep us living a balanced Christian life that will honor Christ.

The Proof of Spiritual Living

Human efforts at goodness without God, however valiant or sincere, can only poorly mimic the graces produced by the Holy Spirit. The difference between the self-righteous life without the Spirit and true spiritual living by the Spirit is like the difference between a Christmas tree and a fruit tree. We can hang fruit, candy and nuts on a Christmas tree, but it bears no fruit. But a fruit tree bears fruit because it is the very nature of its life to do so. In the same way, the Holy Spirit within us will cause us to bear the fruit of the Spirit because this is the very nature of the spiritual life in Christ.

Our response to the Holy Spirit should be to yield ourselves more completely to His holy influence and direction. As we do, the harvest of the Spirit will be more and more evident in our life.—**Daniel L. Black** (*A Layman's Guide to the Holy Spirit*)

Loving Like Christ

Luke 10:38-42; 23:32-43; 1 Corinthians 13:1-13

Unit Theme:
Fruit of Christian Formation

Central Truth:
By word and example, Christ taught us how to love.

Focus:
Consider Christ, the ultimate example of love, and allow His love to be evident in us.

Context:
Selected New Testament passages focusing on godly love

Golden Text:
"Now abideth faith, hope, charity, these three; but the greatest of these is charity" (1 Corinthians 13:13).

Study Outline:
I. Love Is Foundational (1 Corinthians 13:1-13)
II. Love Is Sacrificial (Luke 23:32-43)
III. Love Is Relational (Luke 10:38-42)

INTRODUCTION

A poem written by Annie Johnson Flint sets the tone for today's lesson on Christ's love:

How broad is His love? Oh, as broad as man's trespass,
   As wide as the need of the world can be;
And yet to the need of one soul it can narrow;
   He came to the world, and He came to me.

How long is His love? Without end or beginning,
   Eternal as Christ and His life it must be,
For to everlasting as from everlasting;
   He loveth the world, and He loveth me.

How deep is His love? Oh, as deep as man's sinning,
   As low as the uttermost vileness can be;
In the fathomless gulf of the Father's forsaking;
   He died for the world, and He died for me.

How high is His love? It is high as the heavens,
   As high as the throne of His glory must be;
And yet from that height, He has stooped to redeem us,
   He "so" loved the world, and He "so" loved me.

How great is His love? Oh, it passes all knowledge,
   No man's comprehension, its measure can be;
It filleth the world; yet, each heart may contain it;
   He "so" loved the world, and He "so" loved me.

I. LOVE IS FOUNDATIONAL (1 Corinthians 13:1-13)

A. Love's Surpassing Greatness (vv. 1-3)

1. Though I speak with the tongues of men and of angels, and have not charity, I am become as sounding brass, or a tinkling cymbal.

2. And though I have the gift of prophecy, and understand all mysteries, and all knowledge; and though I have all faith, so that I could remove mountains, and have not charity, I am nothing.

3. And though I bestow all my goods to feed the poor, and though I give my body to be burned, and have not charity, it profiteth me nothing.

The Corinthians had placed much stress on the miraculous gifts of the Spirit listed in the 12th chapter. Paul had stated that the purpose of the gifts was to edify the church, not divide it. Apparently, some believers felt superior to others and wanted to have a place of preeminence; this led to a state of confusion. This was a carnal attitude, and only Paul's prescription of "a more excellent way" (12:31) could reunite the church.

There can be no greater sign of God's grace in a life than the possession of love. It is a far more eloquent method of communication than the gift of words, whether of men or angels. Our words may be misunderstood, but never our love; love is the universal language.

In 13:2, Paul compares love to one of the highest of attainments—the acquisition of knowledge. If one could understand the mysteries of God, see them by the wide range of prophecy, and grasp them by the gift of great faith, which would even move mountains, it would all amount to nothing without love. A person with supernatural insights, but who does not possess love, is personally worthless.

The modern idea of *charity* being the giving of money to help the poor does not express what Paul means by his use of this word. In fact, verse 3 proves that one may give to the poor and still not have love. People have been known to give large sums to charities so they could deduct them on their income tax report, or to appear generous in the eyes of others. A little done because of love is of much greater worth than much done for some other reason (see Mark 12:41-44).

B. Love's Opinion (vv. 4-7)

4. Charity suffereth long, and is kind; charity envieth not; charity vaunteth not itself, is not puffed up,

5. Doth not behave itself unseemly, seeketh not her own, is not easily provoked, thinketh no evil;

6. Rejoiceth not in iniquity, but rejoiceth in the truth;

7. Beareth all things, believeth all things, hopeth all things, endureth all things.

Talk About It:
1. What is wrong with being "as sounding brass, or a tinkling cymbal" (v. 1)?
2. Why is the value of spiritual gifts eroded by a lack of love?
3. When is self-sacrifice of no value to an individual? Why not?

vaunteth not itself (v. 4)—"does not parade itself" (*NKJV*)

unseemly (v. 5)—rudely

Talk About It:

1. List all the things love does *not* do, according to verses 4-6. Why doesn't it do these things?

2. Does "believes all things" (v. 7, *NKJV*) mean love is gullible and blind? Explain your answer.

One of the outstanding characteristics of love is its concern for the well-being of others. It recognizes the other person's weaknesses and failures and expresses itself in patience. Love not only forgives seven times; it forgives "seventy times seven." Passively, love endures the wrongs of others; and, actively, it returns good because it is kind. There is no feeling of "getting even" where true love exists.

Love is always pleased when the one loved is blessed in some manner, and it does not, even secretly, wish to receive the blessing instead. The presence of envy is evidence of the absence of love.

Love recognizes its own limitations and does not boast of its supposed superiority to others. Jesus taught us to "love thy neighbor as thyself." When we think too much of ourselves, it is impossible to have a proper respect for others. This does not, however, mean we are to assume a false humility. Paul expressed this well in Romans 12:3, when he said we are not to think of ourselves "more highly than [we] ought to think; but to think soberly."

The law of love requires good manners (1 Corinthians 13:5). Etiquette was designed out of due respect for the other person. Only the rude, selfish and unloving push ahead of everyone else. The unmannerly assumption on the part of some, that they are due more consideration than others, is the result of pride and a lack of love.

"Seeketh not her own" means love never places her own benefit ahead of the good of others. One who loves would never discredit another in order to attain a higher position.

God is patient with all people, "not easily provoked" with respect to them, even though they are sinful and provoking persons. There is, then, a bad and a good exasperation. Anger may be holy, but generally it is not. Like God, the saint is to be "slow to anger, and plenteous in mercy" (Psalm 103:8). Even in adverse and afflictive circumstances, the loving person maintains his or her calm.

"Thinketh no evil" means love "keeps no record of wrongs" (*NIV*). Love does not credit the other person with a bad motive; it places the best possible construction on the actions of others. Love is not of a suspicious mind. It is not, however, blind to the facts when they are clear. This phrase can also be understood to mean that love does not "plan evil" against another. Love does not think of ways to retaliate.

Love never rejoices when someone falls into sin. Love only rejoices when truth prevails. A person of love will always be heartbroken over the fall of someone else, even if that one is his or her enemy.

Love does not consider the present condition or attitude to

"Love is shown in your deeds, not in your words."

—Jerome Cummings

be the final one, but bears and endures the present state of things, while hoping and trusting for things to improve. Love may be disappointed, but it does not despair. Love is willing to suffer, but it is with the hope that truth will ultimately triumph over evil.

C. Love's Unfailing Nature (vv. 8-13)

8. Charity never faileth: but whether there be prophecies, they shall fail; whether there be tongues, they shall cease; whether there be knowledge, it shall vanish away.

9. For we know in part, and we prophesy in part.

10. But when that which is perfect is come, then that which is in part shall be done away.

11. When I was a child, I spake as a child, I understood as a child, I thought as a child: but when I became a man, I put away childish things.

12. For now we see through a glass, darkly; but then face to face: now I know in part; but then shall I know even as also I am known.

13. And now abideth faith, hope, charity, these three; but the greatest of these is charity.

The word *faileth* means "to fall away as the petals of a withering flower." The idea (as the following context indicates) is that prophecies, tongues and knowledge are only for the present life. They relate to our earthly sojourn and will have no place in the life to come. Notice the contrast between the words *now* and *then* in verse 12. These things are important during the present, but only love will continue to be relevant when "that which is perfect is come" (v. 10).

It is beyond human possibility to have perfect and complete knowledge in this world. We are limited by our nature and the world around us; this is what Solomon meant in Ecclesiastes 3:11 when he said God "set eternity in the hearts of men; yet they cannot fathom what God has done from beginning to end" (*NIV*). Therefore, we can never prove with absolute certainty how God formed the universe; the evolutionists vainly imagine that they can. We may not know *how*, "for we know [only] in part" (1 Corinthians 13:9), but we may know *who*, for "[by] faith we understand that the worlds were framed by the word of God, so that things which are seen were not made of things which do appear" (Hebrews 11:3). It takes far more faith to believe this universe came into being by accident than it does to believe it was created by God. Though our knowledge is not complete, it is sufficient to justify faith.

The most learned, the most intelligent, has only a partial knowledge of things, but the "in part" will give way to "that which is perfect" when human limitations are no longer able to restrict

Talk About It:
1. Why doesn't love fail?
2. When and why will all the blessings listed in verse 8 "vanish away"?
3. What do faith, hope and love have in common? What makes love superior?

or confine. Just as the knowledge of a child is imperfect and limited by comparison with the knowledge of an adult, so our present knowledge is like that of a child. Paul likens our present life to our childhood, and our future life with God to our adulthood. As it is impossible for a child to understand the things that come easily to an adult, so it is impossible for us now to have a correct knowledge of ultimate truth.

No one knows the true nature of God; we have only a dim view of Him. The concept most of us have of Him is formed in our minds by our attributing to Him human parts; therefore, we speak of God's eyes, face, ears, arms, and so forth. By this, we mean that God can see, hear and save, and so forth; but, we have no knowledge of the true essence of God. However, we shall know God as He now knows us. For "now are we the sons of God, and it doth not yet appear what we shall be: but we know that, when he shall appear, we shall be like him; for we shall see him as he is" (1 John 3:2).

Faith, *hope* and *love* remain while all else passes away; but, of these eternal graces, love surpasses all else, in this life as well as in the next.

II. LOVE IS SACRIFICIAL (Luke 23:32-43)
A. "Father, Forgive Them" (vv. 32-34)

malefactors (v. 32)— criminals

32. And there were also two other, malefactors, led with him to be put to death.

33. And when they were come to the place, which is called Calvary, there they crucified him, and the malefactors, one on the right hand, and the other on the left.

34. Then said Jesus, Father, forgive them; for they know not what they do. And they parted his raiment, and cast lots.

Talk About It:
1. How could Jesus pray for the forgiveness of those who were crucifying Him?
2. Why is it significant that Jesus died a criminal's death along with two thieves?

Crime against Rome did not pay, and crucifixion was a very effective method of proving it. The victim was nailed to a stake or cross, and simply left there as an object of ridicule until death eventually came and terminated the awful suffering.

In verses 32 and 33, Luke used a Greek word meaning "evildoers" (KJV: "malefactors"). Matthew and Mark let us know these men were robbers. John did not say who they were or what crime they had committed; he merely recounted that two other men were crucified with Jesus.

The third cross was intended for a thief named Barabbas. However, when given a choice, the Jewish leaders set Barabbas free, and Christ was crucified on the cross that had been prepared for the bandit leader! Not only did Christ take Barabbas' cross; He took the cross each one of us deserved! He died for all of the ungodly throughout the ages!

At the place called *Calvary* ("the Skull") there was a hill considerably higher than those nearby. Adjacent to the main road leading from Damascus, this hill had a very striking resemblance to a human skull. The gaping likeness to an upper palate minus the jaw and the two round openings closely resembling eye sockets were caused by excavations several hundred years before the time of Christ's death.

In verse 34 we see our Lord in His role as the Great High Priest. Looking in compassion upon His persecutors, Jesus extended to them the ministry of intercession. "Father, forgive them" apparently were the first words He spoke after He was raised up on the cross.

In Isaiah 53:12 the ancient prophet foretold that the Messiah "made intercession for the transgressors." The Gospel writers also stated that most of Jesus' words on the cross were for others (see Luke 23:43; John 19:26, 27). It was at this point in the history of God's mighty acts that our Lord's ministry of teaching ceased and His ministry as the great intercessor began.

When the soldiers cast lots for Christ's garments, they fulfilled the prophecy uttered by David more than 1,000 years earlier (see Psalm 22:18). Such a prophecy and its fulfillment is one of the great demonstrations of the divine origin and authority of the Holy Scriptures. The inspired words of Psalm 22 foretold several happenings at the Crucifixion: Jesus' bones being pulled out of joint, Jesus' thirsting, Jesus' hands and feet being pierced, and the soldiers casting lots for Jesus' clothing. The Jews did not practice crucifixion as a way of capital punishment, so such a detailed prophecy of the death of the Son of God could only have been divinely inspired.

> "Ministry that costs nothing, accomplishes nothing."
> —**John Henry Jowett**

B. "Save Yourself" (vv. 35-38)

35. And the people stood beholding. And the rulers also with them derided him, saying, He saved others; let him save himself, if he be Christ, the chosen of God.

36. And the soldiers also mocked him, coming to him, and offering him vinegar,

37. And saying, If thou be the king of the Jews, save thyself.

38. And a superscription also was written over him in letters of Greek, and Latin, and Hebrew, THIS IS THE KING OF THE JEWS.

These four verses recount the mockery of the crowd, the Jewish rulers, and the soldiers whom Pilate delegated to crucify Jesus. The challenge to Jesus to save Himself was in itself a fulfillment of the exact prophecy of David in Psalm 22:8.

The people stood beholding, because some of them had, no doubt, accepted Jesus as the true Messiah. They could understand a powerful militant Messiah, but they had trouble

Talk About It:

1. Compare and contrast the mocking by the religious leaders with the ridicule from the soldiers.

2. On the cross, what kind of king did Christ prove Himself to be?

interpreting the verses of Old Testament prophecy that foretold Jesus' suffering (see 1 Peter 1:10, 11). They stood watching, because many of them would not have been surprised if suddenly an angel would have taken Him down from the cross or if suddenly some other mighty miracle had happened. Certainly many doubted and mocked Him, but there were others who were simply beholding.

The Roman soldiers took great delight not only in mocking Jesus, but in ridiculing the crowd by saying, "If you are the King of these Jews, come down from the cross." There was no love lost between the soldiers and the Jews, and even Pilate took the opportunity to ridicule the Jewish people by the inscription he put on Christ's cross: "THIS IS THE KING OF THE JEWS." He would not alter the inscription when they asked him to add extra words (John 19:20-22).

The usual purpose of a superscription being placed above the head of a crucified man was to signify the charges that were against him. In this case Pilate refused to write, "He claimed to be the King of the Jews." He simply wrote, "This is the King of the Jews." Pilate established that Jesus had made no such claim. Jesus had declared Himself to be the Son of God, but He had not said, "I am the King of the Jews." The people who could have accepted Jesus and crowned Him King had rejected Him.

C. "Remember Me" (vv. 39-43)

39. And one of the malefactors which were hanged railed on him, saying, If thou be Christ, save thyself and us.

40. But the other answering rebuked him, saying, Dost not thou fear God, seeing thou art in the same condemnation?

41. And we indeed justly; for we receive the due reward of our deeds: but this man hath done nothing amiss.

42. And he said unto Jesus, Lord, remember me when thou comest into thy kingdom.

43. And Jesus said unto him, Verily I say unto thee, To day shalt thou be with me in paradise.

Talk About It:

1. Why do you suppose the two thieves responded so differently to Jesus?

2. How are the thieves representative of all people?

Verse 39 records the coarse mockery of one malefactor. His words were said, no doubt, partly in contempt and partly in petition. Death was staring him in the face, and with a mixture of bravado and desperation he repeated the taunt of the crowd. The Greek word translated *railed* is the source of our English word *blaspheme*. This malefactor's request was nothing more than a request to help him break jail. There was nothing penitent in his cry for help.

Verses 40-42 record the remarks of the believing and penitent thief. The word *condemnation* could also be translated "judgment." They had all suffered the judgment of crucifixion, but not all deserved it. The malefactors had heard Christ's prophetic statement to the women and His great priestly prayer for His people and the Roman soldiers who were crucifying Him. Certainly no criminal would pray such a noble prayer!

Suddenly the recognition of who this Man on the center cross was dawned upon the second thief: *Why, this Man must be the true Messiah!* The glorious truth dawned in most unlikely circumstances. Jesus did not look like the King of the Jews. His face was marred and beaten. His back was scarred by the marks of a Roman scourge. But there must have been a majesty and love about Him that shone through all this.

Verse 43 presents Jesus in His role as king. As prophet, Jesus had foretold the destruction of Jerusalem. As priest, He had prayed for His murderers. Now, as king, He opened the gates of paradise to a believing repentant sinner. To the man who had recognized Him for who He really was, He said, "To day shalt thou be with me in paradise."

Up until that time paradise was located in the heart of the earth. It was separated from the place of torment by a chasm or gulf that no one could cross. But before Christ ascended to heaven, He descended into the lower parts of the earth and raised paradise (Ephesians 4:8-10). He took with Him those who had been waiting in the place known as Abraham's bosom. Since that day, paradise has been in the "third heaven," in the presence of God, as the abode of the righteous dead (see 2 Corinthians 5:6-8; 12:2-4).

Jesus preceded the second criminal in death, but just before sundown the Roman soldiers killed the two thieves so they would not be hanging on the crosses when the Passover Sabbath started at 6 p.m. When Jesus arose, the repentant thief was raised into the third heaven with the other righteous dead.

> "When Christ hung, bled and died, it was God saying to the world, 'I love you.'"
> —Billy Graham

III. LOVE IS RELATIONAL (Luke 10:38-42)
A. Mary and Martha (vv. 38, 39)

38. Now it came to pass, as they went, that he entered into a certain village: and a certain woman named Martha received him into her house.

39. And she had a sister called Mary, which also sat at Jesus' feet, and heard his word.

It is apparent that Jesus went to Jerusalem several times in the months before His crucifixion. This is probably the setting for this passage. He was on His way to or from Jerusalem when He went to the home of Mary and Martha. It seems that Martha was the caretaker of the house. Possibly she was a widow, and her brother Lazarus and younger sister Mary lived with her.

Talk About It:
Compare Mary's response to Jesus' arrival (v. 39) with Martha's response (v. 38).

Mary is pictured as sitting at the feet of Jesus. This was the posture of disciples or students in His day. They sat at the feet of their teachers as a sign of humility. We are told that Paul was brought up at the feet of Gamaliel (Acts 22:3).

B. Martha's Complaint (v. 40)

cumbered (v. 40)—
distracted

40. But Martha was cumbered about much serving, and came to him, and said, Lord, dost thou not care that my sister hath left me to serve alone? bid her therefore that she help me.

Martha was serving and Mary was sitting. Mary was tuned in to the supreme value of spiritual feasting, but she was tuned out to helping in the kitchen. This troubled Martha, and she spoke to Jesus about it: "Why don't You tell my sister to help me?"

Talk About It:
Describe distractions that keep people from spending time with Jesus today.

Martha's concern was to provide suitable hospitality for the Savior. Her anxiety was not based on some worldly desire. Her wrong came in being overanxious about hosting Him and being fretful in speaking to Him about Mary. She should have taken the time to sit quietly with Mary at His feet.

Martha's question to Jesus, "Dost thou not care . . . ?" is strong language. It is a reproof of the Lord as if He encouraged Mary in neglecting her duty. Martha paraded before Him how busy she was, how she needed Mary's help, and how Jesus should direct Mary to assist her sister. In so doing, she disturbed the harmony between herself and her sister and between herself and the Lord.

"Cut your morning devotions into your personal grooming. You would not go to work with a dirty face. Why start the day with the face of your soul unwashed?"
—Robert A. Cook

C. Jesus' Answer (vv. 41, 42)

41. And Jesus answered and said unto her, Martha, Martha, thou art careful and troubled about many things:

42. But one thing is needful: and Mary hath chosen that good part, which shall not be taken away from her.

The indications are that Martha had tried to listen to what Jesus had to say. However, she could not concentrate on what He was saying for thinking about the preparations of the meal at the same time.

Talk About It:
1. What was good about Martha's approach to life, and what needed adjusting?
2. Why would Mary's "good part . . . not be taken away from her" (v. 42)?

Jesus addressed Martha in a serious but sympathetic manner. He repeated her name in a fashion that conveyed affection and concern. He described her as *worried* (*NKJV*), a word implying a division and distraction of mind, which believers ought to avoid. Jesus also observed that Martha was "troubled" (v. 41), referring to the outward noise she was making by her excitement. Internally she was distracted, and externally she was in a state of agitation.

On the other hand, Mary had "chosen that good part" (v. 42). Martha was focused on the temporal, but Mary was tuned in to the spiritual. The spiritual blessings Mary would experience by focusing on Christ's words had eternal value.

For us to love like Christ, we must regularly spend time sitting in His presence, growing deeper in our relationship with Him.

CONCLUSION

A church may be made up of the most gifted persons and still fall far short of God's purpose simply because it lacks the one element that would make it truly fruitful—*love*. Paul was aware that the real trouble with the Corinthians was that they did not have the proper respect and concern for others. His cure for their divisions—love—is the only remedy for the problems of modern churches. If all Christians had lived by the principles set forth in 1 Corinthians 13, we would have to rewrite church history.

GOLDEN TEXT CHALLENGE

"NOW ABIDETH FAITH, HOPE, CHARITY, THESE THREE; BUT THE GREATEST OF THESE IS CHARITY" (1 Corinthians 13:13).

Fortunately for us, all three of these abide. *Faith* means a respectful reverence for the unknown when it is related to the integrity of the individual in whom trust is placed. Faith, according to God's plan, will be rewarded with realization. God cannot be pleased with anyone who has no faith in Him. Without God, we are hopeless.

Belief in God and the gospel gives us *hope* not only for this life, but also for the life to come. Hopelessness is a malady that only God can heal.

Love energizes faith and hope, giving them wings with which to travel, a mouth with which to speak, and loving hands with which to help. Love is forever self-giving and forgiving. Love is the fulfillment of the Law, the supreme commandment of Christ. It is the dominant characteristic of every Christian church or community. It is a quality that improves all human relationships. It is a language that all can speak.

The more love you give, the lovelier you become. Faith will be rewarded; hope will be realized; but love, the ultimate reality, flows through time like a mighty stream that conquers malice, enmity, fear and hate. Love is always the winner.

Daily Devotions:

M. Love Your Neighbor
Leviticus 19:16-18

T. Love God Wholeheartedly
Deuteronomy 6:1-9

W. God's Love for His People
Hosea 11:1-11

T. Proof of Discipleship
John 13:33-35

F. Commanded to Love
John 15:9-17

S. Acts of Sacrificial Love
Romans 12:9-21

April 2, 2006

Joy in Christ

**John 15:9-11; Acts 2:41-47;
2 Corinthians 4:17, 18; Philippians 4:4-8**

Unit Theme:
Fruit of Christian Formation

Central Truth:
Joy results from living in spiritual union with Christ and fellow Christians.

Focus:
Recognize and experience Christ as the source of our joy and strength.

Context:
Selected New Testament passages focusing on joy

Golden Text:
"These things have I spoken unto you, that my joy might remain in you, and that your joy might be full" (John 15:11).

Study Outline:
I. The Source of Joy (John 15:9-11)
II. Joy of Christian Community (Acts 2:41-47)
III. Joy of Christian Living (2 Corinthians 4:17, 18; Philippians 4:4-8)

INTRODUCTION

Christianity was born in the saddest of times. With the exception of the Jewish worship of Jehovah, the world was devoted to a sorry assortment of gods, demons and spirits. More than half of the world was in slavery or servitude. Most people had forgotten, if they had ever known, how to laugh. Joy and happiness were not even concepts to most people, who accepted their sadness and absence of spirit as a matter of fact. Human life itself was held in light regard, especially the lives of the enslaved and the poor.

Joy is the state of well-being and assurance that makes us content even in the face of adversity. This virtue is particularly related to the fullness of the Holy Spirit (Acts 13:52). Joy is indifferent to the circumstances that determine happiness and the things upon which pleasure depends, and is frequently most apparent in the face of unhappiness and displeasure. Our joy is to be constant, and in all circumstances.

Paul directed the early church to "rejoice in the Lord alway: and again I say, Rejoice" (Philippians 4:4), and encouraged the people to "rejoice evermore" (1 Thessalonians 5:16). In many ways, the fruit of joy is most conspicuous in times of adversity, a pattern which Jesus set when He "for the joy that was set before him endured the cross, despising the shame, and is set down at the right hand of the throne of God" (Hebrews 12:2). He showed in His crucifixion how joy can be maintained in the absence of either pleasure or happiness.

The early Christians were a happy, joyful people and their message was one of optimism and gladness. Their lives were filled with irrepressible joy, based upon a sure confidence in Jesus Christ, "in whom, though now ye see him not, yet believing, ye rejoice with joy unspeakable and full of glory" (1 Peter 1:8).

For the Christian, life itself is good, and that is a cause for unending joy. The forgiveness of sin and the fullness of the Spirit are causes for joy. Belief that Jesus rose from the dead must bring joy, as does our hope of resurrection. Belief that He stands at the right hand of the Father making intercession for us certainly gives joy. Belief that He is coming again occasions joy for those who are prepared for His coming. And belief that we shall live with Him eternally is reason for our greatest spiritual joy.—Charles W. Conn

I. THE SOURCE OF JOY (John 15:9-11)

A. Love Flowing From the Son (v. 9)

9. As the Father hath loved me, so have I loved you: continue ye in my love.

One purpose of Jesus' coming into the world was to show people what God is like. In His relationship with His disciples, therefore, He showed them how God loved. God's love is selfless, so Jesus gave fully of Himself to His followers. God's love is patient, so Jesus bore with His disciples in their spiritual ignorance and slow growth toward spiritual maturity. God's love is far-reaching—universal, in fact; so Jesus demonstrated to His disciples how love breaks down all barriers—personal, social, psychological, even political.

Now Jesus urged His disciples to apply the lessons, to live and to minister in the spirit of godly love. He also pressed upon them the important element of fellowship as an aspect of that love—their involvement in a love relationship with God and with their fellow believers. The evidence of that love, however, would be seen not in emotional demonstration but in the quality of their relationships with God, with fellow Christians, and with all other human beings.

Talk About It:
1. Describe God the Father's love for God the Son.
2. What does it mean to "continue" in Christ's love?

B. Love Expressed Through Obedience (v. 10)

10. If ye keep my commandments, ye shall abide in my love; even as I have kept my Father's commandments, and abide in his love.

The greatest test of one's love relationship with Jesus and God the Father is obedience. God's own holiness of character mandates certain ethical principles which are the direct outcome of that divine character. Uncompromisingly, those principles are set forth in His Word. If any person would relate to God, he must conform to those principles. Hence, the inseparable connection between obedience and love.

We will not obey if we do not love, and we do not love if we habitually fail to obey. It is possible to substitute emotional experiences for obedience, periodically engaging in "emotional baths" while never yielding the entire personality in obedience to God. Such a substitute for consistent relationship with God is phony and results in powerlessness during crisis and ineffective Christian testimony. Because Jesus followed all of His Father's commands, He can empower us to live in loving obedience to God.

Talk About It:
1. Is this verse saying Christ quits loving us if we disobey God's commands? Explain your answer.
2. How can Christ's obedience to the Father's commands help us?

C. Love Overflowing as Joy (v. 11)

11. These things have I spoken unto you, that my joy might remain in you, and that your joy might be full.

Jesus did not offer His disciples happiness; that is the result

Talk About It:
Where does joy
come from, and what
does it do for us?

Talk About It:
1. What did 3,000
people "gladly"
receive on the Day
of Pentecost
(v. 41)?
2. How did they
grow in their faith
(v. 42)?

of favorable external circumstance. But He did promise joy—if they obeyed Him. Joy is the outcome of a relationship with the Father and the Son undisturbed by disobedience. If, then, we remain in proper relationship, a constant flow of spiritual life is ours—from the Source of life. Joy is an inevitable fruit of that relationship. We will not have to strain for it or resort to artificial means to achieve it. It is the result of abiding in Jesus.

As our lives offer maximum glory to God, we experience the fullest joy. And that joy is not merely the accompaniment to happy circumstance. It is not externally produced; rather, it is the outflow of inner spiritual relationship—in proper balance.

II. JOY OF CHRISTIAN COMMUNITY (Acts 2:41-47)
A. Steadfastness (vv. 41, 42)

41. Then they that gladly received his word were baptized: and the same day there were added unto them about three thousand souls.

42. And they continued stedfastly in the apostles' doctrine and fellowship, and in breaking of bread, and in prayers.

"This passage provides a vivid summary of the life of the new converts [the 3,000 who received Christ on the Day of Pentecost]. Luke describes the direct and immediate results of the outpouring of the Spirit. The distinctive teaching of the New Testament that the church is community comes out clearly in these verses. Luke's description of the believers at Pentecost brings to mind Paul's idea of the church as the body of Christ" (French Arrington, *Acts of the Apostles*, Hendrickson Publishers).

Christian maturity does not happen the moment one accepts Christ. In fact, those who have lived longest for Christ are the first to admit their continued need for teaching from God's Word. A consuming desire to know more about God and His Son Jesus Christ accompanies true conversion.

The word *doctrine* (v. 42) refers to the teaching of the apostles. They had known the Lord intimately. They had witnessed His miracles. They were present when He presented His discourses. What this early teaching was may best be judged not by the later New Testament Epistles but by the sermons recorded in the earlier chapters of Acts. Alexander MacLaren states: "Of course there was necessarily involved a certain amount of what we now call doctrine—because one cannot tell the story of Jesus Christ, as it is told in the four Gospels, without impressing upon the hearers the conviction that His nature was divine and that His death was a sacrifice" (*Expositions of Scripture*).

Luke describes "the fellowship" as the intimate living of the apostles and other Christians. Arrington says, "On the human side it is the fellowship of the believers, but the quality of this fellowship is determined by union and fellowship with Jesus Christ."

Some Bible scholars believe the phrase "in breaking of bread" refers to a common meal and that every such meal in the early days of the church had a religious significance. They believe it became a type and evidence of the kingdom of God among believers. Other scholars say this statement is the common New Testament name for the Lord's Supper. We know the Communion service is intended to promote fellowship or communion with other Christians as well as with Christ.

Prayers were a prominent feature of Christian worship in the early church. Prayers were offered at the Communion service and by groups of Christians in the Temple. And various groups met in the homes of the Christians just for prayer.

> "The Bible knows nothing of solitary religion."
> —John Wesley

B. Influence (v. 43)

43. And fear came upon every soul: and many wonders and signs were done by the apostles.

In commenting on this verse, J. Vernon Bartlet states: "Rather awe began to creep over every soul. This awe, as in the presence of the superhuman, was caused primarily by the Pentecostal outpouring and its results just recorded; but it was enhanced by other signs of divine power among the Christians" (*The New Century Bible*).

Concerning the signs and wonders done by the apostles, Richard B. Rackham observes: "These miracles served the same purpose as those of the Lord. As His works had borne witness to Him, so the works of the apostles were signs of divine approval and the credentials of their apostolate" (*The Expositor's Greek Testament*).

Talk About It:
1. What created *fear* ("awe") among the believers?
2. Should verse 43 also be descriptive of churches today? Why or why not?

C. Unity and Unselfishness (vv. 44, 45)

44. And all that believed were together, and had all things common;

45. And sold their possessions and goods, and parted them to all men, as every man had need.

Having "all things common" was an idealistic sharing among the Jerusalem church and was entered into voluntarily. It was never commanded by the Lord. There is no evidence in the New Testament indicating it is the desire of the Holy Spirit for the entire church.

Most Bible scholars do not believe verse 45 means they divided everything and distributed it evenly among all. It seems, rather, that they took what was their own, sold it, and gave according to the need. Note the clause "to anyone as he had need" (*NIV*).

Talk About It:
1. How were the material needs of believers met in the early church?
2. Should today's church follow the practices described in these verses? Why or why not?

D. Progress and Power (vv. 46, 47)

46. And they, continuing daily with one accord in the temple, and breaking bread from house to house, did eat their meat with gladness and singleness of heart,

47. Praising God, and having favour with all the people. And the Lord added to the church daily such as should be saved.

Talk About It:
1. How often did the believers meet, and what did they do in their meetings?
2. Describe the Christians' inner attitude, their relationship with God, and their impact on the community.

"One hundred worshipers meeting together, each one looking away to Christ, are in heart nearer to each other than they could possibly be were they to become 'unity' conscious and turn their eyes away from God to strive for closer fellowship."
—A.W. Tozer

Notice the steps in the growth of these believers in the early church as they progressed in this second chapter of Acts. First, they had a knowledge they were saved with the accompanying peace with God. Next followed growth in divine truth and meaningful fellowship one with another as they shared their means with those in need. Then they were able to see others being saved. This growth produced gladness of heart. Their behavior also earned the respect of those who had not yet believed in Jesus.

These early Christians praised God for the blessings they were receiving through the gift of His Son. They had communion with God, and they had love one for another.

It has been said that the best proof of Christianity is the Christian life lived in an everyday environment. This the early believers did, and they had "favour with all the people." Such fruits of the Spirit as these early Christians showed are certain to find favor with all.

The pure and simple life of the early Christians commended them to the people and made it easier for them to win confidence, and thus converts. However, the growth of the church, Luke reminds us, was not the work of any human agency or attractiveness, but of the Lord.

III. JOY OF CHRISTIAN LIVING (2 Corinthians 4:17, 18; Philippians 4:4-8)

A. Focusing on Eternity (2 Corinthians 4:17, 18)

17. For our light affliction, which is but for a moment, worketh for us a far more exceeding and eternal weight of glory;

18. While we look not at the things which are seen, but at the things which are not seen: for the things which are seen are temporal; but the things which are not seen are eternal.

Talk About It:
1. In what sense are a Christian's troubles "light"?
2. Why should we and how can we focus on unseen things?

In 2 Corinthians 4, Paul describes Christians as "jars of clay" bearing eternal treasure. Even when we are "hard pressed . . . perplexed . . . persecuted . . . struck down," we have an "all-surpassing power" that enables us to not be crushed, destroyed, nor feel abandoned or hopeless (vv. 7-9, *NIV*).

In fact, when faith triumphs over doubt in our lives, persecution and difficulty work to our advantage and for our improvement. Afflictions then become light and of short life, but they bring to us eternal and "far more exceeding" spiritual glory and triumph. This is why the apostles rejoiced when they were persecuted; persecution identified them with the Lord and made them better men. As Acts 5:41 says, "They departed from the presence of the council, rejoicing that they were counted worthy to suffer shame for his name."

The beauty of the Christian life is that we do not have to be dominated by circumstances and attitudes around us. There is within us strength and power great enough to overcome all obstacles and difficulties. Many of life's greatest opportunities come disguised as difficulties. If we are defeated or deterred by the difficulty, then we never get to the reward of the blessing. Circumstances about us are temporal, which means they are a part of this world. The power within us is eternal, God-given, and perpetually strengthening. This is the confidence, this is the hope, this is the assurance of the child of God. Accepting this truth is faith, and faith is the victory.

B. Rejoicing in Christ (Philippians 4:4, 5)

4. Rejoice in the Lord alway: and again I say, Rejoice.

5. Let your moderation be known unto all men. The Lord is at hand.

moderation (v. 5)—gentleness

Joy and rejoicing is the theme of the Book of Philippians. There are three words in the Greek text of the New Testament that are translated "joy" or "rejoice." One word emphasizes the outward demonstration of joy, while a second emphasizes the personal feeling a person experiences while joyous. The third word, *chairo*, which is the word used in Philippians 4, emphasizes "well-being experienced in response to someone or something."

Paul uses the third word for joy because he is speaking of joy experienced in response to Christ. It is not joy built on outward demonstrations or personal experience, although those qualities may be evident. The center of the joy Paul refers to is Jesus Christ. This is why Paul adds the phrase "in the Lord." Paul's exhortation is not merely to "joy" alone but joy "in the Lord."

In addition to a call to rejoice, Paul exhorts the Philippians regarding their "moderation" ("gentleness," *NIV*). This word means "a humble, patient steadfastness, which is able to submit to injustice, disgrace and maltreatment without hatred and malice, trusting God in spite of all of it" (*Linguistic Key to the New Testament*).

The believers' gentleness was to be known by all persons they encountered. They were to be known for their fairness and equity. And the coming of the Lord was a primary motivation for their gentleness. Christ was the reason they should live in humble and patient steadfastness.

Talk About It:
1. How is it possible to rejoice in Jesus "always"?
2. Why is it important to let people see our gentleness?

C. Praying Instead of Fretting (vv. 6, 7)

careful (v. 6)—
anxious
supplication (v. 6)—petition

6. Be careful for nothing; but in every thing by prayer and supplication with thanksgiving let your requests be made known unto God.

7. And the peace of God, which passeth all understanding, shall keep your hearts and minds through Christ Jesus.

Talk About It:
1. Why do our petitions to God need to be mingled with thanksgiving?
2. What makes the peace of God indescribable?
3. What does God's peace do for believers?

"Be careful for nothing" is rendered "Take no thought" in Matthew 6:25. It means not becoming overly anxious or fretful about anything. Fretfulness is the condition that develops when the Christian fails to foster fellowship with God in prayer. In contrast to fretting, Paul exhorts the believers to let their "requests be made known unto God." Instead of fretting over *nothing*, the Christian in *everything* is to make his or her requests known to God.

The result of letting one's request be made known to God is a "keeping" of the heart and mind. The heart and mind are the areas affected most by a fretful lifestyle. Emotional, mental and spiritual anguish naturally occur when a wholesome prayer life is not developed.

"Peace does not mean to be in a place where there is no noise, trouble, or hard work. Peace means to be in the midst of all those things and still be calm in your heart."
—**Goethe**

Keep comes from a Greek word which indicates "watching over something." This is a military term referring to guards who watch over a city gate or building needing protection. In the same manner, the peace of God, which comes to one's heart and mind, watches over and secures the safety and rest of an individual. God's protection is maximized by a rich prayer life, but is hindered by a fretful lifestyle.

D. Thinking on Right Things (v. 8)

8. Finally, brethren, whatsoever things are true, whatsoever things are honest, whatsoever things are just, whatsoever things are pure, whatsoever things are lovely, whatsoever things are of good report; if there be any virtue, and if there be any praise, think on these things.

Talk About It:
1. List five things that we should meditate upon.
2. List five things we should *not* meditate upon.

Think is from a Greek word meaning to "consider" or "ponder." It emphasizes dwelling upon something rather than casual reflection or mere logical inquiry. Paul exhorts the believer to continually consider things that are "true . . . honest . . . just . . . pure . . . lovely . . . of good report."

True means things that are not hidden and concealed, but open and honest. *Honest* means "grave, venerable or reverent." It refers to someone or something that commands a high degree of respect. *Just* refers to things established by judicial process and found to be right. The word here emphasizes things that have been established to be right under the justice of God.

"It is one thing to be tormented by ideas or images we do not want, but quite another to pursue them intentionally. People

Pure comes from a Greek word referring to being chaste, emphasizing a freedom from moral fault or defilement. *Lovely*

means things that would "attract or draw acceptance and love." *Good report* indicates things that are "well spoken of and praiseworthy."

By filling our mind with thoughts that are excellent and praiseworthy, we can expect the peace and joy of the Lord to guard and bless us.

CONCLUSION

There is a wide and significant difference between *fun* and *joy*. The former is superficial, depending on "things" and circumstances; while the latter is constant, transcending tangibles and mere mundane conditions. Fun is transitory emotion, but joy is a resident quality of life. Fun is self-directed and indulgent; joy is imparted by God himself and to His glory.

The joy Jesus provides is three-dimensional:

1. *It is a joy of initial spiritual experience.* The joy of sins forgiven is a marvelous response to the realization that one has been saved from sin, from self, and from hell. The world cannot give such joy, and it surely cannot take it away.

2. *It is a joy of spiritual development.* Growing in the grace and in the knowledge of Christ is enjoined in Scripture (see, for example, 2 Peter 3:18). Joy attends the maturing process as certainly as it does the impartation of new life. There is joy in applying the means to spiritual growth that the Lord has provided. These means for growth are, among others, Bible study, prayer, and fellowship with other believers in the sanctuary of God. The joy of salvation cannot be maintained apart from these divinely ordained pursuits.

3. *It is a joy of Christian service.* The believer is saved to serve. The busy, responsible Christian is the joyful Christian, for he is in process thereby of sharing Jesus with others, which is, after all, what being a Christian is all about.

GOLDEN TEXT CHALLENGE

"THESE THINGS HAVE I SPOKEN UNTO YOU, THAT MY JOY MIGHT REMAIN IN YOU, AND THAT YOUR JOY MIGHT BE FULL" (John 15:11).

The Christian life is not a cheerless, barren existence devoid of meaning. It is, rather, a happy, rewarding life spent in the wholehearted pursuit of obedience to the Lord's commandments. What Jesus meant here was simply this: As He had the joy of living the completely fruitful life, so He wanted that joy to be in His followers too, as they lived fruitfully. In that sense, then, His joy would be theirs—abiding and full.

who deliberately watch violent films or read pornographic literature for the pleasure it gives them are simply struggling with temptation; they are sinning."
—J. Heinrich Arnold (*Freedom From Sinful Thoughts*)

Daily Devotions:
M. Giving With Joy
   1 Chronicles
   29:6-15
T. Strengthened by
   Joy
   Nehemiah 8:9-12
W. Joy Expressed
   Psalm 66:1-6
T. Reason for Joy
   Luke 10:17-24
F. Heaven's Joy
   Luke 15:4-10
S. Christ Gives Joy
   1 Peter 1:3-9

April 9, 2006

The Peace of Christ

Isaiah 9:6, 7; Matthew 6:25-34; John 14:27; 16:33; Romans 8:1-6

Unit Theme:
Fruit of Christian Formation

Central Truth:
Resting in Christ's presence and promises, we experience His peace.

Focus:
Acknowledge Christ as the Prince of Peace and rest in His presence and promises.

Context:
Selected New Testament passages concerning the peace of God

Golden Text:
"Peace I leave with you, my peace I give unto you: not as the world giveth, give I unto you. Let not your heart be troubled, neither let it be afraid" (John 14:27).

Study Outline:
I. Rooted in Christ (Isaiah 9:6, 7; John 14:27; 16:33)
II. Maintained Through Righteousness (Romans 8:1-6)
III. Reflected in Daily Living (Matthew 6:25-34)

INTRODUCTION

Peace in its most common sense means an absence of war and hostility, but as a fruit of the Spirit it means much more than that and touches every part of life. It is a state of individual harmony with life, which includes God first of all, then other people, and finally ourselves. This harmony of life must reach into the deepest recesses and extend to the farthest reaches of ourselves.

True peace is one of the most difficult virtues to develop and maintain. In fact, it is impossible without the nurture of Christ within us. Peace was associated with Christ's birth, when the angels sang, "Glory to God in the highest, and on earth peace, good will toward men" (Luke 2:14). It was also associated with His death, when He said, "Peace I leave with you, my peace I give unto you" (John 14:27). Observe that it was *His* peace He left us and it is *His* peace we are expected to manifest.

The peace of Christ is not mere passiveness, complacency or absence of involvement—it is peace in the midst of conflict. Jesus lived in a time of gravest conflict and yet His life radiated absolute inner peace, and His peace was communicated to others. Some people seem to have the virtue of peace only because they are unaware of the chaos and disorder about them. The spiritual peace Christians have should live triumphantly in the face of, and with full knowledge of, the turmoil and confusion around them. This is victorious Christian living; this is the Lord's intention for His people.

In his book *New Testament Christianity*, J.B. Phillips, New Testament translator and scholar, says: "As we study New Testament Christianity, we are aware that there is an inner core of tranquillity and stability. In fact, not the least of the impressive qualities which the church could demonstrate to the pagan world was this ballast of inward peace. It was, I think, something new that was appearing in the lives of human beings. . . . It was a positive peace, a solid foundation which held fast amid all the turmoil of human experience."

A person with divine peace in his or her life will manifest it in many ways, of which inner tranquillity is but one. This fruit of the Spirit will be present as a multiple virtue of peace with God, peace with people, and peace with self.—Charles W. Conn

I. ROOTED IN CHRIST (Isaiah 9:6, 7; John 14:27; 16:33)
A. Prince of Peace (Isaiah 9:6, 7)

6. For unto us a child is born, unto us a son is given: and the government shall be upon his shoulder: and his name shall be called Wonderful, Counsellor, The mighty God, The everlasting Father, The Prince of Peace.

7. Of the increase of his government and peace there shall be no end, upon the throne of David, and upon his kingdom, to order it, and to establish it with judgment and with justice from henceforth even for ever. The zeal of the Lord of hosts will perform this.

Isaiah's prophecy reveals that the Messiah, for whom His people had longed, would be born as a child. He comes as the gift of the God of love (see John 3:16). And the government would be vested in Him.

Then Isaiah gives a list of titles which reflect both the character and the mission of the Messiah. He would be *Wonderful* in the whole bearing of His life. Christ would also be called *Counselor*, using His great wisdom to guide and direct human affairs. On numerous occasions, Jesus displayed wisdom that astonished those who heard Him.

The Messiah would also be called *Mighty God*, which is a reference to His divine nature. He would be both God and man. No one else could ever make that claim. Then, the Lord would be called *Everlasting Father*. This name may be more properly rendered "Father of Eternity," denoting His everlasting duration.

Finally, the Messiah would be called *Prince of Peace*. His government would increase continuously, ever growing and expanding (v. 7). The centerpiece of His kingdom would be peace. The earth has not yet seen the kind of prosperity and the quality of peace that He will bring when He sets up His kingdom on earth. The strongest hopes the hearts of people have held will be fulfilled in Him.

Justice and righteousness are the guiding principles of Christ's kingdom. He is never influenced by partiality or prejudice. The constitution under which He governs may be stated in one word—uprightness. In His righteous reign, the Messiah fulfills the ardent desire of God for the establishment of this kingdom.

B. Peace From the Lord (John 14:27)

27. Peace I leave with you, my peace I give unto you: not as the world giveth, give I unto you. Let not your heart be troubled, neither let it be afraid.

Jesus is both the possessor and the source of the peace He describes here. We have the opportunity to have the same

Talk About It:
1. What is significant about Isaiah's two uses of the word *us* in verse 6?
2. If all the information you had about Jesus was contained in these two verses, what would you know about Him?
3. Explain the statement "The zeal of the Lord of hosts will perform this" (v. 7).

Talk About It:
1. What is different between God's gifts and the world's?

2. What is Christ's answer for a troubled, fearful heart? How do we receive it?

"Peace with God is obtained at our conversion and is maintained by our constant submission to His will."
—Charles W. Conn

peace He has. This means we can have a relationship with God that is secure.

Christ has brought about a reconciliation between God and people that results in perfect peace. Paul wrote: "For he himself is our peace, who has made the two one and has destroyed the barrier, the dividing wall of hostility. . . . He came and preached peace to you who were far away and peace to those who were near. For through him we both have access to the Father by one Spirit" (Ephesians 2:14, 17, 18, *NIV*).

Having made His peace available, Jesus encouraged the disciples to find freedom from a troubled heart. Peter Marshall once referred to ulcers as the "badges of our lack of faith." As George Muller said, "The beginning of anxiety is the end of faith, and the beginning of true faith is the end of anxiety."

C. Overcoming Peace (16:33)

33. These things I have spoken unto you, that in me ye might have peace. In the world ye shall have tribulation: but be of good cheer; I have overcome the world.

Jesus wanted to prepare His disciples for the pressure they were about to experience. After referring to the terrible hour that was approaching, He offered a parting word of encouragement and victory. He was concerned about the disciples and reminded them they had peace in Him. He was thinking more of others than of Himself. Even though the bitter cross was near, He forgot His own grief in the grief of the disciples. He offered them the comfort of His own peace. Of course, this peace can only be enjoyed by communion with Him. It is significant that even though He had referred to their forsaking Him, He would never forsake them.

In the words "Be of good cheer; I have overcome the world" is found a great assurance of victory for the believer. The world has a lot of influence and power, but it is not all-powerful. It has been in a battle and has been defeated. One greater than the world has conquered it. It has been said that Noah condemned the world, but Christ conquered it.

Today Christ says to the workers in His kingdom, "Take courage, I have overcome the world." Therefore the storms and persecution that beat fiercely upon the Christian can be used to drive him or her closer to Christ.

II. MAINTAINED THROUGH RIGHTEOUSNESS (Romans 8:1-6)

A. Living Without Condemnation (vv. 1, 2)

1. There is therefore now no condemnation to them which are in Christ Jesus, who walk not after the flesh, but after the Spirit.

Talk About It:
How did Jesus "overcome the world," and how can His triumph help us?

2. For the law of the Spirit of life in Christ Jesus hath made me free from the law of sin and death.

Paul drew a distinct contrast between two lifestyles. He wrote first of life lived according to the flesh. By that expression, he meant human nature in all its weakness and in its vulnerability to sin; human nature apart from Christ; everything that attaches someone to the world instead of to God. One who lives this way is dominated by the desires of sinful human nature instead of by the love of God. In this sinful state, one is moved to sin and goes from bad to worse. On the other hand, when that person becomes a Christian, the surging power of the Spirit of God comes into his or her life and, as a result, that person enters into victorious living.

The believer lives and walks in Christ. He is never separated from Him. As he breathes in the air and the air fills him, so Christ fills him. He has no mind of his own; Christ is his mind. He has no desires of his own; the will of Christ is his only law. He is Spirit-controlled, Christ- controlled, God-focused.

There is no condemnation for the person who lives this kind of life. By that, Paul meant that there would be no calling into court, no judgment. Everything has been taken care of in Christ. The believer is judged in Him.

B. Living in the Spirit (vv. 3, 4)

3. For what the law could not do, in that it was weak through the flesh, God sending his own Son in the likeness of sinful flesh, and for sin, condemned sin in the flesh:

4. That the righteousness of the law might be fulfilled in us, who walk not after the flesh, but after the Spirit.

Paul spoke of the powerlessness of the Law. It was not capable of freeing us from the dominion of sin. It could irritate our sinful nature into more virulent action, but it could not secure its own fulfillment. Our sinful nature stood as a roadblock to the Law in its efforts to effect change for good in us. But what the Law could not do, God did by sending His Son.

Christ not only has the very nature of God, even as a son has his father's nature, but He is essentially of the Father, though that defies explanation. This special relationship is stated here to enhance the greatness and define the nature of the relief provided. It comes from beyond the precincts of sinful humanity altogether; it comes immediately from the Godhead itself.

God accomplished what the Law could not, by the mission of His Son in the likeness of sinful nature. He sent Christ in the character of a sin offering. "He hath made him to be sin for us" (2 Corinthians 5:21). Christ condemned sin in the flesh, that is, He condemned it to lose its hold over us. He forced it to let go its iron grasp, and ultimately to be driven away from the domain of human nature in the redeemed.

Talk About It:
1. What is *condemnation,* and how is a person freed from it?
2. What are the differences between the two laws Paul describes in verse 2?

"It is the unspeakable privilege and comfort of all those that are in Christ Jesus that there is therefore now no condemnation to them. He does not say, 'There is no accusation against them,' for this there is; but the accusation is thrown out, and the indictment quashed."

—Matthew Henry

Talk About It:
1. What can't people obey God's law through their own efforts?
2. What does it mean to live "according to the Spirit" (v. 4, *NIV*)?

Because of the work of Christ in our behalf, we are able to meet the righteous requirements of the Law. But we are only able to do so as we walk in the Spirit.

C. Being Spiritually Minded (vv. 5, 6)

5. For they that are after the flesh do mind the things of the flesh; but they that are after the Spirit the things of the Spirit.

6. For to be carnally minded is death; but to be spiritually minded is life and peace.

Talk About It:
1. How does verse 5 explain the difference between an unbeliever and a Christian?
2. Where does peace of mind come from?

Those who live according to the sinful nature leave God out of their life. Those who live according to the Spirit organize their life around God. This involves every aspect of life, including the mind. The mind-set of the flesh produces hostility toward God and leads to total death. It does not belong to the dominion in which God's Law is obeyed. Indeed, it is unable to obey God, so in its hostility toward God, it is unable to please God. The mind-set ordered by the Spirit produces eternal life, God's life, imparted to those in Christ. In addition to life, it also results in peace.

The Bible says much about the part the mind plays in Christianity. Some people seem to think that when you become a Christian you have to park your brains. But Jesus said we must love the Lord God with all our mind (Mark 12:30).

"The world can create trouble in peace, but God can create peace in trouble."
—**Thomas Watson**

Paul wrote frequently of the importance of the mind in the life of the believer. In Philippians 4:7 he said, "The peace of God, which passeth all understanding, shall keep your hearts and minds through Christ Jesus." In Colossians 3:2 he wrote, "Set your affection [mind] on things above, not on things on the earth." The Spirit-filled mind is focused on Christ and filled with peace.

III. REFLECTED IN DAILY LIVING (Matthew 6:25-34)

A. The Essentials of Life (vv. 25, 26)

25. Therefore I say unto you, Take no thought for your life, what ye shall eat, or what ye shall drink; nor yet for your body, what ye shall put on. Is not the life more than meat, and the body than raiment?

26. Behold the fowls of the air: for they sow not, neither do they reap, nor gather into barns; yet your heavenly Father feedeth them. Are ye not much better than they?

Talk About It:
1. Answer Christ's question, "Is not life more important than food, and the body more important than clothes?" (v. 25, *NIV*).

When you read this passage, you are reminded of the unbounded admiration which Jesus manifested for the world of nature. In the visible creation, Jesus saw the hand of God. He also understood that the human soul is infinitely more precious in God's sight than all these works of His hand. This being the case, all anxiety should be driven from our heart. These creatures are living evidence that anxiety is not necessary. The God who provides for them will provide for us.

Anxiety implies that God cannot do for us what He has promised. It limits "the Holy One of Israel" (Psalm 78:41), which is a grievous sin. It reflects on God's love. What kind of Father is He if He knows our needs, and could supply them, but fails to do so? What injury anxiety brings. We should drive it from our vocabulary, and replace it with trust in God.

The best cure for anxiety is to seek the kingdom of God and His righteousness. When that pursuit has top priority in our lives, we grow in confidence and trust. Paul wrote: "For the kingdom of God is not meat and drink; but righteousness, and peace, and joy in the Holy Ghost. For he that in these things serveth Christ is acceptable to God, and approved of men" (Romans 14:17, 18). Thus, seeking the kingdom of God, and finding it, forces anxiety out of the life. It is replaced by peace and joy in the Holy Spirit.

B. The Futility of Worry (vv. 27-30)

(Matthew 6:27-30 is not included in the printed text.)

What is gained by worry? What advantage does it bring to a person? What value does it offer for your life? Who by being anxiously vexed can add a single step to the length of his life's journey? Who can by worrying add even one hour to his life? How utterly futile worry is.

Not only does God feed the birds, but He also clothes the lilies of the field. Though they do not toil or spin, they are arrayed in greater glory than that of Solomon. If God gives such care to the transient flowers—here today, gone tomorrow (for fuel in the baking oven)—how much more will He clothe His own children? It is unanswerable logic.

C. The Necessities of Life (vv. 31, 32)

31. Therefore take no thought, saying, What shall we eat? or, What shall we drink? or, Wherewithal shall we be clothed?

32. (For after all these things do the Gentiles seek:) for your heavenly Father knoweth that ye have need of all these things.

What are the true riches of life? Do they consist of what we eat, or what we drink, or what we wear? Could there be other matters that are more important? Does not the richness of life lie in a sense of having fulfilled some needs of others? Another of the true riches of life is a friend. A friend is always near. He rejoices in your good fortune; he shares your disappointments; and your problems become his problems. One is never poor, even though her clothes may be worn out and her purse empty, if she still has the love and understanding of loyal friends. Many other items could be listed among the true riches of life. What would your list consist of?

2. What can birds teach us?

"Bishop William Quayle, awake at night because of fruitless worrying, heard God say to him, 'Quayle, you go to bed; I'll sit up the rest of the night.'"

Talk About It:
1. Answer Christ's question in verse 27. What is His point?
2. Who is the person of "little faith" (v. 30)?

Talk About It:
1. What does the heavenly Father know, and why is this important?
2. How should Christians stand out from nonbelievers ("Gentiles")?

The non-Christian is obsessed with the pursuit of things. Since the unbeliever feels no responsibility toward God and entertains no hope in an afterlife, his or her goals are limited to accumulating things. This was especially true of the pagans of Jesus' day. What they had to eat and drink and wear was uppermost in their minds. The Christian must be careful not to fall into that same pattern. Paul wrote: "Set your affection on things above, not on things on the earth" (Colossians 3:2).

We must remember that God knows what our needs are. A loving and caring God desires to meet our every need. Paul wrote, "But my God shall supply all your need according to his riches in glory by Christ Jesus" (Philippians 4:19).

D. The Kingdom of God (vv. 33, 34)

33. But seek ye first the kingdom of God, and his righteousness; and all these things shall be added unto you.

34. Take therefore no thought for the morrow: for the morrow shall take thought for the things of itself. Sufficient unto the day is the evil thereof.

Talk About It:
1. What should our priorities be, and what does God promise if our priorities are in the right order?
2. According to verse 34, why should our focus be on *today* and not *tomorrow*?

Escape from anxiety over things is found in giving first place to God's kingdom and His righteousness. Emphasis upon the rule of God and upon righteousness is characteristic of this gospel. Assurance is given to those who put His kingdom and His righteousness first, that He will give them all the things others seek after as they have need of them.

This promise of provision must be balanced by the warning that sacrifice, privation, and even the cross belong to discipleship. Jesus said, "He that findeth his life shall lose it: and he that loseth his life for my sake shall find it" (Matthew 10:39).

Considering both the promise and the warning, we understand that our part is unconditional submission to the rule of Christ. Thus committed, we have assurance that what we require to fulfill our calling in discipleship will be provided. We may experience "fullness" or "hunger," but in Christ we will find His sufficiency. Listen to Paul: "Not that I speak in respect of want: for I have learned, in whatsoever state I am, therewith to be content. . . . I can do all things through Christ which strengtheneth me" (Philippians 4:11, 13).

In verse 34 of the text, Jesus set forth an important principle for worry-free living. He encouraged His followers to live one day at a time. This means zeroing in on the moment and making the most of it, concentrating all of one's powers and energies on the project at hand, and crossing no bridges before getting to them.

"Men spend their lives in anticipations, in determining to be vastly happy at some period or other, when they have time. But the present time has one advantage over every other: it is our time."

—Charles Colson

When you live in day-tight compartments—24 segments—you discover that life takes on a different perspective. With Christ's enabling power, no problem is so great that you can not handle it until the sun goes down, or until midnight. Tomorrow is a new day and a new opportunity to cope with whatever that day may bring.

CONCLUSION

Worry about the future is wasted effort, and the future of reality is seldom as bad as the future of our fears.

The choice that faces us is whether we will worry needlessly or trust God explicitly. Isaiah said it well a long time ago: "Thou wilt keep him in perfect peace, whose mind is stayed on thee: because he trusteth in thee" (Isaiah 26:3).

GOLDEN TEXT CHALLENGE

"PEACE I LEAVE WITH YOU, MY PEACE I GIVE UNTO YOU: NOT AS THE WORLD GIVETH, GIVE I UNTO YOU. LET NOT YOUR HEART BE TROUBLED, NEITHER LET IT BE AFRAID" (John 14:27).

The secular concept of peace is merely that of the absence of hostilities; the peace Jesus gives is that and more. The disciples of Jesus are indeed at peace in the sense they are no longer at odds with the God of the universe. Hostilities have ceased between them and God. Christians know also a peace which arises out of certitude as to who they are and where they are going, and that bedrock assurance is as continuous as the presence of the Holy Spirit is constantly abiding.

In contrast, the world—people without knowledge of Jesus Christ—can know only that calm which arises out of a fortunate circumstance. When trouble comes, the peace of unbelievers departs and is replaced by fear and uncertainty. Believers in Jesus, however—although they may be temporarily distressed by the inevitable buffets of shifting circumstances—cannot be disturbed at the core of their being, for there dwells eternal assurance.

Daily Devotions:
M. Blessing of Peace
Numbers 6:22-27
T. Prayer for Peace
Psalm 122:6-9
W. Kept in Peace
Isaiah 26:3-9
T. Christ Gives Peace
John 20:19-22
F. Preaching Peace
Acts 10:36-43
S. Peace With God
Romans 5:1-11

Empty Tomb; Living Savior (Easter)

John 20:1-31

Unit Theme:
Easter

Central Truth:
Christ's resurrection is the foundation of Christian faith and practice.

Focus:
Review the events of Christ's resurrection and worship and serve Him as our risen Lord.

Context:
A.D. 30 in Jerusalem

Golden Text:
"Ye seek Jesus of Nazareth, which was crucified: he is risen; he is not here: behold the place where they laid him" (Mark 16:6).

Study Outline:
I. An Empty Tomb (John 20:1-9)
II. The Risen Lord (John 20:10-18)
III. The Great Commission (John 20:19-23)

INTRODUCTION

"One thing is certain—if Jesus had not risen from the dead, we would never have heard of Him. The attitude of the women [on Easter morning] was that they had come to pay the last tribute to a dead body. The attitude of the disciples was that everything had finished in tragedy. By far the best proof of the Resurrection is the existence of the Christian church. Nothing else could have changed sad and despairing men and women into people radiant with joy and flaming with courage. The Resurrection is the central fact of the whole Christian faith" (W. Barclay, *Daily Study Bible, Mark*).

"Had there been no Resurrection, what then? There had been no Christian church, no Christian propaganda, no Christian influence. Everything for which the lonely Nazarene stood lay murdered, dead, in the tomb when they rolled against it a great stone. His disciples had been scattered like chaff before the wind, and the whole movement stamped out. How did it live again? It lived again, and it lives, because He lived again, and lives!" (G.C. Morgan, *The Four Gospels, Mark*).

"Suppose that Jesus, having died on the cross, had stayed dead. Suppose that, like Socrates or Confucius, He was now no more than a beautiful memory. Would it matter? We should still have His example and teaching; would not they be enough?

"Enough for what? Not for Christianity. Had Jesus not risen, but stayed dead, the bottom would drop out of Christianity" (J.I. Packer, *I Want to Be a Christian*).

"The first fact in the history of Christendom is a number of people who say they have seen the Resurrection. If they had died without making anyone else believe this 'gospel,' no Gospels would ever have been written" (C.S. Lewis, *Miracles*).

When the body of Jesus was gently lifted from the cross and tenderly buried by Nicodemus and Joseph of Arimathea in Joseph's virgin tomb, His disciples were overwhelmed with grief and loss. They had thought that it was He who "should have redeemed Israel!" (Luke 24:21). They had failed to understand the scriptures that predicted the passion of Christ before His glory—the cross before the crown.

However, the morning of the third day changed the whole picture. Tragedy turned to triumph with the bodily resurrection of Christ, the best attested fact of the evangelical records.

I. AN EMPTY TOMB (John 20:1-9)

A. Shocking Sight (vv. 1-4)

1. The first day of the week cometh Mary Magdalene early, when it was yet dark, unto the sepulchre, and seeth the stone taken away from the sepulchre.

2. Then she runneth, and cometh to Simon Peter, and to the other disciple, whom Jesus loved, and saith unto them, They have taken away the Lord out of the sepulchre, and we know not where they have laid him.

3. Peter therefore went forth, and that other disciple, and came to the sepulchre.

4. So they ran both together: and the other disciple did outrun Peter, and came first to the sepulchre.

Two lonely men, Peter and John, were probably talking about the recent tragic events which had transpired, when Mary came to them with the strange report that Jesus' tomb was open and empty. Their reaction in words is not mentioned, but they took immediate action. Peter at once took the lead, and John followed his decisive guidance.

Motivated by perplexity, curiosity, concern and devotion, the two disciples raced to the garden tomb to get first-hand facts. The two were equally eager and ran side by side until John pulled ahead of Peter and arrived first at the tomb. Thus, they came to the tomb where loving hands had interred the bruised body of the Lord they both loved, but whom Peter had denied. If John came in love, Peter came with a broken heart. Little did they believe, at the moment, that a new day had dawned—a day of victory, joy and power.

B. Linen Cloths (vv. 5-9)

5. And he stooping down, and looking in, saw the linen clothes lying; yet went he not in.

6. Then cometh Simon Peter following him, and went into the sepulchre, and seeth the linen clothes lie,

7. And the napkin, that was about his head, not lying with the linen clothes, but wrapped together in a place by itself.

8. Then went in also that other disciple, which came first to the sepulchre, and he saw, and believed.

9. For as yet they knew not the scripture, that he must rise again from the dead.

When John arrived at the tomb, he stooped down to take a careful look inside the empty tomb and to observe its contents. The term translated as "looking in" (v. 5) conveys the idea of "looking intently with eager desire and effort at that which is partially concealed" (B.F. Westcott). But for some reason John hesitated to step inside. Perhaps he had already seen enough

Talk About It:
1. Why do you suppose Mary came to the tomb so early?
2. What did Mary think when she saw the rolled-away stone and the empty tomb?
3. How did Peter and John respond to Mary's report? Why?

"The German theologian Jurgen Moltmann expresses in a single sentence the great span from Good Friday to Easter. It is, in fact, a summary of human history, past, present, and future: 'God weeps with us so that we may someday laugh with him.'"

—**Philip Yancey**

Talk About It:
1. Why do you suppose John hesitated before entering the tomb? Why did Peter not hesitate?

2. What did the "folded" and "separate" (v. 7, *NIV*) cloth that had been around Jesus' head seem to indicate?

3. What did John believe, and why?

4. Why did Peter and John not know Jesus "must rise again from the dead" (v. 9) although Jesus had taught them it would happen?

to bring anxiety to his heart. Hence, he "saw" only the linen cloths lying in the empty tomb. Nevertheless, our attention is at once drawn to these shrouds as significant trophies of a mystery that was soon to dawn on the disciples as a supernatural work of God.

When Peter came, he apparently did not hesitate to step into the tomb for a more careful investigation. It is characteristic of this impulsive fisherman to go all the way. "No sensitive qualms inhibited him. Impulsive, he acted, then thought later on, as is so often recorded in the New Testament accounts of him" (J.R. Mantey).

Peter also saw the linen cloths and seemed to be arrested by their presence and arrangement. The word *seeth* in the Greek denotes a critical and careful scrutiny as his eye passed from point to point. The text does not reveal the effect produced upon Peter, but perhaps the naturally vocal disciple was so arrested by the scene that he had nothing to say.

John had evidently not seen the napkin. But Peter did. This rolled-up cloth, lying by itself, is given special attention by the writer, perhaps because its condition and position helped to convince John and kindle his resurrection faith. The fact that this face-cloth was rolled up and lying apart from the main shroud suggests that it had simply collapsed where Jesus' head had lain.

Encouraged by the example of the courageous Peter, John now entered the tomb to behold the mysterious vacancy and the undisturbed graveclothes once wrapped around the body of Jesus. Two verbs in verse 8 express the profound value of John's observation and impression. He "saw, and believed." The Greek verb conveys the idea of seeing with perception. He *saw* with the understanding, and therefore, *believed* the Resurrection.

As G. Campbell Morgan puts it, "Intelligent apprehension produced absolute conviction." John believed that Jesus' body had not been removed by human hands, but had been raised to life by divine intervention. The undisturbed graveclothes convinced John that Jesus had risen in a resurrection body and was, therefore, alive again. One can hardly imagine the profound emotions that now took hold of the beloved disciple. No doubt he felt a great anticipation and hope that he would get to see the living Lord!

John's new faith in the Resurrection was based only on what he had seen in the empty tomb. He confessed that at that time he had not as yet seen or understood the relationship between prophecy and Christ's passion and resurrection (v. 9; see also Psalm 16:10). Not even Jesus' own prediction of these events had registered in the disciples' thinking. Hence,

Empty Tomb; Living Savior

they were unprepared for so great a supernatural phenomenon. This is honesty on the part of the apostle, which makes the reliability of his testimony of Jesus' resurrection and his own faith absolute.

II. THE RISEN LORD (John 20:10-18)
A. Appearance of the Angels (vv. 10-13)

10. Then the disciples went away again unto their own home.

11. But Mary stood without at the sepulchre weeping: and as she wept, she stooped down, and looked into the sepulchre,

12. And seeth two angels in white sitting, the one at the head, and the other at the feet, where the body of Jesus had lain.

13. And they say unto her, Woman, why weepest thou? She saith unto them, Because they have taken away my Lord, and I know not where they have laid him.

Mary returned to the tomb after reporting to the disciples, and she remained after their departure. Overwhelmed with sorrow from bereavement, a circumstance now intensified with the absence of the Lord's body, she was reluctant to leave the garden tomb.

"She was denied the poor comfort even of weeping over His corpse, and paying the last tender rites of reverence and love," said George Keith.

In spite of her blinding tears, Mary was able to see the heavenly messengers who had come to comfort and console her. Their white garments were symbolic of purity and glory.

William Milligan observed, "That one of the angels was 'at the head, and the other at the feet, where the body of Jesus had lain' is to be regarded as expressive of the fact that the body was wholly under the guardianship of heaven."

The angels' asking the reason for her tears was probably intended to draw her out and prepare her for the imminent revelation. In response, Mary repeated the words which she had already addressed to the apostles (v. 2), but there were two significant variations. She probably repeated them in her heart again and again as the sum of all her thoughts; but she now says "*my* Lord" (not *the* Lord), and "*I* know" (not *we* know). Mary regards the relation and the loss as very personal.

B. The Appearance of Christ (vv. 14, 15)

14. And when she had thus said, she turned herself back, and saw Jesus standing, and knew not that it was Jesus.

15. Jesus saith unto her, Woman, why weepest thou?

Talk About It:

1. Why do you suppose the angels appeared to Mary and not to John and Peter?

2. How did the angels communicate God's concern for Mary?

"These angels went into the grave, to teach us not to be afraid of it. . . . Matters are so ordered that the grave is not much out of our way to heaven."

—Matthew Henry

whom seekest thou? She, supposing him to be the gardener, saith unto him, Sir, if thou have borne him hence, tell me where thou hast laid him, and I will take him away.

Talk About It:

1. Why didn't Mary recognize Jesus?

2. Why did Jesus ask Mary a question for which He already knew the answer?

Evidently the presence of the angels had not impressed Mary. Or else the sudden presence of Jesus arrested her attention and cut off any continued conversation with the angels. Even angels could not fill the gap her absent Lord had created.

Aware of someone behind her, Mary turned and saw Jesus, but she did not recognize Him. Several reasons have been suggested for her failure to recognize the Lord: Her eyes may have been dimmed by tears; she was stooping down; she saw His form against the rising sun; He was wearing different clothes; she was only half-turned toward Him; she was too preoccupied with her grief to look carefully; or, perhaps, a cooling off of faith had dulled her spiritual apprehension. Perhaps the real answer is that the risen Christ purposely appeared incognito until He chose to reveal His identity. We read in Luke 24:16 that the two Emmaus disciples "were kept from recognizing him" (*NIV*).

These are the first words spoken by the risen Christ to any human being, as far as is known. They seem to echo the words of the angel, with an added question: Why was she weeping, and whom was she seeking?

Not recognizing Jesus, Mary supposed Him to be the gardener—not because He was so dressed or held tools, but because no one else was likely to be there at that early hour and, logically, no one else would question her as to why she was there. Her answer shows that she thought the custodian, for some reason, had' found it necessary to move the corpse elsewhere. Her offer to take care of the body is unrealistic, and yet it is an expression of her love for the Lord. Loving devotion, such as Mary possessed, does not consider one's lack of strength.

C. The Revelation to Mary (vv. 16-18)

16. Jesus saith unto her, Mary. She turned herself, and saith unto him, Rabboni; which is to say, Master.

17. Jesus saith unto her, Touch me not; for I am not yet ascended to my Father: but go to my brethren, and say unto them, I ascend unto my Father, and your Father; and to my God, and your God.

18. Mary Magdalene came and told the disciples that she had seen the Lord, and that he had spoken these things unto her.

Talk About It:

1. How did Mary

The term of general address, "Woman" (v. 15), awoke no personal response; but "Mary," the symbol of personal knowledge

Empty Tomb; Living Savior

and sympathy, opened her eyes. Her response, "Rabboni [My Master]" indicates full recognition of His identity, and expresses the love and respect of a disciple for her Teacher and Lord.

It appears that Mary, upon recognizing Jesus alive at her side, at once either embraced Him or clung to His feet in reverent and worshipful devotion. His gentle rebuke, "Touch me not" (v. 17), really means "Do not hold on to me" (*NIV*). The prohibition here reminds her that the previous personal fellowship by sight, sound and touch no longer exists and that the final state of glory had not yet begun. He had not yet completed His ascent, but was in the process of arranging a new and spiritual relationship between Himself and His own.

It was Mary's desire to cling to Christ, to hold Him on earth, that she might never lose sight of Him again. Though her weeping had changed to worship, she must learn at once that such devotion and worship must now keep in mind the Resurrection—it must attain a heavenly level and become a spiritual fellowship. This is the most intimate of all communions. Her immediate responsibility was to announce to His "brethren," His disciples, that He was ascending to His Father and God.

The distinction Christ made in the words "my Father, and your Father," and so on, is significant. "We can only call God our God as His creatures, while Jesus himself belongs to the Godhead. Jesus, as the second Person of the Blessed Trinity, is the eternal Son of the Father; Christians only become sons of God by adoption and grace (see 1:12)," wrote R.V.G. Tasker.

Mary at once ran and told the disciples that she had seen the living Lord, and that He had commissioned her to announce the new revelation and His new relationship to them (v. 18).

III. THE GREAT COMMISSION (John 20:19-23)
A. Christ's Appearance to His Disciples (vv. 19, 20)
19. Then the same day at evening, being the first day of the week, when the doors were shut where the disciples were assembled for fear of the Jews, came Jesus and stood in the midst, and saith unto them, Peace be unto you.

20. And when he had so said, he shewed unto them his hands and his side. Then were the disciples glad, when they saw the Lord.

The first 18 verses of John 20 record the testimony of the empty tomb to the early-morning visitors and the appearance of the living Lord to the sorrowing Mary Magdalene. It was now evening of the same first day. The Emmaus disciples had already returned to Jerusalem with hearts still burning from the "highway Bible class" and the revelation of the living Christ (see Luke 24:13-35). How many of the disciples had now gathered, and where they had gathered, is not here made clear. We know Thomas was not with them.

finally recognize Jesus? What does this say about her relationship with Him?

2. What message did Jesus give Mary to deliver to His disciples, and why? What was her response?

Risen Indeed!

In the early 1920s, Nikolai Bukharin was sent from Moscow to Kiev to address a vast anti-God rally. For an hour he ridiculed the Christian faith until it seemed as if the whole structure of belief was in ruins. Questions were invited. A priest of the Orthodox church rose and asked to speak. He faced the people and gave them the ancient Easter greeting, "Christ is risen." Instantly the whole vast assembly stood and thundered the reply, "He is risen indeed!"

—George Sweeting

Talk About It:

1. Why were Jesus' disciples hiding?

2. Why do you suppose Jesus made such a dramatic entrance? What did He show His disciples, and why?

Considering recent Resurrection tidings, it seems natural that the company of disciples should come together to discuss the mysterious events. Perhaps they had gathered in the Upper Room in Jerusalem, secretly, behind closed doors, lest the foes of Jesus might seek them out and give them the treatment already given their Master. In fear, they had gathered, and had shut themselves in. Unexpectedly, Christ appeared to them, and stood in their midst with the greeting of "Peace be unto you." By this miraculous appearance in His resurrection body, the ordinary greeting of peace was intensified, and was intended to calm their fears and to assure them of His personal identity.

The Lord immediately assured them, by showing them His nail-pierced hands and His wounded side, that He was not a phantom, but was the real Jesus Christ standing in their midst, although in the "spiritual body" mentioned by Paul (1 Corinthians 15:44). "Then were the disciples glad." The grief and the gloom of the three days were now exchanged for boundless joy. Their Lord was alive, and they had seen Him. Words cannot describe their joy of fulfillment and exhilaration.

B. Christ's Commissioning of His Disciples (vv. 21-23)

21. Then said Jesus to them again, Peace be unto you: as my Father hath sent me, even so send I you.

22. And when he had said this, he breathed on them, and saith unto them, Receive ye the Holy Ghost:

23. Whose soever sins ye remit, they are remitted unto them; and whose soever sins ye retain, they are retained.

Talk About It:

1. Why did Jesus twice repeat the greeting, "Peace be with you!" (vv. 19, 21, NIV)?

2. Describe the mission Jesus gave His disciples to carry out.

3. What role would the Holy Spirit play in the disciples' mission?

Having dispelled their alarm, Christ repeats His greeting of peace. This was not a static peace, but an inner calm and poise to give boldness for witnessing for Christ in a hostile world. Having identified Himself and calmed the disciples with His greeting of peace, the Lord reminded them of their responsibility as His ambassadors. In verse 21 Jesus used two different Greek verbs for *sent* and *send* in the same sentence. In "as my Father hath sent me," the word denotes delegated authority. In "even so send I you," it denotes a dispatch under authority.

The commission given by the risen Christ to His representatives was confirmed by the enduement of the Holy Spirit (v. 22). This enduement was in harmony with His commission. As Christ had entered upon His ministry as One anointed by the Holy Spirit, so should it be with His apostles. The Greek verb for *breathed* is the same as in the Septuagint translation of Genesis 2:7, where God breathed life into Adam.

This breathing of the Spirit was probably an impartation of the Spirit as the Indweller, in anticipation of the Pentecostal effusion when the Spirit would baptize the believers with spiritual power.

Christ's breathing of spiritual life proves He is of the Godhead. And the imperative "Receive ye" indicates the responsibility of the believers to take or reject what the Lord had to give.

Regarding verse 23, Adam Clarke wrote, "The apostles received from the Lord the doctrine of reconciliation, and the doctrine of condemnation. They who believed on the Son of God, in consequence of their preaching, had their sins remitted; and they who would not believe were declared to lie under condemnation."

What a huge responsibility Christ places on those who teach and preach the gospel! The Lord indwells His ministers with His Spirit and puts His Word in their mouth so they can declare His message of forgiveness to those who repent and judgment on those who refuse Christ's forgiveness. Of course, the God-called messenger's heart is always that those who hear the gospel will receive it.

> "Attempt great things FOR God and expect great things FROM God."
> —**William Carey**

CONCLUSION

All of the Resurrection evidences lay before us in the Gospel records: the rolled-away stone, the empty tomb, the folded linen cloths, the angelic visitation, the appearances of Christ. If we have put our faith in the risen Lord, His resurrection power resides within us (see Romans 8:11). Through His power we can help carry out the Great Commission.

GOLDEN TEXT CHALLENGE

"YE SEEK JESUS OF NAZARETH, WHICH WAS CRUCIFIED: HE IS RISEN; HE IS NOT HERE: BEHOLD THE PLACE WHERE THEY LAID HIM" (Mark 16:6).

The resurrection of Christ was not witnessed by any human being. Neither was the risen Lord himself the first to communicate the news. It was announced by the angel who had rolled the stone away.

There are two features of this announcement: (1) "He is risen," and (2) "He is not here: behold the place where they laid him." These aspects are integrally linked. "He is risen" was proven by the empty tomb—the body of Jesus was gone. And the fact that the tomb was empty is explained by the fact that Jesus was risen.

Liberal thinkers endeavor to explain away the empty tomb and the missing body, claiming these matters do not prove the truth of the Resurrection. However, the Roman and Jewish authorities would have left no stone unturned to trace the body and find the explanation of the empty tomb. The stone was rolled away and Christ's body was not found because He had indeed risen.

Daily Devotions:

M. Living Redeemer
  Job 19:23-27
T. Resurrection
  Hope
  Psalm 16:1-11
W. Jesus Christ
  Lives
  Luke 24:36-48
T. Promise of
  Resurrection
  John 5:19-29
F. Resurrection
  Body
  1 Corinthians
  15:49-58
S. Newness of Life
  Colossians 3:1-
  10

The Long-suffering of Christ

Philippians 3:12-17; 2 Timothy 2:1-7;
James 5:7-11; 1 Peter 2:20-23

Unit Theme:
Fruit of Christian Formation

Central Truth:
Christ is our example of patience and trust in times of suffering.

Focus:
Observe Christ's patience in suffering and follow His example.

Context:
Selected New Testament passages on patience and suffering

Golden Text:
"Christ also suffered for us, leaving us an example, that ye should follow after his steps" (1 Peter 2:21).

Study Outline:
I. Christ: Our Example of Patience (1 Peter 2:20, 21; James 5:7-11)
II. Endure Hardship (2 Timothy 2:1-7)
III. Perseverance Rewarded (Philippians 3:12-17)

INTRODUCTION

Jesus said to the disciples just hours before He was arrested, "If they have persecuted me, they will also persecute you" (John 15:20). As the next day proved, He did suffer terribly, and if we suffer, we are simply following His example. His suffering brought our salvation. Our suffering brings great reward in heaven.

Mel Gibson's motion picture, *The Passion of the Christ,* was controversial because it showed graphically just how much Jesus did endure. The critics hated watching such a visceral view, yet it only portrayed what actually happened. Amazingly, the film showed the Lord literally embracing the cross. He knew His suffering and death would bring salvation for mankind, and He was willing and anxious to see that happen.

Jesus endured rejection by His own people, a trial by religious leaders who had no understanding of real Judaism, lies by false witnesses paid to tell them, mockery and beating by Roman soldiers, and finally a terrible death by crucifixion. Yet, the worst was not what people did to Him, but His having to endure a time of separation from His Father.

Does the fact that Jesus suffered mean that every believer has to go through the same? No, we may not die a cruel death, but we will go through difficulties in this life. When they come, we have the example of Christ to show us how to endure. Like Him, we can "embrace our cross" with peace and trust in God. Jesus said, "If anyone would come after me, he must deny himself and take up his cross and follow me" (Mark 8:34, *NIV*). When one takes up a cross, it is for a death march. Ours may not be a death march to crucifixion, but it is a death to ourselves. With Christ as our example, we can face any injustice or persecution.

I. CHRIST: OUR EXAMPLE OF PATIENCE (1 Peter 2:20, 21; James 5:7-11)

A. Submission to Authority (1 Peter 2:20)

20. For what glory is it, if, when ye be buffeted for your faults, ye shall take it patiently? but if, when ye do well, and suffer for it, ye take it patiently, this is acceptable with God.

The principle of obedience to authority is one of the highest in Scripture. It appears to be even stronger than that of personal anointing. David would not touch Saul, even though he had been anointed as the new king of Israel. Instead, he willingly waited in submission until God removed Saul from the throne. The Christian might not respect the person holding an office, but because he respects the office, he will treat the one holding it with due accord. He will also pray for those in authority (1 Timothy 2:1, 2). "A true Christian submits himself to authority because he is first of all submitted to Christ" (*The Bible Exposition Commentary*). Solomon said, "Fear . . . the Lord and the king" (Proverbs 24:21). In other words, because one fears the Lord, he also fears the king.

In our text, Peter is addressing how Christian slaves should act. His words are in harmony with Paul's teachings on the same subject (see 1 Corinthians 7:20-24; Philemon 8-21). Perhaps as much as half of the population of the Roman Empire was enslaved, and the ratio within the Christian community was likely even higher. Some slaves thought their spiritual freedom in Christ guaranteed them the same in the sociopolitical arena. Peter recognized the reality of slavery without condoning it. The mission of the church was not to overthrow earthly political empires, but rather to establish the Kingdom in the hearts of people.

If a slave was punished for something he was guilty of, then there was nothing to be gained from it. Anyone can take the consequences of actions he has committed. However, if one was punished for something he was not guilty of—and still suffered for it with dignity and no rebellion—then he proved himself as Christ's ambassador. He is acting as Christ acted. First Peter 2:19 says, "It is commendable if a man bears up under the pain of unjust suffering because he is conscious of God" (*NIV*).

We should remember that earlier Peter had been appalled that Jesus said He would have to suffer on the cross. By the time of this writing, however, Peter had realized that believers serve through suffering.

B. Called to Suffer (v. 21)

21. For even hereunto were ye called: because Christ also suffered for us, leaving us an example, that ye should follow his steps.

Talk About It:
1. If you endure suffering because you did wrong, what credit do you deserve?
2. If you endure suffering for doing right, what blessing will you receive?

"Endurance is not just the ability to endure a hard thing, but to turn it into glory."
—William Barclay

Talk About It:
1. Name various ways Christ suffered during His last three years of life on earth.
2. Why must suffering be part of the Christian life?

The believer should never be surprised when suffering comes his way. Why? Partly because he has three great enemies: the devil, the flesh and the world (see Ephesians 2:2, 3). Suffering may come from giving in to any of these. However, here Peter is saying that the believer may suffer for doing good—just as Christ suffered. In fact, included in the privileges of being a Christian is suffering—going through undeserved punishment or judgment for the cause of Christ. Jesus never committed a sin, yet He suffered to bring us redemption and freedom from sin. Likewise, we will face suffering. The goal is to endure it with the same grace that the Lord did. He never fought back. He simply endured it and committed everything to His Father. Since we have Him living inside of us, we can do the same. As Paul said, "I have been crucified with Christ; it is no longer I who live, but Christ lives in me; and the life which I now live in the flesh I live by faith in the Son of God, who loved me and gave Himself for me" (Galatians 2:20, *NKJV*).

Not only did Jesus give an example of how to endure suffering, but He also showed that one can suffer while being fully in the will of God. The Christian life is not a bed of roses. We all go through major problems in this life. Reacting as Christ did will show power, not weakness. It was the weak, immature Peter who drew a sword in the Garden of Gethsemane. It was the strong, faithful Peter who was crucified upside down in Rome.

C. Example of the Farmer's Patience (James 5:7)

7. Be patient therefore, brethren, unto the coming of the Lord. Behold, the husbandman waiteth for the precious fruit of the earth, and hath long patience for it, until he receive the early and latter rain.

Talk About It:
1. What might happen to an impatient farmer?
2. What might happen to a believer who is impatient regarding Christ's return?

Patience is one of the fruit of the Spirit listed in Galatians 5:22, 23. It is also one of the most difficult attitudes to maintain, for everything in the human spirit works against it. James here urges believers to exercise patience while waiting for the coming of the Lord. Those he was specifically addressing were poor people suffering at the hands of rich oppressors (vv. 1- 6). They should keep their eyes on the promise, not on the waiting period. God would bring justice in due time. In the meantime, they were not to sit idly, but rather follow the example of a farmer. A farmer not only prepares the soil and plants the seeds, but also tills the young plants, wards off birds, and makes plans for reaping the harvest. In the same sense, believers should use their time serving God, spreading the gospel, and caring for one another.

The climate of Palestine was such that the early rains came in the fall (October/November). This was planting season. The latter rains came in early spring and helped mature the harvest. There were many weeks of waiting between the two seasons, and these might be very dry. In the Christian life there are the early rains of spiritual blessing, followed by long periods of maturing in what seems like a desert. The faithful believer knows that the latter rains will come—and with them will be great spiritual blessing.

In Deuteronomy 11:14, God promised both the early and latter rains if His people were faithful to Him. However, Zechariah 10:1 says people must "ask the Lord for rain in the springtime" (*NIV*). Even the promises of God require that we be faithful and pray for their fulfillment. James' readers were impatient for the coming of the Lord to end their sufferings. They needed to be patient—and pray. After seeing the vision which we know as the Book of Revelation, John prayed, "Even so, come, Lord Jesus" (22:20).

> "The trouble is that I'm in a hurry, but God isn't!"
> —**Phillips Brooks**

D. Stand Firm in the Meantime (vv. 8, 9)

8. Be ye also patient; stablish your hearts: for the coming of the Lord draweth nigh.

9. Grudge not one against another, brethren, lest ye be condemned: behold, the judge standeth before the door.

stablish your hearts (v. 8)—stand firm

grudge (v. 9)—complain

Instead of dwelling on the problems at hand, people should be aware that the Lord's coming might be at any time. No one can speed up that appointed moment for Him to return, but staying heart-prepared should be the top priority. To *stablish* one's heart means to strengthen it, that is, to take on a solid-rock faith in the promise of Christ. If He said He will return—He will.

Talk About It:
When are believers most likely to grumble against each other, and why must we avoid this trap?

How do you strengthen your heart? (1) Be resolute to resist temptation and sin. Earlier, James said, "Submit . . . to God. Resist the devil, and he will flee from you" (4:7). (2) Get grounded in truth, avoiding "strange doctrines" (Hebrews 13:9), and continue to serve and encourage one another (10:24, 25). (3) Contemplate the lives of saints who have stood firm in the past (12:1), and follow their example. (4) Watch and look forward to the Lord's coming (2 Peter 3:10-13).

In the midst of persecution, James' readers were also prone to be at odds with one another. This could quickly destroy their unity, and thus their effectiveness. He encouraged the people to refrain from such bickering. Paul exhorted the Ephesians to endeavor "to keep the unity of the Spirit in the bond of peace" (4:3). Without unity, the church never reaches maturity (v. 13).

E. Example of the Prophets (vv. 10, 11)

10. Take, my brethren, the prophets, who have spoken in the name of the Lord, for an example of suffering affliction, and of patience.

11. Behold, we count them happy which endure. Ye have heard of the patience of Job, and have seen the end of the Lord; that the Lord is very pitiful, and of tender mercy.

Jewish Christians knew the stories of what the prophets had endured in being faithful to God. The most recent one, John the Baptist, was beheaded for his stand. James reminded his readers that all who speak in the name of the Lord will endure suffering. "Part of his point is that God does not preserve from suffering those he has called; rather, he preserves them in suffering. They are an example to all believers because of their obedience and faithfulness despite the hardships they endured" (*The Life Application Commentary Series*). Even though these great people of faith were reviled by the people of their day, they have become heroes since then. They may have been cursed, but now they were blessed.

It has been many generations since James wrote, but the Lord has yet to return. Does this nullify His promise? By no means. The writer of Hebrews says all the Old Testament heroes of faith saw the promise only from a distance (11:13). Their faith was based on God's character, not on what they could see. Our faith must be based on the integrity of what Jesus has promised, not the timetable by which it occurs.

II. ENDURE HARDSHIP (2 Timothy 2:1-7)
A. Strong in Grace (vv. 1, 2)
1. Thou therefore, my son, be strong in the grace that is in Christ Jesus.
2. And the things that thou hast heard of me among many witnesses, the same commit thou to faithful men, who shall be able to teach others also.

In this final and very intimate letter, Paul was anxious to shore up the faith of his protégé Timothy. Others had defected under pressure (Phygellus and Hermogenes, see 1:15; Demas, see 4:10), and the apostle could not bear to see the same happen to this young man. He passionately exhorted Timothy to hold tightly to the faith—and especially to the teachings he had given him. He exhorted him in the *grace,* or inward source of strength, that is freely given by Christ. Timothy could not rely on his own strength, but on the Lord's. The word *grace* means "undeserved favor," the greatest example being our redemption from sin. After receiving saving grace, however, we are also to live by grace—that is, favor and power that comes from Christ dwelling in us. *The Wycliffe Bible Commentary* says *grace* "is an all-inclusive word for the power and gifts of the Spirit."

Paul asked Timothy to duplicate himself by teaching oth-

Talk About It:
1. Recall the story of an Old Testament prophet who endured suffering for doing right.
2. Why are those who endured suffering considered "happy" (blessed)? What does this reveal about the Lord?

Talk About It:
1. What ministry did Paul commit to Timothy?
2. How could Timothy accomplish this task?

The Long-suffering of Christ

ers—"faithful men" (v. 2)—the doctrines he had learned from Paul. Paul was not self-centered in this command, but was confident that what he had spoken had come by divine inspiration. The people Timothy would teach should then be able to spread the gospel to others.

Paul knew how vulnerable immature believers were. There were plenty of false doctrines and false teachers preying on the ignorant. Much of his writing had been to correct such. Sincere believers must be trained in a thorough understanding of the gospel, or they might be destroyed. Passing on the faith thus involved much more than just simple witnessing. It also included teaching, nurturing and administration. Timothy had to exhibit a well-balanced Christian doctrine. He was well-qualified to do this, having heard Paul teach to many diverse groups. Not only that, he had the example of his mother and grandmother (1:5) to show him the ways of righteousness.

B. Like a Soldier (v. 3, 4)

3. Thou therefore endure hardness, as a good soldier of Jesus Christ.

4. No man that warreth entangleth himself with the affairs of this life; that he may please him who hath chosen him to be a soldier.

In recent years the mass media has made us well aware of the difficulties of a soldier's life. Even with all the modern technology, soldiers on the war front still live in tough circumstances. Not only are their lives at stake constantly from battle, they struggle with few of the comforts of home. The modern soldier, however, knows nothing of difficulty like those did in the ancient world. Theirs was truly a Spartan existence. Paul had spent his share of time in prison, and knew that the guards over him were not in much better condition than he. Godly people have to make the same kind of commitment. In Philippians 2:25, Paul calls Epaphroditus a *fellowsoldier.* It was the toughness of the job that had caused some others to defect.

In our world the role of the Christian soldier has seemed somewhat soft to the eyes of many. Ministers today generally have homes of their own, reasonable salaries, and so on. However, the ministry is not a soft job, and as the times grow more severe, we see more commitment required. As in Paul's day, there are many defections, but those who are true to the gospel are experiencing a greater sense of power and authority.

In wartime, there is no such thing as a reservist, or "weekend warrior." Instead, the soldier leaves civilian priorities behind. He cannot serve two masters. Similarly, as times grow tough, Christians have to put aside entanglements with the world, especially in terms of entertainment, materialism and what we do with

Talk About It:
1. Describe some hardships "a good soldier of Jesus Christ" might face.
2. What kind of "affairs" must a Christian stay away from (v. 4)?

our time. This is not to say we can completely divorce ourselves from the world. Most Christians still have to work secular jobs. Even Paul supported himself as a tentmaker. He wrote to the Corinthians that they were not to remove themselves from society, but were to maintain a witness in the midst of unbelievers (see 1 Corinthians 5:9, 10; 7:17-24). Still, the Christian soldier must be ready to carry out God's orders first, not flinching in the face of life-threatening situations, remaining disciplined, and not becoming too attached to anything in the world.

C. Playing by the Rules (v. 5)

5. And if a man also strive for masteries, yet is he not crowned, except he strive lawfully.

The *New International Version* translates this verse, "If anyone competes as an athlete, he does not receive the victor's crown unless he competes according to the rules." Just as athletes must discipline themselves and have to play the rules of the game, so must Christian soldiers live by the rules of the Cross. Paul frequently used analogies to athletic contests. Both the Greeks and Romans were addicted to sports. As he did in 1 Corinthians 9:25, Paul pictures the Christian life as a period of athletic discipline in preparation for a final match. In the ancient Olympian Games this was a period of 10 months. In the believer's case, it is one's entire life—from the salvation experience to the grave. A single-minded purpose is required of every true athlete—even during injury, exhaustion and pain. He or she must determine never to quit.

What are the rules Christians "play" by? They are the commands and principles laid down in the Word of God. Paul was saying, "The important thing is that you obey the Word of God, no matter what people may say. You are not running the race to please people or to get fame. You are running to please Jesus Christ" (*The Bible Exposition Commentary*).

Paul called Timothy his *son* in verse 1, having begotten him through the gospel into the family of God. Timothy had entered this family by being born of the Spirit (John 3:3, 5). However, Peter says to "love one another with a pure heart fervently: being born again, not of corruptible seed, but of incorruptible, by the word of God, which liveth and abideth for ever" (1 Peter 1:22, 23). We are born of the Spirit, but we are born of the Word as well. God's Word lives forever. It is pure and faultless. It gives us the rules of the game.

D. Like a Farmer (vv. 6, 7)

6. The husbandman that laboureth must be first partaker of the fruits.

7. Consider what I say; and the Lord give thee understanding in all things.

strive for masteries (v. 5)—"competes as an athlete" (*NIV*)

Talk About It:
In using the imagery of an athlete, what is Paul's message to Christians?

"I know a lot of talented ruins. Beyond talent lie all the usual words: discipline, love, luck, but, most of all, endurance."
—**Anonymous**

The Long-suffering of Christ

The farmer keeps the coming harvest in mind throughout the growing season. It is an act of faith to cultivate land, plant seeds, care for the growing crops, and keep them watered. All of these are done in faith that there will be a harvest—one which the farmer is first to enjoy. As Christians, all the work, toil and suffering are made worthwhile when we think of what we will enjoy in the harvest.

Paul also hints at the idea of a worker earning payment. As he said in his first letter to Timothy, "The elders who direct the affairs of the church well are worthy of double honor, especially those whose work is preaching and teaching" (5:17, *NIV*). The faithful farmer is the first to reap the rewards of his labor. In the same sense, the faithful Christian worker benefits from the works he does for Christ.

In verse 7 of the text, Paul exhorts Timothy to take his words seriously. Like all the other words he has heard Paul speak, Timothy is to take these, mull over them, and let the Holy Spirit work them into his character.

> **Talk About It:**
> What should the hardworking farmer receive, and what is the message for Christians?

III. PERSEVERANCE REWARDED (Philippians 3:12-17)

A. Not Having Attained (v. 12)

12. Not as though I had already attained, either were already perfect: but I follow after, if that I may apprehend that for which also I am apprehended of Christ Jesus.

Translating Paul's thoughts from Greek to English can cause some confusion. In the verse just prior to our text (v. 11), Paul spoke of his goal to "attain unto the resurrection," with the word for *attain* meaning "to be a partaker of" or "to arrive at." All his former religious fervor for the Law had brought him nothing, but his faith in Christ had given him everything. "If any man could get to heaven on the basis of character and religion, it was Paul—and yet he was a lost sinner apart from Jesus Christ! When he met Christ, he considered all of his earthly and fleshly attainments mere rubbish!" (*The Bible Exposition Commentary*). His victory in Christ would bring him the special reward of *attaining* the resurrection.

In verse 12, however, the word for *attain* means "lay hold of," or "be perfected," that is, be made mature and complete. He wanted to reach a state of being complete in Christ. In the earlier verse he was taking account of his life—what he had lost and what he had gained. Here he is pressing toward a prize. Paul wanted to take hold of everything Christ offered in the same dramatic way that Christ had apprehended him on the road to Damascus (Acts 9).

> **Talk About It:**
> What did Paul strive to "apprehend" ("take hold of," *NIV*), and how could he accomplish this?

> "Consider the postage stamp: Its usefulness consists in the ability to stick to one thing till it gets there."
> —Josh Billings

B. Pressing Forward (vv. 13, 14)

13. Brethren, I count not myself to have apprehended: but this one thing I do, forgetting those things which are behind,

and reaching forth unto those things which are before,

14. I press toward the mark for the prize of the high calling of God in Christ Jesus.

Paul had earlier used the language and metaphor of an accountant tallying losses and gains. Now he changes to athletic jargon. His single-minded goal as an athlete in competition is to know Christ completely. The Christian life is a process, and even though we are declared righteous upon salvation, we must live with the constant purpose of becoming more like Christ. Every sport has an ultimate hero. In American basketball, young boys for years wanted to be "like Mike" (Michael Jordan). Paul's ambition is to be "like Christ."

From a human perspective, Paul's past would have seemed commendable. He had lived the Law scrupulously. However, his goals had been misplaced. When he was *apprehended* by Christ on the road to Damascus, he realized he had been running his race in the wrong direction. He could not erase that mistake, but he could lay it aside and not let it slow him down now. Many believers are hindered in their Christian walk because of something they did long ago. Even Paul uses the word *forgetting*, indicating that this is still an ongoing process. There is also the implication that we cannot depend on past victories in Christ, but must continue to press on to the future.

There is no one spiritual experience or victory in the Christian life that will permanently sustain us. What happens on Sunday must happen again on Monday, and every day. We never rest on the past, but strive toward the goal of winning our individual races—to be all that Christ has in mind for us.

C. Presenting an Example (vv. 15-17)

15. Let us therefore, as many as be perfect, be thus minded: and if in any thing ye be otherwise minded, God shall reveal even this unto you.

16. Nevertheless, whereto we have already attained, let us walk by the same rule, let us mind the same thing.

17. Brethren, be followers together of me, and mark them which walk so as ye have us for an ensample.

Not having pictured himself as perfect, but still having described his own spiritual goals, Paul now exhorts the Philippians to follow his example and strive for the same. He readily admits that he hasn't attained the full stature in Christ that he desires, but he knows he at least has the right goals. Every fiber of his being is centered on winning the race. No one can live a divided life. There cannot be one foot in the world and one in heaven. We must focus on the race before us.

The word *perfect* (v. 15) means "mature." Those Philippian

Talk About It:

1. Name things of the past believers need to forget.

2. What kind of effort did Paul put into his Christian living? How does this compare with our effort?

Looking Ahead

Many of us know people who were once mighty warriors for the Lord. However, because of some hurt, disappointment, or frustration, they no longer have a passion for the Lord. They saw the failure of a minister whom they had trusted and were devastated.

We cannot run our race toward heaven by looking at anyone else. We must look only to Christ and the finish line.

perfect (v. 15)— mature

Talk About It:

1. How should a mature Christian live?

2. What can be "attained" by believers in this life?

3. Why is it important for Christians to

---

believers who are mature in their thinking will agree with what Paul has said. They have grown to a certain level of spiritual stability in contrast to infants. And, even though they may disagree on some small point, if they open their hearts to Christ, they will be led to see the truth of what he had just declared.

Paul's suggestion that the Philippians follow his example is not egotism. He was simply being practical. The people needed living examples to pattern after. Paul knew his own heart, and though he was not perfect, he knew he had the Spirit in him leading the way—a way that others could pursue.

CONCLUSION

We all have things in our past that can paralyze us, but since we have hope in Christ, we don't let the past destroy us. Christ forgives us of everything. It was He who appeared to Paul on the road to Damascus. Paul had been the greatest persecutor of the church, yet Christ loved him.

Paul spoke of his shame for things he had done, and obviously he could not simply forget it; but he didn't dwell on it. He knew he was forgiven, and he moved on. Let's do the same.

GOLDEN TEXT CHALLENGE

"CHRIST ALSO SUFFERED FOR US, LEAVING US AN EXAMPLE, THAT YE SHOULD FOLLOW AFTER HIS STEPS" (1 Peter 2:21).

We are called to follow the example of Christ, who said we must love our enemies, bless those who curse us, do good to people who hate us, and pray for our persecutors (Matthew 5:44).

These were not only Christ's commands but also His examples to us. He fulfilled in His life all the teachings that came from His lips. And His indwelling Spirit can empower us to imitate His lifestyle.

have strong examples to follow?

Daily Devotions:
M. Reward of Longsuffering Genesis 26:19-29
T. Patient God Exodus 34:5-8
W. Wisdom of Patience Ecclesiastes 7:8-13
T. Longsuffering in Ministry 2 Corinthians 6:3-10
F. Dress for Success Colossians 3:12-17
S. Our Lord's Patience 2 Peter 3:9-15

The Gentleness of Christ

John 8:1-11; 10:11-15; 1 Thessalonians 2:7-12

Unit Theme:
Fruit of Christian Formation

Central Truth:
Gentleness should characterize our attitudes and actions as Christians.

Focus:
Study and follow Biblical examples of gentleness.

Context:
Selected New Testament passages on Christian gentleness

Golden Text:
"He shall feed his flock like a shepherd: he shall gather the lambs with his arm, and carry them in his bosom, and shall gently lead those that are with young" (Isaiah 40:11).

Study Outline:
I. The Gentle Savior (John 8:1-11)
II. The Gentle Shepherd (John 10:11-15)
III A Gentle Ministry (1 Thessalonians 2:7-12)

INTRODUCTION

The three points of our outline wonderfully exemplify the gentleness of the God we serve. First, the religious leaders who attempted to trap Jesus by using the woman caught in adultery were not interested in sin, nor the sinner. All they cared about was their personal power. Isn't this the same thing we are seeing on every level of the political scene today (and in much of the church world as well)? Who really cares for the good of the people? Jesus showed that the individual—no matter how sinful and derelict—is still worthy of redemption and compassion. Sin is terrible, but sinners need forgiveness. When Jesus confronted the poor woman, He didn't condemn. Neither did He condone her sin, but told her to abandon it. His approach brought transformation, not guilt and reproach. He was the only one present who had the right to throw the first stone, but He chose to forgive instead.

The second point of our outline describes Jesus as the gentle Shepherd (John 10). Everyone in Jesus' audience knew the difference between a real shepherd and a hireling. Shepherds loved their sheep and would give themselves in an instant for them. When we place ourselves in the flock of Jesus, we find true freedom and contentment. On our own, all we can do is frantically search for security, but we never achieve it. We discover that life without boundaries is no life at all. In Christ, however, we realize a security that comes from living within His plan and directions for our life.

Our third point uses Paul as an example of Christ's gentleness. Paul ministered to the various churches he founded with the same loving nature Jesus had demonstrated. Paul proved that gentleness was love in action. Each of his letters tempered correction with concern for the people involved. He never bullied or demanded his way, but served those he led.

I. THE GENTLE SAVIOR (John 8:1-11)

A. Back for More (vv. 1, 2)

1. Jesus went unto the mount of Olives.

2. And early in the morning he came again into the temple, and all the people came unto him; and he sat down, and taught them.

Though Jesus had been received with mixed reaction the day before, He returned to the Temple to teach. He was "not willing that any should perish, but that all should come to repentance" (2 Peter 3:9). Even facing rejection, Jesus came back for more. The Feast of Tabernacles had ended the day before, but many pilgrims were still in Jerusalem. They had heard much about Him, had listened to Him the day before, and now anxiously came for more. He taught in the court of the women, at the area where the treasury was situated (see John 8:20). Like other teachers, He sat down as He taught, thus assuming the position of One with authority. This would have likely infuriated His detractors.

Talk About It:
From what you see in these two verses, what would have been challenging about Jesus' earthly ministry?

B. Caught in Adultery (vv. 3-6)

(John 8:6 is not included in the printed text.)

3. And the scribes and Pharisees brought unto him a woman taken in adultery; and when they had set her in the midst,

4. They say unto him, Master, this woman was taken in adultery, in the very act.

5. Now Moses in the law commanded us, that such should be stoned: but what sayest thou?

Two questions naturally arise here: (1) Where was the man who shared the adulterous act? (2) When and how was the woman caught? One simple explanation might be that the scribes and Pharisees hired a man to go to a known local prostitute on the night before. Upon coming to an agreement for her services, the man then turned her over for arrest—much like a modern sting operation. Jesus never questioned the woman's guilt, nor did He ask for the stoning of the male partner (which would have been required by Mosaic Law). Instead, He looked further into the plot to identify all who were guilty. The woman's accusers were merciless in their treatment of her, pushing her in front of the crowd. Of course, she was nothing but a pawn. They cared nothing for her, her soul, or for the Law. They simply wanted to pin Jesus into a legal dilemma. Interestingly enough, they were themselves disregarding the Law, since it required both the man and the woman to be tried (Leviticus 20:10; Deuteronomy 22:22).

The perpetrators thought they had formed a perfect plot with no escape. They phrased their words carefully, fully expecting that any answer Christ gave would alienate some group. If He

Talk About It:
1. What was the motive behind the religious leaders' actions?
2. Why is adultery such a serious offense?
3. What do you suppose Jesus wrote on the ground?

said not to stone her, He would contradict the law of Moses. This would make Him subject to arrest by the Temple guards, since He was teaching in the Temple. If He agreed to the stoning, then they would quickly call in the Romans, who did not allow the Jews to carry out executions. Even though they themselves might have carried rocks in their hands, they had no real intentions of harming the woman. They would have brought the Romans down on themselves. Their only purpose was to embarrass Jesus. The woman meant nothing to them.

Jesus was well aware of what was happening, and it took no deep analysis on His part to figure out what to do. Likely, He had His eyes focused on the poor woman during the entire matter. Tradition holds that she was Mary Magdalene. No matter who she was, however, Jesus ultimately lifted her from her shame and background to redeem her.

What did Jesus write on the sand? No one knows, but it is certainly interesting to hypothesize. "Maybe he was listing the names of those present who had committed adultery (and scaring them to death that he knew it); he might have been listing names and various sins that each person had committed; maybe he was writing out the Ten Commandments to point out that no one could claim to be without sin" (*The Life Application Commentary Series*). The fact that He wrote with His finger was a reminder that the Ten Commandments themselves had been written by "the finger of God" (Exodus 31:18). Amazingly enough, it was His finger that had written those very commandments! Also, this is the only time in Scripture that we see Jesus writing anything. Yet, more has been written about what He had to say than about anyone else in all of history.

Apparently, Jesus was in no hurry, and the silence was deafening. This also gave time for each accuser to ask himself just how far he was willing to participate in this plot. If Jesus had said to throw the stones, they themselves might be arrested, for the Law required that the accusers cast the first stones (Deuteronomy 17:7). "This was in order that the witness might feel his responsibility in giving evidence, as he was also to be the executioner. Jesus therefore put them to the test" (*Barnes' Notes*).

C. Left Alone (vv. 7-9)

7. So when they continued asking him, he lifted up himself, and said unto them, He that is without sin among you, let him first cast a stone at her.

8. And again he stooped down, and wrote on the ground.

9. And they which heard it, being convicted by their own conscience, went out one by one, beginning at the eldest, even unto the last: and Jesus was left alone, and the woman standing in the midst.

Adultery, by its very nature, is done in privacy, and generally will have no witnesses. Could anyone present claim to have seen the act take place? Not likely. "Either the witnesses became such by accident, which would be unusual; or they were present purposely to create the trap for Jesus, in which case they themselves were guilty; or they condoned the deed, and this would make them partners in it" (*Zondervan NIV Bible Commentary*, Vol. 2). Since the witnesses would have to initiate any stoning, these same accusers would suddenly be guilty as well. What they did not know was that Jesus was actually being merciful to them. Their efforts at entrapment entrapped themselves. The poor woman, in the meantime, was likely terrified as to what might happen to her.

When Jesus did make comment, He was not commanding that judicial systems require sinless judges—for that would be impossible. The only sinless judge was Jesus himself, and He refused to make a judgment here. He certainly was not making light of the woman's sin, nor was He contradicting the Law's view of adultery. However, He himself would pay for her sins with His own blood. His blood would buy her forgiveness.

Convicted by their consciences, and likely relieved as well that they did not have to carry out their plot, each man quietly removed himself, beginning with the oldest first. "The older ones either had more sins for which they were answerable or else had more sense than to make an impossible profession of righteousness" (*Zondervan NIV Bible Commentary*, Vol. 2). The entire episode displayed that "the state of public morals was exceedingly corrupt, and justified the declaration of Jesus that it was an adulterous and wicked generation (see Matthew 16:4)" (*Barnes' Notes*).

Though verse 9 says Jesus was left alone with the woman, it appears that the crowd who had come to hear Him teach were still on the sidelines watching. At this time Jesus still had the approval of the common people, so no doubt they were all amazed at the way with which He had handled the accusers. Likely, there was not much love lost between the common folk and the religious elite of the day. They all had felt the same "put-down" that this poor woman had experienced. Their sympathies were probably with her, all knowing that they were guilty themselves of some sin.

D. Freed From Guilt (vv. 10, 11)

10. When Jesus had lifted up himself, and saw none but the woman, he said unto her, Woman, where are those thine accusers? hath no man condemned thee?

11. She said, No man, Lord. And Jesus said unto her, Neither do I condemn thee: go, and sin no more.

Jesus is never as concerned with our past as He is with our future. He is less interested in punishment than He is in restoration

---

Talk About It:
1. Why did the religious leaders continue to press Jesus with their questions?
2. Could Jesus have stoned the woman? Why or why not?
3. What did Jesus' answer reveal about Himself? Why did it leave the Pharisess and scribes speechless?

"Gentleness is not softness except in the finest sense—it is kindness by one who has the power or the position to be harsh and severe."
—**Charles W. Conn**

---

and rehabilitation. If His words sound too lenient for the sin of adultery, they are balanced by His command that she go and sin no more. Even though His words did not specifically state forgiveness, He certainly did forgive her sins. His forgiveness always comes with the responsibility to abandon the sin.

Jesus' handling of the situation might easily be compared to Solomon's handling of the two women with one baby (1 Kings 3:16-28). Solomon was considered to be the wisest man who ever lived. Jesus' wisdom exceeded that of Solomon—for He was both God and man. Here, He had balanced several major truths without compromise. He upheld the Law (the legal penalty of stoning), so no one could accuse Him in that respect. He exposed the evil in the perpetrators' hearts by requiring that the sinless one among them throw the first stone. Also, while not condoning her adultery, He also showed the true spirit of the Law by extending compassion and forgiveness. Most importantly, He showed the woman that she was more important than the sin she had committed.

II. THE GENTLE SHEPHERD (John 10:11-15)
A. The Good Shepherd (v. 11)
11. I am the good shepherd: the good shepherd giveth his life for the sheep.

The Gospel of John was written not as a biography, but rather to present an argument for the incarnation of God into man, showing that Jesus was truly the Son of God sent to earth to redeem lost people. To make his case, John organized his Gospel around seven miracles, each of which demonstrated Jesus' divinity: (1) the changing of water to wine (2:1-11); (2) the healing of the nobleman's son (4:46-54); (3) the healing of the lame man at the Pool of Bethesda (5:1-15); (4) His feeding of five thousand (6:1-15); (5) His walking on the water (vv. 16-21); (6) the restoring of sight to a blind man (9:1-38); and (7) the monumental raising of Lazarus from the dead after several days of decomposition (11:1-44). By this time Jesus had made many enemies among the religious establishment. He was a threat to their sway over the people (not to mention their jealousy that He could do what they certainly could not do). He had shown Himself to have authority over disease and nature, as well as the creative power to change elements and make something out of nothing. By the time He healed the blind man (the sixth miracle), we see the strong parallel to the spiritual blindness of His enemies.

Sandwiched between the last two signs is His teaching on the metaphor of the shepherd. Also, everything between John 7 and 10:21 took place during the Feast of Tabernacles. This includes the incident of the woman caught in adultery. Thus, when He began to teach on the *good shepherd,* there was no

The Gentleness of Christ

doubt that He was contrasting Himself to the religious leaders in Jerusalem—all of which He called *hirelings*.

John also organizes his Gospel around several "I Am" statements that Jesus made, including the "bread of life" (6:35); the "light of the world" (8:12); the "door" of the sheepfold (10:9). In our present text He distinguishes Himself as the Good Shepherd in contrast to the thieves and robbers in charge of the Jewish religion of the day. The word *good* here means "beautiful, fair, intrinsically excellent." *Good* thus means much more than we know it today. In Mark 10:17, the rich young ruler came to Jesus and asked, "Good Master, what shall I do that I may inherit eternal life?" Jesus replied, "Why callest thou me good? there is none good but one, that is, God" (v. 18). Thus, for Jesus to call Himself the Good Shepherd was to call himself God.

The most important character trait of a good shepherd is that he gives his life for his sheep. He cares for them deeply, even to the point of risking his own life. Under the old covenant, sheep constantly had to give their lives (in the sacrificial system) for the sins of their shepherd. Now, Jesus would give Himself as the perfect lamb for the lives of His flock.

B. The Hireling (vv. 12, 13)

12. But he that is an hireling, and not the shepherd, whose own the sheep are not, seeth the wolf coming, and leaveth the sheep, and fleeth: and the wolf catcheth them, and scattereth the sheep.

13. The hireling fleeth, because he is an hireling, and careth not for the sheep.

For the common people, sheep were important commodities. They provided both wool and milk. They were used for sacrifices only as was necessary. Shepherds loved and cared for their sheep. The hireling could never be trusted to look after sheep with the same concern. He looks after them only because he is paid to do so.

By nature, sheep are dumb animals that require constant care. They do not have the instincts to take care of themselves. The Bible constantly uses the metaphor of sheep to describe God's people. David saw himself as a sheep and God as his shepherd in Psalm 23. Likely, those listening to Jesus may have brought this psalm to mind, and recognized that Jesus was making a clear claim for Divinity. "As the Good Shepherd, Jesus fulfilled the Old Testament representation of Jehovah, and also set himself over against the leaders who injured the flock because they were evil in heart. Instead of taking life, this Shepherd was prepared to give his life for the sheep. It is a prophecy as well as an attitude" (*The Wycliffe Bible Commentary*). The prophet Isaiah spoke of the coming Messiah as a shepherd: "He shall feed his flock like a shepherd: he shall

Talk About It:
What is a hired hand unwilling to do, and why?

gather the lambs with his arm, and carry them in his bosom, and shall gently lead those that are with young" (40:11).

Sheep are prone to wander away aimlessly from the flock, get lost, and get caught in briars. A flock of sheep without a shepherd will not last any length of time. A hireling cares nothing for the flock, but only for the payment he receives. The Old Testament prophets frequently criticized the religious leaders of their day because they acted like hirelings instead of shepherds. Ezekiel in particular spoke with hard words: "Thus saith the Lord God unto the shepherds; Woe be to the shepherds of Israel that do feed themselves! should not the shepherds feed the flocks?" (Ezekiel 34:2). "The hireling counts the sheep his own, no longer than they are profitable to him; the good shepherd looks upon them as his, so long as he can be profitable to them" (*Adam Clarke's Commentary*).

C. A Relationship of Trust (vv. 14, 15)

14. I am the good shepherd, and know my sheep, and am known of mine.

15. As the Father knoweth me, even so know I the Father: and I lay down my life for the sheep.

There is a mutual relationship between the Good Shepherd and His flock. The word *know* carries a much greater connotation than simple acquaintance. The relationship is comparable to that between Jesus and His Father in heaven. This is an admonition to each of us. If we truly belong to Christ as His sheep, then we can know Him as intimately as He knows His Father. Few of us have dedicated ourselves to this extent, but clearly it is possible. Jesus later said, "And this is life eternal, that they might know thee the only true God, and Jesus Christ, whom thou hast sent" (John 17:3). The greatest blessing of eternal life will be that we can know both Jesus and the Father.

There is nothing more endearing to our ears than to have someone important call us by name. Success gurus will say that the quickest way to making a solid impression is to remember a person's name. John 10:3 says Jesus "calls his own sheep by name" (*NIV*). Jesus also knows each of us by our individual natures, and responds to us accordingly.

Psychologists are very much in the business of personality "typing." They label one person as sanguine, another as melancholy, and so on. Even though someone may "put on" a face, his basic nature doesn't change. The 12 disciples were a perfect example of this. What a varied group of personalities! Most likely, anyone reading the Gospels could relate their own nature to at least one of these men. Jesus loved each of them (as He loves us all), and gave Himself freely for them.

Because He knows our natures, Christ also works with us according to our needs. Remember the disciple Thomas.

Talk About It:

1. How should our relationship with Jesus be like Jesus' relationship with the heavenly Father?

2. How could Jesus say "I lay down my life for the sheep" before He was arrested and crucified?

The Gentleness of Christ

Virtually everything we can learn about this disciple (or sheep) comes from John's Gospel. Mostly we remember that he was a skeptic by nature (14:5; 20:24, 25). However, he was willing to risk himself for the Lord. At one point he said, "Let us also go, that we may die with him" (11:16). He was among those whom Jesus met by the seaside after the Resurrection (21:2), and also waited in the Upper Room for the Holy Spirit (Acts 1:13). Thus, to judge Thomas purely because of his skeptical nature would miss his greater qualities. Jesus knew Thomas, and responded to him accordingly (John 20:27-29).

III. A GENTLE MINISTRY (1 Thessalonians 2:7-12)
A. A Cherished Church (vv. 7, 8)

7. But we were gentle among you, even as a nurse cherisheth her children:

8. So being affectionately desirous of you, we were willing to have imparted unto you, not the gospel of God only, but also our own souls, because ye were dear unto us.

This first letter Paul wrote to the Thessalonian church was likely the second of all his epistles. Written around A.D. 51, it reviews the basics of the faith that he taught the converts he had made in that city. He had started the Thessalonian church by preaching three Sabbaths in a row at the local synagogue (see Acts 17). He had great success, both with the Jews and the Greek proselytes— until jealous Jews rose up against him. Paul and Silas left the city and went to Berea, where they also had success, but soon the jealous Jews from Thessalonica appeared on the scene again. Paul moved on to Athens, and then to Corinth. From there he sent Timothy back to Thessalonica to check on the believers. Timothy brought back to Paul all the questions they had about their faith. This letter is Paul's gentle reply. It reinforces the basics of the gospel message, instructs them further in their faith, and then provides practical applications of spiritual truths.

Later in our text (v. 11) Paul sees himself as the father of this congregation, but here he uses the imagery of a nursing mother. "New Christians need love, food, and tender care, just as a mother would give to her own children. Newborn babes need the milk of the Word and then must graduate to the meat, the bread, and the honey" (*The Bible Exposition Commentary*). When Paul says that he and Silas had been *gentle*, this was to contrast themselves to the behavior of certain other traveling preachers and teachers. Paul frequently defended his ministry in light of the charlatan nature of some high-minded teachers who fleeced the flocks. Paul knew his own team's pure motives. "They had come with the authority of the God of heaven, yet they had served among the people with the kind gentleness of a loving and nurturing mother" (*Life Application Commentary Series*).

nurse (v. 7)—nursing mother

Talk About It:
1. When Paul was with the Thessalonians, how did he show a "motherly love" to them? Why?
2. Can a person be an effective teacher or preacher of the gospel without getting involved with the lives of those he or she serves? Why or why not?

"The churches would soon be filled if outsiders could find that people in them loved them when they came. This love draws sinners! We must win them to us first, then we can win them to Christ. We must get people to love us, and then turn them over to Christ."

—D.L. Moody

The fact that Paul and Silas had left Thessalonica prematurely was testimony to their gentleness. The convert who had hosted them, Jason, had been dragged into the streets along with several others by jealous Jews. To protect these men, Paul and Silas moved on, but did not abandon those they left there. Throughout his ministry Paul maintained a certain dual relationship with his converts. They were his brethren in the faith, but they were also his children, having brought them to trust in Jesus. Because he loved these converts, he gave himself totally and freely for them.

B. Labor of Love (v. 9)

9. For ye remember, brethren, our labour and travail: for labouring night and day, because we would not be chargeable unto any of you, we preached unto you the gospel of God.

Talk About It:

Why did Paul work so hard when he was with the Thessalonians? Why was he now calling them to remember his "toil and hardship" (v. 9, *NIV*)?

Paul's affections were demonstrated by his hard work for them. How many of us remember a father who might not seem very affectionate, yet spent countless hours working to make sure we had our needs met? Paul not only worked for the people he served, but he also worked to provide for his own needs, never letting himself become dependent financially on those he served. He was a tentmaker. Every Jewish boy learned a trade, no matter what their status in the social structure. Tentmaking was a viable occupation that could be carried anywhere, much like computer specialties are today. The Romans used tents to house soldiers, and the Romans were everywhere. Paul was always able to provide for himself. "The 'double duty' of earning a living while trying to preach, teach, and build up a body of believers in Thessalonica called for exhausting labor and toil as they worked night and day" (*The Life Application Commentary*). Still, Paul (and Silas) gladly made the sacrifice so he would not be a burden on his converts.

C. Fatherly Advice (vv. 10-12)

10. Ye are witnesses, and God also, how holy and justly and unblameably we behaved ourselves among you that believe:

11. As ye know how we exhorted and comforted and charged every one of you, as a father doth his children,

12. That ye would walk worthy of God, who hath called you unto his kingdom and glory.

Talk About It:

1. Describe how Paul lived before the Thessalonians, as described in verse 10. Why was this important?

The Thessalonians were witnesses to the upstanding way Paul and Silas had carried themselves. Accusing Jews might say otherwise, but facts were facts. Today we watch biased newscasts in which honest national leaders are skewered by lies and misconstrued facts. The best way for leaders to defend themselves is to live honorably. Ultimately, their own record will stand for itself. Paul's consistent example had to have affected the Thessalonians, despite criticisms they heard otherwise. If he had lived carelessly among them, they would have seen the hypocrisy, and his message would not have touched them. But the message had won their hearts. The best witness for Christ is a life lived honorably.

Just as fathers must set a good example for their children, so Paul had lived a dedicated life before His converts. He taught them by encouragement, comfort and strong admonition to excellence. In addition, he was interested in the individual— "every one of you" (v. 11). He had apparently spent much time in counseling with different converts on a one-on-one basis. Like Jesus, Paul was never so busy that he forgot the individual, something we must remember today. We count our church congregations not by numbers, but rather by individual members.

CONCLUSION

In His extended metaphor on shepherding, Jesus said, "I have come that they may have life, and that they may have it more abundantly" (John 10:10, NKJV). This immediately brings to mind David's words, "My cup runneth over" (Psalm 23:5). Many of the wonderful blessings of being a Christian are not realized until we make it to heaven, but many others are realized in the present. In essence, David said, "My cup is running over right now!"

Our gentle Shepherd wants us to live a "more abundant life" every day—and not have to wait until eternity. If we fully trust Him, our worst day is still a great day. On the surface it may not seem such, but when we look deeper, we can see that He is showering us with good things, and has many more blessings in store.

GOLDEN TEXT CHALLENGE

"HE SHALL FEED HIS FLOCK LIKE A SHEPHERD: HE SHALL GATHER THE LAMBS WITH HIS ARM, AND CARRY THEM IN HIS BOSOM, AND SHALL GENTLY LEAD THOSE THAT ARE WITH YOUNG" (Isaiah 40:11).

A good shepherd knows his individual sheep and provides the type of care each one needs. He is especially gentle with mother sheep who are leading their young. When leading lambs, the caring shepherd sometimes carries them in his arms.

In the same way, our Good Shepherd knows each of His children. It is within His heart and ability to provide the type of care all Christians need. Christ carries His lambs (new believers) close to His heart to nurture them. When mature believers need added strength because of heavy responsibilities, the Good Shepherd is especially gentle with them.

The Good Shepherd will be everything to us that we allow Him to be.

2. How did Paul treat them as if they were his own children?

3. What was Paul's deep desire for the Thessalonian believers (v. 12)?

"A man who lives right, and is right, has more power in his silence than another has by his words."

—Phillips Brooks

Daily Devotions:

M. The Gentleness of God
   2 Samuel 22:31-37

T. A Gentle Rebuke
   2 Chronicles 30:6-9

W. The Shepherd's Tender Care
   Psalm 23:1-6

T. Jesus' Gentle Touch
   Mark 10:13-16

F. Gentle Leadership
   2 Timothy 2:23-26

S. Gentle Wisdom
   James 3:13-18

The Kindness of Christ

Luke 10:30-37; John 19:25-27;
Romans 12:10; Ephesians 4:25-32

Unit Theme:
Fruit of Christian
Formation

Central Truth:
Kindness is Christ's
love in action.

Focus:
Perform acts of kind-
ness through the love
and power of Christ.

Context:
Selected New
Testament passages
giving insight on com-
passion, love and
kindness

Golden Text:
"Be ye kind one to
another, tenderheart-
ed, forgiving one
another, even as God
for Christ's sake hath
forgiven you"
(Ephesians 4:32).

Study Outline:
 I. Christ
    Demonstrates
    Kindness
    (John 19:25-27)
 II. Christ Teaches
    Kindness
    (Luke 10:30-37)
 III. Show Christian
    Kindness
    (Romans 12:10;
    Ephesians 4:25-32)

INTRODUCTION

A kind, sweet spirit should be the standard for every believ-er. The old adage "You can accomplish more with honey than you can with vinegar" applies to us all. Certainly no one is to put on a false face, but we shouldn't have to. The transform-ing power of Christ can change our spirits to express gentle-ness and kindness naturally.

Our lesson gives three Scriptural perspectives on kind-ness. The first shows how Jesus treated His mother when He was dying on the cross. Crucifixion was the worst possible death sentence. It was a slave's punishment, and thus added even greater humiliation to our Lord. Deuteronomy 21:23 says anyone hanged on a tree was cursed. Of course we know the curse Jesus took on Himself ultimately brought Him exaltation, and also brought us redemption from sin. Scripture records seven sayings Jesus spoke while on the cross. The third of these showed great kindness to His mother. Even in dying He made sure she would be cared for, and not just by anyone, but rather by His most devoted disciple, John—the only one who dared go to Golgotha.

The second passage is a lesson on kindness Jesus gave in the form of a parable. The story of the Good Samaritan is one of the most famous in the world. What the hated Samaritan did as an act of kindness shows us what it means to extend mercy. This man identified with the needs of a stranger and had compassion on him. He sacrificed his time and resources simply because he was kind. At the same time, those who should have done the same thing were selfish in their pursuits. At the end of the story, Jesus asked the ques-tion, "Which man was the better neighbor?" He proved that kindness goes beyond nationality, religion, creed or race. We simply should be kind to everyone. It is a trait of godliness.

The third passage is teaching from Paul on loving others and being kind at all times. God has called us to real love that goes beyond simple politeness. True Christian character demands our time, money and personal commitment to others.

I. CHRIST DEMONSTRATES KINDNESS (John 19:25-27)
A. Faithful Women at the Cross (v. 25)

25. Now there stood by the cross of Jesus his mother, and his mother's sister, Mary the wife of Cleophas, and Mary Magdalene.

The Romans didn't invent the crucifixion, but they certainly perfected it as a means of execution. Only under certain extreme cases, however, could a Roman citizen be crucified. Rather, this was reserved for the worst criminals, and mainly in the conquered territories. Most often the victims of crucifixion were rebels against Roman rule. Though today we see the cross as a beautiful symbol, in ancient times it stood for something very ugly.

Talk About It:
Why do you suppose these women were more faithful to Jesus during His crucifixion than were His disciples?

Modern executions in the civilized world are carried out privately. Usually, if there are witnesses, they are family members of the person the criminal murdered or injured. These observers are there to see for themselves that their loved one has been avenged. In contrast, crucifixion was a public event. Jesus was required to carry His cross the mile-long distance from Pilate's hall to Golgotha. Carrying a cross was a symbol of shame and a mark of guilt. Since Jesus was a well-known rabbi, the spectacle that day was even greater. Jesus began the journey, but somewhere along the way Simon the Cyrene was drafted to help Him.

Except for John, none of the other disciples were present at Golgotha. Judas had likely already hanged himself. Peter was too ashamed to show his face, and the rest were frightened for their lives. But the women came. They were not afraid. John counts four faithful followers who stood weeping at the foot of the cross (though there might have only been three, if Salome and Mary, the wife of Cleophas, were the same person). They included Mary, the Lord's mother; her sister, Salome, who was also the mother of James and John (see Matthew 27:56; Mark 1:19; 15:40); Mary, the wife of Cleophas; and Mary Magdalene. Their willingness to stand by Jesus must have encouraged Him, even though He was shamed at their seeing Him so humiliated. No one enjoys being paraded naked and vulnerable—not even the Son of God.

In his Gospel, John first introduces Mary (mother of Jesus) at the wedding Jesus attended with the disciples at Cana of Galilee (2:1-11). From that account, we know she was a strong-willed woman who could take charge of a situation. (She somewhat demanded that Jesus take charge, for which He mildly rebuked her.) On another occasion, we see her with Jesus' brothers asking to speak to Jesus while He was teaching the multitudes (Matthew 12:46-50). Jesus again rebuked her, declaring that the relationship He had with His disciples was stronger than family bonds. Apparently, Mary accepted His words as simply part of God's plan. It was no accident that she was in Jerusalem when He was crucified. She must have joined the other women later in His ministry and went wherever He went.

At the cross, Mary remained quiet. She might have wanted to scream to all who would listen what she knew of her Son—how the angel Gabriel had appeared to her . . . how Jesus had been born in Bethlehem as the Scriptures had predicted . . . how she had conceived Him as a virgin. But no, she knew this was the time for quiet surrender. What Simeon, the old man at the Temple, had told her 33 years earlier was now coming to pass: "A sword shall pierce through thy own soul" (Luke 2:35). Though we do not venerate Mary in the same way Catholics do, much still needs to be said about her. "As the first member of the human race to accept Christ, she stands as the first of the redeemed and as the flagship of humanity itself. She is our enduring example for faith, service to God, and a life of righteousness" (*Nelson's Illustrated Bible Dictionary*).

We might also wonder what was going through the minds of the other women. Mary Magdalene had been delivered from demon-possession by Jesus. Since that time, she had dedicated herself to following Him and using her financial resources to assist His ministry. Salome was Jesus' aunt, and she had selfishly asked for major positions for her two sons in Jesus' kingdom (see Matthew 20:20-28). Did she feel guilt now for that selfish request? Or did she suspect that there would be no kingdom at all?

B. A New Son, a New Mother (vv. 26, 27)

26. When Jesus therefore saw his mother, and the disciple standing by, whom he loved, he saith unto his mother, Woman, behold thy son!

27. Then saith he to the disciple, Behold thy mother! And from that hour that disciple took her unto his own home.

Seeing two of the people who obviously were most dedicated to Him, Jesus directed His mother toward John, the beloved disciple. Even in His agony, His thoughts were not for Himself but for others. Earlier in His ministry, He had told His mother that Kingdom relationships were more important than blood ones (Matthew 12:49, 50). Now she would see living proof of this. John would take her and care for her as his mother, and he would be her son. The natural question arises: Why wasn't one of Mary's other four sons (13:55) assigned this responsibility? Obviously, none of them were at the Cross, but were still in Galilee. Jesus' brothers had rejected Him, though

"If Jesus Christ died and died for me, then no sacrifice can be too great to make for Him."

—C.T. Studd

Talk About It:
What did Jesus ask John to do for Mary? How did he respond?

The Kindness of Christ

two of them—James and Jude—would later become pillars in the church. Apparently, Mary had at some point taken a stand for Jesus in opposition to her other sons.

Whether John immediately took Mary away from the terrible scene is not known, but we know that both of them were part of the gathered believers who waited in the Upper Room (Acts 1:14). "Even while He was performing the great work of redemption, Jesus was faithful to His responsibilities as a son" (*The Bible Exposition Commentary*). At the same time, Jesus was breaking ties with earthly relatives. From now on, even those who had been blood relatives would see Him as Savior, not as a human family member. When He cried, "Woman, behold thy Son!" one might misunderstand this to be disrespectful. Why didn't He call her "Mother"? Probably to spare her feelings and not draw undue attention to her. We must remember that there were scoffers present. Feelings of hatred toward Him could be redirected toward her.

History shows that John was the only disciple to have died a natural death, though he went through his share of trouble. Many believe he was spared because he took responsibility for Mary. Though nothing is said later in the New Testament, John himself here (since he wrote this Gospel) took full responsibility for Mary's welfare. She likely remained in Jerusalem as part of the early church there, and eventually told her story, possibly to Luke while Paul was incarcerated in Caesarea. Though for many years she had quietly kept everything "in her heart" (Luke 2:19, 51), she now let the world know of the miraculous nature of the Son of God's birth.

> "God cares about not just spiritual things like salvation, justification, sanctification, and glorification, but also about everyday, practical things."
>
> —William Lyon Phelps

II. CHRIST TEACHES KINDNESS (Luke 10:30-37)

A. Jesus, the Storyteller (v. 30)

30. And Jesus answering said, A certain man went down from Jerusalem to Jericho, and fell among thieves, which stripped him of his raiment, and wounded him, and departed, leaving him half dead.

Jesus was the master storyteller. His extended use of short illustrations to drive home His teachings captured the attention and imagination of His listeners. Of course, He wasn't the first to use this form. One excellent parable was told by Nathan in the Old Testament to point King David to his own sin (2 Samuel 12:1-4). Still, Jesus perfected the art of parables more so than any teacher before—or since. Along with the parable of the Prodigal Son (Luke 15:11-32), this story of the Good Samaritan stands out as the most prominent of His stories.

In Jesus' approach to telling stories, the real meaning was not always clear. The central point of the Good Samaritan is fairly obvious—the hated Samaritan proved to be the good

Talk About It:
How often do we come across people who have been beaten and bruised—physically, emotionally, and/or spiritually? How do we respond?

neighbor, while those who should have exhibited kindness passed by the wounded man. In other words, we cannot judge people by nationality, race, religion or occupation. What counts is how we treat other people.

Many of Jesus' other stories weren't so clear in intent. Even the disciples came to Him and asked, "Why do you speak to the people in parables?" (Matthew 13:10, *NIV*). Jesus responded that parables both reveal and conceal a truth. Most of those listening to Jesus couldn't understand the spiritual nature of the Kingdom He came to reveal. Only those who accepted Him would be given the understanding. To others, the message would remain a mystery.

The basic story Jesus told His listeners that day, in Luke 10, was easy to relate to. Most of them at one time or another had to make the 17-mile trek from Jerusalem down to Jericho. The route was notoriously dangerous, full of hiding places for crooks. Stories of injuries and robberies were common. What caught their attention, however, was the intensity of this crime. Not only did the robbers steal from the poor man, but they stripped him, and beat him severely. Without help he would certainly die in the baking sun.

B. Those Who Should Have Helped (vv. 31, 32)

31. And by chance there came down a certain priest that way: and when he saw him, he passed by on the other side.

32. And likewise a Levite, when he was at the place, came and looked on him, and passed by on the other side.

This part of the parable could be understood by all who heard. There was plenty of hypocrisy in the priesthood of the Temple. Everyone knew that. There was even hypocrisy in the lawyer who posed questions to Jesus that led to this parable. He wasn't so interested in finding truth as he was in simply engaging Jesus in a debate (vv. 25-29). His questions revealed a "profound ignorance about central issues of the faith—eternal life and the basic command to love one's neighbor" (*The Life Application Commentary Series*).

The priest and Levite were both meticulous in the observance of every jot and tittle of the Law, but had little common decency about them. They mistakenly thought their religiosity had brought them righteousness. Both priests and Levites had to come from the tribe of Levi, but the priest had to be specifically from the lineage of Aaron. Their duties in the Temple were different. A priest could offer sacrifices, while Levites were set apart as helps to the priesthood. Both groups were "supported by Israel's tithes and by revenues from certain cities that had been given to them. Worship in the Temple could not have taken place without the combined efforts of the priests and

Talk About It:
Do you think the priest and Levite would have acted differently if they had come across the suffering man in front of a crowd? Why or why not?

The Kindness of Christ

Levites" (*The Life Application Commentary Series*). The difference between the two might be compared to the difference today between a registered nurse and a practical nurse, or between a medical doctor and a physician's assistant, or even between a pastor and a Sunday school teacher. Both have serious duties—and both should show compassion.

It is speculated that the reason neither man stopped to help the poor soul was the possibility of defilement. Had the man been dead (as he perhaps looked), then they would have been deemed as unclean. However, since both were on their way from Jerusalem, they would have already finished their Temple duties, thus negating this possibility.

"It is impossible to adore God and abhor one of His children at the same time."
—*Quotable Quotes*

C. The Unlikely Minister (vv. 33-35)

33. But a certain Samaritan, as he journeyed, came where he was: and when he saw him, he had compassion on him,

34. And went to him, and bound up his wounds, pouring in oil and wine, and set him on his own beast, and brought him to an inn, and took care of him.

35. And on the morrow when he departed, he took out two pence, and gave them to the host, and said unto him, Take care of him; and whatsoever thou spendest more, when I come again, I will repay thee.

Jesus' listeners knew that the two earlier men should have stopped to help, but they weren't prepared for the next turn of events in the story. They likely suspected that Jesus would tell of a poor, humble Jew (someone like themselves) who ultimately did the good deed. Instead, it was a hated Samaritan. Jews despised Samaritans for their half-breed status, and the feeling was equally returned. Jews saw themselves as the rightful descendants of Abraham, while Samaritans were a mixed breed of northern kingdom Jews and foreigners. Not only that, their religion was a mixture of worship of both Jehovah and pagan gods. Thus, in the Jews' mind, the Samaritans were contaminated both by foreign blood and pagan idolatry. "The Jewish historian Josephus indicates that the Samaritans were also opportunists. When the Jews enjoyed prosperity, the Samaritans were quick to acknowledge their blood relationship. But when the Jews suffered hard times, the Samaritans disowned any such kinship, declaring that they were descendants of Assyrian immigrants" (*Nelson's Illustrated Bible Dictionary*). The Samaritans did believe God was the Creator of all things, and they also celebrated certain feasts prescribed by the law of Moses. This would certainly make them all the more accursed to the Jews.

Jews hated to have to go through Samaria, but sometimes

Talk About It:
1. What is compassion? Why do you suppose the Samaritan was compassionate while the priest and Levite were not?
2. Describe various costs the Samaritan incurred because of his compassion.

had to use that route. They were frequently robbed and beaten on their journeys. Thus, every ear listening to Jesus perked up when He said it was a Samaritan who actually stopped to help the injured man. Jesus went to great detail to show all the good things the Samaritan did. He even stayed overnight with the wounded man at the inn—and paid the innkeeper in advance for his services. The *two pence* was enough to pay for several weeks' stay. He even agreed to pay more upon his return, if needed. All of this pointed to the Samaritan putting forth tremendous effort, concern and personal resources.

D. The Good Neighbor (vv. 36, 37)

36. Which now of these three, thinkest thou, was neighbour unto him that fell among the thieves?

37. And he said, He that shewed mercy on him. Then said Jesus unto him, Go, and do thou likewise.

Finishing the story, Jesus asked the lawyer which of the three travelers had been the good neighbor to the injured man. The priest and the Levite were committed by occupation to helping people, but their lack of genuine spirituality and compassion allowed them to violate Leviticus 19:18, which commands, "Love thy neighbour as thyself." The Samaritan, however, responded with kindness. The lawyer had no choice but to answer that the Samaritan had been the better neighbor. Jesus then told him to go on his way and show the same kind of kindness.

The Samaritan had demonstrated more love to the injured man than those of the lawyer's own religion had shown. Was Jesus belittling Judaism? No, and neither was He saying that good deeds can bring righteousness. Jesus' story was a prelude to the truth that salvation would be only in His name. As Peter would later preach before the Sanhedrin, "Neither is there salvation in any other: for there is none other name under heaven given among men, whereby we must be saved" (Acts 4:12).

III. SHOW CHRISTIAN KINDNESS (Romans 12:10; Ephesians 4:25-32)

A. Christian Devotion (Romans 12:10)

10. Be kindly affectioned one to another with brotherly love; in honour preferring one another.

There are several Greek words that can be translated as *love.* The highest form of love is *agape,* or self-sacrificial love. That is the love Christ had for us, but is not used in this verse. The word translated here as "kindly affectioned" is *philostorgoi,* or "devoted in love and affection." It is connected with "brotherly love" (*philadelphia*).This love allows for weaknesses and imperfections in those loved; it affirms and demonstrates loyalty.

No matter which form of love we are talking about, each requires that we put others above ourselves. There is no room in the Christian life for selfishness. In fact, Christianity is best lived out in community. None should live as islands to themselves. Willingness to share our lives with others is the trademark of Christian fellowship. Neither should we search out only those of our economic or social status. The foot of the Cross is a place where we all come as equals.

B. Kindness Through Truthfulness (Ephesians 4:25)

25. Wherefore putting away lying, speak every man truth with his neighbour: for we are members one of another.

Jesus said Satan is "a liar and the father of lies" (John 8:44, *NIV*). Since this is true, for believers to lie to one another would be playing right into the devil's devices. Jesus said of Himself, "I am the way, the truth, and the life" (14:6). We belong to Jesus, so we belong to the truth; therefore we should always be truthful. We are no longer of the world, so our actions must change to reflect the new creations we have become. "Like putting off the old self and replacing it with the new self, so believers put off falsehood and put on the willingness to speak the truth" (*The Life Application Commentary Series*). The only way one can tell a lie is for someone else to hear it. However, once a lie is told, the truth eventually comes out—and the liar is left with a reflection on his character. Lying disrupts the unity of the Christian body and tears relationships apart. Therefore, believers must be truthful.

Talk About It:
Why is dishonesty so damaging to the body of Christ?

C. Footholds and Hand Checks (vv. 26-28)

26. Be ye angry, and sin not: let not the sun go down upon your wrath:

27. Neither give place to the devil.

28. Let him that stole steal no more: but rather let him labour, working with his hands the thing which is good, that he may have to give to him that needeth.

Anger is not necessarily sinful. Paul makes this clear in verse 26: "Be ye angry, and sin not." There are times when anger is justified. Still, we are not to let it continue for long. We have the right to respond in controlled reaction to wrongs and sin, but we cannot allow our anger to consume us. If we do, we are as guilty as the one who caused the anger. We must remember we are always being watched. It is never a question of what happens to us, but rather how we handle those things. The more we let something stew, the more the devil has opportunity to invade our thinking.

The only time the Gospels record Jesus as showing anger

Talk About It:
1. When does anger become sinful?
2. How can a Christian "give place to the devil"?
3. Describe and explain the turnaround commanded in verse 28.

Time-out

Next time you feel the surge of anger, say to yourself, "Is this really worth what it's going to do to me and others emotionally? I will make a fool of myself. I may hurt someone, or I might lose a friend." Remember Seneca, who said, "The greatest cure of anger is delay."

—Norman Vincent Peale

Talk About It:

1. Describe the type of words that should and should not come from our mouth.

2. What has the Holy Spirit done for believers, and how can we grieve Him (v. 30)?

"Words—so innocent and powerful as they are, standing in a dictionary, how potent for good and evil they become, in the hands of one who knows how to combine them!"

—Nathaniel Hawthorne

clamour (v. 31)—
"brawling" (*NIV*)

Talk About It:

1. Why must Christians get rid of "all" the things listed

was when He twice overturned the tables of the moneychangers in the Temple. However, this was righteous anger (because they were stealing from the people), and He did not sin.

Paul's words in verse 28 seem redundant, since stealing is prohibited by the Ten Commandments. However, he is saying that those who have been redeemed from a lifestyle that included such vices as theft should never let their own natures control them. The inference here is toward believers who had once used thievery as a livelihood. Now they should work honestly, and God will bless them.

D. Righteous Words, Holy Spirit (vv. 29, 30)

29. Let no corrupt communication proceed out of your mouth, but that which is good to the use of edifying, that it may minister grace unto the hearers.

30. And grieve not the holy Spirit of God, whereby ye are sealed unto the day of redemption.

Christians should maintain a high standard of speech. We should avoid slander, gossip, coarse language, or any word that is insensitive to others. We should be wise in our choice of phrasing, ever aware that we are witnesses for Christ. Words have power for good, and evil as well. We are the church, and the church is Christ's body on earth. Our words should build up one another.

Because we belong to Christ, the Holy Spirit is living in us. Imagine Jesus standing in person next to us at all times. Anything we might do that would embarrass or sadden Him also grieves the Holy Spirit. The Holy Spirit's power in us empowers us to live for Christ. We either yield to Him or to our old sinful nature. If we say yes to the Holy Spirit, He will guide our speech and actions, making sure they express kindness to everyone.

It is amazing to think that our words and deeds have an impact on the Lord himself. We are of utmost importance to Him, so how we live, speak and act can either sadden Him or make Him proud of us. His Spirit living within us is our guarantee of eternal salvation.

E. Christlike Relationships (vv. 31, 32)

31. Let all bitterness, and wrath, and anger, and clamour, and evil speaking, be put away from you, with all malice:

32. And be ye kind one to another, tenderhearted, forgiving one another, even as God for Christ's sake hath forgiven you.

As long as we have contact with people, there will be disagreements and opportunity for conflict. No two persons—even the most devout believers—will agree on everything. However, we can agree to disagree on certain issues and still maintain brotherly fellowship. All the sins listed in verse 31 are part of our old nature, the nature we are to put away. None of them have any place in the heart of the believer who has the Holy Spirit living inside. Instead, God's indwelling Spirit helps us to be kind, compassionate and forgiving, as Christ has been to us.

CONCLUSION

In the story of the Good Samaritan, there are four different attitudes we should check in ourselves. First, the thieves saw the traveling Jew as someone to exploit. They cared nothing for him. Exploitation comes in many forms today. A friend just told me how a certain "Christian" organization had used a tele-marketer to call her, and demanded that she give a certain amount as a donation. When she refused, the caller became almost belligerent.

Second, the priest and Levite saw the poor man as a ministry nuisance, so they avoided him. How many times do we get irritated at having to make a hospital visit, or get frustrated when some poor soul asks for a handout?

Third, there was the Samaritan, who saw the injured man as one of God's children in need of help. Finally, there was the injured man himself. Helpless and unconscious, he could make no choice. Sometimes we don't need to be selective in whom we allow into our lives. The very person we might despise may prove to be our greatest friend.

GOLDEN TEXT CHALLENGE

"BE YE KIND ONE TO ANOTHER, TENDERHEARTED, FORGIVING ONE ANOTHER, EVEN AS GOD FOR CHRIST'S SAKE HATH FORGIVEN YOU" (Ephesians 4:32).

The late Martin Luther King once preached a sermon called "Hard Heads and Soft Hearts." His message pointed out the necessity of being tough-minded and resilient, not soft-minded and gullible, while remaining tenderhearted at the same time.

Throughout the Bible this warning is sounded. In our efforts to be tough-minded, we must not become calloused and cynical, insensitive to the feelings of a hurting world.

in verse 31? How is this possible?
2. For whose sake have we been forgiven, and for whose sake must we forgive others?

Daily Devotions:
M. Unkindness Demonstrated 1 Samuel 25:5-12
T. Kindness Displayed 1 Samuel 25:23-33
W. A Friend's Unkind Accusations Job 4:1-8
T. A Plea for Kindness Job 6:22-30
F. The Kind Neighbor Acts 9:36-43
S. Transformed by Christ's Kindness Titus 3:1-7

Living by Faith in Christ

Matthew 8:5-13; John 11:38-44; Hebrews 11:1-3, 6

Unit Theme:
Fruit of Christian Formation

Central Truth:
Pleasing God requires living by faith in Christ.

Focus:
Comprehend and experience the power of faith in Christ.

Context:
Selected New Testament passages regarding faith

Golden Text:
"Without faith it is impossible to please him: for he that cometh to God must believe that he is, and that he is a rewarder of them that diligently seek him" (Hebrews 11:6).

Study Outline:
I. Faith Defined (Hebrews 11:1-3, 6)
II. Faith of Christ Demonstrated (John 11:38-44)
III. Faith in Christ Rewarded (Matthew 8:5-13)

INTRODUCTION

Faith is a major theme of both the old and new covenants. Despite the fact that Israel as a nation was called to be God's chosen people, only those individuals who trusted Him were covered by that covenant. Circumcision and outward obedience to the Law did not displace devotion, love and faith in the God of the covenant. Every Old Testament king, prophet, priest, judge, and so on, who pleased God did so by faith. It was faith in God's integrity that caused them to obey.

Though our three lesson texts are taken from the New Testament, the first one gives us examples of faith from the Old. Hebrews 11 is called the great faith chapter of the Bible. It paints a picture of faith through a roster of men and women who trusted God in ancient days. Each one believed God in spite of circumstances, and acted accordingly. They never had the benefit of the Holy Spirit dwelling in them (as we do), and the Lord's visits with them were sometimes few and far between. For instance, after God spoke to Noah to build the ark, there is no record of another word from heaven until it was time to enter the ark. Genesis 6:22 says, "Noah did according to all that God commanded him" (*NKJV*). The next verse says, "Then the Lord said to Noah, 'Come into the ark'" (7:1, *NKJV*). Amazingly, Noah spent 120 years obeying God without hearing another word! That's faith. The faithful heroes of the Old Testament simply believed God.

The story of the raising of Lazarus shows the ultimate expression of faith on the part of Jesus during His earthly ministry. Though He was God in the flesh, He was human as well, and had to move by faith. His dependence on the Spirit's leading was no different from ours except that He was filled "without limit" (John 3:34, *NIV*). He raised Lazarus because He was led by the Spirit to do so.

Our third text tells the story of the healing of the Roman centurion's servant. We see two important truths here. First, Jesus responds to desperate faith. He doesn't respond to doubt. Second, Jesus responds to whoever looks humbly to Him for help. "The first degree of humility is to acknowledge the necessity of God's mercy, and our own inability to help ourselves; the second, to confess the freeness of his grace, and our own utter unworthiness, ignorance, unbelief and presumption will ever retard our spiritual cure" (*Adam Clarke's Commentary*).

I. FAITH DEFINED (Hebrews 11:1-3, 6)

A. Definition of Faith (v. 1)

1. Now faith is the substance of things hoped for, the evidence of things not seen.

This verse gives the most basic definition of Biblical faith, yet it is not a definition at all, but rather a description of how faith works. *Faith* is not a positive feeling or optimism. It is confident trust in what God has said—no matter what the circumstance. "Faith is that pause between knowing what God's plan is and seeing it actually take place" (Chuck Pierce and Rebecca Wagner Systema, *Possessing Your Inheritance*).

When looking through eyes of faith, we see what God sees as already happening or completed. Biblical faith is not wishful thinking, but rather an inner conviction that is based on the Word of God and the Holy Spirit working in us. Can we have faith for something that is against God's will for us? Certainly, but it won't come to pass. True faith is exercised in harmony with the Spirit to accomplish God's will.

The writer of Hebrews was intent on encouraging weary believers who were ready to return to Judaism. Major sections of the book deal with the superiority of the new covenant over the old covenant (8:8-13; 9:15-22). To go back to the old covenant and its rigid obedience to the law of Moses was a step away from God, not toward Him. The new covenant is entered into by simple faith in Jesus. To back away from faith in Him is to back away from the only way to God.

B. Power of Faith (vv. 2, 3)

2. For by it the elders obtained a good report.

3. Through faith we understand that the worlds were framed by the word of God, so that things which are seen were not made of things which do appear.

The great heroes of faith from the Old Testament enumerated in this chapter were not heroes because they lived up to a certain code of ethics, nor because they were members of God's chosen people, nor because they always acted wisely. They were who they were because they chose to live by faith. God considered them righteous because they believed and trusted Him, not because they were perfect in their obedience of the Law. They all held to unwavering confidence in who God is. They knew their personal limitations, their inability in themselves to live flawlessly. They understood that only their faith in God's character could carry them through this world. They held to an inner conviction that God was all they needed. "The presence of God-given faith in one's heart is conviction enough that He will keep His Word" (*The Bible Exposition Commentary*).

Faith perceives something in the mind's eye before it is seen

Talk About It:
Why do we need to be sure of what we hope for and confident of what we cannot see?

"Living without faith is like driving in a fog."
—*Quotable Quotes*

Talk About It:
1. What is the fate of people whose beliefs are limited to what their eyes can see?
2. How can nature encourage our faith in God?

by the physical eye. God created the universe by faith. He saw it in its completed form before He spoke it into existence. He made everything out of nothing, yet saw it all before the fact. Verse 3 supports the Christian view that there was a single Creator, and that nothing happened by chance or accident. Also, all things visible had to spring forth from something that was not visible. Just how God did this we do not know, but He saw it all before He did it.

The intended readers of Hebrews were on the verge of returning to Judaism because its rituals and sacrifices were easier to grasp. That cop-out appeal is just as powerful today. Millions try to earn righteousness by doing penance for their wrongs. The idea that one can perform some deed to prove his worthiness before God somehow seems more logical than simply trusting by faith that a prayer of repentance will remove one's sin. The writer's use of the pronoun *we*—"we understand"—lays a burden of responsibility on all to live by faith in the words and promises of God. "Faith is a present reality, not exclusively the property of past heroes" (*Zondervan NIV Bible Commentary*, Vol. 2).

> "Faith is more than thinking something is true. Faith is thinking something is true to the extent that we act on it."
>
> —W.T. Purkiser

C. The Necessity of Faith (v. 6)

6. But without faith it is impossible to please him: for he that cometh to God must believe that he is, and that he is a rewarder of them that diligently seek him.

If we refuse to act by faith, then we are incapable of seeing beyond the temporal circumstances around us. We are blinded spiritually to what God is doing. Jesus said to the woman at the well in Sychar, "God is spirit, and his worshipers must worship in spirit and in truth" (John 4:24, *NIV*). Spirit cannot be seen, and often cannot be felt either—but is real nevertheless. There is no possible substitute for faith.

There are two elements that make up faith: first, we must believe God is real; second, we must believe God responds to those who earnestly seek Him. In the previous verse, Enoch is used as a demonstration of faith. Enoch walked with God in a close relationship. Obviously, he believed God was real, but this was not enough. Even the demons in hell believe in God's existence (James 2:19). Enoch went beyond assent to personal interaction.

This was the message the Jewish believers needed to hear. Ritual, sacrifice and diligent adherence to meaningless behavior could never substitute for laying oneself before the Lord in earnest supplication and worship. Seeking God brings His presence. Also intimated here is a certain hope for those who have never heard the gospel. "To 'earnestly seek' means to act in faith on the knowledge of God that one possesses, and then

Talk About It:

1. Are there people who pray to God without believing in Him? If so, why do they pray?

2. What does it mean to "diligently seek" God?

Living by Faith in Christ

to determine to devote oneself to him" (*The Life Application Commentary*).

II. FAITH OF CHRIST DEMONSTRATED (John 11:38-44)
A. The Groaning of Jesus (vv. 38, 39)
(John 11:38, 39 is not included in the printed text.)

This was the second time Jesus *groaned* (see v. 33), a word that conveys the idea of anger at something. Certainly Jesus wasn't irritated at the two sisters, even though they had displayed frustration at His not coming sooner. More likely, He was expressing a divine reaction to the chaos that sin had brought to humanity. After all, God had made people for perfect fellowship, yet Adam's fall had alienated the friendship. On the way to the tomb Jesus broke into weeping, thus showing His ability to relate to the grief and anguish all people face. "Perhaps Jesus was weeping for Lazarus, as well as with the sisters, because He knew He was calling His friend from heaven and back into a wicked world where he would one day have to die again" (*The Bible Exposition Commentary*). The watching Jews saw this as weakness on His part, smugly thinking He could do nothing.

Talk About It:
1. Why was Jesus "deeply moved" (v. 38, *NIV*) as He came to the grave?
2. Why does Jesus sometimes challenge people's faith in a difficult time?

Judaism held strong belief in a life after death, though the ideas about that life were vague. Martha had stated that she knew Lazarus would rise some day. She had also opened the door of her own faith by saying, "But even now I know that whatever You ask of God, God will give You" (v. 22, *NKJV*). She certainly was aware that Jesus had raised the widow of Nain's son (Luke 7:15), though that boy had been dead only a matter of hours. That Lazarus' body had been decaying for four days likely flooded her thoughts to dispel hope of a similar miracle. Jesus had spurred her on to believe for what looked impossible by stating, "I am the resurrection, and the life" (John 11:25). What He was about to do would bring resurrection to present reality, not just a distant hope.

The fact that Lazarus was buried in a cave indicates a level of family wealth, though most of those who followed Jesus were the poor. This tells us there is certainly nothing wrong with material blessing. We also see that the two sisters and brother were also the most gracious and giving of people. God blesses as we bless others.

"The middle verse in the Bible says, 'It is better to trust the Lord than to put confidence in men' (Psalm 118:8, *TLB*). Take either direction from there. Walk backwards to Genesis 1:1 or forward to Revelation 22:21 and on every page you will find the faithful God of the covenant."
—**T. David Sustar**

B. The Glory of God (v. 40)
40. Jesus saith unto her, Said I not unto thee, that, if thou wouldest believe, thou shouldest see the glory of God?

Jesus had told the disciples upon receiving message of Lazarus' illness that this entire episode would reveal the glory of

Talk About It:
What did Jesus
promise Martha if
she would only
believe (see vv. 25-
27)?

God (v. 4). By saying the sickness was "not unto death," He meant death was not the final result. Christ's delay in coming was to show that He meets our needs perfectly, but according to His schedule and purpose. His delay builds patience, and patience builds trust. Though Martha had earlier expressed faith in His ability to raise Lazarus, she now waned. Jesus reminded her of who He was and what He could do. Her protest against opening the grave was a natural but human response. The thought of the stench of a decaying body went against all that seemed sane. However, for Jesus this made the potential of showing the glory of God all the more convincing.

C. Jesus' Prayer (vv. 41, 42)

41. Then they took away the stone from the place where the dead was laid. And Jesus lifted up his eyes, and said, Father, I thank thee that thou hast heard me.

42. And I knew that thou hearest me always: but because of the people which stand by I said it, that they may believe that thou hast sent me.

Talk About It:
1. Why did the
mourners decide to
move the stone?
2. Explain why
Jesus prayed as He
did.

Something is implied that takes place between verses 40 and 41. Jesus had asked Martha a question, and she must have answered by assenting to the stone being rolled away. "Such an act would demonstrate her faith and remove her uncertainty and hesitancy so that the glory of God might be revealed to her and all present" (*Zondervan NIV Bible Commentary*). Martha had done her part. She had taken the last step of faith to meet the conditions for Jesus to act. However, Jesus had not said just what He would do. Too often we are guilty of trying to tell Jesus just what He should do—and how He should do it. True faith expects an end result, but leaves the exact method to Him.

Jesus' prayer here is not a request, but an offering of thanksgiving to the Father for having already heard Him. Likely He had prayed for Lazarus upon first hearing the news of his illness. That had been a prayer of faith. The present prayer was simply an affirmation of that expressed faith. The fact that He prayed at all was possibly for the sake of all who were watching—to prove that He had indeed come from heaven.

"If God did everything for us just as we wished Him to do, then we would see Him as our servant boy—and that is the opposite of faith. We are the servants, and He is the Master. Living by faith means that we humble ourselves and trust not only for God's provision, but for His timing and His method."
—Rodney Hodge

D. The Resurrection (vv. 43, 44)

43. And when he thus had spoken, he cried with a loud voice, Lazarus, come forth.

44. And he that was dead came forth, bound hand and foot with graveclothes: and his face was bound about with a napkin. Jesus saith unto them, Loose him, and let him go.

Jesus said in John 5:28, "The hour is coming in which all who are in the graves will hear His voice and come forth"

(*NJKV*). We note that He called Lazarus by name. To have made a general command would have brought all the dead of times past back to life. That is the power and authority He has at His disposal! However, to the scoffers who were present, even a greater demonstration of divine power would not have changed their hearts. This was demonstrated with the Israelites coming out of Egypt. At Mount Sinai, God showed Himself mightily to them, but that never turned their hearts toward Him. Miracles of themselves do not produce godly faith and worship. As Jesus told Thomas later, "Because you have seen Me, you have believed. Blessed are those who have not seen and yet have believed" (John 20:29, *NKJV*). Faith is believing without having to first see.

The cry Jesus made might either have been out of emotion, or simply for the multitude to hear. Three miracles resulted. First, Lazarus was brought back to life. Second, the decay of his body was reversed. Third, because he was bound and wrapped, divine power had to have moved him out of the tomb to public view. An interesting reflection can be made about his graveclothes. Even as we are given the second birth, we are not perfect. We are still often bound and wrapped by habits, proclivities, unhealed hurts, and so on. These call for ministry from those around us. Jesus commanded people to unwrap Lazarus' body. He requires the family of believers to reach out to each other.

III. FAITH IN CHRIST REWARDED (Matthew 8:5-13)
A. The Roman Centurion (vv. 5, 6)
5. And when Jesus was entered into Capernaum, there came unto him a centurion, beseeching him,
6. And saying, Lord, my servant lieth at home sick of the palsy, grievously tormented.
A Roman centurion was the leader of 100 soldiers. Centurions were the backbone of the Roman military and were generally respected by all. Every mention of a centurion in the New Testament is in a positive light. Luke's account of this story (7:1-10) says the centurion sent local synagogue leaders to appeal to Jesus rather than coming himself, "perhaps because he believed the appeal would be more acceptable coming from Jewish elders rather than from a Gentile" (Ed Glascock, *Moody Gospel Commentary—Matthew*). Matthew apparently saw this as unimportant, because the man still reached out to Jesus in faith.

Everything about this man seems noble. He showed respect for Jesus by calling Him "Lord." Though from a heathen background, he saw something divine in Jesus. Next, the centurion's concern for a servant shows a tender heart. The term *palsy* could have been any of a variety of diseases, all with

Talk About It:
1. Why did Jesus call for Lazarus "with a loud voice"?
2. Why did Jesus have to tell the people to take the graveclothes off Lazarus?
3. Have you ever witnessed Jesus performing a spiritual resurrection? If so, when?

Talk About It:
1. List some unusual traits about this Roman commander.
2. Should we seek for Jesus or should we wait for Him to come to us?

symptoms of muscle and organ paralysis. It was apparent that the servant was dear to the centurion and was also near death. "While this soldier's concern about a servant may seem unusual, the Jewish historian Josephus wrote that Roman soldiers had many servants who actually trained and fought with them" (*Life Application Commentary Series*).

B. Jesus' Offer (v. 7)

7. And Jesus saith unto him, I will come and heal him.

Though Jesus waited to go to the side of Lazarus to heal him, He here agrees to go immediately to a Gentile's servant with the promise of healing the individual. Jesus responds to desperate faith. Whether we can make a comparison to the case of Lazarus is disputable, but the message sent by Martha and Mary concerning their brother's illness did not sound desperate. Does this mean Jesus never responds until things look hopeless? No. It is certainly best to pray in faith before things reach such a state. How many times has God provided for us before the problems reached a distressed point! Yet, the first simple truth to be learned here is that He responds when we desperately reach out to Him.

Jesus had just touched a leper (something against the Law) and healed him before the centurion arrived (vv. 1-4). Now, to agree to go to a Gentile's house and heal his servant was an even more radical move. There is no recorded instance of Jesus entering a Gentile's home—but He was willing. Compassion and doing good were His priorities, not worrying about what anyone thought. Thus, the second truth garnered from this incident is that it doesn't matter who we are, Jesus still responds to faith.

C. A Man Under Authority (vv. 8, 9)

8. The centurion answered and said, Lord, I am not worthy that thou shouldest come under my roof: but speak the word only, and my servant shall be healed.

9. For I am a man under authority, having soldiers under me: and I say to this man, Go, and he goeth; and to another, Come, and he cometh; and to my servant, Do this, and he doeth it.

There are two recorded instances of Gentiles coming to Jesus in desperation. Matthew 15:21-28 tells the story of the Canaanite woman whose daughter was demon-possessed. Just as in this case, Jesus responded to desperate faith. In both cases Jesus performed the healing miracle from a distance. This would parallel what Paul said to the Ephesians (who were Gentile believers): "But now in Christ Jesus ye who sometimes were far off are made nigh by the blood of Christ"

Living by Faith in Christ

(Ephesians 2:13). Jesus was preparing the way to show that the gospel is for all people who believe.

Luke's account tells us that the centurion was a worthy individual, having built a synagogue for the local Jewish residents (7:4, 5). Whether he was a Jewish proselyte is not known, but obviously he held a respect for the God of the Jews. The statement "I am not worthy" expressed great humility. He may not have understood all of who Jesus was, but he knew Jesus had come from God. Still, everything about his being a man of war would seem to prevent him from appealing to Jesus. Soldiers were hard and rough, whereas Jesus was gentle and peaceful.

This soldier understood authority. There were those whom he held command over, while at the same time, he was under the command of higher authorities in the Roman military. He had likely heard enough about Jesus to know He was under a higher authority from heaven. As such, he knew Jesus also held authority over sickness. "All Christ had to do was speak the word and the disease would obey Him the way a soldier obeyed his officer" (*The Bible Exposition Commentary*).

Talk About It:
1. What does verse 8 reveal about the centurion?
2. According to verse 9, what was similar between Jesus and the centurion?

"Faith is to believe what you do not yet see; the reward for this faith is to see what you believe."
—**Augustine**

D. Jesus' Amazement (vv. 10-13)

10. When Jesus heard it, he marvelled, and said to them that followed, Verily I say unto you, I have not found so great faith, no, not in Israel.

11. And I say unto you, That many shall come from the east and west, and shall sit down with Abraham, and Isaac, and Jacob, in the kingdom of heaven.

12. But the children of the kingdom shall be cast out into outer darkness: there shall be weeping and gnashing of teeth.

13. And Jesus said unto the centurion, Go thy way; and as thou hast believed, so be it done unto thee. And his servant was healed in the selfsame hour.

One might make the point that if Jesus is God, how could anything amaze Him? The word for *marvelled* here is used many times to show how people responded to Jesus' teachings and miracles. For Jesus to marvel somehow seems to go against His omniscience as God. However, we must remember that Jesus was also fully human, experiencing all the same emotions we experience. He chose not to exercise His rights as God, but to live on our level (such as having to live by faith) so He could experience life just as we do.

Marveling at a Gentile's faith was in direct contrast to the skepticism of the Jews. In verses 11 and 12, Jesus warned Israel that their failure to respond to the Messiah would cause them to be displaced by Gentiles. Though the Jews knew from the Old Testament that some Gentiles would be included when

Talk About It:
1. What caused the Son of God to "marvel"?
2. What will cause people to be eternally punished?
3. How could a stronger faith in Christ affect your life?

the nation was finally reunited (see Psalm 107:3; Isaiah 25:6; 43:5, 6), still they never dreamed that Gentiles could have a prominent role. Jesus here speaks of Gentiles sitting at the same table with the great patriarchs, something unthinkable to the average Jew's mind. The obvious warning for us all is that their spiritual pride should never be allowed among us. We all should carry the humble attitude of the centurion.

Because of the centurion's great faith, Jesus healed the servant without actually going to him and touching him. Did the centurion believe his servant had been healed as he left Jesus' presence? Yes, because he himself had just affirmed Jesus' authority over illness. The likelihood is that the centurion returned home in great expectation of seeing a well servant.

CONCLUSION

Our varied texts in the lesson tell us that though we must live by faith, we cannot live by assumption. We must not assume that God will answer exactly as we wish Him to, nor on our time schedules. The patriarchs of old recognized this. God promised Abraham that his descendants would receive the land of Canaan (Genesis 12:7), but Abraham knew this wouldn't happen while he was on the earth. Jacob was promised that his seed would be as the "sand of the sea" (32:12), but this would require many generations. These men simply trusted God to work things out as He please.

In contrast, Martha and Mary were distressed that Jesus had not come quickly to heal their brother. Mary's refusal to come outside when Jesus arrived might indicate pouting on her part (see John 11:20). Jesus did things His way, though, and showed them an even greater miracle than they might have ever expected. In contrast again, the centurion came to Jesus with open faith. He didn't put limitations on Jesus, but rather simply sought His help in total desperation. However Jesus answers us is up to Him. Our responsibility is to trust Him completely with our total lives. He is forever faithful and will never disappoint us—as long as we trust Him.

GOLDEN TEXT CHALLENGE

"WITHOUT FAITH IT IS IMPOSSIBLE TO PLEASE HIM: FOR HE THAT COMETH TO GOD MUST BELIEVE THAT HE IS, AND THAT HE IS A REWARDER OF THEM THAT DILIGENTLY SEEK HIM" (Hebrews 11:6).

Faith is the only thing that gives God His proper place and puts people in their place. Faith lifts up God because it proves we have more confidence in His eyesight than in our own.

Faith not only believes God exists, but it also trusts Him to reward those who seek Him. This diligent seeking of Him will be exhibited in prayer, patience and worship. All faith that does not set people on a diligent search for God is vain.

Daily Devotions:
M. Faithless Generation
Deuteronomy 32:16-21
T. Results of Unbelief
Psalm 78:18-33
W. Faith for Provision
Matthew 6:30-34
T. Faith for Healing
Matthew 9:18-29
F. Faith for Salvation
Romans 10:4-13
S. Faith's Reward
1 Peter 1:3-9

The Meekness of Christ

Isaiah 53:7, 8; Matthew 11:28-30; 26:47-54; Acts 7:54-60

INTRODUCTION

One of the most important fruits to be developed in the Christian life is that of a humble, meek spirit. Meekness is an attitude of gentleness toward God and people. It does not come automatically, but rather is developed in a heart that recognizes `God is in control. A prime Old Testament example was Moses. Numbers 12:3 says, "Moses was very meek, above all the men which were upon the face of the earth." Meekness must not be equated with weakness, however. Though Moses was meek, he was a man who spoke with God "face to face" (Exodus 33:11), and could carry out God's commands with tremendous authority.

Weakness indicates a lack of strength, while meekness is a sign of strength emanating from conscious choice. Meekness is power under control. Paul exhorted church leaders in the New Testament to exercise their authority over their congregations wisely, restraining themselves with meekness. He said to the Galatians, "Brethren, if a man be overtaken in a fault, ye which are spiritual, restore such an one in the spirit of meekness; considering thyself, lest thou also be tempted" (Galatians 6:1). Meekness recognizes personal limitations, while counting on the unlimited capabilities of God.

Jesus included the *meek* in the Beatitudes when He said, "Blessed are the meek: for they shall inherit the earth" (Matthew 5:5). He also practiced perfectly what He preached. He is our example to follow. He allowed Himself to be beaten and crucified, taking on the sins of all people, while not uttering the first complaint. For those who would follow Him as disciples, He declared that He would be a gentle master, whose yoke is easy to bear. He came to free us from the weight of our sins, while not loading us down with a set of impossible religious rituals and responsibilities.

Besides Jesus as our example of meekness, we will also look at Stephen, a man who was bold to preach the gospel in power, but not out of spite. Even while he was being stoned to death, Stephen prayed for the souls of those throwing the stones. Though his words had been harsh, his motivation was a sincere desire to see people come to God. This is meekness in action.

Unit Theme:
Fruit of Christian Formation

Central Truth:
Christian meekness is power under control.

Focus:
Consider Christ's response to opposition and emulate His example of meekness.

Context:
Selected Scripture passages regarding the spiritual fruit of meekness

Golden Text:
"Take my yoke upon you, and learn of me; for I am meek and lowly in heart: and ye shall find rest unto your souls" (Matthew 11:29).

Study Outline:
I. Christ: Our Example of Meekness
(Isaiah 53:7, 8; Matthew 11:28-30)
II. Strength Under Control
(Matthew 26:47-54)
III. Facing Hostility With Meekness
(Acts 7:54-60)

I. CHRIST: OUR EXAMPLE OF MEEKNESS
(Isaiah 53:7, 8; Matthew 11:28-30)

A. The Lamb (Isaiah 53:7, 8)

7. He was oppressed, and he was afflicted, yet he opened not his mouth: he is brought as a lamb to the slaughter, and as a sheep before her shearers is dumb, so he openeth not his mouth.

8. He was taken from prison and from judgment: and who shall declare his generation? for he was cut off out of the land of the living: for the transgression of my people was he stricken.

Talk About It:

1. Why did Jesus keep quiet during His suffering?

2. How was Jesus "stricken," and why?

In the verse prior to these two, humanity is seen as "sheep gone astray," thus implying that the Messiah is the ultimate Shepherd. John 10:11 affirmed Jesus' willingness to give Himself for His flock when He said, "I am the good shepherd: the good shepherd giveth his life for the sheep." In our text, Isaiah changes metaphors and pictures the Holy One as the actual lamb sent to the slaughter. Sheep are the meekest of animals, thus speaking of Jesus' compliance to die. Isaiah is looking forward prophetically to the Lord's death by crucifixion. Unlike lambs slaughtered in the Temple, however, we see the cruelty and torture this Lamb is put through before finally being killed. Crucifixion victims under the Romans were usually totally exhausted from beatings by the time they reached their execution site. The actual nailing to the cross was enough to cause one to lose consciousness. The subsequent grueling hours (and sometimes days) on the cross were the worst form of horror. Death was a relief.

It is interesting that the Lord's quiet endurance of pain is compared to the shearing of a sheep. Of course, sheep are not slaughtered during shearing time, but the endured fear is just as real. This is the only place in Scripture where the sheep's quiet endurance of shearing is mentioned.

As a criminal with no human rights, Jesus was treated in the most inhumane way, thus robbing Him of all dignity as a living person (v. 8). The term *cut off* suggests "not only a violent, premature death but also the judgment of God" (*Zondervan NIV Bible Commentary*, Vol. 1). This was the passage the Ethiopian eunuch was pondering when Philip joined him on the desert road (see Acts 8:26-40). Philip showed that Isaiah's words described what Jesus had just recently endured in Jerusalem. This was the ultimate sacrifice one person could make for others. The phrase "my people" indicates that God's motive was to bring back to Himself those who were His own people. It was His own who had deserted Him, and it was His own for whom the Messiah would die.

Sacrifice means giving up something. Sacrifice for others

"The Christian teaching about who crucified Christ is not that the Romans or the Jews or whatever people happened to be there did, but that you and I did, and that all human societies without exception are involved in the crucifixion of Christ."
—Northrop Frye

means giving up something for the sake of others. Parents regularly sacrifice personal cares and comforts so their children will have advantages in the future. True sacrifice, however, means taking on a burden for someone else that you don't want to bear. No one could possibly want to suffer the kind of horror and death that Isaiah describes, yet this is just what Jesus did. He took on Himself the horror of what we deserved so we would not have to bear it.

B. Our Burdens (Matthew 11:28)

28. Come unto me, all ye that labour and are heavy laden, and I will give you rest.

Jesus wasn't the kind of Messiah the Jews had expected. The true nature of His mission and ministry was lost on them. Even at a point early in this chapter, John the Baptist had sent word to Him, expressing his own doubts and second thoughts. Jesus' answer of miracles and the poor receiving the gospel affirmed that Jesus knew exactly what He was doing. He then pointed out just how vacillating Israel had always been toward God's messengers. He used the analogy of children playing games (v. 16). "Like children at play in the marketplace while their parents did business, the Jews were more interested in their own entertainment than in the serious business going on around them" (Ed Glascock, *Moody Gospel Commentary— Matthew*). They were playing religious games while refusing to see the redemptive plan Jesus was showing them. He then threw stinging remarks, or "woes," against villages and cities that had rejected Him (vv. 20-24). His reason was clear. These cities had seen more of the miraculous ministry of Jesus than any others, yet were aloof to His message. "These cities remained dependent upon the dead religion of Israel with all its traditions and rabbinical legalism instead of recognizing their Messiah and His kingdom standards" (Glascock). Interestingly, both Jewish and Gentile cities were named. He was prophetically speaking of a time to come when both Jew and Gentile were equally responsible for how they responded to the gospel. Also, those who had been more privileged (as these He named had been) would face a stronger judgment, for "to whom much is given, from him much will be required" (Luke 12:48, *NKJV*).

Jesus then offered up praise to the Father because the Father had revealed truth to the simple people who believed the message. It wasn't the "wise and prudent" (Matthew 11:25), that is, those who are self-sufficient and see themselves as wise, but rather those who are "dependent and love to be taught" (*Zondervan NIV Bible Commentary*, Vol. 11). In other words, those who pride themselves in their religion and wisdom are really fools, while those who understand little but are hungry for Jesus see spiritual realities.

Talk About It:
1. To whom does Jesus want to minister?
2. What kind of "rest" does Jesus offer?

"I have read in Plato and Cicero sayings that are wise and very beautiful; but I have never read in either of them: 'Come unto me all ye that labour and are heavy laden.'"

—Augustine

Having said all this, Jesus reaffirmed that the message He brought was straight from the Father, and that no one could know the Father except through Him. He then reached out to the common people with an offering of relief from the burdens of sin—and religiosity as well—that they suffered under. In other words, all who recognized their own weaknesses and needs were welcome. He would bring rest to them from their labor.

C. Christ's Yoke (vv. 29, 30)

29. Take my yoke upon you, and learn of me; for I am meek and lowly in heart: and ye shall find rest unto your souls.

30. For my yoke is easy, and my burden is light.

Talk About It:
1. How do we "learn of" Jesus? What will He teach us?
2. What is a yoke? What makes most yokes heavy?

A yoke was the piece of equipment used to connect two animals (oxen, horses, etc.) together for sharing a workload of plowing or pulling a cart. Cultural tradition says that a young, inexperienced animal would be trained by being hitched beside an older, more experienced one. The older was actually carrying the bulk of the load for both of them, while helping the younger adjust to the burden. In the same sense, Jesus walks alongside the believer. To "take my yoke" also meant to become His disciple. When we give our lives to Jesus, we become yoked to Him. The word *easy* means "well-fitting," indicating that His plan for us is individually and perfectly suited to us. His yoke isn't difficult because of His gentleness toward us. "His service flows from grace, not legalism; from love, not judgmentalness; and from gratitude, not trying to earn what is unattainable by human effort" (Glascock).

To "learn of me" means to yield completely to Him. When the crises of life deepen, if we will depend on Him, we will learn more of His heart and find a greater peace. "Life is simplified and unified around the person of Christ" (*The Bible Exposition Commentary*).

II. STRENGTH UNDER CONTROL (Matthew 26:47-54)

A. Self-Restraint in the Face of Betrayal (vv. 47-50)

47. And while he yet spake, lo, Judas, one of the twelve, came, and with him a great multitude with swords and staves, from the chief priests and elders of the people.

48. Now he that betrayed him gave them a sign, saying, Whomsoever I shall kiss, that same is he: hold him fast.

49. And forthwith he came to Jesus, and said, Hail, master; and kissed him.

50. And Jesus said unto him, Friend, wherefore art thou come? Then came they, and laid hands on Jesus, and took him.

As Jesus was admonishing the disciples for not remaining awake and praying (for their own sakes, not for His safety),

Judas came on the scene, leading a contingent of Temple guards to arrest Him. The guards apparently expected resistance, and thus brought clubs and swords. This may have been at Judas' instigation, since the other disciples had often made known their intense loyalty to Jesus. Judas was likely fearful for his own safety. One as explosive as Peter was could easily be provoked to turn his strength on the betrayer. The reference to "the chief priests and elders" (v. 47) indicates they had planned the arrest. It is possible that Judas had first led the mob to the Upper Room, expecting that Jesus was still there. Finding it empty, he would have easily guessed the next place to look.

A kiss was a common mode of greeting, but here was used by the guards to distinguish Jesus from the others. This indicates that for all His celebrity, Jesus was not necessarily known to everyone. In retrospect, we see that Judas made a mockery of all that He touched. A kiss that normally indicated affection now became a kiss of betrayal. "In that day, it was customary for disciples to kiss their teacher. But in this case, it was not a mark of submission or respect. The Greek verbs indicate that Judas kissed Jesus repeatedly" (*The Bible Exposition Commentary*). Judas' name was a derivative of *Judah*, the fourth son of Leah to Jacob. *Judah* meant "praise," but now the name would henceforth be tainted.

Jesus responded to Judas initially by calling him *Friend.* The word used here does not carry an intimate meaning, but more of a polite cordiality. He had already identified Judas as the betrayer, so there was no reason to extend affection. The question Jesus then asked might also be translated as "Do what you have come to do" (*The Nelson Study Bible*). Jesus never winced at what was happening. He did not try to run but was fully prepared to fulfill what Isaiah had predicted about Him. In meekness He would allow Himself to be crucified. The Lord's demeanor seemed to be giving Judas permission to carry out the treachery he had planned—and that had been seen in heaven eons before. Everything was happening on the Lord's timetable.

B. Restraint of Peter (vv. 51, 52)

51. And, behold, one of them which were with Jesus stretched out his hand, and drew his sword, and struck a servant of the high priest's, and smote off his ear.

52. Then said Jesus unto him, Put up again thy sword into his place: for all they that take the sword shall perish with the sword.

All four Gospels record Peter's impetuous effort to defend Jesus, but only John (18:10, 11) identifies the man as Peter. There was no way the small band of disciples could defend Jesus from such a force of Temple guards, but Peter was willing

Talk About It:
1. What did Judas call Jesus, and why (v. 49)?
2. What did Jesus call Judas, and why (v. 50)?

Releasing Hurt
The only people who can really hurt us are those with whom we have relationship. President Ronald Reagan was shot in an assassination attempt in 1981. He spoke later of praying for his own recovery, but was reminded by the Lord that he first had to pray for the misguided young man who had tried to harm him. He didn't know the man, so he had no pent-up feelings of resentment toward him. Had he been a colleague or former friend, however, it would have hurt so much more.

Jesus' reaction to Judas in calling him "friend" gives us an example to follow. When a friend hurts us, we should do as Jesus did and remind him of the friendship. Jesus didn't reject Judas. In fact, He gave him an opportunity to repent.

Talk About It:
Explain the meaning of Jesus' statement about violence in verse 52.

to die trying. Jesus had earlier told the disciples to get swords (Luke 22:36-38), but He was speaking figuratively. Peter apparently misunderstood His intent, thinking it was his duty to protect Jesus. All he accomplished was to cut the ear off one guard. Although this was foolish, it was fully in character for Peter at this time. None of the disciples had real spiritual depth. Fortunately for Peter, Jesus put the ear back on the man and healed him, or "there probably would have been four crosses at Calvary" (*The Bible Exposition Commentary*). Still, we can all identify with Peter. We'd like to think we'd be the one who would be gallant at such a time, willing to defend the Lord at any cost.

C. Suspension of Power (vv. 53, 54)

53. Thinkest thou that I cannot now pray to my Father, and he shall presently give me more than twelve legions of angels?

54. But how then shall the scriptures be fulfilled, that thus it must be?

Talk About It:
1. Describe the power at Jesus' disposal.
2. Why didn't Jesus take advantage of this power?

Despite Peter's noblest effort, Jesus did not need nor want to be defended. He set a precedent here: The Kingdom need not be defended with physical force. However, over the centuries since then, many have forgotten. Many of the scars on the face of the church have been caused by men "fighting for God." As Christians, most of our battles with others need to be fought on our knees.

Jesus had no reason to defend Himself or have others defend Him. He knew He had to die to achieve the mission the Father had given Him. All was taking place in the Father's perfect timing. He knew also that He could easily call on the forces of heaven to defend Himself. This puny force of soldiers was nothing. However, that would defy His own mission in giving His life as a sacrifice—and the fulfillment of Scripture (v. 54). Jesus let Peter know that He was in control.

"Meek endurance and obedience, the accepting of His dealings, of whatever complexion they are and however they may tear and desolate our hearts, without murmuring, without sulking, without rebellion or resistance, is the deepest conception of the meekness which Christ pronounced *blessed.*"

—**Alexander MacLaren**

Paul later reminded us that our battles in this world are primarily spiritual, not fleshly (Ephesians 6:12). We thus fight with spiritual weapons. Our sword is the "sword of the Spirit, which is the word of God" (v. 17). We might also note that Moses initially was just as impetuous as Peter. He killed an Egyptian, and that one misguided action cost him 40 years of training in the wilderness.

III. FACING HOSTILITY WITH MEEKNESS (Acts 7:54-60)
A. Reaction to the Word (v. 54)

54. When they heard these things, they were cut to the heart, and they gnashed on him with their teeth.

Those who heard Stephen's sermon regarded his words as pure apostasy. Their bigoted eyes were shut off to the truth. Stephen was more daring than anyone else to say that Israel's rejection of Jesus was a rejection of the Messiah and the result of callous hearts. Peter's words in Acts 3:13-15 had been strong, but the religious leaders' attitudes had not yet had time to harden. They were more taken aback by his boldness. Now, Stephen's frontal attack brought on a harsh reaction. This was not Stephen's intent. He wanted them to see what they had done—and repent.

There is no middle ground when one hears the gospel. Either the heart is convicted and moved to repentance, or the heart is convicted and moved to harden itself. Those who try to put off a decision and wait for a more "convenient season" (24:25), as Felix did, are simply allowing the heart to harden even more.

Talk About It: How did Stephen's accusers respond to his message, and why?

B. Heaven's Approval (vv. 55, 56)

55. But he, being full of the Holy Ghost, looked up stedfastly into heaven, and saw the glory of God, and Jesus standing on the right hand of God,

56. And said, Behold, I see the heavens opened, and the Son of man standing on the right hand of God.

Stephen was full of the Holy Spirit. His intent was not to hurt anyone, but to draw them to Jesus. We notice that he was in control of himself, though his listeners were not. As the crowds began to react angrily toward him, his attention was suddenly focused far beyond the present situation. He saw heaven opening up and Jesus standing at the right hand of the Father. He was likely unaware of the crowd drawing closer to stone him, for his gaze was upward toward heaven. His vision "confirmed Jesus' claim and condemned the council for having rejected him" (*Zondervan NIV Bible Commentary*, Vol. 2). The fact that he saw Jesus simply further infuriated his accusers. They were faced with the ultimate decision—either repent of their sin of rejecting the Messiah, or deepen their resentment toward Jesus' claim of deity and condemn Stephen for blasphemy. "Had he been judged only as impertinent apostate, the thirty-nine lashes of Jewish punishment would have been appropriate" (Zondervan). However, his actions were seen as openly rebellious. They demanded death.

Talk About It:
1. Why is it important to be "full of the Holy Ghost"?
2. Explain God's response to Stephen's ministry.

This was the first time since His ascension in Acts 1 that Jesus made an earthly appearance. Also, He would normally be sitting at the right hand of the Father. Psalm 110:1 says of Him, "The Lord said unto my Lord, Sit thou at my right hand, until I make thine enemies thy footstool." The writer of Hebrews said, "Let us fix our eyes on Jesus, the author and perfecter of our faith, who for the joy set before him endured the cross, scorning its shame, and sat down at the right hand of the throne of God" (12:2, *NIV*). Other passages denote the same

"Humility of soul makes us willing to leave our cause and our destiny in the hands of God. We will not fight or scrap in our own interests."
—**Charles W. Conn**

stance, but in this case Jesus stood. Apparently this was done in honor of Stephen's selfless sacrifice. Jesus had said in Luke 12:8 that those who honor Him, He would in turn honor. This should be the highest goal of our lives—honoring Christ with our every action and attitude.

C. Death Sentence (vv. 57-60)

57. Then they cried out with a loud voice, and stopped their ears, and ran upon him with one accord,

58. And cast him out of the city, and stoned him: and the witnesses laid down their clothes at a young man's feet, whose name was Saul.

59. And they stoned Stephen, calling upon God, and saying, Lord Jesus, receive my spirit.

60. And he kneeled down, and cried with a loud voice, Lord, lay not this sin to their charge. And when he had said this, he fell asleep.

Talk About It:
1. Describe the two prayers of Stephen during his stoning.
2. Why is "he fell asleep" a meaningful phrase regarding Stephen's death?

We note that, just as it had been in Jesus' case, the Romans did not allow the Jews to condemn a man with a death sentence. Still, they were so infuriated that they chanced bringing reprisal on themselves. However, they were so entrenched in their petty obedience to the Law that they carried Stephen outside the city to execute him. Watching all this was the young Christian persecutor—Saul of Tarsus. Though he would continue for a time to rage against believers, this episode made an indelible mark on the man. When it came his turn to be confronted by a vision of Christ, he would turn from his hatred of Christianity and become its greatest proponent.

Though he had preached a harsh message against them, Stephen held no animosity toward his persecutors. Instead, he prayed for them, just as Jesus had done at His crucifixion. He did what we should do—imitate Christ. It might be mistakenly thought that Stephen died prematurely, but the fact is that he accomplished more in death than he might have in life. The example of his meek spirit was etched on the heart of Saul, who was soon converted. This reminds us that we never know how our life is touching others. The smallest kindness might have the greatest impact.

CONCLUSION

If someone says or does something awful toward you, is your first impulse to strike back? It is for most of us, and despite the fact that we want to be controlled in our responses, we often are not. Taking on the meekness of Christ is not an achievement we can make on our own. It is a fruit of the Spirit working in us. That's why we must daily submit our lives to the Holy Spirit to mold our characters and give us direction.

The Meekness of Christ

GOLDEN TEXT CHALLENGE

"TAKE MY YOKE UPON YOU, AND LEARN OF ME; FOR I AM MEEK AND LOWLY IN HEART: AND YE SHALL FIND REST UNTO YOUR SOULS" (Matthew 11:29).

Jesus invites us to willingly exchange yokes. Instead of being "heavy laden" with the impossible task of trying to be righteous through our own power, Jesus says, "Come unto me" (v. 28). As the "meek and lowly" ("gentle and humble," *NIV*) Savior, Jesus will fit us with His yoke of grace and peace. His yoke is refreshing, inspiring us to serve Him wholeheartedly.

Jesus' yoke does not offer an escape from responsibility, but instead provides the only way to have a full and eternally meaningful life. His meekness means He will demand from us only what He empowers us to do.

Daily Devotions:

M. A Meek Leader
  Numbers 12:1-15
T. Responding With
  Meekness
  2 Samuel 16:5-
  12
W. The Meek Are
  Teachable
  Psalm 25:1-9
T. Restore Others
  With Meekness
  Galatians 6:1-7
F. Put On
  Meekness
  1 Peter 3:1-7
S. Witness With
  Meekness
  1 Peter 3:13-18

Christ-Controlled Living

Matthew 4:1-11; 1 Corinthians 9:24-27; Galatians 5:16-25

Unit Theme:
Fruit of Christian Formation

Central Truth:
A life of temperance is possible when we allow Christ to fulfill our deepest longings.

Focus:
Study Christ's response to temptation and live a Christ-disciplined life.

Context:
Selected New Testament passages on Spirit-led living

Golden Text:
"Walk in the Spirit, and ye shall not fulfil the lust of the flesh" (Galatians 5:16).

Study Outline:
I. Overcoming Temptation
 (Matthew 4:1-11)
II. Walking in the Spirit
 (Galatians 5:16-25)
III. Practicing Self-Control
 (1 Corinthians 9:24-27)

INTRODUCTION

Self-control is a fruit of the Spirit. It comes with Christian maturity as a believer turns his reliance from himself to the Spirit's guidance. Jesus gave us the perfect example of self-control with His resistance to the devil during His wilderness temptation. This is the first point of our lesson outline. Satan did not doubt that Jesus was the Son of God. What he doubted was whether Jesus would hold out under pressure because of the human nature He had taken on. In other words, he challenged the Lord's mission. It would have been nothing for Jesus to change the stones to bread. However, that would have compromised the Father's plan for Him to live a perfect life, a plan they had conceived together in eternity past. Neither would Jesus compromise by jumping from the pinnacle of the Temple and having angels catch Him (thus bringing all of Jerusalem's attention to Himself). Jesus did nothing out of vanity and self-exaltation. Finally, Jesus would not succumb to Satan's offer of the kingdoms of the earth—the very domain Adam had possessed before giving in to temptation. Jesus refused, partly because He came to earth to restore people to their rightful position—which includes eventually ruling and reigning with Him. To have succumbed to Satan would have resulted in humanity being excluded from the glory God intended for us.

The second point of our lesson's outline tells us that self-controlled living can be accomplished only by yielding to the Holy Spirit inside us. Our old sinful nature is always battling against the redeemed new man. Paul said the believer is "controlled not by the sinful nature but by the Spirit, if the Spirit of God lives in you" (Romans 8:9, *NIV*). Even with the Spirit's presence, however, we will not naturally have self-control. There has to be a daily conscious yielding to the Spirit. The flesh is strong and doesn't give up easily. When we do yield to the Spirit, however, the results are marvelous. We are transformed into people who truly resemble Christ.

Our last point in the lesson outline has to do with seeing the Christian life as a race to be won. Paul used comparisons to athletic contests in much of his writing. In order to win a race, one has to be disciplined and self-controlled. The runner cannot pursue other things, but rather must keep his or her eyes on the finish line. Outside of Jesus himself, Paul probably provides us with the best model of Christian self-control in all the New Testament.

I. OVERCOMING TEMPTATION (Matthew 4:1-11)

A. The Place of Temptation (v. 1)

1. Then was Jesus led up of the Spirit into the wilderness to be tempted of the devil.

From the time we see Jesus at the Temple at age 12 when He confounds the religious teachers (Luke 2), to the time He begins His public ministry at about age 30, we hear nothing. This was a period of divine protection while He grew physically and also in wisdom and knowledge. There were no miracles, nor interactions with great teachers. He simply was allowed to grow into early adulthood. Some feel this might have been necessary because one's manhood wasn't respected until about this age. The baptism by John set the stage for His entrance into ministry in the public arena, and also identified Him as the Messiah (Matthew 3:13-17).

All three persons of the Trinity were represented at His water baptism. God the Father spoke from heaven, God the Son was baptized, and God the Holy Spirit descended from heaven to anoint the Son. Jesus' willing humiliation is seen in the Father's delight in Him, and the Spirit's desire to glorify Christ.

It was the Holy Spirit who led Jesus into the wilderness to face temptation from the devil. There was nothing coincidental about the matter. Matthew's use of the word *led* is not as strong as the one used by Mark. In dramatic fashion, Mark says the Spirit literally "sent him out" (1:12, *NIV*). Jesus did not make this decision on His own, but was forcefully led to the desert by the Spirit. The word translated as *tempted* carries the connotation of being sifted for genuineness or sincerity. The word can also mean "entice someone to evil." "Accordingly, 'to be tempted' here is to be understood both ways. The Spirit conducted Him into the wilderness simply to have His faith tried; but as the agent in this trial was to be the wicked one, whose whole object would be to seduce Him from His allegiance to God, it was a temptation in the bad sense of the term" (*Jamieson, Fausset, and Brown Commentary*).

Thus, Jesus can know exactly what we go through in our lives because He felt the pressure of His human side in conflict with His divine nature. Also, even though He is God's Son, Jesus had to depend on the Holy Spirit to stand up to the devil. No wonder, then, that this confrontation with Satan came after His baptism and filling by the Spirit.

B. The First Test (vv. 2-4)

2. And when he had fasted forty days and forty nights, he was afterward an hungred.

3. And when the tempter came to him, he said, If thou

Talk About It:
1. Why did the Holy Spirit lead Jesus into the wilderness?
2. Why did the devil tempt Jesus?

"Jesus' spiritual anointing was the beginning of a new era, the age of the Spirit. This event initiated Jesus' ministry and continues to serve as a model for a Spirit-anointed ministry."

—French Arrington

be the Son of God, command that these stones be made bread.

4. But he answered and said, It is written, Man shall not live by bread alone, but by every word that proceedeth out of the mouth of God.

Talk About It:

1. What was the purpose of Jesus' long fast?

2. Why did Satan use the word *if* in this first temptation? Did he believe Jesus was God's Son?

3. What does it mean to "live on . . . every word that comes from the mouth of God" (v. 3, *NIV*)?

We have established that Satan did not lead Jesus into the wilderness. The devil didn't arrive on the scene until after 40 days of fasting. Just what kind of fast was this? Jews usually practiced partial fasts, which allowed for occasional bits of food, and drinking water. Daniel's three-week fast (Daniel 10) was one where he had at least some sustenance. A fast of this nature simply focused the heart on God and away from physical nourishment. Total fasting from all food and drink usually was for only one day, or perhaps two, in a week. The full fast that Jesus endured required divine help. His 40 days parallel Israel's 40 years in the wilderness. They failed the test—but He passed.

After so long without food or water, one would likely be too depleted to even think about food. Jesus, however, was indeed hungry, indicating that He was still in control of His wits. Satan recognized who He was and tried to persuade Him to use divine power to prove Himself. This was total arrogance, but what Satan was really challenging was the mission Jesus had taken on, not whether He was actually able to change the molecular structure of stones to that of bread. He didn't think that Jesus, having taken on humanity, could resist using His divine side to make things easier for Himself. Jesus didn't have to prove who He was, but rather prove that He was willing to be fully obedient to the Father. Satan was trying to use Jesus' weakened state to make Him feel that God the Father was unnecessarily putting Him to a test. "For Christ to use His divine powers out of the will of God would be defeat" (*The Bible Exposition Commentary*). Jesus knew the plan of the Father and had no qualms about what it required of Him. He said later, "He that sent me is with me: the Father hath not left me alone; for I do always those things that please him" (John 8:29).

Jesus met the devil head-on by answering with the Word of God. Centuries earlier, God had tested the Israelites in the desert to show them the wickedness of their hearts. They were like selfish animals, looking only for their next meal. God had said through Moses, "He humbled you, causing you to hunger and then feeding you with manna . . . to teach you that man does not live on bread alone but on every word that comes from the mouth of the Lord" (Deuteronomy 8:3, *NIV*). God had taught Israel that physical provision was from above. There was nothing the people could do on their own to make the manna appear and provide for themselves. Not only that, they had to learn they were more than mere physical beings. They

Christ-Controlled Living

were spiritual as well, and spiritual needs are answered through the words that come from the mouth of God. "The manna thus taught Israel that only as man stands obediently under his Lord's sovereign word, the ultimate source of life, does he find true and lasting life" (*The Wycliffe Bible Commentary*).

Feeding the inner soul is ultimately more important than being fed physically. If we focus on our relationship with Christ, then physical needs will be met. Jesus said in Matthew 6:33, "But seek ye first the kingdom of God, and his righteousness; and all these things shall be added unto you." The manna in the wilderness never failed to appear for 40 years, thus giving proof that God does provide for physical needs. This gives credence to the next verse in Matthew, which says, "Therefore do not worry about tomorrow, for tomorrow will worry about itself" (v. 34, *NIV*).

> "Temptations discover what we are."
> —Thomas à Kempis

C. The Second Test (vv. 5-7)

5. Then the devil taketh him up into the holy city, and setteth him on a pinnacle of the temple,

6. And saith unto him, If thou be the Son of God, cast thyself down: for it is written, He shall give his angels charge concerning thee: and in their hands they shall bear thee up, lest at any time thou dash thy foot against a stone.

7. Jesus said unto him, It is written again, Thou shalt not tempt the Lord thy God.

In this test Satan set the stakes higher. He took Jesus to the highest point of the Temple, which would have been about 500 feet above the floor of the Kidron Valley. He said to Jesus, in essence, "Throw Yourself off the Temple and let the angels catch You. All the people of Jerusalem will be watching, and that will immediately prove to them who You are!" Satan wanted Jesus to perform a selfish miracle—one that did no good for anyone else. Jesus saw exactly what the devil was doing. The appeal to human vanity is enormous, but He would have no part of that.

Satan was quoting Psalm 91:11, 12, but only the part that served his purposes. He left out the phrase "to guard you in all your ways" (*NIV*). He always either leaves out or adds to the Word. Neither is legitimate. The devil's motive is to "give carnal Christians Biblical reasons to support their foolish actions. Beware of taking promises out of their context, or claiming promises when you have not met the conditions" (*The Bible Exposition Commentary*). We cannot live by excerpts of the Word, but by the "whole counsel of God" (Acts 20:27, *NKJV*).

To deliberately put God to a test just to see if He will protect

Talk About It:
1. What did the Temple represent to the Jews? Why do you suppose the devil chose this as the second place of temptation?
2. How did Satan twist the meaning of Psalm 91:11, 12 in this test?
3. How can people "put the Lord . . . to the test" (v. 7, *NIV*)? Why is this wrong?

us is a sin. Daring God to intervene is an invitation to pain. Certainly there is nothing wrong with putting God to the test when we are moving by faith to carry out His will. Faith does include a measure of stepping into the unknown. However, faith and presumption are radically different. Jesus here referenced Deuteronomy 6:16: "Do not test the Lord your God as you did at Massah" (*NIV*). Israel was always testing God, but never in faith. They always demanded more, yet never believed God. We should be careful when we proposition God by saying, "Lord, I will do, but only if You do for me first." That is using God for selfish means.

D. The Third Test (vv. 8-11)

8. Again, the devil taketh him up into an exceeding high mountain, and sheweth him all the kingdoms of the world, and the glory of them;

9. And saith unto him, All these things will I give thee, if thou wilt fall down and worship me.

10. Then saith Jesus unto him, Get thee hence, Satan: for it is written, Thou shalt worship the Lord thy God, and him only shalt thou serve.

11. Then the devil leaveth him, and, behold, angels came and ministered unto him.

Jesus knew the plan He and the Father had put together in eternity past for the redemption of humanity. It required that He give His life as a sacrifice. Now Satan was offering a shortcut— one without pain and bloodshed. All He had to do was bow down and worship Satan. This would have been the ultimate insult to the Father, and the one thing Satan wanted (see Isaiah 14:12-14). Jesus knew this would not work. There is no short route to accomplishing God's will.

Satan had carried Jesus to a high mountain peak where He could view the kingdoms of the world. An old hymn says, "This is my Father's world," but the fact is that the world presently is under the dominion of Satan. Adam handed that dominion to him when he fell in the Garden. Jesus himself acknowledged Satan as "the prince of this world" (John 14:30), and believers are encouraged not to love the things of this world (1 John 2:15, 16). This is why we eagerly await the new heavens and new earth. God will ultimately have victory of all things, but Satan did have the authority to make his easy-out offer to Jesus. He promised Jesus the very same kingdoms of the earth which the Father will give Him, but without death. An old adage applies here: "There are some things worse than dying." Living in dishonor is one of them.

Jesus had resisted Satan long enough and simply told him to go away. This is the same command He later gave to Peter

Talk About It:

1. How could the devil "give" God's Son "all the kingdoms of the world" (vv. 8, 9)?

2. Describe different ways people "worship" Satan today. What do they hope to gain?

3. Compare Jesus' reply to Satan (v. 10) with the way we are instructed to reply in 1 Peter 5:8, 9. What makes this strategy successful?

Christ-Controlled Living

when the bewildered disciple tried to suggest He would not have to die (Matthew 16:23). Jesus was not actually rebuking Peter personally as being a devil, but rather the demonic suggestion he was making. Here, Jesus rebuked the real devil for asking for worship—something only God deserves—and referenced Deuteronomy 6:13.

This had been the ultimate test, and thus the confrontation ended. Angels then came to minister to Jesus (Matthew 4:11). He had been successful in relying on the Spirit to handle Satan's ploys. "He did not conjure up His own food but, like Elijah in the wilderness, received God's supernatural care" (*Moody Gospel Commentary—Matthew*). Remember, He was living by the power of the Spirit—just as we must do. We trust by faith that God has "ministering spirits" (Hebrews 1:14) watching over us.

II. WALKING IN THE SPIRIT (Galatians 5:16-25)
A. The Spirit Versus the Flesh (vv. 16-21)
(Galatians 5:19-21 is not included in the printed text.)

16. This I say then, Walk in the Spirit, and ye shall not fulfil the lust of the flesh.

17. For the flesh lusteth against the Spirit, and the Spirit against the flesh: and these are contrary the one to the other: so that ye cannot do the things that ye would.

18. But if ye be led of the Spirit, ye are not under the law.

There is a constant war going on inside of the believer. Like two fighting brothers, the spirit battles against one's flesh. By flesh (*sarx*) we do not mean the physical body, for it is neutral, but rather the fallen Adamic nature with its lusts and desires. The spirit (*pneuma*, or breath) is the "incorporeal part of a person, which (like breath) leaves at death" (*Zondervan NIV Bible Commentary*, Vol. 2). The spirit person knows to do right, but the evil nature constantly fights to sway the believer in the opposite direction.

For the believer, however, there is the added strength of having the Holy Spirit, or third person of the Trinity, living inside. Every believer has a measure of the Holy Spirit. When Jesus appeared to His disciples the evening after His resurrection, He "breathed on them and said, 'Receive the Holy Spirit'" (John 20:22, *NIV*). The infilling of the Spirit's baptism (as occurred on the Day of Pentecost in Acts 2) is a more intense empowerment by the Spirit for service in the Kingdom.

The only way for believers to consistently rise above the fleshly desires is to walk daily in harmony with the Spirit. The power of the Spirit gives us the ability to overcome the flesh. Otherwise, we fail miserably. Paul spoke of the fleshly believer when he said, "I do not understand what I do. For what I want to do I do not do,

"Only he who flings himself upward when the pull comes to drag him down, can hope to break the force of temptation. Temptation may be an invitation to hell, but much more is it an opportunity to reach heaven. At the moment of temptation, sin and righteousness are both very near the Christian; but, of the two, the latter is the nearer."

—Charles H. Bren

Talk About It:
1. How can you tell if you are walking in the Spirit?
2. Why does the flesh fight against the Holy Spirit?
3. Who will not inherit the kingdom of heaven? Why not?

but what I hate I do" (Romans 7:15, *NIV*). However, he also said that if we yield to the Spirit's leading, we are not bound by the Law (Galatians 5:18). In other words, it is hopeless to fight the flesh on our own; instead, we should surrender our will to the will of the Spirit. As we do this, we fulfill what the new covenant promises to us: "I will put my laws into their hearts, and in their minds will I write them" (Hebrews 10:16).

Verses 19-21 of the text list the ugly works that come from yielding to the flesh. "The flesh is able to manufacture sin but it can never produce the righteousness of God" (*The Bible Exposition Commentary*). This list includes many vices we normally would attribute to the devil. However, he doesn't have to be present for fleshly people to sin. The flesh is fully capable of conceiving wickedness on its own.

Paul says that the person who practices these things will not inherit God's kingdom. Obviously, we all fail sometimes—but we don't have to make a habit of doing so. Even though we are under grace, we cannot use this as an excuse to feed the fleshly desires. The flesh is determined to keep us bound by sin. We must live by the Holy Spirit, who wants us free from sin.

> "In the New Testament, *walking* emphasizes a way of life. As we walk in the power of the Spirit, we march in line with Him and walk the steps that the Spirit walks. As we follow the Spirit, the fruit of the Spirit flourishes in our life."
> —**French Arrington**

B. The Fruit of the Spirit (vv. 22, 23)

22. But the fruit of the Spirit is love, joy, peace, long-suffering, gentleness, goodness, faith,

23. Meekness, temperance: against such there is no law.

In stark contrast to the consequences of living by the flesh, we see here the wonderful results of actively yielding to the Holy Spirit. Note that the last of these, *temperance,* is the same as *self-control.* The fruit of the Spirit is not the same as the good works we do for Christ; rather, they are the attitudes developed by the Spirit's working in us. Fruit is not just the fact we are able to resist fleshly desires; it is the positive character qualities that blossom from the cooperation of human spirit with the Holy Spirit. Jesus used the metaphor of the vine and branches to illustrate this: "No branch can bear fruit by itself; it must remain in the vine. Neither can you bear fruit unless you remain in me" (John 15:4, *NIV*).

We should also distinguish the "fruit of the Spirit" from the "gifts of the Spirit." The fruit is manifested in the graces that come with character development by the Spirit's involvement. The gifts of the Spirit are special empowering abilities for service in the Kingdom.

The other eight aspects of the fruit of the Spirit are contained in the word *love. Joy* is love celebrating; *peace* is love at rest; *longsuffering* is love on trial; *gentleness* is love in society; *goodness* is love in action; *faith* is love on the battlefield; *meekness* is love in submission; *temperance* is love in process. Love is the cohesive force that blends all the fruit into one.

Talk About It:

1. Why is there "no law" against the fruit of the Spirit?

2. How is the fruit of the Spirit expressed in our emotions? Our relationships? Our attitudes?

> "Fruit of the Spirit is our identification as the body of Christ; it reveals to the world and to us that we are the disciples of Christ."
> —**Charles W. Conn**

C. Living by the Spirit (vv. 24, 25)

24. And they that are Christ's have crucified the flesh with the affections and lusts.

25. If we live in the Spirit, let us also walk in the Spirit.

Since the Galatian believers to whom Paul was writing already had the Holy Spirit, they certainly should be walking by the Spirit. To *walk* in the Spirit is to follow the nudgings and promptings He gives us. The believer must get in line with the Spirit if there is to be fruit. We might compare this to a marriage. A man may be married and wearing a wedding ring—while still letting his eyes wander, or engaging in flirtation with another woman. The fact of marriage doesn't automatically mean full devotion to the marriage. For there to be a true union, the marriage partners must look to each other and no one else. So we must look to the Holy Spirit and yield everything to Him.

Talk About It:
What does it mean to *crucify the flesh*? How can this be accomplished?

III. PRACTICING SELF-CONTROL (1 Corinthians 9:24-27)

A. Racing for the Prize (vv. 24, 25)

24. Know ye not that they which run in a race run all, but one receiveth the prize? So run, that ye may obtain.

25. And every man that striveth for the mastery is temperate in all things. Now they do it to obtain a corruptible crown; but we an incorruptible.

Paul pictures the Christian life as a race for a prize. The prize comes at the end of the race; therefore the race must be finished. And, though it is not a race against other people, it still must be won. He who runs a race has to put aside all other interests and live a self-controlled, focused life. "If athletes can give up their rights in order to win a fading olive-leaf crown, certainly Christians can lay aside privileges to win an eternal crown!" (*The Bible Exposition Commentary*). Believers must take on the mind-set of running like a champion. We aren't running just for the benefits of exercise. We want the prize. Paul had clearly defined his own personal race. He had to discipline his body, mind and spirit—focusing everything on the crown he would receive. What is the race? It is the calling that God puts on a life. Paul was called to be an apostle. Others are called to other tasks. Paul sacrificed everything for his apostolic calling.

striveth for the mastery (v. 25)— "competes in the games" (*NIV*)

Talk About It:
Compare the effort Christians should exert in following Christ to the physical training done by committed athletes. What is similar? What is different?

B. Beating the Air (vv. 26, 27)

26. I therefore so run, not as uncertainly; so fight I, not as one that beateth the air:

27. But I keep under my body, and bring it into subjection: lest that by any means, when I have preached to others, I myself should be a castaway.

Was Paul afraid of losing out completely with Christ if he stumbled and didn't finish the race? Probably not, though he

castaway (v. 27)— disqualified for the prize

1. How is Christian living like a race? Like a boxing match?

2. How could a believer become a "castaway"?

Self-Control Defined

The fruit known as *temperance* comes from a Greek term meaning "to hold oneself in, to have inner power"— hence, *self-control*.

Self-control implies the rational restraint of all natural impulses. It may, therefore, crown the list of virtues mentioned in connection with the conflict between the flesh and the Spirit.

—**T. David Sustar**

Daily Devotions:

M. Integrity and Self-Control
   Genesis 39:5-12
T. Disciplined Vigilance
   Nehemiah 5:16-23
W. Disciplined Speech
   Psalm 141:1-5
T. Love's Constraints
   2 Corinthians 5:14-20
F. Cure for Anxiety
   Philippians 4:4-9
S. Character Improvement
   2 Peter 1:3-11

was disappointed in those who had forsaken their race (see 2 Timothy 4:10). Paul was most concerned for doing the best he could. Nothing less was satisfactory. His passion was to fulfill what Christ had given him to do. If Christ had trusted him with such a calling, then he needed to live up to that trust. In his last letter to Timothy, we see that he was satisfied with how he had run. He wrote, "I have fought a good fight, I have finished my course, I have kept the faith" (4:7). He was looking forward to the crown of righteousness he had run so hard to obtain.

The phrase "beateth the air" is a boxing metaphor, but it has no connection to what we see today when one pretends to be boxing an invisible opponent. Paul was talking about making wild misses while in an actual boxing match. It means making dumb mistakes, detours, and side steps into selfish pursuits. Paul refused to lose focus and hurt his race.

CONCLUSION

In Romans 7, Paul describes the war between flesh and spirit that goes on in the heart of believers. Here he pictures the terrible conflict a person goes through when attempting to live righteously on his or her own. That person channels the energies of his flesh into obeying the Law, and fails terribly. Righteousness simply cannot be achieved by human merit. The flesh is too strong an adversary.

Praise God that Paul went on to show there is another way—living by the Spirit. He said, "Therefore, there is now no condemnation for those who are in Christ Jesus, because through Christ Jesus the law of the Spirit of life set me free from the law of sin and death" (8:1, 2, *NIV*).

GOLDEN TEXT CHALLENGE

"WALK IN THE SPIRIT, AND YE SHALL NOT FULFIL THE LUST OF THE FLESH" (Galatians 5:16).

Walking in the Spirit conveys the idea of continuous activity, motivated by, energized by, enabled by, and for the benefit of the Holy Spirit. It is living unceasingly for the glory of God. This walk indicates a calm and steady progress that is pleasing to God and productive in His service.

The alternative to this kind of life is the walk in the flesh, which is a self-centered, pleasure-seeking lifestyle that disregards the will of God and yields to temptations easily. It is neither victorious nor productive, and its only consistency is in the constant trouble that characterizes such a life.

Introduction to Summer Quarter

The first lesson for this quarter—"Why the Holy Spirit Came" (Pentecost Sunday)—was written by the Reverend Keith Whitt (see biographical information on page 129).

Unit 1 (lessons 2-6) was compiled and written by Lance Colkmire, editor of the *Evangelical Sunday School Lesson Commentary*. Those studies, under the theme "Living in Light and Love," are taken from the apostle John's three epistles.

The second unit of studies (lessons 7-13), "Christ in the Revelation," were written by the Reverend Keith Whitt. Here we see Christ reigning forever, speaking to the churches, redeeming His people, judging the world, triumphing over evil, establishing His kingdom, and making all things new.

Additional resource available from Pathway Press:

Apocalypse! A New Look at the Book of Revelation
by David C. Cooper
$10.99
Item # 087148-0433

Call 1-800-553-8506 or go to *www.pathwaybookstore.com*

June 4, 2006

Why the Holy Spirit Came (Pentecost)

John 14:15-26; 15:26, 27; 16:7-14;
Acts 2:1-4; Romans 8:26, 27

Unit Theme:
Pentecost

Central Truth:
The Holy Spirit enables us to live for Christ and make the gospel known to the world.

Focus:
Understand God's purpose in sending the Holy Spirit and rely on the Spirit's help for Christian living and witness.

Context:
Various New Testament passages concerning the Holy Spirit

Golden Text:
"When the Comforter is come, whom I will send unto you from the Father, even the Spirit of truth, which proceedeth from the Father, he shall testify of me" (John 15:26).

Study Outline:
I. The Spirit Came at Pentecost
(John 14:15-25; Acts 2:1-4)
II. The Spirit Helps Believers
(John 14:26; 16:12-14; Romans 8:26, 27)
III. The Spirit Convinces the World
(John 15:26, 27; 16:7-11)

INTRODUCTION

As we become more familiar with someone, there is a greater tendency to take that person for granted. This can be a problem for Pentecostals. As we become more accustomed to the Holy Spirit's presence, power and movement, we tend to take Him for granted. Subconsciously, we think we fully understand the Spirit's person and power. However, the Spirit is neither easily categorized by human terms nor contained by human motives. In accordance with the divine will, He goes where He pleases and works as He chooses (John 3:8).

In today's Scripture texts, "the Spirit of God" is called the "Spirit of truth," the "Holy Spirit" or "Holy Ghost" (both are from the same Greek word), and the "Comforter." This last term is rather complex. The Greek word (*parakletos*) is quite diverse in meaning. Its basic meaning is "one who is called alongside of another," a fitting description of the Spirit's activity in our lives. It also depicts one who is "an advocate, defender, intercessor" or "a helper, counselor, comforter." While the term is not applied to the Spirit in the Old Testament, the background for the term is there. First, there is the powerful relationship between a principal figure who leaves a successor to continue and expand his work (Moses and Joshua; Elijah and Elisha), just like Jesus and the Spirit. Second, the Spirit empowered individuals to interpret the activity of God in history, just as the Spirit today empowers believers to interpret the words of Jesus and His redeeming role in the world. Third, God broke into history to reveal His plans and purpose through various means, just as the Spirit breaks into our lives and unveils to us the significance of Jesus, His activity and words.

History reveals that the Spirit abides with and works through those who seek and assist Him. If He does not have the liberty in a church or denomination to fulfill His will, He finds others to use who are submitted fully to Him. History also reveals that the present move of God usually is persecuted by those who were part of the previous move of God. Instead of trying to put the Spirit in a box and tell Him what He can or cannot do (domesticate Him), let us reaffirm our commitment to humbly allow Him to release His power, fulfill His plan, and accomplish His purpose in and through us.

I. THE SPIRIT CAME AT PENTECOST
(John 14:15-25; Acts 2:1-4)

A. The Conditions of the Promise (John 14:15, 19-25)

15. If ye love me, keep my commandments.

19. Yet a little while, and the world seeth me no more; but ye see me: because I live, ye shall live also.

20. At that day ye shall know that I am in my Father, and ye in me, and I in you.

21. He that hath my commandments, and keepeth them, he it is that loveth me: and he that loveth me shall be loved of my Father, and I will love him, and will manifest myself to him.

22. Judas saith unto him, not Iscariot, Lord, how is it that thou wilt manifest thyself unto us, and not unto the world?

23. Jesus answered and said unto him, If a man love me, he will keep my words: and my Father will love him, and we will come unto him, and make our abode with him.

24. He that loveth me not keepeth not my sayings: and the word which ye hear is not mine, but the Father's which sent me.

25. These things have I spoken unto you, being yet present with you.

Interestingly, Jesus' teaching on the Holy Spirit begins with a commandment that stands out from the context: "If ye love me, keep my commandments" (v. 15). The implication is that the Spirit comes conditionally. We must be obedient to the commandments of Jesus (fulfill the conditions) to receive the Spirit. It is a theme that is repeated throughout this opening passage (vv. 15, 21, 23, 24).

An axiom of Pentecostal wisdom—"The Holy Spirit will not dwell in an unclean vessel"—is being challenged these days. Some whose lifestyles remain unchanged still claim to be Spirit-filled. Later in this lesson we find that the Spirit does help us purge things from our lives that are not pleasing to God. Perhaps the saying should be changed to "The Holy Spirit does not dwell in a vessel that remains unclean."

Jesus makes it clear that character and conduct do count and that reception of this gift of the Spirit is contingent upon continued submission to the Word of God. In verse 24, He states it negatively: If we do not love Him, we will not keep His sayings. The conclusion is that continued disobedience of His sayings brings the quality of our love into question. In other words, our love is demonstrated by our persistent submission to the Word and will of God. The grammar reveals that Jesus is talking about continued obedience and disobedience, not temporary failures or isolated acts of disobedience. He is addressing the lifestyle of Christians. To further emphasize the

Talk About It:
1. How do we prove our love (or lack of love) for Jesus Christ (vv. 15, 24)?
2. What two promises did Jesus make to His followers in verse 19, and how are they related?
3. How did Jesus promise to "manifest" Himself to His followers (vv. 20-23)?

importance of conduct based on a transformed character, He notes that these words are from the Father.

B. The Promise of the Comforter (vv. 16-18)

16. And I will pray the Father, and he shall give you another Comforter, that he may abide with you for ever;

17. Even the Spirit of truth; whom the world cannot receive, because it seeth him not, neither knoweth him: but ye know him; for he dwelleth with you, and shall be in you.

18. I will not leave you comfortless: I will come to you.

Talk About It:
1. Why did the disciples need "another Comforter" (v. 16)?
2. Why can't the world receive "the Spirit of truth" (v. 17)?

Jesus promises to "pray the Father" for "another Comforter." *Pray* carries the idea of requesting something, usually with a sense of urgency. He knows believers *need* this Comforter—One who will replace Him on the face of the earth. The ministry of the Holy Spirit does not replace that of Jesus' but rather complements Jesus' ministry, as *another* means "of the same quality or kind." The Spirit is given to us as a result of Jesus' request to the Father. He is entrusted to us as an investment from which the Father expects a profit. This profit is not money or earthly treasure, but an expansion of the Kingdom, both in us (to produce fruit) and through us (to produce disciples).

The Spirit abides with believers (v. 16). This is not a mere existence, nor just a reliable presence alongside of believers, though that is true. The Spirit (who is the presence of God) sojourns with us everywhere we go—through the mountaintop *and* valley experiences. This abiding presence of the Spirit also serves as a continual, sanctifying force in the life of the believer, enabling him or her to persevere regardless of the circumstances faced. His living presence makes us true worshipers, for true worship requires worshiping in the Spirit and truth (John 4:24). True worship is not ritual confined to a physical location, but an experience which demands that the world and its forces release their grip on us. The Spirit ushers us into the very presence of God. We meet God, commune with Him, and rededicate ourselves to Him. We are transformed and empowered through this experience and the steadfast presence of the Spirit. He not only dwells *with* us, but resides *within* us! The assurance of continual presence is reinforced throughout John (7:37-39; 15:26, 27).

The Comforter is "the Spirit of truth" (14:17), whom the world cannot receive. There is a great contrast depicted here. The kingdom of God operates on the basis of truth, while the world operates on the basis of deceit; consequently, the world itself is deceived. For that reason, the world is not able to receive the Spirit, because they neither perceive God ("see") nor have a relationship with Him ("know"). In emphatic language, Jesus

Why the Holy Spirit Came

reminds the disciples they do know God. *Know* conveys intimate knowledge and relationship that is progressive in nature. The more time we spend with God, the more we become like Him, for we "see" Him as He is. It is knowledge that encompasses mind, body and soul. Every realm of life is transformed by this knowledge.

The last part of verse 17 gives us insight into the role of the Spirit before Pentecost. He was dwelling with the disciples, but inhabitation or infilling was forthcoming. At salvation, we are baptized by the Spirit into the body of Christ (1 Corinthians 12:13; see also Romans 8:9). The Spirit dwells within us. In Spirit baptism, Jesus baptizes us into the Spirit, who then fills us with His power and presence (Matthew 3:11). A person can dwell in a house with limited amenities, but filling the house requires moving all of his or her possessions into it and filling it with his or her personality and presence. Let us be full of the Spirit!

Jesus also promises He will not leave believers "comfortless" (John 14:18). This is a twofold promise. First, He says He will not leave believers as "orphans" (the literal translation). Because of the Spirit's abiding presence and power, believers are not abandoned, deprived or unprotected. While we should not press the analogy too far, the Spirit is the presence of Jesus in Jesus' absence. He continues the ministry of Jesus in us and through us. Second, Jesus promises that He has not deserted believers, for He will return again (vv. 1-3).

Falling on God

In many relationship seminars, the participants are encouraged to close their eyes and fall back into the arms of another person. This is done to establish trust. It goes against the grain of human nature (or experience) to place ourselves in the hands of another. Yet, this is exactly what we must do in our Spirit-filled walk. The Spirit is there to lead, establish, and hold onto us, if we will trust Him fully. We must "fall" into His waiting arms.

C. Fulfillment of the Promise (Acts 2:1-4)

1. And when the day of Pentecost was fully come, they were all with one accord in one place.

2. And suddenly there came a sound from heaven as of a rushing mighty wind, and it filled all the house where they were sitting.

3. And there appeared unto them cloven tongues like as of fire, and it sat upon each of them.

4. And they were all filled with the Holy Ghost, and began to speak with other tongues, as the Spirit gave them utterance.

The New Testament presupposes that all believers are (or will be) Spirit-filled (John 7:39; Acts 19:2; Ephesians 5:18). This experience was not an option for the early believers, nor should it be for believers today. Instead, we should keep being filled with the Spirit on an ongoing basis. It is not a onetime event. The promises of the Spirit as recorded in John's Gospel (and elsewhere) are fulfilled in the Book of Acts. The first recorded fulfillment (ch. 2) highlights at least five important aspects.

First, *there is the emphasis on unity* (v. 1). The believers were where Jesus told them to be (Luke 24:49). They anticipated

Talk About It:
1. What does it mean to be in "one accord" (v. 1), and why was this important?
2. Why are the words "all" (v. 4) and "each of them" (v. 3) important?

3. Explain the term "as the Spirit gave them utterance" (v. 4).

"The sound of wind signified that the Spirit was with the disciples; the fiery tongues that rested on each of them were a manifestation of God's glory.... Speaking in tongues —an outward, visible, audible sign— attested that the disciples had been baptized with the Spirit. The sound of wind and the sight of fiery tongues pointed to the uniqueness of the occasion, but tongues marked the enduement of the disciples with supernatural power."

—French Arrington

receiving the promise of the Father (Acts 1:4). They were of one heart (1:14; 2:1). Unity is not uniformity. We do not have to be alike or even agree on everything, including minor doctrine. Scripture is full of diversity. However, we must have an agreed-upon purpose. We can be a diverse people, holding to a common purpose—to worship God to the best of our ability and provide Him vessels through which to accomplish His purpose.

Second, *there is the prominence of power* (v. 2). There was loud noise and a violent, forceful wind, whose origin is clearly identified as divine. The word *Spirit* is translated from the same word that is used for "wind" or "breath." Here, however, a different word is used for *wind*, a word that can also mean "to exhale" (see John 20:22). When God exhales, there is power (Genesis 2:7; Job 4:9).

Third, *purity is emphasized through the disbursed ("cloven") tongues of fire that rested upon each of them* (v. 3). Fire is a symbol of God's purification process (Matthew 3:12). In fact, God himself is a consuming fire (Hebrews 12:29). When His fire touches us, the impure is purged out, and His character and image are burned in (Isaiah 6:6, 7).

Fourth, *they were all "filled with the Holy Ghost"* (v. 4a). The word *filled* carries two distinct ideas. It can refer to the fulfillment of prophecy (Luke 21:22), and it can mean "to be filled with, or experience completely." The promise was fulfilled and the disciples experienced the power of that promise. Do we?

Finally, *as the Spirit gave them the ability, they spoke in tongues* (v. 4b). Speaking in tongues is evidence, not the totality of the experience. There is more to being Spirit-filled than glossolalia, though this is an important element that provides *edification* (builds up the inner person), *inspiration* (motivates enthusiasm), *intercession* (improves the effectiveness of prayer), *revelation* (enables us to hear the voice of God), and *a sign to unbelievers*. Yet, the Spirit-filled life must not stop here. We must offer ourselves as vessels through which God can work.

II. THE SPIRIT HELPS BELIEVERS
(John 14:26; 16:12-14; Romans 8:26, 27)
A. The Wise Teacher (John 14:26)

26. But the Comforter, which is the Holy Ghost, whom the Father will send in my name, he shall teach you all things, and bring all things to your remembrance, whatsoever I have said unto you.

Jesus promises that the "Comforter" ("one called alongside to help"), whom He clearly identifies as the Holy Spirit, will be dispatched from heaven to earth. The unity and cooperation of the Trinity are clearly displayed in this verse, as the Spirit is sent by the Father in the name of the Son. The Spirit's mission includes

Talk About It:
According to this verse, what ministries would the Holy Spirit perform?

illuminating and enlarging or extending the words of Jesus. He instructs those who are willing. The Spirit creates an environment that enables us to learn those things that are necessary for a vital relationship with God and His creation. Also, He helps us understand our place of ministry in the Kingdom. Further, He causes us to think again on ("remember") the things which Jesus has spoken. Every time we reflect on the Word, new insight and understanding occurs, and the Spirit is given the opportunity to make them relevant for our time and circumstances.

B. The Master Guide (16:12-14)

12. I have yet many things to say unto you, but ye cannot bear them now.

13. Howbeit when he, the Spirit of truth, is come, he will guide you into all truth: for he shall not speak of himself; but whatsoever he shall hear, that shall he speak: and he will shew you things to come.

14. He shall glorify me: for he shall receive of mine, and shall shew it unto you.

In a little over three years Jesus said and did some phenomenal things in the presence of the disciples. It had to be difficult to comprehend all of this, and there was more to come; but Jesus knew they were unable to receive more at this point (v. 12). Human limitations require that revelation be progressive or revealed at a pace we can absorb. We receive and learn truths about God "precept upon precept, line upon line, here a little, there a little" (Isaiah 28:10, NKJV).

Jesus promised that "the Spirit of truth" would guide His followers into truths and along paths that would be beneficial to them and the Kingdom (John 16:13). The Holy Spirit only speaks the truth, as opposed to the spirit of lies and deceit in the world, and He speaks that which He hears from God. As such, He serves as an example for believers, guiding us to be like Jesus Christ.

His primary purpose is to glorify Jesus, by taking the things of Christ and expounding them to believers (vv. 14, 15). He reveals to us the words, works and character of the Son. Through the activity of the Spirit in our lives, we in turn have deeper insight into Jesus and the things He did, which serve as an example of what we are to do. In brief, the Spirit reveals the Son. The Son reveals the Father. The disciple or believer is to receive deeper insight, wisdom and ability, which allows us to reveal the character of God through our living witness (words and activity) to those in our lives.

C. The Perfect Intercessor (Romans 8:26, 27)

26. Likewise the Spirit also helpeth our infirmities: for

Talk About It:
How does the Holy Spirit carry on and expand Jesus' ministry?

"The Holy Spirit is not a blessing from God, He is God."
—**Colin Urquhart**

we know not what we should pray for as we ought: but the Spirit itself maketh intercession for us with groanings which cannot be uttered.

27. And he that searcheth the hearts knoweth what is the mind of the Spirit, because he maketh intercession for the saints according to the will of God.

Talk About It:
1. Why do we sometimes "know not what we should pray" (v. 26)?
2. What is so wonderful about the Holy Spirit's intercession on our behalf (vv. 26, 27)?

Paul's inspired teaching concerning the Spirit in these verses builds upon the foundation of the previous verses. He notes that "likewise," or "in the same way," the Spirit helps us to have hope in the midst of things that we anticipate and believe, yet have not seen come to fruition (see vv. 22-25). The Spirit literally comes alongside of us and takes hold of us ("helpeth") in the midst of our powerlessness, sickness and inability. In those times that words seem to fail or our minds fail to comprehend our circumstances, He is there to help us. He intercedes exceedingly or above what we are able to do, going directly into the throne room to represent us as an advocate and intercessor. Further, He also interacts with our spirit, helping us to express through spiritual means ("groanings which cannot be uttered," v. 26) emotions so intense that we cannot express them through normal human faculties.

With the aid of the Holy Spirit, we are able to pray according to the perfect will of God (v. 27). As God intently examines ("searcheth") our hearts, we are brought into conformity with the will of God. The Spirit intercedes for us and prays for the perfect will of God to be accomplished, and He helps us to pray the same.

III. THE SPIRIT CONVINCES THE WORLD
(John 15:26, 27; 16:7-11)
A. Divine Witness for Believers (15:26, 27)

26. But when the Comforter is come, whom I will send unto you from the Father, even the Spirit of truth, which proceedeth from the Father, he shall testify of me:

27. And ye also shall bear witness, because ye have been with me from the beginning.

Talk About It:
How should believers partner with the Holy Spirit in ministry?

Again, the unity and collaboration of the Trinity is highlighted. The Spirit of truth is sent "from" the presence of the Father (from whom He proceeds) by Jesus (cf. 14:16) to testify of Him. The complexity of the Trinity is revealed in this verse. There are not three Gods, but one God eternally existing in three persons. No illustration explains sufficiently the nature of the triune Godhead; however, the analogy of a triangle is helpful. There are three sides to a triangle, yet there are not three triangles. If one side of the triangle ever ceases to serve its function or is absent, there is no longer a triangle. The three sides make it what it is.

The sending of the Spirit from the Father parallels the sending of the Son by the Father on a divine mission to humanity. The Spirit's mission is to testify of Jesus, and He fulfills this in part through the anointed ministry of the disciples. Testimony or witness is a key theme in the Gospel of John, where several testify or bear witness of Jesus, including John the Baptist (1:15), the Father (8:18), the disciples (15:27), the crowds (12:17), the Scriptures (5:39), Jesus' works (10:25), and Jesus himself (18:37).

B. Abiding Comforter for Believers (16:7)

7. Nevertheless I tell you the truth; It is expedient for you that I go away: for if I go not away, the Comforter will not come unto you; but if I depart, I will send him unto you.

In John 16, Christ shared with His disciples that He was going back to the Father. The disciples were filled with grief at the news of Jesus' soon departure. He explained to them it was for their good He was going away. This was hard for them to understand. How could it be for their good that He leave them? He had been their Comforter, their Counselor, their Helper, and now He spoke of leaving them for their good.

Then Christ told them that if He did not go away, the Holy Spirit would not come to them, but if He departed, He would send the Spirit. Thus Peter could say of the outpouring of the Spirit on the Day of Pentecost: "This Jesus . . . having received of the Father the promise of the Holy Ghost, he hath shed forth this, which ye now see and hear" (Acts 2:32, 33).

While the disciples could only be with Jesus as long as they were in His physical presence, the Holy Spirit would come to live in them and abide with them forever. Thus, it could be said it was for their good that Jesus go away.

C. Divine Witness for Unbelievers (vv. 8-11)

8. And when he is come, he will reprove the world of sin, and of righteousness, and of judgment:

9. Of sin, because they believe not on me;

10. Of righteousness, because I go to my Father, and ye see me no more;

11. Of judgment, because the prince of this world is judged.

One function of the Holy Spirit is to make the world conscious of sin, righteousness and judgment. It is His business to make the people of this world aware that there is such a thing as sin. When the Spirit convicts people of sin, they are stirred to action. When Peter preached in the power of the Spirit on the Day of Pentecost, the crowd was made to feel guilt for their sin: "Now when they heard this, they were pricked in their heart, and said unto Peter and to the rest of the apostles, Men and brethren, what shall we do?" (Acts 2:37).

expedient for you (v. 7)—"good for you"

Talk About It:
1. Why would "the Comforter" not come to the disciples until Jesus went away?
2. Describe the Holy Spirit's ministry to the world.

Not only did the Holy Spirit come to convict people of sin; He came to declare that the essence of sin is the refusal to believe on Christ. This was the heart of Peter's sermon. He accused his hearers of failure to believe on Christ and of crucifying the promised Messiah and Redeemer. When this truth was brought home by the Holy Spirit, many of the hearers sought divine mercy.

The Holy Spirit also convicts the world regarding righteousness. Outside of Him, there is no righteousness that is acceptable to God. The evidence of our acceptance comes when He sends His Spirit into our heart to bear witness to the righteousness of Christ in us. Someone has said, "The presence of the Spirit in the midst of the church is the proof of the presence of Christ in the midst of the Throne."

The Holy Spirit also thereby convicts the world of judgment, assuring us that righteousness will be victorious. The prince of this world—Satan—has been judged. Christ gained total victory over him at Calvary. He is an eternally defeated foe. Every believer has victory over the entire evil empire through Christ. The Spirit bears witness to this truth.

CONCLUSION

The Spirit is an advocate, intercessor, comforter and encourager, and He is more. It is the Spirit who takes the words and works of Christ and gives them meaning, both in and through our lives. There is a parallel here for those who desire to be filled with the Spirit. There must be obedience to the Father, reliance upon the Son, and surrender to the Spirit. We must be in unity with those in our lives, and we must believe that God's Word can be actualized in our lives through the abiding presence of the Spirit.

GOLDEN TEXT CHALLENGE

"WHEN THE COMFORTER IS COME, WHOM I WILL SEND UNTO YOU FROM THE FATHER, EVEN THE SPIRIT OF TRUTH, WHICH PROCEEDETH FROM THE FATHER, HE SHALL TESTIFY OF ME" (John 15:26).

The outpoured, indwelling Holy Spirit changed fearful, disturbed, impotent disciples (see John 20:19) into courageous, powerful proclaimers of Christ. They became apostles fulfilling His mission—spreading the gospel of the Kingdom, healing the sick and lame, cleansing the lepers, casting out devils, raising the dead.

During Jesus' last personal teaching session with the disciples before His death, He gave them a short discourse on what they could expect from the world—hatred and persecution (15:18-25). He quickly followed His warning with a promise: "When the Comforter is come . . . " (v. 26).

The Pentecostal experience (Acts 2:4) brought to the confused disciples the fulfillment of His promised, empowering comfort. Fears were dispelled; confusions were clarified; the revelation of Jesus Christ as King of a spiritual kingdom was opened to His followers by the Holy Spirit's ministry. In today's world, where Jesus' followers are often confused, persecuted, abused, misused, mistreated and hated, the promise of John 15:26 is as much for sanctified believers as it was to those earliest disciples who needed His comfort.

The ministering Holy Spirit occupies a prominent place in the New Testament (mentioned 93 times—50 times in Acts alone). He therefore, should occupy a conspicuous place in the church and in the lives of individual members. When that happens, the name of Jesus Christ is lifted up and people are drawn to Him, for that is the Holy Spirit's purpose.

Daily Devotions:

M. Anointed by the Spirit
1 Samuel 16:10-13

T. Led by the Spirit
Ezekiel 3:10-14

W. Born of the Spirit
John 3:1-8

T. Ministry by the Spirit
Acts 6:8-15

F. Witness of the Spirit
Romans 8:12-17

S. Filled With the Spirit
Ephesians 5:15-21

Fellowship in the Light

I John 1:1 through 2:16

Unit Theme:
Living in Light and Love (1, 2 and 3 John)

Central Truth:
As we walk in His light, Christ makes possible fellowship with God and other believers.

Focus:
Understand that the Christian life is fellowship with God and other believers, and walk in His light.

Context:
Written to an unnamed audience by the apostle John

Golden Text:
"If we walk in the light, as he is in the light, we have fellowship one with another, and the blood of Jesus Christ his Son cleanseth us from all sin" (1 John 1:7).

Study Outline:
I. The Word of Life (1 John 1:1-4)
II. Walk in the Light (1 John 1:5—2:2)
III. Walk in Obedience (1 John 2:3-16)

INTRODUCTION

The apostle John is the author of five New Testament books: the Gospel that bears his name, three epistles, and the Revelation. John does not use his name in the three epistles and does not identify the destination of the first two. From the earliest Christian tradition, however, all three letters have been accepted as the work of the apostle.

The first letter is a statement of doctrine concerning the person and work of Jesus Christ, the love of God, and the effect of that love in believers' lives. The epistle is a warm, intimate writing that explains what it means to be a Christian. The intent of the letter is to lead believers into a deeper spiritual life. John wants his spiritual children to be firmly established in the truth. Twice he states the reason for writing: "that your joy may be full" (1:4) and "that ye may know that ye have eternal life, and that ye may believe on the name of the Son of God" (5:13).

The letter was also written to warn the readers against the heretical influences that were gaining sway at that time. The Gnostics denied that Jesus had a physical body, but was only a spirit-like appearance of God on earth (2:22; 4:2, 3, 15). John wrote in order to affirm that Jesus had lived and suffered in the flesh (5:6). John declared he knew these facts because he had seen Jesus with his own eyes and had touched Him with his own hands (1:1-3).—Charles W. Conn

I. THE WORD OF LIFE (1 John 1:1-4)
A. God in the Flesh (vv. 1, 2)
1. That which was from the beginning, which we have heard, which we have seen with our eyes, which we have looked upon, and our hands have handled, of the Word of life;

2. (For the life was manifested, and we have seen it, and bear witness, and shew unto you that eternal life, which was with the Father, and was manifested unto us;)

When John wrote his three letters (1, 2 and 3 John), he confronted a growing gnostic influence and heresy. This heresy was the belief that Jesus was merely a phantom of sight and that the Son of God was not truly man.

This is why John's defense of the gospel in these letters has a similar beginning to his Gospel record. John 1:1 and 1 John 1:1 have very similar opening clauses, focusing on the beginnings of the gospel message in Jesus. The beginning is a reference to the eternal life Jesus had with the Father.

The passage in 1 John 1:1 has four main verbs. The first two, "we have heard . . . we have seen," denote a present condition based on a prior fact or action. Thus, John can say as a present reality that what he, and others (note the *we*), actually heard and saw was truly the Son of God.

The last two verbs focus on the historical reality of what they saw and heard. The phrase "we have looked upon" denotes an attentive viewing of Jesus. In other words, they actually saw Him and not some ghostlike form of the Messiah. The verb phrase *have handled* has the sense of the hands touching a surface. It means to actually feel. It is the same word used in Luke 24:39, when the risen Jesus spoke to His frightened disciples: "Behold my hands and my feet, that it is I myself: *handle* me, and see; for a spirit hath not flesh and bones, as ye see me have."

Jesus is the eternal Word of God. When He became flesh, He was fully accessible to humanity. John knew beyond a shadow of doubt that the divine Logos, "which was with the Father" (1 John 1:2), had been manifested to the disciples. At the end of the first century, there was no doubt among Christians that Jesus was the eternal Son of God.

B. Divine Fellowship (v. 3)
3. That which we have seen and heard declare we unto you, that ye also may have fellowship with us: and truly our fellowship is with the Father, and with his Son Jesus Christ.

Christ was the revelation of God. This is the glory, and the mystery, of the Incarnation: The clearest revelation of God is

Talk About It:
1. What title is Jesus given in verse 1? What does it signify?
2. What was John's testimony (v. 2)?

"All that I am I owe to Jesus, revealed to me in His divine book."
—David Livingstone

Jesus Christ. If you know Jesus, you know God. The people in Judea and Galilee who saw Jesus with their eyes were actually seeing God. God's desire to be known and to fellowship with humanity was so great that He was willing to allow His Son to take human flesh and become as one of us.

The verbs *have seen* and *heard* are in the Greek perfect tense, denoting a present reality based on a prior action. Thus, John was saying that what he presently declared was based on the fact that he, and others, actually saw and heard the Word made flesh (see John 1:14). He was an eyewitness to the glory of God in Christ. He also preached only what he had seen and heard from Christ. The preaching of the gospel is not the preaching of our ideas; it is what we have seen and heard in Jesus. For John that was first-person, eyewitness preaching. For us, it is the preaching of Jesus as He is revealed in the Bible and as we have personally experienced Him. The Bible is our source for knowledge of Jesus. To hear Him speak today is to listen to the Word of God. To see Him act today is to recognize that His same power to save and deliver illustrated in the Gospels is still working among those who believe.

The theme of "fellowship" is important in 1 John. John indicated that the purpose of proclaiming the gospel was to enable people to be in fellowship with God and with other believers. The Bible does not know of a fellowship with God that excludes fellowship with other Christians. Neither does it know of genuine Christian fellowship without fellowship with God. The person who wants to have a real relationship with God must do so in conjunction with the Christian community.

"A habit of devout fellowship with God is the spring of all our life, and the strength of it."
—H.E. Manning

Some skeptics say they believe in God but don't want to have anything to do with the church. They think church people are hypocrites. But sadly, what they experience as a relationship with God is actually not a relationship at all, because they are cut off from genuine Christian fellowship.

C. Full Joy (v. 4)

4. And these things write we unto you, that your joy may be full.

Talk About It:
What is joy, and
how does one
receive it?

"These things" refers to all the material in John's first epistle. Under the inspiration of the Holy Spirit, he had written this letter for the purpose of fulfilled joy. If believers would hear his words and obey them, the result would be "complete" joy (*NIV*).

Whose joy is he talking about? In studying the original language, it is hard to determine if the phrase should read "your joy" or "our joy." For John, probably one could not have existed without the other. If the readers would believe in the incarnation of Jesus, enter into fellowship with Him, and have fellowship with one another, they would experience a fullness of joy that cannot otherwise be known. And this would bring complete joy to John's heart.

In John 15:11, Jesus described the joy that comes from abiding in Him as the life-giving Vine: "These things have I spoken unto you, that my joy might remain in you, and that your joy might be full."

The sense of completeness and fulfillment that comes from serving Christ is available from no other source. To those of us who have never seen Christ, yet believe in Him, Peter wrote, "Though now you do not see Him, yet believing, you rejoice with joy inexpressible and full of glory, receiving the end of your faith—the salvation of your souls" (1 Peter 1:8, 9, *NKJV*).

II. WALK IN THE LIGHT (1 John 1:5–2:2)
A. The Declaration (v. 5)

5. This then is the message which we have heard of him, and declare unto you, that God is light, and in him is no darkness at all.

John gave us three statements in his writings that are revelations of the nature of God. In the Gospel of John, he declared that "God is spirit" (4:24, *NIV*); in 1 John 1:5, "God is light"; in 4:8, "God is love."

Talk About It:
Why is "Light" an appropriate name for God?

What did the apostle mean when he said God is light and does not have any darkness in Him? We have to remember the kind of world John lived in at the time he wrote. People believed in all kinds of idols and false gods. They did not expect these to be any more perfect or holy or pure or good than themselves. In fact, they expected to find all the evil things in their gods that they found in themselves and in one another. But then John said we have a message from Jesus Christ informing us that in God there is no darkness of sin, for He is perfectly holy. There is no darkness of error in Him, for He is perfect wisdom. There is no darkness of deceit in Him, for He is all truth. There is no darkness of hatred in Him, for He is love. There is no darkness of any kind in Him, for it is His nature to be light.

B. The Conclusion (vv. 6-8)

6. If we say that we have fellowship with him, and walk in darkness, we lie, and do not the truth:

7. But if we walk in the light, as he is in the light, we have fellowship one with another, and the blood of Jesus Christ his Son cleanseth us from all sin.

8. If we say that we have no sin, we deceive ourselves, and the truth is not in us.

John includes himself with those to whom he is writing when he says, "If we say." He recognized that all people are capable of making the error he is going to talk about.

Talk About It:
1. What does it mean to "walk in darkness" (v. 6)?
2. What are the benefits of walking "in the light" (v. 7)?
3. According to verse 8, how do some people deceive themselves? Why is this serious?

The error John refers to is professing fellowship with God while walking in darkness. Fellowship is equal to communion with God, such as Adam and Eve had with God in the Garden before the Fall. The word *walk* in the New Testament refers to one's total way of life.

Concerning the statement "We lie, and do not the truth," Alfred Plummer wrote, "This is not mere repetition, for lying is falsehood in speech, but not doing the truth includes false actions as well as false words. A life in moral darkness can no more have communion with God than a life in a coalpit can have communion with the sun. Light can be shut out, but it cannot be shut in" (*The Cambridge Bible*).

"God is light; we walk in it. The requirement for fellowship is to let the light reveal right and wrong and then to respond to that light continually. The Christian never becomes light until his body is changed, but he must walk in response to light while here on earth. Two consequences follow—first, 'fellowship with one another,' then cleansing," comments Wycliffe.

"Walking in the light shows up our sins and frailties; thus we need constant cleansing, and this is available on the basis of the death of Christ. The verb is in the present tense and it refers to the cleansing in sanctification."

Dr. H.G. Woods, in his book *At the Temple Church*, wrote concerning verse 8: "Perhaps we do not sufficiently realize our sinfulness because our standard of conduct is too low. Perhaps our self-examination is not strict enough to enable us to know ourselves thoroughly. Perhaps we underestimate the area of our accountability. Think of the sins of omission. How seldom people take themselves sufficiently to task for the good which they have left undone!" All these are methods of self-deception, leaving us thinking of ourselves more highly than we ought to think.

> "A man who believes himself a sinner, who feels himself sinful, is already at the gates of the kingdom of heaven."
> —Francois Mauriac

C. The Confession (vv. 9, 10)

9. If we confess our sins, he is faithful and just to forgive us our sins, and to cleanse us from all unrighteousness.

10. If we say that we have not sinned, we make him a liar, and his word is not in us.

John did not tell us how, when or where to confess our sins. This is not as important as it is to confess. The emphasis is on the fact that we must admit and acknowledge our sins to God. True Christians want to do this in order to obtain remission and forgiveness.

In forgiving our sins, God is faithful because He is keeping His promise; at the same time He is just and right because we are pleading the atonement for sin which satisfies infinite justice.

God does two things for us when He forgives us. He remits

Talk About It:
1. How do we receive forgiveness (v. 9)?
2. Explain the phrase "make him [God] a liar" (v. 10).

the punishment due us because of our sins, and He cleanses us from the guilt and pollution caused by our sins. He saves us from the past, and He introduces us to a future of purity.

Denying our sinfulness is more than just lying (v. 6), more than self-deception (v. 8). It is charging God himself with lying (v. 10). God has declared that we are sinners. He has asserted our need for salvation from our sin by sending His Son to die on the cross for us.

We have God's Word in us when we receive it in our hearts, hold it in faith, and are governed by it. But when we close our hearts to it and believe, hold and follow something else, His Word is not in us. When this happens, we are making God a liar.

D. The Advocate (2:1, 2)

1. My little children, these things write I unto you, that ye sin not. And if any man sin, we have an advocate with the Father, Jesus Christ the righteous:

2. And he is the propitiation for our sins: and not for ours only, but also for the sins of the whole world.

Calling his readers "my little children," John is obviously speaking to those who have been cleansed from sin and have fellowship with God. He does not now speak of the sinful nature of humanity but of the occasion of sin in those who are cleansed. He uses the word *if* in raising the question, and identifies the remedy if sin should appear in the life of one who has been cleansed. His acknowledgment that sin is possible does not in any way justify or encourage sin among Christians. He simply acknowledges its possibility and gives direction in the event a sin is committed.

If a Christian should lapse into an act of sin, he should not regard it as being fatal to his relationship with God. Instead, he has an Advocate, the Lord Jesus Christ, with God the Father. An advocate is one who stands at the bar of justice to intercede for another. The picture John gives us is one of sublime power and beauty. He pictures Jesus as a lawyer, at the bar of justice, appealing to the Judge of the universe for mercy on our behalf. His advocacy is on the grounds of His blood that was shed for the redemption of our sins. The motivation is His love that caused Him to shed His blood for us.

Jesus died for all of our sins, and for the sins of the whole world, so surely this will cover any momentary shortcoming that a Christian may have. His work is not to drive away but to restore people to fellowship with God in spite of failures. The entire sense of this assurance is that God does not cast us aside every time we disobey or displease Him. This is great reassurance without being a condonement of sin in the life of the Christian.

"Confession is always free. But that doesn't mean that confession is always easy. Sometimes it is hard. Incredibly hard. It is painful (sometimes literally) to admit our sins and trust ourselves to God's care."
—Erwin Lutzer

propitiation (v. 2)— atoning sacrifice

Talk About It:
1. Why do people need an *advocate*?
2. Whom is Jesus Christ willing to represent before His Father?

III. WALK IN OBEDIENCE (1 John 2:3-16)

A. Keep His Commands (vv. 3-6)

3. And hereby we do know that we know him, if we keep his commandments.

4. He that saith, I know him, and keepeth not his commandments, is a liar, and the truth is not in him.

perfected (v. 5)—
matured

5. But whoso keepeth his word, in him verily is the love of God perfected: hereby know we that we are in him.

6. He that saith he abideth in him ought himself also so to walk, even as he walked.

Talk About It:

1. Who is a liar (v. 4)?

2. How do we "know" we are in" God (v. 5)?

The first proof that we know God is that we keep His commandments. The preceding verses show the advocacy of Jesus Christ in the event of sin in our lives, but verse 3 reveals that we cannot keep on sinning, or live a life of sin, and expect to have fellowship with God. If we truly know and love God, our greatest desire in life will be to do His will.

In John's day, as well as our own, some claimed to know God but violated His will and Word. Verse 4 is similar to John's statement in 1:10, but there is a difference. In 2:4, there are some who claim to be Christian and yet fail to adhere to the will or purposes of God. In both instances, the pretense is a lie. If a person knows God and has fellowship with Him, he or she will abide in the truth of God.

The love of God is "perfected" in those who adhere to the Word of God (v. 5). As love is made complete in us, we come to have knowledge and assurance that we are in Him. John speaks of spiritual assurance several times in this epistle: such as in 3:14; 4:13; 5:13, 18-20. In fact, John speaks so much of the things "we know" that this could well be called the "epistle of assurance."

Verse 6 of the text says the proof that we are in Christ is that we walk like Him. Our lives must be patterned after Him, our words an amplification of His words, our love an extension of His love, our works a continuation of His works. Peter tells us that we should follow His steps (1 Peter 2:21). It was Jesus himself who first said we should follow His example (John 13:15). A true Christian is always known because he follows in the steps of his Lord.

B. Love One Another (vv. 7-14)

7. Brethren, I write no new commandment unto you, but an old commandment which ye had from the beginning. The old commandment is the word which ye have heard from the beginning.

8. Again, a new commandment I write unto you, which thing is true in him and in you: because the darkness is past, and the true light now shineth.

9. He that saith he is in the light, and hateth his brother, is in darkness even until now.

10. He that loveth his brother abideth in the light, and there is none occasion of stumbling in him.

11. But he that hateth his brother is in darkness, and walketh in darkness, and knoweth not whither he goeth, because that darkness hath blinded his eyes.

12. I write unto you, little children, because your sins are forgiven you for his name's sake.

13. I write unto you, fathers, because ye have known him that is from the beginning. I write unto you, young men, because ye have overcome the wicked one. I write unto you, little children, because ye have known the Father.

14. I have written unto you, fathers, because ye have known him that is from the beginning. I have written unto you, young men, because ye are strong, and the word of God abideth in you, and ye have overcome the wicked one.

John emphasizes that he is giving no new commandment but is simply repeating an old commandment that Christians had heard from the beginning. It was Jesus himself who gave the commandment that our lives must be filled with love:

- "A new commandment I give unto you, That ye love one another; as I have loved you, that ye also love one another" (John 13:34).
- "This is my commandment, That ye love one another, as I have loved you" (15:12).

Even though the commandment of brotherly love had been firmly stated by Christ, in verse 8 of the text John states the commandment in new words. He calls it "a new commandment," which means that he expresses it in terms explicit to his present time. The Lord's commandment had been given by Him for His followers, but now the Lord has returned to glory and His light shines only through His followers. Whereas Christ was the light of God while He was on the earth (John 1:4-9; 1 John 1:5-7), now the true light shines through those who are in Him. This is a beautiful and powerful statement: Jesus, the Light of the World, shines so brightly through His followers that the world is lighted and the darkness is past. Unbelievers are supposed to look at Christians and see Christ in them. The world should look at our lives and see us following in the steps of Jesus.

In verse 9 John again comes back with a reference to those who claim to be Christians and are not. Christian pretenders have been a problem to the church from its beginning. This is not surprising, for the devil frequently endeavors to overcome the work of God by imitations and counterfeits. In this instance,

Talk About It:

1. Explain the statement "the darkness is past, and the true light now shineth" (v. 8).

2. Explain the statement "there is nothing in him to make him stumble" (v. 10, *NIV*).

3. Describe the overcoming power believers have in Christ (vv. 13, 14).

John refers to those who claim to be in the light of Christ and yet have hatred for others. This is an impossibility, and the pretender is in darkness. Love is a commandment and a fruit of the Spirit (Galatians 5:22); it is not something that can be pretended or successfully imitated. John's use of the word *hate* is a vigorous and extreme way of describing the emotions that are possible for those who do not truly know Jesus Christ. Hate is an emotion so intense that it translates itself into harmful actions.

Love and hate are the antithesis of each other; they are the extremes of the range of human emotions; they are the most active of the whole emotional structure; and they are as different as light and darkness. The person who loves is in light, for it is Christian light that creates the condition of love. There is no occasion of stumbling in the person who loves, because love always expresses itself in positive benefits toward its object. It is our love for one another that indicates our fellowship with God. Jesus said, "By this shall all men know that ye are my disciples, if ye have love one to another" (John 13:35).

The very opposite is true of hate. Hatred is proof that the hater lives in darkness and walks in darkness, for there is no light in hate (1 John 2:11). Hatred is the darkness of life, the emotion that blinds a person's eyes to all truth.

The proofs of fellowship with God are twofold: our obedience to His Word and our love for His children. By obedience to the Word and love for the brotherhood, we have full assurance of our own place in Christ Jesus. Because of God's relationship to us as Father, His purpose is to give assurance in a time when many pretenders of Christianity are not Christians at all. It is necessary for us as believers to have the assurance that our sins are forgiven and that the Wicked One has no authority over us.

Verses 12-14 reveal the tenderness and compassion of John. He seems not to be able to say in enough ways how confident we can be of our place in Jesus Christ. To maintain that place, he reminds us, we must "overcome the wicked one" (vv. 13, 14). This is to be done by the Word of God in us, by the light of God that illuminates us, and by the presence of God with us.

> "A person who really cares about his or her neighbor, a person who genuinely loves others, is a person who bears witness to the truth."
>
> —Anne Graham Lotz

C. Hate the World (vv. 15, 16)

15. Love not the world, neither the things that are in the world. If any man love the world, the love of the Father is not in him.

16. For all that is in the world, the lust of the flesh, and the lust of the eyes, and the pride of life, is not of the Father, but is of the world.

Fellowship in the Light

In the Christian life there are some things so incompatible that they must not exist. One of these is to love both God and the world. The word *love* in this instance suggests a strong attachment and affection for. The double expression of "the world" and "things that are in the world" speaks of the present world system (v. 15). This is a love of such extraordinary degree that the person guilty of it actually prefers the world to God. Demas is said to have loved the world in this fashion (2 Timothy 4:10). Such enmity exists between God and the world that it is said true Christians will be hated by the world (1 John 3:13).

Talk About It:
Why can we not love both God and the world?

It is possible for people to become so attached to the world that they lose their taste or desire for the world to come. They find in this world all the things that appeal to them and satisfy them: pleasure, riches, fame, favor and a suitable lifestyle. When such a love of the world as this possesses a person, it is not likely that he or she can maintain an appropriate love for God. "Ye adulterers and adulteresses, know ye not that the friendship of the world is enmity with God? Whosoever therefore will be a friend of the world is the enemy of God" (James 4:4).

The appeal of the world is threefold: it appeals to the flesh, to the eyes, and the pride of life (1 John 2:16). The term *flesh* speaks of natural appetites; the term *eyes* refers to things pleasant or pleasures; the term *pride* refers to a vaulting human ambition. This formula of worldliness is seen in the case of Eve, who "saw that the tree was good for food [lust of the flesh], . . . it was pleasant to the eyes [lust of the eyes], and a tree to be desired to make one wise [pride of life]" (Genesis 3:6).

In the same way, the devil tempted Jesus to turn the stones into bread (the flesh), to leap from the pinnacle of the Temple (the eyes), and to seek sovereignty over the nations (pride of life) (Matthew 4:3-10).

Worldliness generally shows up in one of these three forms. Each temptation of the world is the appearance of something that will draw our attention and affection from God. Anything that diverts our love from Him can be said to be worldliness. We must be separated from all that is in the world and separated unto the Lord.

"A whole new generation of Christians has come up believing that it is possible to 'accept' Christ without forsaking the world."

—A.W. Tozer

CONCLUSION

Many people live their entire lives in darkness, never responding to the light of Jesus Christ. Other people see His light and begin to walk in it, but then allow worldliness to draw them back into the cold darkness. Where are you walking today?

GOLDEN TEXT CHALLENGE

"IF WE WALK IN THE LIGHT, AS HE IS IN THE LIGHT, WE

HAVE FELLOWSHIP ONE WITH ANOTHER, AND THE BLOOD OF JESUS CHRIST HIS SON CLEANSETH US FROM ALL SIN" (1 John 1:7).

If is the "big" little word in this scripture. It indicates something that may or may not happen. Here the power of choice lies with men and women, boys and girls.

"If we walk" indicates we must decide whether we will live in darkness or light. There is no middle ground—no partially lit paths. Either we follow Christ according to the light of the Scriptures or we walk in darkness.

If we are walking in the Light, we have a kinship with fellow believers that is not experienced elsewhere—not even in the bonds of human families—because this fellowship is spiritual and eternal. When we are adopted into relationship with God through faith in His Son, we become a brother or sister of every other believer in the world. And the blood of Jesus will keep on cleansing us—allowing us to lead a holy life—as we dedicate ourselves to His purposes.

Living in God's Love

1 John 2:17-29; 4:7-21

INTRODUCTION

God's love motivates our love. His love is unfathomable. Many of us are not really very lovable. Full of faults, by nature rebels against God, essentially selfish, often a burden to others, we feel like asking, "Who am I that God should pour out His amazing love upon me? Who am I that Jesus should give His life for me?"

Until I have a true appreciation of myself as the unworthy recipient of God's grace, I cannot properly appreciate others. Until I realize how much the Lord loves me just as I am, I cannot love others just as they are.

A love that picks and chooses, that includes the likable but excludes the unlikable, is natural human love. But the love of God shed abroad in our hearts is something quite different. When we can bless those who curse us, pray for those who injure us, and do good to those who hate us, then indeed we are exemplifying the love of God.

Love is thoughtfulness of others. Its rule is, "Treat men exactly as you would like them to treat you" (Luke 6:31, *Phillips*). It makes the Golden Rule the standard for day-by-day living.

Love means helpfulness—attention to the needs and problems of others and the use of appropriate means to help find the solution. It means sharing the burden of others' woes and doing what I can to alleviate them. It means visiting the sick, feeding the hungry, and clothing the naked, not for people's applause but for Jesus' sake.

Love takes risks. Jesus had to endure the slights and persecution of ungodly people; so will we as we show His love to others. When we turn the other cheek, we may get it slapped. When we offer the wrongdoer our shirt after he has seized our coat, we run some risk of losing our shirt. When we offer a helping hand, we may be imposed on. Love is not always returned.

Unit Theme:
Living in Light and Love (1, 2 and 3 John)

Central Truth:
Love for God and others is evidence of a Christian life.

Focus:
See the contrast between the way of evil and the way of love, and live in God's love.

Context:
Written to an unnamed audience by the apostle John

Golden Text:
"Beloved, let us love one another: for love is of God" (1 John 4:7).

Study Outline:
I. The Antithesis of Love
(1 John 2:17-29)
II. The Genesis of Love
(1 John 4:7-13)
III. The Command to Love
(1 John 4:14-21)

A. Temporary World (v. 17)

Talk About It:
Contrast the world
with the Christian
(v. 17).

"Exhalation is as
necessary to life as
inhalation. To accept
Christ it is necessary
that we reject what-
ever is contrary to
Him."
—A.W. Tozer

17. And the world passeth away, and the lust thereof: but he that doeth the will of God abideth for ever.

The world and its desires are real. "The cravings of sinful man, the lust of his eyes and the boasting of what he has and does" (v. 16, *NIV*) crowd in on us day by day. We can see, touch, taste and feel the things the world offers, and they are appealing to the flesh. The ever-present temptation is to *conform* to the world—to be shaped by it, as the Bible warns us. Overcoming worldly lusts requires eyes of faith that foresee the eternal day when the world and its desires will have passed away. In the eternal world, those who have led "transformed" lives (Romans 12:2), following the will of God, will be with Him forever.

B. Many Antichrists (vv. 18-23)

18. Little children, it is the last time: and as ye have heard that antichrist shall come, even now are there many antichrists; whereby we know that it is the last time.

19. They went out from us, but they were not of us; for if they had been of us, they would no doubt have continued with us: but they went out, that they might be made manifest that they were not all of us.

unction (v. 20)—
anointing

20. But ye have an unction from the Holy One, and ye know all things.

21. I have not written unto you because ye know not the truth, but because ye know it, and that no lie is of the truth.

22. Who is a liar but he that denieth that Jesus is the Christ? He is antichrist, that denieth the Father and the Son.

23. Whosoever denieth the Son, the same hath not the Father: [but] he that acknowledgeth the Son hath the Father also.

Talk About It:
1. Where did the
antichrists John
mentions come
from? What was
their purpose?
2. According to
verse 23, who has
the Son? Who has
the Father?

Here John warned that in "the last time"—the era that will climax with Christ's second coming—"many antichrists" will rise up to deceive believers (v. 18). "This is how we know it is the last hour," John said (*NIV*). Antichrists are those who deny Jesus is the Messiah or who, like the Gnostics, deny that the Son of God became human.

Many more antichrists have emerged in the centuries since John wrote. This will eventually culminate in the coming of *the* Antichrist—whom Paul identified as the "man of sin" (2 Thessalonians 2:3-10). This person will work "with all deceivableness of unrighteousness in them that perish; because they received not the love of the truth, that they might be saved" (v. 10).

The "spirit of antichrist" (1 John 4:3) was working in the hearts of individuals who had "gone out" from the church (see 2:19).

John said these people had never been true Christians—"they were not of us"—as was proven by their apostasy.

The genuine believers could stay true to God because they had an "unction," or anointing, from the "Holy One," or Holy Spirit, whose indwelling presence would help them discern truth from error (v. 20). Just as Jesus had promised, "the Spirit of truth" had come to lead God's children "into all truth" (John 16:13). The same indwelling Spirit helps believers today understand the Word of God and discern right from wrong.

John explains anyone who denies Jesus is the Christ (the Messiah or Anointed One) is antichrist (1 John 2:22). By refusing to accept Jesus, this person is also rejecting God the Father. "No one who denies the Son has the Father; whoever acknowledges the Son has the Father also" (v. 23, *NIV*).

C. Abiding Realities (vv. 24-29)

24. Let that therefore abide in you, which ye have heard from the beginning. If that which ye have heard from the beginning shall remain in you, ye also shall continue in the Son, and in the Father.

25. And this is the promise that he hath promised us, even eternal life.

26. These things have I written unto you concerning them that seduce you.

27. But the anointing which ye have received of him abideth in you, and ye need not that any man teach you: but as the same anointing teacheth you of all things, and is truth, and is no lie, and even as it hath taught you, ye shall abide in him.

28. And now, little children, abide in him; that, when he shall appear, we may have confidence, and not be ashamed before him at his coming.

29. If ye know that he is righteous, ye know that every one that doeth righteousness is born of him.

To continue in relationship with the Father and the Son, John urged his readers to "abide in" (v. 24) those basic truths of the gospel they had been taught from the beginning: truths such as the incarnation of Christ, the death and resurrection of Christ, the way of salvation, and Christ's second coming. Those who are committed to Christ and His gospel are guaranteed the promise of eternal life (v. 25).

John was writing "these things" because of the false teachers who were trying to "seduce" (lead astray) true Christians (v. 26). The Gnostics, who claimed to have superior knowledge because of a superior revelation, had nothing to say that Christians needed to hear. Instead, the believers had received an anointing that was "real, not counterfeit" (v. 27, *NIV*) from the

Talk About It:
1. What are the "beginning" truths (v. 24) to which believers must cling, and what will the result be?

2. What difference does the Holy Spirit's anointing make in a believer's life (vv. 26, 27)?

3. What is the greatest "confidence" a person can have (v. 28)?

Holy Spirit. He was their teacher, and nothing He would reveal would contradict the Word of God. "All things" necessary for their salvation had been revealed to them, and they needed to walk therein.

Paul warned Timothy "that in the latter times some shall depart from the faith, giving heed to seducing spirits, and doctrines of devils; speaking lies in hypocrisy; having their conscience seared with a hot iron" (1 Timothy 4:1, 2). He advised Timothy, "Take heed unto thyself, and unto the doctrine; continue in them: for in doing this thou shalt both save thyself, and them that hear thee" (v. 16).

If we will follow Paul's and John's advice by abiding in sound doctrine, we will stand confident and unashamed at Christ's return (1 John 2:28). The public evidence of our readiness for His coming is His righteousness, which is revealed in our actions. We act righteously because we have been covered and empowered by His indwelling righteousness.

II. THE GENESIS OF LOVE (1 John 4:7-13)
A. A Spiritual Birth (vv. 7, 8)
7. Beloved, let us love one another: for love is of God; and every one that loveth is born of God, and knoweth God.
8. He that loveth not knoweth not God; for God is love.

Talk About It:
Why is love an essential part of the Christian life?

John is not only giving sound counsel to his readers about spiritual truth in general, but he is also answering some false teachers who were plaguing the churches of Asia Minor at this time. The fully developed Gnostic believed: (1) God as spirit is wholly good and the world as matter is wholly evil—thus, God could neither have made the world nor have come into contact with it. From God there came a whole series of "emanations," spiritual beings, less and less spiritual and less and less powerful as they got farther from God. One of these made the world. (2) Salvation comes by *gnosis*, or knowledge supernaturally given to a select few, and involves the liberation of the spirit from the body. (3) The spiritual Christ could have only been loosely connected with the human Jesus. (4) The outward life of the Gnostic could go in one of two ways: Since the spirit is good and the body evil, some Gnostics would deny the body in an extreme asceticism; but others looked upon the body as unimportant and allowed it to indulge in whatever it wanted!

John exhorts his readers to love one another. He declares that love finds its origin in God. And he points out that true salvation is not in some knowledge limited to the privileged few, but is characterized by love. The person who has divine love at work in his heart is the one who has experienced the new birth and who really knows God.

The Gnostic was more interested in knowledge than in

Living in God's Love

love—he was quite conceited, exclusive, and contemptuous of those who did not have his "light." John says that such a person is a stranger to God rather than a "knower" of Him. The truth is that God and love are to be identified together. This does not mean God and love are synonymous, nor justify the reversing of the clause—"love is God." God's nature is not exhausted by the concept of love, but every attribute of God is characterized by love. There is nothing about Him that is unloving or opposed to love.

> Compassion is love, plus a desire to share
>   The trouble and tears that come from despair;
> Compassion is love, plus sympathy, too,
>   With a will to help, to heal and renew.
> Compassion is love, plus pity enough
>   To walk with the weary when the going is rough;
> Compassion is love, plus the spirit to do
>   For others; our Lord had compassion, do you?
>   —James A. Sanaker

B. A Sacrificial Act (vv. 9, 10)

9. In this was manifested the love of God toward us, because that God sent his only begotten Son into the world, that we might live through him.

10. Herein is love, not that we loved God, but that he loved us, and sent his Son to be the propitiation for our sins.

John stresses three aspects of the origin of divine love: it begins in the nature of God itself (v. 8); it is made known to us through the gift of His Son (v. 9); and it becomes immediately effective in the individual life through the new birth (v. 7). The love of God was made real by His sending Jesus into this world. The purpose of His coming was "that we might live," not in some undeveloped power of our own, but "through him" (v. 9).

In verse 10, John sums up what he has said. Love of the kind he is discussing is not something springing out of the nature of humanity, not a divine spark such as the Gnostic found in every spirit, not our interest in God. Instead, it is God's act, reaching out for us.

Sin defiled people in God's sight and disqualified us from fellowship and relationship with our Maker. God's greatest act of love removed the defilement and disqualification by assuming the penalty Himself in the form of His Son. The only condition we have to fulfill to receive this benefit of God's love is to genuinely believe in the Son, receiving Him wholeheartedly while rejecting all previous loves.

Love is . . .
  Slow to suspect—quick to trust,
  Slow to condemn—quick to justify,
  Slow to offend—quick to defend,
  Slow to expose—quick to shield,
  Slow to reprimand—quick to forbear,
  Slow to belittle—quick to appreciate,
  Slow to demand—quick to give,
  Slow to provoke—quick to help,
  Slow to resent—quick to forgive.
      —**Author Unknown**

Talk About It:
Why did God love us first? How did He prove His love?

C. The Duty to Love (v. 11)

11. Beloved, if God so loved us, we ought also to love one another.

The word *ought* denotes obligation. God did "so" love us that He sacrificed His Son to bridge the gulf of sin that separated us from Him. If we have Christian love today, it will show in our willingness to go out of the way to build bridges of rescue and love between ourselves and others. No sacrifice should be too great to establish and preserve these relationships of love.

Love is not complete unless reciprocated and communicated. God's reign of love is intended to be constantly expanding and intensifying in and through His people.

D. The Certainty of Salvation (vv. 12, 13)

12. No man hath seen God at any time. If we love one another, God dwelleth in us, and his love is perfected in us.

13. Hereby know we that we dwell in him, and he in us, because he hath given us of his Spirit.

No one has ever beheld God in His total, triune existence, nor has anyone ever been able to comprehend God completely in his own intellect. But it is possible to know God even more intimately and completely than if we were able to examine Him visually, for He is capable of dwelling within us.

God's nature is best described as *love* (v. 12). Therefore, when we have genuine love in our hearts, we are capable of knowing Him and fellowshiping with Him as never before.

The word *know* (v. 13) is one of the author's favorite words. Assurance of salvation should be the normal experience of every believer in Christ. One may legitimately question whether he has been saved if he is not certain of it.

The main way in which God has chosen to assure us of salvation is by imparting to us His Holy Spirit. The Holy Spirit is active in our spiritual birth when we first believe, and He comes to dwell in our cleansed hearts. The consecrated believer's spirit is so permeated with the Spirit of God that the spiritual union is as complete as when oxygen unites with hydrogen to become water. The result of God's Spirit uniting with our spirit produces a spiritual life that is as marvelous and useful as water is in the material universe.

III. THE COMMAND TO LOVE (1 John 4:14-21)

A. The Confession of Christ (vv. 14-16)

14. And we have seen and do testify that the Father sent the Son to be the Saviour of the world.

15. Whosoever shall confess that Jesus is the Son of God, God dwelleth in him, and he in God.

Talk About It:

Why must we love other people? Does this include people we don't like?

Talk About It:

1. How do we know if God is living in us?
2. How can we live in God while He lives in us?

"God is looking for imperfect men and women who have learned to walk in moment-by-moment dependence on the Holy Spirit."

—**Charles Stanley**

Living in God's Love

16. And we have known and believed the love that God hath to us. God is love; and he that dwelleth in love dwelleth in God, and God in him.

Someone is certain to ask, "Isn't there a contradiction between John's statement that he had seen Christ and his statement that no man had seen God at any time? Does not Colossians 2:9 state that 'in him dwelleth all the fulness of the Godhead bodily'"?

John means no contradiction but intends to convey the idea that God is more fully and perfectly understood through His indwelling presence than through visual perception. John should know, and undoubtedly he is comparing his experience with Christ before the Resurrection and his experience with Christ and the Holy Spirit following the Resurrection and Pentecost. The result of all John's experience points up his conclusion that Christ was sent by the Father to save people from their sins. John was probably the most intimate of all Jesus' friends and followers and was with Him even at His crucifixion, yet John never saw God in all His glory. John's driving passion was to tell the world what he had come to know about Christ.

In verse 15, the idea of confession includes belief that Jesus is God and trust in Him as Savior. If this is the experience of the "whosoever" in question, then it will mean so much to him that he will be compelled to share Christ with others. To attempt to contain Christ or confine Him within one's heart without allowing Him expression in our lives is to quench His presence eventually. Christ lives, and therefore He must be expressed in living and loving actions and words.

Verse 16 reveals that we need not be unsure of whether we are united with God. If we can be sure of the presence of another person by sight, then we may be a hundredfold more certain of our relationship with God because of His presence within our heart. As Paul said in Romans 8:16, "The Spirit itself beareth witness with our spirit, that we are the children of God."

B. Holy Boldness (v. 17)

17. Herein is our love made perfect, that we may have boldness in the day of judgment: because as he is, so are we in this world.

John assumes "perfect" (complete) love to be a definite possibility, even the normal experience for a Christian. In 2:5 he had explained, "Whoso keepeth his word, in him verily is the love of God perfected: hereby know we that we are in him." Here John makes plain that love of fellow believers, as well as love of God, is required of the child of God. So love, knowledge and obedience work hand in hand to complete and maintain God's work of grace in us, being the indwelling and outworking

Talk About It:
1. What is the message the Holy Spirit wants to communicate through us? How can we communicate it?
2. What does it fully mean to "confess that Jesus is the Son of God" (v. 15)?

Who Saved Him?

A tramp, obviously under the influence of alcohol, approached evangelist D.L. Moody. "Mr. Moody," said he, "you're the man who saved me."

As Moody observed the man's awful condition, he replied, "Yes, it looks as if I did save you. If the Lord had, you wouldn't be in this condition."

Talk About It:
How can we have confidence *now* ("in this world") about the coming "day of judgment"?

of His Spirit. There is therefore no need to fear the "day of judgment," for God will not judge against His own nature; and a part of His nature dwells in the true believer.

C. Defeat of Fear (vv. 18, 19)

18. There is no fear in love; but perfect love casteth out fear: because fear hath torment. He that feareth is not made perfect in love.

19. We love him, because he first loved us.

Talk About It:

Why do love and fear not live together?

Fear and love are mutually exclusive. One cannot coexist with the other. Either can displace the other, if we allow it to happen. Fear of torment, judgment or punishment is present in many people because of their sins which have left guilt feelings on sensitive consciences. Only as we allow the blood of Christ to wash away our sins and let the Holy Spirit occupy our heart's throne does love replace fear and continue to grow.

Verse 19 reminds us that God loves us first, and He made it possible for us to love Him and others. There is spiritual security in the love of God just as there is security for a child as he experiences the love of his parents. God's love drives away fear.

D. Breaking of Barriers (vv. 20, 21)

20. If a man say, I love God, and hateth his brother, he is a liar: for he that loveth not his brother whom he hath seen, how can he love God whom he hath not seen?

21. And this commandment have we from him, That he who loveth God love his brother also.

Talk About It:

Why can we not love the unseen God without loving our next-door neighbor?

We cannot be selective with our Christian love. Just as God's love is for all, our love that originates in Him and flows through us also is for all.

John's question is very persuasive. It follows that all people who claim to love God should be showing love for their Christian family also. How else can we tell if they have any love at all, if they say they love God but show no love to their brothers and sisters?

The commandment in verse 21 would be unreasonable if the Lord had not made us with the capacity to respond to it obediently. Naturally, this command is not obeyed by people in the way that a robot obeys the command of its human master. The robot can do no other, but we can resist God's commands. Therefore, it is possible to obey God's commands to love others only if we have received God's love in our hearts to begin with. If there is no love there, then there is no love with which to obey the commandment.

"I have decided to stick with love. Hate is too great a burden to bear."

—Martin Luther King Jr.

CONCLUSION

The Lord's exemplary act of love has made it possible for

people's lives to be changed to conform to His will through the response of faith and obedience and love. God expects His people to love one another and treat one another just as He does, just as He showed us in Christ. Love is the one most important characteristic or virtue of a Christian life and experience.

GOLDEN TEXT CHALLENGE

"BELOVED, LET US LOVE ONE ANOTHER: FOR LOVE IS OF GOD" (1 John 4:7).

Beloved is the beautiful word that John begins with. It appears five times in 1 John (3:2, 21; 4:1, 7, 11). The word is beautiful because it tells us as believers in Christ that we are being loved. Jesus proved once and for all that God loves all people. And there is nothing that can separate us from His love (Romans 8:35-39).

John knew God loved us and he in turn was directed by the Holy Spirit to tell us that we ought to love one another. We know what love is if we know God. And if we know what love is, we know how to love. If we relate to others as God relates to us, we are showing love. God through Christ is our example.

Daily Devotions:

M. God Commands
   Our Love
   Exodus 20:1-6

T. God's Faithful
   Love
   Isaiah 63:7-9

W. God Loves the
   World
   John 3:14-21

T. God
   Demonstrated
   His Love
   Romans 5:1-11

F. Love, the
   Greatest Virtue
   1 Corinthians
   13:1-13

S. Rooted and
   Grounded in
   Love
   Ephesians 3:14-
   19

Life in Christ

1 John 3:1-24; 5:14-20

Unit Theme:
Living in Light and Love (1, 2 and 3 John)

Central Truth:
Living in Christ inspires pure conduct and loving service.

Focus:
Examine the believer's relationship with God and celebrate life in Christ.

Context:
Written to an unnamed audience by the apostle John

Golden Text:
"He that keepeth his [God's] commandments dwelleth in him, and he in him" (1 John 3:24).

Study Outline:
I. Living as God's Children
(1 John 3:1-10)
II. Evidences of Life in Christ
(1 John 3:11-24)
III. Benefits of Life in Christ
(1 John 5:14-21)

INTRODUCTION

The apostle John experienced a dramatic change of temperament during his life with the Lord. By nature, he was of such tempestuous disposition that he and his brother James earned the title "The Sons of Thunder" (Mark 3:17). They were once ready to call fire down upon a city of Samaritans who were inhospitable to Christ and His disciples (Luke 9:51-56). John eventually earned the recognition of "beloved disciple" because of his deep love for Christ and the dominant loving side of his nature.

At the Crucifixion, John was directed to assume care of the Lord's mother, Mary (John 19:27). After the resurrection of Jesus, John and Peter rushed first to the empty tomb (20:2-8). From that time on, Peter and John, who had once been rivals in the circle of apostles (21:20- 22), became close companions in the work of the Lord (Acts 3:1-4; 4:13; 8:14).

The Book of Acts deals mainly with the ministry of Peter and Paul and does not provide any details of the later ministry of John. Early tradition says that after the fall of Jerusalem in A.D. 70, John settled in Ephesus and became the acknowledged leader of the churches there. Also, according to early tradition, John was the only one of the 12 apostles to escape martyrdom. He was miraculously spared death, although he suffered much persecution during his lifetime. He died a natural death at Ephesus, where he returned after being set free from a period of exile on the isle of Patmos.

John's writings are the latest of the New Testament books. Evidence indicates that his letters may have been written 15 or more years after the other New Testament epistles. He was apparently an elderly man at the time of their writing. The letters have the tone of a father speaking to his little children.—Charles W. Conn (*The Bible, Book of Books*)

I. LIVING AS GOD'S CHILDREN (1 John 3:1-10)

A. Purifying Hope (vv. 1-3)

1. Behold, what manner of love the Father hath bestowed upon us, that we should be called the sons of God: therefore the world knoweth us not, because it knew him not.

2. Beloved, now are we the sons of God, and it doth not yet appear what we shall be: but we know that, when he shall appear, we shall be like him; for we shall see him as he is.

3. And every man that hath this hope in him purifieth himself, even as he is pure.

Divine love is of such nature and depth that it makes humans into children of God. Because of God's love for us, He was not willing that we should remain alienated from Him through sin, but He sent Jesus Christ, His only begotten Son, to redeem us. Through the acceptance of Christ we become the children of God, born of His Spirit and bearing His name, receiving His holiness and sharing His life.

Sonship to God is not an accidental circumstance but the result of His love and design for us. Because He was not willing for us to perish (2 Peter 3:9), God brought us into this relationship. In Ephesians 2:4-6, Paul says God was "rich in mercy, for his great love wherewith he loved us . . . and hath raised us up together, and made us sit together in heavenly places in Christ Jesus."

Because the world could not understand the love of God, it cannot understand those who follow God. Jesus said of His followers, "The world hath hated them, because they are not of the world, even as I am not of the world" (John 17:14).

Our relationship as children of God at this time presupposes what glories and advanced relationships we shall enjoy at His appearing. Human understanding is incapable of grasping the glory of His appearing and the transformation that event will work in us. We shall see Him in His glorified form, which is the way the disciples saw Him following His resurrection (John 20:19, 20, 27; 21:1, 4). At that time He was not subject to the limitations or pain of this life. At His appearing we shall be like Him, transformed from mortality to immortality, released from the frailties of this life. John recognized the impossibility for us to fully grasp the majesty of what we shall be. So he simply says "we shall be like him; for we shall see him as he is" (1 John 3:2).

Such an eternal hope should have a telling effect in the lives of those who hold it. Who can be possessed by such a hope without being greatly changed by it? The hope of immortality should drive carelessness and foolishness out of believers: they will purify themselves in preparation for the future (v. 3).

Talk About It:
1. Why can't the world understand Christians?
2. What does it mean to be a child of God in this life? What will it mean after this life?
3. How does someone "purify himself" (v. 3)?

"It is not after we were reconciled to God by the blood of His Son that He began to love us, but He loved us before the foundation of the world, that with His only begotten Son we too might be sons of God before we were any thing at all."
—Augustine

John again declares that Jesus must be the pattern for our lives. We cannot redeem ourselves from sin, but we can follow purity and love and mercy as He manifested these virtues before us. In 2:6 John says we should walk even as He walked; in 3:3 he says we should purify ourselves even as He is pure. This means we should lay aside those things that are unlike Him and follow those things that are like Him.

The apostle did not say Christ purified Himself but that "he is pure." It is believers who have to purify themselves. We who hope to be like God hereafter must rely on God, and purify ourselves after the example of Christ. Christ conformed to the Father; we are to conform to Christ.

B. Identifying Mark (vv. 4-6)

4. Whosoever committeth sin transgresseth also the law: for sin is the transgression of the law.

5. And ye know that he was manifested to take away our sins; and in him is no sin.

6. Whosoever abideth in him sinneth not: whosoever sinneth hath not seen him, neither known him.

Talk About It:

1. What is sin (v. 4)?
2. Why is Jesus able to take away our sin (v. 5)?

John wanted his readers to know it is possible for the believer to sin under pressure of the Enemy, and for such a one there is the advocacy of Jesus Christ, the righteous (2:1). However, it is not possible for a genuinely born-again believer to habitually practice sin (3:6).

John explained that committing sin is the same as disregarding the law of God (v. 4). *Lawlessness*, in both the English and the Greek, means not the absence of law but the disregard of it. It is not just that sin manifests itself in ignoring God's law, but that sin is in its very nature lawless.

The focus in verse 5 is not the mode in which Christ took away sins. Instead, the focus is how His becoming incarnate in order to take away sins shows that sin is incompatible with the divine relationship of being children of God. In John 1:29 our Lord is said to take away "the sin of the world," while here (1 John 3:5), He is said to take away sins. "The sin of the world" may be understood as the condition of sin—that is, the *root* of sin or the sinful nature. "Our sins" may be considered as the result of sin or the *fruit* of sinfulness in our lives.

Jesus lived a sinless life, and because He was sinless, the devil had no hold on Him. Therefore, Jesus was able to destroy the works of the devil, one of which is sinning. John implied that as the Son of God is sinless, so the believer must oppose sin with all his might and strive for holiness.

Both the verbs *abideth* and *sinneth* (v. 6) are in the present continuous tense and express the normal state. To abide in Christ involves the habit of communion with God and the habitual fulfillment of His will. Since there is no sin in Christ, it is obvious that if one abides in Him, he or she should not sin either. Although the believer sometimes sins, opposition to sin is the ruling principle of their life. If a believer sins, he or she must confess it, obtain forgiveness, and persevere with their self-purification.

C. Pure Seed (vv. 7-10)

7. Little children, let no man deceive you: he that doeth righteousness is righteous, even as he is righteous.

8. He that committeth sin is of the devil; for the devil sinneth from the beginning. For this purpose the Son of God was manifested, that he might destroy the works of the devil.

9. Whosoever is born of God doth not commit sin; for his seed remaineth in him: and he cannot sin, because he is born of God.

10. In this the children of God are manifest, and the children of the devil: whosoever doeth not righteousness is not of God, neither he that loveth not his brother.

In verse 7 John issues a solemn warning to his "little children." The peril of the situation is shown by the tenderness of the address the writer used. The warning "Do not let anyone lead you astray" (*NIV*) appears to have been directed against false teachers in the community. The false teachers were seeking to lead believers astray not only theologically but morally as well. Therefore, he warned Christians to be on guard.

John asked his readers to apply the standard of truth by which they would be able to detect deception. Here is the criterion: "He that doeth righteousness is righteous, even as he is righteous" (v. 7). It is he who habitually does righteousness, not he who simply does a righteous act. The doing of righteousness reveals the character but does not create it. However, the person who is righteous is recognized by his or her actions.

"He that committeth sin is of the devil" (v. 8) links sin not with the law of God, which it breaks, but with the devil, in whom sin originates. The devil's sinful action is continuous and present—he "sinneth from the beginning." This means, presumably, from the moment of his proud rebellion against God—the beginning of his devilish career. The devil is the source of the evil that rules the person who is a habitual doer of sin.

If the characteristic work of the devil is to sin, the characteristic work of the Son of God is to save. Morally, Satan's work is enticement to sin; physically, the infliction of disease; intellectually, seduction into error. Christ came to undo these sins, to take away both sin and its consequences. The word *destroy* occurs frequently in the New Testament, with the sense of "to undo, to pull to pieces." The two objectives of the manifestation

Talk About It:

1. How did Jesus Christ "destroy the works of the devil" (v. 8)?

2. Compare the children of God with the children of Satan (vv. 9, 10).

of Christ cover the whole work of redemption—"to take away our sins" and to "destroy the works of the devil" (vv. 5, 8). Of course, we know from experience that they are not in an absolute sense destroyed, because the devil is still busy doing his wicked works; but he has been defeated, and in Christ we can escape from his tyranny.

In verse 9, John made two startling statements. He first said that a Christian *does not sin*. (Earlier in this epistle he had said he was writing "that ye sin not" [2:1]). He then went on to say that a believer *cannot sin*. These expressions have sometimes been taken as teaching that a true Christian—one who is born of God—is incapable of sinning. But such an interpretation cannot be maintained unless we are to suppose that John contradicted himself within this epistle.

The word *seed* (3:9) has a figurative connotation: "God's nature" or "God's principle of life." This new seed, new life or new nature abides in the believer, and therein lies his or her secret weapon against sin. The principle of life that Christ has given continues to be the ruling principle of growth.

It is the abiding influence of this seed within everyone born of God that allowed John to affirm without fear of contradiction that the born-again individual cannot go on living in sin. Divine sonship and sin are mutually exclusive. As long as the relationship with God remains alive, sinful acts are but mishaps or fallings.

Verse 10 is both a summary and a conclusion of what has been said before as well as a transition to what follows. It is not a theoretical consideration of the nature of sinlessness or the possibility of sinlessness that occupies the author but the concept of community. How are the children of God to be recognized, and how are the children of the devil to be discerned? Life reveals the children of God. They bear characteristic marks, stamping their actions, their feelings, their conduct and their motives as distinctively Christlike.

John divided the world sharply into two classes. Our parentage is either divine or diabolic. God's children (v. 9) and the devil's (v. 8) may both be recognized by their moral behavior. The distinction of being children of God, as opposed to being children of the devil, consists of two great facts—doing what is right and loving one's brother.

> "Satan is neither omnipotent nor free to do anything he pleases. Prince of the world he may be, but the Prince of Peace has come and dealt him a death blow."
>
> —Harold Lindsell

II. EVIDENCES OF LIFE IN CHRIST (1 John 3:11-24)
A. Not Like Cain (vv. 11-15)

11. For this is the message that ye heard from the beginning, that we should love one another.

12. Not as Cain, who was of that wicked one, and slew his brother. And wherefore slew he him? Because his own works were evil, and his brother's righteous.

Life in Christ

13. Marvel not, my brethren, if the world hate you.

14. We know that we have passed from death unto life, because we love the brethren. He that loveth not his brother abideth in death.

15. Whosoever hateth his brother is a murderer: and ye know that no murderer hath eternal life abiding in him.

The manifestation of love in our lives is the fulfillment of the earliest Christian commandment. John here looked back to the first human family in the Garden of Eden. From the beginning God intended that the family should be bonded together in love. Because God is love, it would be His nature for love to be manifested throughout His creation.

Satan's assault on the law of love was evident in the first family when Cain killed his brother, Abel. Evil does not hesitate to take active steps to destroy righteousness. Verse 15 says, "Whosoever hateth his brother is a murderer." This proves that hate is more than a negative emotion—it is such ill intent that it will actively work to the destruction of its object. Cain had become so filled with wrath and hate because of Abel's righteous offering to the Lord that he was willing to snuff out his brother's life (Genesis 4:3-8). This shows the vast difference between righteousness and unrighteousness, and why there is no middle ground between the two.

Verse 13 of the text says one should not wonder at the world's hatred of righteousness. Righteousness is a rebuke to worldliness, and worldliness, under the influence of Satan, is not reluctant to put an end to righteousness in any way it can. Hate is intolerable in a Christian, for hate is the domain of the devil. Verse 15 states that one who hates another is a murderer and does not have eternal life abiding within.

There is more than an emotional step between love and hate, for love is active good and hate is active evil. The fact that the world hates righteousness means the world is quite capable of violence toward righteous people. Hate is unreasonable and unreasoning, without conscience in its destruction of what is good.

Once we understand the dreadful nature of hate, we can understand why love is the surest mark of a Christian. Observe how the latter part of verse 14 and the first part of the next verse show the progression of evil in one who does not have love. In the former it is said where there is an absence of love there is no life—this does not yet mean hate. But in the latter verse we see that when the absence of love progresses to active hate, it is comparable to murder.

On the contrary, the one fact above all others that demonstrates to ourselves that we are true Christians is the love in our heart. Jesus said it is by love that others know we are

Talk About It:

1. What motivated Cain to murder his own brother?

2. Why should Christians expect to be hated by the world?

3. How serious is the sin of hatred (v. 15)?

An Enemy's Face

When Leonardo da Vinci was working on his masterpiece *The Last Supper*, he painted the face of a man he hated as Judas. But when he came to paint the face of Jesus, he tried again and again but failed. It was only when he painted out the face of the man he hated and put another in its place that he had a clear picture of the Lord's countenance. His hatred, you see, had created a "dead spot" between him and the work he was doing, and this had to be put right before even his marvelous ability could produce the finished work.

—**Kenneth Budd**

Christians (John 13:35). The fact that love identifies us as Christian, to ourselves as well as to others, also indicates that love is something that can be seen. The world cannot judge an emotional feeling we might have, and yet the world knows by our love that we are indeed the disciples of Christ. Love is seen by good acts and hate is seen by all evil acts.

B. Like Christ (vv. 16-21)

16. Hereby perceive we the love of God, because he laid down his life for us: and we ought to lay down our lives for the brethren.

17. But whoso hath this world's good, and seeth his brother have need, and shutteth up his bowels of compassion from him, how dwelleth the love of God in him?

18. My little children, let us not love in word, neither in tongue; but in deed and in truth.

19. And hereby we know that we are of the truth, and shall assure our hearts before him.

20. For if our heart condemn us, God is greater than our heart, and knoweth all things.

21. Beloved, if our heart condemn us not, then have we confidence toward God.

Talk About It:

1. How should we "lay down our lives for the brethren" (v. 16) in Christian living?

2. Why is it so much easier to "love in word" than "in deed and in truth" (v. 18)?

3. What should give us "confidence toward God" (v. 21), and why?

Verses 16-21 establish the truth that love is something you do and not merely something you feel. We are first able to understand the nature of love when we see that Christ laid down His life for us. Love made Him willing to die for us (v. 16).

Just as James drew a parallel between faith and works (James 2:17), John drew a parallel between love and works. In the same way it is impossible to have faith without translating it into good deeds, so it is impossible to have love without translating it into beneficial action. No one who has provision for himself and withholds assistance from a destitute brother can be truly classified as a Christian. The Bible is very strong in this regard.

It is in this expression of love that we have the assurance of what we are in Christ (1 John 3:19). If in this matter of loving others and opening our heart to them we feel guilt and condemnation (v. 20), then this should be corrected before God. Where there has been negligence, we need not flounder in guilt, but simply correct the deficiency. God is greater than the guilt in our hearts and waits only to see an improvement in our action through His grace.

If, on the other hand, we have practiced such charity toward others that there is no feeling of guilt in us, then we have established a strong and active love that will sustain us in all areas of Christian living. Our confidence in God has been as strong as the manifestations of His love in our hearts and lives (v. 21).

Life in Christ

C. In His Name (vv. 22-24)

22. And whatsoever we ask, we receive of him, because we keep his commandments, and do those things that are pleasing in his sight.

23. And this is his commandment, That we should believe on the name of his Son Jesus Christ, and love one another, as he gave us commandment.

24. And he that keepeth his commandments dwelleth in him, and he in him. And hereby we know that he abideth in us, by the Spirit which he hath given us.

Verse 23 sums up the commands of God—we are to believe on Jesus and love one another. In Matthew 22:37-40, Jesus identified these as the two greatest commandments. If obeying these commands is our way of life, we can expect to receive what we request in prayer, for our prayers will not be selfish, but instead will be focused on the will and glory of God and the good of others (1 John 3:22).

In verse 24 John gives another identifying mark of the true Christian—the indwelling presence of the Holy Spirit. It takes the Holy Spirit for us to be able to keep God's commands. When we are able to forgive instead of fight, give instead of grab, and obey instead of oppose, we realize there is a higher power living and working in our heart.

Talk About It:
1. Who can expect to have their prayers answered (v. 22)?
2. What is the basic commandment from which all others flow (v. 23)?
3. How does God's Spirit assure believers (v. 24)?

III. BENEFITS OF LIFE IN CHRIST (1 John 5:14-21)

A. Answered Prayer (vv. 14-17)

14. And this is the confidence that we have in him, that, if we ask any thing according to his will, he heareth us:

15. And if we know that he hear us, whatsoever we ask, we know that we have the petitions that we desired of him.

16. If any man see his brother sin a sin which is not unto death, he shall ask, and he shall give him life for them that sin not unto death. There is a sin unto death: I do not say that he shall pray for it.

17. All unrighteousness is sin: and there is a sin not unto death.

As we saw in 3:22-24, life in Christ gives us the assurance of answered prayer. John makes it clear that our petitions are to be according to God's will. This means we should pray for that which is in agreement with God's Word; otherwise, we are praying according to self-will. We should have full confidence that when we pray as His children and according to His will, the heavenly Father will answer in love.

Believers are specifically directed to pray for any brother or sister who has fallen into sin, with the promise that those prayers can deliver the erring Christian from judgment (5:16). How powerfully this should motivate our prayer lives—knowing

Talk About It:
1. How do we know if we are praying according to God's will?
2. How should we reach out to a believer who falls into sin?

that God wants to use our intercession to help someone experience spiritual life instead of spiritual death!

Regarding the statement "There is a sin unto death: I do not say that he shall pray for it" (v. 16), there are various opinions. Many believe the "sin unto death" is the "unpardonable sin" Jesus describes in Mark 3:29—namely, blasphemy against the Holy Spirit. Even if someone has committed such a sin, we probably won't know it for sure. After all, Jesus has saved countless hard-hearted sinners whom many thought would never be saved. But someone kept interceding, and God did the impossible!

B. Deliverance (vv. 18, 19)

18. We know that whosoever is born of God sinneth not; but he that is begotten of God keepeth himself, and that wicked one toucheth him not.

19. And we know that we are of God, and the whole world lieth in wickedness.

Now as then, "the whole world is under the control of the evil one" (v. 19, *NIV*). Believers are pitted "against principalities, against powers, against the rulers of the darkness of this world, against spiritual wickedness in high places" (Ephesians 6:12). The situation sounds bleak, but John declares that the "wicked one" cannot *touch*—cannot hold on to and harm—those who are "born of God" (1 John 5:18).

The believer is protected because he or she has been adopted into God's family and "keepeth himself" safe through prayer and obedience to God's will. The devil will attack the Christian, but no lasting harm can be done because of the believer's standing in Jesus Christ.

Talk About It:

How do these verses compare the status of the world with the condition of Christians?

C. Spiritual Insight (vv. 20, 21)

20. And we know that the Son of God is come, and hath given us an understanding, that we may know him that is true, and we are in him that is true, even in his Son Jesus Christ. This is the true God, and eternal life.

21. Little children, keep yourselves from idols. Amen.

Not only do Christians experience answered prayers and divine deliverance; we also are given spiritual understanding that the world does not have. The indwelling Holy Spirit enables us to discern truth from error "that we may know him that is true" (v. 20). In a society where we are continually confronted with misleading ideas and doctrines from secularists, cultists, and even some "Christian" leaders, we must have spiritual discernment. Only Jesus is the "true God" and the way to "eternal life."

John refers to the tender phrase "little children" in closing

Talk About It:

1. Why must God give us "an understanding" (v. 20)?

2. Why do you suppose John ended his letter by writing, "Keep yourselves from idols" (v. 21)?

this letter. His final plea is that the believers will keep themselves from idols. Wycliffe says the word *keep* means to "guard as a garrison does." He adds, "An *idol* is anything which occupies the place due to God. [The ancient world] abounded with idols and idolatrous practices; so the warning was most appropriate." And the warning is just as appropriate today.

CONCLUSION
Philip Schaff said, "Without Christ, life is as the twilight with dark night ahead; with Christ, it is the dawn of morning with the light and warmth of a day ahead."

GOLDEN TEXT CHALLENGE
"HE THAT KEEPETH HIS [GOD'S] COMMANDMENTS DWELLETH IN HIM, AND HE IN HIM. AND HEREBY WE KNOW THAT HE ABIDETH IN US, BY THE SPIRIT WHICH HE HATH GIVEN US" (1 John 3:24).

As Christians, we live in Jesus Christ by obeying His commands, and He lives in us. We know He lives in us because of His Spirit's presence. The Holy Spirit speaks to us, guides us and comforts us. He helps us discern right from wrong, and He enables us to choose the right. God's Spirit grows His fruit in our lives, empowers us to witness, helps us pray, and unifies us with other believers.

It is because of the Holy Spirit's wooing that we came to Christ for salvation; it is through Him we are able to keep God's commands; and it is His abiding presence that will keep us until the end.

Daily Devotions:
M. Holy Conduct
   1 Samuel 26:5-12
T. Acknowledging God
   Proverbs 3:1-12
W. Doing Right
   Matthew 12:9-13
T. Overcoming Evil
   Romans 12:9-21
F. Forbearing One Another
   Colossians 3:12-17
S. A Pure Heart
   2 Timothy 2:19-26

Faith in God's Son

1 John 4:1-6; 5:1-13

Unit Theme:
Living in Light and Love (1, 2 and 3 John)

Central Truth:
Having faith in Christ results in eternal life.

Focus:
Know that faith in Christ brings victory and live an overcoming life.

Context:
Written to an unnamed audience by the apostle John

Golden Text:
"This is the record, that God hath given to us eternal life, and this life is in his Son" (1 John 5:11).

Study Outline:
I. Confession of Faith (1 John 4:1-6)
II. Object of Faith (1 John 5:1-5)
III. The Threefold Witness (1 John 5:6-13)

INTRODUCTION

A personal relationship with Jesus Christ begins with hearing His claims. Paul asked, "How, then, can they call on the one they have not believed in? And how can they believe in the one of whom they have not heard? And how can they hear without someone preaching to them?" (Romans 10:14, *NIV*).

Hearing about Christ must be followed by receiving Him. It is not enough to only accept the witness of God concerning His Son. John wrote, "God has given us eternal life, and this life is in His Son. He who has the Son has life; he who does not have the Son of God does not have life" (1 John 5:11, 12, *NKJV*).

Traveling by ship in Norway, you sail slowly through the beautiful and silent *fjords* (narrow inlets of the sea between cliffs or steep slopes). You see the grand mountains rising all around, and beautiful waterfalls make sweet music as they hurry down the steep cliffs on their way back to the sea. Standing on the deck of the vessel, you see the channel in front narrowing until it looks like a dead end. You seem to be sailing straight into the mountain. A few hundred yards farther and you are sure the front of the ship will strike on the iron cliffs. But just when progress seems impossible, the channel opens up and the steamer glides out upon another fjord of entrancing beauty.

So it is with the iron gates we encounter on the pilgrimage of life. Faith swings the gates open, and we pass into the beautiful life God has provided in His Son. As we start the journey by faith, so we continue by faith and gain ultimate triumph by faith. By faith our travels will end as did Christian's in John Bunyan's book, *Pilgrim's Progress*: "So he passed over, and all the trumpets sounded for him on the other side."

Since Jesus Christ, the Son of God, is both the way to heaven and the rewarder of the saints in heaven, people who question Christ's claims and identity cannot inherit everlasting life.

I. CONFESSION OF FAITH (1 John 4:1-6)

A. Testing the Spirits (vv. 1-3)

1. Beloved, believe not every spirit, but try the spirits whether they are of God: because many false prophets are gone out into the world.

2. Hereby know ye the Spirit of God: Every spirit that confesseth that Jesus Christ is come in the flesh is of God:

3. And every spirit that confesseth not that Jesus Christ is come in the flesh is not of God: and this is that spirit of antichrist, whereof ye have heard that it should come; and even now already is it in the world.

From the beginning of the Christian era, false teachers have tried to overcome the gospel of Christ by means of confusion. What the devil cannot deny he imitates, and by this imitation he does more harm than he could do by mere denial.

The false teachers mentioned here do not deny that Christ has come; they simply represent Him in an erroneous way. It's the same issue believers today face with the "Jesus" of the Muslims, Jehovah's Witnesses and Mormons. They say Jesus was a great prophet or an enlightened teacher or one of the sons of God; but none of them accept Jesus as the one and only Son of God who created the world, died for humanity, rose again and reigns forever.

As born-again children of God, we are called upon to put spirits to the test. The most effective way to test the truth of any prophet is to judge his word by the Word of God. And one of the cardinal Biblical doctrines declares, "The Word [God's Son] became flesh and made his dwelling among us" (John 1:14, *NIV*).

Anyone speaking by inspiration of the Holy Spirit will confess that Jesus came in the flesh and *continues* to live as the Son of God ("is of God," 1 John 4:2). Not only will the faithful teacher proclaim this truth in words; he or she will also abide under Christ's lordship in their daily lives.

Verse 3 says any spirit or attitude that professes to be Christian yet denies the incarnation of God's Son is actually "antichrist" (against Christ). Those who deny this truth are false teachers no matter how much they may claim to be followers of Jesus. Such false teachers may even use the name of Jesus freely, but this does not make them true disciples of the Lord.

The early church was constantly warned that people would arise who would deny the deity of Jesus. Before the death of all the apostles there were already false teachers, claiming to be Christians, who denied that Jesus was the incarnation of God on the earth. Jesus himself had warned of such false prophets (Matthew 24:5).

Talk About It:
1. How can a Christian "test the spirits" (v. 1, *NIV*)? Why is this necessary?
2. To be a Christian, what must a person believe and confess concerning Jesus Christ?

"The Spirit of truth is divinely sensitive to anything that even hints of deception."
—Charles Stanley

B. Overcoming the World (vv. 4-6)

4. Ye are of God, little children, and have overcome them: because greater is he that is in you, than he that is in the world.

5. They are of the world: therefore speak they of the world, and the world heareth them.

6. We are of God: he that knoweth God heareth us; he that is not of God heareth not us. Hereby know we the spirit of truth, and the spirit of error.

The child of God is to have no fear of the spirit of antichrist because truth overcomes the power of error. The secret of the Christian's protection and power is Christ's Spirit living within. Christ lives in our hearts and dominates our lives so we can live without fear in a dangerous world.

"Greater is he that is in you, than he that is in the world" is one of the most powerful statements in Scripture. If Christ abides in our lives, we need not fear being overwhelmed by sin, heresy or any ungodly work. The devil is behind all of those things, but the Spirit of God is infinitely greater than him.

Verse 5 says teachers who deny Christ's incarnation are "of the world." They speak those things the people of the world want to hear. Paul warned Timothy that "the time will come when they will not endure sound doctrine; but after their own lusts shall they heap to themselves teachers, having itching ears; and they shall turn away their ears from the truth, and shall be turned unto fables" (2 Timothy 4:3, 4).

The world does not want to hear the truth because the truth condemns its evil. Sinful people then provide for themselves false teachers whose words will give them a sense of security and well-being. Think of any antichrist lifestyle—from homosexuality to polygamy, from relativism to materialism—and you can find a "religious" group that endorses it. Worldly people want a worldly doctrine.

However, true followers of Christ are "of God" (1 John 4:6). They gladly receive the full Christian message. "The spirit of truth" accepts that Jesus Christ has come from God in the form of human flesh, while "the spirit of error" rejects this fact.

II. OBJECT OF FAITH (1 John 5:1-5)

A. Born of God (v. 1)

1. Whosoever believeth that Jesus is the Christ is born of God: and every one that loveth him that begat loveth him also that is begotten of him.

Belief that Jesus is the Christ is the core of Christianity. This single belief is the difference between life and death, light and dark, salvation and damnation. Spiritual life begins with the belief that Jesus of Nazareth was indeed the Son of God, sent

---

Talk About It:

1. Whom must believers "overcome" (vv. 4, 5), and how can this happen?

2. How will "he that is not of God" respond to Christian teaching or witnessing (v. 6)?

Trapped but Triumphant

Imagine a city under siege. The enemy that surrounds the city will not let anyone or anything leave. Supplies are running low, and the citizens are fearful. But in the dark of the night, a spy sneaks through the enemy lines. [He tells] the people that in another place the main enemy force has been defeated; the leaders have already surrendered. . . . It is only a matter of time until the besieging troops receive the news and lay down their weapons. Similarly, we may seem now to be surrounded by the forces of evil . . . but the Enemy has actually been defeated at Calvary.

—**Richard J. Mouw**
(Uncommon Decency)

Faith in God's Son

from heaven as a sacrifice for the sins of the world, whose blood cleanses us from sin. According to John, anyone who believes this cardinal fact about Christ is born of God. This means belief in Christ is the watershed between life and death: those who believe have life and those who do not believe remain in death.

Talk About It:
Who is "born of God"? What is the born-again person's relationship with Jesus Christ? With God the Father?

The love for God the Father and Christ the Son are so intertwined that they amount to the same thing. To love one is to love the other, and to reject one is to reject the other. Jesus himself said, "He that hateth me hateth my Father also" (John 15:23). In the days of John the Christian church was made up mainly of Jews who had been converted to Christ. Yet the great multitude of Jews rejected Christ and still professed to love God. John's statement here is that anyone who truly loved the Father would also love the Son.

B. Obedient to God (vv. 2, 3)

2. By this we know that we love the children of God, when we love God, and keep his commandments.

3. For this is the love of God, that we keep his commandments: and his commandments are not grievous.

grievous (v. 3)— burdensome

Talk About It:
1. How do God's children live?
2. Why are God's laws not considered burdensome?

The love we have for God and His Son reaches to all the children of God. If we truly love God, we will love our fellow Christians as well. Proof that we love God is the fact that we love one another. The phrase "and [we] keep his commandments" means in its broadest sense that we keep all His commandments, but in its strictest sense, it means that we obey the commandment of love (John 13:34; 15:12, 17; 1 John 4:21).

Jesus does not *recommend* that we love one another, nor does He *suggest* it might be a good idea for us to do so, but He *commands* us to do so (5:3). The fruit of love goes further, however, and is seen in full obedience to all the commandments of Christ.

"Come to me, all you who are weary and burdened, and I will give you rest. . . . For my yoke is easy and my burden is light."

—Jesus Christ (Matthew 11:28, 30, NIV)

In 1 John 3:23, belief on Christ is identified as a commandment along with loving others. Such a commandment is liberating and life-giving, not burdensome.

C. Overcomers by Faith (vv. 4, 5)

4. For whatsoever is born of God overcometh the world: and this is the victory that overcometh the world, even our faith.

5. Who is he that overcometh the world, but he that believeth that Jesus is the Son of God?

There is a constant battle between the Christian realm and the worldly realm. The world never makes peace with Christianity. Thus the world must be overcome. The word *overcome* shows that Christians must come to grips with the world

Talk About It:
Who overcomes the world, and how is it accomplished?

and bring it under their subjection. We cannot expect to be delivered from the conflict, for conflict is necessary for victory. Only those who are genuinely born of God are able to be victorious in this spiritual conflict. The means of triumph is steadfast faith.

In verse 5 John repeats for emphasis the same assurance he has just spoken. No one can overcome the world except one who has faith that Jesus is the Son of God. Faith that Jesus is God's Son is power and triumph and life. This is a truth already asserted in verse 1, and which will be repeated in verse 10. Belief that Jesus is the Son of God is a stabilizing, sustaining force. A person cannot truly believe this great spiritual reality without having his or her life changed and fortified by it.

III. THE THREEFOLD WITNESS (1 John 5:6-13)
A. Perfect Agreement (vv. 6-9)

6. This is he that came by water and blood, even Jesus Christ; not by water only, but by water and blood. And it is the Spirit that beareth witness, because the Spirit is truth.

7. For there are three that bear record in heaven, the Father, the Word, and the Holy Ghost: and these three are one.

8. And there are three that bear witness in earth, the Spirit, and the water, and the blood: and these three agree in one.

9. If we receive the witness of men, the witness of God is greater: for this is the witness of God which he hath testified of his Son.

Talk About It:
1. What is the testimony of Jesus' blood, His baptism, and the Holy Spirit concerning Jesus Christ?
2. Why should we believe their testimony?

It is a Scriptural precept that all truth should be established by two or three witnesses (Matthew 18:16; 2 Corinthians 13:1; 1 Timothy 5:19). In verses 6 and 8 of our lesson text, there are three witnesses listed—the water, the blood and the Spirit. The blood obviously represents the crucifixion of Christ, while the Spirit is of course the Holy Spirit, or Holy Ghost. But what does the water signify? There are various interpretations. Some believe the water refers to Jesus' natural birth, while others see it as a reference to the "blood and water" that was poured out when Jesus' side was speared (John 19:34). Perhaps the most common idea is that the water refers to the baptism of Jesus.

All three of these—"the Spirit, and the water, and the blood" (1 John 5:8)—testify that Jesus is the Son of God. At Jesus' baptism, the Holy Spirit descended like a dove, lighting on Him; and a voice from heaven declared, "This is my beloved Son, in whom I am well pleased" (Matthew 3:16, 17). At the crucifixion of Jesus, the Holy Spirit was present with convicting power. Thereby a Roman soldier cried out, "Truly this was the Son of God" (27:54).

Faith in God's Son

Still today it is the Holy Spirit, now present among us, who bears witness to the truth of Jesus' identity and plan of salvation. His presence affirms to us that Jesus is indeed the Son of God and His blood cleanses us from all sins.

Verse 7 of our text says "the Father, the Word, and the Holy Ghost" testify together, "and these three are one." There are many clear Biblical expressions of the Trinity, including Matthew 28:19, where Jesus commanded His followers to baptize believers "in the name of the Father, and of the Son, and of the Holy Ghost." In 2 Corinthians 13:14, Paul prayed, "The grace of our Lord Jesus Christ, and the love of God, and the communion of the Holy Ghost, be with you all. Amen."

Different from the Father, Son and Holy Spirit, the "three that bear witness in earth" are not one, but they "are in agreement" (1 John 5:8, *NIV*). These three work together in the manifestation of God on the earth. They have an identical purpose but individual functions. They agree as witnesses on the earth to the divinity of Christ and His power to redeem lost people.

In verse 9 John likens the threefold witness required in Deuteronomy 19:15 with the threefold witness of the Spirit, the water and the blood in declaration of His Son. If three witnesses among people were sufficient for a matter to be accepted as true, certainly a threefold witness from God should certainly be enough to establish the truth that Jesus is His Son.

B. Internal Witness (v. 10)

10. He that believeth on the Son of God hath the witness in himself: he that believeth not God hath made him a liar; because he believeth not the record that God gave of his Son.

The previous verses show there is a threefold witness to Christ, but this verse shows an inner, personal witness in the life of every believer. This inner witness is one that comes to every person who believes on Christ. The three-part record is theological, but the witness within our hearts is intensely personal. The greatest verification of the reality of Christ is the fact that He transforms the lives of men and women and gives them newness of life. Every child of God is living proof of the reality of Christ. Paul commended Roman Christians because their faith was spoken of throughout the whole world (Romans 1:8).

The Pharisees engaged in long theological disputes about the identity of Christ, but one thing they could not deny was that a blind man had received his sight when Jesus touched him. The man who had been healed could say, "One thing I know, that, whereas I was blind, now I see" (John 9:25). A life that is touched by Christ remains to this day the greatest confirmation of His reality.

> "In the great mystery of the Incarnation, God does not merely bring fire to earth to ease the cold and dark of mortal life, but sacrificially gives the divine Life itself, that we may live with God forever. . . . God chooses not only to save the world, but to do so by becoming one of us, by becoming human."
>
> —Deborah Smith Douglas
> *(Weavings)*

Talk About It:
1. What is the "record" mentioned here?
2. What inward witness do believers have?

Those who do not accept Christ make God a liar, for they respond with disbelief to God's gift of His Son for the sins of the world. Intellectual acceptance of the fact of Christ is not enough; we must accept Him in our heart.

C. Eternal Living (vv. 11-13)

11. And this is the record, that God hath given to us eternal life, and this life is in his Son.

12. He that hath the Son hath life; and he that hath not the Son of God hath not life.

13. These things have I written unto you that believe on the name of the Son of God; that ye may know that ye have eternal life, and that ye may believe on the name of the Son of God.

Life in Christ improves the quality of our present lives and gives eternal life to us. The scripture says God *has* given us eternal life, not that He *will* give us eternal life. This places eternal life in the present tense. Eternal life begins for us when we accept Jesus Christ. The seed of Christ brings us into the beginning of eternity.

Verse 12 makes this truth even more emphatic. Every person who has Christ also has life, which means eternal life; whoever does not have Christ does not have life, even though he still lives in the present world. Jesus said, "He that believeth on the Son hath everlasting life: and he that believeth not the Son shall not see life; but the wrath of God abideth on him" (John 3:36).

When John writes "These things have I written unto you" (v. 13), he is referring to the entire epistle. The Holy Spirit had inspired him to write this letter to help believers understand they already had received eternal life, and to hold on to it dearly, as well as to challenge unbelievers to give themselves to Christ.

Talk About It:

1. Why is there no life without the Son?

2. According to verse 13, why did John write this letter?

"Jesus died on the cross—that's history. Jesus died for me—that's salvation."
—Church sign

CONCLUSION

It is possible for us to think of eternal life only as the incredible future that awaits us in heaven. And we should be thrilled about living and reigning with Christ, saying goodbye to sickness and sorrow and death, and experiencing a world with no evil influences. At the same time, God wants His children to experience life "to the full" (John 10:10, *NIV*) while here on earth. The deeper our faith in Christ reaches, the fuller our life in Him will be.

GOLDEN TEXT CHALLENGE

"THIS IS THE RECORD, THAT GOD HATH GIVEN TO US ETERNAL LIFE, AND THIS LIFE IS IN HIS SON" (1 John 5:11).

Faith in God's Son

Testimony services used to be a staple of Pentecostal worship. Individuals would take turns telling of God's goodness to them. Many people would start their testimony by saying, "I thank God for saving me and . . . "

In this verse, the word *record* means "testimony" or "witness." It's a testimony of salvation. However, rather than speaking in first person, saying, "God has given *me* eternal life," John uses the word *us*. So he presents a testimony that all Christians can repeat together: "God has given us eternal life, and this life is in his Son" (*NIV*).

Daily Devotions:
M. Showing Mercy
   1 Samuel 24:1-10
T. Maintaining Integrity
   Job 2:1-10
W. Demonstrating Faithfulness
   Malachi 3:16-18
T. Willing to Sacrifice
   Matthew 26:7-13
F. Boldness in Ministry
   Acts 4:1-13
S. Steadfast in Faith
   Acts 16:22-32

Knowing and Telling the Truth

In his three epistles, John urged his readers to understand and follow God's truths in the face of false teaching. In the following article, Christians today are urged to do the same.

Noted Christian apologist G.K. Chesterton once warned that when people stop believing anything, they are prepared to believe everything. Perhaps this time has come in America with an invasion of world religions, pseudo-Christian movements, cults, the occult and unchristian philosophies.

Pollster George Gallup Jr. said, "The problem is not that Americans don't believe, it's that they believe everything. Thus, we find in the extreme cases the weekly churchgoer who believes in channeling and the born-again Christian who believes in ghosts and witches. The question is, how can churches help people discern what is of God and what is not?"

Humanity is incurably religious. Sigmund Freud even tried through psychoanalysis to cure us of what he called the "universal obsessive neurosis"—or our belief in God. He didn't succeed. Reinhold Niebuhr said, "Irreligion is a luxury which only those who observe life rather than live it may allow themselves. Those who live virtually must base their life upon an act of faith that life has meaning, and seek to conform their actions to that meaning" (*Christian Clippings*).

All religions share three common characteristics: beliefs, a code of conduct and worship. Religion boils down to our concept of God and how we experience Him. How we think about God, in turn, shapes our attitudes, values, beliefs, philosophy of life and, ultimately, our lifestyle.

There are three monotheistic religions in the world: Judaism, Christianity and Islam. (Monotheism means the belief in one God.) They all have their origins in the Old Testament patriarch, Abraham. He was the father of the Hebrew people. From Israel came Jesus the Messiah. His followers were later called Christians, although most early believers, like their Master, were Jewish. Christianity, then, is the natural outflow and fulfillment of Judaism. Finally, Muhammad blended elements of Judaism and the teachings of Christ along with his own religious roots to pioneer a new religion known as Islam.

The Eastern religions of Hinduism and its later offshoot, Buddhism, are polytheistic religions. *Polytheism* means the belief in many gods, which includes everything from deities to inanimate objects to the elements of the universe. In Eastern mysticism, God may be seen as personal or impersonal, depending on the particular religious viewpoint. New Ageism, mysticism, astrology, transcendental meditation, and the belief in karma and reincarnation, all find their roots in the ancient Eastern religions.

The American culture has also been influenced by two pseudo-Christian movements that began in the 1800s: Mormonism and Jehovah's Witnesses. Because they are unaware of the real beliefs espoused by these movements, many individuals believe they are Christian denominations. But a great divide exists on many fundamental points between orthodox Christian faith and these two particular movements.

America has its share of religious cults. There are about 700, according to one research study, with each one headed by a formidable leader claiming to be a prophet of God, or even worse, the Messiah himself. What is a cult? A cult is a religious movement that deviates from Biblical truth about the nature of God and His provision of salvation through Jesus Christ.

Cults share three basic characteristics. First, a cult is led by a charismatic leader claiming to be a representative of God. Second, cults claim secret revelations of truth known only to the adherents of the movement. Third, cults manipulate, exploit, and control the thinking, lifestyle and financial resources of their members. Such groups often recruit followers by offering seminars on self-fulfillment rather than salvation on campuses and in corporate settings.

The most frequent sign Jesus gave of His second coming was the proliferation of false christs and false prophets: "Many false prophets will appear and deceive many people. . . . For false Christs and false prophets will appear and perform great signs and miracles to deceive even the elect—if that were possible" (Matthew 24:11, 24, *NIV*).

The issue is not whether all religions have some good points. Many do. There exists an obvious sharing of a collective morality among many religions. In addition, all the major religions welcome Jesus into their faith and ascribe to Him a status greater than that of an ordinary man. Even the Koran acknowledges His virgin birth, and considers Him to be one of the seven great prophets.

The issue is one of truth. What is the truth about God? About Jesus Christ? About life after death? About morality? And what is the source of truth? We must measure world religions and pseudo-Christian movements in light of the truth of the Bible. As we better understand the Christian faith along with other religious viewpoints, we will be better equipped to share our faith when those special "divine opportunities" come our way.

Witnessing should not intimidate a believer. Think of it as simply sharing your personal testimony of what Christ means to you. You are the greatest living witness to the risen Christ! God not only wants you to be His witness, but to be an expert witness. Like a lawyer gets an expert witness to support his case in a court of law, so Jesus wants you to be an expert witness for Him. Expert witnesses are knowledgeable.

When God gives you the opportunity to share your faith, be considerate and respectful of the viewpoints of others. Try to see life from their vantage point. Most people are raised in a particular religion. They have no reason to question its validity. Show the same respect and desire to listen as you have for wanting to share your faith.

Sharing one's faith requires a certain amount of courage. Religion is a sensitive subject and difficult to talk about. The Holy Spirit will give courage and the right words to say when the opportunity arises.

It is a privilege to share our faith. Cherish every opportunity that comes your way. I often think of Paul's encouragement when I have the opportunity to talk with someone about religious matters and to share Christ with them: "Be wise in the way you act toward outsiders; make the most of every opportunity. Let your conversation be always full of grace, seasoned with salt, so that you may know how to answer everyone" (Colossians 4:5, 6, *NIV*).—Adapted from *Faith Under Fire*, by David C. Cooper

Faithfulness to the Truth

2 John 1-11; 3 John 1-12

INTRODUCTION

John's second epistle is addressed to a church greatly loved by the apostle. John warns the church especially about the danger of receiving and giving audience to heretical teachers. He was writing from another local church (possibly Ephesus, also in Asia Minor) which he called an "elect sister" (v. 13).

John rejoices that the members are steadfast in the truth, as a father rejoices when his children do well. He reminds the readers of the commandment to love one another, a theme that is prominent in John's Gospel and his first epistle.

John expresses a desire to visit the church soon, when he can say all the things in person that he presently is unable to write (v. 12). He closes with Christian greetings from the church where he is writing (v. 13).

John's third epistle is a short letter to a person named Gaius. It is a personal note similar to Paul's letter to Philemon and reveals one of the ways church guidance was provided in those days. Gaius was probably one of John's converts, for he calls him one of his children (vv. 2-4).

John had written to the church earlier, but Diotrephes, a self-willed, ambitious church leader, rejected both the letter and the authority of John (vv. 9-11). Diotrephes was not only adamant against accepting those who came to the church, but he excommunicated those who did receive them. John declares strongly that when he comes to the church later, he will deal with this evil man, who despite his position in the church has never seen God.—Charles W. Conn

Unit Theme:
Living in Light and Love (1, 2 and 3 John)

Central Truth:
Christians must resist error and follow the truth.

Focus:
Understand the challenges to the gospel and follow the way of truth.

Context:
The second and third epistles of John warn and encourage believers.

Golden Text:
"I have no greater joy than to hear that my children walk in truth" (3 John 4).

Study Outline:
I. Commendations (2 John 1-4)
II. Commandments (2 John 5-11)
III. Exhortations (3 John 1-12)

I. COMMENDATIONS (2 John 1-4)

A. Indwelling Truth (vv. 1, 2)

1. The elder unto the elect lady and her children, whom I love in the truth; and not I only, but also all they that have known the truth;

2. For the truth's sake, which dwelleth in us, and shall be with us for ever.

The author of this brief letter must have been so well-known to those whom he was writing that the title "elder" identified him. The word *elder* is translated from the Greek *presbyteros*, which can mean an old man, a senior person deserving of respect, or a senior church leader.

There are two views regarding the identify of the "elect lady" to whom John wrote. Some feel that because of the formal style of the letter, the word *lady* (v. 1) refers to a specific church and *children* refers to its individual members (cf. v. 13). Others think it's more natural to view the designation as that of a literal lady and her Christian family. In either case, this little letter is packed with spiritual counsel.

John said he loved this group of believers "in the truth . . . because of the truth" (vv. 1, 2, *NIV*). The truth of the gospel bound John in love to this church and to all other believers. This truth was not said to abide "in you" or "in them," but "in us." The apostle was identifying himself with the whole society of the faithful.

For John, truth was more than objective knowledge. This truth he spoke of indwells believers, permeates their existence, and therefore is the ground of their loving fellowship. Through Christ, the truth gives believers a personal power that "shall be with us for ever" (v. 2). When Jesus called Himself "the way, the truth, and the life" (John 14:6), He also said, "I will come again and receive you to Myself; that where I am, there you may be also" (v. 3, *NKJV*).

B. Walking Truth (vv. 3, 4)

3. Grace be with you, mercy, and peace, from God the Father, and from the Lord Jesus Christ, the Son of the Father, in truth and love.

4. I rejoiced greatly that I found of thy children walking in truth, as we have received a commandment from the Father.

The blessings of grace, mercy and peace belong to those who are of the truth. The phrase "grace . . . mercy, and peace" marks the order from the first action of God to the final satisfaction of people.

Grace is the favor of God toward sinners that comes to them in their helpless condition. *Mercy* is the compassion of God for the misery of sinners. It is the manifestation of divine grace. *Peace*

Talk About It:

1. What must Christians do "for the truth's sake" (v. 2)?

2. What two qualities does verse 2 reveal about truth?

Here is the Truth in a little creed,
Enough for all the roads we go;
In Love is all the law we need,
In Christ is all the God we know.
—Edwin Markham

Talk About It:

What brought great joy to the apostle John? Why?

refers to the harmonized relationship between God and those who through faith become His children. It also means the sense of rest and contentment which results from this relationship.

In verse 3 John affirmed the deity of Jesus by joining "the Lord Jesus Christ" with "God the Father" and by calling Jesus "the Son of the Father." One cannot walk "in truth and love" without acknowledging the deity of Jesus, as the apostle emphasized in his first epistle (1 John 4:2, 3).

In verse 4 of our text we see John had somehow learned that "some" of the elect lady's children were "walking in truth," and he "rejoiced greatly" in their authentic Christianity (*NKJV*). The truth here is likened to a path which believers should walk without deviating. Indeed, to go astray from revealed truth (whether in doctrine or morals) is not just an unfortunate error but an active disobedience, for we have been commanded by the Father to walk in the truth.

Love, truth and obedience are three elements that must work together. Love without obedience is mere sentiment and lacks reality. Obedience without love is heartless slavery. Love and obedience must be founded on and directed by truth. Neither can flourish outside its realm.

II. COMMANDMENTS (2 John 5-11)
A. Love One Another (vv. 5, 6)

5. And now I beseech thee, lady, not as though I wrote a new commandment unto thee, but that which we had from the beginning, that we love one another.

6. And this is love, that we walk after his commandments. This is the commandment, That, as ye have heard from the beginning, ye should walk in it.

The commandment "which we had from the beginning" probably means the one they had from the start of their experience with the Lord. "Love one another" was not a new commandment when John was writing; it was as old as the gospel. It was not even new to his readers; they had known it from the first days of their Christian walk. It is possible to fake belief, and confession can be made with the lips only, but love is more difficult to counterfeit.

In verse 6 John declared the interrelationship of love and obedience. Obedience finds its expression in love, and love finds its expression in obedience. "Walk in it" refers to God's command to love. When all of God's precepts have been condensed into one, we are left with the command to love God and one another.

B. Watch Out! (vv. 7, 8)

7. For many deceivers are entered into the world, who

Talk About It:
We know God's command to love each other. Why can it be difficult to "walk in it" (v. 6)?

confess not that Jesus Christ is come in the flesh. This is a deceiver and an antichrist.

8. Look to yourselves, that we lose not those things which we have wrought, but that we receive a full reward.

Talk About It:
1. What is the goal of the "deceivers" mentioned here (v. 7)?
2. Explain the warning in verse 8.

Five Legs?

Once, when a stubborn disputer seemed unconvinced, Lincoln said, "Well, how many legs has a cow?"

"Four, of course," came the reply disgustedly.

"That's right," agreed Lincoln. "Now suppose you call the cow's tail a leg; how many legs would the cow have?"

"Why, five, of course," was the confident reply.

"Now, that's where you're wrong," said Lincoln. "Calling a cow's tail a leg doesn't make it a leg."

—*Sermon Illustrations.com*

The word *for* (v. 7) indicates there is a special reason for walking in truth and love. Christians, John attested, need to walk in the path of light and love because many false teachers are at work. False teachers are filled with a spirit of deception and seek the spiritual destruction of Christians. In his first letter, John branded false teachers as liars (2:22), seducers (v. 26), false prophets (4:1), and the mouthpiece of Antichrist (2:18, 22; 4:3); he now labeled them as deceivers.

In this reference, *deceivers* has two meanings: (1) those who lead people astray or cause them to wander and (2) vagabonds, hence charlatans or impostors. The phrase "are entered into the world" (v. 7) marks a particular crisis. They are the ones who "confess not that Jesus Christ is come in the flesh." These deceivers denied not merely the fact of the Incarnation but even its possibility.

The truth is that unless Jesus Christ was God incarnate, there would be no salvation. John therefore said any who taught this false doctrine was "a deceiver and an antichrist" (v. 7). There is in this heresy a double offense—it deceives people and opposes Christ. The word *antichrist* means "against Christ" and "instead of Christ."

After announcing the fact and indicating the danger of itinerant false teachers, John issued his first warning: "Look to yourselves" (v. 8). The importance of such watchfulness is twofold: negatively, "that we do not lose those things we worked for," and positively, "that we may receive a full reward" (*NKJV*).

The phrase "those things we worked for" does not refer to their winning or losing salvation (which is a free gift), but to their reward for faithful service. Apparently John was referring to the result of their labors, which were as talents entrusted to their charge to be used for the Kingdom (see Matthew 25:14-30). The phrase "a full reward" means one in which no element is lacking. Therefore, rewards for faithfulness, obedience and diligence include blessings and satisfaction in our earthly life as well as special recognition in the life to come.

C. Deny Deceivers (vv. 9-11)

9. Whosoever transgresseth, and abideth not in the doctrine of Christ, hath not God. He that abideth in the doctrine of Christ, he hath both the Father and the Son.

10. If there come any unto you, and bring not this doctrine, receive him not into your house, neither bid him God speed:

11. For he that biddeth him God speed is partaker of his evil deeds.

The danger spoken of in verse 9 is that of going beyond the Word of God by adding to it. The word translated *transgresseth* means "goes beyond, runs ahead too far, passes beyond assigned limits." It speaks of teaching that goes beyond Christian doctrine.

"The doctrine of Christ" (v. 9) means not only the teachings concerning the person and works of Christ but also what He taught. The false teachers proposed to enter new regions of "truth" and leave the old.

To acknowledge that Jesus Christ has come in the flesh is fundamental to the faith, and to love one another is also fundamental. To confess the former requires that we do the latter, for Christ desires to love through us.

The phrase "hath not God" (v. 9) means people do not have Him as their God; therefore, they do not hold Him in their heart as the One they adore, trust and obey. By denying Jesus' claims, they cannot *have* God—they cannot be in relationship with Him. On the other hand, "he that abideth in the doctrine of Christ, he hath both the Father and the Son."

John's second warning is found in verse 10. The phrase "if there come any unto you" anticipates a visit of a false teacher to the church. If one should come teaching any other doctrine, "receive him not," John urged.

If these deceivers were treated as if they were Christians, their opportunity of doing harm would be multiplied, and they might never be brought to see their errors. Such teachers should not be received as people who could justly claim the privilege of Christian hospitality. They should not even be welcomed with a sympathetic greeting. The injunction "neither bid him God speed" covers any act that might be seen as giving sanction to the false doctrine or showing sympathy with it.

We should construe John's words as forbidding hospitality to all unbelievers. The prohibition concerns those who are actively engaged in teaching a false view of Christ and seeking approval among Christians. John then gave an explanation for his mandate: "Anyone who welcomes him shares in his wicked work" (v. 11, *NIV*).

The word for *evil* (KJV) is often used to describe Satan, and implies an active program of corrupting others. To say that one who welcomes a deceiver would be a partaker of his evil deeds indicates that the individual has a share in the deceptive teaching.

III. EXHORTATIONS (3 John 1-12)

A. Great Report (vv. 1-4)

1. The elder unto the wellbeloved Gaius, whom I love in the truth.

---

biddeth him God speed (v. 11)—welcomes him

Talk About It:
1. How can someone have "both the Father and the Son" (v. 9)?
2. How should the church and individual Christians respond to false teachers (vv. 10, 11)?

Gaius (GAY-yus)—v. 1—a convert of John known for his hospitality

2. Beloved, I wish above all things that thou mayest prosper and be in health, even as thy soul prospereth.

3. For I rejoiced greatly, when the brethren came and testified of the truth that is in thee, even as thou walkest in the truth.

4. I have no greater joy than to hear that my children walk in truth.

Talk About It:

1. How did John respond to the news of Gaius' spiritual condition?

2. Why should the good spiritual health of people we have influenced for Christ be a source of great joy?

John's third epistle is addressed to Gaius, who seems to have been a man of position and influence in the Christian community. John wishes for him prosperity and well-being (v. 2). This appropriate Christian benediction has come to be widely misunderstood in modern times, which results in spiritual error. Some have espoused from this simple verse an elaborate notion that all Christians should attain wealth in this life. Such a belief is inaccurate and leads to disillusionment. The Lord promises to supply our need (Philippians 4:19), but not to make us wealthy. If we are blessed with wealth, then we should understand it is a blessing of God, and not a promise or obligation of God. John would certainly not set forth such a teaching when he himself was not a partaker of it. In Acts 3:3-6 it is said that John, along with Peter, had neither gold nor silver. If he is here preaching divine prosperity, then he is guilty of preaching what he did not practice.

In verse 3 of the text we see word had been brought to John of Gaius's faithfulness to the Lord. John now declares he is greatly refreshed and blessed by hearing of Gaius's spiritual welfare. As he said to the elect lady in 2 John 4, he asserts that a spiritual father can have no greater blessing than to hear that his children in the Lord do well. Every person who has ever worked for the Lord or has ever brought souls into the kingdom of God knows the truth of this sentiment. The effect on a Christian who hears that his spiritual children do well is like that of a natural parent who rejoices in the success of his children.

B. Christian Hospitality (vv. 5-8)

5. Beloved, thou doest faithfully whatsoever thou doest to the brethren, and to strangers;

6. Which have borne witness of thy charity before the church: whom if thou bring forward on their journey after a godly sort, thou shalt do well:

7. Because that for his name's sake they went forth, taking nothing of the Gentiles.

8. We therefore ought to receive such, that we might be fellowhelpers to the truth.

In the early days of Christianity, the message was carried forth by itinerant preachers who depended on the hospitality of other Christians for housing, food and support in their mission.

This was more important in those days than in this time when housing and food are so easily come by in commercial institutions. In those days the traveling preachers had to depend on the hospitality and charity of Christians they encountered along the way. Gaius was one of those who became well known for having performed such duties. This was regarded as a special mark of distinction and worth throughout the Christian church (read Acts 16:15; 1 Timothy 5:10; 2 John 10).

Those preachers who came back from their travels testified to the charity and hospitality of Gaius (3 John 6). In this way he had become well known for his good works. There was benefit in hospitality, however, only when it was extended to people of truth. John did not suggest that hospitality of itself is a blessing. If Gaius should lend strength to error by his hospitality, then he would be a participant in that error. The early days of Christianity were days when Satan did everything possible to impede the progress of the church and defeat its efforts to reach the world. The same thing is now true in the last days, when apostasy is once again rampant, and the occasion to lend strength to false causes is again widespread. There is no good consequence to the giving of support to error.

In verse 7 we see what dependence the early church placed on this individual hospitality. Paul and other itinerant preachers did not stop in the homes of Gentiles and unbelievers, but with those who were of the faith. When they stopped in private homes, they were refreshed and blessed and supported by their host. But the hosts were also blessed by the fellowship, enlightenment and encouragement of their visitors. This custom therefore laced the church together in bonds of fellowship and love. There came to be a virtual network of Christian houses along the way where Christian travelers might stop for rest in their labors.

Verse 8 says the example set by Gaius should be followed by all, as much in our day as it was in his. Those who participate in assisting laborers in the gospel are themselves participants in the gospel. Those who send the gospel are participants with those who carry it (Romans 10:15).

C. Opposite Examples (vv. 9-12)

9. I wrote unto the church: but Diotrephes, who loveth to have the preeminence among them, receiveth us not.

10. Wherefore, if I come, I will remember his deeds which he doeth, prating against us with malicious words: and not content therewith, neither doth he himself receive the brethren, and forbiddeth them that would, and casteth them out of the church.

11. Beloved, follow not that which is evil, but that which

Talk About It:
1. Describe the reputation of Gaius (vv. 5, 6).
2. Describe the ministry of those to whom Gaius was a "fellowhelper" (vv. 7, 8).

"Hospitality is the art of making people want to stay without interfering with their departure."
—*Quotable Quotes*

Diotrephes (die-OT-rih-feez)—v. 9—a domineering church leader

Demetrius (dih-
ME-tree-us)—
v. 12—a faithful
believer

Talk About It:
1. Describe Diotrephes' attitude and the actions that flowed from it.
2. What was the reputation of Demetrius, and how did John confirm it?
3. Why is verse 11 an appropriate bridge between the descriptions of Diotrephes and Demetrius?

is good. He that doeth good is of God: but he that doeth evil hath not seen God.

12. Demetrius hath good report of all men, and of the truth itself: yea, and we also bear record; and ye know that our record is true.

Early in the history of the church there were many who showed carnal attitudes. Near the top of such a list would have to be Diotrephes, a domineering, overbearing "church boss." He resisted John and others in their work for the Lord, closing his home to them and obstructing those who wished to help. Moreover, it seems that he interfered with their acceptance in the church itself. Even written appeals by John were scorned by this malicious, prating man.

John did not deal gently with the contemptible Diotrephes but said, "If I come, I will remember his deeds which he doeth" (v. 10). This was a more vigorous proposition than merely criticizing him. It meant John would deal with Diotrephes with spiritual strength. There come times when this must be done, such as in the case of Ananias and Saphira (Acts 5:1-10).

In verse 11 of the text John dismisses the sorry example of Diotrephes and moves on to the positive Christian teaching of good works. The true Christians were not to be discouraged or adversely influenced by the example of Diotrephes, but they should follow that which is good. God calls His people to good works, not because they are saved by good works, but because the gospel is strengthened by them (see James 2:14-18). In his appearance before King Agrippa, Paul said he preached that men "should repent and turn to God, and do works meet for repentance" (Acts 26:20).

Verse 12 of the text introduces Demetrius. Like Gaius, Demetrius had a good report for the good he did. He was the opposite of Diotrephes and was a grace to the Christian church.

This verse includes the words *report* and *record*, which lets us know that people become known for their good works. They are known both on earth and in heaven because their works for the benefit of others are a service to God. Demetrius did not do his works in order to be recorded in the Holy Scriptures and reported widely through the Christian church. He worked because it was in him to work and to bless others. In consequence, he was known both then and now, both on earth and in heaven. The same is true with today's Christians and churches. They become known widely for their good works and their faithful lives. Their report goes before them and it blesses all who hear of them.

"To disregard what the world thinks of us is not only arrogant but utterly shameless."
—Cicero

CONCLUSION

It is possible to obtain a large body of knowledge without

coming to an understanding of truth. People are interested in three major questions: *Where did I come from? Why am I here?* and *Where am I going?*

Truth in all three areas can be found in Jesus Christ. He knew He had come from the Father. He also knew why He was here—to seek and save the lost. There was no doubt in His mind as to where He was going. Often He spoke of returning to His Father.

If anyone will earnestly seek the Lord Jesus Christ for the truth, Christ will reveal the truth in these areas. "Ye shall know the truth, and the truth shall make you free" (John 8:32).

GOLDEN TEXT CHALLENGE
"I HAVE NO GREATER JOY THAN TO HEAR THAT MY CHILDREN WALK IN TRUTH" (3 John 4).

An elder statesman of the gospel was now entering the final stages of this life, looking forward with assurance to being present with his Beloved. John had begotten many children and many churches by preaching the truth of Jesus Christ. Like any father, he found joy and satisfaction in knowing that those whom he had begotten by the Word of God were living out their lives as a witness to God.

When Christian believers walk in the truth, they are walking in the will of God, in righteousness before God and people, in holiness. For the children of God to walk in the truth is to be completely dependent on God's guidance and purpose for life—no secret places, no hidden closets, no private sins, but open to the light and presence of God. The apostle John had heard a report that his spiritual children were living out their lives, individually and corporately, faithful to the teachings they had received regarding the Son of God. He was rewarded for his labor; he was proud of their accomplishments.

Let us be like John, seeking to beget children of faith and seeking the joy of hearing that our children are walking in the truth. God is yet available to forgive sinners and bring them into the family of God as obedient children. God desires to give us children of faith with a good report. Don't stop begetting children—win the lost to Christ!

Daily Devotions:

M. Walking in Godliness
   Genesis 17:1-8

T. Walking in Obedience
   Leviticus 26:1-12

W. Walking in Love
   Ruth 1:11-17

T. Walking in Humility
   1 Chronicles 29:10-17

F. Walking in Courage
   Acts 20:22-32

S. Walking in the Spirit
   Galatians 5:16-25

Understanding the Revelation

At first glance the Book of Revelation seems to be little more than a series of bizarre and meaningless visions written by an aged apostle. But when we read the opening verses we suddenly realize the book contains a vital message for our times:

> The revelation of Jesus Christ, which God gave him to show his servants what must soon take place. He made it known by sending his angel to his servant John, who testifies to everything he saw—that is, the word of God and the testimony of Jesus Christ. Blessed is the one who reads the words of this prophecy, and blessed are those who hear it and take to heart what is written in it, because the time is near (Revelation 1:1-3).*

People look at the Book of Revelation in different ways. Some view it as a book of confusion. They struggle to sort out the meaning of its symbolism and get lost in its imagery.

Others see it as a book of controversy. They like to debate different theological positions regarding the last days and assert their personal opinions with unabashed dogmatism. Still others view it as a book of consternation. They find themselves filled with fear and apprehension about the future when they read the Revelation. In reality, however, the Revelation was inspired by God, written by the apostle John and given to us as a book of peace to encourage and strengthen our faith. Let's take a close look at its message of peace.

Pay careful attention to the title of the book—*The Revelation*. It is a "revelation," not a "concealment." I point this out because many people think the Revelation is full of deep, hidden secrets that we cannot comprehend. But the word *revelation*, or *apocalypse*, simply means to openly disclose and make known that which was previously hidden.

In the Revelation, God pulls back the veil and shows us His eternal throne, power and glory as He works out His will for the world in the final chapter of history. This is why John says that the revealing was given "to show his servants [that's us] what must soon take place."

In a very real way the Revelation transports us into heaven itself so we can see everything that happens in human history—past, present and future—from the vantage point of eternity.

The Book of Revelation gives to us an eternal perspective in a temporal world. This is by far its greatest blessing. It enables us to see such awe-inspiring scenes as the throne of God; Jesus Christ reigning triumphantly and returning in glory; and the Holy Spirit, who is represented as "the seven spirits before his throne" (1:4).

It also shows us the four living creatures, or cherubim, crying, "Holy, Holy, Holy," around God's throne; the raptured church in heaven; and countless multitudes around the throne, joyfully praising God. We are even shown the horrific works of the devil on earth and the final judgment of God against evil. In the Revelation, God reveals all things to us about both the natural world of man's inhumanity against man, and the supernatural realm of angels and demons. He leaves nothing uncovered.

Several important words and phrases in the opening statements put the book into its proper perspective.

Not only is it a revelation, it is a specific revelation—*the revelation of Jesus Christ*. Jesus, then, is the central figure of the drama. He is referred to as the Son of Man, the Lion of the tribe of Judah, the Root and the Offspring of David, the Lamb of God, and the King of kings and Lord of lords. This means that the Revelation is all about Him and His ministry as our Redeemer and Judge.

The phrases "what must soon take place" and "the time is near" leap off the page. They tell us that the contents of the book not only concern the distant future of the last days but also the condition of the times in which the book was written—the first century.

So the Revelation is more than a collection of secret clues about the future; it is a message for the people of God here and now. As John says, the time is near.

Finally, how can we overlook the word *blessed*? It means "Oh, how happy!" What a paradox: Oh, how happy are those who read and understand and take to heart the message of the horrors of the Revelation! This makes us want to read further to find out what wonderful message is contained in the book.

When you read "blessed . . ." you think of the Beatitudes given by Jesus in His Sermon on the Mount in Matthew 5:3-10: "Blessed are the poor in spirit. . . . Blessed are the merciful. . . . Blessed are the peacemakers . . . ," and so forth.

But in the Revelation we find another series of His beatitudes that have been overlooked far too long. Altogether there are seven beatitudes given by Jesus in the Revelation:

- "Blessed is the one who reads the words of this prophecy, and blessed are those who hear it and take to heart what is written in it, because the time is near" (1:3).

- Then I heard a voice from heaven say, "Write: Blessed are the dead who die in the Lord from now on." "Yes," says the Spirit, "they will rest from their labor, for their deeds will follow them" (14:13).

- "Behold, I come like a thief! Blessed is he who stays

awake and keeps his clothes with him, so that he may not go naked and be shamefully exposed" (16:15).

- Then the angel said to me, "Write: 'Blessed are those who are invited to the wedding supper of the Lamb!'" And he added, "These are the true words of God" (19:9).

- "Blessed and holy are those who have part in the first resurrection. The second death has no power over them, but they will be priests of God and of Christ and will reign with him for a thousand years" (20:6).

- "Behold, I am coming soon! Blessed is he who keeps the words of the prophecy in this book" (22:7).

- "Blessed are those who wash their robes, that they may have the right to the tree of life and may go through the gates into the city" (22:14).

These beatitudes give a positive message of hope about the future.

The Revelation also contains good news for our times. To tap into its message of good news, we must view the book as a threefold revelation:

- A revelation to the church
- A revelation of Jesus Christ
- A revelation of the future

—David C. Cooper (*Apocalypse!*)

*Scriptures are from the *New International Version*.

July 16, 2006

Christ, the Forever-Living Lord

INTRODUCTION

The Book of Revelation is one of the most intriguing books of the Bible. It is usually one of the first books people want to study after they are saved. Individuals who care little about religion and the Bible are attentive when Revelation is discussed, because a major portion of it deals with the future and end-time events. We all want to know what is going to happen.

It is also one of the most complex books of the Bible, and it is apocalyptic in nature. Apocalyptic literature (taken from the Greek word *apokalypsis*, meaning "revelation" or "unveiling") usually contains many types, symbols and figurative language. This is the literature of crisis, written to people suffering oppression, adversity and persecution. It is God's response to those who question the suffering of the righteous and the seeming prosperity of the wicked. Apocalyptic writings remind the reader that history is moving in a divinely ordained course and that the end is already predetermined. As such, it is prophetic and eschatological in nature, revealing things that must come to pass before God deals dramatically and decisively with the presence of evil in His creation. From the beginning of time, God knew how everything would turn out—and He planned for it!

Revelation's first readers were Christians facing extreme persecution and hardship from the culture in which they lived and the often-brutal Roman government. History and Scripture record incidents of believers being beheaded, burned alive, torn apart by wild animals, crucified, boiled, even sawn in half. Believers in our society also face persecution—albeit more mental, emotional and spiritual, than physical.

Hollis Gause, whose lectures and writings have enhanced these lessons, likens the study of Revelation to the examination of a painting. It is easy to become so engrossed with the brush strokes (details) that we miss the beauty of the painting. There are some elements of the book that we may not fully comprehend this side of eternity. Our goal is to glean what we can and allow the Holy Spirit to make it alive and applicable to our lives and witness.

Unit Theme:
Christ in the Revelation

Central Truth:
Because Christ was resurrected, Christians have eternal life.

Focus:
Acknowledge that Jesus Christ lives forever and worship Him as Savior and Lord.

Context:
Written by the apostle John from the island of Patmos around A.D. 96.

Golden Text:
"I am he that liveth, and was dead; and, behold, I am alive for evermore, Amen; and have the keys of hell and of death" (Revelation 1:18).

Study Outline:
I. All-Sufficient Savior (Revelation 1:1-8)
II. Glorified Son of Man (Revelation 1:9-16)
III. Christ: Alive Forever (Revelation 1:17-20)

I. ALL-SUFFICIENT SAVIOR (Revelation 1:1-8)
A. The Revelation Revealed (vv. 1-3)

1. The Revelation of Jesus Christ, which God gave unto him, to shew unto his servants things which must shortly come to pass; and he sent and signified it by his angel unto his servant John:

2. Who bare record of the word of God, and of the testimony of Jesus Christ, and of all things that he saw.

3. Blessed is he that readeth, and they that hear the words of this prophecy, and keep those things which are written therein: for the time is at hand.

In the opening verse, the writer reveals that the *revelation* is a "laying bare" or "unveiling" that originates from God and is mediated through Jesus Christ. It is the unveiling of the glory of Jesus Christ, the sovereignty of God, the activity of the Spirit, the hope of the believer, the corruption of this world order, and the final vindication of God's promises—good for the saints, bad for the sinners. The revelation comprises the entire book, sent to help the servants of God understand there are things which, of necessity, must come to pass suddenly and quickly ("shortly") before the full revelation of Jesus Christ upon His throne. However, we must understand this in terms of eternity and God's plan, not our limited view of time. We must live and work, however, as though it will be fulfilled in the near future. It is an authoritative message that is authenticated by the presence of a heavenly messenger (22:16).

The authorship and date of this book are often questioned. The author had to be well known, since he is identified only as John, a fellow servant. While authorship does not affect inspiration, John the apostle is the most likely candidate and the one the early church accepted as the writer of Revelation. It was most likely written in the last decade of the first century.

The recording of this revelation is by one who has the authority and experience to do so (v. 2). John tells us in his first epistle that he heard, saw and experienced firsthand the earthly ministry of Jesus (1:1-4). He is a witness in the fullest sense of the word. The world is not looking for easy answers and memorized presentations. The world needs to hear from those who have engaged and experienced Jesus Christ and His redemptive power.

A beatitude or blessing is promised for the one who reads and those who hear this "prophecy" (Revelation 1:3). This is more than happiness, though it certainly includes joy (hopeful exuberance in spite of present circumstances). It is living in a state of continual provision and blessings from God. When this letter was first received by the churches, a person would read it to the entire congregation. The reading was an act of corporate worship. It was not just the presentation of a literary document, but an encounter with the living Word of God and all of its power, provision, blessings and warnings (see 22:18, 19).

B. Greetings, Grace and Glory (vv. 4-6)

4. John to the seven churches which are in Asia: Grace be unto you, and peace, from him which is, and which was, and which is to come; and from the seven Spirits which are before his throne;

5. And from Jesus Christ, who is the faithful witness, and the first begotten of the dead, and the prince of the kings of the earth. Unto him that loved us, and washed us from our sins in his own blood,

6. And hath made us kings and priests unto God and his Father; to him be glory and dominion for ever and ever. Amen.

With the notable exception of the four Gospels and Acts, the remainder of the New Testament is composed of epistles or letters written to churches (e.g., Romans, Hebrews) or individuals leading churches (e.g., 1 & 2 Timothy, Titus). The greeting and the pastoral nature of the book mark Revelation as an epistle. The seven churches receiving this letter (named in chs. 2, 3) were located in Asia Minor, an area governed by Rome. There are dozens of churches recorded in the New Testament, yet these seven are chosen by Jesus to be the first recipients of this magnificent letter. The number *seven* in Scripture usually represents perfection or completion. As with all Scripture, though this letter may have been sent originally to these seven churches, God intended for it to be received by and beneficial for the church across the ages.

Dispensational theology views these seven churches as representative of seven church ages, or periods of history, that correspond to circumstances associated with each church in chapters 2 and 3. For example, according to this view, the first church age would be the "Ephesian age" and the conditions of the church at the time of this writing would correspond to those ascribed to the church in Ephesus (2:1-7). Succeeding periods of history would correspond with the other churches listed in Revelation 2 and 3. According to many, we would be living in the "Laodicean age," a time when the church is lukewarm, rich, naked and blind (see 3:15-18). Some see merit in this view. Others reject this because the descriptions of the "church ages" have to be forced to correspond with church history. For example, the supposed Laodicean age is the age that has seen the phenomenal growth of the Pentecostal Movement and the greatest missionary effort in the history of the Kingdom, hardly a church that is blind and lukewarm.

first begotten
(v. 5)—firstborn

Talk About It:
1. Why do you suppose Jesus is called "the faithful witness" (v. 5)?
2. How did Jesus prove His love for people (v. 5)?
3. In what sense are God's children "kings and priests" (v. 6)?

In 2:4 John expresses his (and God's) desire for the readers to be blessed with "grace" (undeserved favor that saves and sustains us) "and peace" (a restoration of harmony with God that produces a continual confidence in God regardless of the circumstances). The source of these blessings is clearly identified as the Godhead.

First, though not mentioned by name, the Father is identified as the One who controls and owns time and eternity, the great I AM of Exodus 3:14. He was with us in the past, is with us now, and is already in the future, waiting with all His power and provision to accompany us through whatever it brings.

Second, the Spirit is identified as "the seven Spirits which are before his throne" (Revelation 2:4). This phrase has Zechariah 4:2, 10 as its foundation, where the Spirit is represented by the number seven. Some also see a connection with Isaiah 11:2, where a sevenfold manifestation of the Spirit enables the Messiah to accomplish His ministry (abiding presence, wisdom, understanding, counsel, strength, knowledge, reverence of the Lord). There are not, however, seven Holy Spirits.

Third, "Jesus Christ" is clearly named and identified by a threefold title and description of His ministry of salvation (Revelation 1:5, 6). Drawing from Psalm 89:26, 27, John declares that He is (1) "the faithful witness," who manifested the truth and love of God even in death as the ultimate witness or martyr (John 18:37); (2) "the first begotten of the dead," who is the Resurrection and the Life (John 11:25) and, as the firstfruits (1 Corinthians 15:23), the pattern by which believers are made alive; and (3) "the prince [or ruler] of the kings of the earth," who legitimately has received through obedience and death what the devil offered Him as a reward for false worship (Matthew 4:8-10). He is the "King of kings, and the Lord of lords!" (Revelation 19:16).

John's appropriate response to these verses and their implication is to break out in praise or a doxology (1:5, 6). First, He is the One who loved us while we were in sin and continues to love us even now. Second, on the basis of His love, He set us free ("washed") from our sins, breaking the chains of guilt and bondage by virtue of His own blood. Third, because of this freedom we are established ("made") as a kingdom of priests unto God. This is a fulfillment of the promise at Sinai (Exodus 19:5, 6), which the church has inherited (Acts 7:38). Israel failed in its commission. The work and power of Jesus Christ assure that the church will not fail (see Matthew 16:18). As priests, one of our functions is to bring people into the presence of God. We cannot take someone to a place with which we are unfamiliar. Our ministry as priests is dedicated unto God. There are two ways this can be understood: unto God and His Father (dedicated to Jesus); or, unto His God and Father (dedicated to the Father).

> "Christ has outlasted the empire that crucified Him 20 centuries ago. He will outlast those who defy Him now."
> —Ralph Sockman

Christ, the Forever-Living Lord

Ultimately, the result is the same, for Jesus does that which brings the Father glory (John 8:49, 50). In light of the context, the first is preferable. Because of His magnificent love and provision, to Him belongs praise and honor ("glory") and power and might ("dominion"), both now and throughout all the ages of time and eternity. With John, we must declare, "Amen!"

C. The Focus of the Revelation (vv. 7, 8)

7. Behold, he cometh with clouds; and every eye shall see him, and they also which pierced him: and all kindreds of the earth shall wail because of him. Even so, Amen.

8. I am Alpha and Omega, the beginning and the ending, saith the Lord, which is, and which was, and which is to come, the Almighty.

Verse 7 records the primary theme of the Book of Revelation—the return of Jesus Christ. The imagery of this prediction is drawn from Zechariah's prophecy (ch. 12) and Daniel's vision (ch. 7), as well as the Gospels. It is not just those who personally participated in His humiliation and death that are in mind here, but all of humanity, whose sin He bore, shall see Him. Every one of us participated in His piercing and pain. His return is a day of judgment that will cause wailing from those who are unprepared (see Isaiah 2:12).

In the prophecies and the records of Christ's life, there is a strong connection between the suffering and the glory, the Crucifixion and the return, the personal poverty and the provision for the saints. In other words, His marks of suffering become His medals of vindication and glorification. The same is true for the saints.

The language of Revelation 1:8 is reminiscent of the Father's description in verse 4. The announcement that He is "Alpha and Omega," the first and last letters of the Greek alphabet, is a declaration of eternality. All things begin and end in Him. He is "the Almighty," the All-Powerful One, who holds all power and rules all things.

II. GLORIFIED SON OF MAN (Revelation 1:9-16)
A. A Revelation of Learning (vv. 9-11)

9. I John, who also am your brother, and companion in tribulation, and in the kingdom and patience of Jesus Christ, was in the isle that is called Patmos, for the word of God, and for the testimony of Jesus Christ.

10. I was in the Spirit on the Lord's day, and heard behind me a great voice, as of a trumpet,

11. Saying, I am Alpha and Omega, the first and the last: and, What thou seest, write in a book, and send it unto the seven churches which are in Asia; unto Ephesus, and

Talk About It:
1. Who will "wail" when Jesus comes again (v. 7)? Why?
2. What is similar about the titles attributed to Jesus in verse 8?

Patmos (PAT-mus)—v. 9—a small rocky island in the Aegean Sea

Ephesus (EF-eh-
sus) . . . Smyrna
(SMUR-nuh) . . .
Pergamos (PER-
guh-mus) . . .
Thyatira (THIGH-
ah-TIE-rah) . . .
Sardis (SAR-dis) . . .
Philadelphia (fill-
uh-DEL-fee-uh) . . .
Laodicea (lay-ah-
deh-SEE-uh)—v.
11—These were
seven principal
towns in Asia Minor
(now Turkey) in
which there were
Christian congrega-
tions.

Talk About It:
1. In what ways did
John say he was a
"brother" to his read-
ers (v. 9)?
2. What does it
mean to be "in the
Spirit" (v. 10)?
3. What was John
instructed to do
(v. 11)?

**unto Smyrna, and unto Pergamos, and unto Thyatira, and
unto Sardis, and unto Philadelphia, and unto Laodicea.**

In verse 9, John, who expects his identity to be readily iden-
tifiable, distinguishes four ways in which all who are in Christ
are joined together: (1) brotherhood—a blood kinship of identity, closeness and equality; (2) "companion in tribulation"—part-
nership in suffering for the name of Christ (even apostles are
not exempt from affliction and oppression); (3) "the kingdom"—
life in the reign of God's rule and all of its benefits; and (4)
"patience of Jesus"—steadfast maturity that comes from obedience, experience and suffering (see Hebrews 5:7-9). The
church historian Eusebius tells us that in A.D. 95, John was
sent to the island of Patmos (in the eastern Aegean Sea) by
Domitian the Roman emperor and held there for about 18
months. The island is relatively small (approximately 6 miles
wide and 15 miles long at its largest points), rocky, and was
very barren in the first century. It was the place Rome kept prisoners who, because of the nature of their crimes, must not
escape. According to tradition, John found shelter in a cave
and there wrote the Book of Revelation. John is explicit in the
reason for his exile: "for the word of God, and for the testimony of Jesus Christ" (Revelation 1:9).

As John was worshiping in intimate communion with God
through the anointing and empowerment of the Holy Spirit, his
attention was turned to "a great voice, as of a trumpet" behind
him (v. 10). Trumpets (or their sounds) signify announcements
or warnings in Scripture (Isaiah 58:1; Matthew 24:31). The
voice instructed John to record what he was about to see and
distribute it to the seven churches listed.

B. A Revelation of Glory (vv. 12-16)
    (Revelation 1:14-16 is not included in the printed text.)
    **12. And I turned to see the voice that spake with me.
And being turned, I saw seven golden candlesticks;**
    **13. And in the midst of the seven candlesticks one like
unto the Son of man, clothed with a garment down to the
foot, and girt about the paps with a golden girdle.**

girt about the paps
with a golden
girdle (v. 13)—
"dressed . . . with a
golden sash around
his chest" (NIV).

John heard the voice and now turned to discover the One
speaking. His first recorded observation is not concerning the
source of the voice, but the "seven golden candlesticks," or
lampstands (v. 12). Candles as we know them did not exist in
this era. These lampstands, reminiscent of Zechariah 4, are later
revealed to represent the church (v. 20) and serve to remind us
that the church is to bear and, in a sense, be the light of God's
presence to a world of darkness. As individual members of the
church let their light shine (Matthew 5:14-16), the collective light
of the church burns brightly. Light reveals things as they truly are,

Talk About It:
1. Describe the ap-
pearance of Christ
(vv. 13-15) in two
words.

not as we mistakenly perceive them to be. It also reveals imperfections and flaws, but illuminates the pathway that leads to God. If the light does not shine brightly, a congregation has no reason to exist (Revelation 2:5).

Standing in the midst of the churches, John saw "one like unto the Son of man" (1:13). This first part of this verse reminds us of two things. First, the church is the church because of the presence of Jesus Christ. He must be the center of who we are and what we do. Second, Daniel 7:13, 14 is coming to pass. Jesus, often called "the Son of man" in Scripture (e.g., Matthew 16:13), is subduing all kingdoms and receiving the dominion promised Him.

In verses 13-16 of our text, John describes the Son of Man. The description is symbolic and points to the characteristics of Jesus and His ministry. First, the long robe is associated in Scripture with the priesthood (Exodus 28:4) and kings (Esther 6:8). Second, the robe is bound to His chest with a belt that was inlaid (or overlaid) with gold. This belt usually served three purposes: It fastened a garment for labor or service, offered protection in battle, and had a pocket for carrying money. It reminds us of Christ's dignity, honor, provision and protection. Third, the whiteness of His hair points to His purity, stability and wisdom associated with age. Fourth, His eyes penetrate to the heart of the matter in righteous judgment. Fifth, His feet of shining brass (an alloy of fine gold and silver) radiate His glory. Sixth, His voice is one of majesty, power and authority. Seventh, in His hand He holds seven servants ("stars" or "angels") that do His will and work (Revelation 1:16; see v. 20). Eighth, out of His mouth proceeds the sword of the Lord, the Word of God, which both judges and heals (see Hebrews 4:12). Finally, His outer appearance ("like the sun shining in its strength," *NKJV*) reflects not only His glory, but also His authority over all creation.

III. CHRIST: ALIVE FOREVER (Revelation 1:17-20)

A. The Keys Reclaimed (vv. 17, 18)

17. And when I saw him, I fell at his feet as dead. And he laid his right hand upon me, saying unto me, Fear not; I am the first and the last:

18. I am he that liveth, and was dead; and, behold, I am alive for evermore, Amen; and have the keys of hell and of death.

John's response was the only appropriate one. The magnitude of Christ's glory and presence emptied him of all physical strength (v. 17; see also Joshua 5:14; Ezekiel 1:28). The Person in his vision laid His right hand upon John, an action and symbol of imparting strength, power and a commission. He then heard words he had heard many times from the lips of Jesus—"Fear

---

2. What is the significance of the seven stars Christ held? The sword in His mouth? His shining countenance (v. 16)?

"The greatest need in the church today is a sense of the living presence of Christ. It is His presence that gives Christianity its power, its enthusiasm, and its hope."

—Homer Rhea

Talk About It:
1. How did John respond to this vision of Christ? Why? How did Christ help him?

---

2. What does Christ
mean by saying He
holds "the keys of
hell and of death"
(v. 18)?

not!" (see Matthew 10:26-31). Jesus then identified Himself as the Sovereign One in whom all things begin and end.

The Speaker was clearly the Living One who had conquered death. Jesus was not the first One to be raised from the dead. In Scripture, seven others were also raised. Jesus, however, was the only One to remain raised from the dead and is alive for all time and eternity. He truly made an open spectacle of death and those behind its power (Colossians 2:15). As such, He alone now possesses the keys of hell and death. In Jewish literature (non-Biblical), the keys belong to God alone. Jesus, both as God and liberator from death, has the power to possess the keys.

B. The Mystery Revealed (vv. 19, 20)

19. Write the things which thou hast seen, and the things which are, and the things which shall be hereafter;

20. The mystery of the seven stars which thou sawest in my right hand, and the seven golden candlesticks. The seven stars are the angels of the seven churches: and the seven candlesticks which thou sawest are the seven churches.

Talk About It:

1. What did Christ say he would show John, and why (v. 19)?

2. What was revealed to John in verse 20?

John's commission was to record this vision of the revelation of Jesus Christ (v. 19). The seven stars are revealed as "the angels of the seven churches" (v. 20). This could mean the churches had angels assigned to the members (see Daniel 10:13), for this is certainly a Biblical truth (Psalms 34:7; 91:11). However, *angel* also means "messenger," and as such, it is viewed as a reference to the pastors of the congregations (see Matthew 11:10), especially since John was to write to the angel in charge of each church (Revelation 2:1, 8, 12, 18; 3:1, 7, 14). May God grant that all of our churches are surrounded by heavenly hosts and our pastors are securely in the right hand of Jesus Christ.

"The hand that holds the seven stars is as loving as the hand that was laid in blessing upon the little children; the face that is as the sun shining in its strength beams with as much love as when it drew publicans and harlots to His feet. The breast that is girt with the golden girdle is the same breast upon which John leaned his happy head."

—Alexander MacLaren

CONCLUSION

In studying the Book of Revelation, the focus must be kept upon Jesus Christ. He is the Revealer of and the reason for the book. As the Son of Man, He is able to identify with our human temptations, fears and concerns. As the Son of God, who has received glory, honor and power, He is able to protect us in and deliver us from the worst of times. He still stands in the midst of His church. Does His church celebrate and embrace or disregard and take for granted His presence?

GOLDEN TEXT CHALLENGE

"I AM HE THAT LIVETH, AND WAS DEAD; AND, BEHOLD, I AM ALIVE FOR EVERMORE, AMEN; AND HAVE THE KEYS OF HELL AND OF DEATH" (Revelation 1:18).

The eternal changelessness of God as revealed in Jesus Christ is expressed in these words. Jesus was alive before anything was created.

In spiritual substance, Jesus is coequal with God the Father and the Holy Spirit. In the flesh, our Savior was born of a virgin; He was crucified and buried. After a brief suspension of continuity, He came out of the grave victorious. He laid down His life that He might take it up again, showing Himself to be the Living One.

As the resurrected Savior, Jesus holds the master keys of death and hell and paradise with all their mysteries.

There is a Light shining from the empty tomb that time will never put out. Everyone who walks in the Light will one day say with Christ, "I am alive forevermore!"

Daily Devotions:

M. The Almighty
   Psalm 89:1-3

T. Promised
   Deliverer
   Isaiah 9:1-7

W. Jesus,
   Emmanuel
   Matthew 1:18-25

T. Eternal Lord
   John 1:1-5

F. Exalted Lord
   Philippians 2:9-11

S. Coming Lord
   1 Thessalonians
   4:13-18

Christ Speaks to the Churches

Revelation 2:1 through 3:22

Unit Theme:
Christ in the Revelation

Central Truth:
Christ still speaks to the church by His Word and Spirit.

Focus:
Hear and obey what Christ says to the church by His Word and Spirit.

Context:
Written by the apostle John around A.D. 96 from the island of Patmos

Golden Text:
"He that hath an ear, let him hear what the Spirit saith unto the churches; To him that overcometh will I give to eat of the tree of life, which is in the midst of the paradise of God" (Revelation 2:7).

Study Outline:
I. Christ Reproves (Revelation 2:1-7, 12-29)
II. Christ Warns (Revelation 3:1-6, 14-22)
III. Christ Encourages (Revelation 2:8-11; 3:7-13

INTRODUCTION

Revelation 2 and 3 record Christ's words to seven churches of the first century. This letter is not a dated message addressed solely to the churches listed, but was to be read in other churches of that day. This is the pattern for all the New Testament books (see Colossians 4:16). The inspired Word was deemed precious, beneficial and applicable to believers of other congregations and believers of all ages. Great care was taken by the early church to preserve the Word of God. Revelation, also called the Apocalypse, is not a message to the early church alone. It is a message to the church throughout the ages (Revelation 22:18, 19).

The lesson does not examine each of the churches in order, though that is highly recommended for personal study. Rather, it focuses on three particular aspects: reproof, warning and encouragement. Under these three headings, the churches are listed according to the primary emphasis of the message to that particular congregation. Six of the seven churches receive commendations, as well as warning or rebuke, and a promise of reward to the victorious. The lone exception is Laodicea (3:14-22), which receives stinging criticism, no commendation, but does receive a promise of reward to those who overcome. As Jesus closes each section of the letter addressed to a particular church, there is the admonition "He that hath an ear, let him hear what the Spirit saith unto the churches" (2:7, 11, 17, 29; 3:6, 13, 22). The material contains a message much deeper than human capabilities can discern. It takes the revealing insight and guidance of the Spirit for us to "hear" truly what Jesus is speaking to the church in the first century as well as the 21st century.

An examination of these churches provides a window into the culture and ethos, or mind-set, of the first century. The words spoken to these churches reveal the struggles, temptations and trials that all the congregations and believers faced and had to overcome through the power of the Lamb. Scripture reminds us that Satan utilizes the same basic weapons and schemes, though they may be clothed in different garb (see Ecclesiastes 1:9). Our culture may not be under the dominion of Rome, but through these chapters we certainly understand that the world system is not designed to promote Christian living. Like the churches of Asia Minor, we must choose to reject evil and embrace God.

I. CHRIST REPROVES (Revelation 2:1-7, 12-29)
A. The Church in Ephesus (vv. 1-7)
(Revelation 2:1, 5-7 is not included in the printed text.)

2. I know thy works, and thy labour, and thy patience, and how thou canst not bear them which are evil: and thou hast tried them which say they are apostles, and are not, and hast found them liars:

3. And hast borne, and hast patience, and for my name's sake hast laboured, and hast not fainted.

4. Nevertheless I have somewhat against thee, because thou hast left thy first love.

The church in Ephesus received commendation from Christ, who was in the midst of the churches (v. 1), for two areas of faithfulness. First, Jesus knew their works (v. 2). It is not a commendation for scattered acts, but an obedient lifestyle. Actively, they labored to the point of exhaustion. Passively, they steadfastly waited on deliverance and maintained faithfulness in spite of persecution and trials. They did this for the sake of Christ's name (v. 3). Second, they withstood false workers (vv. 2, 6). Correctly, the congregation examined the character, attitudes and conduct of those claiming to be sent from God for consistency with the Word and example of Jesus.

They were, however, sharply reproved (vv. 4, 5). Their lifestyle was missing the love that first characterized this church (see Acts 19). They were doing the right things, but with a wrong heart (see 2 Chronicles 25:1, 2). Their sin could have happened willfully or through neglect. The result is the same. Good works and proper theology are no substitute for love. Good works are accompanied by right reasons and right attitudes. To do less is to be out of harmony with God's grace and love and brings judgment (Revelation 2:5). Repentance (renouncing sin and embracing God) is the only acceptable response.

The letter closes with a call to let the Spirit convict them of their sin, convince them of the message's validity, correct their hearts, and guide them into greater revelation knowledge (v. 7). It also contains a promise. Those who are victorious to the end will be permitted to eat from the Tree of Life. The Tree of Life is symbolic of God's perfect will that was impeded by sin in the Garden of Eden (Genesis 3). Partakers of this fruit shall never die, for it is the Tree of Life and healing (Revelation 22:2).

B. The Church in Pergamos (vv. 12-17)
(Revelation 2:12, 16, 17 is not included in the printed text.)

13. I know thy works, and where thou dwellest, even where Satan's seat is: and thou holdest fast my name, and hast not denied my faith, even in those days wherein Antipas was my faithful martyr, who was slain among you, where Satan dwelleth.

Nicolaitanes (NIK-oh-lay-ih-tanz)—
v. 6—a group of people whose works were hated by both the Ephesian church and the Lord

Talk About It:
1. How did the angel commend the church of Ephesus?
2. How did this church need to change?
3. What promise is made to overcomers (v. 7)?

Balaam (BAY-lamb)—v. 14—a seer who led Israel astray (see Numbers 31:16)

Balak (BAY-lack)—v. 14—a Moabite king who hired Balaam to pronounce a curse on the Israelites (see Numbers 22:4-7)

Talk About It:

1. Describe the difficult situation faced by the church in Pergamos (v. 13).

2. What warning were they given (v. 16)?

3. What was promised "to him that overcometh" (v. 17)?

14. But I have a few things against thee, because thou hast there them that hold the doctrine of Balaam, who taught Balac to cast a stumblingblock before the children of Israel, to eat things sacrificed unto idols, and to commit fornication.

15. So hast thou also them that hold the doctrine of the Nicolaitanes, which thing I hate.

Pergamos ("citadel") probably derived its name from its location high on a hill. John received instruction for this church from Christ, who held a sharp two-edged sword, depicting the Word of God (Ephesians 6:17; Hebrews 4:12) and divine judgment (Revelation 19:15, 21).

The church was commended for "hold[ing] fast [to] my name," even though they dwelt "where Satan's seat is" (2:13). Pergamos had shrines dedicated to Zeus, Athena, Dionysus and Asklepios (the god of healing), which brought many to the city. Also, there was a temple dedicated to the worship of the caesar. Here, worshipers declared, "Caesar is lord." For believers to declare, "Jesus is Lord" (1 Corinthians 12:3) brought accusations of blasphemy and cries against the "heretics" and "atheists" (denying the deity of Caesar). These charges were punishable by death. Yet, the believers of Pergamos were faithful to their beliefs. Antipas was martyred, perhaps even in their presence ("among you") for the faith. According to tradition, he was slowly roasted to death inside a brazen bull by Domitian. The language here is not that of faithfulness to a stale doctrine or a memorized creed, but a vibrant belief in the lordship of Jesus Christ.

A few individuals were guilty of embracing the doctrines of Balaam (v. 14) and the Nicolaitans (v. 15). These two beliefs were practically identical. Numbers 31:16 explains how Balaam, who had earlier pronounced blessings on Israel, now enticed them into idolatry. Here is the pattern of false teachers: they (1) cause the person to have fundamental reservations about their beliefs, (2) introduce a new belief system that appeals to the carnal nature, and (3) provide an opportunity for gratifying the flesh. It is a system of deception that Jesus hates (Revelation 2:15).

Without repentance, sinners would be judged. Also, the church would be disciplined for allowing false teaching to continue in its midst. The judgment would come quickly and decisively (v. 16).

Finally, the promise of "hidden manna" and "a white stone" engraved with a "new name" was made to those who overcame (v. 17). *Manna* is symbolic of spiritual sustenance (1 Corinthians 10:1-4) and the covenant relationship we have with God (Psalm 78). We give our all to Him (our lives) and He gives His all to us (everything we need). It is "hidden" to those with spiritual blindness. Also, *stones* are symbolic of God's covenant with us (see

444   Christ Speaks to the Churches

Exodus 28:21) and are used to commemorate victories through His power (Joshua 4:20-24). The color *white* in Revelation symbolizes purity and victory (7:9, 13; 19:11, 14). In the first century, names represented character, conduct and hope (see Matthew 1:21, 23). Here, it is a "new name" that is given, a Kingdom name that perfectly represents the nature of the One who gives it and the one who receives it!

C. The Church in Thyatira (vv. 18-29)

(Revelation 2:18, 21-29 is not included in the printed text.)

19. I know thy works, and charity, and service, and faith, and thy patience, and thy works; and the last to be more than the first.

20. Notwithstanding I have a few things against thee, because thou sufferest that woman Jezebel, which calleth herself a prophetess, to teach and to seduce my servants to commit fornication, and to eat things sacrificed unto idols.

In verse 19, three commendations were given to this church living in a pagan society. First, Jesus knew their "works," or their good deeds done as unto Christ. Second, these works were motivated by a deep love ("charity"), confident trust ("faith"), and were evident in a dedicated ministry ("service"). This was done with a steadfast hope evident even in times of great duress. The economy of the city depended on the trade guilds (somewhat like a labor union). Participation in a trade guild required embracing pagan worship. Yet, these believers held to their beliefs and trusted in God to provide for them. Third, their present works were more plentiful than earlier works ("the last to be more than the first"). Instead of allowing hardship to diminish their work for the Lord, it increased in the face of this persecution.

Yet, the Lord declared that He had "a few things against" them (v. 20). The rebuke was severe and centered on a false prophetess called "Jezebel." First, note that the reproof was not because she was a prophetess, but because she was a *false* prophetess, leading people astray. The New Testament clearly recognizes and embraces the role of prophetesses (see Luke 2:36; Acts 2:17, 18; 21:9; 1 Corinthians 11:5). It was Queen Jezebel who led King Ahab astray and polluted the minds and hearts of many in Israel with the worship of Baal (1 Kings 16:30, 31). Her evil deeds were consistent with the same types of sin found in the church at Pergamos (Revelation 2:14, 15).

Second, she had been given the opportunity to repent, but had rejected it (v. 21). Every rejection of the grace of God hardens the heart, and continued rejection results in a depraved heart (an unfit heart that rejects God without regard for the consequences). Third, judgment would fall upon her and her followers

Talk About It:
1. Describe the works of the church in Thyatira (v. 19).
2. What was this church wrongfully tolerating (v. 20)?
3. What did Christ promise those who rejected false doctrine and followed Him (vv. 26-28)?

("her children," vv. 22, 23). A source of pleasure ("a bed") now became an instrument of certain judgment ("will kill . . . with death"). This is the nature of sin and its judgment.

Finally, the judgment would be public, righteous and true. Christ promised that through His judgment "all the churches" would know His character. His judgment is not based on whim or an incorrect view of predestination, but on the basis of the deepest feelings, intents, thoughts, and will of the person ("reins and hearts," v. 23). This judgment will be only upon the guilty (v. 24).

The victorious will receive "power over the nations" (v. 26). As we live in Him, we shall also rule with Him over His enemies, who shall be subdued finally and eternally (v. 27). Also, the victorious shall receive "the morning star" (v. 28). Christ himself is the Morning Star (2 Peter 1:19; Revelation 22:16). Thus, believers are incorporated into the glory of God and the glory of God into believers.

II. CHRIST WARNS (Revelation 3:1-6, 14-22)
A. The Church in Sardis (vv. 1-6)
(Revelation 3:1, 4-6 is not included in the printed text.)

2. Be watchful, and strengthen the things which remain, that are ready to die: for I have not found thy works perfect before God.

3. Remember therefore how thou hast received and heard, and hold fast, and repent. If therefore thou shalt not watch, I will come on thee as a thief, and thou shalt not know what hour I will come upon thee.

This letter emphasizes Christ's continual relationship with the Holy Spirit. As noted in lesson 7, the phrase "seven Spirits of God" has Zechariah 4:2, 10 as its foundation, where the Spirit is represented by the number *seven*. Some also see a connection with Isaiah 11:2, where a sevenfold manifestation of the Spirit (abiding presence, wisdom, understanding, counsel, knowledge, strength, reverence of the Lord) empowers the Messiah's ministry.

Whereas other churches were commended because Christ knew their works, this church was rebuked because of its works (3:1). Though it had a reputation ("name") as a church that was alive, it was powerless and lifeless. The term used here for "livest" refers to spiritual vitality, not biological life. It did not draw its spiritual strength from the Source of Life—God. The emphasis on the "seven Spirits of God" indicates it was not a Spirit-empowered church. Like the city, the church was complacent, so much so that they probably did not even realize they were dead. The situation could change. If they would arise and shake off the complacency ("be watchful") and firmly

---

"We must never be guilty of thinking our good works can off-set sin. The Christian life is not a balancing of good and bad. Any violation of God's Word violates God's authority in our lives—and ultimately leads to destruction."
—Rodney Hodge

Talk About It:
1. What was the reputation of the Sardis church, and what was the reality?
2. What was the remedy?
3. Whom does God consider "worthy," and what are they promised (vv. 4, 5)?

Christ Speaks to the Churches

establish ("strengthen") the things that still showed signs of life, a renewal could take place (v. 2).

Revivals begin with desire. Desire can be motivated by spiritual experiences in our past that need to occur again. Revival requires repentance, turning away from anything that hinders our relationship with God and turning to Him. Revival involves proper stewardship of the spiritual graces we receive from God. If we do not allow God to work through us, He will raise up a people to replace us. This can happen so quickly that we may not be aware of the action (v. 3).

The commendation for Sardis was for "a few names," not the entire church. A limited number were living a life of purity (v. 4). They had not allowed their lives to become influenced by the culture around them. Their lifestyle was not stagnant or complacent, but was based on a vibrant and continually growing relationship with Christ.

For those who kept on overcoming, the promise was three-fold. First, they would be clothed by God in garments of purity and victory. Second, their names would not be removed (the language is very emphatic) from the Book of Life, the record of all those who had been redeemed by the blood of the Lamb. Third, Christ himself would publicly acknowledge their faithfulness in the presence of "my Father, and before his angels" (v. 5). It was a proclamation of complete redemption, vindication from the accusations of the Enemy, and a declaration of ultimate success.

B. The Church in Laodicea (vv. 14-22)

(Revelation 3:14, 15, 20-22 is not included in the printed text.)

16. So then because thou art lukewarm, and neither cold nor hot, I will spue thee out of my mouth.

17. Because thou sayest, I am rich, and increased with goods, and have need of nothing; and knowest not that thou art wretched, and miserable, and poor, and blind, and naked:

18. I counsel thee to buy of me gold tried in the fire, that thou mayest be rich; and white raiment, that thou mayest be clothed, and that the shame of thy nakedness do not appear; and anoint thine eyes with eyesalve, that thou mayest see.

19. As many as I love, I rebuke and chasten: be zealous therefore, and repent.

The letter to the church in Laodicea came from "the Amen" (v. 14), a title of deity and power (2 Corinthians 1:20); the Witness who is both faithful and genuine; and the Origin ("beginning") of all creation. The church had no works worthy of commendation. Like Sardis, it was a reflection of the city in which it existed—rich and self-sufficient.

Talk About It:
1. What does it mean to be spiritually lukewarm?
2. What wrong idea did the Laodiceans have about their possessions (v. 17)?

3. What is one way
Christ proves His
love for us (v. 19)?

Mild Christianity

Millions of Christians
live in a sentimental
haze of vague piety.
. . . Their religion is a
pleasant thing . . .
demanding little ex-
cept lip service to a
few harmless plati-
tudes. I suspect that
Satan has called off
his attempt to con-
vert people to ag-
nosticism. After all, if
a man travels far
enough away from
Christianity, he is
liable to see it in per-
spective and decide
that it is true. It is
much safer, from
Satan's point of view,
to vaccinate a man
with a mild case of
Christianity so as to
protect him from the
real disease. (Taken
from *Early Chris-
tians of the Twenty-
first Century,* by
Chad Walsh)

Talk About It:
1. What did Christ
mean by saying,
"Yet you are rich!"
(v. 9, *NIV*)?

There was no rebuke for false teachers or corrupt doctrine;
rather, the church's works revealed its complacency. First, Jesus
said the church was "neither cold nor hot" (v. 15). Traditionally,
this has been understood to mean He would rather the church
be on fire spiritually or be a spiritual icicle than to be lukewarm.
Another view avoids the obvious contradiction. Cold waters
refresh and reinvigorate (see Matthew 10:42), while hot water
soothes and heals. Lukewarm water does neither. It is distasteful and repulsive (Revelation 3:16). Jesus is stating that
this church neither refreshes nor heals. What it offers is not
worth having.

Second, Christ addressed the prideful and self-sufficient
attitude of the church (v. 17). Laodicea was a very wealthy city,
noted for its banking, fine black wool, and school of medicine
that produced an eye salve. Yet, the church did not realize that
it was shameful, miserable, destitute, wandering in spiritual
darkness, and humiliated by their spiritual nakedness. They
confused material possessions with spiritual standing.

Mercy always precedes judgment. An invitation was given
to the church to obtain pure gold, garments of purity and victory, and eye salve that healed spiritual blindness (v. 18). The
implication was that renewal and purity come by process and
the process is not always pleasant. Those whom Christ loves
can expect correction and discipline (v. 19). His goal is always
restoration to a right relationship. He will not violate our free will,
but stands at the door waiting to gain attention and entrance
(v. 20). Those who open the door (the victorious) receive fellowship, communion and participation in the Kingdom. They
also are permitted to participate in Christ's victory, power,
authority and inheritance (see Romans 8:17).

III. CHRIST ENCOURAGES (Revelation 2:8-11; 3:7-13)
A. The Church in Smyrna (2:8-11)
(Revelation 2:8, 11 is not included in the printed text.)
**9. I know thy works, and tribulation, and poverty, (but
thou art rich) and I know the blasphemy of them which say
they are Jews, and are not, but are the synagogue of
Satan.**
**10. Fear none of those things which thou shalt suffer:
behold, the devil shall cast some of you into prison, that
ye may be tried; and ye shall have tribulation ten days: be
thou faithful unto death, and I will give thee a crown of life.**

The One who has power over death directed John to write
the letter to the church at Smyrna (v. 8). By His very nature, He
is Life (John 11:25). The church itself received no reproof, and
the brief commendation was powerful.

In verse 9 of the text, the church was characterized by its
"works"—an outward expression of an inward condition. They

were suffering "tribulation." The idea behind this word is outward circumstances that surround and severely press against a person. As well, they suffered "poverty." There are two definitions for *poverty* in the New Testament: (1) having no more than what is absolutely necessary for the sustenance of life, and (2) having nothing. Jesus used the latter word to describe their condition, yet He reminded them that they were "rich" with spiritual virtues and eternal possessions. Apparently, their tribulation and poverty were caused by those who were in the Jewish community. Christ highlighted three things about these Jews: (1) their slanderous speech against God and His people has not escaped His attention; (2) they may have been "Jews" by ethnic identification and religious practice, but they were not true Jews (Romans 2:28, 29); and (3) they worshiped profanely in the synagogue of the adversary of God.

In verse 10 of the text, Christ encouraged the church and prepared them for the future. First, they were to stop being afraid of the suffering they faced. We are not to live in an atmosphere of fear. God's people have always faced suffering in some form or another. It is part of this fallen world system. To *suffer* literally means "to experience life." One person's suffering is another person's growth experience. We take life as it comes, but never alone!

Second, some of them might be placed in prison by the devil. This probably meant a literal imprisonment by Roman authorities, but could also be spiritual oppression. Clearly, the instrument behind it was the devil. Third, the tribulation had a specified duration of "ten days," or a relatively brief period of time for their persecution. This is not, however, the Great Tribulation from which believers are sealed (3:10).

Finally, the victorious would receive a "crown of life" (2:10). There are two types of crowns in the New Testament: (1) the *diadem*, the crown of royalty; and (2) the *stephanos*, used here, which is the crown given to the victorious. Also, the victorious will not be harmed by the "second death" (v. 11). This is a rabbinic term indicating death beyond the grave. It is a reference to the final judgment of God, where one's eternal destiny is determined. Faithfulness unto death results in true life. For the believer, death loses its sting and victory because of the triumph of Jesus Christ (1 Corinthians 15:53-57)!

B. The Church in Philadelphia (3:7-13)
    (Revelation 3:9, 10, 13 is not included in the printed text.)
    7. And to the angel of the church in Philadelphia write; These things saith he that is holy, he that is true, he that hath the key of David, he that openeth, and no man shutteth; and shutteth, and no man openeth;
    8. I know thy works: behold, I have set before thee an

2. What warning did Christ give the Smyrna congregation? Why?

"Many a man's reputation would not know his character, if they met on the street."
—Elbert Hubbard

open door, and no man can shut it: for thou hast a little strength, and hast kept my word, and hast not denied my name.

11. Behold, I come quickly: hold that fast which thou hast, that no man take thy crown.

12. Him that overcometh will I make a pillar in the temple of my God, and he shall go no more out: and I will write upon him the name of my God, and the name of the city of my God, which is new Jerusalem, which cometh down out of heaven from my God: and I will write upon him my new name.

Talk About It:

1. Explain Christ's talk about open and closed doors (vv. 7, 8).

2. What command had the Philadelphia church kept, and what promise did God make them (v. 10)?

3. What "new name" will Christ give His faithful ones (v. 12)?

The letter to the Philadelphians centered upon the theme of opening and closing doors. Christ alone has the keys and ultimate authority over all doors (v. 7). He has opened the door of the Kingdom and no one can close it (v. 8).

The church was commended for three things. First, their works revealed that in spite of diminished strength, they had been diligent workers in the Kingdom. They may have been small in numbers, but that did not impede their ministry. Second, they had kept His word (vv. 8, 10). The language indicates a particular trial or time. They were steadfast in their doctrine. Third, they did not renounce the name of the Lord in this trial. They were firm in their faith. Consequently they were promised a threefold reward: (1) vindication before their enemies (v. 9); (2) preservation in the hour of God's Great Tribulation upon the earth (v. 10); (3) a crown of victory (v. 11). The overcomers shall be people of stability, in a position of prominence, and secure eternally (v. 12).

CONCLUSION

Each of the letters to the churches begins with a depiction of Jesus Christ that either reinforces or expands the description of Jesus in chapter 1. In these chapters He is (1) the Son of Man, who understands our struggles with the flesh; (2) the King, ruling in dominion, righteousness and glory; (3) God, able to subdue any attack of the enemy of His people; (4) Messiah, the anointed Savior of those who look to Him; (5) Light, Life and Lord of the church. It is His church and must be subject to His will, not ours. As the church, we must accept His reproof, hear His warnings, and embrace His encouragement.

GOLDEN TEXT CHALLENGE

"HE THAT HATH AN EAR, LET HIM HEAR WHAT THE SPIRIT SAITH UNTO THE CHURCHES; TO HIM THAT OVERCOMETH WILL I GIVE TO EAT OF THE TREE OF LIFE, WHICH IS IN THE MIDST OF THE PARADISE OF GOD" (Revelation 2:7).

Each of the seven letters ends with a promise to the person

who obeys the message of the letter and overcomes in the conflict with evil. To the church at Ephesus the promise was that the overcomer would have free access to the Tree of Life in God's paradise, whose fruit had previously been forbidden to people. Eternal life would become the everlasting feast of the conqueror in the paradise of God.

The word *paradise* occurs three times in the New Testament (Luke 23:43; 2 Corinthians 12:4; Revelation 2:7). The "paradise of God" is the expression of heaven's blessedness. It is an actual place, of which the earthly garden (Genesis 2) was but a shadow. Here the blessedness is fixed and eternal. Paradise is the sum of all enjoyment, the aggregate of all pleasure, promised to the converted dying robber, and "into" it Paul was caught. It is the special and unique promise held out to the overcomer in Christ.

Daily Devotions:

M. Hearing God's Voice
Deuteronomy 5:22-27

T. Listening to God
1 Samuel 3:3-12

W. Disobeying God's Command
1 Kings 11:4-13

T. Wisdom of Hearing Christ
Matthew 7:24-29

F. Arrested by Christ's Voice
Acts 9:1-8

S. Encouraged by the Lord
Acts 18:5-11

Christ Is the Redeemer

Revelation 4:1 through 5:14

Unit Theme:
Christ in the
Revelation

Central Truth:
Christ redeems from
sin all who trust in
Him.

Focus:
Appreciate the fact
that Christ is the
Redeemer and praise
Him for redemption
from sin.

Context:
Written by the apostle
John around A.D. 96
from the island of
Patmos

Golden Text:
"Thou [Christ] art wor-
thy to take the book,
and to open the seals
thereof: for thou wast
slain, and hast redeem-
ed us to God by thy
blood out of every kin-
dred, and tongue, and
people, and nation"
(Revelation 5:9).

Study Outline:
I. The Redeemer
   Needed
   (Revelation 4:1-11;
   5:1-4)
II. The Redeemer
   Provided
   (Revelation 5:5-10)
III. The Redeemer
   Worshiped
   (Revelation 5:11-14)

INTRODUCTION

On a human level, we can only imagine what John was feeling. He is worshiping by himself on a barren prison island (Patmos). He has been exiled there because of his preaching and witness. Suddenly, the risen Lord begins to instruct him to record what he sees and send it to the seven churches of Asia Minor. He turns and sees Jesus standing there in all of His glory. His vision is full of symbolism, which Jesus clarifies for him. He begins to write what is spoken to him, while trying to gain his mental composure, and still get the details right in the letters to the churches. The personal aspects of the letters come to an end. His mind must have raced, wondering, *Is this the end of the vision? What happens now? Am I dead or alive?*

Suddenly there is a shift in his perspective. Earth is no longer in view. He is transported through heaven's open door into the very throne room of God. He sees the omnipotent and omniscient One sitting upon the throne. He hears the resplendent praise of the angels and other attendants in the throne room. He feels the power and glory of the Lord in a way never before experienced by any mortal. He sees the multitude of the heavenly hosts and everyone is keenly aware of his presence. What he sees is almost beyond human ability to fathom, much less describe, yet this is what he must write about. We feel for John, yet yearn for a similar experience.

Revelation 4 and 5 record the phenomenal throne-room vision of the apostle John. In these two chapters there is one focus—the sovereignty of God over all creation, whether in history, the present or the future. He is the God of power and judgment; He is also the God of mercy and redemption. Mercy and redemption are presently offered. The power of His judgment is about to be revealed.

I. THE REDEEMER NEEDED (Revelation 4:1-11; 5:1-4)
A. A Shift in Perspective (4:1-3, 5, 6a)
(Revelation 4:5 is not included in the printed text.)
    1. After this I looked, and, behold, a door was opened in heaven: and the first voice which I heard was as it were of a trumpet talking with me; which said, Come up hither, and I will shew thee things which must be hereafter.
    2. And immediately I was in the spirit: and, behold, a throne was set in heaven, and one sat on the throne.
    3. And he that sat was to look upon like a jasper and a sardine stone: and there was a rainbow round about the throne, in sight like unto an emerald.
    6a. And before the throne there was a sea of glass like unto crystal.
    In Revelation, "After this I looked" indicates a shift in focus and introduces something important (v. 1a; see also 7:1, 9; 15:5). John saw a door that had been opened by someone else, presumably for him. The "first voice" (see 1:10) speaks to him again (4:1b). On both occasions, the voice sounds like a "trumpet," the sound used for announcements and warnings in eschatology. The voice belongs to Jesus Christ. John is instructed to "come up here" to see the future order of events, all of which are under God's control. The course has been determined and shall be brought to pass by Him.
    The shift in perspective is not only for John's benefit but also for ours. Often we view things solely from an earthly perspective, while God is trying to shift our focus to a heavenly perspective of His majesty, sovereignty, power and provision. Some see this verse as symbolizing the Rapture, the catching away of the saints from earth to heaven (see 1 Thessalonians 4:13-18).
    Consistent with the prophets Isaiah and Ezekiel, John sees the throne and the One who sits upon it (Revelation 4:2). Like these prophets, there is no attempt to describe God in great detail, for He is indescribable. His glory is depicted in terms of the colors radiated by "jasper" and "sardius" (*NKJV*) stones (v. 3). *Jasper*, though usually red, can contain several colors, including yellow and green. *Sardius* is usually a deep red or orange. However it is viewed, the imagery is bright, colorful and glorious. God's throne has been firmly, decisively and permanently established ("was set," v. 2). This clearly indicates that the One who established it has the right to sit upon and control it (3:21). The power of this throne cannot be overthrown nor usurped (see Isaiah 14:13-20). Behind the throne is a "rainbow" that resembles the green radiance of an "emerald" (Revelation 4:3). It is a visible symbol of God's covenant with Noah and serves as a reminder that God keeps His word (Genesis 9:8-17).

Talk About It:
1. How is the throne of God unlike an earthly king's throne (vv. 2-4)?
2. Describe the sounds heard by John (vv. 1, 5). What are their significance?

"The open door of heaven means that God is giving us a glimpse of what life on earth looks like from the balcony of heaven."
—**David Cooper**

The noises coming from the throne, generated by the thunder and voices, and the lightning activity symbolize God's power and sovereignty over creation. They also recall the scene on Mount Sinai when God came down to meet with Israel (Exodus 19:16). Further illumination is provided by the Spirit. The floor of the throne room is described as "a sea of [transparent] glass, like. . . crystal" (Revelation 4:6). The imagery is that of beauty, glory and dominion.

B. A Shift in Worship (vv. 4, 6b-11)

4. And round about the throne were four and twenty seats: and upon the seats I saw four and twenty elders sitting, clothed in white raiment; and they had on their heads crowns of gold.

6b. And in the midst of the throne, and round about the throne, were four beasts full of eyes before and behind.

7. And the first beast was like a lion, and the second beast like a calf, and the third beast had a face as a man, and the fourth beast was like a flying eagle.

8. And the four beasts had each of them six wings about him; and they were full of eyes within: and they rest not day and night, saying, Holy, holy, holy, Lord God Almighty, which was, and is, and is to come.

9. And when those beasts give glory and honour and thanks to him that sat on the throne, who liveth for ever and ever,

10. The four and twenty elders fall down before him that sat on the throne, and worship him that liveth for ever and ever, and cast their crowns before the throne, saying,

11. Thou art worthy, O Lord, to receive glory and honour and power: for thou hast created all things, and for thy pleasure they are and were created.

In the throne room two groups of worshipers are described, the 24 elders (vv. 4, 10, 11) and the four living beings ("beasts," vv. 6-9). These two groups represent the blending of the heavenly with the earthly to bring praise sufficient for God. These also provide a heavenly pattern for earthly worship.

Seated around the throne are 24 elders, clothed in white (purity and victory) and wearing gold crowns (v. 4). These are not diadems reserved for a king, but crowns given to the victorious. Elsewhere, these represent the "crown of life" (2:10), the "crown of righteousness" (2 Timothy 4:8), the "crown of glory" (1 Peter 5:4), and the "crown of thorns" worn by Jesus (Matthew 27:29). Since these are gold, they probably indicate a special honor (cf. Revelation 14:14).

The identity of these elders is debated. Some view them as representative of the 24 divisions of the Aaronic priesthood

Talk About It:

1. How should our worship resemble the way the four beasts worship (vv. 8, 9)?

2. What do the 24 elders do with their crowns, and why (v. 10)?

3. According to verse 11, why is God worthy of all worship?

Christ Is the Redeemer

(see 1 Chronicles 24:1-5), who now bestow upon God the perfect priestly worship which the earthly priests failed to do. Some believe they are an exalted order of angels. This view is unlikely since they are called *elders*, a term reserved for humans. Others assert that they are representative of the redeemed of all ages. This view has merit. In the Old Testament there are the 12 tribes that compose Israel, the people of God. In the New Testament there are the 12 apostles, through whom the gospel has been disseminated. These two groups represent the redemptive work of God in both testaments and all of history. The redeemed in the Old Testament looked forward to the Cross. The redeemed in the New Testament look backward to the Cross. The same Blood, however, frees every repentant person from sin's guilt, shame, bondage and penalty.

First, in an ultimate act of worship, the elders prostrate themselves before the throne. Thus, they acknowledge His deity. Second, they lay their crowns at the feet of the One seated upon the throne. They give back to God that which they received from Him. He enabled them to overcome, and they acknowledge their dependency. Third, they "worship Him who lives forever and ever" (Revelation 4:10, *NKJV*). They acknowledge their life that emanates from Him. Worship begins with a decision of the will (mind), moves to the emotions (heart), and is expressed in the physical (body). It encompasses the entirety of our being and existence. It is praise to God for who He is and thanksgiving for what He does. It is dedicated to an audience of One—God. It will bless those around us, but it is dedicated solely to God. Our concern must be to please Him, not others.

Fourth (v. 11), in worship directed to Him they acknowledge (1) God's distinctive and sacred worthiness ("Thou art worthy"); (2) His sovereignty over their lives and the intimate, redemptive relationship they have with Him ("our Lord and God," *NIV*); (3) His splendor and majesty ("glory and honour and power"); (4) His primacy above all creation, for it originates from Him ("created all things"); (5) His dominion and design—we exist to bring Him glory and accomplish His will ("You called all things into being, and because of Your will, they exist and were created," author's translation).

In the midst of and around the throne are the four "living beings" (v. 6b, *NLT*). Some translations call them "beasts" (KJV) or "living creatures." This does not do justice to them, the God who created them, or the word used to describe them. The Greek word finds its root in the word for "life." This root is used to describe God as the living One (v. 10). It usually designates the part of living creation that is outside of the classification of "humanity."

The appearance of the living beings is similar to the seraphim

Ugly but Loved

In Louisa May Alcott's classic *Little Women*, a doll is passed down through the family until it is battered, ugly and broken. Beth, the youngest daughter, takes the doll, dresses it, provides it a blanket, and smothers it with love. In her eyes, it is a beautiful doll.

This is similar to what Christ has done for us. Through His blood we have been accepted and cleansed. We are clothed in His righteousness, and we are the object of His love. The only appropriate response is worship from a new heart.

described by Isaiah (6:2, 3) and the cherubim by Ezekiel (1:5-14; 10; 11:22). In verse 7 of the text, they reflect God's creation and His characteristics: (1) a "lion" is symbolic of majesty and omnipotence; (2) a "calf" denotes patience and labor; (3) a "man" represents intelligence and omniscience; (4) a "flying eagle" depicts supremacy and sovereignty in motion. Thus, they are a class of angels whose function is to glorify God (v. 9). Continu-ously, they declare the perfect holiness, eternality and dominion of the Almighty One (v. 8). In Hebraic thought, a three-fold repetition was the highest superlative one could offer.

C. A Shift in Need (5:1-4)

1. And I saw in the right hand of him that sat on the throne a book written within and on the backside, sealed with seven seals.

2. And I saw a strong angel proclaiming with a loud voice, Who is worthy to open the book, and to loose the seals thereof?

3. And no man in heaven, nor in earth, neither under the earth, was able to open the book, neither to look thereon.

4. And I wept much, because no man was found worthy to open and to read the book, neither to look thereon.

Talk About It:
What do you suppose was in the sealed book, and why could no one be found to open it?

John's attention shifts from the scene of worship to the "book" (scroll) in the hand of God, seated in a place of power and judgment—"the throne" (v. 1). The scroll is in His right hand of authority and might. Both sides of the scroll have been written and sealed by God prior to John's arrival. In the early world, it was customary to write the contents on the inside of the scroll, seal it for authenticity and security, then write a summary of the contents on the outside. It may be, however, that the events to come are so extensive that it took both sides of the scroll to record them. It is an official document of the Kingdom, and He alone chooses the One to open and execute its contents. As the remainder of Revelation reveals, the seven seals not only emphasize the perfection and completeness of the scroll's contents—the seals also represent seven stages of judgment.

A mighty angel, serving as God's spokesperson, cries out to all creation to determine if anyone is worthy to execute the contents of the scroll (v. 2). No one in all the realms of creation steps forward to break the seals, read and execute the contents (v. 3). Inside is the destiny of all humanity. The prospects of knowing about the scroll's existence but not knowing its contents are bad enough for John. But understanding there is no one worthy to look at the contents, much less carry out God's divine decrees, overwhelms John with deep emotion. The fulfillment of the Kingdom hinges upon this one unopened document. For John, the scene has changed from worship to sorrow.

Christ Is the Redeemer

II. THE REDEEMER PROVIDED (Revelation 5:5-10)

A. Comfort Provided (v. 5)

5. And one of the elders saith unto me, Weep not: behold, the Lion of the tribe of Juda, the Root of David, hath prevailed to open the book, and to loose the seven seals thereof.

On Mount Moriah, both Abraham and Isaac learned that God always provides (Genesis 22:14). He is never without a solution to any problem. One of the elders, in a command of comfort, not rebuke, speaks to John, "Stop weeping!" It is the human counterpart of Jesus' "Stop fearing!" The elder understood God had a solution. John need not weep in vain. "Behold" is a call for close consideration. It can also be translated "Listen!" or "Remember!" He may have been appealing to John's memory of the time spent with Jesus. In the midst of our sorrows, trials, tribulations and temptations, this is not bad advice. We need to remember that the Redeemer of the past, who never failed us, is the Redeemer of the present circumstance. His nature and power have not changed.

The elder reminds John there is "the Lion of the tribe of Judah." This designation not only recalls Jesus' human lineage from the tribe of Judah (which means "praise"), but that He is a mighty conqueror ("Lion"). Further, He is the Descendant of David ("Root"). In Him the promises of a legitimate heir to the throne (Jeremiah 23:5), a rod of Jesse who rules with the anointing and wisdom of the Spirit (Isaiah 11:1-5), and an everlasting kingdom (2 Samuel 7:12- 17) are fulfilled. This One has conquered so that He can open the scroll and its seven seals. The imagery in Revelation 5:5 is that of a mighty Warrior-King, whose past victory makes Him worthy to be King, receive and open the scroll, and execute its contents.

B. The Redeemer Revealed (vv. 6, 7)

6. And I beheld, and, lo, in the midst of the throne and of the four beasts, and in the midst of the elders, stood a Lamb as it had been slain, having seven horns and seven eyes, which are the seven Spirits of God sent forth into all the earth.

7. And he came and took the book out of the right hand of him that sat upon the throne.

The search in heaven, earth and under the earth could not produce anyone worthy to open the scroll. The One who steps forward is not from any realm of creation, for He is not created. He is God. He steps out of the middle of the worshiping elders and praising beings (see Psalm 22:3). The midst of the throne room is His rightful place. Remarkably, John does not see the fierce Lion, but the sacrificed Lamb. Slain lambs do not stand

Talk About It:
1. Why is Christ called a Lion? Why is He called a Root?
2. How did Christ "prevail" or "triumph"?

Talk About It:
1. Does a Lamb seem like the likely one to step forward here? Why or why not? Why is Christ called the Lamb of God?

2. How does the Lamb show His authority to open the book (v. 7)?

"What a paradox—the Lion who is a Lamb. The angel announces the entrance of the Lion of the tribe of Judah, and a Lamb steps onto the stage."
—David Cooper

odours (v. 8)—incense

Talk About It:
1. How are the prayers of godly people received by Him (v. 8)?
2. According to the "new song" (v. 9), why was Christ worthy to open the sealed book?

unless they have conquered death! Neither do lambs have horns, let alone seven of them, or seven eyes. Horns in prophetic literature represent power and victory over kingdoms, while the eyes of the Lord represent all-seeing wisdom (see Zechariah 4:1-10). The number *seven* emphasizes perfection and completeness. These paradoxical images reveal the dual natures of Jesus as Victor and Sacrifice, as God and the Son of Man. Only He is worthy to take the scroll out of the right hand of the Enthroned One.

Revelation 5:7 also reveals the Trinitarian relationship of the Father on the throne, the Son in the midst of the elders and living beings, and the Spirit, who is an integral part of the Redeemer's ministry. All three Persons are equally involved with the formation and execution of the scroll and its seals. In Scripture there are four "tests" of Deity or "Godness": (1) He receives titles reserved for God, (2) does the works of God, (3) has all the attributes attributed to God and (4) is worshiped. Thus, in the Book of Revelation and throughout Scripture, we find that only God—in the persons of the Father, the Son, and the Holy Spirit—meets these criteria.

C. Worship Revived (vv. 8-10)

8. And when he had taken the book, the four beasts and four and twenty elders fell down before the Lamb, having every one of them harps, and golden vials full of odours, which are the prayers of saints.

9. And they sung a new song, saying, Thou art worthy to take the book, and to open the seals thereof: for thou wast slain, and hast redeemed us to God by thy blood out of every kindred, and tongue, and people, and nation;

10. And hast made us unto our God kings and priests: and we shall reign on the earth.

The Father has concluded that the Son is worthy to receive the scroll. This is confirmed through the actions of the four living beings and the 24 elders (v. 8). Previously, the elders fell before the feet of the Father (4:10). Now, accompanied by the living beings, they fall before the Lamb. It is an expression of their humility in His presence and His worthiness to receive their worship. Further, each one has two items: a harp (a stringed instrument of worship) and a golden bowl containing incense, "the prayers of saints" (5:8). It is a sober reminder that our prayers are an offering of worship unto God (Psalm 141:2; Hebrews 13:15). Are our prayers a worthy offering, or are they hurried ramblings of need and want?

The group of worshipers break out in a "new song" (Revelation 5:9). The song is a recognition of the new covenant enacted through His death and the mercy it brings. It is a song of redemption through the provision of the Lamb. It is a recognition of His worthiness to receive and open the scroll because (1) He laid down His life as a sacrifice for others; (2) He has purchased what was forfeited through sin ("redeemed"); (3) He has made us to be a kingdom of priests. His redemption of our souls has loosed us from the bondage of sin and transformed our identity from slaves of the devil to servants of the Most High. This redemption was secured through His blood, shed that we might live and not die. It is available and efficacious for any person, anywhere, anytime who sincerely accepts His offer. Even the vilest of sinner has the opportunity to reign with Him (see 20:6).

III. THE REDEEMER WORSHIPED (Revelation 5:11-14)
A. Heavenly Worship (vv. 11, 12)

11. And I beheld, and I heard the voice of many angels round about the throne and the beasts and the elders: and the number of them was ten thousand times ten thousand, and thousands of thousands;

12. Saying with a loud voice, Worthy is the Lamb that was slain to receive power, and riches, and wisdom, and strength, and honour, and glory, and blessing.

The elders and living beings are joined by a group of worshipers that includes the host of angels John could not number—literally, "myriads of myriads and thousands of thousands" (see v. 11). Their praise declares a sevenfold blessing unto the slain Lamb (v. 12), who is entitled to accept (1) supernatural power (Matthew 28:18); (2) abundant wealth of glory, mercy and grace (Romans 9:23; Ephesians 2:7); (3) the embodiment of God's wisdom (1 Corinthians 1:24); (4) strength that prevails (Ephesians 6:10); (5) earned dignity (Hebrews 2:9); (6) the manifestation of divine radiance (Revelation 21:23); (7) the manifestation of divine blessing and provision (Ephesians 1:3). The heavenly hosts are not bestowing these qualities on Him, but recognizing these characteristics that He embodies.

B. All-Encompassing Worship (vv. 13, 14)

13. And every creature which is in heaven, and on the earth, and under the earth, and such as are in the sea, and all that are in them, heard I saying, Blessing, and honour, and glory, and power, be unto him that sitteth upon the throne, and unto the Lamb for ever and ever.

14. And the four beasts said, Amen. And the four and twenty elders fell down and worshipped him that liveth for ever and ever.

The scene of worship shifts from heaven to all creation. Every aspect of creation cries out in worship unto Him. It is the

"As we ponder the awesome scene of the throne of God, the seven-sealed scroll and the Lamb, we learn first and foremost that the God who is sovereign over prophetic history is also sovereign over our personal life. . . . He is in control."

—David Cooper

Talk About It:
1. What is the focus of heaven?
2. What is the Lamb of God worthy to receive (v. 12)?

"When Handel composed the *Messiah* after 24 days of seclusion, someone asked him how he was able to write such a brilliant masterpiece. He replied, 'I saw heaven open before me, and God Almighty seated on His holy throne.'"

—David Cooper

Talk About It:
1. Who will someday worship God?

John's Eyeview

While studying Revelation, one must keep in mind that John is describing things on the basis of his language, knowledge, perspective and perception. Much of John's description portrays symbolism, rather than literal imagery. It is similar to asking someone in the first century to describe all they would see in a visit to the 21st century.

Daily Devotions:

M. The Redeemer Promised
   Genesis 3:9-15

T. Redemption Foreshadowed
   Exodus 12:3-13

W. The Redeemer's Sufferings
   Isaiah 53:1-12

T. Redemption Symbolized
   Luke 22:7, 8, 14-20

F. Justification Through Redemption
   Romans 3:19-26

S. Redemption by Christ
   1 Peter 1:13-21

fulfillment of the prayer of creation to be released from the effects of sin that it might give greater glory to God (Romans 8:21, 22). It is the ultimate acknowledgment of the Lamb's provision and supremacy (Philippians 2:9-11).

The worship scene began with the four living beings (Revelation 4:8), moved to the 24 elders (vv. 10, 11), was joined by the heavenly host (5:11, 12), and encompassed all creation (v. 13). Appropriately, the four living beings bring this scene of worship to the eternal One (though not the worship itself) to a conclusion (v. 14).

CONCLUSION

The unveiling of all of the events depicted in the Book of Revelation began during the worship of one man, our fellow servant John (1:10). Worship is a powerful instrument when directed appropriately. People "worship" (ascribe honor to) many things. Consequently, these become idols. God, our Redeemer, is the only One worthy of our deepest praise and our worship. It is by God's grace that we are able to recognize the need for a Redeemer. It is by the Blood that redemption has been provided. It is through our worship that we acknowledge our acceptance of and His worthiness in the plan of redemption.

GOLDEN TEXT CHALLENGE

"THOU [CHRIST] ART WORTHY TO TAKE THE BOOK, AND TO OPEN THE SEALS THEREOF: FOR THOU WAST SLAIN, AND HAST REDEEMED US TO GOD BY THY BLOOD OUT OF EVERY KINDRED, AND TONGUE, AND PEOPLE, AND NATION" (Revelation 5:9).

Singing is a vital part of Christian worship, a natural expression of joy and praise. The subject of the new song here is the worthiness of Christ. He is worthy to open the seals and to reveal a new epoch of divine action in the universe because He has completed the action and purpose of God's plan of redemption up to that point. He has fulfilled the purpose of God; therefore, He is worthy.

Redemption also motivates this song of praise. The redeemed are from every possible cultural background in the world. There will be no prejudice or discrimination in heaven.

Christ Will Judge the World

Revelation 6:1-8; 7:9-17; 10:1-7

INTRODUCTION

Revelation 1 introduces John and the central figure of the vision, Jesus Christ. The risen Savior is standing in the midst of the churches, and its ministers are in His right hand. The church is the church only because of His presence and power. He instructs John to write to the seven churches of Asia Minor (chs. 2, 3). Each letter begins with a description of Christ that speaks to the situation of the church and prepares the way for commendation, reproof and promise. They motivate us to examine our own lives. The scene shifts from earth to heaven in chapters 4 and 5. John sees the throne room of God and heavenly worship. He also becomes aware of a scroll that contains the destiny of humanity. From the midst of the throne room emerges a victorious Lion who is a slaughtered little Lamb. He alone is worthy to break the seven seals and execute the contents of the scroll.

Each broken seal releases another judgment of God. The first six of these seals are opened in chapter 6. The seventh seal is broken and the scroll opened in chapter 8. The judgments are old and new. They are old in that they are a record of God's continual judgment upon the effects of sin in the world since the beginning of time (death, famine, war, etc.). They are new because they are poured out with greater intensity, and are designed to move the world toward God's predetermined end for this present evil age.

Judgment contains God's anger, but is not motivated by anger. It is the consequence of sin. In a sense, judgment is motivated by love and mercy and is always redemptive in nature. God judges sin that sinners might repent and be brought into a right relationship with Him (see Deuteronomy 30:1-3). Even the Great White Throne Judgment is motivated by love. While it does determine the eternal destiny of sinners, it also vindicates the saints and their faithfulness to God and His Word. Thus, it is an act of His love for His saints.

Unit Theme:
Christ in the Revelation

Central Truth:
Christ the Savior will also judge the world.

Focus:
Be informed about end-time judgments bringing punishment and reward, and trust Christ for salvation.

Context:
Written by the apostle John around A.D. 96 from the island of Patmos

Golden Text:
"The Lord Jesus Christ . . . shall judge the quick [the living] and the dead at his appearing and his kingdom" (2 Timothy 4:1).

Study Outline:
I. End-Time Judgments (Revelation 6:1-8)
II. End-Time Salvation (Revelation 7:9-17)
III. End-Time Consummation (Revelation 10:1-7)

I. END-TIME JUDGMENTS (Revelation 6:1-8)

A. The White Horse Rider (vv. 1, 2)

1. And I saw when the Lamb opened one of the seals, and I heard, as it were the noise of thunder, one of the four beasts saying, Come and see.

2. And I saw, and behold a white horse: and he that sat on him had a bow; and a crown was given unto him: and he went forth conquering, and to conquer.

Talk About It:
When the sealed book is opened, what is set into motion?

The Lamb alone is worthy to open the seven seals (v. 1). The first four seals are commonly known as the Four Horsemen of the Apocalypse: (1) Each is called forth ("Come!") by a living being; (2) their mission is reflected in the horse's color; (3) their power is not their own but "was given" by God; thus, they can do no more than God permits; (4) therefore, they are instruments of God and, like Cyrus (Isaiah 45:1) and Pharaoh (Exodus 3:10), their personal agendas are used for God's purpose; (5) their activities are the consequences of and judgment for sin; (6) the effects are worldwide. They are similar to the horsemen and chariots of Zechariah (1:8-17; 6:1-8).

The white horse rider emerges, representing conquest, probably both military and political domination. The means of his conquest is force. He is armed with a bow, the symbol of warfare. The rider receives a crown of victory, not royalty. The rider of the white horse has been identified as Christ by some, going forth with the gospel ("conquering in order to overcome," see Revelation 6:2). This is unlikely because (1) the rider is dispatched, yet Christ continues to open the seals; (2) the purpose here is world domination, not holy war (see 19:11-16); (3) this mission is accomplished by force, which violates humanity's free will—something God himself does not do. The rider has also been identified as the Antichrist, the prince of Daniel 9:26, 27, who leads a resurrected Roman Empire.

"A sealed scroll was a document containing sensitive material and could only be opened by the owner. . . . In John's vision the seven-sealed scroll represents God's ultimate plan for humanity to bring all things together under Christ."

—David Cooper

B. The Red Horse Rider (vv. 3, 4)

3. And when he had opened the second seal, I heard the second beast say, Come and see.

4. And there went out another horse that was red: and power was given to him that sat thereon to take peace from the earth, and that they should kill one another: and there was given unto him a great sword.

Talk About It:
What is unleashed with the opening of the second seal?

This rider is mounted upon a fiery red horse, an appropriate color for his mission (v. 4). The rider receives power from God to take peace from the earth. The result is widespread slaughter as the inhabitants of the earth violently butcher ("kill") one another. The rider also receives a "great sword" from God. Some see in this a prophecy of widespread civil war. Others see a foretelling of religious persecution. Regardless, it is consistent with 2 Thessalonians 2:6, 7, where restraint has been removed from the earth and devastation follows.

C. The Black Horse Rider (vv. 5, 6)

5. And when he had opened the third seal, I heard the third beast say, Come and see. And I beheld, and lo a black horse; and he that sat on him had a pair of balances in his hand.

6. And I heard a voice in the midst of the four beasts say, A measure of wheat for a penny, and three measures of barley for a penny; and see thou hurt not the oil and the wine.

The black horse rider's mission of spreading famine is indicated by the pair of scales ("balances") in his hand and the horse's color. A quart ("measure") of wheat could feed one person for one day. Three quarts of barley would feed a small family for one day. The cost for this provision in this famine is a denarius ("a penny"), or a normal day's wage (Matthew 20:2, 9). Based on information in Cicero's writings, these prices are approximately 11 times the normal price of that day. The severity of this famine is emphasized in that every dollar a normal person makes will be spent on food just to survive. Nothing is left for the other necessities of life. Protection, however, is put upon "oil and wine." These are the foods of the rich. Because of their wealth, they can survive the famine. Food is available for a price, so the famine is a greedy manipulation of the food source to drive up prices. Wealth can temporarily shield a person from the consequences of sin, but it cannot protect them indefinitely (Revelation 6:15).

Talk About It:
Why is famine such a terrible plague?

"Christ stands before no man to be judged, but every man stands before Him."
—Signposts

D. The Pale Horse Rider (vv. 7, 8)

7. And when he had opened the fourth seal, I heard the voice of the fourth beast say, Come and see.

8. And I looked, and behold a pale horse: and his name that sat on him was Death, and Hell followed with him. And power was given unto them over the fourth part of the earth, to kill with sword, and with hunger, and with death, and with the beasts of the earth.

Christ opens the fourth seal to reveal a "pale" (yellowish-green) horse. Appropriately, it has been described as the color of a corpse. In contrast to the other riders, this one is named "Death." This cessation of life results in spiritual death. The term is not used in the New Testament to describe a natural process, but a destructive power resulting from the consequences of sin. This force and power is now personified. It is this death that Christ came to abolish (Luke 1:79). His companion is "Hell" (Hades), the place in the New Testament where the souls of the unrighteous dead await judgment (Luke 16:23).

Talk About It:
How do these verses show Christ's power over death and hell?

Those who are righteous are immediately with Christ (2 Corinthians 5:6-8). These two are permitted to kill one-fourth of those who remain on the earth. They perform their tasks through a fourfold plague, an intensification of the first three judgments: (1) a large two-edged "sword" that can subdue and inflict physical and spiritual pain; (2) a deprivation of food ("hunger"); (3) physical and spiritual "death"; (4) death by means of the wild creatures ("beasts") of the earth.

God's desire is to touch the hearts of those on the earth. Many will attribute these judgments to natural circumstances. Such is the nature of fallen humanity, who fail to see the hand of God in their lives. Yet, God continues to offer salvation in love.

II. END-TIME SALVATION (Revelation 7:9-17)

A. The Appearance of the Redeemed (vv. 9, 10)

9. After this I beheld, and, lo, a great multitude, which no man could number, of all nations, and kindreds, and people, and tongues, stood before the throne, and before the Lamb, clothed with white robes, and palms in their hands;

10. And cried with a loud voice, saying, Salvation to our God which sitteth upon the throne, and unto the Lamb.

Talk About It:

1. What does verse 9 reveal about the redeemed ones pictured here?

2. What will be the focus of heaven?

As the events and judgments of Revelation are unfolding, there is a break in the judgment events. Chapter 7 comprises two visions: (1) the sealing of the 144,000 on earth (vv. 1-8) and (2) the appearance of a multitude in heaven (vv. 9-17). The first vision contains a specific number of people who are "sealed"— who are consecrated to Christ and put under His protection for the coming persecution. They are identified on the basis of their Jewish lineage, and they are clearly on the earth. There are no works, persecution or activity recorded before the perspective changes from earth to heaven. Also, they make their appearance in heaven in chapter 14, not here. The second vision deals with a host that John is incapable of numbering (7:9). They come from "all nations, tribes, peoples, and tongues" (*NKJV*), who have come out of tribulation. Most importantly, they are in the throne room of God. There are several points made in verses 9 and 10 that characterize the multitude.

First, *their numbers are so significant that human capability of John's time cannot number them.* While this verse does not promote universalism (the belief that everyone will go to heaven, even those who do not repent while on earth), it does reveal that the number of the redeemed is extremely large. According to creationists, approximately 51 billion people have lived on earth since the beginning of time. This provides a significant number of people who could have been in right relationship with God.

Christ Will Judge the World

Second, *this multitude encompasses all national, ethnic, racial and language groups.* Christ's blood cleanses "whosoever will" (see Romans 10:13). Further, it reveals the unity that is found in the body of Christ through the blood of the Lamb. A true worshiper of God is unconcerned about a fellow worshiper's color or ethnicity, for we are all created by Him and are one in Him (Galatians 3:28).

Third, *they stand in the presence of the Father ("before the throne") and the Son ("the Lamb").* Through the redemptive plan designed by the Father and the execution of that plan by the Son on the cross, they are able to stand in the throne room of God. That they are in the throne room signifies their redemption is complete. No more pain, grief, fear, temptation or trials. Mind, body and soul is what God originally intended. They made it!

Fourth, *they accepted God's gracious redemptive provision and clothed themselves in robes of white that He has provided.* He made it possible. They made it happen. Through the help of the Spirit and the continual cleansing available through the Blood, they determined within themselves to remain pure and keep their garments unspotted. This emphasizes the dual aspects of salvation. It is a free gift, but we must live out its conditions.

Fifth, *they are worshipers.* They have palm branches in their hands. Unlike those in the crowds with palm branches who worshiped Jesus as He entered Jerusalem on the way to the cross (Matthew 21:8), but forsook Him during the Crucifixion (Mark 14:50), these have worshiped Him even in the worst of times.

Finally, *they have one focus now that they are in heaven— to give glory to God.* It is not with a subdued whisper, but with a loud shout that they praise God for His works of salvation. The language indicates excitement and enthusiasm. It is from the heart, but expressed through every faculty necessary to bring forth praise appropriate for the Father and the Lamb.

B. The Reception of the Redeemed (vv. 11, 12)

11. And all the angels stood round about the throne, and about the elders and the four beasts, and fell before the throne on their faces, and worshipped God,

12. Saying, Amen: Blessing, and glory, and wisdom, and thanksgiving, and honour, and power, and might, be unto our God for ever and ever. Amen.

The angels and the four living beings, who cannot echo thanksgiving for salvation, because they have never experienced such, fall upon their faces. They are joined by the 24 elders as they honor and worship God. Falling before Him is an act of humility, submission, profound reverence and, for humanity, remembrance symbolized. Genesis 2:7 records humanity's

Not Home Yet

The story is told of a missionary who was returning on a ship from a lifetime in Africa, where he spent his life and buried his wife. Also on the ship was President Teddy Roosevelt, returning from a hunting expedition. When the boat docked, the crowds rushed to greet the president. The battered and frail missionary was stunned. All that he suffered and there was no one there to greet him. "Where is my greeting party, Lord?" he asked. To which God responded, "You're not home yet, My son!" The celebration will be celestial!

Talk About It:

How can the angels' worship of Christ never be the same as our worship of Him?

creation. Adam was formed from the dust of the ground. God breathed the breath of life into him, he became a living soul, dust lived, and gave glory to God. It is appropriate that humanity remembers from whence we came—and how we came to be.

The elders' song is one of confession—acknowledging who God is. Appropriately, it begins with *Amen*, a word of confession and profession. They confess that He is true; they profess that He has been true in their lives. It is true that He is and deserves recognition from Creation for His blessings (benefits bestowed by a Greater upon one lesser). He is, has, and bestows glory. All wisdom comes from Him. He is deserving of thanksgiving for all He does, and honor for who He is. Power and strength belong to "our God" now and forever! He is *our* God! And we are His redeemed people!

C. The Identity of the Redeemed (vv. 13, 14)

13. And one of the elders answered, saying unto me, What are these which are arrayed in white robes? and whence came they?

14. And I said unto him, Sir, thou knowest. And he said to me, These are they which came out of great tribulation, and have washed their robes, and made them white in the blood of the Lamb.

In the midst of this most glorious moment, John's attention is pierced by an elder's twofold question concerning the multitude's identity and origin (v. 13). Note the emphasis on their robes and how they are white. Redemption cannot and must not be separated from the blood of the Lamb. Reminiscent of Ezekiel's answer to God's question (Ezekiel 37:3), John politely and wisely defers to the elder. Some suggest that he did not know the answer. The elder answers, "These are they who have come out of the great tribulation (persecution) and have washed their robes and made them white in the blood of the Lamb" (Revelation 7:14, *Amp.*).

This is the church raptured from the earth! They have experienced great afflictions and trials in their lives and have been brought to heaven before the seventh seal is unfolded, which represents the Great Tribulation. They have been caught away from the earth before that tribulation starts, a fulfillment of Christ's promise (Revelation 3:10). Also, it is important to note that not all the events of Revelation are sequential. They are recorded in the order that John saw them, not necessarily as they occur.

Editor's note: Some Bible scholars believe those "arrayed in white robes . . . which came out of great tribulation" are those people who became Christians during the Great Tribulation period and are martyred for their faith.

Talk About It:

1. Who will be saved during the coming "great tribulation"?

2. How will they suffer for their testimony (see Revelation 6:9-11)?

"The world despises a clear-cut testimony based on the Word of God. During the Tribulation period hatred will be given free reign, resulting in an agonizing time of persecution for God's people."

—Homer Rhea

Christ Will Judge the World

D. The Care of the Redeemed (vv. 15-17)

15. Therefore are they before the throne of God, and serve him day and night in his temple: and he that sitteth on the throne shall dwell among them.

16. They shall hunger no more, neither thirst any more; neither shall the sun light on them, nor any heat.

17. For the Lamb which is in the midst of the throne shall feed them, and shall lead them unto living fountains of waters: and God shall wipe away all tears from their eyes.

The elder continues to inform John of their destiny and provision. Because of the whiteness of their robes and all it represents, they now stand before the throne of God to "serve him" (v. 15). They serve Him through their ceaseless worship in His temple (place of His glory). Worship is bestowed upon the One who deserves it, and from those who understand intimately how precious is our salvation. Consequently, He "dwells," or "tabernacles," among them—the idea is that of pitching His tent over them. Thus, they suffer no more the effects or consequences of sin (v. 16). The One who defeated sin and its power now becomes a Shepherd to them (v. 17). This is a final fulfillment of Jeremiah 23:1-8. All that they have suffered will be healed as the Father wipes the tears, and all that caused the tears, from their eyes!

Talk About It:
1. Whom will God "dwell among" in heaven (v. 15)?
2. What will not be experienced in heaven (vv. 16, 17)?

III. END-TIME CONSUMMATION (Revelation 10:1-7)
A. The Prophetic Scroll (vv. 1-4)

1. And I saw another mighty angel come down from heaven, clothed with a cloud: and a rainbow was upon his head, and his face was as it were the sun, and his feet as pillars of fire:

2. And he had in his hand a little book open: and he set his right foot upon the sea, and his left foot on the earth,

3. And cried with a loud voice, as when a lion roareth: and when he had cried, seven thunders uttered their voices.

4. And when the seven thunders had uttered their voices, I was about to write: and I heard a voice from heaven saying unto me, Seal up those things which the seven thunders uttered, and write them not.

As we have seen in this and previous lessons, there are many parallels and patterns in Revelation. For example, there are seven seals which secure the contents of the scroll the Lamb receives from the Father (5:1-7). This scroll contains the destiny of all humanity and the future of the world itself. The seventh seal contains seven trumpets (8:1, 2). There is a pause between the opening of the sixth and seventh seals, which allows for two visions to be presented—the sealing of the 144,000 and the introduction of the redeemed in heaven to

Talk About It:
1. Describe the angel's appearance and its significance.
2. What authority has the angel been given?
3. What is John not allowed to do?

John and the readers (ch. 7). There is also an interlude of two visions between the sounding of the sixth and seventh trumpets—the angel with the little scroll (10:1-11) and the two witnesses (11:1-12). This interlude presents the prophetic role. The sixth trumpet has sounded (9:13), but the seventh does not sound until Revelation 11:15. The activity and judgment that precedes these literary interludes does not cease. They allow the reader to receive more information concerning the intricate and decisive plan of God and the end of time.

John's vantage point from chapter 4 through chapter 9 has been in heaven. His location may change here or, more probably, it is a redirection in his perspective and attention as he sees a mighty angel descend from heaven (10:1). The identity of this angel is difficult to determine. He is powerful ("mighty") and "clothed with a cloud." A "rainbow," a sign of God's faithfulness to His covenants (Genesis 9:13), is upon his head. A rainbow also is found at the throne of God (Revelation 4:3). His face shines with the radiance of the sun itself, and his legs recall the pillars of fire that represented God's presence, protection and guidance in the wilderness (Exodus 13:21, 22; 14:19, 24). All of these attributes are associated with God; thus, this would seem to indicate this is Christ. However, John never refers to Jesus as an angel anywhere else in the book. Further, his use of an oath (Revelation 10:6) seems inappropriate for Christ. On the basis of parallels with Daniel 8:16 and 12:7, some identify this angel as Gabriel. This identity is credible and teaches us a powerful truth: those who are in God's presence reflect His glory and image. The longer we are there, the more like Him we become.

In the angel's hand is a small book or scroll that is open (Revelation 10:2). This scene recalls images of Ezekiel 2:8—3:3, where the prophet receives a scroll from an angel. The angel in Revelation sets one foot on land and the other on the seas. This is a stance of universal authority over all of earth and its inhabitants. This image stands in stark contrast with the idolatrous and rebellious behavior of humanity revealed in the verses just prior to this chapter (9:20, 21). The angel's authority comes from the One who sent him and is represented by the scroll he holds. This is true of all messengers from God. The authority is not their own; it is God's. Those who hear the messenger and the one who speaks the message should not lose sight of this fact.

The angel cries out "with a loud voice," which sounds like the roar of a lion (10:3). A lion's roar is associated with victory and warning. The cry results in the sound of seven thunders. It is evident that these thunders contain messages which John understood, for he is about to write them down when he is prevented from doing so by a voice from heaven (v. 4). The content of those

"Christians should never fail to sense the operation of an angelic glory. It forever eclipses the world of demonic powers, as the sun does a candle's light."
—Billy Graham

Christ Will Judge the World

messages are sealed from us at this point in time. Their magnitude in the scheme of end-time events is illustrated by the scene that follows. God is bringing the events to His desired end.

B.The Prophetic Message (vv. 5-7)

5. And the angel which I saw stand upon the sea and upon the earth lifted up his hand to heaven,

6. And sware by him that liveth for ever and ever, who created heaven, and the things that therein are, and the earth, and the things that therein are, and the sea, and the things which are therein, that there should be time no longer:

7. But in the days of the voice of the seventh angel, when he shall begin to sound, the mystery of God should be finished, as he hath declared to his servants the prophets.

The angel raises his right hand toward heaven in the stance of an oath, and he swears by the eternality of God and His sovereignty over all aspects of creation that time should cease (vv. 5, 6). The cessation of time is fulfilled in the sounding of the seventh trumpet (11:15). This is a declaration that God is bringing all things to an end (10:7). He is in control of the circumstances and their timing. It is a summary of what God's prophets have declared through the ages.

Talk About It
1. How does the angel show where his allegiance lies?
2. What does the angel announce?

CONCLUSION

The events of this lesson reinforce the sovereignty of God. He is in control of the course of this world. It is a world under judgment. Those who are His have been judged at the Cross (Romans 8:1) and are under His protection (Revelation 3:10) and provision (Deuteronomy 8:9). God's purpose is not to annihilate humanity, but to bring repentance. Even if it is not accepted, He still offers.

Charles Spurgeon said, "There is no attribute more comforting to His children than that of God's sovereignty. Under the most adverse circumstances, in the most severe trials, they believe that sovereignty has ordained their afflictions, that sovereignty overrules them, and that sovereignty will sanctify them all. There is nothing for which the children ought to more earnestly contend to than the doctrine of their Master over all creation--the kingship of God over all the works of His own hands--the throne of God and His right to sit upon that throne . . . for it is God upon the throne whom we trust."

GOLDEN TEXT CHALLENGE

"THE LORD JESUS CHRIST . . . SHALL JUDGE THE QUICK [THE LIVING] AND THE DEAD AT HIS APPEARING AND HIS KINGDOM" (2 Timothy 4:1).

This verse is the beginning of Paul's charge to his protégé, Timothy, to preach and teach the Word of God. This mission must be carried on with an awareness of Christ's imminent return and the judgment to come. Paul commissions Timothy by God the Father, by Christ the future Judge, by Christ's second coming, and by His kingdom, to be sincere and faithful in preaching.

At the judgment seat of Christ, the believers in Christ will be judged according to their faithfulness in ministry (Romans 14:10; 2 Corinthians 5:10). At the white throne judgment, the unbelievers will be judged according to their works. These two judgments underline the immeasurable importance and seriousness of teaching and preaching God's Word (Revelation 20:11-15).

Christ Will Triumph Over Evil

Revelation 12:1-10; 14:6-20; 17:1-18; 19:1-21

INTRODUCTION

Revelation is often understood as a chronology of end-time events. Certainly, it is an account of God's end-time activity; however, it is not always chronologically arranged. There are interludes that allow for new or revisited material to be brought to the attention of the reader. The events are recorded as John saw them, not as they actually occurred. Also, there are sections interspersed that bring meaning to history and other events in the book.

Chapter 12 is such an account. It is the record of history itself, recording the continual battle between God's kingdom and Satan's misguided attempts to overthrow the throne. In a sense, it is a summary of Revelation and the entire Bible. The chapter gives meaning to the events prior to and following this account. Jesus' words to His believers ring true throughout Revelation 12: "If they have persecuted me, they will also persecute you" (John 15:20). The struggles are real and, at times, almost overwhelming, yet the end is in sight and its outcome is certain—God and those in Him will prevail. Satan has been cast down once and it will happen again.

Chapters 14 and 19 record the events that occur at the closing of this present evil age (Galatians 1:4), and the introduction of the age of God's rule and reign without the effects or consequences of sin. Chapter 14 is an announcement of defeat, not the record of that defeat. That comes later in the lesson. This announcement is made through the proclamations of three angels. These proclamations are connected and progressively more intense in their consequence. Chapter 19 reveals the King of Glory in a militaristic mode. The enemies of God have blasphemed Him and badgered the saints. The time has come to deal with them decisively and definitively.

An earlier lesson noted that we can become so engrossed with the meaning of every symbol that we miss the big picture. This lesson has sections that can be understood in several different ways. This may be by design. It has a verse or two that is difficult to comprehend. As we stand back and look at the big picture, the view is clear—God will prevail over His enemies, and all creation is and will be subject to Him.

Unit Theme:
Christ in the Revelation

Central Truth:
By His death, resurrection and ascension, Christ demonstrated His victory over evil.

Focus:
Know that Christ will put an end to all evil, and live daily in the assurance of His victory.

Context:
Written by the apostle John around A.D. 96 from the island of Patmos

Golden Text:
"He [Christ] must reign, till he hath put all enemies under his feet" (1 Corinthians 15:25).

Study Outline:
I. Satan Cast Down (Revelation 12:1-10)
II. Worldly Powers Defeated (Revelation 14:6-20; 17:1-18)
III. Christ, the King and Lord (Revelation 19:1-21)

I. SATAN CAST DOWN (Revelation 12:1-10)

A. The Marvelous Woman (vv. 1, 2)

wonder (v. 1)—sign

1. And there appeared a great wonder in heaven; a woman clothed with the sun, and the moon under her feet, and upon her head a crown of twelve stars:

2. And she being with child cried, travailing in birth, and pained to be delivered.

Talk About It:

Why is there so much symbolism in Revelation?

John records the appearance of a great "wonder," or sign, in heaven (v. 1). The woman's origin is heavenly, even though the events transpire on earth. Her glory is highlighted by a series of characteristics. She (1) is arrayed with the glorious light of the sun; (2) has the moon beneath her, depicting her dominion; (3) wears a victor's "crown of twelve stars," recalling Joseph's dream (Genesis 37:9). Her appearance is breathtaking. She is not divine, but of supernatural origin and surrounded by the glory of God. Some identify her as Israel, others as the church. Credible arguments can be made for both. The 12 stars could represent the 12 tribes or the 12 apostles. She begins as Israel, but transforms into the church (see v. 17). Thus, she is the radiant bride of Christ, the redeemed of all ages. Believing Israelites and saints are all saved by the Blood, which makes us His people and the Bride.

The woman's glory includes her pregnancy and pangs of labor (v. 2). She is struggling to give birth. Isaiah 66:8 teaches that without travail and pains of labor, there are no births. In times of distress people are receptive to the gospel. However, souls need to be saved in between national disasters and personal misfortune. "In pain" (*NKJV*) depicts something that brings great anguish until it is fulfilled. May the church regain this pain, longing for lost people to be saved.

B. The Red Dragon (vv. 3, 4)

(Revelation 12:3, 4 is not included in the printed text.)

Talk About It:

Why is a mythological creature—a dragon—used to portray Satan, who is real?

Another sign appears in heaven—an enormous red dragon (v. 3). His color represents his desire for glory, prideful attitude and murderous nature. In Scripture, dragons inflict fear and bring chaos or disorder (see Job 41:1-10; Isaiah 27:1). They are a symbol of evil and opposition against the kingdom of God. This dragon's description is unnatural and hideous. His seven heads represent completion and the universality of his power. The 10 horns represent 10 kings (Revelation 17:12). On his heads are seven crowns (diadems) claiming royalty over the kingdoms of the world. Diadems were linen bands worn about the forehead. A king could wear a diadem for each kingdom controlled. The dragon's claim of supremacy is false, for only Christ—who will be revealed with a multitude of diadems—is King (19:12). Later, John makes it plain that this dragon is Satan (12:9).

Christ Will Triumph Over Evil

The dragon is powerful and influential. He is able to draw one-third of the stars of heaven and cast them to earth (v. 4; see Daniel 8). Some see this as descriptive of his physical power. Others believe it is rebellious Lucifer's removal from heaven prior to Creation, along with the angels who chose to follow him (Ezekiel 28:1-19; 2 Peter 2:4; Jude 6; Revelation 9:1). His mission is clear: he stands prepared before the woman to devour her Child at birth. The reference is clearly to Jesus (see Matthew 2; 4:1-11), but reminds us that Satan stands ready to devour all "children" born into the Kingdom (Jeremiah 31:15; John 10:10). The church must protect the little ones of the Kingdom through prayer, instruction, encouragement and a fitting example (Matthew 18:14).

> "That there is a devil is a thing doubted by none but such as are under the influence of the devil."
> —Cotton Mather

C. The Birth of the Child (vv. 5, 6)

5. And she brought forth a man child, who was to rule all nations with a rod of iron: and her child was caught up unto God, and to his throne.

6. And the woman fled into the wilderness, where she hath a place prepared of God, that they should feed her there a thousand two hundred and threescore days.

The glorious woman brings forth a male Child, whose destiny is to shepherd the nations. This is the birth of Jesus (see Psalm 2:9). Israel was commissioned to minister to the nations as a kingdom of priests (Exodus 19:6). She failed to fulfill the mission (Isaiah 1, esp. vv. 16, 17). Where Israel failed, this Shepherd will succeed. His rule is characterized by a shepherd's staff of iron. This seems to indicate a harsh reign, as staffs were normally made of wood. However, it is revealing a powerful and comforting truth. The shepherd's crook was placed over the neck of straying sheep stranded in crevices, bringing them to the safety of the shepherd. The staff was also used as a weapon to kill or dispel attackers. The iron staff assures the sheep that it will not break in times of rescue or protection. His shepherding is strong and sure.

Talk About It:
Christ will one day "rule all nations with a rod of iron." What does this mean?

Without great detail, John records Jesus' ascension into heaven and to the throne (v. 5). The Child is "caught up," which means "forcefully seized away." The term most often depicts a rescue. Here the Child is removed from the dragon's attacks. He is also exalted when He takes His rightful place at God's right hand (Ephesians 1:20-22).

The woman flees into the "wilderness" (Revelation 12:6), usually viewed as a place of barrenness and isolation. Here it is the place of God's provision, protection and preparation (Israel's wilderness wanderings). It is also a place of intimate fellowship with God. The wilderness event is for a specific period of time. Some view the 1,260 days as part of the Antichrist's reign. Others view it as representing God's protection of His people through all ages, yet signifying that He has a prescribed period in mind. The end is predetermined.

D. A Heavenly War (vv. 7-10)

7. And there was war in heaven: Michael and his angels fought against the dragon; and the dragon fought and his angels,

8. And prevailed not; neither was their place found any more in heaven.

9. And the great dragon was cast out, that old serpent, called the Devil, and Satan, which deceiveth the whole world: he was cast out into the earth, and his angels were cast out with him.

10. And I heard a loud voice saying in heaven, Now is come salvation, and strength, and the kingdom of our God, and the power of his Christ: for the accuser of our brethren is cast down, which accused them before our God day and night.

Talk About It:

1. Compare the strength of Satan and his demons with God's angels.

2. Why is Satan called "the accuser of our brethren" (v. 10)?

A Defeated Enemy

Many nations are engaged in fighting terrorism. It is proving difficult to fight a war that has no structure, location or uniforms. The enemy is almost invisible and formless. Such is the enemy that Christians fight. Satan does not appear in a red suit with a pitchfork. It takes the discerning of the Holy Spirit, the blood of Christ, and the provision of the Father to

War erupts in heaven (v. 7). Michael and God's angels fight Satan and his fallen angels. In Jewish literature, Michael is the mighty warrior angel who protects Israel from Satan. As the archangel, Scripture confirms that he confronts and contends with Satan (here and in Jude 9). Satan and his minions are permanently cast out of heaven (Revelation 12:9). The dragon, who is also "that old serpent," is *Satan* ("adversary") and the *devil* ("slanderer"). He is a continual deceiver who opposes God and His people. He deceives "the whole world," a phrase used exclusively in Revelation to refer to unbelievers (3:10). Satan attempts to deceive believers, but is unsuccessful. However, he deceives those who serve him. Agreements and promises mean nothing to him, for he never fulfills his promises. He and his angels are cast to earth, the place of their activity.

Four explanations of the event's significance are proposed by commentators: (1) This is the record of Satan's fall from heaven after his rebellion against God. This, however, seems to be recorded in 12:4. (2) It is an attempt by Satan to regain his place in heaven after the Crucifixion. It is Michael and the angels, though, who initiate the conflict. (3) It is symbolic of the end-time events and the all-out war between Satan and the forces of God. (4) This reveals the power of the Crucifixion. Job teaches that Satan had access to the throne room before the Cross (Job 1:6-12; 2:1-7; also see Zechariah 3:1-10). After Satan was defeated through the Cross, he no longer was permitted access to accuse believers in the presence of God (Revelation 12:10). It seems illogical that Satan could accuse the saints in the presence of the One who died for them. Thus,

Christ Will Triumph Over Evil

after Christ's ascension to the throne room (v. 5), Satan was denied access to God's presence, a fulfillment of John 12:31.

This interpretation seems to be confirmed by verse 10 of the text. There is the declaration that salvation has come through God's reign, which is characterized by deliverance, manifested power, the sovereignty of God, and the authority of Christ. The accuser can now only slander the saints to one another and themselves (see 2 Corinthians 2:11).

> subdue this enemy in our lives. We cannot do it alone. He is defeated, but not ready to concede. We must be diligent, prepared and equipped.

II. WORLDLY POWERS DEFEATED
(Revelation 14:6-20; 17:1-18)

A. A Vision of Impending Judgment (14:6-13)
(Revelation 14:8-12 is not included in the printed text.)

6. And I saw another angel fly in the midst of heaven, having the everlasting gospel to preach unto them that dwell on the earth, and to every nation, and kindred, and tongue, and people,

7. Saying with a loud voice, Fear God, and give glory to him; for the hour of his judgment is come: and worship him that made heaven, and earth, and the sea, and the fountains of waters.

13. And I heard a voice from heaven saying unto me, Write, Blessed are the dead which die in the Lord from henceforth: Yea, saith the Spirit, that they may rest from their labours; and their works do follow them.

The first angel is flying in mid-heaven. It is also the location of the other two angels who follow. He has the message of Christ ("everlasting gospel") to preach to all the unbelievers in the Tribulation ("them that dwell on the earth"). His voice will resonate around the earth. The unholy trinity (Satan, Antichrist and the False Prophet) has been revealed in chapter 13 and demanded that worship be given to the Antichrist ("the beast," 13:4, 15). In stark contrast, this angel calls the earth to worship God (14:7). The people are to fear God, something they have failed to do even in the midst of these terrible conditions, and give Him glory. The angel announces that it is the hour of His judgment and His creation is subject to Him.

The second angel announces, as part of the judgment previously announced, that "Babylon is fallen, is fallen" (v. 8; see also Isaiah 21:9). Babylon was a city of the Chaldeans (modern Iraq). John does not give a specific identity for the city. Here it is symbolic of widespread corruption, false worship and void of morals. She is not only under judgment for her character but also her actions: she has spread her sinful decay to "all nations," because she has "made them drink from the wine of the passion of her immorality" (writer's translation). *Wrath* can mean "anger" or "intense feelings." *Fornication* normally refers

Talk About It:
1. What message is delivered by the angel, to whom is it given, and why is it called "everlasting" (vv. 6, 7)?
2. Why does Babylon fall (v. 8)?
3. What judgment is pronounced against those who received the Beast's "mark in his forehead, or in his hand" (vv. 9-11)?
4. Why are God's people commended (v. 12)?

to any sexual activity outside of God's will, but here it includes religious infidelity.

The third angel warns everyone to reject the mark of the Beast (v. 9). Receiving this mark is more than receiving an image, number, or implanted computer chip, though it may include these. It is offensive to God because it is an act of worship dedicated to the Antichrist. It is a rejection of the redemptive provision through the blood of God's Son and an embrace of everything that God opposes. The one who does this has drunk from the wine of Babylon and will now drink from the undiluted wrath of God's wine (v. 10). Their suffering includes the torment of fire and brimstone in the presence of the holy angels and the One who died that they might not suffer such a fate. The suffering is compounded by the holiness of God. It is an eternal and painful reminder of God's love rejected (v. 11).

In contrast, the angel declares blessings upon the saints (vv. 12, 13). In spite of trials, troubles and tribulations, they have patiently kept the Word of God. A further blessing is bestowed from God. Their labor instills peace and their works illustrate their character.

B. The Harvest of the Earth (vv. 14-20)
(Revelation 14:15-20 is not included in the printed text.)
14. And I looked, and behold a white cloud, and upon the cloud one sat like unto the Son of man, having on his head a golden crown, and in his hand a sharp sickle.

Talk About It:
1. What does the Son of Man's crown represent? His sickle?
2. How terrible will be "the great winepress of the wrath of God" (v. 19)?

Upon a symbol of divine presence, "white cloud" (cf. Matthew 17:5), one "like unto the Son of man" is revealed with a golden crown of victory (not royalty) and an instrument for reaping (Revelation 14:14). Some view this as a depiction of the Rapture. Others view it as an angel reflecting the Son's glory and serving as His agent of judgment (see 10:1). It does not seem proper that the Son of God would receive instruction from an angel concerning the time of the Rapture (14:15), even if that angel comes from the presence of God ("temple"). The harvest is described as dried, withered and overripe. This does not seem to be an appropriate description of the redeemed. Rather, it is indicative of a world that has been given ample opportunity to repent, but has chosen to reject God's grace. The result is severe judgment (vv. 19, 20).

C. The Scarlet Harlot (17:1-18)
(Revelation 17:1-12, 15-18 is not included in the printed text.)
13. These have one mind, and shall give their power and strength unto the beast.
14. These shall make war with the Lamb, and the Lamb shall overcome them: for he is Lord of lords, and King of

admiration (v. 6)—
wonder
perdition (v. 8)—
destruction

Christ Will Triumph Over Evil

kings: and they that are with him are called, and chosen, and faithful.

Chapters 17 and 18 record the fall of Babylon. Judgment is upon her because of (1) her activity and influence (17:1, 2); (2) her relationship with the Beast (v. 3); (3) her ostentatious appearance designed to seduce others with her immorality (v. 4); (4) the pride with which she reveals her character and perpetuates that character through her offspring (v. 5); (5) her murderous opposition of the saints (v. 6a). The power of her seductiveness is apparent in John's intense amazement and wonder, for which he was rebuked (vv. 6b, 7a). The mystery of the woman and the Beast are interrelated, for they both desire world domination (vv. 7b-11).

The nations of the world, represented by the 10 kings controlled by the Antichrist (v. 12), come together in a stunning display of unity to make war with the Lamb (vv. 13, 14a). However, it is a futile effort. He is the King of all the kingdoms of creation! He is the Lord over all masters! Those who follow Him are His and they are loyal (v. 14b). This stands in contrast to the relationships in the Beast's government. The woman is destroyed by those whom she seduced (v. 16). Turmoil is in the camp, but God is still in control (v. 17).

III. CHRIST, THE KING AND LORD (Revelation 19:1-21)
A. The Marriage Supper (vv. 1-10)

(Revelation 19:1-4, 7-10 is not included in the printed text.)

5. And a voice came out of the throne, saying, Praise our God, all ye his servants, and ye that fear him, both small and great.

6. And I heard as it were the voice of a great multitude, and as the voice of many waters, and as the voice of mighty thunderings, saying, Alleluia: for the Lord God omnipotent reigneth.

Chapter 19 is a prelude to the Great White Throne Judgment (see 20:11-15). It begins with praise and worship to God because Babylon is destroyed (vv. 1-4). The praise continues from the angels around the throne (v. 5), a rejoinder from many voices (v. 6), and the announcement of the Marriage Supper of the Lamb (v. 7). The Bride (the redeemed) is arrayed appropriately (v. 8). The Supper begins here (v. 9), but is not consummated until the descent of the New Jerusalem in chapter 21.

B. The Bridegroom King (vv. 11-16)

11. And I saw heaven opened, and behold a white horse; and he that sat upon him was called Faithful and True, and in righteousness he doth judge and make war.

12. His eyes were as a flame of fire, and on his head

Talk About It:
1. How can sin take on such a beautiful appearance (v. 4)?
2. Describe the unity and strength of the kings who will make war against the Lamb of God (v. 13).
3. Who will be with the Lamb, and who will win the battle (v. 14)?

"Jesus is portrayed as the Lion of the tribe of Judah, who has conquered. The church is pictured as being victorious over Satan, the Antichrist and the False Prophet. God the Father is revealed as the One who will complete His eternal plan for the ages."
—David Cooper

Talk About It:
1. Why are the redeemed people called "both small and great" (v. 5)?
2. Who is the bride in the Marriage Supper of the Lamb, and how will she prepare herself (vv. 7-9)?

"What a paradox— the book that unfolds the terrible future and the judgments of God is a book of praise!"
—David Cooper

were many crowns; and he had a name written, that no man knew, but he himself.

13. And he was clothed with a vesture dipped in blood: and his name is called The Word of God.

14. And the armies which were in heaven followed him upon white horses, clothed in fine linen, white and clean.

15. And out of his mouth goeth a sharp sword, that with it he should smite the nations: and he shall rule them with a rod of iron: and he treadeth the winepress of the fierceness and wrath of Almighty God.

16. And he hath on his vesture and on his thigh a name written, KING OF KINGS, AND LORD OF LORDS.

The Bridegroom appears in military garments, not wedding apparel. Reminiscent of His baptism (Matthew 3:13-17), the heavens open in an act of divine revelation. He is sitting on a white horse of conquest. His character is revealed in His covenant names, *Faithful* and *True* (see also Revelation 3:14; 21:5). He is a warrior-judge, but His motivation is righteousness, not a desire for power. *Righteousness* here means "legitimacy" and "right relationship with God." He is conducting a war that is right and commissioned by the Father.

Recalling 1:14, His eyes discern, judge correctly, and reflect His glory (19:12). He wears many diadems of royalty. As noted, a ruler was entitled to wear a diadem for each kingdom he controlled. He has a name that can be seen, but not understood by anyone but God. Thus, it is (1) reflective of His power (unfathomable by humanity); (2) a name above every name (Philippians 2:9-11); (3) one that cannot be usurped or stolen; (4) consistent with His mysterious nature.

His garments were given to Him and were dipped in blood (Revelation 19:13). Some see a reference to the Blood of atonement here, but the imagery is reflective of the impending victory (v. 15), and consistent with Isaiah 63:1-6. He is "the Word of God." This is (1) His divine nature as the Word incarnate (John 1:1-14); (2) a promise that the Word will be fulfilled completely (2 Corinthians 1:20); (3) an assurance of protection (Ephesians 6:17). He is accompanied by the army in heaven dressed in fine linen, brilliant white and clean, riding white horses. This army could be the redeemed. The manner of dress is consistent with the redeemed in Revelation 7. Some believe it is the angelic host, since they are associated with conquest (Matthew 26:53). Regardless, the imagery is majestic and stunning.

Verse 15 of the text records the dual role of Christ as the Judge, from whose "mouth goeth a sharp sword," and as a Shepherd with the unbreakable staff of iron. These reflect two complementary aspects of His nature. Each is governed by the other. Here His concern is judgment and the establishment of God's will and kingdom.

---

smite (v. 15)—strike down

Talk About It:

1. What will Jesus Christ do "in righteousness" (v. 11), and what does this mean?

2. Why is Jesus called "The Word of God" (v. 13)?

3. How will Jesus Christ prove Himself to be King of kings and Lord of lords?

Christ Will Triumph Over Evil

Written on His garment and draped across His thigh (close to where a sword normally hangs) is a name that depicts who He is, both in identification and nature—King of Kings and Lord of Lords (v. 16). All rulers, governments, principalities and powers—human or spiritual—are subject to Him!

C. The Supper of the Great God (vv. 17-21)
(Revelation 19:17-19 is not included in the printed text.)
20. And the beast was taken, and with him the false prophet that wrought miracles before him, with which he deceived them that had received the mark of the beast, and them that worshipped his image. These both were cast alive into a lake of fire burning with brimstone.
21. And the remnant were slain with the sword of him that sat upon the horse, which sword proceeded out of his mouth: and all the fowls were filled with their flesh.

This section details the final defeat of the Beast and fulfills Revelation 16:16. In stunning imagery, an angel is profiled against the sun and calls the vultures to assemble for "the supper of the great God" (19:17). This is not the Marriage Supper of the Lamb. It is a feast for the vultures, who shall consume the flesh of those who opposed God (v. 18). The Antichrist, kings and their armies gather to engage in war against the King and His army (v. 19), commonly called Armageddon.

The battle is swift and the outcome certain. The Beast and False Prophet are violently seized and thrown alive into a lake of fire, burning with brimstone (v. 20; a fulfillment of 14:10). The lake of fire is the place of everlasting punishment (20:10). The remnant of the opposing army is slain by the sword that proceeds from the mouth of Christ (19:21). This should not be interpreted, however, to mean they escape the lake of fire (see 20:15), nor that all unbelievers are slain at this time (vv. 7-9).

Talk About It:
1. What will this terrible "great supper" be (vv. 17, 18)?
2. What will be the fate of Satan's forces (vv. 20, 21)?

"The forces of evil are no match for the Son of God. The Resurrection proved that."
—H. Bert Ames

CONCLUSION
The passages examined here reveal that the enemies of Christ are determined, but defeated. The Beast (Antichrist) and his forces seek power and dominion, but encounter the sovereignty of God. Just as Satan has been cast from heaven to earth, he will be cast from earth to the lake of fire (20:10). Those who believe his lies will suffer his fate, unless they accept God's continued call to repentance. Jesus died to bring life. Let not His death be in vain for those in your life.

GOLDEN TEXT CHALLENGE
"HE [CHRIST] MUST REIGN, TILL HE HATH PUT ALL ENEMIES UNDER HIS FEET" (1 Corinthians 15:25).
Who and what are the enemies of Christ? We've seen many of them in today's study: Satan, Satan's angels, immorality,

M. Lucifer's Fall
   Isaiah 14:12-17
T. Victorious
   Warrior
   Isaiah 63:1-6
W. Gog Defeated
   Ezekiel 39:1-7
T. Victory Over
   Satan
   Luke 10:17-22
F. Victory by Christ
   2 Corinthians
   2:14-16
S. The Blessed
   Hope
   Titus 2:11-15

godless political systems, the Antichrist, the mark of the Beast, pride, the followers of Satan, hell and death.

Christ's enemies are always active, fighting Him and His purposes every moment of every day. But they will not stand. Christ is reigning now, and at the end of time all of His enemies—including the final one, death—will be crushed under His feet. Those who serve Him *now* will reign with Him *then*.

Christ's Kingdom Will Come

Revelation 11:15-18; 20:1-15

INTRODUCTION

Most of Revelation is built around the seven seals of judgment. The first four seals release horsemen upon the earth to accomplish their designated missions (6:1-8). The fifth seal reveals the souls under the altar—martyrs who were killed because of their witness (v. 9). The opening of the sixth seal shakes all of creation (v. 12). The seventh seal is so awesome that for the only time in recorded history, the attendants of the throne cease praising God (8:1). This seal contains seven trumpets, each of which announces another judgment upon the rebellious.

The seventh trumpet announces a different type of judgment (11:15). It is not a plague or calamity like the others. It announces the end of the battle. All the kingdoms of the world will become the kingdoms of Christ. The wicked have rebelled, blasphemed and antagonized the kingdom of God. Now they will be subdued by the King whose kingdom is forever.

Following Christ's decisive battle with the Beast and his kingdoms, Satan is banished to a bottomless pit for 1,000 years (20:1-6). This is known as the *millennial* (Latin for 1,000 years) reign of Christ. It is a literal period where peace reigns on the earth because the Prince of Peace governs with those who rejected the seduction of the enemies of God. The Lord's Prayer includes petitions which declare, "Come Your kingdom! Be done Your will, as in heaven also on earth!" (Matthew 6:10, literal translation). These petitions are fulfilled in this period. Of course, these petitions must be fulfilled in our lives every day. We willingly submit our wills to His, allowing the King to sit upon the throne of our heart and rule our lives in power.

After the end of the thousand years of peace, the battle of Gog and Magog—the final battle of history—takes place, and Satan's kingdom is subdued (Revelation 20:7-15). For centuries he has deceived and destroyed. Now he has to bow his knees before the throne of Christ and admit in front of every soul that has ever lived on the earth that, indeed, Jesus is Lord (Philippians 2:9-11). Satan then joins the Beast and False Prophet in the lake of fire and remains there forever. Those who followed him are judged at the White Throne Judgment. As they followed him in life, they shall follow him in eternity.

Unit Theme:
Christ in the Revelation

Central Truth:
Christ's kingdom will come in its fullness when He returns.

Focus:
Understand that Christ's kingdom has not yet come in its fullness and pray for His kingdom to come.

Context:
Written by the apostle John around A.D. 96 from the island of Patmos

Golden Text:
"The kingdoms of this world are become the kingdoms of our Lord, and of his Christ; and he shall reign for ever and ever" (Revelation 11:15).

Study Outline:
I. Christ's Kingdom Is Forever (Revelation 11:15-18)
II. Christ's Millennial Kingdom Will Come (Revelation 20:1-6)
III. Satan's Kingdom Will Fall (Revelation 20:7-15)

I. CHRIST'S KINGDOM IS FOREVER (Revelation 11:15-18)

A. The Announcement of All Announcements (v. 15)

15. And the seventh angel sounded; and there were great voices in heaven, saying, The kingdoms of this world are become the kingdoms of our Lord, and of his Christ; and he shall reign for ever and ever.

Talk About It:
What will "the kingdoms of this world" become (v. 15)? What does this mean?

Revelation 11:15-19 is a proclamation of what follows in the remainder of the book. It is an interlude to help orient John and the readers to the events that ensue.

Verse 15 is a summation of the entire Bible; indeed, all of history. Every event in the record of humanity and every oracle of the prophets of God are brought to understanding and completion in the fulfillment of this verse. "Great voices in heaven" make this hymnic declaration. *Great* emphasizes the magnitude of the number and the resonating sound. The speakers are taken to be the angelic host of heaven and the redeemed. It is a declaration that the kingdoms usurped from God through the wiles of the Enemy will be returned to their rightful King. Everything will reach its culmination in "our Lord, and . . . his Christ" (Messiah). This universal kingdom shall be His forever (Zechariah 14:9; Daniel 2:44).

B. The Announcement's Reception (vv. 16-18)

16. And the four and twenty elders, which sat before God on their seats, fell upon their faces, and worshipped God,

17. Saying, We give thee thanks, O Lord God Almighty, which art, and wast, and art to come; because thou hast taken to thee thy great power, and hast reigned.

18. And the nations were angry, and thy wrath is come, and the time of the dead, that they should be judged, and that thou shouldest give reward unto thy servants the prophets, and to the saints, and them that fear thy name, small and great; and shouldest destroy them which destroy the earth.

Talk About It:
1. What do the elders call God, and what do they praise Him for doing with His "great power" (v. 17)?
2. Why are the nations angry, and why should the Christians rejoice (v. 18)?

At the end of the declaration, the 24 elders, seated upon thrones before the throne of God, fall on their faces and worship God. First, they remove themselves from the thrones they have received. This in itself is an act of worship, as it is a recognition of the One from whom they received the thrones. Second, they bow themselves before God. This is an act of great reverence, humility and recognition that life comes from God. Third, they worship God. Worship in its most basic sense is being a living sacrifice dedicated to Him. It also means enjoying God. These elders are being blessed, even as they bless. Thus, worship is reciprocal.

First, their hymn of redemption begins with thanksgiving, a

recognition of and gratitude for the things God does for His own (v. 17). Second, it recognizes God's covenant activity. This is done by recalling His Old Testament names. He is "Lord," whose name is so holy and special that it was not to be uttered in its purest form. It comes from the verb of existence. Succinctly, *He is who He is.* Thus, He is true to His character and nature. "God" signifies He is the true and sovereign God. It especially emphasizes His loving actions toward humanity. He is also "the Almighty"—the all-powerful One who is more than sufficient to remove His enemies, vindicate His saints, and reveal His glory.

Third, their hymn recognizes the eternality of the God who has always been, is, and always will be. Fourth, He held "great power" in the past. That power has not diminished through the passing of time. Fifth, even in the midst of rebellious spiritual beings and kings, He "reigned." They were under His control, even when they did not recognize or acknowledge that sovereignty. The same is true of rebellious humanity today. People are subject to Him even in their rebellion against His authority.

The second half of the hymn takes on a different but related tone (v. 18). It reveals how God's nature governs His actions. The "nations were angry" at the sovereignty of God. Their anger reveals that even they realize they did not have full dominion over "their" kingdoms. The declaration of verse 15 intensifies their anger. Thus, the time has come for God to exercise justice: the guilty will be punished, the innocent will be rewarded and vindicated, and the fear of the Lord restored to the earth. The Lord God Almighty will right the wrongs of this earth.

> "In all ages God has pre-announced certain things which He purposed to do. These announcements are termed *prophecies.* Prophecy is history pre-written."
> —Selected

II. CHRIST'S MILLENNIAL KINGDOM WILL COME
   (Revelation 20:1-6)
A. The Imprisonment of Satan (vv. 1-3)

1. And I saw an angel come down from heaven, having the key of the bottomless pit and a great chain in his hand.

2. And he laid hold on the dragon, that old serpent, which is the Devil, and Satan, and bound him a thousand years,

3. And cast him into the bottomless pit, and shut him up, and set a seal upon him, that he should deceive the nations no more, till the thousand years should be fulfilled: and after that he must be loosed a little season.

The events of chapter 20 are connected to those in chapters 19 and 21, but arise from separate visions. This is revealed through John's use of the phrase "and I saw" (20:1; also see 19:11, 17, 19; 20:4, 12; 21:1). John sees "an angel descend out of heaven, holding the key of the Abyss and a great chain was in his hand" (writer's translation). The Abyss is depicted as a deep, dark cavern in the earth that imprisons the rebellious

Talk About It:
1. What do verses 1 and 2 reveal about the devil's power?
2. According to verse 3, what is the chief purpose of Satan? Why is he so successful at it?

angels until judgment (Luke 8:31; 2 Peter 2:4; Jude 6). Notice that it is not Michael, Gabriel, or even a strong angel, but "an angel" that descends.

The angel "laid hold" (forcibly seized) Satan and imprisoned him for a thousand years (Revelation 20:2). So that the reader does not miss the nature of the one seized, several of his names are mentioned here. First, he is "the dragon" of 12:3, who stood in front of the radiant woman (the redeemed) to kill Christ at His birth. The Resurrection was a public triumph of Christ's power over physical and spiritual death (Colossians 2:15). Second, he is "that old serpent" from the beginning, who led Adam and Eve into sin (Genesis 3:1-13). His desire was to destroy God's plans for humanity. Yet, the Lamb was slain from the foundation of the world (Revelation 13:8). Third, he is "the Devil," the slanderer or false accuser, whose access to God was terminated through the Cross (12:9). Finally, he is "Satan," the adversary of God and His people (1 Peter 5:8). He is now in chains and under the control of "an angel," fulfilling the plan of God. His situation proves that, in all these attempts to thwart the plan of God, he failed. His "carnal sacraments"—the lust of the flesh, the lust of the eyes, and the pride of life—are proven to be illusions and lies (1 John 2:16).

Satan is securely placed in the bottomless pit for a thousand years, with "a seal upon him" (Revelation 20:3). Kings often placed their seal upon that which was not to be opened without the king's knowledge or permission. It also identified his property. Christians have the assurance that we have the seal of the Holy Spirit (Ephesians 1:13). Here, even Satan knows that he is not his own, but is subject to the King.

B. The Age of Peace (vv. 4-6)
4. And I saw thrones, and they sat upon them, and judgment was given unto them: and I saw the souls of them that were beheaded for the witness of Jesus, and for the word of God, and which had not worshipped the beast, neither his image, neither had received his mark upon their foreheads, or in their hands; and they lived and reigned with Christ a thousand years.

5. But the rest of the dead lived not again until the thousand years were finished. This is the first resurrection.

6. Blessed and holy is he that hath part in the first resurrection: on such the second death hath no power, but they shall be priests of God and of Christ, and shall reign with him a thousand years.

In verse 4, another vision is introduced ("and I saw") that is separate from, but connected to, the preceding account. The millennial reign does not begin because the devil is bound. The devil is bound so that God's plan for the millennial reign can begin. John saw thrones, whose occupants have been given the right to govern and judge. The exact identity of those who sit on the thrones is debated. Some limit them to those who were martyred. Others suggest these are the thrones of the apostles (Matthew 19:28). Some view these as the saints, who will judge fallen angels (1 Corinthians 6:2, 3). The passage reveals that the enthroned number is quite large. The souls of those who were martyred because of their testimony are clearly present, and verse 5 reveals that all the righteous dead have been resurrected. Thus, the thrones are for all the redeemed, whether apostles, saints or martyrs. All the promises of judging and ruling to each of these groups are fulfilled in the millennial reign with Christ.

Talk About It:
1. What can those who give up their life for Christ expect to receive?
2. What is the "first resurrection," and why is it a blessing?
3. What is the "second death," and why is it a curse?

Those who are part of the first resurrection receive one of the seven blessings pronounced in Revelation (v. 6; see 1:3; 14:13; 16:15; 19:9; 22:7, 14). This is a real, bodily resurrection of the righteous dead. First, these are "blessed" because they are free from the threat and power of the second death, for over them it has "no power." Second, they are "holy." The term's *etymology* (word from which it derives) has mistakenly been identified as "to cut" and "to shine." A better understanding of the word's origin and meaning reveals it is a word of relationship. If we are holy, we are "whole in our relationship with God." It is not a part-time relationship, or a one-sided relationship. It is a covenant relationship that allows us to participate in and continually be transformed by the character and provision of God. This makes us distinctive from the world. Holiness is first and foremost "perfect or complete love for God." God's essential character is love, life and holiness. These three primary characteristics are interconnected and revealed in the character of the resurrected righteous ones.

Third, these are also "priests of God and of Christ." This is not a restoration of the Levitical priesthood and sacrificial system, as some suggest. This is clearly condemned in the New Testament (Galatians 4:9). One Sacrifice has been offered for the sin of humanity and that sacrifice is eternally effective (Hebrews 10:12). There remains no other sacrifices that God desires than mercy (Matthew 9:13), living sacrifices (Romans 12:1), and the sacrifice of praise (Jeremiah 33:11; Hebrews 13:15). Thus, to be "priests of God and of Christ" relates to reigning as royalty with the Lord for 1,000 years.

"In Christ even the most ordinary man becomes a king."
—William Barclay

III. SATAN'S KINGDOM WILL FALL (Revelation 20:7-15)
A. The Battle of Gog and Magog (vv. 7-9)
7. And when the thousand years are expired, Satan shall be loosed out of his prison,

Magog is the name
of the descendants
of Noah's son
Japheth, who settled
the regions of the
earth north of Israel
(Genesis 10:2). In
the Revelation, Gog
and Magog repre-
sent all the heathen
opponents of the
Messiah.

Talk About It:

1. Why do you think
Satan will be freed
one last time?

2. How successful
will Satan be in
recruiting an army?

3. How will God
destroy His ene-
mies?

8. And shall go out to deceive the nations which are in the four quarters of the earth, Gog and Magog, to gather them together to battle: the number of whom is as the sand of the sea.

9. And they went up on the breadth of the earth, and compassed the camp of the saints about, and the beloved city: and fire came down from God out of heaven, and devoured them.

At the end of this thousand-year period, Satan is released from the bottomless pit. He does not escape or overcome the power that held him captive, but is released by God for an undesignated period of time. In our limited understanding, it may be difficult for us to know why God permits this. Simply, it is a necessary part of His plan. Some view the Millennium as the restoration of the earth's order prior to the Fall (Genesis 1:28-30). With that promise fulfilled, God can now bring all things to a close. Thus, Satan is loosed by God, but is still subject to God's will.

Revelation 19 closed with the defeat of the Beast, False Prophet, and the kingdoms that followed them. Apparently, there are those who submit to the Shepherd's staff of iron (see 19:15), but are later deceived by Satan. These are called "Gog and Magog" (20:8). The background for this passage is Ezekiel 38 and 39. Briefly, these terms represent those who oppose Israel (38:16). Attempts have been made to identify them as Turkey, Russia, Afghanistan, Europe, China, or a combination thereof. John simply identifies "Gog and Magog" as those who rise to oppose God and His people. Four things are highlight-ed: (1) they are deceived; (2) they come from all regions of the earth ("four corners"); (3) they are numerous; (4) they are preparing for battle.

"Breadth of the earth" is probably a reference to the "width of the earth" (v. 9). It indicates the number of the unholy army is expansive and encompasses "the camp of God's people, the city he loves" (*NIV*). These are viewed as references to Jerusalem. It is not the saints who fight, but rather "fire," whose origin is clearly God, and it consumes the enemy. His rebuttal of their attack is swift, powerful and decisive. Ezekiel 38:19-23 says that every living thing on earth will tremble because of the fierceness of His wrath in this battle, which judges His ene-mies, protects His saints, and reveals His holiness.

"A thousand years in the Abyss will not change Satan."
—Homer Rhea

B. Satan's Righteous Reward (v. 10)

10. And the devil that deceived them was cast into the lake of fire and brimstone, where the beast and the false prophet are, and shall be tormented day and night for ever and ever.

With his deluded army destroyed and the other members of

his unholy trinity (the Beast and the False Prophet) sentenced to the lake of fire, Satan is thrown into the lake also. He had 1,000 years to contemplate his future, but he remained rebellious to the end. He will suffer torment 24 hours a day forever. Such is the end of all those who oppose God.

Talk About It:
What will be the eternal condition of Satan after his final judgment?

C. The White Throne Judgment (vv. 11-15)

11. And I saw a great white throne, and him that sat on it, from whose face the earth and the heaven fled away; and there was found no place for them.

12. And I saw the dead, small and great, stand before God; and the books were opened: and another book was opened, which is the book of life: and the dead were judged out of those things which were written in the books, according to their works.

13. And the sea gave up the dead which were in it; and death and hell delivered up the dead which were in them: and they were judged every man according to their works.

14. And death and hell were cast into the lake of fire. This is the second death.

15. And whosoever was not found written in the book of life was cast into the lake of fire.

John sees "a great white throne" and the throne's Inhabitant. The scene is so awesome that heaven and earth flee, leaving an empty horizon (v. 11). These are removed in anticipation of the new heaven and earth (21:1). The background for this scene is Daniel 7:9, 10, where the Ancient of Days is seated upon His throne. Here, it is Christ seated upon the throne (see John 5:22). "White" symbolizes the character of the judgment. "Throne" represents the seat of government, and as such, a place of judgment. Individuals approach the throne to receive justice. The Hebrew idea of *justice* is "making the wrong right." The innocent are vindicated, and the guilty are dealt with in a manner consistent with their crime.

Talk About It:
1. How will human beings be judged (vv. 12, 13)?
2. Who will be "cast into the lake of fire" (v. 15), and why?

Standing before this throne are "the dead," from the powerful to the weak (Revelation 20:12). The passage indicates that the dead from every realm of life, including those lost at sea, and those removed from Death and Hades, are resurrected in the second resurrection and judged (v. 13; cf. v. 5). The judgment is based on the evidence written in "the books" (or scrolls) and the "book of life" (v. 12). The Book of Life is the record of all the names of the redeemed (Philippians 4:3; Revelation 21:27). The other books contain a record of the deeds or works of individuals (see Jeremiah 17:10; Romans 2:5, 6; 1 Peter 1:17). On the basis of these books, the dead are judged.

A question that often arises in connection with this judgment is, will this be a judgment of the resurrected unrighteous only or all the resurrected dead? There is evidence for both views. Some believe that since the Book of Life is present and because we all must give an account of our works, the righteous dead will also appear. Others contend that the righteous and the unrighteous are separated (Matthew 25:31, 32) and the righteous are judged at the coming of Christ (see Revelation 22:12). Also, here only the dead are judged. There is no mention of the raptured saints. It seems unlikely that they would escape a judgment that the righteous dead have to face. Further, there is only one verdict issued at this judgment (20:15).

If the righteous do appear at this judgment, there is nothing to fear. The faithful redeemed are assured that their names will not be removed from the Book of Life (3:5). Further, the One who laid down His life for the redeemed and intercedes for them is the One who sits upon the throne (Hebrews 7:25; 8:1). The only aspect of their lives that would be judged at this point is the quantity and quality of their fruit, not their salvation (1 Corinthians 3:10-15).

The lake of fire is the place that ultimately receives "Death and Hades" (Revelation 20:14, *NKJV*). "Death" is the consequence of sin, the last enemy to be destroyed (1 Corinthians 15:26). "Hades" is the place where unbelievers are held until judgment. "Hell" (or "Gehenna") is the term in the Gospels for the lake of fire (Matthew 10:28). It is the place where fallen spiritual beings and unrepentant humanity spend eternity. Those whose names are not written in the Book of Life are cast therein (Revelation 20:15). It is the second death from which there is no escape.

The doctrine of annihilation is popular with some. This view asserts that after a period of time, those in the lake of fire will be burned up and cease to exist. This is not the image that Scripture presents. Jesus and the Book of Revelation make it plain that the torment, suffering and confinement are *forever* (Matthew 25:46; Revelation 14:10, 11)—literally "into the ages of the ages." This is the New Testament way of expressing something that has no end.

The Last Word

Voltaire, the French philosopher who died in 1778, was unrelenting in his condemnation of the Bible. He stated that in less than 100 years no one would know what a Bible was. Less than 50 years later, the Geneva Bible Society was using Voltaire's house and his printing press to print the Bible. His house became a major distribution point for God's Word. The devil and his followers may rant and rave, but God is still in control—and He will have the last word.

CONCLUSION

The announcement of the end of evil and the establishment of God's complete and unhindered reign brings peace and comfort to those in trials and tribulation. Satan's kingdom, though strong, is no match for the power of God, who is so powerful that "an angel" under His authority is able to bind Satan and cast him into the Abyss. Martin Luther declared that the devil is God's devil. That is, he is under God's dominion and can travel no farther than God permits. Satan's time is limited. The same power of God that saved us from sin will protect us as we call upon His name.

Christ's Kingdom Will Come

GOLDEN TEXT CHALLENGE

"THE KINGDOMS OF THIS WORLD ARE BECOME THE KINGDOMS OF OUR LORD, AND OF HIS CHRIST; AND HE SHALL REIGN FOR EVER AND EVER" (Revelation 11:15).

The kingdom and power of God will subdue all earthly kingdoms. The reign of Christ will be an actual, physical reign over the nations and kingdoms of the earth. The kingdoms of the world will come under the visible reign of Jesus Christ.

This reality affirms the completeness of God's power. That reality is first experienced within the heart and character of every believer. Eventually, with the fulfillment of Scripture's end-time prophesies, that reality will be completed with Christ's reign on earth.

Christ Makes All Things New

Revelation 21:1 through 22:21

Unit Theme:
Christ in the Revelation

Central Truth:
Believers in Christ have a glorious, everlasting future.

Focus:
Consider the glorious, eternal future awaiting Christians and give priority to things eternal.

Context:
Written by the apostle John around A.D. 96 from the island of Patmos

Golden Text:
"He that sat upon the throne said, Behold, I make all things new" (Revelation 21:5).

Study Outline:
I. New Heaven and Earth (Revelation 21:1-8)
II. New Holy City (Revelation 21:9-27)
III. New Paradise (Revelation 22:1-21)

INTRODUCTION

The Book of Revelation begins with the appearance of Christ and His commission to John (ch. 1). The seven letters to the churches of Asia Minor, which contain commendation, reproof and promise, are recorded in chapters 2 and 3. Chapters 4 and 5 reveal the throne room, heavenly worship, and the revelation of the Lion who is a slaughtered Lamb. The opening of the seven seals found on the scroll containing the destiny of creation is accomplished in chapters 6 and 7. The seventh seal consists of seven trumpets, sounded in chapters 8 through 11. Chapters 12 through 14 are a record of conflict and evil chaos. The last seven plagues are found in chapters 15 and 16. Babylon is depicted and destroyed in chapters 17 and 18. The final victory of God and His people begins in chapter 19 and ends in chapter 20 with the Great White Throne Judgment. Chapters 21 and 22 comprise the last section, the new heaven and new earth revealed.

Interspersed in this broad outline are three interludes, presented through visions. These help the reader make sense of what is happening and how it fits into the broad plan of God. These interludes offer visions of security and salvation (7:1-17), the prophetic role (10:1–11:14), and final judgment (14:6-20).

The final two chapters (21 and 22) present the fulfillment of God's plan for His people. The plan is given in marriage imagery. Thus, this is the consummation of the marriage between the Bridegroom and the Bride. The Bridegroom receives His bride (new Jerusalem), the Marriage Supper of the Lamb is completed, and the Bridegroom and Bride reside in their completed home, the kingdom of God.

The letter closes with encouragement and admonition. The reader is encouraged through assurance that the Book of Revelation is the inspired Word of God and that Jesus is coming quickly. It also warns that the unveiled material is not to be altered. This warning is deeper than a prohibition to alter words. It means we must accept God's revealed decrees even if they challenge human sensibilities and we don't fully understand them. God is in control, and we must choose to submit ourselves to Him, His plan and His timing—both for His kingdom and for our lives.

I. NEW HEAVEN AND EARTH (Revelation 21:1-8)
A. A Terrestrial and Celestial Transformation (vv. 1, 2)

1. And I saw a new heaven and a new earth: for the first heaven and the first earth were passed away; and there was no more sea.

2. And I John saw the holy city, new Jerusalem, coming down from God out of heaven, prepared as a bride adorned for her husband.

Following the Great White Throne Judgment, another vision is introduced through the phrase "and I saw." The object of John's vision is "a new heaven and a new earth," for the old have "passed away" (v. 1). In this verse a multitude of promises and prophecies are fulfilled. At the conclusion of a servant song depicting Messiah's ministry, God declared, "Behold, the former things have come to pass, and new things I declare; before they spring forth I tell you of them" (Isaiah 42:9, *NKJV*). He also promised to "create new heavens and a new earth" (65:17), which shall endure forever (66:22). Second Peter 3:10-13 reveals that at the end of this age all things will be transformed, including heaven and earth. Sin's presence and effects on earth, caused by humanity's sin, are removed by fervent heat; while sin's presence and effects in the heavens, caused by Satan's rebellion and dominion therein (Ephesians 3:10; 6:12), will also be eradicated. Creation will be returned to its original sin-free state. Thus, it is a redeemed heaven and earth.

The absence of the sea in the new order has provoked discussion. Some say the ancient people's fear of the sea is behind this declaration. John, however, was a fisherman before his calling (Matthew 4:21). In Scripture, the sea is associated with turmoil (Isaiah 57:20) and the rise of wickedness (Revelation 13:1); thus, it is an assurance that evil and turmoil will never arise again in the new order.

John also observes "new Jerusalem" descending from heaven (21:2). The origin of this "holy city" is God himself. The city has been understood as (1) a physical city; (2) the abiding place of the righteous dead, who now descend to the new heaven and earth; (3) a symbol of the church. Here, the city is depicted as "a young bride who has been made beautiful for her husband" (writer's translation). There is an emphasis on preparation prior to the unveiling. The bridal description is consistent with that of the church espoused to Christ (Isaiah 54:5; 2 Corinthians 11:2; Ephesians 5:23-27). Yet in Revelation 21:11–22:5, the physical description is of a city. It is best understood as the fulfillment of Zion, the city of God and the abiding place of the people of God (see Galatians 4:26; Hebrews 11:10, 16). Also, it is a symbol of the saints, for there they dwell. It is not the corrupt Jerusalem, but a redeemed community where God abides.

Talk About It:
1. Why will God create "a new heaven and a new earth" (v. 1)?
2. How will "the holy city" be "prepared as a bride" (v. 2)?

Letting Go
One particular greeting card contains a truth that has to be inspired by Biblical truth. It states: "Sometimes we have to let go of the past in order to enjoy the present, and be able to dream of the future." The devil wants to shackle us to past failures and obscure the future with the false promise of pleasure in the present. God, through the Book of Revelation, inspires us to examine the present, use it wisely, and anticipate the future age of glory. Since we know the end, whose word shall we take?

B. An Emotional Transformation (vv. 3-5)

3. And I heard a great voice out of heaven saying, Behold, the tabernacle of God is with men, and he will dwell with them, and they shall be his people, and God himself shall be with them, and be their God.

4. And God shall wipe away all tears from their eyes; and there shall be no more death, neither sorrow, nor crying, neither shall there be any more pain: for the former things are passed away.

5. And he that sat upon the throne said, Behold, I make all things new. And he said unto me, Write: for these words are true and faithful.

Talk About It:
1. How does verse 3 describe the eternal relationship God will have with His people?
2. List the "former things" that will pass away.

This passage contains one of the most touching and powerful promises in Scripture, consisting of three aspects. First, now that "the tabernacle of God" is with humanity, God himself will tabernacle ("dwell") with the redeemed (v. 3). This announcement comes from heaven and ultimately from God, regardless of the speaker (see v. 5). He "pitches His tent" or "overshadows us" with His presence, giving us power (see Luke 1:35), protection (Isaiah 4:5, 6), perfection (John 17:23), and provision (Jeremiah 33:7-9). Thus, the covenant relationship, as illustrated especially in the Tabernacle topology, comes to its perfect fruition—He is ours and we are His!

Second, God promises to transform our emotions (Revelation 21:4). As the hand of God wipes away tears and their stains, He also removes the source of the tears found in the old order (see Isaiah 25:8). In this new redeemed order, there is no possibility of death. There is no more grief, for we are reunited with loved ones who died in the Lord. Wailing has no place, for there are no tragedies in His presence. All afflictions have been healed. Every negative aspect of the sin-cursed age is subdued by His redemptive provision. They cease to exist any longer (Isaiah 65:17). Some see in this a promise to remove every painful memory.

Third, we have the personal guarantee from the Father that all this will be accomplished (Revelation 21:5). His throne represents the seat of His government, His right to rule, and His sovereignty over all aspects of life. His promise to "make all things new" speaks to the quality of the newness. It is not just different; it is better. To emphasize the surety and eternality of His promise, He commands John to record it for all to read.

C. A Relational Transformation (vv. 6-8)

6. And he said unto me, It is done. I am Alpha and Omega, the beginning and the end. I will give unto him that is athirst of the fountain of the water of life freely.

7. He that overcometh shall inherit all things; and I will be his God, and he shall be my son.

8. But the fearful, and unbelieving, and the abominable, and murderers, and whoremongers, and sorcerers, and idolaters, and all liars, shall have their part in the lake which burneth with fire and brimstone: which is the second death.

The Father speaks directly to John (v. 6a). The Father speaks on a limited number of occasions in Revelation (see 1:8; 16:1, 17). It is usually Christ, the elders or the angels who speak with John. God's declaration here is the same as 16:17, "It is done." When God speaks, it is not just the utterance of words. It becomes an event within itself without regard to time. In other words, when He speaks it is accomplished in eternity, even if we do not see the manifestation of the spoken word in the present. He is the "Alpha and Omega [first and last letters of the Greek alphabet], the beginning and the end" (21:6b). As the Alpha and Omega, He was the Creator of the old order and is now the Judge who ends it. Further, He is the originator of the new age and the One who completes it. It is everlasting, therefore it will not end, but it cannot exist apart from Him. It is a promise of eternality.

God is love, life and holiness. Out of these issue all that God is. Therefore, it is His nature to promise and provide these things. First, He "freely" gives life to those who earnestly desire it (thirst), through the imagery of "the fountain of the water of life" (v. 6c). In an age before bottled or purified water, people had to be careful from which source of water they drank. A standing pool of water could be deadly, whereas water bubbling up from the earth assured the drinker it had been naturally purified, was cool and refreshing (see Jeremiah 2:13). Second, those who overcome—the continually victorious—receive all the inheritance associated with the kingdom of God (Revelation 21:7). It is a promise not only of provision, but also relationship. Children, not strangers, receive inheritances. To further clarify the nature and quality of the relationship, God notes it is not one of distant relatives, but that of Father and child.

Those who are "cowardly, the unbelieving, the vile, the murderers, the sexually immoral, those who practice magic arts, the idolaters and all liars" have no place in redeemed Zion or the bride of Christ (v. 8, *NIV*). "Fearful" (cowardly) includes an element of shame (see Luke 9:26). Those who are "abominable" (vile) have offended the holiness of God. "Sorcerers" (those who practice magic arts) often used drugs to manipulate others or enhance their magical experience. In brief, these have rejected the provision of God and relied upon something false and unfulfilling. They reject the life offered by the Father and will suffer the "second death" and its inheritance—the lake of "fire and brimstone."

fearful (v. 8)—cowardly

abominable (v. 8)—vile

whoremongers (v. 8)—sexually immoral

Talk About It:
1. How does God show Himself to be "the beginning and the end" in Revelation 21?
2. What inheritance awaits God's children?
3. Why will all those listed in verse 8 experience "the second death"?

"Neither science nor learning can quench the fires of judgment in that day, but a Christian can steal a quick look at Calvary and know that his judgment is past."
—*Signposts*

II. NEW HOLY CITY (Revelation 21:9-27)
A. The Glory of the City (vv. 9-21)
(Revelation 21:15-21 is not included in the printed text.)

9. And there came unto me one of the seven angels which had the seven vials full of the seven last plagues, and talked with me, saying, Come hither, I will shew thee the bride, the Lamb's wife.

10. And he carried me away in the spirit to a great and high mountain, and shewed me that great city, the holy Jerusalem, descending out of heaven from God,

11. Having the glory of God: and her light was like unto a stone most precious, even like a jasper stone, clear as crystal.

12. And had a wall great and high, and had twelve gates, and at the gates twelve angels, and names written thereon, which are the names of the twelve tribes of the children of Israel:

13. On the east three gates; on the north three gates; on the south three gates; and on the west three gates.

14. And the wall of the city had twelve foundations, and in them the names of the twelve apostles of the Lamb.

The angel that poured out the last plagues (ch. 15) instructed John to join him for a view of "the bride, the Lamb's wife" (21:9). This is probably the same angel that summoned him to see Babylon (17:1). The contrast between the two cities is striking. The language here can indicate that a processional is in place or that the marriage ceremony is complete. Since the Bride is being displayed, it is taken to be her processional walk. That she is the Lamb's wife emphasizes the redemptive action and character that allows the marriage to take place. Truly, she is redeemed (cf. Hosea 3) and transformed (Isaiah 1:18).

Through the Spirit, the angel carries John to "a great and high mountain" (Revelation 21:10). Mountains are often places of revelation in Scripture (see Matthew 5:1, 2; 17:1-5). This is not a second descent of the Holy City, but rather the same descent from a different vantage point. John's first vision revealed the relationship the redeemed have with the Father (Revelation 21:2-7); this second vision emphasizes the relationship the redeemed have with the Lamb (v. 9).

The splendor of the city is not in the materials used for construction. Rather, the splendor and materials reflect the glory of God, as illustrated by the character of the light (v. 11). It is a glorious city because God is there (see Ezekiel 48:35). Space prevents a detailed analysis, so the three characteristics emphasized in the passage will be examined.

First, the redemptive nature of God is reflected in the city (vv. 12-14). Verse 12 records there are 12 angels guarding 12

---

lieth foursquare (v. 16)—"was laid out like a square" (*NIV*)

twelve thousand furlongs (v. 16)— about 1,400 miles

Talk About It:

1. Describe the New Jerusalem in three words.

2. Why do you suppose the names of the 12 apostles are written on the city's foundations?

3. Why will the holy city have walls?

Christ Makes All Things New

gates, which have the names of the tribes of Israel written on them. The wall of the city sits upon 12 foundations that have the names of the 12 apostles written in them (v. 14). Entrance into the redemption of God was introduced through Israel (John 4:22), but sits firmly upon the teaching of the apostles (Ephesians 2:20)—salvation through Christ alone (Acts 4:12). Thus, Old and New Testament saints alike are redeemed by the blood of the Lamb and form an integral part of that city, the Bride, and the Kingdom.

Second, the perfection of the city is reflected in its size and symmetry (vv. 15-17). It is approximately a 1,400-mile cube (12,000 furlongs). Surrounding it is a wall that is about one-half mile high (144 cubits). All the measurements are multiples of 12. The protective measures (wall, angels, etc.) are there for reassurance, not because there are enemies seeking to enter (v. 25).

Third, the glory of the Lord is emphasized by the quality of the materials (vv. 18-21). The purity of the materials are reflected through their transparency. The gold from which the city is constructed is so pure that it is like "clear glass" (v. 18). The stones with which the city is adorned are vibrant, pure and glorious. With God's glory shining upon them, the splendor is beyond comprehension. Each gate is constructed out of one pearl (v. 21). The singular "street of the city" could be an emphasis on the main street. Since the city is made of gold, the other streets would be the same.

> "This city [the New Jerusalem] has a capacity for more people than could be born on this earth in 10,000 years; for it is estimated that every human being from Adam until now, if they were all saved, would hardly fill one corner of this enormous structure."
> —Joseph A. Seiss

B. The Presence in the City (vv. 22-27)
(Revelation 21:24-27 is not included in the printed text.)

22. And I saw no temple therein: for the Lord God Almighty and the Lamb are the temple of it.

23. And the city had no need of the sun, neither of the moon, to shine in it: for the glory of God did lighten it, and the Lamb is the light thereof.

In Ezekiel's vision, several chapters are spent on the temple (Ezekiel 40–47). Here there is no temple, because Ezekiel's symbolism is fulfilled with the reality of the presence of the Father and the Lamb. Here the entire city is the abiding place of God, whose glory illuminates it completely (Revelation 21:23). Because of the divine presence, there is no fear. This allows free access in and out of the city (vv. 24-26). The only inhabitants are those whose name is written in the Lamb's Book of Life (v. 27).

Talk About It:
1. Why will there be no temple in the new city?
2. Why will the 12 gates never be shut (v. 25)?
3. How does a person's name get recorded in the Lamb's Book of Life?

III. NEW PARADISE (Revelation 22:1-21)
A. The Provision in the City (vv. 1-5)

1. And he shewed me a pure river of water of life, clear as crystal, proceeding out of the throne of God and of the Lamb.

2. In the midst of the street of it, and on either side of the river, was there the tree of life, which bare twelve manner of fruits, and yielded her fruit every month: and the leaves of the tree were for the healing of the nations.

3. And there shall be no more curse: but the throne of God and of the Lamb shall be in it; and his servants shall serve him:

4. And they shall see his face; and his name shall be in their foreheads.

5. And there shall be no night there; and they need no candle, neither light of the sun; for the Lord God giveth them light: and they shall reign for ever and ever.

Talk About It:

1. Why do the nations need healing (v. 2)?

2. Explain the statement "And there shall be no more curse" (v. 3).

3. Why is seeing "his face" significant (v. 4)?

The glory of the city, along with its provision, continues in 22:1, where John sees the crystal-clear river of life. The source of the river is God. It originates from His throne. The foundation of God's throne is righteousness and justice (Psalm 89:14). Everything that flows from God is consistent with His nature, gives Him glory, and benefits humanity.

The nature of this water reflects its Source. It is clear, pure, and imparts life. As it flows from the throne through the main street of the city, it causes trees of life to spring forth on each side (v. 2). The singular "tree" is a collective noun, emphasizing the quality and nature of the trees, not the quantity. Some see this as a reference to the Holy Spirit flowing from the throne; others see it as abundant life, while others view it as immortality. Each of these is true. The focus, however, is on the availability of this life-giving stream. The centrality of the river reveals it is easily accessible to the inhabitants of the city. It imparts health to the people ("nations") through its fruit and leaves. This is the nature of life. Life imparts life, just as death begets death. Freely we have received life; let us give life freely.

Because of the fall of Adam and Eve and the stark account associated with the tree of life in the Garden of Eden (Genesis 3:22-24), many associate the tree with the curse of sin. Revelation 22:3 specifically dispels that association—there is "no more curse." The first Adam brought the curse and lost paradise. The Second Adam removed the curse and brings paradise reclaimed. The assurance of this truth is emphasized by noting that "the throne of God and of the Lamb shall be in [the city]" (v. 3). Consequently, those whom He has redeemed minister unto Him.

Four benefits of ministering unto Him are given in verses 4 and 5. First, the redeemed are in face-to-face relationship with Him. Humanity has not been able to look on the face of God and live (Exodus 33:20; 1 Timothy 6:16). The new order changes that. The redeemed will look upon Him (Matthew 5:8) because we shall be like Him (1 John 3:2). Second, His name is written upon their foreheads. It is continual proof that the redeemed are overcomers (Revelation 3:12). Third, all darkness is dispelled. Darkness is associated with sin (John 3:19), fear (Genesis 15:12), and death (Job 10:21, 22). The continual light and the Source of that light remove all darkness and the negativity associated with it. Fourth, according to the last part of verse 5 of the text, "these shall serve as royalty forever" (writer's translation). This is not the world's concept of kingship, which Jesus clearly condemned (Matthew 18:1-5; 20:20-28). To reign with Him is to serve Him. The new order is patterned in part after the redeemed order now. That is to say, what we are and do in part now as the redeemed shall be perfected in the Kingdom.

> "Within the new heaven and on the new earth is the Holy City—the new home for the saints of God."
> —William Evans

B. Faithful and True Sayings (vv. 6-15)

6. And he said unto me, These sayings are faithful and true: and the Lord God of the holy prophets sent his angel to shew unto his servants the things which must shortly be done.

7. Behold, I come quickly: blessed is he that keepeth the sayings of the prophecy of this book.

8. And I John saw these things, and heard them. And when I had heard and seen, I fell down to worship before the feet of the angel which shewed me these things.

9. Then saith he unto me, See thou do it not: for I am thy fellowservant, and of thy brethren the prophets, and of them which keep the sayings of this book: worship God.

10. And he saith unto me, Seal not the sayings of the prophecy of this book: for the time is at hand.

11. He that is unjust, let him be unjust still: and he which is filthy, let him be filthy still: and he that is righteous, let him be righteous still: and he that is holy, let him be holy still.

12. And, behold, I come quickly; and my reward is with me, to give every man according as his work shall be.

13. I am Alpha and Omega, the beginning and the end, the first and the last.

14. Blessed are they that do his commandments, that they may have right to the tree of life, and may enter in through the gates into the city.

15. For without are dogs, and sorcerers, and whoremongers, and murderers, and idolaters, and whosoever loveth and maketh a lie.

"He said" (v. 6) is probably a reference to the angel that beckoned John to see the Bride in 21:9. Ultimately, it is God's voice of assurance concerning the trustworthiness of these truths that is heard, regardless of the speaker. God has spoken

Talk About It:

1. What was John's response to the Revelation (v. 8)? Why?

2. What was John not to do, and why not (vv. 9, 10)?

3. How will Christ return, and for what purpose (v. 12)?

4. What is the significance of "the tree of life" (v. 14)?

through Old and New Testament prophets. He continues to speak today. We must not confuse the speaker with the message, nor reject the message because we do not like the speaker. There are but two questions: (1) Is it the Word of the Lord? and (2) How do we act upon if it is?

Christ verbalizes the theme of Revelation: "Behold, I come quickly" (22:7). This same message occurs two more times in this chapter (vv. 12, 20). There is an emphasis on the lack of delay and the swiftness with which it will occur. Also, there is the connection between obedience and reward. To take part in His coming, one must be faithful to the words of the book.

At this point, John affirms the veracity of the things recorded and is overwhelmed. He falls before the angel to worship him and is strongly rebuked (vv. 8, 9). The next phrase has two possible interpretations: (1) the angel is a fellow servant and a brother in the family of God, but not a human; (2) "angel" is better translated "messenger" (the word carries both meanings) and is one of the prophets. It is not teaching that the redeemed become angels. The angel informs him that only God is worthy of worship. Further, the message is not to be locked away, but shared with the church (v. 10). If the message is rejected, the opportunity for repentance is past.

Christ speaks again and reaffirms His coming along with His reward (v. 12). The obedient will be blessed with access to the Tree of Life, while the disobedient will be denied access to the new order (vv. 14, 15).

C. The Testimony of Jesus (vv. 16-21)

(Revelation 22:16-21 is not included in the printed text.)

In this passage, Jesus again assures the seven churches of Asia Minor (chs. 2, 3) and everyone else who reads the book that the contents are inspired. We enter into agreement with the Spirit and John and pray, "Come! . . . Even so, come, Lord Jesus!" (22:17, 20).

Talk About It:

1. Why was John given the Revelation (v. 16)?

2. Why would it be serious to try to alter the prophecies of Revelation (vv. 18, 19)?

3. Why is verse 21 a fitting conclusion to the last book of the Bible?

"The word *come* may be the most important word in the Bible, because it is God's word of invitation."

—David Cooper

CONCLUSION

The Book of Revelation evokes many feelings for believers. We are motivated to examine our hearts, pray for and witness to unbelievers, and worship with greater passion. The judgment scenes fill us with compassion. The workings of the enemies of God anger us. In the end, it is the hope of eternal life with and becoming more like our Savior that encompasses all of these feelings and provides the greatest motivation. Transformation and God's love await us now and in eternity.

GOLDEN TEXT CHALLENGE

"HE THAT SAT UPON THE THRONE SAID, BEHOLD, I MAKE ALL THINGS NEW" (Revelation 21:5).

"Daddy, I want some new toys." "It's time to buy a new car." "Let's vote for a new leader."

The demand everywhere is for the new—new conditions, new technology, new ideas, new methods, new houses, and so on.

God has always been in the business of creating the new. He will ultimately make over everything Satan has touched. God never deals in secondhand merchandise—His products are always new.

In salvation God gives us a new spirit, new attitude, hew hope, new peace, new love, and new ambitions. It is true we have these in an old body whose senses and systems are warped and suffering from the Fall and its ravages. But we will eventually inherit a new body living in a new world perfected by the Lord Almighty.

Daily Devotions:

M. New Song
   Psalm 40:1-5

T. New Creation
   Isaiah 65:17-25

W. New Covenant
   Jeremiah 31:31-34

T. New Commandment
   John 13:31-35

F. New Person
   2 Corinthians 5:17-21

S. New Life
   Ephesians 4:23-32